The Good People

The Fort, Ballyclare, Co. Antrim, Northern Ireland. (Ulster Folk and Transport Museum)

The Good People

New Fairylore Essays

Peter Narváez, Editor

THE UNIVERSITY PRESS OF KENTUCKY

To Anne

Publication of this volume was made possible in part by a grant
from the National Endowment for the Humanities.

Published by arrangement with Garland Publishing, Inc., by
The University Press of Kentucky

Scholarly publisher for the Commonwealth,
serving Bellarmine University, Berea College, Centre
College of Kentucky, Eastern Kentucky University,
The Filson Historical Society, Georgetown College,
Kentucky Historical Society, Kentucky State University,
Morehead State University, Murray State University,
Northern Kentucky University, Transylvania University,
University of Kentucky, University of Louisville,
and Western Kentucky University.
All rights reserved.

Editorial and Sales Offices: The University Press of Kentucky
663 South Limestone Street, Lexington, Kentucky 40508-4008
www.kentuckypress.com

Library of Congress Cataloging-in-Publication Data

The good people : new fairylore essays / edited by Peter Narváez
      p.   cm.
  Originally published: New York : Garland, 1991, in series: Garland reference
library of the humanities; vol. 1376
  Includes bibliographical references (p.) and index.
  ISBN-10: 0-8131-0939-6 (paperback : alk. paper)
  1. Fairy tales—History and criticism. I. Narváez, Peter.
[GR550.G66   1997]
398.2—dc21   97-25305
ISBN-13: 978-0-8131-0939-8 (pbk. : alk. paper)

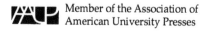

Contents

Illustrations

Acknowledgments

Many persons have assisted in the development of this book. In particular I would like to thank John D.A. Widdowson at the Centre for English Cultural Tradition and Language, the University of Sheffield, for his enthusiastic encouragement at the initial stages of the project. All my colleagues and student friends in the Department of Folklore, Memorial University of Newfoundland, have been supportive but special gratitude goes to Barbara Rieti for her knowledgable and thoughtful comments regarding this topic. The hard work and good humor of Department Secretaries Sharon Cochrane and Karen O'Leary have been indispensable during a long and sometimes confusing process. Colleagues from Memorial, Michael Staveley (Dean of Arts), Gerald Thomas (Folklore), Gary McManus and John Mannion (Geography), and Christopher Youé (History), have contributed in very direct ways. For a variety of assisting tasks I would additionally like to thank Richard Blaustein, John Doyle, Rosalind Gill, Sandy Morris, Colin Neilands, Judy Piercey, Robyn Gardner, and Holly Everett.

Grateful acknowledgment is also extended to the following persons for permission to reprint cited materials: Jonathan Bell, Editor, *Ulster Folklife* (article by Richard Jenkins); Jacqueline Simpson, Hon. Editor, *Folklife* (article by Susan Schoon Eberly); J.D.A. Widdowson, Editor, *Lore and Language* (article by Peter Narváez); Duncan Williamson and Linda Williamson, and Alan Bruford, Editor, *Tocher* (Duncan Williamson's variant of "Thomas Rymer").

For the permission to print photographs and graphic materials I would like to thank Patricia Lysaght (University College Dublin), Jonathan Bell and Linda-May Ballard (Ulster Folk and Transport Museum), Robin Gwyndaf (National Museum of Wales), George Bennett, Tom McKean, Joan Mann, Ian MacKenzie (School of Scottish Studies), Daniel C. Postellon, Nancy J. Hopwood, the Librarian of the Brotherton Library (University of Leeds), Rosemary Wells, Rob Browne, Brian Ajhar, and Vivienne Flesher.

Finally, I want to express my greatest appreciation to my good friend Anne Budgell to whom I have dedicated this work. Her sustaining interest, patient efforts, and insightful criticisms have been invaluable in making it a reality.

Introduction

The authors of the essays in this book generally focus on the *living traditions* of the supernaturally powered "little people" from North Atlantic countries and regions, not fairies in literature. They provide a wealth of orally transmitted knowledge in the form of informational testimonies, personal experience narratives, legends, ballads, and place-names. The variety of fairy behaviors depicted in these accounts renders any single definition of "fairy" lacking. In part this diversity of meanings reflects the complex etymological development of the Modern English term fairy, a growth well traced by Noel Williams in his essay, "The Semantics of the Word *Fairy*." Deriving from the conceptually related terms *fatua, fatum* (Latin), *fee* (Old French), *fagan, faege* (Old English), and *fay* (Middle English), fairy in the British Isles, Ireland, and the English-speaking world has become a generic term that incorporates the meanings of many previous regional supernatural rivals, such as *boghost, bugalug, thurse,* and *shuck,* while subsuming marvelous creatures that have been maintained in oral tradition like *elf, pixie, goblin, lutin,* and the twentieth century *gremlin,* all of which are commonly thought of today as kinds of fairies. Interestingly, many people who participate in living fairy traditions refuse to use the term. Because of a traditional taboo against saying "fairy" aloud, fairies on both sides of the Atlantic are often referred to with a variety of euphemisms, including "the good people," "the gentry," "the people of peace," and "them."

The development of fairy meanings has not been arbitrary, however. Whether they be "little people," which most of them are, monsters, supernatural creatures, partially human entities, mortals, or immortals, these beings share a characteristic with similar entities encountered in cultures throughout the world—they represent challenging, "significant other" societies of *liminal personae,* creatures "betwixt and between," possessing supernatural powers that can be used for evil or good. Thus, the folkloristic, ethnographic, and anthropological essays in the "Regional Fairylore" section of this volume situate fairies between heaven and hell (fallen angels), between the dead and the living (restless dead), or between purity (a mortal's home or home community) and danger (deep woods, barrens, bogs, cliffs) in areas such as barns, gardens, and berry grounds. Confronting humans as solitary beings or in groups (trooping fairies), on land, water, or the air, fairies engage people competitively and must be dealt with. They demand appropriate responses rooted in traditional knowledge, for if ignored they may wreak havoc and disaster. Regional cultures, therefore, have evolved intricate rules of behavior on the basis of long experience with fairy habits, living spaces, likes, aversions, and ultimate designs. Fairy liminality has prompted mortals to be cautious, observe prohibitions, and practice defensive and remedial magicoreligious customs and rituals (see Anne Helene Bolstad Skjelbred, "Rites of Passage as Meeting Place: Christianity and Fairylore in Connection with the Unclean Woman and the Unchristened Child").

As oral depictions of fairies attest, fairies appear in all manner of garb (red suits, flowing gowns, blue velvet knee britches, long caps with peaks). Although such portrayals have sometimes been influenced by mass culture, they usually have not included the diaphanous-winged, effeminate fairy images of literature and feature-length cartoons. Accounts of visual encounters further disclose fairies engaging in a spectrum of both festive (dancing, playing musical instruments, feasting, riding horses) and solemn (funerals) activities. The complex conflation of fairy motifs and beliefs from literature and oral tradition as expressed in a popular culture legend concerning two young women who allegedly encountered and photographed winged fairies is closely examined in Paul Smith's treatment of "The Cottingley Fairies: The End of a Legend."

On the other hand, oral narratives sometimes describe the *presence* of fairies as involving extraordinary natural circumstance (fairy winds), or psychological influence, more than visible, physical interaction. In Newfoundland, for instance, to be "in the fairies," "fairyled," "led astray," or "taken astray" refers to a form of disorientation sometimes resulting in getting lost in dangerous areas, frequently while berry picking or cutting wood in a forest. While in this mental state, an individual may experience being in one place and then in another without temporal or spatial transition. As in Europe, one of the most popular counteractant magical practices in such circumstances has been to reverse one's fate by turning articles of clothing (cap, shirt, coat) inside out.

In other circumstances, physical disorders have been attributed to fairies, again, often without actual human-fairy encounters. Barbara Rieti shows in her article, "'The Blast' in Newfoundland Fairy Tradition," that the fairy "blast" in Newfoundland parallels the European "elf shot," a wound that commonly becomes tumorous. It is inflicted by angry fairies in contexts where individuals intrude on fairy territory or cross fairy paths. Narrators maintain that when medical doctors have lanced such tumors they have found objects such as feathers, pins, straw, hair, and teeth. Similarly, changeling accounts cite the presence of an abnormal, often old, fairy "child"; yet, as a rule, the fairy abductors of the human child are not caught in the act. Susan Schoon Eberly's and Joyce Underwood Munro's interpretations of European changeling traditions stress the parental importance of such beliefs in assigning moral responsibility for the advent of disabled infants to fairy activities rather than to personal deficiencies. Thus, strong community beliefs in fairies have provided opportunities for changeling parents to coalesce with fairies by using fairy explanations in order to avoid the sanctions, embarrassment, and shame of other, more condemning traditional interpretations (e.g. the "cursed child"—a child cursed by the sins of its parent[s]). On a related theme, I suggest in my article, "Newfoundland Berry Pickers 'In the Fairies,'" that oral testimonies reveal the possibility of fairy explanations being used as alibis to mask a variety of deviant behaviors, such as extreme tardiness, premarital sexual relations, infidelity, incest, child molestation, wife battering, and sexual assault.

With the possible exception of the Tooth Fairy, a being receiving extensive attention in essays by Tad Tuleja and Rosemary Wells, the fairylore of the New World, particularly Atlantic Canada, has clear European antecedents. Perhaps the greatest distinction between Old and New World fairylore is the spatial emphasis of the latter, a characteristic that has expressed the need of dealing with potential tragedies of getting lost or encountering mortal dangers in vast wilderness areas through magico-religious means. Conversely, in Europe it has frequently been familiar places associated with death or unknown habitants, for example Early Iron Age ring forts in Ireland (see Diarmuid Ó Giolláin's, "The Fairy Belief and Official Religion in Ireland"), that have fostered fairy taboos. On both continents, however, orally circulated accounts concerning dangerous zones, and the tragic encounters of specific individuals with fairies in such places that have resulted in permanent physical stigma (awkward demeanor, disfigurement, premature aging, lameness, speech impairment) or psychological disability ("strange" behavior, retardation, "sinful" tendencies, insanity), have served as geographical warnings on the cognitive maps of community residents. In addition, such accounts have left moral imprints as explanatory, cautionary tales and have functioned as agents of social control. These social functions are well demonstrated in Richard P. Jenkins's analysis of "Witches and Fairies: Supernatural Aggression and Deviance Among the Irish Peasantry." Fairylore has maintained traditional values, therefore, by stressing the importance of subordinating individual desires to collective needs (obedience to community norms), and by underscoring the necessity of yielding to the wisdom of generational pressures (the admonitions of one's elders concerning fairies as threatening figures).

Today fairy beliefs are often relegated to the past or thought of as moribund. Informants cite a variety of causes for the demise of fairy traditions including the advent of roads, cars, electric light, television, and other contemporary electronic media. Some contemporary students of fairylore maintain, however, that fairies have not disappeared, they have simply transformed into the growing numbers of "little green" inhabitants of unidentified flying objects (UFOs) who continue their traditional practice of abducting humans with impunity, an intriguing point of view linked with an epistemological explanation by Peter M. Rojcewicz ("Between One Eye Blink and the Next: Fairies, UFOs, and Problems of Knowledge"). Others, such as Linda-May Ballard ("Fairies and the Supernatural on Reachrai"), observe that for centuries there have been reports of fading fairy traditions and that the idea of the fairies' disappearance itself is part of the fairylore belief complex.

The Good People

A few words concerning the origins of *The Good People* are in order. This book has evolved as a direct result of my initial contact with Newfoundland fairylore at Memorial University in the fall of 1974. Having assigned folklore collections to my undergraduate introductory folklore class, one student included an item of fairylore in her paper. She explained that members of her family had espoused and practiced the belief of carrying a piece of bread while berry picking in order to keep the fairies from "leading you astray." A little astonished, my reaction was whimsical surprise at what I considered to be a curious anomaly. After all, during my graduate training at Indiana University's Folklore Institute, Richard M. Dorson, a leading North American folklorist, had informed his classes that fairies were traditional supernatural creatures "rooted in the soil" of the Old World; they were not evident on this side of the Atlantic. The experience of my own upbringing in a small industrial town in New Jersey supported Dorson's view. The only fairies I confronted there were winged sprites on pop bottle labels, the Tinkerbell-fare served up by Walt

Disney, and the dimly recalled, enigmatic Tooth Fairy who had prowled my bedroom on several occasions in early childhood. But my Canadian experience proves Dorson wrong. Fairies *have been and are* in the New World. Atlantic Canada is not like the New Jersey of my childhood, for after over twenty years of teaching in Newfoundland my folklore students continue to submit items of fairylore with startling regularity.

My growing interest in fairylore over these years resulted in a study published in the British folklore journal, *Lore and Language,* and an hour-length radio program, "The Fairy Faith Today," which aired on *Ideas,* a national broadcast of the Canadian Broadcasting Corporation. Both of these projects put me in contact with a large number of scholars from North America and Europe who were actively collecting, examining, and assessing fairylore of past and present. It is their exciting work which is presented in this anthology. Sixteen of the essays have been contributed especially for this volume.

The Good People is divided into six sections. The first section, entitled "Regional Fairylore," is the lengthiest. Here a large number of traditional beliefs, customs, and narratives from Newfoundland, Ireland, Scotland, and Wales, are presented and analyzed. In the second section historical and cultural issues involving the intermingling of fairylore and official religion in Ireland and Norway are considered. The essays in the third section, "Physical Disorders: Changelings and the Blast," concern the darker manifestations of fairy-human encounters and their meanings in social and medical terms. The social consequences of fairylore for believing, practicing communities, particularly in regard to aggression and worldview, are the focus of the fourth section. The fifth section presents analyses of the Cottingley Fairies and the Tooth Fairy, fairies whose histories reflect the commingling of traditional and mass-mediated elements along the folklore-popular culture continuum. A final section combines the past and the present, one article tracing the historical meanings of the word "fairy," another positing how data pertaining to human-fairy encounters and human-unidentified flying object (UFO) encounters may contribute to our understanding of human knowledge.

Some of these articles are more technical than others, but generally they are accessible to the general reader and provide a fine introduction and overview of fairylore scholarship today. The extensive notes and references supplied with many of these essays furnish viable avenues for those who wish to pursue further research in this stimulating area of folklore studies. To update these references for this paperbound edition, a selected bibliography of significant fairylore publications which have appeared since the book's first printing is provided here. Most of these are fairy narrative studies published in a splendid special volume (59) of the Folklore of Ireland Society journal *Béaloideas* entitled "'The Fairy Hill Is on Fire!' Proceedings of the Symposium on the Supernatural in Irish and Scottish Migratory Legends, Dublin, 7-8 October 1988," edited by Pádraig Ó Héalaí, which appeared in 1991.

Selected Bibliography of Recent Fairylore Publications

Almqvist, Bo. "Irish Migratory Legends on the Supernatural: Sources, Studies and Problems." *Béaloideas* 59 (1991): 1-43.
Breatnach, Deasún. "The Púca: A Multi-Functional Irish Supernatural Entity." *Folklore* 104.1-2 (1993): 105-10.
Lövkrona, Inger. "'Det är bestämt en byting.' Dordi Larsdotter och hennes vanföra barn. En studie utifrån ett gotländskt domstolsfall. ['The Child is Surely a Changeling.' Dordi Larsdotter and her Disabled Child. A Study of a Court Case in Gotland, Sweden]." *Budkavlen* 68 (1989): 5-18.
MacCárthaigh, Críostóir. "Midwife to the Fairies: The Irish Variants in Their Scottish and Scandinavian Perspective." *Béaloideas* 59 (1991): 133-43.
MacPhilib, Séamas. "The Changeling: Irish Versions of a Migratory Legend in Their International Context." *Béaloideas* 59 (1991): 121-31.
Ó Catháin, Séamus. "Tricking the Fairy Suitor: A Rare Peripheral Relic?" *Béaloideas* 59 (1991): 145-59.
Ó Giolláin, Diarmuid. "Capturer of Fairy Shoemaker Outwitted: The Multiple Marker Versions." *Béaloideas* 59 (1991): 161-6.
Ó Héalaí, Pádraig. "The Priest in Irish Fairy Legends." *Folk Narrative and World View*. Vorträge des 10. Kongresses der Internationalen Gesellschaft für Volkserzahlungsforschung. Innsbruck 1992. Ed. L. Petzoldt. Innsbruck: International Society for Folk Narrative Research, 609-21.
O'Neill, Aine. "'The Fairy Hill is on Fire!': A Panorama of Multiple Functions." *Béaloideas* 59 (1991): 189-96.
Selberg, Torunn. "Det magiske landskapet [The Magical Landscape]." *Tradisjon* 1 (1996): 15-22.
_____. "Male and Female in the Narrative Tradition about Fairies." *ARV* 52 (1996): 99-106.
Uí Ógáin, Ríonach. "Music Learned from the Fairies." *Béaloideas* 60-1 (1992-3): 197-214.
Wood, Juliette. "The Fairy Bride Legend in Wales." *Folklore* 103.1 (1992): 56-72.

Peter Narváez
Memorial University of Newfoundland
St. John's, Newfoundland   1997

The Good People

I. Regional Fairylore

Living folklore, the traditional artistic communications that circulate informally in small groups, cannot be found in library stacks or in folklore archive cabinets. To make such interstitial knowledge accessible the folklorist generates texts by "collecting" them in the social contexts of fieldwork. What *can* be found in the library and in the archive are previously collected texts in published and stored collections and these materials are constantly being reevaluated in the light of new data and methods of analysis. Both procedures, the collecting of folklore in the field and the assessment of previously collected folkloric materials, involve folklorists learning from people, attempting to understand the content of folklore and the meaning that it possesses for its bearers. This section of regional fairylore studies from North Atlantic cultures exhibits folklorists in the midst of such inquiries.

One of the thorny problems in collecting extraordinary and anomalous folklore concerns approaching levels of belief and disbelief, the humorous and the solemn, empirical truth and cultural truth. Gary Butler's portrayal of his attempts to comprehend the *lutin* (fairy) tradition of French Newfoundland develops from initial surprise to illuminating perceptions of the complexity of worldview. Through every juncture in his fieldwork experience he candidly depicts the intellectual struggle involved in understanding belief as a dynamic form that is reified in discourse.

Also derived from fieldwork and concerning belief, the next two pieces by Patricia Lysaght and Linda-May Ballard display the position of traditional fairy narratives amongst a pantheon of remarkable beings in two Irish contexts, Co. Laois in the Midlands and Reachrai, or Rathlin Island. In the first instance, a close examination of a tradition-bearer's narratives, combined with her own evaluations of the items in her repertoire, reveal *repertoire dominants* thematically linked to ghosts and fairies. On Rathlin Island Linda-May Ballard's broad collecting net presents fairylore enmeshed in repertoires of narratives concerning omens, ghosts, wise-women and witches, the devil ("Old Nick"), and the power of the priest. The vitality of speculation regarding fairies on the Island prompts her to pose the possibility of a traditional fairy belief that may not always be obvious: "Might it be that the idea that fairy belief is fading and belongs to the past is part of [the fairylore] complex?"

The vitality of fairy belief in Balquhidder, Scotland, a former heartland of fairy activity, is the focus of the essay by Margaret Bennett, who herself retains vivid memories of fairylore from her upbringing on the Isle of Skye and the Isle of Lewis. Balquhidder was the home of Robert Kirk, the parish minister who in the seventeenth century wrote one of the most famous treatises about fairies, *The Secret Common-Wealth*. Bennett's fieldwork with various age groups demonstrates that the community's history and fairy landscape continues to sustain belief, particularly among children.

Again from Scotland, Alan Bruford offers a richly detailed fairylore survey in his account of the "good neighbors" in the Northern Isles of Orkney and Shetland, areas with an intricate past and Nordic cultural links. Here, abundant and complex reports concerning the land and sea interactions of humans with fairies, *trows* ("a variant of the Norse *troll*"), and related inhabitants of the Otherworld show that these remarkable creatures have frequently been dangerous, but when properly placated they have proved helpful, served useful purposes, and afforded good fortune.

Scrutinizing supernatural British balladry through a structural method pioneered by Vladimir Propp,[1] David Buchan's "talerole analysis" of a "preponderantly Scottish" cluster of traditional ballads featuring Otherworld beings unveils fascinating commonalities that highlight important cultural messages. To fully appreciate Buchan's method of narrative analysis the reader is encouraged to read the variant texts of the ballad story-type numbers (CH 19, CH 39, etc.) referred to in the essay. These can be found in Francis James Child, *The English and Scottish Popular Ballads* (5 volumes, 1882–98).[2]

The final regional presentation is from Wales. Fairylore scholar Katharine Briggs once noted that "Welsh fairies seem to have been rather unusually high-souled."[3] After reading Robin Gwyndaf's intriguing collection of oral fairylore texts concerning the many activities of *Y Tylwyth Teg* (the fairies) one may be inclined to agree. Gwyndaf's similar assessment is that generally, "Welsh fairies were believed to be benevolent by nature." In some of these accounts, however, Welsh fairies do betray the same malevolence as their Celtic fairy neighbors.

Notes

1. See Vladimir Propp, *Morphology of the Folktale*, American Folklore Society Bibliographical and Special Series, Vol. 9, Indiana University Research Center in Anthropology, Folklore, and Linguistics, Publication 10, trans. Laurence Scott, rev. Louis A. Wagner (orig. 1928; Austin: U of Texas P, 1968) and David Buchan, "Propp's Tale Role and a Ballad Repertoire," *Journal of American Folklore* 95 (1982): 159–72.

2. Francis James Child, ed., *The English and Scottish Popular Ballads*, 5 vols. (1882–98; New York: Dover, 1965).

3. Katharine Briggs, *A Dictionary of Fairies* (Harmondsworth: Penguin, 1977) 55.

The *Lutin* Tradition in French-Newfoundland Culture: Discourse and Belief

Gary R. Butler

A tradition can have a changing body of adherents, changing in size, changing in membership, and changing in their beliefs too. The boundaries of a tradition are in one respect the boundaries of adherence of collectivities defined by their community of belief; in another respect they are the boundaries of symbolic constructions.

Edward Shils, *Tradition*

The Lutin Tradition

"What?!"

I almost shouted at the white-haired man with the sparkling eyes sitting in his armchair opposite me. Between us a cassette tape recorder continued to run, impassively noting our conversation. I had just asked a question I had already posed without success to twelve other people since my arrival on the Port-au-Port Peninsula of Newfoundland: "And uh, have you ever heard any stories about *lutins*?" Unperturbed, Joseph Bozec repeated the reply which had prompted my reaction: "Oh, dame, j'en avais un dans ma grange." As if commenting on what a nuisance mosquitoes were, this seventy-five-year-old resident of the French Newfoundland community of L'Anse-à-Canards had just told me that he used to have a fairy in his barn.[1]

It is not known for certain when the first French-speaking settlers established themselves permanently in the Bay St. George/Port-au-Port Peninsula area of Newfoundland, but historical sources indicate that inmigration had begun by the last quarter of the eighteenth century.[2] The majority of the francophone settlers arrived from two primary source areas. The first group, consisting of Acadian families from the east coast of Cape Breton Island, Nova Scotia, began to arrive in significant numbers after 1820, attracted by the rich cod and herring fishery. By 1856, it was estimated that the total population of this area consisted of approximately 1500 people.[3] In many cases, the Acadian settlers brought with them their cattle and domestic possessions and subsisted on a combination of fishing, farming, and raising livestock, thereby effectively transplanting the rural domestic economy and way of life they had known in their previous home. The second group of French-speaking settlers consisted of single adult males from source areas in continental France. In most instances, these men had been employed as menial laborers involved with the full-scale fishing operation conducted on Newfoundland's "French Shore"[4] by companies working out of ports in northwestern France, primarily in Brittany and Normandy. After their arrival, some of the crew members, many of whom had been recruited from farming villages in their home country and who in most cases were little versed in the skills of a large-scale fishing enterprise, chose to desert their ships rather than return to France or St. Pierre upon the termination of operations in the fall.[5] These men subsequently married into the Acadian families already present and pursued the way of life to which they were better accustomed. The result was the establishment of settlements such as L'Anse-à-Canards, Cap-St-Georges (English usage Cape St. George), La Grand'Terre, Stephenville, and Kippens, and many of the present inhabitants of these communities are able to trace their ancestry to both continental French and Cape Breton Acadian sources.

On June 15, 1980, I arrived in Cape St. George, situated on the southwestern tip of the peninsula, about thirty miles from L'Anse-à-Canards, to begin folkloristic fieldwork to collect information on the supernatural belief tradition in the area. My intention was to conduct general preliminary surveys in all four of the principal francophone communities and eventually to focus my efforts on a single community. By the end of my doctoral fieldwork four years later, I had spent nearly a full year in residence in L'Anse-à-Canards and compiled a collection of almost one hundred hours of sound recordings dealing with most aspects of the traditional culture in French Newfoundland, with an emphasis on supernatural belief and the social context of its expression. A large portion of this collection consists of beliefs and belief narratives dealing with supernatural beings, such as the devil, revenants, witches, and *marionnettes.* Included in this category was the French *lutin* [lyt~], a being corresponding in many ways to a species of fairy or elf in Anglo-Irish tradition. By the end of the first week of what was to be a two-month period of fieldwork, I had interviewed and recorded four informants and spoken less formally with at least eight others, none of whom was able to offer any information concerning the *lutin* tradition. Some of the people I spoke with told me that while they recognized the word as one they remembered having heard many years ago, they could not identify its referent. This situation seemed to suggest that the *lutin* tradition had once existed in French-Newfoundland culture, but was in the final stages of disintegration, apparently having been reduced to the status of a meaningless lexical item. It was for these reasons that Joseph Bozec's offhand remark in response to my question, posed more in passing than with the hope of eliciting a positive commentary, momentarily startled me. Regaining some poise, I leaned forward and prompted: "Yes?" Bozec continued:

> I used to have a, I used to have a little mare. And, uh . . . And I couldn't comb her, I couldn't comb her . . . her mane. It was always so . . . so tangled, I couldn't comb it. No. You couldn't.[6]

Anticipating what was to come, I asked how that could be? What could have caused it? Then the lesson began:

> Oh, well now, I, it—this is how the story goes. There were those who used to tell you that it was the *lutins* who did it, you see? Because—they used to say that. And if they braided something like that, well, you weren't supposed to undo it, you see, eh? But this one, something tangled her, her mane. Mmm. But whether it was *lutins* or whether it's uh . . . No, she was too lazy to comb herself [laughs]. I tried to untangle them. I couldn't. No, I couldn't untangle them! No.

By this point, it was becoming increasingly evident that here was a man possessing a knowledge of the cultural tradition and speaking of a personal experience in terms of this tradition; yet, in an apparently paradoxical way, he had absolutely no belief in the tradition's contents. Bozec appeared to be finished, but the contradiction between the direction of his discourse and the expectations established by his response to my initial question prompted me to ask him what exactly a *lutin* was.

"A *lutin*!" His response was marked by surprise, almost astonishment, that I would ask such a thing. Then, laughing, he answered:

> The devil only knows! I don't know. They say that it's people, "little people." [du petit monde] Just like the, the Irish now. They have their fairies there and their . . . ah? Their "little people," they call them.

To be sure that I had correctly read my informant's meaning, I finally asked: "Were there ever any around here? Do you believe—?" I got no farther.

> Nah! No! I never heard of any. It's only me, me and my horse . . . Do you see? It's . . . the mane, her mane was tangled like that. There are, there are—you take some animals or something you know? The hairs were all tangled together, you see? Or something like that. No, I wouldn't believe in that, either.

Bozec chuckled, while I smiled. He laughed at my mistaken assumption that he had been serious when he mentioned the *lutin* that used to live in his barn; he was clearly amused to discover that I had listened, all the while thinking that here was a man talking about *lutins* as supernatural beings while he was talking about *lutins* as a quite natural problem involving his horse's mane. My initial disappointment at having lost an example of positive belief regarding a supernatural tradition was quickly replaced by a greater interest as I began to realize the communicative complexity of what had transpired between us and how Bozec had signified what he meant to communicate. The status of this tradition in L'Anse-à-Canards suddenly revealed a whole new dimension and my research perspective was never to be quite the same.

In the analysis of naturally occurring discourse, the context-oriented researcher is primarily concerned with what the speaker is doing with words and, more specifically, with "the relationship between the speaker and the utterance, on the particular occasion of its use. . . ."[7] What a speaker attempts to communicate is based largely upon the notions of *reference*, the relationship between words and things,[8] and *presupposition*, that which is "taken by the speaker to be the common ground of the participants in the conversation."[9] When reference is shared between speaker and hearer and when the speakers' presuppositions accurately conform to their interlocutors' knowledge, the result is successful communication.

The study of oral tradition is a specialized investigation, one oriented towards a particular variety of speech acts and communicative events and involving the researcher in the context-sensitive analysis of a complex transaction of mind. The folklorist's raw material is the uttered discourse which has as its primary referential framework a body of traditional knowledge, a complex system of "multiform folk ideas."[10] As cognitive elements of worldview, these ideas are available to the individual as communicative resources, to be related to the interactional situation and molded to the speakers' perception of the context of discourse. This context of discourse involves speakers in determining what they wish to do and how best to do it with the communicative resources at their disposal. The measure of their communicative competence[11] is determined by the success of their speech acts, by their skill in knowing "how to do things with words."[12]

My informant's initial response had been made on the basis of his understanding of the situation and his definition of "what was going on." I had asked about something which for him possessed two quite different referents, but which for me possessed in this context only one. I was referring to the traditional supernatural belief once widely known and believed both in France and in regions of French North America. More specifically, I had intended reference to the tradition noted by the prominent French folklorist Paul Sébillot, who wrote in 1905:

> ... vers 1830, on disait dans La Manche lorsqu'un cheval avait les crins mêlés ensemble, qu'il avait servi de monture aux fées qui aiment à courir la nuit sur les chevaux dont elles nouent la crinière pour se faire des étriers ... [13]

> [... in La Manche, in 1830, when a horse had its mane braided together, they used to say that it had served as a mount for fairies who like to ride horses at night and that they would knot the mane to make stirrups ...]

In the past, this tradition was especially widespread in northern France, particularly in Celtic Brittany and Normandy, and while the French fairy tradition consists of a complex wealth of details and elements which rivals the Irish tradition, the particular aspect described by Sébillot seems to be among the few which have survived transplantation to the New World. In his study of the folklore of the Upper Peninsula of Michigan, Richard M. Dorson noted the presence of a similar tradition amongst the French-speaking population whose ancestors had arrived from Quebec during the lumber boom in the last quarter of the nineteenth century.[14] And in the Acadian culture of Maritime Canada, French-Canadian folklorist Père Ansèlme Chiasson noted:

> Ces êtres minuscules à formes humaines, s'introduisaient la nuit dans les étables des chevaux. Ils choisissaient les meilleurs, les sortaient deshors et galopaient avec eux dans les champs. Les lutins s'asseoient toujours sur le cou de leur coursier et tressent le crin pour s'en faire des étriers. Les lutins femelles tressaient le crin d'un seul côté. Les chevaux ainsi lutinés, malgré leurs courses, étaient toujours bien nourris par les lutins. Mais si le propriétaire du cheval défaisait les tresses des lutins, ces derniers se mettaient en colère et traitaient durement les chevaux.[15]

> [These tiny humanlike beings would enter a horse's stable by night. Choosing the best, they would take it outside and gallop through the fields with it. The *lutins* would always sit on their steed's neck and braid the mane to make stirrups for themselves. The female *lutins* would braid only one side of the mane. These horses were always well treated and fed by the *lutins*. But if the horse's owner untied the braids, the *lutins* would become angry and treat the horse harshly.]

Given that the French population of Newfoundland's Port-au-Port Peninsula descend from French fishermen from northern France who settled there in the mid- to late nineteenth century and from Nova Scotia French Acadian families who arrived perhaps as early as the eighteenth century, it is natural to expect reference to the *lutin* tradition to reflect these dual origins. And given that Bozec's father had come from Quimper, in Brittany, and that his mother had been of Acadian descent, it seemed that I had encountered a clear example of this tradition.

However, for this particular informant, the term *lutin* no longer served the primary function of communicating information related to his culture's traditional belief system. With the evolution of the concept over time, this traditional referent had been replaced by a new primary referent and it was inevitable that this change should be reflected by a different use in natural discourse. To Joseph Bozec, my question about *lutins* was the same as asking if he had ever had any problems with his horses' manes being tangled. When he answered that he used to have one (i.e., a *lutin*) in his barn, he was answering the question as he had understood it from this new, non-traditional perspective. That is, from the outset, the illocutionary force underlying his discourse had been determined by a case of what Grice refers to as the "Irony Principle."[16] On the other hand, I was reading his response as paired with and reflecting what I had intended by my original query. Our frames of reference did not correspond and neither of us was aware that we each had constructed different definitions of the context of discourse, of "what was going on."

It was not until I clearly expressed my desire for him to elaborate on how the horse's tangled mane related to his initial statement about the *lutin* in his barn that my informant saw the focus of my initial question as referring to his secondary frame of reference (i.e., the belief tradition of previous generations of French Newfoundlanders). At the same time, realizing that I had interpreted his response literally, Bozec shifted the direction of his own discourse accordingly to talk about the stories people used to recount and what they used to believe about the *lutins*. His present view of the tradition is made adequately clear:

GB: Did any people believe in . . .?
JB: Oh . . . only, it was only the French [i.e., the original French settlers] who spoke about such things.
GB: Did your father?
JB: Yes, yes! Yes! He used to speak about it, too.
GB: What would he say?
JB: He'd say that it was uh . . . the *lutins* were like fairies, you know? *Des fées*, yes.
GB: He believed this?
JB: He believed it! Yes!
GB: And your mother, as well?
JB: Oh, yes, because she didn't have, she had no education. No. A person without any education, you can make them believe almost [laughs]. . . . People are more uh—Nowadays, they, they don't believe in anything!

The matter seemed to have been settled definitively. Few people I talked to had ever heard of the term *lutin* and the one individual who possessed a knowledge of the tradition dismissed it out of hand. However, this served to establish a time-depth indicating that the belief in *lutins* had been accepted by at least some community members as recently as sixty years ago.

Subsequent inquiries failed to turn up any further information related to the *lutin* tradition. Then, on July 9, 1980, having interviewed another seven informants since talking with Bozec, I visited an elderly couple in Cape St. George.

When I first met them, Philomène and Joseph Simon were both well into their seventies and had been married for nearly sixty years.[17] Having established, I thought, the status of fairy belief in contemporary French Newfoundland society, my question concerning *lutins* was posed with the intention of gauging to what extent the knowledge of this disappearing tradition had persisted. The Simons' response again demonstrated the perils of drawing conclusions about the status of a particular tradition before conducting a thorough investigation:

GB:	Have you ever heard of *lutins*?
PS:	Oh, yes. There used to be *lutins*.
GB:	Yes?
JS:	*Lutins*, yes.
GB:	And what were they?
JS:	They used to believe they were enchanted people.
PS:	Oh, yes [agreeing with her husband].
GB:	Yes? And what did they do?
JS:	They, they, they braided the . . . the manes.
PS:	Braided the—
PS/JS:	[together] horses' manes.
PS:	Yes. Horses' manes. They'd braid them.

Uncertain as to whether the Simons were referring to their own belief or that of past generations, I asked them if this was true. Joseph Simon answered as if it were the most natural thing in the world:

JS:	Oh, yes. My dead father used to have a mare whose mane was braided.
GB:	Yes?
JS:	By *lutins*.
PS:	Yes, yes.
JS:	Yes, braided and uh, you couldn't undo it.
GB:	No?
JS:	[vehemently] No! No, no, no, no! No!

Although less directly than had Bozec, Simon also implied the taboo against untying the horse's braided mane and his description added some new details unmentioned by Bozec, referring to the *lutins* as "enchanted."

But, unlike my previous informant, the couple's manner in answering my questions, particularly Joseph Simon's example about his late father's horse, seemed to confirm their belief in the existence of these supernatural beings. However, closer examination shows how this case is marked by an interesting set of relationships between this specific tradition, the couple's current worldview and the nature of their belief. Clearly, the Simons accept what they had been told by past generations concerning *lutins* and have retained a knowledge of at least some of the details of the tradition. Nevertheless, they do not regard the *lutin* as a reality in their present environment, but see it as a phenomenon which ceased to exist at some point in the past. This is quite different from the situation where individuals come to reject as false a belief traditum[18] they once accepted as true. In a very real sense, the Simons both believe and do not believe in fairies, an interesting combination of acceptance and rejection which has been given little consideration in contemporary studies of traditional belief.

While the Simons differed from Bozec in their attitude towards the *lutin* tradition, all three shared the common view that these creatures did not exist in their cultural present. After spending a month in fieldwork, I had encountered only two instances where informants expressed a relatively detailed knowledge of the tradition; and both reflected an attitude of rejection, albeit for different reasons and from different perspectives, of the tradition's relevance in the contemporary context.

On July 16, 1980, I returned to L'Anse-à-Canards to visit Emile Benoit, a sixty-seven-year-old man whom I had met and interviewed the previous summer. Benoit is as close to being a living repository of all aspects of his tradition as is anyone I have met in the course of my fieldwork. Not only is he a gifted fiddler and composer, he is one of the very few individuals who is able to perform the traditional wonder tales, or Märchen, which in the past were a vibrant part of the oral culture in French Newfoundland. In addition to this, he possesses an extraordinary depth and breadth of knowledge about all aspects of his people's traditions and is highly respected in his community.

While I had not dropped by with the intention of interviewing Benoit for the purpose of my fieldwork, our after-supper conversation inevitably turned towards the general topic of the beliefs and worldview of Benoit's community. I brought out the tape recorder,[19] which he ignored completely and our conversation continued as before. It was not until over two hours had passed that I said, "You know, Emile . . . there are some people, I've heard them speak of *lutins*." Benoit's eyes brightened and, with some excitement, he responded:

EB: *Lutins?* Ah! Oh, yes! Yes! Ah, well now! Now, I can tell you a story about that too, me!

And then, almost triumphantly, he continued:

EB: That, that happened to me too! I had heard about that. Yes. I had heard about that. Well, but, I never used to believe it. No, I didn't believe that there were such things as *lutins*. . . . Yes. But now, one morning I was in the barn, I noticed that my horse . . . his mane, his mane was all laced! There now! There! Well, my friend! I really would have liked to have had a camera to take a picture! It wasn't braided a lot. It wasn't braided a lot. But there was a little braid here, and a little braid there, and a little braid there, and it was braided about four inches long.

GB: Yes?

EB: But it wasn't finished right to the end. Well now, if you could have seen that, eh! Ah? I noticed that. Now, I examined that! Well, there . . . ah, now, I thought about the *lutins*, that I'd heard my father speak about. Ah ha! So, now, that's it! Well, there you have your proof, ah! And I untangled it, but my friend, I had a lot of trouble!

GB: Yes, eh?

EB: Oh, it was all tangled together! It was all hooked together like that! Was it ever laced! And there were three all laced. But my friend! And that was all hairs, eh? Shoelaces or things like that, they aren't hard to undo, eh? But that! That's hard to untangle, my friend!

Much of what Benoit knew about *lutins* he had learned from his father, who according to Benoit, had never witnessed this phenomenon. *Lutins* were "little people" with wings resembling those of bats. Benoit then mentioned that he had seen a television show about flying saucers containing "little people" and while he laughed at the memory of this show, which he dismissed as ridiculous, he went on to say that such flying saucers and their occupants probably did indeed exist. I asked if he believed this and very gravely he answered:

EB: Oh, yes! Oh, yes! Oh, yes! Oh, yes! Yes, I believe that! Yes, I believe it. Well, so okay. I combed my horse, but my friend, I was there a while before I was able to untangle it! I had the, the, the comb, you know? With the big teeth? And I tried to—I untangled it. . . . You talk about a job! It wasn't naturally braided, you know! But it—it was braided! It was braided!

I then asked Benoit why the *lutins* would do such a thing, to which he replied that it was said that the *lutins* mounted the horses and rode them, although why they did this, he did not know. Finally, I asked him where they came from:

EB: Ah, I don't know! But I know they come from somewhere!
        Another planet or . . . somewhere.

Emile Benoit's account corresponds to the general description of the
nature of *lutins* outlined by Sébillot and Chiasson and offers several
additional details to the comments of my previous informants. However,
his personal attitude toward this tradition is quite unlike that of the
previous two informants. He believes the traditional notions concerning
lutins to be true and he uses this belief to support his interpretation of the
observed state of his horse's mane. However, it is noteworthy that his
belief is not simply the result of traditional enculturation, for he admits
not having believed in *lutins* until he had seen the evidence with his own
eyes. Only then did he apply to the witnessed phenomenon his knowledge
of traditional propositions and arrive at a conclusion as to the probable
cause and effect relationship.

A significant and fascinating aspect of this man's commentary is his
incorporation of elements of popular culture regarding flying saucers and
extraterrestrial beings into his discourse. While not professing to know the
origin or provenance of the *lutins* which he knows to exist, he suggests
quite clearly that there may exist an extraterrestrial connection. It is
evident that Benoit rejects the traditional supernatural explanation which
describes these creatures as spiritual or enchanted beings. Moreover, his
statement of rejection cannot be attributed to a hesitation to admit belief in
supernatural causality. Over a period of ten years, other researchers[20] and
I have documented Benoit's exceptionally strong acceptance of many
aspects of his tradition's magico-religious belief system and there would
be no reason for him to hide his belief in this instance. Rather, obviously
feeling his own traditional worldview did not offer adequate explanatory
information, Benoit constructed a possible alternate explanation based on
information appropriated from the channels of popular culture and media
and this personal merging of sources has resulted in Benoit's syncretic
recontextualization of the *lutin* tradition.

A little over a week later, on July 24, 1980, I again travelled to Kippens
to interview another elderly couple, John and Clara White,[21] and although
I did not realize it at the time, this was to be my last encounter with a
detailed description of the *lutin* tradition in French Newfoundland. When
I brought up the topic, John White immediately reacted with a mixture of
amusement and interest, visibly surprised by my mention of something he
hadn't heard spoken of in many years. He immediately oriented his
discourse towards the past, explaining in general terms how people used
to say that *lutins* were "little people" ("petit monde") who would braid
horses' manes, but adding that the exact nature of these fairies was never
clearly understood or explained. At this point, Clara White, who had been

listening with amusement, offered a specific example of an individual whose belief in this tradition had been very strong.

CW: There used to be [laughs]—There used to be a young girl who was in charge of the school in Kippens.
GB: Yes, yes.
CW: She didn't live here [in Kippens] but she didn't stay far from here. Oh, she believed . . . she, she had a strong belief in . . . in fairies!
GB: Yes?
CW: Oh! When she would go out in the evening, she always carried something in her pocket to give to the fairies! Some [unclear], or lettuce!

When I asked how long ago this had been, the Whites discussed it for a moment and agreed that it had been at least sixty years ago. This was the only example Clara White was able to recall, a fact that suggests that even sixty years ago, the fairy tradition was on the decline; still she added, this particular individual was convinced of the tradition's validity:

CW: Yes. Yes, she had a strong belief in fairies. [laughs]

When I asked whether people in general used to believe in *lutins,* John White again repeated his knowledge of the tradition. "Oh, yes! They used to believe they braided the horses' manes!" He then went on to narrate a story relating a particular example of this.

JW: There was one time—Now, I didn't see it personally, but I heard about the story, it's a story. [This fellow] apparently put a, a pail full of oats. He had some oats and he put them there so that the fairy would knock it over, you know? To take the—because they, they used to say that the fairies fed the horses. They'd feed the horses!
GB: Yes?
JW: Well, the ones they braided, well they'd feed them. So he put that on . . . so that the fairy would knock it over and when the fairy went to—because if he knocked it over, well he was forced to pick it up! All the oats! And the man, the man ate his dinner. And [the fairy] hadn't finished picking up the oats when the man arrived. So, now that's a story that I heard.
GB: Yes, yes.
JW: That wasn't true, though!

John White never discovered what the supposed fate of the *lutin* was, saying with some amusement that he didn't know "whether the man ate him or what!"

White's narrative also introduces some new details concerning the *lutin* tradition which Sébillot noted in Auvergne:

Les paysans emploient, pour les chasser, sans compter l'eau bénite et les talismans catholiques, des procédés variés. Le plus habituel consiste à placer, dans un recipeint en équilibre, des pois, du millet ou de la cendre: le lutin, en arrivant à l'étourdie, le heurte et le renverse, et comme il est obligé de remasser une à une ces innombrables graines, il est si ennuyé de cette besogne qu'il ne se risque plus à revenir.[22]

[To drive off *lutins*, country people used, in addition to holy water and Catholic talismans, a variety of methods. The most common consisted of placing in a balanced vessel, some peas, grain, or ashes: the *lutin* ... would tip the vessel over and as he is obliged to pick up the many grains one grain at a time, he becomes so annoyed that he is likely never to return.]

Auvergne is located in western France, a region which was the original source area of a large part of the North American Acadian population. This would help to explain the presence of this detail in the predominantly Acadian settlement of Kippens.[23]

Like Emile Benoit, the Whites made use of narrative to make a statement about the belief tradition in general and their own belief in particular. However, where Benoit used personal experience narrative to support his belief, they used narrative examples to provide a background for the expression of their personal disbelief in this tradition. Each presented a story relating the belief of other individuals and the way in which this belief subsequently influenced the way these people behaved. In effect, these stories provide a body of referential content which the Whites use as a backdrop against which to contrast their own negative attitudes, rather than to support the validity of the tradition. This is particularly true in the case of John White's narrative, the text of which, if taken in isolation, might be seen as an affirmation of belief. It is only when placed in the discourse and interactional situation as a whole that the text is transformed by context and its actual communicative function becomes clear. Such functional transformation and flexibility is the essential feature which differentiates narrative as text from narrative as pragmatic discourse and clearly demonstrates the superior interpretive power of this latter perspective.

The Nature of Belief

There exists a considerable body of literature dealing with the subject of traditional belief and its relationship to oral expression. However, most work makes use of the perspective on belief outlined by folklorist Ray B. Browne in the mid-1950s.[24] In the course of his research on the relationship between items of belief and individual reactions to them,

Browne identified three categories of attitude. First there are those who unconditionally accept the truth of a traditional belief. Then, there are those individuals for whom "[rationally] the old ideas are thought nonsense, but [who] emotionally . . . are not ready to abandon them completely." Still others find the beliefs humorous and quite incredible and treat them as sources of amusement.[25] To these, Goldstein later added a fourth category which applied to those community members who totally reject a certain supernatural belief and consequently dissociate themselves from it, at times going so far as to deny any knowledge of the traditional ideas.[26]

While they serve to provide a general overview, it is obvious that the process of attitude formation regarding supernatural belief traditums is much more complex than that suggested by these four stances. For although they identify the general range of possible individual attitudes (i.e., total acceptance, uncertainty, total rejection, total dissociation), they do so only within a restricted framework defining belief tradition as moving linearly from a correspondence of knowledge and belief to a state of opposition between knowledge and belief. And while Goldstein's category introduces a consideration of the effects knowledge-belief discordance exert at the level of communication (in this case, the result is non-communication), it is merely an extension of Browne's continuum and suggests the logical consequence of the decontextualization of tradition. By positing the possible co-temporal presence of all four attitudes within the same community culture, this research correctly dispels the outdated notion of the homogeneous tradition, which suggested uniformity in diachronic and synchronic states of belief acceptance and attitude evolution. However, the premise underlying all these considerations of belief is that natural cultural evolution moves from full acceptance to total rejection and ultimate dissociation, a sequence which suggests a logical final phase where the knowledge of the tradition ceases to be transmitted in any form whatsoever and passes out of the culture entirely.

I have no quarrel with the general applicability of this devolutionary perspective; no doubt it accurately reflects the route followed in the demise of belief traditions in many cultures. But it fails to consider that along the way, certain individuals may actually appropriate a moribund belief traditum and revive it within a personal cognitive framework. Such was the case with Emile Benoit, who moved from a state of total rejection of the *lutin* as defined by his tradition to an acceptance of this traditum within a new interpretive context. Similarly, the Simons do not believe in *lutins*, not because of a change in their attitude from acceptance to rejection of the tradition, but because of the division of their worldview into synchronic and diachronic folk models, each of which they accept as correct. Joseph Bozec is representative of the category of individual who sees the old traditions as sources of amusement, but even he has found a metaphorical, pragmatic way to use traditional ideas for the communication of quite non-traditional information. Of the four cases examined, only the Whites seem to correspond exactly to one of the phases outlined by Browne and Goldstein. This is not intended as a criticism of categories essentially designed to define variation in belief acceptance, but rather to suggest the equal importance of considering *how* people believe, including not only the nature of their attitude, but also the process by which it is developed and the radiants of meaning which become associated with—or detached from—the ideational complex itself.

The Relation of the Part to the Whole

A study such as this which highlights a single aspect of traditional belief can unintentionally give the impression that this aspect is more prominent in a culture than is actually the case. Within the larger complex of supernatural belief traditums, the *lutin* is, at best, a very minor component. For example, of the one hundred and forty narratives containing supernatural elements which I collected in L'Anse-à-Canards alone, only two dealt with the *lutin*, making it by far the least frequently occurring of the eleven supernatural belief categories comprising the total corpus.[27] Moreover, the *lutin* tradition is the only domain of supernatural belief I have never heard mentioned in naturally occurring discourse and I have never encountered it unelicited in the course of an informal interview. The youngest individual who professed general knowledge of the tradition was over fifty years of age and all informants who could actually provide details concerning the *lutin* were over the age of sixty. No French speaker under thirty had ever heard the word.

A body of cultural lore which seems to have derived originally from the French fairy tradition continues to exist, but in the Newfoundland context, has lost the supernatural connection. This is the tradition of the *feu follet*, or "Jack the Lantern," mysterious balls of light, or "fire," with which most of my informants, old and young alike, are familiar. Sébillot and Jolicoeur mention the *feu follet* as being a flame carried at night by the *lutin*, who uses it to confuse unwary travellers and lead them astray.[28] And Devlin observes that in Berry, France, the *follet* was "supposed to take horses galloping in the pasture-lands at night and to knot the animals' manes to make stirrups so that the little elves could ride them,"[29] a description remarkably similar to the accounts of the *lutin* noted earlier in this study. No general consensus exists among French-Newfoundlanders concerning the origin of these *feux follets*. Most regard it as a purely natural, albeit unexplained phenomenon, although some claim that those who follow the light risk being deliberately lead into a hazardous situation, such as onto thin ice or near the edge of the cliffs which in some areas overlook the ocean. However, on no occasion did my informants draw an association between the *follet* and the *lutin*-fairy tradition.[30] There is little doubt but that the *lutin* tradition is in the final stages of disappearing entirely from French Newfoundland culture. Nevertheless, even the study of such moribund traditions can offer substantial insight into the dynamics of cultural evolution by illuminating the ways in which individuals react to and accommodate such cultural change, each eventually incorporating it into her or his unique construction of shared worldview. As folklorist Henry Glassie points out, culture "is not owned equally. Some have thought harder than others and have sought wisdom with more energy . . . [and some] have developed richer modes of expression."[31] Knowledge, belief, and discourse are the central foci in this complex process of cultural creation and maintenance.

Notes

1. Recorded 23/06/80; Memorial University of Newfoundland Folklore and Language Archive (MUNFLA) accession number 80-144; tape F3489c/C4827; personal designation B10 (Butler 10). All interviews were initially recorded in French; the English translations are my own.
2. Charles de la Morandière, *Histoire de la pêche française de la morue dans l'Amérique septentrionale* (Paris: Maisonneuve et Larose, 1966). For details on early settlement patterns see John J. Mannion, "Settlers and Traders in Western Newfoundland," in John J. Mannion, ed., *The Peopling of Newfoundland: Essays in Historical Geography*, Social and Economic Papers No. 8 (Toronto: U of Toronto P, 1977) 234–75.
3. *Newfoundland House of Assembly Journal* (1857): 247.
4. The so-called "French Shore" or "Treaty Shore" was that area of the west coast of Newfoundland where France had been granted, first by the Treaty of Utrecht (1713) and later by the Definitive Treaty of Versailles (1783), exclusive rights to conduct large-scale fishing operations. The French government eventually relinquished these rights in 1904.
5. The prospect of a lengthy period of compulsory military service awaiting them upon the completion of their contract of work in the fishery was a deciding factor in the desertion of many of these French workers.
6. Recorded 23/06/80; MUNFLA 80-144; F3489c/C4827.
7. Gillian Brown and George Yule, *Discourse Analysis* (Cambridge: Cambridge UP, 1983) 27.
8. Brown and Yule 28.
9. R. Stalnaker, "Assertion," *Syntax and Semantics 9: Pragmatics*, ed. P. Cole (New York: Academic P, 1978) 315.
10. See Alan Dundes, "Folk Ideas as Units of World View," in Américo Paredes and Richard Bauman, eds., *Toward New Perspectives in Folklore* (Austin: U of

Texas P, 1972) 93–103. This same notion is treated in Barre Toelken, *The Dynamics of Folklore* (Boston: Houghton Mifflin, 1979).

11.   Based on the syntactic model of performance and grammatical competence developed by Noam Chomsky, "communicative competence" is defined as not only the "rules for communication . . . and shared rules for interaction, but also the cultural rules and knowledge that are the basis for the context and content of communicative events and interaction processes." See Muriel Saville-Troike, *The Ethnography of Communication* (Oxford: Basil Blackwood, 1982) 3.

12.   See for example, John Austin, *How To Do Things With Words* (Oxford: Oxford UP, 1962).

13.   Paul Sébillot, *Le Folklore de France*, 5 vols. (Paris: Maisonneuve et Larose, 1968) 3: 116. The translations of French citations from this and other works in this study are my own.

14.   Richard M. Dorson, *Bloodstoppers and Bearwalkers: Folk Traditions of the Upper Peninsula* (Cambridge: Harvard UP, 1952) 78–9.

15.   Père Ansèlme Chiasson, *Chéticamp: histoire et traditions acadiennes* (Moncton: Editions des Aboiteux, 1962) 263–4.

16.   H.P. Grice, "Logic and Conversation," *Syntax and Semantics 3: Speech Acts*, ed. P. Cole and J. Morgan (New York: Academic P, 1975) 41–58.

17.   Recorded 09/07/80: MUNFLA 80–144: F3497c/C4835c: B18.

18.   A "traditum" is defined by Shils as "anything which is transmitted or handed down by the past to the present. . . . The conception of tradition as here understood is here silent about whether there is acceptable evidence for the truth of the tradition or whether the tradition is accepted without its validity being established . . ." Edward Shils, *Tradition* (Chicago: U of Chicago P, 1981) 12.

19.   Recorded 16/07/80; MUNFLA 80–144; F3506c/C4844c; B27.

20.   In particular, Thomas' monograph on storytelling in French Newfoundland culture devotes two complete chapters to Emile Benoit. See Gerald Thomas, *Les deux traditions: le conte populaire chez les Franco-terreneuviens* (Montréal: Bellarmin, 1983).

21.   Recorded 24/07/80; MUNFLA 80–144; F3509c/C4847c; B30.

22.   Sébillot 1:141.

23.   This particular element is not restricted to Acadia. For French Ontario, see Germain Lemieux, *Les jongleurs de Billochet: conteurs et contes franco-terreneuviens* (Montreal: Bellarmin, 1972) 119. J.C. Dupont describes similar methods where grain and ashes are used to trick the *lutin*. See J.C. Dupont, *Héritage de la francophonie canadienne: traditions orales* (Québec: Presses de l'Université Laval, 1986) 128–9.

24.   Ray B. Browne, *Popular Beliefs and Practices from Alabama* (Berkeley: U of California P, 1958).

25.   Browne 4–5.

26.   Kenneth S. Goldstein, "The Collecting of Superstitious Beliefs," *Keystone Folklore Quarterly 9* (1964): 13–22.

27.   The total distribution was as follows: Revenants (32); Devil (18); Death Tokens (18); Witch Figure (18); Magic (17); Marionnettes/Spirits (10); Seventh Sons (9); Signs (7); Forerunner (5); Healing Priests (4); *Lutins* (2).

28.   Sébillot 2: 89. For Acadia, see Catherine Jolicoeur, *Les plus belles légendes acadiennes* (Montréal: Stanké, 1981) 31.

29.   Judith Devlin, *The Superstitious Mind: French Peasants and the Supernatural in the Nineteenth Century* (New Haven: Yale UP, 1987) 84.

30. A final traditum bears mentioning here, and this deals with the *Marionnettes,* a term applied to the Aurora Borealis, or Northern Lights. According to my informants, a number of supernatural explanations were applied by past generations of French Newfoundlanders to explain this spectacular phenomenon. The most commonly held notion suggested that the lights were the souls of infants and children who had died without having been baptized, a belief which is often used to explain the origin of fairies in European tradition.

31. Henry Glassie, *Passing the Time in Ballymenone: Culture and History of an Ulster Community* (Philadelphia: U of Pennsylvania P, 1982) 644.

Fairylore from the Midlands of Ireland

Patricia Lysaght

In his well-known monograph *The Gaelic Storyteller* (1945), James Hamilton Delargy[1] vividly describes storytellers of *Gaeltacht* or Irish-speaking[2] areas of the countryside he knew and had collected from in the early decades of the present century, and other storytellers from whom the fieldworkers of the Irish Folklore Commission were still garnering rich harvests of oral narrative tradition. For the collectors of folklore at the time, the teller of the long, elaborate and demanding tales (international and national *Märchen*, hero tales and Fenian lore) was still the storyteller par excellence, a *scéalaí* and successor of the medieval *scélaige*. Delargy's descriptions of those storytellers, many of whom possessed repertoires remarkable by any standards in terms of size and variety, shows that they were usually men of advanced years, native Gaelic speakers, whose art had become largely irrelevant in a changing society less appreciative of and sympathetic to the storyteller and his tales.[3] In Delargy's experience women storytellers who could tell the long tales were in general less numerous than men,[4] and in this connection he mentions in particular Peig Sayers, the noted Gaelic-speaking storyteller, who spent most of her life on the Great Blasket Island off the west Kerry coast. In addition to *Märchen* and also, exceptionally, some Fenian tales,[5] she possessed a great store of other traditional genres such as folk songs, prayers, and a large body of socio-historical material.[6]

As well as the oral literature specialists, there existed also in any given community tradition-bearers, far more numerous in number, who told short tales, family sagas or genealogies, social and historical tradition, prayers and songs, as well as short realistic stories dealing with fairies, ghosts and other supernatural beings.[7] These traditional genres were usually associated more with women than with men,[8] a distinction found also in other societies,[9] and according to Delargy, the women excelled the men in those branches of tradition.[10] The tradition-bearer I am concerned with in this essay belongs to this latter category of narrator in terms of her repertoire content, but she differs in most other respects from the tradition-bearers of the earlier decades described by Delargy and on whom the collection efforts of the Irish Folklore Commission were primarily focused.[11]

Plate 1. Mrs. Jenny McGlynn, Co. Laois, Ireland. (Patricia Lysaght)

Mrs. Jenny McGlynn, a fifty-year-old housewife from Mountmellick,[12] County Laois, is the product of an English-language environment in terms of domicile and cultural milieu (see Plate 1). By the middle of the nineteenth century the county was virtually anglicized. Only one percent of the population were still native Gaelic speakers and these were mainly old people living in the southern end of the county.[13] Although she learned the Irish language in primary school, which she attended until the age of fourteen, Jenny's vernacular language is English. The stories and traditions which she heard and learned were narrated in English and she narrates them in that language.

Jenny was born in 1939 into a working-class family living in a laborer's cottage in Manor Lane, affectionately known as "the Lane," an area at the southwestern edge of the town. She has never left her home area for any significant period of time and prior to her marriage she had lived virtually all of the time in the family home.

Certain aspects of her local environment were of fundamental importance for Jenny's later emergence as an active bearer of tradition. Circumstances in her home milieu contributed to a climate in which beliefs and narratives were transmitted and the affairs of the time, both family and local, social and economic, were broached and discussed. The fact that her home was number six in a row of ten cottages meant that the neighbors on either side—many of them related—visited. Her home was in fact a "rambling"[14] house, a house where the neighbors felt welcome to come and while away the evenings and nights and according to Jenny, "they all had their stories." On New Year's Eve 1983 Jenny described to me how the neighbors used to gather in her old home in the Lane, when she was growing up in the 1940s and 50s, to welcome in the New Year:

> Our house was the middle house in the Lane. There was ten cottages and everyone rambled to our house. And we'd have the dance and a singsong and tell stories. We'd bring in the New Year! It would end up about two o'clock in the morning. That would go on every year as long as the old crowd was around.[15]

Thus Jenny learned many of her narratives in her own home from her parents and neighbors. She recalled how on rainy days her mother told them stories and how she sat enthralled by the fire in wintertime listening to ghost stories.

> I used to love the ghost stories and especially on the winter nights! It would be grand! We'd all be sitting around the fire and the embers burning—we'd be sitting close to the hearth and listening to them all going on . . . [16]

It is also significant that during the formative years of her repertoire, Jenny's family lived with her maternal grandmother and Jenny attributes some of her traditions to her. It was from her grandmother that Jenny learned a version of the well-known Irish treasure guardian legend about the Leipreachán's pot of gold.[17]

> My granny used to tell the story that if you caught a leipreachán or fairy you'd have to ask them for their wealth. Anyhow, they usually had a crock of gold and it was buried under a *buachalán* [ragwort]. And there was a lot of *buachaláns*, but this one was the biggest in the field. And the man dug it up and saw that it was the fairy gold. He tied a piece of his red handkerchief around the *buachalán* and went home for to get a spade for to dig down deeper to see if there was any more of them there. . . . And when he came back with the spade every *buachalán* in the field was tied up with a red string.[18]

In her home Jenny was hearing the stories, learning and memorizing them and also repeating them. This she often did for the younger children while playing games like "House" in which she, as the "Mammy," told the stories she had heard in her own kitchen the night before to the children to put them to sleep.[19]

In 1961, at the age of twenty-two years, Jenny married into a working-class family and crossed the town to live with her family-in-law[20] in their cottage on the Bay Road, an area also on the edge of the town, this time at its southeastern end. To Jenny, this house known as "the Bay" was in the country, it being just beyond the town lighting limits (see Plate 2).

The Bay was also a rambling house of some repute where "all the chaps used to ramble in and bring their friends with them." Jenny further described it in the following terms:

> It was a kind of rambling house and everyone rambled in. You see we had no television or anything like that, so there was no distraction. . . . And it was a place to go for a chat and a laugh and a cup of tea to break the monotony of the night . . . [21]

It was at this stage—as late as the 1960s—that Jenny became an active bearer of tradition and performed for seasoned adult audiences. She described occasions in the Bay at that time when fifty or more people sat around the kitchen at night while she and her husband Tom sat at either side of the fire, neither being necessarily a master of ceremonies, though Tom might start the sessions off depending on the circumstances on the particular occasion.[22] The ensuing session, as Jenny described it, was usually one of participation and interaction between teller and audience, where no one narrator dominated the floor, but each person present was welcome to contribute.

Plate 2. "The Bay," the cottage in which Jenny lived for many years after her marriage in 1961. (Patricia Lysaght)

Very often Jenny was the only female present at these sessions[23] since her elderly mother-in-law usually retired to bed on the night of a large session as "she was not able for a crowd at that stage." On these occasions Jenny was not the tea-maker, but rather an interested member of the group or a narrator who was considered an equal by the predominantly male audience. She was also called upon to contribute her story and she would do so if the theme being discussed was suitable. Her preferred genre was and is supernatural lore in all its variety and complexity, especially ghost lore, and in this area she was regarded as an expert. At sessions with a large attendance she usually told only one story so as to allow the others present the opportunity to participate.[24]

She also learned many narratives on these occasions. She heard many of her stories about the devil and nocturnal evil spirits and phenomena from the men who rambled in the Bay who were often out late at night. Also from these men she learned some of her fairylore concentrated on the landscape.[25] Thinking back on those occasions, she gleefully remembered that by the following morning she often had her own version of a story heard the night before, provided it was about ghosts or fairies, because, as she said, she would have such an interest in that type of story that she would "take them in." She might repeat the story two nights later, perhaps at a session and have it sanctioned by the person she heard narrating it in the first place!

Some of Jenny's traditions of the supernatural arose out of her own experiences. This is particularly so in relation to the banshee. She has many memorates or personal experience stories about the supernatural death-messenger.[26] Others relate to the fairies. Thus Jenny's store of supernatural lore is, on her own assessment, based partly on her own personal experiences. Some of it is also inherited from her family. Her narratives are "kind of family stories coming down from Granny to mother to daughter," partly consisting of stories she "heard and registered" from others which she then put in "her own words."[27]

The fairylore component of her repertoire is the focus of this presentation.

Aims and Method of Study

Although I have collected from Jenny McGlynn on a fairly regular basis since the summer of 1976, I have not specifically collected just fairylore from her on any occasion.[28] It is thus possible that her knowledge of this genre is greater than indicated by what I have collected from her to date. I visited Jenny initially in connection with my study of banshee traditions,[29] but even during our very first recording session, tales of the fairies and of the ghost world naturally followed on the heels of the banshee. In the intervening years I also collected much valuable socio-economic and socio-historical information including details of her own life history. However, since ghost lore is Jenny's favorite genre, it came up for discussion on most occasions and fairylore then invariably followed. This means that some of the fairy legends have been collected more than once and in terms of style and structure there is a high degree of consistency among the various tellings; there is also a remarkable consistency in ideas about some of the fairy phenomena she describes. This is especially so, as we shall see, in relation to the fairies' aversion to blood.

On re-reading the transcripts of my interviews with her over the years I was increasingly struck by the extent to which they revealed Jenny's attitude to the supernatural. It became more and more obvious to me that she reacted critically to phenomena and experiences described as being supernatural and that her attitude supports Lauri Honko's assertion that tradition-bearers adopt a much more critical attitude towards supernatural experiences than they are usually credited with.[30] For Jenny, stories of supernatural phenomena such as the Pooka (*Púca*)[31] were only myths told to frighten children in order to get them in out of the dark and to keep them away from dangerous places. She also feels that the traditionally recognized supernatural light phenomenon, known in her area as "Jackie-the-Lantern,"—if indeed such phenomenon ever really existed—was used by adults as a culturally acceptable explanation, or even excuse, for their having gone astray at night in circumstances and for reasons not in the least supernatural.[32]

There are, however, certain aspects of the supernatural which she believes implicitly. These include the supernatural being known as the banshee,[33] because she is convinced she has experienced both aural and visual manifestations of this death-messenger. She also believes that the dead "can and do, return." The basis for her belief here is the biblical passage referring to the tombs opening and the dead issuing forth at the moment of Christ's death on the cross,[34] as well as her own experiences and those of family members. (As we shall see, there are also aspects of fairylore which she believes implicitly.) In general terms, therefore, it is correct to assert that she tends to give full credence only to those experiences that she or people she knows and trusts have undergone. For example, her reply to my query about phantom funerals was, "I didn't hear it for genuine, I just heard it being spoken of, but I never heard anyone who witnessed it."[35] Even with those she knows, she can still be skeptical and will take many factors into account since she feels some people are such "wonder makers," they can actually make themselves believe they have experienced something supernatural.

In view of Jenny's attitudes to certain supernatural beings and phenomena, I was curious to know if she applied the same critical standards to fairylore in particular. Although the indications in the material already recorded were that she did, I decided to interview her specifically about her attitudes to the fairy faith, in order to clarify the position. Since some observers have had the impression that belief in supernatural beings is on the wane[36] and others have had the idea that rural people were and are in the grip of foolish "superstition," I was anxious to know to what extent this female tradition-bearer from a rural town in the Midlands of Ireland believed in the various reflexes of the fairy faith. In relation to fairy legends, I also wished to discover if personal belief on her part and on the part of the audience was a necessary prerequisite for communication of the legend. These two problems are interrelated and will be discussed together in the following pages.

Although the material I had already recorded from her contained some pointers in these regards, the texts and in some cases, the additional elucidating comments by Jenny were not sufficient to allow me properly to discern the existence of belief, or disbelief, let alone ambivalence or fluctuations in belief on her part, or to judge the belief criterion in terms of legend transmission. I accordingly arranged to visit Jenny at her home in Mountmellick on the eighteenth of August 1989; and since my aim was to find answers to these questions rather than collect further material, my interview was based on the fairylore I had already recorded.[37] It was evening, she was very relaxed and she was interested in talking to me about her attitudes to the various beliefs and legends. As the interview drew to a close and over a parting cup of tea, she commented several times on how much she had enjoyed the discussion.

In order to discover Jenny's attitudes to the fairy faith and from that to discern the status which she, as a legend teller, accords the belief component in terms of her communicating the legend, we must now analyze the main themes of Jenny's fairy tradition. To exemplify these themes and also to elucidate the discussion, liberal quotation from the primary interview material will be presented.

Fairylore and the Belief Component

Jenny's accounts of the fairies include the following themes: locations of the fairy world, fairy origin and hope of salvation; social organization of the fairy world; fairy physique and dress; fairy aversions; interaction between the human world and the fairy world.

All these are themes commonly met with in Irish fairylore in general and are also part of the fairy faith complex of other Celtic countries, as W.Y. Evans-Wentz has so ably pointed out.[38] All are of importance in terms of revealing Jenny's attitudes to the fairy tradition, but of pivotal significance in Jenny's case is the *location* of the fairy world, that is, the identification of a feature of the human landscape as a physical

manifestation of the fairy realm. Jenny's professed belief in the existence of
the fairy world and of the interpenetration of the human and fairy worlds
is centered around the existence in her immediate neighborhood of a rath
or mound, traditionally considered a dwelling place of the fairy race,
about which are told legends of revenge arising from interference with it.
It is probably fair to say that this particular landscape feature is a *sine qua
non* for Jenny's fairy beliefs. Its existence and status are also in harmony
with, and are probably an expression of Jenny's still firmly held belief in
the existence of places which have "something" about them that "sets
them apart." To Jenny these are sacred places and should be treated with
respect.

The rath which so impinges upon Jenny's worldview and is of such
mnemonic significance for her is called the "Rusheen," and she describes it
as "a bit of a hill with a rath on top of it, covered with bushes." The status
of the Rusheen as a "gentle" place was well-known to the locals, to her
father and father-in-law and to those who rambled in the Bay. It is
exemplified by legends detailing the harmful results of human
interference with it.[39] One such legend, which is known elsewhere in the
folklore of Laois,[40] is the following:

> It [the Rusheen] is supposed to be a place for the fairies. And this man
> had cattle that used go in around it to graze and he took a brang [branch]
> off one of the trees for to *hois*[41] the cows ahead of him and when he was
> going through the gate with his cattle a little man handed him one of the
> cattle's tails and said: "There's a lash for your whip." And one of the
> cow's tails was cut off. You know, if you do harm on them, or their
> property, they will do harm on you. I mean, that was a big loss to that
> man, the tail gone off his cow on the way home to be milked.[42]

Another legend Jenny tells concerns the loss of a limb as a result of
interfering with the Rusheen.

> There was a man, now, sent out—he didn't know it was a rath—and he
> was sent out to clean up. And he went and he cut old thorny bushes out
> of the way for to make room to till. And he got a splinter in his hand.
> And the hand decayed; he had to have the hand taken away. And it was
> the one he had hit the thorny bush with. He heard it was a rath and he
> wouldn't let anybody else go near it.[43]

Both these legends confirm the *sacred* nature of the Rusheen since
Jenny considers both to be objectively true. Of the first she said, "Well, the
man was still there when I was living down 'the Bay.' He is dead now, the
Lord have mercy on him! But it was himself who told the story. . . ."

She is equally convinced of the truth of the second one. When I asked
if she thought this incident really happened she replied most
emphatically, "Well, he's dead since. He was at the rath; he did get a

splinter; he did lose the power of his hand and he had to have it taken away!"

Jenny's acceptance of the truth of the contents of these legends has no doubt been facilitated by her conviction, arising out of an incident in her own life, that the Rusheen was certainly a place that should not be interfered with in any way, even with the permission of the landowner on whose farm it stood. She makes an emotional association[44] between a streak of bad luck and the eerie reputation of the Rusheen.

> I feel there is something, something there, because Tom got a firing—the people that owned the Rusheen told Tom to get a fire out of it—and he went in and got the firing. And from the day he got it until the last stick was burned we were in want and hardship. And I believe it happened because of that place.[45]

Both of these legends, and Jenny's interpretation of her own experience, confirm the traditional recognition of places on the landscape associated with the fairy race as liminal places. It is also implied that ownership of these places rested not with the human landowners, but that it was vested in some way, depending on their social organization, on the fairy inhabitants whose power structure was often a reflection of earlier stages of the human social organization of the country. The ambivalent status of these places guaranteed their survival to a large degree[46] and may be compared with the immunity conferred on modern day diplomatic missions in foreign countries by virtue of their recognized special status.

It is clear from many references by Jenny that the Rusheen is considered to be inhabited. Although she referred to the residents as "the fairies" and told that they were heard to play music as well as engage in revenge activities, actions typical enough of the fairy race, yet she was unsure about their origin. Even though she knew and had told me on more than one occasion the explanation of the origin of the fairies found generally in Irish tradition, that is, that they are the bad angels cast out of Heaven by God during the war with Lucifer, yet, she was hesitant to extend this explanation to the inhabitants of the Rusheen. According to Jenny "that is the origin of the fairies if you believe the old folk." This implied that she herself does not so believe. Her suggestion that the Rusheen may have been an old burial ground is a suggestion which may in fact contain more than a grain of truth since the Gaelic word *ros*, of which Rusheen may well be a diminutive form, is often applied to an old burial ground as well as to a growth of small bushy trees or underwood,[47] a description most appropriate to the Rusheen. In her view, the fairies are the ancient dead who live on in the mounds and hills.[48]

A further mingling of beliefs about the dead and the fairies, characteristic of Irish tradition in general,[49] was evident in Jenny's inability to ascribe with certainty a personal experience, which involved the actualization of the belief[50] that to leave the house untidy at night invites the intervention of the fairies or the dead. It was the norm (and also evidence of good housekeeping) to leave the kitchen tidy and warm and to have fresh water available. The accompanying memorate describes the sanction which resulted from a breach of that norm.

> Well, I was always made to do that down here in the Bay from the time I married in. I was never to leave anything on the table but a cup of water and the kettle left on the hook; the house had to be left spotless. One night I was just too tired after a day's work and I didn't wash up after the supper. I said I would just leave it in the basin until morning and I thought every cup that was in the basin was going to be broken with the racket that went on in the house that night. I've never left the house dirty at night since.[51]

Initially Jenny was inclined to believe her mother-in-law and ascribe this incident to the fairies, but on later reflection she feels it might well be attributed to the dead. Jenny's dilemma is understandable because in Irish tradition both the fairies and the dead are believed to visit houses at night and both liked to find a clean warm kitchen with a supply of fresh water on their arrival.

Jenny is also ambivalent in her attitudes to traditional ideas about the social organization, physique, dress and pastimes of the fairy race.[52] The reason is because she "has never seen the fairies." Despite her ambivalence, however, she was quite prepared to tell me or anybody else her version of the traditional descriptions of the inhabitants of the fairy world and their way of life: the fairies are social beings living within raths and mounds and are ruled over by a King and Queen. They each have their own trade and their food consists mainly of fruit and vegetables, milk and honey, but "they don't eat meat because, of course, blood is associated with meat." They are small in stature, about the height of a two- or three-year-old child, but "old featured." Perhaps in order to indicate that fairies are not too different in physique from humans and thus not always recognizable, the common perception of the fairies in Irish tradition, she adds, "but there are small people too in the human world." Her description of their clothes as fancy colored, red and green, with shiny buttons and leaf-shaped shoes, is literary in origin, and is probably influenced from children's books. This probability is strengthened by Jenny's reference to an "owl's feather" as part of the garb of the fairies, since this is a feature mentioned in a very popular poem about the fairies still found in children's school books. "The Fairies," by William Allingham,[53] describes fairies' dress as green jacket, red cap, and white owl's feather. The Irish fairies are known to be very keen sportsmen and Jenny tells a legend about a human playing football with them at night.

... it was a man by the name of Con. I don't know what his surname was, but Con was his Christian name. He was celebrating with me Daddy on the birth of his child, his first child. And Daddy went on home and this man had to go on a few miles further to go to his place. And he was all the time about football and hurling, all the games you could think of, he was all the time talking about them. And he looked in over a fence and there was, as he thought, a team of boys kicking football. He got interested in it and he got in over the fence and started to watch them playing. He was shouting at them what to do. And one of them said "Tip the ball to Con" and he did. He took the ball and he started to play with them. And he came to his senses at the far side of Tullamore after being playing all night long right across the country! That's fifteen miles as the crow flies![54]

The human involvement here is not, however, as a helper whose assistance is needed to secure victory for one side or the other, a favorite motif in Irish, both in early literature and in modern folklore.[55] Rather, he is just being led astray. Jenny's remark in this particular legend that the man was "celebrating the birth of his first child" hints that he might have gone astray on his way home from the public house for a more mundane reason than playing football with the fairies.

Linked to the question of the origin of the fairies is their final fate on the Day of Judgment. In Irish tradition their fate is inextricably linked to their origin; as the fallen angels there is no hope of salvation for them.[56] Although Jenny is ambivalent about their origin, she knows and tells a legend common in Ireland which confirms the hopelessness of the fairy people's continuing expectations of readmittance to Heaven.

The story went that a fairy met a priest and his assistant; it was during the time of the hedge-Masses. And he was a little small man and he says he'd like to know if he could get to Heaven, himself, the fairy. So the priest asked him if he had a penknife. And he [the priest] gave him a penknife and he says, "Now," he says, "I want you to take the penknife and cut your finger." And the fairy cut his finger, but no blood came and the priest says, "No, there's no redemption for you, because you are not a human being, you're a spirit." And the fairy went screaming across the fields and there were no more fairies in that area after that.[57]

A marked feature of Jenny's attitude to her narratives is that she seeks to understand and tends to declare, their meanings. This tendency is quite obvious in the legend just quoted; she understands that the fairies' basic deficiency, according to the legend, is their lack of a human nature— exemplified by their want of blood—and that consequently they cannot achieve the salvation in store for human beings. Jenny's realization that the central point of the legend is the fairies' lack of a human nature, is further emphasized in her telling of another version of the same legend which actually revolves around this issue and leaves the question of redemption in abeyance. She states that the little people were put to the test one time to find out if they were human.

> They tried to make out that they were equal to the human race and they were tormenting an old man and telling him that they were as good as he was, that they could do anything he could do and even more so. And he said, "Ye couldn't because ye haven't got blood in ye'r veins. . . ."[58]

Jenny has also taken the interpretations a step further and states that the fairies' ultimate problem is that, unlike human beings, they cannot die to achieve redemption. Fairies, according to Jenny, "have no death, fairies don't die."

The motif of the fairies' lack of blood has been further developed by Jenny. Around it she has built a theory about the fairies' aversion to the color red. She maintains, very consistently, that the fairies' hatred of the color and their desire to avoid it is because it reminds them of their own bloodless state and their hopeless quest for reinstatement in Heaven. Not only will the fairies avoid anything which is red in color, such as red cloth, red fire, meat, even the red comb of the farmyard cock, but they will also avoid sharp, pointed objects such as knives, pins, needles and the thorns of the fairy thorn tree, which might prick them, remind them of their lack of blood and "make them hysterical." Red has, therefore, apotropaic qualities which can be used by humans for protective purposes against fairy invasions of domestic human space and abduction.

The theme of fairy abduction has several reflexes in Irish tradition.[59] Jenny mentions two; the abduction of young children in whose places changelings are left and which are usually, but not invariably, banished; and the attempted abduction of a bride. Both of these beliefs have found expression in legends. Jenny has told me the Changeling Legend several times. Here is a version I recorded in July 1981.

> A child was about a year old and it was taken and there was a changeling put in its place, a terrible cross child left in its place. It was crying. . . . was getting no bigger and at night they used to hear music in the room. And the mother and father were wore out walking the rooms with the child, crying, crying, crying. And it used to cry while the mother was there, but when the mother would go it would be real quiet and the music would be coming from the room.
>   It went on for twelve years and some relative said it must have been a changeling. And they asked the mother to go . . . and they rescued their own child back.
>   So this man seemingly knew about the way to do it; he got the man of the house to redden the fire iron, to have it very red . . . and to sharpen a pointed knife or a skewer or something like that, very, very sharp and to start cursing. And there was some terrible curses had to be said! And

the woman [mother] went out and they got around the cot and they began to put the iron towards the child. The child never grew you see; it was a twelve year old in the shape of an infant. And they were cursing and they were prodding at the child—they didn't actually prod the child—and holding the iron. And there was an awful scream and there was a beautiful girl left back in two minutes. When the curses were all finished the girl was left back. They had changed her back again, got her back.[60]

As with most of her other narratives, Jenny's personality shines through in this well-developed *fabulate*[61] or migratory legend. In addition to the significant motifs normally found in versions of this legend in Ireland, it also contains some very human details springing no doubt from Jenny's own experiences as a mother of three children; walking the room at night with a crying child is the experience and nightmare of most parents! Details such as these create empathy between narrator and audience and contribute to Jenny's status as a convincing narrator who enjoys performing and captivating her listeners.[62]

Jenny's very persuasiveness as a narrator when telling legends such as these added fire to the already smouldering question in my mind—did she actually believe that human children were exchanged for fairies? The indications were that she did not believe; however, I decided on my last visit to discuss the question with her. When I asked if she thought little children were exchanged, she replied, "I don't think so; I think that was a myth. . . ." Then I asked her why she thought people told that story about children being taken away by the fairies.

It is possible that the child was a contrary baby. It was alright for the first few weeks. Babies do change and it could have been an unwell baby. It wasn't getting the right food or something. And the child that is not getting the right food does naturally be contrary and cross. And in those days they hadn't got the same technology as they have now. So I think that's what the thing was and when they got the children on the right food . . . they just got back to normal again, you know![63]

Thus, the changeling belief could have arisen to account for the sudden or unexpected return to normality of a child considered abnormal in terms of behavior and appearance—an abnormality which could have occurred, according to Jenny, from *natural* causes, such as an incorrect diet.

Although Jenny does not give credence to the changeling belief herself she feels that "the old folk," like her grandmother, definitely did believe. She bases her assertion on the fact that her grandmother (with whom they lived) always ensured that the children wore something red at night.

Granny always had the red flannel on us. She had it stitched on to us with the safety pin. And she'd make sure the red flannel would be put on us before we'd be put down at night. "Don't forget the red flannel," she would say, a little square of red flannel pinned onto our chests before we'd go to bed.[64]

Jenny's pragmatic attitude to the changeling belief is also evident in her explanation of the factors which she considers gave rise to the belief that the fairies abduct brides. This belief finds expression in her version of a legend known widely in Ireland—the Attempted Abduction of a Bride.

Well, they had this man helping them for to get at the bride so that they could take her and he was there and they were having high tea the evening before the wedding. And she was to fit on her clothes and let them all see her—the family that is—before she went to church next day. And the little people you see got in while the old man [the human helper] was making his greetings and they were up in the rafters. And they used to do terrible funny things you see to distract the neighbors and family from the bride so as to be able to take her. And one of them was moving over and seemingly there was dust and she sneezed and the fairies vanished. So they couldn't take her; you see they wouldn't take her unless she was perfect. They couldn't have anyone that was sickly in their tribe because otherwise they'd all get sick. So they had to have everyone perfect especially the humans they had taken.[65]

Jenny's reaction to my query if she thought brides were stolen was to declare "No! I think it was an old wives' tale." And she went on to explain that the belief arose

. . . because people change; they have to get used to a new way of life when they get married. And some can take it and some can't. Some women can be good wives and mothers. Others can't take it and they are irritated and they break up their own happiness. So I think it is just like today's broken marriages; you hear more about them today than you did then. They would say that she [the wife] was a demon, that she wasn't from this earth at all, that she was one of the changelings. I think that's what it was all about.[66]

As with the changeling belief, Jenny is of the opinion that people formerly believed that brides could be and were, stolen. As she indicated, the belief could have arisen to explain and perhaps even excuse[67] what was perceived as altered behavior on the part of some women after marriage.[68] In this way a legend such as this could have been of value in helping to provide useful explanations for some tragic human problems in the course of life.

With our discussion of the abduction theme, we have reached a state of professed *disbelief* on Jenny's part. On her own admission, she believes neither in changelings, nor in attempts to abduct brides by the fairies. Nevertheless, as the analysis shows, she tells both of the legends in her repertoire arising from this belief in the same way as she narrates the legends she believes and those she is uncertain about. Commenting on her own different qualities of belief in relation to the various facets of fairylore and at the same time acknowledging that people genuinely did believe the manifold reflexes of the fairy faith, she explains that she also believed at one stage in life. She says: "I remember at one time I believed everything they told me. Well, I think I must have been eighteen or nineteen years of age before I realized that some of them were only stories!"[69] This realization dawned on Jenny just a couple of years before her marriage in 1961, at which time she became an active bearer of the traditions she then knew. Her lack of belief in some legends and her ambivalence in relation to others has never prevented her from telling them on appropriate occasions. She is still telling some of them almost three decades later! This is also her position in regard to legends with religious themes. Although she positively disbelieves a personal narrative of her father's concerning the Holy Family, she will still tell it in appropriate circumstances. Her explanation can be regarded as a declaration of her position in relation to legend communication in general.

> I'd tell that story, definitely. I'd tell that story if I thought people wanted to hear it. The fact that I don't believe it doesn't mean that I won't tell it, because there are people who do believe in things like that as well as people who don't. And everyone is entitled to their own opinions.[70]

Thus Jenny was aware, both as narrator and member of the audience, that people might want to hear a particular legend not necessarily because they believe it, but because they simply like it, or in the case of a religious legend, because it has a nice devotional ring to it. She knew also that some may not have reached any decision in their reaction to it. She was also well aware that some of the audience were narrators like herself, who were there simply to get new themes which they could adapt and develop to add to their repertoires. Her purpose therefore, as a good narrator, is to convince her audience of the truth of the legend despite the fact that she does not believe in the legend herself. Jenny acknowledges that the lack of belief or ambivalent belief on her part, acts as a catalyst for, or a challenge to her ability, because in many narrating situations, she is unsure about the belief position of her audience. Thus, in attempting to convince her audience of the truth of the legend she uses many of the devices concerning setting, time and characters which are typical of *Sage* transmission.

Jenny conceals her own disbelief from her audience, while at the same time conferring on her narrative the sanction of tradition by using the opening formula, "Well, me mother used to tell me this" or "me Granny used to tell me . . ." depending on the tradition-bearer from whom she had learned the legend in the first place.[71] As cited earlier in her version of the Changeling Legend, Jenny's persuasive use of details touching on human anxieties and conditions are likely to dispose at least some listeners towards acceptance of the legend. Other details which may evoke belief in her audience are the setting of the legend at a pre-wedding "hen party" at which the attempted abduction takes place and the references to dust and sneezing which have a modern health-conscious tone to them. Furthermore, her explanations and elaborations of certain motifs, such as the persistent and consistent interpretation of the fairies' aversion to the color red in terms of their own lack of blood, must have had its impact on audience reaction. All of these factors, together with the opening gambit of traditional sanction for her narratives and the post-performance comments by the audience and teller, must, in combination, have made her performance if not fully convincing for everybody, at least capable of creating doubt about the truth of the legend, or maintaining indecision in the minds of those wavering in their fairy faith.

To create doubt in the audience's mind was good enough for Jenny. She puts it neatly; she says, "Keep them in doubt; it keeps the stories going; it keeps the old traditions alive!"[72] For doubt ruptures curiosity and curiosity keeps people listening, perhaps even hoping to be convinced. As Jenny McGlynn demonstrates, conviction about the truth of a legend is not necessary for the formation or communication of a legend; what is of much more importance is the relationship of the specific legend to folk belief systems.[73]

Summary and Conclusion

In terms of tradition area, language, gender and genre, the foregoing analysis of the fairylore component of the repertoire of a female tradition-bearer from English-speaking Midlands of Ireland is in stark contrast with the geographical, linguistic, gender and genre bias of Irish folklore scholarship evident in the published repertoires of tradition-bearers to date. These are mainly the repertoires of male tradition-bearers from the Gaelic-speaking areas of Ireland with the scéalaí or oral literate specialist and his tales having pride of place. The study of the repertoires of extra-Gaeltacht tradition-bearers is not only valid, but necessary, for reasons too numerous to be mentioned here. In the context of this paper, however, suffice it to say that such a study should at the very least broaden our understanding of the complex interactive processes of repertoire formation and narrative performance in Irish tradition in general.

In addition, analysis of the different components of an individual tradition-bearer's repertoire, combined with that tradition-bearer's own evaluation of the various tradition categories and themes comprising the repertoire, should reveal the existence of, and also help to explain *repertoire dominants.*

Some of the factors—human, social, temporal, and spatial—which have interacted and combined in the formation of Jenny McGlynn's repertoire have been isolated and discussed. These factors have influenced the acceptance or rejection, the adaption and transmission of certain traditional items at her disposal. One of the significant factors mentioned was that she spent her formative years in a marginal community located in a marginal area at the edge of the town. In this scenario, both the situation and the arrangement of the houses was of interactive consequence. In addition to their physical location as an isolated group of cottages which resulted in strong social bonding in the community as a whole, the arrangement of the cottages in one long row of ten, with Jenny's house more or less in the middle, meant that the neighbors gravitated toward her house which had the reputation of being a rambling house. In that house Jenny assimilated beliefs about the supernatural world and learned many narratives, including most of her fairy legends.

On her marriage, she left one rambling house and married into another in a marginal area at the opposite end of the town. Here she became an active bearer of tradition with the encouragement of her father-in-law and here too, she listened and learned, selected and adapted, and thus expanded her repertoire.

In the atmosphere which surrounded Jenny before and after her marriage, traditions of the supernatural held a strong and important place. For Jenny, supernatural lore is a repertoire dominant and includes ghost and fairy traditions, with ghost lore being more important to her than fairylore. Her own evaluation of these two aspects of supernatural lore shows that the relative importance of the one over the other hinges on the question of belief. Her belief in ghosts is uncomplicated. She believes firmly in ghosts which she considers to be the returning dead. On the other hand she is ambivalent in her belief of the fairy faith.

As this analysis of the main themes in her fairylore has shown, Jenny's attitudes to them range from firm belief in the existence of the fairy world and a conviction of the inadvisability of interfering with it or its denizens in any way, through uncertainty and fluctuation of belief about the origin and final fate of the fairy race and details of their daily life, until finally, a state of total disbelief is reached on Jenny's part in relation to the abduction of humans by the fairies.

She explains that her different qualities and quantities of belief in relation to the fairy faith arose as she grew older and gained experience in life. As we have also seen, she ceased to believe in some aspects of the faith and became or remained indecisive about other facets of it. These developments are of significance for an illumination of belief criteria in relation to legend definition and legend transmission. It is abundantly clear, from Jenny's legend texts and also from her comments, that lack of belief in some legends and ambivalent belief in others has not prevented her from telling them over the years, and her position is the same in relation to legends with religious themes.

In terms of communicating these legends, she will, as in the case of legends she fully believes, perform them with vigor, verve, and artistry in order to convince her audience of their veracity. She realizes that audiences too, share different qualities and quantities of belief in relation to the fairy faith. She does not expect to convince them all and is satisfied if she can at least, by the dint of her performance, cause disbelievers to wonder if the story of the legend could possibly be true.

In the course of this essay I have spoken, almost casually perhaps, of Jenny's actual belief in aspects of the fairy faith. In general terms, there can be little doubt that the fairy faith remains strongest in Ireland where it is tied to a landscape feature, as Jenny's is. For her, firm belief in the existence of the fairy world is linked to a dominant local landscape monument, the rath or mound called "the Rusheen," which has powerful mnemonic significance for her. But the very fact that a monument such as this retains its ancient mythic significance and influences the worldview of an intelligent and discerning woman in the latter half of the technological and space-oriented twentieth century is surely unusual, if not remarkable. In addition, her reluctance to disbelieve other facets of the fairy faith, combined with her firm belief in further aspects of the supernatural, are facts of life for Jenny and must be acknowledged in any assessment of the fairy faith in contemporary societies.

Old faiths die hard in anglicized Ireland as well as in Gaelic Ireland and although the fairy faith has faded into the evening it has not yet settled into the long night of extinction.

Notes

1. "The Gaelic Story-teller" was published initially in the *Proceedings of the British Academy* 31 (1945): 177–221. The study was also published separately (1945) and subsequently reprinted by the American Committee for Irish Studies, *Reprints in Irish Studies* 6 (1969). Citations hereafter refer to the separate publication. Works by Delargy are also published in Irish under his name Séamus Ó Duilearga.

2. B. Ó Cuív, *Irish Dialects and Irish-Speaking Districts* (Dublin: Institute for Advanced Studies, 1951).

3. Even by the end of the nineteenth century, storytellers capable of performing the folk- and hero-tales in the Irish language were getting ever fewer in number and even in the *Gaeltacht* areas such storytelling was no longer a familiar feature of the social life of the people. In Cillrialaig, Co. Kerry, where Delargy worked in the 1920s "storytelling was only a memory" (6, 12, 14). Also Douglas

Hyde, *Beside the Fire: A Collection of Irish Gaelic Folk Stories* (London: David Nutt, 1910) xlii–xliii, mentions in particular the effect of the decline of the Gaelic language on the storytelling tradition. While those gifted old-time storytellers have passed away, the genres which they so artistically performed, such as the long *Märchen* and heroic romantic tales in the Gaelic language are still known to a few tradition-bearers in Gaeltacht areas. However, they perform them mainly now for the professional folklore collector. One such tradition bearer is Seán Ó hEinirí, a Mayo storyteller, whose very substantial repertoire covers the narrative spectrum from short anecdotes to long hero-tales. See S. Ó Catháin, *Scéalta Chois Cladaigh/Stories of Sea and Shore* (Dublin: Comhairle Bhéaloideas Éireann, 1983) xiv. It would be of interest to know what proportion of the repertoire of a modern day storyteller like Ó hEinirí consists of folk- and hero-tales. A few storytellers can also still perform Fenian tales, but rarely more than one or two each. For recent discussions of the *Fiannaíocht* tradition common to Ireland and Scotland see B. Almqvist, S. Ó Catháin, P. Ó Héalaí, *The Heroic Process* (Dublin: The Glendale Press, 1987); *The Proceedings of the International Folk Epic Conference, 2–6 September 1985* (Dublin: U College, 1985) 1–243; *Béaloideas* 54–5 (1986–7).

4. Seán Ó Súilleabháin (Sean O'Sullivan), *Storytelling in Irish Tradition* (Cork: Mercier, 1973) 11; Delargy 15. Most of the storytellers described by Delargy are men. This preponderance of male storytellers is also reflected in published studies of tradition-bearers and their repertoires. Cf.: the publications of The Folklore of Ireland Council (Comhairle Bhéaloideas Éireann) in Dublin; the bibliography in S. Ó Duilearga, *Leabhar Sheáin Í Chonaill* (Dublin: The Folklore of Ireland Society, 1948) 399–407 (English translation by Máire MacNeill: *Sean Ó Conaill's Book* [Dublin: Comhairle Bhéaloideas Éireann, 1981] 363–72); and C. Ó Danachair, *A Bibliography of Irish Ethnology and Folk Tradition* (Cork and Dublin: Mercier, 1978) 44–9.

5. Delargy states: "The recital of Ossianic hero-tales was almost without exception restricted to men. 'A woman *fiannaí* or a crowing hen!' the proverb runs. There are exceptions to this rule, but still the evidence is unmistakable that the telling by women of Fenian tales was frowned upon by the men"(7). Two other women storytellers from whom Fenian tales were collected in the early days of the Irish Folklore Commission's work are mentioned there.

6. Peig Sayers, 1873–1958. For an indication of the contents and size of her repertoire, see Delargy 15 and Kenneth Jackson, *Scéalta ón mBlaoscaod* (Dublin: The Folklore of Ireland Society, 1938). For description of her life and times see Robin Flower, *The Western Island* (Oxford: Oxford UP, 1945). See also Peig Sayers' autobiography *Peig, Clólucht on Talbóidigh, Tta* (Dublin, 1936) and English translation of it by Bryan MacMahon, *Peig: The Autobiography of Peig Sayers of the Great Blasket Island* (New York: Syracuse UP, 1974); her reminiscences have been translated by Seamus Ennis in *An Old Woman's Reflections* (1939; London: Oxford UP, 1962). See also the further biographical data from Peig's son Micheál Ó Gaoithín, *Beatha Pheig Sayers* (Dublin: FNT, 1970).

7. That active tradition-bearers tended to specialize in different categories of tradition is pointed out by Ó hEochaidh, a full-time folklore collector in Donegal (1935–1983). He tells us that the active tradition-bearers of Teilionn, a Gaelic-speaking fishing community in southwest Donegal "belonged to three classes (1) those who could tell the long folktales; (2) those who specialized in *seanchas* (socio-historical tradition and shorter narrative items of a realistic nature) and (3) the singers. . . ." and he adds significantly, "These three distinct groups of tradition are

rarely found in one person." In the *céilidhe* (or rambling) house each of the three types of tradition-bearers were expected to contribute to the night's entertainment (Delargy 19). Delargy also mentions an outstanding Co. Kerry storyteller "who had no regard for oral material other than the long folktales" (Delargy 16). As public performers these tradition-bearers were specialists; but the published repertoires of individual oral literature specialists (*an scéalaí*) show that they also knew *seanchas*. Indeed in Seán Ó Conaill's repertoire, collected and published by S. Ó Duilearga (see note 4) *seanchas* are also substantially represented. This is to be expected when living in a traditional community in which beliefs and legends of the kinds discussed in this paper were part of the very fabric of life and concerned with the processes of daily living.

8. Delargy 7.

9. According to Proinsias Mac Cana in *The Learned Tales of Medieval Ireland* (Dublin: Institute for Advanced Studies, 1980) 3, the distinction "has to do with the fact that men were generally the custodians of the sacred traditions of the tribe or community and women were often expressly excluded from direct knowledge of them."

10. Delargy 7.

11. The brief of the Irish Folklore Commission was to collect, preserve, index and publish the folklore of Ireland. Due mainly to lack of resources the Commission did not concentrate its personnel in the English-speaking areas of Ireland as it did in the *Gaeltacht* or Irish-speaking areas of the country. For an assessment of the Irish Folklore Commission and its work see B. Almqvist, *The Irish Folklore Commission: Achievement and Legacy* (Dublin: The Folklore of Ireland Society, 1979) 21 and also *Béaloideas* 45–7 (1977–9): 6–20.

12. Mountmellick, which originated as a Quaker town and was at one stage an important linen spinning center, is situated about fifty miles roughly westward from Dublin.

13. Laois was formerly known as Queen's County in honor of Mary Tudor who partly "planted" the county in the sixteenth century and the principal town (now Portlaoise) was called Maryborough. See Very Rev. John Canon O'Hanlon and Rev. E. O'Leary, *History of the Queen's County* (Dublin: Sealy, Breyers & Walker, 1907) 1: 436–9; T.W. Moody, F.X. Martin, *The Course of Irish History* (Cork: Mercier, 1967) 190. For the situation in regard to the Gaelic language in Laois, see Ó Cuív 17 .

14. Rambling or the social custom of night visiting is known by many different names in various parts of Ireland. Its importance for the preservation of the oral literature and traditions has been emphasized by Delargy (1945) 17–20.

15. Patricia Lysaght transcript (hereafter PL), tape 10, 31 December 1983.

16. PL, tape 20, 18 August 1987.

17. Migratory Legends-Suggested Irish Type (MLSIT) 6011 under the title "Capturer of Fairy Shoemaker Outwitted" has been suggested by B. Almqvist in *Crossing the Border. A Sampler of Irish Migratory Legends about the Supernatural* (Dublin: Department of Irish Folklore, 1988) 45. See also D. Ó Giolláin, "The Leipreachán and Fairies, Dwarfs and the Household Familiar. A Comparative Study," *Béaloideas* 52 (1984): 85–91.

18. PL, tape 8, 25 July 1981.

19. PL, tape 20, 18 August 1989.

20. Her father-in-law lived for only ten months after Jenny's marriage but it was essentially with his encouragement that she became an active bearer of

tradition. She ascribes some of her lore to him and to her mother-in-law, from whom she learned much supernatural lore as they sat by the fire at night.

21. PL, tape 20, 18 August 1989.

22. But according to Jenny it was usually somebody who came in who started the session off by relating a recent experience (PL, tape 20, 18 August 1989).

23. "I might be the only woman among all the lads sitting there. Me mother-in-law she'd be gone to bed because she wasn't very strong. She'd ramble off into her own room.... Oh yeah!, I was kind of taken as an equal—just another storyteller" (PL, tape 20, 18 August 1989).

24. Jenny's description of the legend telling occasions in "the Bay" points to the interactive nature of the event with the narrator being one of the group and sharing in the same background of belief; he or she may be considered especially competent in some area. Cf. also Linda Dégh and Andrew Vázsonyi, "Legend and Belief," *Genre* 4.3 (1971): 287–8.

25. On occasion when I have enquired about "wild nature" phenomena she commented, "Now, you'd want to get some of the men to tell you that" (PL, tape 1, June 1976).

26. Patricia Lysaght's *The Banshee. The Irish Supernatural Death-Messenger* (Dublin: Glendale, 1986) includes much of Jenny's banshee lore.

27. PL, tape 20, 18 August 1989.

28. I have made approximately seventeen hours of audio tape recordings of Jenny McGlynn in addition to 2 1/2 hours of video tape recordings. I have also recorded material from her late mother and from a neighbor who regularly rambled in "the Bay."

29. See Lysaght.

30. Lauri Honko, "Memorates and the Study of Folk Beliefs," *Journal of the Folklore Institute* 1 (1964): 10. The complexities involved in measuring the degree or depth of belief of tradition-bearers are discussed by Lysaght (218–9).

31. See Seán Ó Súilleabháin, *A Handbook of Irish Folklore* (1942; Hatboro, Pa.: Folklore Associates, 1963) 485–6. See also T. Crofton Croker, *Fairy Legends and Traditions of the South of Ireland*, 2nd ed., 3 vols. (London, 1826–8) 1: 241–9.

32. For Jackie-the-Lantern, see Ó Súilleabháin 498. Jenny has a couple of legends about people led astray at night by a light phenomenon known traditionally as Jackie-the-Lantern. Her father features in the following version. "I've heard of Will o' the Wisp or Jackie-the-Lantern. ... It's a light that can bring you astray. Me father followed it. He was out—he was fond of the drink and he was out—I think he was in Killeigh [Co. Offaly] and he thought he'd come home be the fields and he kept following the light. And instead of coming in the direction of Mountmellick he ended up the other side of Tullamore [Co. Offaly] in daylight!" PL, tape 1, side 1, June 1976. Jenny's skepticism about the causes of his *seachrán* or wandering, is evident in the remark that her father was fond of the drink and this skepticism was confirmed in a recent interview. Cf. Type 330 "The Smith Outwits the Devil" in S. Ó Súilleabháin and Reidar Th. Christiansen, *The Type of the Irish Folktale*, Folklore Fellows' Communications 188 (Helsinki: Academia Scientiarum Fennica, 1963–7). Her tendency to look for logical explanation for phenomena considered supernatural is also evident in her interpretation of a legend, very common in Ireland, about the old woman who turns herself into a hare in order to suck milk from cows, especially on May mornings. The "hare" is shot at, or is chased by a black hound with no white rib of hair, is injured and escapes into a

nearby house. On investigation, an old woman with a bleeding limb is found in the house. Jenny's explanation of this is that the trail of blood followed by the protagonists may not have come from a hare at all, but rather from an actual old lady who needed a sup of milk and who looked like a hare in the distance as she milked the cow early in the morning to avoid detection because of the risk of being thought to be "stealing" the profit of the milk or even of being a bewitched hare.

33. It should be remarked that Jenny has also a strong belief in the Devil.

34. Matthew (27. 51–4). At the death of Christ "the veil of the Temple was torn in two from top to bottom; the earth quaked; the tombs opened and the bodies of many holy men rose from the dead and these after his resurrection came out of the tombs, entered the Holy City and appeared to a number of people." Many of the themes concerning the return of the dead mentioned in Ó Súilleabháin (244–50) are known to Jenny. She also tells a good version of the Irish redaction of the migratory legend "The Midnight Mass of the Dead" (ML 4010) and tells also "Dead Mother Revisits her Children" (ML 4030). These legends and their corresponding type numbers are mentioned in Reidar Th. Christiansen, *The Migratory Legends. A Proposed List of Types with a Systematic Catalogue of the Norwegian Variants*, Folklore Fellows' Communications 175 (Helsinki: Academia Scientiarum Fennica, 1958).

35. PL, tape 1, June 1976. For phantom funerals see "Supernatural funerals" in Ó Súilleabháin 491–2.

36. This opinion was expressed by a number of nineteenth and early twentieth century writers such as Maria Edgeworth (1800), T.C. Croker (1826), Mr. and Mrs. S.C. Hall (1854), D.R. McAnally Jr. (1888), and W.G. Wood-Martin (1902) in relation to the banshee. See Lysaght 230–1, 403.

37. However, while discussing the theme of some of the legends in the course of the interview, Jenny tended to repeat them in order to better illustrate her point and even told a few I had not heard from her before.

38. W.Y. Evans-Wentz, *The Fairy Faith in Celtic Countries* (Oxford: Oxford UP, 1911).

39. "Gentle" is the anglicized form of the Gaelic adjective *uasal* and is used to describe spatial ambivalence such as the so-called "sacred" places in the landscape, places associated with the dead or the fairies. See N. Ó Domhnaill, *Foclóir Gaelige-Béarla, Oifig an tSoláthair* (Dublin, 1977). Peter Narváez has shown in a recent article (revised in this volume) "Newfoundland Berry Pickers 'In the Fairies': The Maintenance of Spatial and Temporal Boundaries through Legendry," *Lore and Language* 6.1 (1987): 15–49, that in folk communities in Newfoundland in the past, particular mechanisms of a folkloric kind, such as the fairies "established proximic boundaries. . . . which demarcated geographic areas of purity, liminality and danger. . . ." A liminal area is defined as an area between known space (purity) and unknown space (danger) (cf. Mary Douglas, *Purity and Danger*, [London: RKP, 1976] and Narváez 17). This concept of liminality seems to be equivalent to the Gaelic concept of *uasal* or "gentle." Thus "the Rusheen," which lies between purity and danger can be regarded as gentle, a liminal area or ambivalent realm, inhabited by the fairies, creatures of ambivalent status and inclination, an area which can be traversed by humans and where one might experience the benign or the malignant, depending on one's conduct.

40. For the occurrence of the legend in Laois folklore see Helen M. Roe, "Tales, Customs and Beliefs from Laoighis," *Béaloideas* 9 (1939): 22, "The Whip and the Lash."

41. *Hois* is a Gaelic expression used when driving cows. See Rev. P.S. Dineen, *Foclóir Gaedhilge agus Béarla* (Dublin: Irish Texts Society, 1927).
42. PL, tape 1, June 1976; tape 20, 18 August 1989.
43. PL, tape 20, 18 August 1989. That physical disability or even death can result from interference with fairy property such as a rath is well attested in Irish tradition. Many examples are evident in the subject index of the Archive of the Department of Irish Folklore, U College Dublin.
44. *Die Emotionalassoziation*, a concept elucidated by C.W. von Sydow to describe irrational cause and effect explanation of the type mentioned here. See von Sydow, "Die Psychologischen Grunde der Manavorstellung," *Vetenskapssocietetens i Lund årsbok* (Lund: 1929) 63–73. See also Carl-H. Tillhagen, "Die Zaubermacht des Ungewohnlichen," *Festschrift für Robert Wildhaber*, eds. W. Escher, T. Gantner, H. Trumpy (Basel: Verlag G. Krebs AG, 1973) 666–7.
45. PL, tape 20, 18 August 1989. When I asked Jenny if she thought her extreme caution in relation to raths arose from a certain unfamiliarity with the landscape, she replied, "No! Because I seen farmers now that had land with raths on it and they wouldn't go next or near them ... you know, there's Keating's rath up there and nobody would go next or near it; they'd plough all round it. They wouldn't go next or near it; they'd leave a good furrow between them and the rath."
46. There is no doubt that the association of these raths, mounds and other antiquities with the fairies was the principal reason for the preservation of such large numbers of them in the Irish countryside. The principal prehistoric and early historic monuments of the Irish countryside are discussed by S.P. Ó Ríordáin, *Antiquities of the Irish Countryside*, 4th ed. (London: Methuen, 1976).
47. See under *ros* in Dinneen. See also *ros*, "Rusheen" in P.W. Joyce, *The Origin and History of Irish Names of Places*, 7th ed. (Dublin: Longmans, Green and Company, 1901) 1: 495–6.
48. This is a very old idea in both Gaelic and Norwegian traditions. See Reidar Th. Christiansen, "Some Notes on the Fairies and the Fairy Faith," *Béaloideas*, 39–41(1971–3): 104–5.
49. Cf. Ó Súilleabháin 450.
50. This supernatural experience lends itself to analysis on the basis of the model developed by Honko for experiences which begin with the violation of a norm (cf. Honko 10–9).
51. PL, tape 1, June 1976.
52. For details of these ideas see Ó Súilleabháin 450–79.
53. W. Allingham, *Songs, Ballads and Stories* (1877; New York: AMS Press, 1972) 158–60.
54. PL, tape 7, April 1981.
55. The motif also occurs in the Welsh tale of Pwyll. See P. Mac Cana, *Celtic Mythology* (London: Hamlyn, 1970) 126.
56. Christiansen, "Some Notes" 96–7. S. Ó hEochaidh, M. Ní Néill, S. Ó Catháin, *Síscéalta Ó Thír Chonaill/Fairy Legends from Donegal* (Dublin: Comhairle Bhéaloideas Eireann, 1977) 36–7, 373.
57. PL, tape 20, 18 August 1989. Scandinavian and Irish traditions of fairy origin and hope of salvation may be compared by reference to Christiansen, "Some Notes" 95–111, Christiansen, *The Migratory Legends* ML 5050 and ML 5055, and Christiansen's *Folktales of Norway* (London: Routledge & Kegan Paul, 1964) 87–92.

According to a study of the fate of the fairies on Judgment Day in Irish tradition, our legend belongs to one of five separate redactions of it known in Ireland to date. See M. Bríody, "Súil na Síog le slánú," student essay, Dept. of Irish Folklore, U College, Dublin, 1977. These versions from Laois are to be added to those mentioned in the essay. In view of the absence of salvation prospects for the fairy race in Irish tradition another title "No Prospect of Salvation for the Fairies" with Type 5051 has been suggested for this legend by Almqvist 61.

58. PL, tape 20, 18 August 1989.

59. See Ó Suilleabháin 470–6 and Ó hEochaidh et al., especially legends 1–21.

60. PL, tape 8, July 1981. See a study of the Changeling Legend in Irish tradition in S. MacPhilib, "Iarlaisí: Símhalartú i mBéaloideas na hÉireann," MA thesis, U College Dublin, 1980. This legend is ML 5085 in Christiansen's *The Migratory Legends*.

61. The term *fabulate* was coined by von Sydow to describe well-constructed legends with a surprise effect such as the version of the Changeling Legend just quoted. See von Sydow, "Kategorien der Prosa-Volksdichtung/The Categories of Prose Tradition," *Selected Papers on Folklore*, ed. L. Bødker (1948; New York: Arno P, 1977) 74–6, 87.

62. Jenny says, "I enjoyed it. I really enjoyed it; and I did get the interest of the group and they liked to hear what I had to say" (PL, tape 20, 18 August 1989).

63. PL, tape 20, 18 August 1989.

64. PL, tape 20, 18 August 1989.

65. Although no study of this legend as it occurs in Ireland has yet been undertaken, there are some samples from the four provinces and these show that the two basic motifs are: the bride sneezes three times and at the third sneeze she is saved from abduction by the pious exclamation, usually *Dia linn!* (God with us!), of the human helper. Such a combination of motifs was also found in Leinster as a mid-nineteenth century example of the legend shows. (See Noleen McLaughlin, *'Old, New, Borrowed, Blue.' A Classification of some Irish Marriage Customs*, MA thesis, U College Dublin, 1986) 572. Jenny's insecurity in relation to this legend may be due to the fact that it belonged to her *memory* repertoire until her daughter got married when it became part of her *active* repertoire. For discussion and application of the concepts of *memory* repertoires and *active* repertoires see I.G. Carpenter, *A Latvian Storyteller* (New York: Arno P, 1980) 37–8 and works quoted there.

66. PL, tape 20, 18 August 1989.

67. Unfortunately, being considered a changeling could also prove tragically fatal for the "altered" wife. See Thomas McGrath, "Fairy Faith and Changelings: The Burning of Bridget Cleary in 1895," *Studies* (Summer 1982): 178–84.

68. According to Jenny (tongue-in-cheek, I think), the changeling belief also explained changed behavior in men after marriage, men who perhaps were dissatisfied with their choice of wife and "stepped out of line, especially after they came in and give the wife a clatter" (PL, tape 20, 18 August 1989).

69. PL, tape 20, 18 August 1989.

70. PL, tape 20, 18 August 1989.

71. Jenny heard versions of the Changeling Legend from her mother and father; she learned the Attempted Abduction of the Bride from her mother and as already stated, she learned the Leipreachán's Crock of Gold from her grandmother.

72. PL, tape 20, 18 August 1989.

73. I am thus in agreement with Dégh and Vázsonyi's conclusions (301–2).

Fairies and the Supernatural on Reachrai[1]

Linda-May Ballard

Reachrai, or Rathlin Island, is the only populated island off the coast of the state of Northern Ireland. It sits like a punctuation mark on the northeastern extremity of County Antrim and at one point in its history it was considered to be one of the Western Isles of Scotland. L-shaped, it measures approximately four and a half miles from end to end, and its width varies from approximately three quarters of a mile to one and a half miles across. Before the great famine of the 1840s, its population was in excess of a thousand but this has been in decline for more than a century and today the figure is closer to a hundred.[2]

The island is possessed of tremendously imposing natural beauty, but its climate like its geology can be extremely inhospitable. Its history suggests that it has not been continuously occupied. Clark's list of significant dates in the island's history includes massacres in 1274, 1557 and 1572.[3] In those unruly times, the island may have offered a retreat to anyone wanting to keep a low profile for a period without actually settling there.[4] With the arrival of the Gage family from mainland County Antrim, who bought Reachrai in the mid-eighteenth century, a more systematic approach to subsistence agriculture and farming developed on the island and a period of relative stability began.[5] Culturally, the heritage of the islanders reflects strong influences from the northwestern seaboard region. Until early this century many islanders spoke a type of Gaelic related to the forms spoken in both Ireland and Scotland, as might be expected from both their history and their geographical position.[6]

It is not surprising that tales of the otherworld, of fairies, ghosts, the devil and other supernatural beings abound, today told in English. Although on Rathlin as in other places, patterns of living are changing, these stories may still with justification be described as the contemporary legends of this tiny island. The stories on which this paper is based were collected by the author for the archive of the Ulster Folk and Transport Museum during the course of several field trips to Rathlin conducted between 1978 and 1984, the most intensive recording being done between 1979 and 1982. The narratives were recorded in a series of interviews arranged to be most convenient to the storytellers. Mr. and Mrs. T. Cecil were recorded in their home, and were often joined by one of their young

children. Mrs. Cecil was not born on the island. Mr. Cecil learned his tales
from his father, the late Dougal Cecil, whom I often met and to whom I
frequently talked, but who was not prepared to be interviewed, although
he occasionally told stories to his son specifically so these could be passed
to me. He also learned tales from his elderly Uncle Robert and is highly
aware of the importance of his repertoire. As the social life of the island
has changed, opportunities to tell stories are few, and Mr. Cecil keeps a
notebook in which many of his tales are preserved.[7] Mr. J. McFaul was
interviewed both in his café and at his mother's home at the Upper End of
the island, sometimes alone, sometimes with his wife and his mother, as
time and work permitted. Neither his wife, nor his mother was born on
the island. Mr. McFaul's mother, Mrs. P. McFaul, is herself a good
storyteller, and both of them learned many of their tales from the late Mr.
McFaul who, like Mr. Cecil senior, was a fisherman. Both Mr. T. Cecil and
Mr. J. McFaul are fishermen, in addition to following other occupations,
but Mr. McFaul has always lived on the island while Mr. Cecil (like
several other islandmen of the present generation) has been a member of
the Merchant Navy. I have spent many very happy evenings in Mrs. P.
McFaul's home, recording stories from her and her son. Other members of
the family often passed through the kitchen, or stayed to listen, while the
stories were recorded. Mrs. McFaul's home is situated in a place called
"Lart Aoibhinn," the Beautiful Hollow.[8] The late Mrs. B. McKenna, when I
met her a very elderly and bedridden lady, was interviewed at her
daughter's home in Belfast. The late Mr. Alec Anderson, an elderly
gentleman at the time of our first meeting in 1978, was interviewed in his
garden and in his home, sometimes in the presence of his brother, a poet,
now also dead. Although I have had the privilege of recording other
islanders, it is from these storytellers that the narratives included in this
paper were collected.

Fairylore

Many tales of the fairies still circulate on Rathlin, although it is
probably true to state that fairies are less part of the actual belief system of
the islanders than they were a generation ago.[9] However, as in other rural
areas of Ireland, the fairies have not become totally irrelevant. People are
still prepared to speculate on their existence, which accounts for the
sustained vibrancy of tradition on the island.

Thematically, Rathlin fairy stories have much in common with
fairylore from other regions which share a strong Gaelic heritage. Thus
fairies are conceptualized as a parallel race of beings, capable of helping
humans, but capricious and best avoided. Island lore includes many
common fairy motifs: fairy habitations, especially fairy thorns, should not

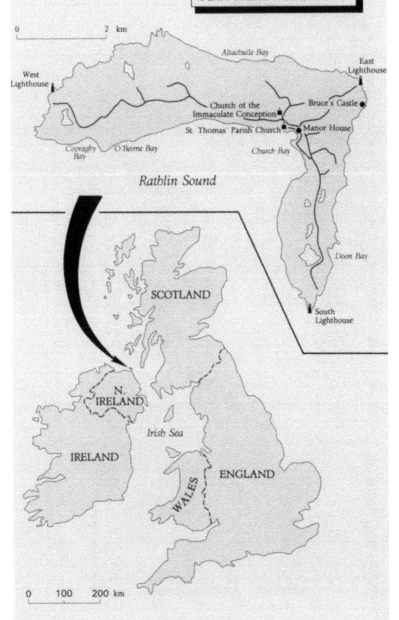

RATHLIN ISLAND

0   2   km

Altachuile Bay

East
Lighthouse

West
Lighthouse

Church of the
Immaculate Conception

Bruce's Castle

St. Thomas' Parish Church

Manor House

*Cooragby
Bay*   *O'Beirne Bay*

Church Bay

Rathlin Sound

SCOTLAND

Doon Bay

South
Lighthouse

N.
IRELAND

Irish Sea

IRELAND

WALES

ENGLAND

0   100   200 km

Plate 1. The Manor House occupied by the Gage family and situated at Church Bay commands a clear view of the pier and most craft departing from and returning to the island, ca. 1905. (Ulster Folk and Transport Museum)

Plate 2. Storyteller James McFaul, with two of his children, Anne and Jim, 1954. It was from James McFaul that both his wife Peggy and his son Jim learned many of their stories. (Ulster Folk and Transport Museum)

Plate 3. Until the 1940s some island men climbed the island's steep cliffs and rocky stacks in search of sea birds and their eggs. Storyteller James McFaul is shown with rope at the right, his brother is on the left and Charlie Fulton, a farm laborer and good friend of the family, is in the middle, ca. 1936. (Ulster Folk and Transport Museum)

be interfered with; musical ability, or at least a new tune, is sometimes learned from the fairies; the fairies may lead people astray, or may leave gifts (which as usual must not be spoken of) for those whom they favor. They are sometimes believed to play tricks on people, as the following account illustrates.

> They played a trick on my grandfather one time. He came out to fodder the horses, and he went round the stable a dozen times, couldn't get the door. He was an hour out, and they went out to look for him, and they asked him what kept him. He said, "Them wee buggers!" Made a fool of him! And he could hear them laughing up in the hill. He couldn't see them. That was some of the wee folk.[10]

Rathlin fairylore provides an aetiological account of the fairies similar to that found elsewhere, although the following example of the well-known tale ascribes a similarly mystical origin to the seals.

> I heard a yarn in the time of the rebellion in heaven, they were cast out, and some fell on the land, some fell in the sea, and the seal, he's the one that fell in the sea.[11]

On Rathlin, the fairies are generally visually conceptualized as small, and as dressed in red and green, although one recorded account illustrates that deductions might be drawn from the dress of a manifested fairy.

> You nearly always seen this one, if there was going to be a birth in the family, and they could tell, if he was wearing red, you know, at that time, a lot of babies died, maybe fifty percent of them, maybe more died if you seen a fairy wearing red . . . if there was a birth concerning the family you knew it was going to be alright.[12]

The idea that fairies may depend on humans, especially for the skills of the midwife, is also current on the island.

> Years ago, maybe even today, they used to believe in the fairies and used to see them quite a lot. In fact there's some ones'll tell you even yet that they've seen them. But this was a very stormy, a very stormy night you see, blowing a gale, and rain, sleet, and there was a woman lived at the far end of the island. She was a nurse-cum-midwife. She done everything, you see.
> So, she was in bed this night and a knock came to the door, and I said it was a very, very stormy night, and she went to the door, and there was—at that time there was no such thing as a four-wheeled coach on the island. The only ones had a carriage was the Gages—and she went to the door and this team of four horses and a four-wheeled coach was outside the door, and there was a man with it, and she thought it very strange. At first she thought she was dreaming, but then she knew, she realized there

was something strange about it and the man, she couldn't see him in the darkness. He said that she was needed, there was a woman in labour and they needed her very urgently, and, so she knew, and decided that no harm would come to her, that she'd get into the coach.

So, she got into the coach, and it set off down the road, and if I was at the far end of the island I could point out the place to you. Set off across bogs, round the side of the hill where there was no road, and across a bog you know, a very marshy place. It didn't sink in the bog. And they arrived at this hill at the back of Brockley. And as they come to the hill, the side of the hill opened up and the horse and carriage went into the hill. And inside it, you know it was the most beautiful place, it was like a palace inside it. There was everything you could imagine in it. And before this there was a lot of islanders going missing, and young girls, and young men in the island going missing. And nobody ever knew what was happening, they thought that they were maybe being kidnapped, you know somebody coming to the island by boat and taking them off it. It was put down to this.

But anyway inside the hill; there was a palace inside the hill, the woman recognized a lot of them. And anyway she attended to the woman that was giving birth and everything was sorted out. But I forgot to add here, that there was a lot of fairies running around, the wee folk, there was a lot of them in this hill you see. And they went to her and they said to her that they would give her anything to stay. So, "No," she said. "No." She wouldn't. And then they offered her something to eat and she was going to, she was quite hungry, so she decided it wouldn't do any harm, she would take something to eat. But just by the side of the fire there was a young girl sitting nursing a small baby and she was singing to it in Gaelic. Now unfortunately I don't know, don't remember the words in Gaelic, what she was singing, but in English what she was singing to the baby was, "eat nothing, drink nothing, or don't stay the night." She was repeating this over and over again in Gaelic. So, this was a warning, you see, to the nurse. So she insisted that they take her back home. So she got into the carriage again, and they left her back to her own door. So she was very upset about all this and, she didn't know what to do about it, so she went down to the landlord, the Gages. She went down to him and she told him about this, and he warned her on peril of her life she was never to mention this to anybody or he would banish her off the island. So she must have mentioned it or the story wouldn't have got out. So that was that. I always thought that was a very nice tale. I used to like to listen to that a lot.[13]

This tale brings into focus the role and powerful position of the midwife or handywoman in a community dependent upon her skills. Her pivotal position, emphasized by the fact that she was often responsible both for assisting at childbirth and for laying out the dead, was not only one of great power, it was one which made it appropriate for her to be associated with the creatures of the other world. In Rathlin fairylore, as in such stories from other regions, there is no absolute and clear distinction between the world of fairies and the world of the dead.

This issue underlines the most dreaded aspect of fairy behavior, their ability to "change" or "take" people, especially young children. The awareness of the vulnerability of children and of infant mortality has already emerged from the account quoted above. The following anecdote implicates the fairies in the death of a small child, and again includes the motif that predictions may be based on the appearance of the fairies.

There was an old woman here on the island, when she was a young girl, she was, [it] was a Sunday. She'd been visiting relatives up at the other end of the island, she lived down the middle of the island there, and she was coming home, it was in the summertime in the evening and ah, she heard this music. Ah, you know she couldn't describe it, it was lovely music, but she went to the top of the hill and was supposed to be if you hear the fairies playing this music you're not to look, you know, you'd to go on, you're not to stop and look at them, because it'll bring bad luck to the family. But anyway she went to the top of the hill and looked down into, she knew there was a wee hollow, a wee valley down below and she went up had a look and she hid in the heather up at the top of the hill and there they were, all down in the hollow dancing around having great times.

So she went home and she told grandmother, and the grandmother said to her not to tell anybody that she'd seen this. She says, "You know," she says, "you shouldn't have looked at them, but maybe they didn't see you." And she says, "Oh aye," she says, "they seen me alright, because before I run away one of them came running up the hill towards me." And they all dressed, all these fairies dressed in different clothes, but just depending on what the one that runs towards you, what he's wearing, that usually signifies whether it's good luck, bad luck or death they're going to bring you. And she says, the grandmother says, to her, "Well what was it wearing? What was he wearing?" Well she says, "It was all dressed in black." "Oh my God," she says, "that's death that he's brought us."

So that was alright. A few days after that they were away, all the ones of the house were away at the shore gathering seaweed and used to make it, for making the kelp you know, the whole family was away and this girl was left behind to look after her brother and of course, she was only about twelve and as she was looking after the brother but she'd all the baking for the whole family to do, and the cows to milk, and the hens to feed, and the whole household chores to do, and the brother was only about, he'd been about three or four and aw, damn, but, suppose she wasn't paying any heed to him, he disappeared anyway and she searched high up and low down for him, couldn't be found anywhere. But then she thought maybe that while she was working about the house, some of them had come back and took him to the shore along with them. So they came home, she said, (I don't remember his name) but she said, did they see him and they said, "No," that she was left to look after him. And they searched everywhere for him and he couldn't be found, so all the neighbors gathered to search from him. Well then they discovered, you know the big long tongs in the old houses, great big long pair of tongs they used to have hanging at the side of the fire, they discovered that the pair of tongs was missing and they searched around, round where the byres was the barns was, it was sort of muddy and they seen his tracks, he was in his bare feet, they seen his tracks in the mud and he was trailing the pair of tongs along with him because they could see the mark they made in the ground, so they followed this right along and here and there they would see it, you know where there was a damp patch or muddy place, they seen the track of the tongs or his bare feet and they followed it right over to very near the cliffs and they searched around, they couldn't find, and somebody looked over the particular place, looked over the edge of the cliffs and there he was lying down below.

And you see where they used to go down to the shore there was a path down and there's two places look exactly the same and they reckoned that he must've been following the mother and father to the shore and he mistook the first place as the place you went down, and he walked down and he walked down there and then it just, there was a wee bit of a path down there, it was just sheer cliffs and they got him lying down there.[14]

The story illustrates the commonly held belief that the fairies should not be sought out or interfered with, that it is dangerous to enquire into their nature and by implication, into their elemental and fundamental significance. The irony of the tale is that the child is carrying the tongs, which normally protect children from danger from the fairies. Following his sister's vision, his death is inevitable, while she, as a consequence of the vision rather than of her domestic responsibilities, is to a degree absolved.

In the following tale, the direct involvement of the fairies in the abduction of children is explicit. The story is an unusual variation on the abduction theme.

There was this small boy on the island. He disappeared from home and they didn't know where he had got to, they put it down that he had fallen over the cliffs or he'd fell down a well, or fell into one of the lakes. And they searched the island for two or three days, and they couldn't find him. Searched everywhere, high and low, streams and wells and bogs, everywhere and there wasn't a trace of him to be got and you know, the parents were naturally very upset and on the third morning . . . they were in a pretty bad way and they'd put him down as being dead and he turned up at the door, spic and span, he was as clean as a new pin and they asked him where he was. And he said he went over the mountain for a walk and this particular place there's a wee valley in it and he said he seen a lot of small children playing and he went down to them, and they took him in through (told them the place), took him in through this hill and it wasn't children at all but it was the fairies you see. So they took him into the hill anyway and they wanted him to stay, so they scrubbed him and they cleaned him. . . . To get him to stay they had to take every earthly sign off him, everything off him, any earthly thing he had on him, they had to take off him. Only after they had done that they could keep him you see, . . . he would never get back to his own people again. He would be one of them. So they scrubbed him and they cleaned him and they washed him and they done everything. Took his own clothes off him and they give him other clothes and still he wanted to go back home, and they finished up, they couldn't keep him by the third day you see, they had, this was the thing, if the fairies keep you, by the third day they must let you go. So they had to let him go on the morning of the third day and I forgot to add that the wee boy was away gathering blackberries you see, this is what he was doing when he disappeared, and he arrived back home and he was telling them all this in the house, and they were giving him something to eat and all, and he says, "Mammy," he says, "my hand is very sore," he says, "when I was gathering the blackberries," he said, "I got a jag under me finger nail." And he showed it to her and she says, "Well the Lord be praised," she says, "that you got that under your finger nail," she says, "for only that," she says, "the fairies would have been able to keep you." And this was the only thing they couldn't remove.[15]

The inability of the fairies to divest the child of his humanity is in direct contrast to the idea stated in the midwife tale, that to ingest fairy food is to partake of their nature and to be incapable of leaving them. This tale appears to be a Rathlin oicotype, perfectly consistent with the broad range of Irish fairy belief but unrecorded in other areas so far as I am aware. The irony of this tale, in which it is a thorn which protects the child, seems to counterbalance the irony of the tongs in the preceding story, told on a different occasion by the same narrator.

The danger of attempting to trick the fairies is illustrated in this story:

Just above Cooraghy . . . [there are] two very funny shaped stones, they're V-shaped stones and to look at them you would think it was alright to stick your head in and get a drink out of the well. Nobody has ever tried this, but the fairies used to use this well one time, and they were always using it for their drinking water. Nobody else was supposed to use it, but there was this herdboy up there and he decided he would play a trick on them and he went and he got butter. There was a wee flat stone where they used to kneel down and get a drink out of, so he went and he got butter you see and he spread it on this stone for the fairies. So they didn't know anything about this and at their usual time they went to get a drink and one of them slipped and went into the well and was supposed to have got drowned. So they cursed the well then and they took the remains of their mate out of it. Anyway the herdboy, he didn't know anything had happened but whenever the fairies cursed anything, that's it. You daren't go near it. So he went and had a look at it and there was nothing happened, on top it was OK so he went in to take a drink out of it, now there's two V-shaped stones, looks alright and he stuck his head in to take a drink but whenever he put his head in, he found that he couldn't get his head back out, so he drowned in the well.[16]

This tale also reflects the idea that the fairies are themselves subject to ultimate mortality and strongly reinforces the belief that they are best left to their own devices. On Rathlin, stories of harm from fairies far outnumber tales of benefit from them, a point which no doubt reflects the often inhospitable environment which they symbolize.

Omens, Warnings, and Signs of Coming Death

Death, an understandably major preoccupation of Irish folklore, is a common theme in Rathlin stories. It features as an important sub-theme in fairylore and there is a significant amount of material dealing with warnings that a death is about to occur. Generalized warnings associated with death are well-known on Rathlin. The following story bears an unusual relationship to the common idea that the period between death and funeral is subject to rules of time different from those which normally prevail, and is, therefore, marked by the stopping of the clock.

Inf. 1: The clocks always stopped [at the time of a death].

Inf. 2: Well, I had never heard that story about clocks or anything else to do with clocks. And there was a man here died . . . he was very ill, and he died this night. . . . And here, Francis had not long got that clock and it kept excellent time, only had it a few weeks. And for some reason, what time . . . did he die? And here the clock had stopped at that exact time. Well . . . I thought that was a bit funny, the clock should stop then you know. I was standing, the day of the funeral and he'd to go by that way you see, to go up to the chapel, the body was to go up there and Francis was away at it, and I was standing here, . . . I was watching them going by up there, you know, following the funeral. Honest, I'll never forget it, and the clock all of a sudden, just as the body went by started "tick tock tick tock," it started up again. It scared me stupid. I says, "Why should it start up again then?" You know, this was about two days later, the clock started. It was the weirdest thing.

Inf. 1: You see, it was always the custom, they always stopped the clock whenever somebody died in the house, they used to stop it as soon as they died.

Inf. 2: So as you wouldn't go into the house and ask them.

Inf. 1: Aye, that was the reason, that, when you went in, you just looked at the clock and then you knew what time they died at.[17]

In addition to the pragmatic reason given for stopping the clock, the story suggests a deeper reason for the practice.

The banshee is also known on Rathlin.

> I've heard the older ones say it. I don't know why you never hear it now.
> There was just a grey shape . . . up where we used to live, in that house,
> where the banshee used to follow them. That man I was telling you
> about, that had been dead for a long time, McMenamin was their name,
> and the . . . evening they took him to the chapel, the banshee! They heard
> the banshee . . . just in the cliffs above the house, a grey form, like
> somebody dressed in a grey robe, and this merciful cry just drifting along
> the edge of the cliffs, you know, they'd be about thirty or forty feet high.
> Just drifting along the cliffs.[18]

In the following story, the banshee's cry is transferred to the natural
world, but the implication of a supernatural expression associated with
death is retained.

> There was a woman died across there, McFarlane was her name, and the
> day they were taking her . . . down to the graveyard, it's not really the
> banshee, it's normally maybe a dog howling or a cat screaming, you
> know, a cat's mournful howl, and they were taking her down to the
> graveyard, and some of the ones stood talking, having followed the
> funeral down, and they heard this merciful crying of cats, and there's
> only one or two of them heard it . . . some of the ones couldn't hear, but it
> turned out that the only ones that heard it were . . . the ones that were
> related . . . but ones that were no relations to her at all didn't hear it.[19]

Familial proximity is often an issue in tales of the banshee. The idea
that animals are attuned to human death is also widespread. The
repertoire of the teller of the above story also includes an account of the
cry of seals as an omen of impending death.[20] It is worth noting that in
this narrative, the frequently heard disclaimer that hearings reputedly of
the banshee are merely of animals is turned to the advantage of the
storyteller.

Rathlin death lore includes belief in an ominous boat.

> Inf.: Well there's this family on the island, before any of them died
> there's usually a boat seen, and I have seen it myself, and other
> people on the island have seen it, and there's a boat with six
> oarsmen in it and you know it's seen at different times, and not so
> very long ago it was seen on the island and you'll get ones on the
> island would tell you about it. One particular instance of it, two
> men were working at the forest away at the far end of the island
> and they seen the boat putting out from the harbor here. So they
> were waiting on their pay coming by the post and one of them set
> off, you know he allowed how long it would take the boat and he
> knew it must have been [time]; they thought it was the mail boat
> and they come down and there was no boat ever left the quay and

there was no boat ever in at the quay and yet and all they had seen a boat going out with the sail on it and all, sailing out the bay, and within a couple of days one of this particular family had died.

LB: Did you say you saw it yourself?

Inf.: Aye, seen it myself and you know a number of other people seen it at the same time and yet and all there was never any. It was very very bad weather and there was no small boat would have been out in it, and when, when I went to the top of the hill to see with the glasses, to see what boat it was, because I thought it was unusual, there was no sign of anything anywhere, and you know it had completely disappeared.[21]

In common with other areas on Rathlin, certain families are "followed" by individualized death omens.

There was another thing that was supposed to follow a particular family, was a fire, you know, if anybody seen it, the family never seen it, but if there was an impending death in the family, they used to live over there, it was the X family, and if there was fire seen around their house, you know, a mass of flames and fire, and maybe the whole house engulfed in fire, and before X died over there, somebody going to the Upper End, the top part there just above where you took that photograph, and they looked back and they saw the whole place in flames, the whole house in flames, and they run back and they run back to the turn in the road there, and they got as far as there, there wasn't a sign of anything. The lights was on in the house and there weren't any, and a few days after that Joe died. It suddenly dawned on them that that's what it was.[22]

Examples from other regions of such individualized beliefs include the strange landslide which is believed to occur before a death in a particular family from the Ards peninsula of Co. Down.[23] These stories represent a development of the system of generalized belief in death omens affecting a family in the same way that families are said to be "followed" by the banshee, but distinct from the belief in wraiths, which are essentially associated with a particular individual.

Wraiths as death warnings are well-known on Rathlin, and there are several examples of wraiths being seen at the time of death of the individual concerned. Wraiths are usually associated with the precise point of death, but a wraith might fairly be described as the spirit of the dead seen before the funeral, while a ghost is a spirit manifested after the funeral has occurred. Generally, the wraith functions as a signifier that death has occurred, but in the following story, the wraith performs a different purpose.

There was a man fishing down on the shore and there was a neighbor who he knew was quite ill, you know they were actually waiting on him to die and this neighbor had a horse that was going to foal, or a mare that was going to foal I should say. And he was fishing on the rock, the neighbor that was ill had said to him, he says, "When this mare's going to foal," he says, "I'll come and give you a shout," you know, "because I'll need a hand with her." So he said that was alright, but in the meantime the neighbor took ill and they were waiting on him to die, so all the goings on the man forgot about the mare that was going to foal.

So that was alright, he was fishing at the rock you know, about, maybe might have been about three or four mile about where the house was and he seen his neighbor coming down the path down to the shore and all of a sudden it came into his head you know, "By God he's coming for me, he must have got alright, and I bet you," he says, "the mare's going to foal."

So he wound up his line and he set off up the path up the cliff to meet him, and he met the neighbor and he says, "Is the mare going to foal?" "Aye," your man says, "it is." He says, "I'll go ahead of you." So he went back and got his rod and string of fish, he said to him that he'd a lot of fish to string. Strung the fish and the neighbor went away on up ahead of him and he set off after him, he maybe only a minute or so after, but when he got to the top there was no sign of his neighbor about, and you know he should have seen him because it was a straight walk down to where the house was, and he thought it very strange and anyway he went on. The stable was a bit away from the house and he decided, "Well," he says, "I'll go and see how the mare is," and he went into the stable and by jove wasn't the mare just going to have the foal, she was foaling and there were no sign of your man about, his neighbor about and he says, "Well I know now," he says, "he's away for somebody else for help." So he stayed with the mare, and damned but she foaled and the foal was alright. And he seen her, got the foal fixed up and all and he set to for the house and he thought it very funny that all the neighbors was about the house whenever he arrived at the house, and the priest was there and wasn't your man just after dying and had never left the house at all.[24]

Wraiths usually have visual form, but the following account is unusually of an aural manifestation.

Inf. 1:   I don't know whether it happened, maybe it was after you were there the last time, but that house over there I was building out at the back. . . . And I was working and this unmerciful crashing and falling in it, you know, and nobody had been working or anything in it, so I run into Martin's, that's Martin's mother that's next door . . . I run in and I thought somebody, like somebody falling down a stairs, this unmerciful thumping and groaning and shouting and I thought, Martha hadn't been well, and I run in and I thought she'd fallen down the stairs because that's what it sounded like, and she was sitting having a cup of tea at the table. And I said "Did you hear anything?" And of course I was white as a sheet for I was sure she was killed, and "No," she says, "no, I never heard anything." And with that, her daughter had been out, Susan had been out the front, and she come in. She heard the wild crashing but she knew where it was, it was in next door. She says "There's somebody has fallen down the stairs in the old Post Office." And her mother says "You are doting." I said "I'm telling you." And I even went in and told Martin, you know, Martin was in the house and I even went in and told him. So I never put any more pass on it. I thought you know, put it off as something else, and by jove within the hour the word come that, the two old ladies that lived in it had been taken to the old people's home in Ballycastle, and one of them had died, the older one had died. She must've been nearly ninety. But she always used to take turns and it was always whenever she would go up, she was sort of epileptic, you know, she would take these turns, and three or four times she'd fallen down the stairs and nearly broke her neck and this is what I heard as sure as God that's what it was. And I seen her, Martin seen her as well, she used to be, she would fall down, she'd be bruised and she'd be as black as the coal, you know, her face with bruises.

Inf. 2: I know . . . I don't know how she didn't kill herself.

Inf. 1: I think it must've been the effort of her going up the stairs and yet they always persisted, they had rooms downstairs, but they always persisted.

Inf. 2: Oh, just on going up the stairs.

Inf. 1: And just within the hour the word had come that she'd died.

Inf. 3: That's right next door to you, Linda.

LB: Oh stop it.

Inf. 2: If you hear a crash the night, it's the other old doll's popped off![25]

Rathlin oral lore also includes tales of people to whom supernatural warnings are given enabling them to avert death.

Another story about a man that was . . . he was clipping sheep in a place called Altachuile, it's round the other side of the island, you know, there's good grazing below the cliffs. And he'd made a pen below the cliffs and he was clipping the sheep in it, and he had them all in it, he'd about twenty or thirty sheep in it and he was about half way through them, and this man ran one of the boats from the island, to the mainland and he was called on fairly often, to take ones either over to the mainland or back to the mainland. And while he was clipping the sheep, his mother came to the cliff top and shouted down to him that he had to go to Ballycastle. And it wasn't so many years ago that this particular thing happened. Anyway he let all the sheep out of the pen, and gathered up what wool he had and carried it home with him. This was in the morning you know, he'd just started his work, and he arrived home at the house and he says to his mother, he says, "Who wants me to go to Ballycastle?"

She says, "I haven't left the house all day." "Well damn it," he says, "that was you at the top of the rocks." "Well," she says, "it wasn't me."

So anyway he said he would stay for his dinner, so he stayed for his dinner and then went back again. And the place that he was clipping the sheep, that he had the pen there was a big overhang, a big nose as we would call it, jutting out of the cliffs, and he went back to the place where it was, where he had the pen, and here wasn't there thousands of tons of the cliff face had fallen down just where he had the pen. And this was supposed to be some warning to him to leave it, and you know it was my father told me this story and he said that he remembers the man that it happened to and you can still see the place. It's all grass all around it but at this particular place, it's all just big rocks with the cliffs and all fallen down. It's supposed to be quite true.[26]

This is an unusual but not a unique account, for as is evident especially from the release of tension through teasing and laughter at the end of the aural manifestation of the tale, few stories of this kind offer comfort. There is resistance to experiencing a "warning," and in Rathlin lore, tales of death omens are generally concerned with confronting the unknown.

Ghost Stories

Rathlin's ghost lore shares many features with ghost belief in the northern part of Ireland. One feature of the island's ghost stories is, however, more typical of Scotland, for in Ireland there are few stories of ghosts associated with battlefields. As the following account shows, this idea is well-known on Rathlin. It clearly illustrates the fact that the island's traditions show a strong Scottish influence.

One night there was two or three going to fish at the place called Gunner's Rock. Why they called it Gunner's Rock is another story. Used to be a gun at the lighthouse that they fired every so often during fog, it was actually fired every twenty minutes, like a big cannon, and they had a special man at the lighthouse, a gunner . . . and this particular man always used to fish at this rock, so that's how it got the name the Gunner's Rock. But these people were going to the Gunner's Rock, you see they had been down fishing and there was two or three of them, two or three islanders, and they heard this awful screaming and terrible goings on, so they were young, you know young fellows and they didn't know what under heavens it was, you know, it was getting dark, it was the winter time, about October, it was getting dark, so, they set off, you have to come up a path up the cliffs up to the top. And they set off, and they come up, and as they come up the path this screaming and shouting and terrible goings on got louder as they come up to the top. So, they were in two minds what to do, whether to stay where they were, or to come on up, you know, they thought there was a terrible slaughter going on, you see. So they decided to come on and they come onto the top and just when you come to the top of the cliffs there's a sort of a wee hollow and they had never heard any of the stories about the massacre at Bruce's castle or anything, but, they come up and they seen these people in this hollow, you know, they said there was women and children and people in uniform and all, and they could see them and they were getting killed, and then when they come a bit further everything disappeared. So they come home and they told it and this particular place, they told some of the older ones this particular place . . . is actually where all the people at one time were all killed in the castle. It was actually Drake come and got them all out of the castle and they were all murdered in this hollow. And they were supposed to have seen this all taking place. So . . . nobody was ever too keen on going after night again, to fish there. I know I have fished there and I never seen anything like that.[27]

Tales of massacres as well as of subsequent hauntings are important elements in island lore.[28]

Many elements of Rathlin ghost tradition are common to other parts of Ireland. Some tales are straightforward statements, usually secondhand, of sightings, offered as evidence of the existence of ghosts. Others are developed narratives, often on familiar themes. The association between mysterious lights and ghosts is represented in the following two accounts of the same incident told on different occasions by the same storyteller.

That was the house that was up beside where we used to live. The old man had been dead for about a fortnight before anybody found him in it, and . . . he was a very odd sort of a boy and he had the house all, you never seen him for weeks on end and you know that's maybe about fifty years ago he died. But you used to never see him for weeks on end and nobody ever put any heed to it, but he'd been dead for about a fortnight before anybody had got him, and they say that he haunted the house. Oh, my mother seen the lights and all on and you'd go to one window and you could see the lights shining through, at that time there were a thatched roof and all on it. Nice, very nice wee cottage it was and . . . the light would go from one, as you went to one window the light would be in the next room, although you couldn't see a light, it was just the glow of the light shining through. And it happened, it happened a lot.[29]

After he died, he was dead nearly a week in the house before anybody found to him, he had the doors all propped from the inside and everything; and nobody had found him and he had been dead a week or so. But anyway my mother, we used to live next door to it, this house, it was derelict, and the roof was still on, the windows and doors and all still quite, you know, was even liveable, but it was during war time and at that time you weren't supposed to have a naked light in the window or anything, you know you were supposed to have dark curtains and all on. And she went out to take washing in off the line and my grandfather was in the house, and she said to him, she says, "Come on out till you see this," she says. "There's a light in Paragh Beg's." "Awk, not at all," he says, "there wouldn't be." And, "Oh aye," she says, "there is." I remember her at different numerous times telling me this, you know, telling us about there was a light on the house alright but you know you couldn't see like a flame or anything although the whole inside of the room inside of the one room was lit up, so my grandfather went down, he thought maybe somebody had been . . . working in it during the day and had left a dropped match or a light or something, and he went down and when he went down to look in the window, (there was like, different rooms in the house) we would look in one window and the light would be in the next room, and it was only a matter of walking a step to look in the other window and it would be in the room that he was just after looking in.

. . . so he never put any more heed on it and came up and didn't want to scare my mother she was on her own, my father was fishing over in Ballycastle, fishing salmon so he said, "Aye," he says, "it was some of them," he said, "had been in it and they had left a candle." But it was after he was telling my father about it, another night my father was coming home and he seen the same and he looked all round that house, and he said, "There's no. . . ." There was a light in it alright but there was no visible sign of flame you know or torch or anything, there was no such thing as electricity and yet and all he could never see, he could see the light in the room he'd move to that window and it would then be in the opposite end.[30]

Despite some difference in the circumstantial details, these two accounts, recorded from an experienced storyteller, are basically consistent. Their relative lack of formalization suggests that the account is freshly offered at each telling, as a matter of personal belief, rather than recounted as a more distanced narrative. The widely known theme is thus highly particularized and individualized.

Other well-known ideas which circulate on Rathlin include the belief that horses are sensitive to ghosts.

A horse, you know, will see something unnatural before a human being will. And if you're riding along on a horse . . . at night, you know, sometimes a horse will stop along the road there, but they say if you look out between the horse's ears, if you . . . look exactly between the horse's ears you'll see what the horse sees. So that is a sure way of seeing the ghost.[31]

Island lore forges close links between the supernatural and natural worlds. Seals and sometimes seabirds are said by some to be the ghosts of dead fishermen, while other stories tell that fishermen lost in heavy seas can be seen fishing from their boats on stormy days.

Another story, widely told in Ireland and Scotland, is remembered on Rathlin.

> The West Cave they call it. It's supposed to go right through the island, this cave, and supposed to be a piper and his dog went into it one time, now for what reason I couldn't tell you. But the dog was supposed to come out, this cave went right through the island, right under Ushet Lough, and out at Doon, and this piper and his dog came out. He was playing his pipes and the dog came out at the other end, but he never come out, and they say if you go down there on a big stormy night you can still hear the man in the cave, piping away, playing his pipes.[32]

Many stories deal with the reason why a ghost is impelled to appear. Both accidental death and murder are frequently given as the cause of a haunting.

> There was two people going to the shore to gather driftwood, there used to be great competition a long time ago to get the driftwood that was washing up, and this is a very steep grassy slope that runs right down to the shore and they seen some timber washed up and they were running down to get it. This one chap, I suppose maybe he was a bit greedier than the other fellow, he decided to run down the slope so, you know naturally enough if you start running down a slope you'll find it very hard to, you just go faster and faster and you find it very hard to stop. And at the bottom of it there's a wild pile of rock and stone, so he started going faster and faster and he couldn't stop, so when he did hit this pile of stones, his head was supposed to have been cut off him, you see. So that was alright, he was killed anyway. So a few years later there was some going to fish off the rock round the same area and it was just getting dusk and they seen this person coming up the cliff path and thought there was something in it, they thought there was something unusual about him, and as they come near they discovered that this bloke had no head.[33]

The following story includes the motif of the appearance of the ghost leading to the revelation of the murder.

> Well, talking about fishing, there was this man and he was fishing you see, he went out in the boat. Every day he went out this wee boy would appear up in the bow of the boat, you know—laughing at him, sitting there crossed legged in the bow of the boat laughing at him. And this in broad daylight! But if he took anyone else with him the boy never appeared. So, damn it, he didn't know what the hell it was. It was a new boat he got, it was a new boat to him, it was a secondhand boat, you see. And she had come from Scotland, and by Jove, he thought this very strange and every day that he would go out on his own, he would see this. So he thought to himself, you know, that it was sort of getting him worried, and he was catching fish and doing alright, but this boy he

never said anything, just sat laughing at him on the deck of the boat. So he decided that he would go and he would say to the priest did he want to go out and fish—the priest was very keen to go to fish—they always used to go to the priest for everything. But anyway they went for him and he says to him, "Do you want to come out to fish with us?" and "Oh aye, I wouldn't mind a day's fishing," he says, "I'll go with you surely, I'll be down in the morning." So he came down in the morning and he says to him when they set off, "Where will I sit?" "You sit there up in the bow of the boat." So that was alright, the priest went up. They fished and nothing happened. On the way back, he says to him, he says, "You never seen anything when you were fishing the day up there?" And the priest said, "No, no just fish and birds and that about, why?" Well he says, "Father, every day," he says, "I've been out," he says, "there's a wee man appears up there on the bow of the boat," he says. "That's why I took you with me today, to see if you would notice anything or see anything." He says, "Is that so?" he says, "where did you get the boat?" He says, "I got her over in, she come from Scotland." And he says, "Aye, that's funny." He says, "I don't know," he says, "anything you can do about that." He says, "I thought you might have been able to do something, maybe bless the boat or something." "Well," he says, "I can do that surely for you."

But the priest done it, but it didn't make any difference. The next day he went out on his own the same thing happened. And it was beginning to get him down. Anyway, he says "To hell with that," he couldn't stick this any longer, "I'll take the boat back." So he took the boat back and says to the man he bought it off, he says, "I don't want that boat" he says, "you may give me my money back, and you can keep the boat." The man says to him, he says, "Why?" he says to him, "what's wrong with it, is there anything wrong with it? Is it a bad boat or is she rotten or anything?"

"Oh no," he says, "there's nothing wrong with the boat. She's a good boat and sails well . . . but . . ." he says, "I have no peace in her," he says, "and every day I go out to fish," he says, "there's a wee man appears up there in the bow of her." And he got him to describe the wee man to him, "Oh," he says, "I see, well," he says, "I'm sure we can put that right, I'll see what we can do." And that was alright, the man stood there a couple of nights and the boy came back to him and he said (he'd been away to Campbelltown or somewhere and he came back) and he says to him, "That's alright, you take the boat home," he says, "and you'll have no more bother." He says, "You'll never see that boy again." "Well," the man says to him, he says, "What did you do?" "You know," he says, "I'd like to know what you done, or I'd like to know why that man was there." "Well" he says, "it's like this, . . . that boy that you seen in the bow of the boat," he says, "was a sort of a half-wit that used to live about here and he went out to fish with another man in that boat one day . . . but . . ." he says, "he went out with him to fish one day," and he said, "the half-wit fell over the side and he got drowned," he said, "whenever I left you the other night," he says, "I went," he says, "and I got the police," he says "and we went to the house and we told the man that we knew what happened and," he said, "he confessed to the whole thing." He had

thrown the boy over the side and drowned him and that was why he kept
appearing to him and he would never rest until the other boy was caught.
Whether your man ever seen him afterwards or not I don't know.[34]

Sudden, violent death is not the only reason given in island lore for
ghostly manifestation. In the following account, the ghost appears in order
to redress a wrong done by the living to the dead.

There's a story that there was these two brothers, aye, they were two
brothers from the island. They went over to Isla with some produce; it
was either produce or they went for something. Now, I think it was
probably they were taking something over to the island, or over to Isla, it
was probably grain for the distilleries. And that was alright, they had
nothing to come back with and the boat was light and there was a fair
breeze of wind in it and you needed ballast in the boat, and they had
nothing to take back with them, and they didn't know what to do, you
know, what to take for ballast. And they didn't want to take sand, you
see, because sand was too hard to take out of the boat if they needed to
put it out quick, and it was too dead when it got wet. So round where
they were I suppose there were no stones or anything, but not very far
away there was a graveyard. And it was early in the morning, or maybe
late at night whenever they decided to go, they went to the graveyard
and they broke the headstones and they took the headstones and put
them in the boat. And that was alright, they set off for home, and they
were sailing across and she was going good on and the next thing this old
woman appeared in the bow of the boat and she said to them, "Turn
back." And one of them said to her, "What will we turn back for?" She
said, "Turn back, these gravestones, you know, they are marking peoples'
graves, you must turn back with them." "Oh, no." They went on, and
"Well," she said, "I'm telling you now, turn back or you'll never make it."
That was alright, they decided to go on. "Well," she says, "you may go on
but you'll not be able to put the stones out, you know that's what's going
to happen, you'll not be able to put the stones out." The boy took the
hammer, I suppose he had a hammer or something on the boat and he
broke the stones up in wee lumps, you see it was the big slabs they took,
they just broke them level with the ground to put into the boat. "Aw," he
said, "we'll put them out." And he took a hammer or something and
broke them into nice handy pieces in the boat and they sailed on, and
they got caught in a tide race away off the West Lighthouse and . . . they
had to put some of this ballast out or shift it maybe to the other side and
when they went to lift the stones they couldn't budge them, they were
solid. They couldn't move them, and the boat was overwhelmed, but
anyway there was another boat fishing off the back of the island and she
seen the boat capsize and they sailed out to them. I forgot to say that one
of the brothers wanted to turn back and the boy that wanted to turn back,
of course, he wasn't steering the boat. It was the elder brother was
steering the boat. And by the time that they got out, the other boat got
out, the elder brother was drowned and the young fellow was saved, and

that's how they knew what had happened. So that's why you should never use headstones for ballast. And that's happened, you know, in a lot of places that's what they used to do. You know, because usually graveyards were fairly close to the shore and they used to take them.[35]

This statement of the need to respect the dead and their physical and literal domain in addition to their spiritual realm is related to the broader belief that it is unwise to seek to enquire closely into the supernatural.

The next narrative also deals with the issue of respect, but in this case a Protestant woman has transgressed by mocking the elevation of the host at the Mass, and is consequently denied rest and condemned to "walk" after her death.

Inf. 1: Oh, the keeper's wife. She was a lass. She used to get a sheet, and tie it round her, and a spoon, you know, and ring round the tin with a spoon . . . like at the consecration. Then my uncle Paddy was a very strong man, and he was coming home one night, and she appeared to him with the tin, the sheet and the tin. And was ringing it. And you may guess, he was a strong, strong able man.

Inf. 2: Was this Paddy the Cliff Climber?

Inf. 1: Aye, that's his name, and when he came home, when he went in, he fainted, after seeing the keeper's wife.

Inf. 2: And did anybody else ever see her?

Inf. 1: Yes, another fellow, called Willie Black. He saw her. And there was three of them. My brother, and my cousin, and Willie Black. And they were wondering what was making him shift from one side to the other. And it was because the keeper's wife was appearing to him. And when he would go to one side, she would go after him.[36]

The elderly storyteller refers to her uncle, who approximately a century ago was noted for his great strength and bravery as a cliff climber.

A moral issue of a different type is contained in the next story, which deals with the need both to obey natural laws and to accept the possibility of the supernatural.

This fisherman could talk to the wind (a very useful thing, nowadays). He could talk to the wind anyway and he always knew when there was a gale coming up you see. And he always knew when it was safe to go out to fish and he was always very lucky at fishing, because he knew what the weather was going to do. And of course naturally enough the advice of this man was very much sought after and you know all the island, the other island fishermen heeded him and listened to what he had to say, and there was one day a young fisherman arrived from Scotland you see, the fishing's very good around the island, and even people from the Irish side used to come over here and fish, you know from the County Antrim side, and they used to live in the caves, you know, maybe for the summer

or the autumn when the fishing was good, they would set up in the caves
and the caves were quite dry and plenty of firewood and all in them.
They were comfortable enough and they'd maybe go home you know, at
the weekends, come and stay two and three days at a time. And they
used to come from Scotland as well. And there was this young man come
from Scotland and of course was full of new ideas, and never paid any
heed to this old man at all you see, he said this talking to the wind was a
lot of baloney. And one particular day the young boy was getting the
lines ready to go out to fish and the old man came to him and told him
not to go, he said, "because there's a bad gale coming up." And there
was, when the young Scotsman arrived, there was an islandman teamed
up with him. He'd a fairly big boat and he needed another hand, so an
island man went fishing with him and damn it when the island man
heard the old boy saying this, he says, "Well," he says, "you know," he
says, "I'll not go." And the Scotsman says, he says, "Well, he's talking a
lot of baloney," he says, he says, "I'll go on my own," and he says "you
know," he says, "I don't believe in these old superstitions," he says. He
says, "That's fair enough," he says, "you can stay and I'll go." So anyway
the old boy was kind of angry about this you see, because they wouldn't
listen to him, and he cursed him and the young fellow laughed at him
and away he went to fish and this very bad gale blew up, blew out of the
east and it blew for three days and then it changed around to the west,
what it usually does, and the young Scotsman never came back. And they
always say on the island, if you talk to any of the older men on the island,
they'll say that the east's never in debt to the west, and usually if you do
get a bad gale out to the east it will shift into the west, and it'll blow just
as hard out of the west. And they say that's why this happens, that the
young man, this Scotsman, the boy with no sense, that he'll never get
land anywhere, that when it blows him this way, the wind'll shift and it'll
blow him back and he'll never make it.[37]

Most of the preceding stories express a sense of fear of death and of
the dead, but in this tale, the haunting is motivated by romance.

This man used to go *ceilidh* every night and, two or three nights in a row,
going home, this woman appeared in front of him. And he knew it was a
ghost and he was very upset about it. It happened in the Upper End. And
she always appeared to him in this particular place on his way home, and
he was very upset about it and all, and went to the priest about it, you
see. So he never told the priest that he knew who it was, but he says he
seen this woman, he says, "What will I do?" "Well," he says to him, he
says, "I don't know what you may do," he says, "the only thing I can
suggest is to come home another way and maybe you'll not see her." This
was alright, he done this for a while but something was always tempting
him to go back, you know, it was a short cut home, tempting him to go
back this way. So anyway this night, he was going home and he came to
the spot where it was, and he was married, this man was married, and
had a family and all. Anyway, going home this night, he seen this woman

again, and he went on home, he went in and he was very upset. His wife said to him what was wrong. "Well," he says, "I've seen the ghost of Jane." So the wife knew who it was. This was a girl that this man used to go with, when he was a young man, he used to go with. And in this particular spot where he seen her, she had been going home one evening after herding cows or sheep or something and slipped, hit her head on a stone, and she didn't die right away, but she lay for a long time, she was bad, and she died some months after it, and he was quite brokenhearted after her. But anyway, he told the wife about it and he said, "Aye, I know who it is." So she said, "Go back to the priest, and tell him. Tell him you know who it is and see what he says." So he went back and the priest says, "All we can do," he says, "is say a Mass for her, and maybe that will be alright." And that was alright, everything was OK for awhile, and another night he was going home, again she appeared in front of him. "Well," he says, "I can't put up with this any longer," and he stopped. She always walked in front of him you know, she would look back. So he stopped. . . . "Look Jane," he says, "what can I do for you, or what's bothering you that you're appearing in front of me every night? Can I do something for you?" She says to him "Yes, John," she says, "you can." She says (and it must have been in the springtime), "that bunch of flowers, that bunch of primroses at your feet there," she says, "take them and plant them at my grave," she says, "and I'll never appear to you again," she says, "that will put me at ease and I'll never appear in front of you again." So he took the flowers, and the next day he took these flowers and he planted them in the graveyard on her grave and from that day to the day he died, she never appeared to him again.[38]

This tale holds the promise that the appearance of a ghost can be comforting and may offer unthreatening evidence of the afterlife. In this respect it is in strong contrast to the most typical ghost narratives of the island, whose purpose is to create frisson and to express fear.

Wise Women and Witches

The power of the midwife entitles her to be characterized as a wise-woman, one who may even be required to help the fairies. Wise-women appear in other Rathlin tales—one of them is able to advise the young man who falls in love with the mermaid on how to trap his bride.[39]

According to some aetiological tales, a witch is responsible for the very origin of the island.

There was a witch one time, she lived on the mainland and she was getting up to all sorts of tricks and all, so they decided they would banish her to Scotland. So she wanted to take some things with her and they wouldn't let her take anything with her, "Well," she says, "give me just a wee bit of soil, a wee bit of sod of Ireland to take with me." So they allowed her take that and when she was passing over the sea over where Rathlin is now, damn it wasn't there a hole in her apron, and the sod dropped out and it went into the sea, and that's how Rathlin was formed. And the unfortunate thing she wasn't a wee bit nearer Scotland or a wee bit nearer Ireland![40]

In other variants she is responsible only for the origin of a particular landmark on the island.

Another story including a wise-woman offers an explanation for an unusual feature of island topography. It also includes rare reference to mythological tradition, dealing as it does with the ancient tale of the Children of Lir, whose journeying in swan-form took them to the Sea of Moyle which surrounds Rathlin.[41]

These children they were turned into swans, they could get nowhere to shelter, you know, from the bad weather and all, they tossed about on the seas out there between here and Scotland, you see, so there was an old fisherman on the island and he knew about it, and ah, of course, they couldn't come to land on the island, but at that time swans were a great source of food, you see. So they couldn't come to land here on the island or they couldn't come to shelter on the island anywhere anybody would see them, because they'd be killed. But there was this old fisherman, he was out fishing and he seen them, you know, and he heard them crying, you see, and he knew that they were enchanted. So . . . he went up in his boat to them and he says, you know . . . what was wrong and they said that they were cold and they were swept about by the storms and that they needed somewhere to shelter, that they couldn't go to Scotland and they had to come to . . . you know, they had to get shelter somewhere. So, he says, "Well," he says, "I know a place where you won't be caught and where the sea won't get you." He says, "It's a cave," he says, "a cave on the island." And they said "Oh, but if we go to the island, they'll [sic] know." And he said, "Where I'm going to take you," he said, "is a cave, it's a sea cave." And they said to him, "Well, that'll be no good because the sea will wash up in to it and we'll be washed out of it, and . . . that'll be no good, we wouldn't get any shelter there." So, "Well," he said, "I'll take you to it anyway," and he said, "I know a person," he says, "that'll make the cave safe for you." So the cave is Avaragh, that's over below the east lighthouse, I couldn't tell you what Avaragh means, but he took them to this cave and it was a sea cave, the sea went right into it and you could go right into it with a boat. And they told him it was a nice cave and all, they could shelter in it, but that wouldn't stop . . . when there'd come an easterly gale or that . . . wouldn't stop the sea going into it. So he went away home, he says, "Well," he says, "I know a woman that can put that right, but," he says, "now you'll have to do something for her, you know, we'll have to find some way of repaying her." And . . . he went home . . . and told this woman what about the swans, about the Children of Lir, and he told her the whole tale about it and she says, "Well, I can help them as regards the cave." So she went and worked this spell over the cave and out of the bottom of the sea there rose this bar of rock come across the whole entrance of the cave so as that there was water on the inside and with high tide you could get out, you see. So that was alright, that was done, they were quite safe in the cave, nobody knew about them, nobody could get to it, and . . . Yes it is, it's the only cave there's a big bar of rock across the mouth of the cave, and there's quite . . . very deep water in the inside, and ah . . . you can get out with high tide, but you can't get into it at low tide. . . . But, anyway, this woman had to be repaid and she said to them that . . . how could they . . . they said to her . . . how can she be repaid. And, ah, she said that she had a son at home and he was blind, he was born blind, that he could never see. So . . . in thanks for what she done to them they told her to go home and not to worry about it any more. So, when . . . her son was only a small, you know, a small boy, he was about seven or eight, and, ah . . . he had never been out of the house in his life because he was blind and she couldn't take him anywhere. So she went home, and when she went home, when she was coming up to her house, the wee boy came running out of the house and down the loanen towards them and he could see quite clearly and that was her reward for making their cave safe.[42]

This story incidentally confirms the possibility of reciprocity between supernatural beings and humans with special gifts.

Subsistence on Rathlin is a precarious issue, and many tales reflect the difficulties presented by island terrain and the susceptibility of the islanders to the elements. The following story, well-known along the northwest seaboard area (which embraces the west coasts of Scandinavia, and the north and west coasts of Scotland and Ireland), remains popular on Rathlin, where even today a change in the wind may mean that no one leaves or comes to the island for days.

It was fishermen that were over in Isla. They went across there one time to fish, they used to salt the fish and dry them. And take them across there and sell them. And they kept friendly with a lot of people over there, and they were always complaining about the weather, you know, as fishermen do, and it never suited them, there was never enough wind or if there was enough wind there was too much, sort of thing. And they used to get very annoyed about this. But they were across this time, suppose maybe it must have been the summertime—there was very little wind in it, and they set off from Isla and no wind to sail the boat back and they probably had a lot of foodstuffs and all back with them. But they were going to have a long row home, so they decided to turn back and wait for a bit of a breeze. And they went back again, you know, they told the Isla folk why they turned back and they said, "Well, there's an old woman that lived over there." If they went to see her, and of course they had to take something with them, you know, in payment for it. She said, "Aye, certainly." She could help. And she went away out of the house and after about a half an hour she came back and she gave them a leather bag with a piece of string hanging out of it, and she said to them, she said, "Now when you want a breeze, just pull that string out and there'll be a knot on it, loose the knot out." And she said, "You'll get a breeze," she says, "if it's not enough, pull a bit more out, take another knot out of it." You know, this must have been an endless piece of string!

But anyway, they set off and they were a bit wary, about this, and anyway, they said, "We'll try it." So there was very little wind, hardly any wind at all, so they pulled out a piece of string out of the bag, loosed a knot off and up sprung the breeze. And that was alright, they'd a wee bit of breeze, not enough, and they decided they'd try another knot out. Tried another knot, the wind puffed up a bit more. And damn it they said, "This is working. You know, it was worth the money that we gave the old woman." So that was alright, tried another knot out of the string, fair enough—just got a nice sailing breeze and they sailed the whole way home, and this was great, you know, it worked the best for them, they could get wind whenever they wanted it. But I never heard in the story how they stopped the wind!

But anyway, they went back this time to Isla and there were some fair or something like that on, and some of them had their families across. And they stayed there for a few days and there was just this one boat had the leather bag with the string from it, bag of tricks! But anyway, on their way back again, they loosed out sufficient amount of knots to get whatever wind they wanted, and they left the leather bag with the string in the bow of the boat, and the families were in there, you know, the wives and the children, I suppose two or three of them or whatever amount was in it. And they had a sail over the top of them, you know to keep the spray off them, and they were sitting huddled in there, and one of the kids started playing with this bag of string and started pulling the string out, and loosed the knots and all. And the wind got worse and worse and worse, sprung up until there was a living gale in it, really bad, and the men in the boat couldn't understand what was wrong, what had happened. You know this thing had gone haywire, blowing a real storm. There was a boat coming behind them anyway, another boat, and funnily enough, she was just in a light sailing breeze, but it was real turmoil where this other boat was. And eventually the boat capsized and they were all thrown into the sea, and the other boat sailed up alongside them, and picked one or two of them out of the water, the most of them were drowned, they picked one or two of them out of the water, and that's how the story got out, nobody knew they had this bit of string, and they picked them up. Nobody ever went back near the old woman again for another piece of string.[43]

The common theme of witchcraft interfering with dairying was well-known on Rathlin, although now that little churning is done on the island, these stories are less commonly told. They are known to some older narrators.

That's the morning they be all out, May morning, gathering the dew for some purpose, witchcraft or something. Well, they don't exactly gather it.

They'd be out in the morning before the sun would get up, they must have had a wee rhyme of some kind. . . . "Come all to me, come all to me."

And then I heard a yarn, this woman was churning, and this other woman was [?] away in the water, and she would say, "Milk to my eyes and butter to my elbows." It was a good one, aye, "Milk to my eyes and butter to my elbows." . . . Awk, those times is; nobody believes in that now . . . Awk, it was superstition. Aye. But there were such things.[44]

The same story teller also knew the tradition of the woman who transforms herself into a hare in order to steal milk. The transformation theme is popular in contemporary island lore, although here the thrust of the tale has changed.

There's another story about years ago, when the landlord, the Gages they were the landlords, they owned the island, they used to take friends out from the mainland for a day's shooting on the island. You know, shooting the ducks and shooting the hares, and they had pheasants and all on the island. It was well stocked and they were going to the Upper End to shoot some hares you see. So on the way they met a small boy you see, and they said to him, they had dogs with them, and they said to him, "If you can find a whin bush with a hare in it, and tell us on the way back down, we'll give you a half-crown." You see?

So you know, at that time a half-crown was a small fortune. The wee boy went home and he told his granny. And she said to him, (there's a hillock on the way to the Upper End, it's called Doage) she said to him, "You go up to Doage and wait for them coming back," and she said, "you know the bush, the whin bush growing along the road," she says, "and in the whin bush there'll be a hare." You see? So, anyway the wee boy done this and went up and waited for it. But now in telling his granny about getting the half-crown for the hare and all, he forgot to tell her that the Gages had the dogs with them, these hounds with them for hunting the hares. So on the way down again, the wee boy pointed out you know where the bush was, with the hare in it. And they surrounded the bush you see, with the dogs, and the hare bolted out of the bush and the dogs set off in pursuit. Anyway, the hare run down the hill, right down Doage and down the back where the church is up there, and back down, and disappeared in this wee boy's grannie's door. And when they caught up with it, the dogs were going mad, the door closed you see and the dogs were going mad at the door, and the Gages run up and opened the door, and there the granny was sitting at the fire, she hadn't a breath, she was gasping, at the fire and the wee boy says to her, he says, "By God Granny," he says, "you beat the dogs," he says, "and I've got the half-crown." So, that was supposed to be, the granny could turn herself into a hare you see.[45]

Underlying many of these stories is, of course, the implication of diabolical connection.

The Devil

Stories of "Old Nick" abound on Rathlin, expressing fear and awareness of the power of evil. Some anecdotes are abbreviated to a comment on his appearance, actualizing and validating belief.

> He appeared at a farm as a dog, . . . a big black dog with red eyes. There's quite a few people have seen that.[46]

The "devil's footprint," a mark rather like one which might have been made by a hoof, clearly visible in a well-known position, is also cited as evidence of the physical presence of the devil.

> There is a stone down there and there's a mark of a cloven hoof on it. I suppose it must have been some time the priests earned their money on the island, but anyway, the devil was down that end too, so they sent for him, and he banished him. But on his way out, he stepped on this stone, his cloven hoof on the stone, and they said that was a sign that he would be back. So it's said that if he ever came back to the island, to that end of the island, this cloven hoof mark would disappear. So, I'd been looking a while ago, and I see it's still there. You can see it, it's just quite plain to be seen, cloven hoof mark.[47]

The following story deals with the common theme of the devil's association with card playing. Apart from the evils of gambling which may be associated with the activity, the cards themselves are often believed to be possessed of potential evil.

> There's supposed to be, devils supposed to be around Gage's a lot. The Manor House, and years back the young people of the island, they used to maybe get together for the night and they'd go to an old byre or an old stable or something to play cards. I suppose, maybe the people that owned these buildings they were always frightened of them, they'd thatched roofs and all, and maybe in smoking, you know. They were sitting with a candle, and they always had visions of them getting burnt down. In fact I think at one time there was one of these outhouses, was burnt down, and this is what it was put down to, somebody playing cards had left a candle or a cigarette end or something.
>
> Anyway they decided that they would go round to Gage's, one of Gage's outhouses, and they went round there, and they had a candle of course, and a tea chest and they started to play cards. And anyway they were sitting playing cards and the door opened. And this man walked in and sat down, and was playing cards with them. Now this was the wintertime you see, and nearly any of the boats that come to the island always lands round the area of harbor here. And the weather was bad it was winter time and they knew there was no boats. And of course like everyone on the island knows if there's any strangers on the island and

they knew this man didn't arrive by boat. And in them days, there was no other way to come you see. So he sat down and put his couple of pence on the table along with everyone else, so they'd no option but to deal him a hand of cards along with everyone else and anyway the game was in progress and all of a sudden, the candle went out. So, by this time, they began to get very nervous, and somebody struck a match and lit the candle, and when they lit the candle again the hand of cards that this stranger had was lying on top of the tea chest and they were burned, and the door had been bolted from the inside you see, whenever the fellows went in, they bolted the door on the inside so as nobody else could come in. And this was the strange thing. The door opened, and it had been bolted on the inside, and when they lit the candle again, there was no sign of the stranger, his hand of cards was lying on the tea chest and they were burned, and the door was still bolted on the inside. So I'm sure these boys that was in there, they made a very hasty retreat outside . . . this was supposed to be old Nick himself.[48]

Devil stories may also express anxieties arising from the presence of strangers or outsiders on the island. As shown in the previous narrative, stories and anecdotes hint at or openly state a relationship between the landlord's family and the devil.

LB: I've heard that the devil was in the Manor House at one time.
Inf.:   Aye, so they say he was, and he left his (they called him the *gruagach*), he left, is supposed to have left the marks of his fingers round a window case, where he was going out through the window.
LB: Why was he going out the window?
Inf.:   He was exorcised by a priest. I suppose the window was the only opening available to him. He's supposed to have been seen several times in the room where they were in the habit of playing cards. Again you don't know whether these stories are true or not. He was banished for ninety-nine years. I think the ninety-nine years are nearly up, so he's due a return trip! Alright, no mocking, I mean, you believe in God, you believe in the devil. You can't say you believe in one and not the other.[49]

This story, in addition to suggesting that the landlord was compelled to submit to the power of the priest, also links the devil to the *gruagach*, who is more usually an "ugly" or "hairy" fairy (*gruagach* literally translates from Gaelic as "hairy" or "ugly"). Thus the devil is sometimes conceptualized as a hobgoblin. This aspect of the devil, less threatening than in other accounts, occurs in a number of stories told by another narrator.

Inf.:   I was telling you that there used to be a watch hut up where, the
        coastguards kept a watch on it, and you know, any ships in
        distress, or I think it was actually to prevent smuggling. I think
        that was actually what their job was. But they used to change the
        watch up in my grandfather's house, a man coming off would
        meet the man coming on there and then he would walk on up
        over the mountains to, as they called it, the look out. And they
        had a wee stove and fire and all that and there was one particular
        night this man coming off watch met the chap coming on, and he
        said to him you know, passing the time of night and he said, to
        him, he says, "Did you leave a fire on?" "Oh aye," he says, "I
        did," he says, "and I left the wee man sitting beside it." Now the
        wee man, everybody talks about them on the island and that is
        the *gruagach* is another name for Old Nick. And so the man
        laughed about it, and he went on and he went into the watch hut,
        he opened the door and went in there was a fire, a roaring fire on,
        and the stool beside the fire, here wasn't the wee man sitting on it.
        So the boy closed the door and beat a hasty retreat and there was
        never a watch kept in the hut after it, they closed the place down.
LB: Aye! Are there other stories about the *gruagach* then?
Inf.:   Oh aye, you see he's been seen a lot. He's supposed to be
        harmless, he'll not do you any harm but you know, I don't think
        it does your nerves very much good. There was a crowd coming
        from a dance one night, coming down from the hall, or maybe
        from a ceilidh in some house and they were coming down the
        back of Gage's there, you see, so they decided that they would get
        up to some devilment, there. Once in Gage's, they'd get up to
        some devilment you see, so they were going to come down to the
        back of the house, and maybe throw stones on the roof or get up
        to some roguery. They were coming down you see, so they were
        up the back of the house, and one of them said, he said to the
        fellow beside him, he says, "You clod stones up on the roof." So
        he never answered him and he was digging a scraw out of the
        ditch, you see to throw on the roof, he says, "Here you throw
        that." And the fellow beside him never answered him, and here,
        the other ones further along the way, you see they were throwing
        stones up, so he turned round to look at the fellow who was
        standing beside him, you see, and he turned round and he sees
        here this wee man was sitting, here the *gruagach* was sitting
        beside him. So they didn't stay too long round the house. But it
        was supposed to be this *gruagach* that the priest banished out of
        the house, so I doubt he didn't make a very good job of it.[50]

In the following variant, the devil's activities are more akin to
poltergeist than to fairy.

Gage's house, I was telling you, was haunted, you see, so, Old Nick
himself was supposed to be down in it. The dresser the dishes was in

would clatter unto the floor but the dishes wouldn't get broken, and beds would be lifted and it used to be, they weren't getting any peace in the house at all. So they decided there was nothing for it but to get the minister down. So they sent for the minister and he came down, and had a look around and he says, "Well," he says, "there's not much," he says, "I can do with that," he says. He says, "You may send up for the boy up above," he says, "the priest." At that time there was no chapel in the island, there was nowhere, it was just an old mill and they said mass in this old mill and it didn't even belong to them, you know, Gage relented a wee bit and said they could use it, and the priest hadn't a house, he used to stay in houses you know, say I would keep him for a week and you would keep him for a week, that's the way he went around the island. And so Gage went up for the priest, told him what was going on and the priest came down and he was supposed to have banished the devil out of the house and I remember the old brigadier showing me the mark on the wall; there was a big burnt mark on one of the corners of one of the rooms. This was supposed to be the devil went through the stones, burnt, and the plaster and the wall was burnt. And he used to paper over the top of it and the paper would be scorched on the wall. And he banished it for three hundred years and in gratitude for what he done, Gage gave them the ground to build a chapel on, ground to build a house and he got also gave him another bit of ground to graze the cow in and all on. So that's how they got the land for the chapel and the house and all. So whether that's right or not I don't [know].[51]

This story establishes the priest's power as superior to landlord and Protestant clergyman, as well as over the devil, and allows the priest to secure the right to build a Catholic church on the island in spite of the establishment.

Some tales of the devil subvert rather than uphold the satanic idea. The following narrative contrasts an apparent tendency of the laity to leap to supernatural conclusions to the common sense of the priest in the simple pursuit of evidence.

When I'm talking about that cloven hoof (the mark left in the rock), there was one time, I think it was around the First War. There was one night there was very heavy snow. There was lots of mysterious things heard and seen through the island, and the devil was supposed to be rife and all. But anyway, there was snow this night and it was blowing out of the east, you know, blowing from the east, and some got up in the morning and went out, and I suppose went out to feed the cattle, and there was a good covering of snow on the ground, and sometime during the night it must have stopped snowing anyway. But the man went round to get some fodder to feed the cattle, and as he went round the end of the barn, he seen the cloven hoof in the snow. And he knew right away what it was. So that was alright, there was a great to-do, they followed this cloven hoof along the snow, and when it would come to the top of the mountain, it would disappear, and maybe even a lake or a pond or something, and it then would reappear on the other side of it, they just walked right across the water. Funny, it was only one mark. Anyway, they were very upset about this, the people that found it, and nearly half the island knew about it. So they went for the priest. And it came in the east side of the island and it was going up, right up over the middle of the island. And they went and got the priest about this, that the devil had appeared, and you know, that he would have to come and do something about it. So the priest came down, and he says, "We'll just have to see." And he seen the cloven hoof mark in the snow too. "Well," he says, "we'll just have to go and see where he went to." So the whole crowd of them got together and away they goes after this mark in the snow, this cloven hoof, and they followed it right up over the mountain, disappeared at the top of the mountain, reappeared at the far side, same with a lake and all. They come away up to the other end of the island there, and there was a wild lot of bushes and trees, old trees and all, and here caught in one of these trees! Well, you know, the barrage balloons that they had, one of these barrage balloons was caught in the trees and there was a big lump of rope trailing from it with a shackle on the end of it! This was the cloven hoof! And the old shackle was travelling and hitting the ground every time. So there you are. If they hadn't got that, they'd have sworn it was the devil and he went out over at the far side of the island.[52]

Like devil tales, stories of ghosts are also sometimes subverted in this way. While this may help to release tension, the underlying issues are seriously regarded.

The devil's ability to transform into an animal was cited previously in the instance of a black dog. Similarly, the devil which is believed to haunt the Gage Manor is said in one account to have taken the form of a cat. Again, a priest takes care of the matter.

That was a cat that used to come in and sit on Mr. Gage's table, whenever they would go to their dinners, whenever they would go to dine. This black cat would come in and sit in the middle of the table. But Father Eddie Magowan, he banished her. . . . They were afraid of the cat.[53]

The devil in the form of a cat is the theme of another story, three versions of which provide important points of contrast regarding belief.

Another time he appeared as a cat, a big black cat. Ah, this was a man that was coming home from the east side, he'd been out in the boat fishing on the east side of the island, and he'd a big string of fish, you know, maybe a couple of strings of fish in fact, and maybe be about three dozen on every string and, on his way home, it was a dark winter's night, about maybe November time, and on his way home, he lived away up near Ballyconaghan, away up in that direction, and on his way home he was going up a hill they called Tromore, and it was dark you know, and there was a breeze of wind on it. This cat appeared in front of him, and you know it was larger than a normal cat, and you know, he was a bit afraid of it. So he says to himself, he said, "If I throw the fish now, I'll get by it." So he threw it a fish and the cat ate the fish and he still couldn't get by it, and he threw it another fish, and the cat kept moving ahead of him, and he kept throwing the fish to the cat until he was about maybe half a mile from home and he was running out of fish you see, so damn it but he finished up, he threw all the fish he had to the cat, the cat ate, and all of a sudden he tried to run by and the cat attacked him and he got badly torn with it and badly mauled, but something told him, that he wasn't to tell anybody. You see, this cat or whatever it was told him he wasn't to tell anybody.

Well, he went home. The man was very ill and they got the priest to attend to him and the priest tried to find out what had happened. Everybody said he'd fallen over the cliffs and he'd been drunk and what not, but the same time his family knew he'd been out fishing you see, and yet in all he wouldn't tell them what had happened, because he knew something dreadful would happen to him if he said what had happened. So at the finish up, the priest was that persistent about it and all, he decided, (after a couple of weeks he still wasn't on his feet) but he decided nothing could happen him, he was at home and all, he decided he would tell the priest, so he told him. The priest says, "That's a lot of nonsense," he says, "you'll be alright," he says, "I wouldn't worry any more about it." But by God, the next morning when the wife went to call the man, wasn't he lying dead. He had died during the night. So this is a tale, I heard this from my father.[54]

In the above account, the cat is a demonic force brought into conflict with the priest. The informant is unequivocal in maintaining the protagonist's physical encounter with the devil. The following version, recorded on a different occasion from another storyteller, is more equivocal.

Whatever it was, it had been sighted by people mostly at night, this is why it would have seemed more like a ghost story because people's imaginations would be inclined to run away with them at night. But the last time it was ever sighted, it was a man who lived in Shandragh, that would be Ballygill Middle, on to that townland, you know. And about the middle of the island, and he went away off down to the east side, some fishing rock, that he decided to fish from the rock, one evening. He was coming back and the thing followed him, growling and snarling, and it was this huge cat, and he started to throw some of his fish that he'd caught to it. Every time he threw a fish, he'd run as hard as he could, and the thing would be behind him before very long, and he'd throw another one. It was getting quicker and quicker, gobbling his fish up and he was running out of fish. He threw the last one as he was going up his own lane, up to the house, and he made it to the house anyway, but he left his dog outside, and he wasn't very long in until he heard the fighting and the dog starting in. The fighting went on a while round the house, and moved away across the fields, but he allowed the dog would probably chase whatever it was. The next morning he got up and he found the dog all torn in pieces, lying somewhere. But they never saw the beast again either.[55]

The above version of the story was introduced as follows, by a comment made by the storyteller's wife.

There's supposed to be, again talking about sailing ships, there's supposed to be one time, through the last century there was a big yellow cat on the island, was attacking things. And at the time it was treated very much as, "I wonder what this yellow cat was?" Nowadays they'd probably realize it would have been a lion cub, dropped off a sailing ship, that it was getting too big. You told me a story about a lion, about the man throwing it fish to keep it away.[56]

By this further rationalization, the historicity of the story is preserved at the expense of its supernatural quality, illustrating the mutability of narrative and belief, and the urge to identify an acceptable framework in which this piece of traditional island lore may be maintained.

Despite subversion and rationalism, however, tales of the devil are persistently told, and exorcism is an important issue in island narrative, as many of the above stories show. Exorcism is the theme of the following story, a variant on the custom of turning one's clothes to avoid being fairy-led.

This house on the island, the devil was in it, you know, creating a wild uproar and as usual they went to the priest and the priest came and he got rid of him, he put him out. And they sent for him again, and he got rid of him, he came back in a week or so. So that was alright, they decided they would try the minister. Sent down for the minister, and he came up and he done the same thing and he got rid of him, but just came back again. So, anyway, they sent word to the parish priest on the mainland about this and he came over and he was a very elderly man, the priest that was on the island was only a young man, I suppose he didn't know all the tricks of the trade. But anyway, the old parish priest came over and he banished him as well, but he says "Now," he says, "I'll get rid of him," he says, "and we are going to have to stop him going back in." And he made them take out all the windows in the house and turn the windows, you know, inside out, and the door was always, say on that side of the house, the door was shifted to the other side of the house, that was so that he couldn't find his way back in. And the windows, you see, were turned inside out so that he couldn't come in so that's how they got rid of him.[57]

The following account also parallels the devil and the fairies. It was told in response to a query about protecting children from the fairies.

> I remember seeing it now, I seen a piece in my grandmother's, a string with three knots in it, and you used to see it hanging up at the side of the fire, and I always wondered what it was, you know just an ordinary piece of twine, three knots in it, and I remember asking her what it was. You see, you get this piece of twine and you take it and you get the priest to bless it. Now, the idea you put that across the cot or the cradle and that'll protect the baby from evil, you know, from the devil. And the idea of the three knots in it, the three knots are supposed to represent the Trinity, you see, and this was the idea of the three knots.[58]

Potential danger to children is a significant theme, one which can be understood in practical terms as a consequence of the high rate of infant and neo-natal mortality in Ireland. This account suggests that underlying practical concern is another, deeper issue, that infant mortality may be the result of retribution for moral failure. The account can, therefore, be understood on several levels; at face value, that a baby needs supernaturally to be protected from evil (traditionally this is especially true of unbaptized children); or, that the child needs to be protected from evil influences which might seek to steal him from his parents (in this case, the influences are specifically demonic, although this behavior is more usually attributed to the fairies); or that the child's life may be at risk purely as the consequence of the perceived moral frailty of his parents. The frequency with which the theme of loss of children to supernatural forces recurs in Irish narrative hints at the issue of potential anguish contained in this idea.

In many Rathlin tales, the devil is associated with the complex of belief which surrounds the protection of the capacity to catch fish (an important source of livelihood on the island). This is fundamental to the narratives which follow.

> . . . he was coming home one night, they were fishing, they were doing a net up at Cooraghy, fishing a net up there, and there's a house up there, the haunted house they call it, and it was supposed to be that the devil used to appear in it in the form of a woman. But anyway, they had got the priest up and he banished her, for I just don't remember the number of years, but this man, he's coming home and he'd been fishing the net, he'd fished with them you see. This woman appeared in front of him and she was dancing in the middle of the road, spitting fire at him, so he was an elderly man and there was no way that he could get round her. But he set back, some of them were still working at the net and he went back to them and he said, you know, about seeing this, so they thought, "Well, he's an old man maybe with the cold and the wet he's imagining it." And they sent the young fellow with him. So the young fellow went with him and he come to the top and went along through the gate and by Jove, the old boy says to him, he says, "This is where I seen her," and by Jove didn't he see her too. The young fellow seen her, she danced down in

front of the road, down nearly to the house ahead of them and spitting
fire and whatnot at them.

So they went for the priest and they told him what had happened,
and he said he would come up the next night and he would put an end to
it. So the next night they come, they went to the net again, they had the
priest with them, and whatever he done, anyway, he was supposed to
have banished her for a number of years. I don't know how many
hundred years, but they say Cruckanturragh is the name of the hill, that
she disappeared out over, as a ball of fire. And they say that in Irishtown
that they seen this very brilliant light disappearing out over
Cruckanturragh, so whether that happened or not I couldn't tell you.

But there's another, about this one I'm talking about, Cooraghy,
there's a cave there, and used to be, I was telling you before, that the
fishermen used to come and stay in this cave. Well, there was three island
men in it one night and they had lines out, it was during the war time,
they had lines out and they would set them when it was getting dusk. It
was the summertime, and they would lift them when it was getting clear.
And nobody had ever stayed in this cave for a number of years, so they
decided for handiness to save themselves walking from home in the
morning, the good weather, nice warm weather and the summertime and
it wasn't dark for that long, that they would stay in the cave, you see?
Because it was only a matter of a few hours they would be down there,
for the night. So they lit a fire and made themselves tea, and there was a
big stone in it, a great big flat stone, they used as a table. There maybe
were a lot of wooden boxes and all. There was only three of them in it, so
whichever one of them made the tea, the three mugs was sitting on the
table and the only light that was in the cave was a fire that they'd lit at
the entrance, that they'd been boiling their tea pot on. And he was
pouring out the tea into the three mugs and all of a sudden they heard
the clump of another mug on the stove and they seen the hand, they
couldn't see anybody, but they seen the hand and they seen the mug! So
there was nothing for them but to fill this other mug as well. They filled
the other mug and it disappeared. But somebody said to them after it
(you know they took their tea and that was all, they didn't stay the night
in it, you know?) this was the old boy again. Nobody ever stayed in it
after.[59]

The idea that the devil seeks human souls is represented in Rathlin
narrative. The following account of a demonic experience at Cooraghy is
more developed and more sinister than the last.

There was one night there was this boat from Donegal came in, sail boat
came into the island, very rough night and they tried to haul the boat,
(there was a couple of islanders there) a fairly big boat, they tried to haul
her up. You know, there was no harbor here at the time. They tried to
pull her up and they couldn't budge her, you know she was that heavy
and there was only three or four in the boat from Donegal and there were
a couple of islanders down. So, one of the boys, said, one of the Donegal

boys said, "We need more help." And it was up at the other end of the island, up there at Cooraghy. . . .

"You go and get help and I'll stay with the boat, or we'll stay with the boat." So they were setting off to go and get more help and that was alright. One of the boys says, he says, "I'll stay with her, you go on up there and get something to eat and get some dry clothes, there's no point in us all staying." So that was alright, away they went, they said that was okay, they thought he could manage, they had her a wee bit out of the water you know, she was safe. And away they went, and the next half an hour or maybe an hour after that, they came back and there the boat was, your man was sitting there and the boat was high and dry up at the grass, hauled right up to the grass. They said, "My God! How did you get the boat up there?" And well he says, "It come very bad, and I knew, you see a big swell started to come in," he says, "while you were away, and," he says, "I knew we were going to lose the boat, and," he says, "there were a man come down out of the cave there and he says did I want a hand up with her, and I says I did, and he says, 'That's alright,' he says, 'will you pay me for giving a hand?' 'Aye,' [I] says, 'I'll give you whatever I have.' And well, he says, 'Will you give me what I want?' I says, 'I will.' And he says, 'Just went on the other side the boat with me,' he says. And as true as I'm standing here, I never put a bit of strength on her," he says. He just pulled her up himself and he says, "He went away up the pad there." And they were sitting wondering who it was, and they described the lightkeepers to him, and they described this one to him and they described that one to him but it wasn't any of them.

So that was alright, they were all setting off back home, they made sure the boat was safe, they went all up the path and these people were taking them back to the house, they had been fishing the net in Cooraghy and they said they'd take them back and give them a bed for the night. And on the way back, your man fell behind the rest of them and he said that he was kind of tired, so they waited on him and he came on a bit, but he fell behind again. And they were walking on along the road talking and damn it, but they missed him and they turned back and they got him lying by the side of the road. They seen he fainted or passed out or something, and they lifted him up and they said to him what had happened. He says "That man caught up with me again," he says "and he has took now," he says, "what he wants." And that was alright, this boy died on the spot.

So they rushed down for the priest, they knew he was dying anyway, they rushed down for the priest, and the priest come up and went to see the man and put them all out of the room, he says to him you know, I suppose he was talking to the boy, and he came up and he said "Well," he says, "there's nothing that I can do for him now," he said, "because I've come too late." And they said to him, "Are you not going to give him the last rites?" He says, "The last rites will be no good to him," he says, "do yous know who that was that hauled the boat with him?" And they said they didn't. "Well," he says, "that was the Devil himself, and," he says, "what he wanted was that man's soul, and," he says, "there's nothing I can do for him." So, the boy died and there was nothing anybody could do for him. That was claimed, that was where the boy came with the extra tin, or put the extra mug out.[60]

Many social and moral issues may be explored through the medium of tales of the devil. As one quoted storyteller remarked, belief in formal religion requires a belief in the force of evil, and the complex of traditional supernatural beliefs in Rathlin lore are ultimately inseparable from concepts of God, the church and the priest.

The Power of the Priest

Many of the stories so far considered have referred to the power of the priest, particularly to exorcise and to combat the force of evil. The story of the ghost of the mocking Protestant woman also attests to the power of the Roman Catholic church. In the nineteenth century, when the Gage family (who were members of the Church of Ireland—at one point the Rev. Robert Gage was both rector and landlord) dominated the island, many islanders were Protestant. Today the population is almost entirely Roman Catholic. The power of priests is an important theme of island lore, and a substantial number of these stories (some dealing with a figure more accurately described as a "holy man"), which illustrate their magical skills are still current in the oral lore of the island.

Many issues are considered when this theme arises during storytelling sessions. In the following example, island topography is an issue. More than considering the power of the priest, the story deals with the shortage of material resources, particularly fuel, a problem which has caused considerable hardship for the islanders. In the past, imported coal was expensive, and islanders exploited resources such as heather and cow dung for fuel, in addition to burning sods, a practice which was ruinous to the already meagre top soil.

They used to cut just the scraw on the top of the mountain, you know, the heather in it, and they used to burn it on the fire. And Gage never allowed this, you know, I mean it was a sensible thing because people would have dug the mountain, whole top of the mountain away and it would just have been a barren waste. And there'd be nothing on it, nothing growing on it. And he never allowed them to do this. Probably another reason was he sold coal on the island and if they could burn the top of the mountain they wouldn't be buying the coal off him. And anyway there was this one particular old man, he didn't listen to Gage, he dug away, he used to dig it in a circle, you see, start in the center and dig round to they'd have a big circle, you see. This was how they used to dig the sods off the top of the mountain. So Gage used to have his keepers that went round the different parts of the island to see that nobody was cutting the sods, as we call them. And he went to this particular house or particular farm, and it was people called X lived in it. And he seen on the top of the mountain it was all cut, the big circle where they were cutting the sods, so he went down to them and he said, "Yous were cutting sods from the top of the mountain." They said they were, they had no fire and they hadn't any money, they hadn't anything to sell to buy coal. And they owed the rent and they said they couldn't do without a fire, they had a young family in the house, and it was coming on to wintertime. And he said, "You're not allowed to do that, you know, and if you continue doing it, Gage will put you off the island, put you off your farm." So they were in a really desperate plight and they didn't know what the heck to do, so they went to the priest and they said to him, what would they do. And he said, "Gage says you're not allowed to do it, you're not allowed to do it," he says, "that's all that's to it, you'll have to do without a fire," he says, "go along the shore and you might get some wood, or timber washed in." But they went along the shore, but damn all they got, a wheen of bits of stuff for the fire, but it was no good. It just kept it burning for a short time.

So, in the meantime there was an old missioner come to the island, you know, they used to come quite regular, and he was staying up along with the priest and he heard of this. He went and visited the people, and Gage's keepers, they had measured the piece that was cut on the top of the mountain you see, to make damn sure they didn't cut any more off it. So he said to them, "Never listen to Gage," he said, "on my way home," he said, "I'll go and have a look at this place." He said, "Just take me up and let me have a look at this place where you get the sods for the fire," he says. "You can't do without a fire," he said, "you need to keep the children warm." So he left the house that evening, the man of the house took him up and he showed him where they were cutting the sods, and they say that the old missioner, he knelt down where they were working, and is supposed to have said a prayer and all, and blessed the bit of ground. "Now," he says, "as long as you live on that farm," he says, "cut you away at that bit of ground," he says, "and Gage will not say a word to you." So, the old man of the house, you know, he was kind of worried about it, you know he didn't want to lose his bit of land for he had nothing else, he didn't have a boat, he couldn't fish and he just had the wee bit of ground. But that winter again, he left it and didn't bother, just tried and survived as best he could. But that winter again there came very heavy snow and he was really desperate, he had no fire, so he said, "Well no matter what the consequences," he says, "I'll go up and get something to keep the place warm." So up he goes and cuts the bag of turf or a creel of turf, sods off the top of the mountain, and comes down with it. His wife was in a very bad way, they would be thrown out of the land and all. And a neighbor seen him doing this you see, and they had an eye to the farm, they allowed that if he was thrown out they'd have a wee bit extra ground, that Gage might give it to them. So that was alright, away they goes and tells Gage, and Gage sends his men up and the people that lived in the house, they seen Gage's men coming and they were in a bad way, they said, "This is it, we're finished."

They went up and measured it, and the bit of ground was the same size. So that was alright. The man swore black and blue, the neighbor swore black and blue that they seen them taking turf or sods down off the top of the mountain, and there was no doubt about it, they seen them. So the boy came down to the house and seen the sods burning and said, "Where did you get them?" "Ah, they're ones I had stacked away from when I cut them on it before," he said. So that was alright, here the boy continued cutting away at the sods, and the bit of ground never got any bigger, he cut away and burned away. And there was never anything about it, Gage couldn't do anything about it.[61]

Political opposition between priest and landlord is an issue in this story which also gives expression to friction between neighbors; differences of this kind are sometimes intensely experienced in the environment of the small island.

Inevitably, some tales of the priest bring him into even more direct conflict with the authority of the family of the landlord.

There was one . . . in particular . . . was very, very bigoted against the Catholic religion, against the priest . . . he forbad the priest to be boated into the island altogether. . . . They used to smuggle him in at that time.[62]

The same informant provided this account.

They tell a story about the first old Mrs. Gage, or the second old Mrs. Gage. It couldn't be the first, because they didn't allow the priest on the island. She was very severe on the priest. And on one particular occasion the priest was going to give the last rites to someone who was dying away down at the other end of the island. She met him along the road up there, and she was going to take him to task about something. In those days, when the priests were carrying the Blessed Sacrament and going to attend the sick, they didn't speak to anyone, they just went on about their business. She stepped out in front of him you know, to tackle him about some trivial thing, I'm sure. And he pushed her to the one side and says, "Stay there till I come back." And she was unable to move. Well now, again the truth of that, I don't know, but that was one of the stories that they do tell.[63]

Despite, or perhaps because of, the disclaimer this story allows the focus to be placed on the superior power of the priest especially when reinforced by the presence of the Host. As in several of the stories so far quoted, when landlord and priest are brought into conflict, the priest prevails. This allows for a degree of stereotyping, the priest as champion, the landlord as villain.[64] It would be easy to draw oversimplified conclusions from this point. However, not all landlord tales are necessarily tales of opposition or resentment. Many acknowledge that the relationship between landlord and tenant is symbiotic by giving the tenant the advantage. The landlord's authority is nonetheless a problematical issue, and tales of the above type allow an expression of tension and resentment. This story recurs in the repertoire of a number of island storytellers. In another variant of the narrative Mrs. Gage is victimized without apparent reason.

> Father Eddie Magowan left Mrs. Gage, Mrs. Captain Gage, standing at the big garden till he went home and got his dinner, and went back down again.[65]

In a final, detailed variant the priest is again depicted as the righteous protagonist.

> It was about Mrs. Gage and a priest that was here on the island fell out over something ... I think it was probably something over land ... but it was old Mrs. Gage, the landlord's wife. She was going up the road. ... The priest, he wouldn't move off the road for her. He was coming down on the horse, you see, you had to, in them times, you daren't get in their way. But this priest, he wouldn't get out of the road, so she ... gave out hell to him.
> "Well," he says, "I'm in a hurry," he says, "I'm going to attend somebody that's dying." And he says, "It's you should have got out of my way." And she gave out hell to him.
> "Well," he says, "I haven't time to stop and argue with you now," he says, "but you'll be here," he says, "when I'll be going back."
> And that was alright. He was away a good while, whoever he went to see took longer dying than he thought, and it was away late at night. And whenever he was coming back anyway at the same spot that he had the argument with Mrs. Gage, wasn't she still there waiting on him, and she couldn't move from the spot until he said so.[66]

A related theme which is acknowledged in some island stories is the priest's power to curse.

> There's a lot of tales about the priests on the island, the powerful things they could do and the curses they could bring to bear on people. ... There was one time, you know, the Gages didn't allow any priests on the island ... they didn't encourage them, and at that time, the Gages had their own boats, and they controlled who come to the island, and who left the island, and all. So, there was this priest wanted to get across to the island, and this story has been handed down, and it's quite true; it did happen. This priest come down to the pier in Ballycastle, and asked to get a passage to the island. And ... it was Gage's boat, and Gage's boatmen, and it was more than their job was worth to take the priest across, because they knew when they arrived on the island, that was the end of the job, and at that time, money was very scarce, and jobs were hard to get, and they refused him. So the priest ... was supposed to curse them. There and then, he said, "Before you're home," he says,

"maybe you'll be glad of me." And thank heavens there have been very few boating disasters round the island with island boats. But this particular boat hit a rock at the back of the Rue on the way home, and all the crew, and everybody on the boat was drowned. So, whether the priest had anything to do with it or not, I don't know. But that did happen anyway.[67]

This ability of the priest, implicit in his power, has been a source of social tension in that it can be directed alike against apparently innocent and apparently guilty. As the priest is a figure of authority, the attitude expressed to him in island folklore is also fraught with ambiguity.

Conclusion

It is plain from this selection of narratives collected on Rathlin that the supernatural is a central issue of contemporary legend on the island. These stories are threaded together and related in that they all explore different aspects of the same question; all are concerned with vital issues of living belief in which formal religion is assigned a place, but in which other potent forces are also assessed.

It may be claimed that these stories are related to a particular landscape and climate; they express a physical domain, and in this way they accord with Evans-Wentz's view of Celtic fairy faith.[68] They are also related to a social landscape which is moral and emotional. They express resentment toward the landlord, suspicion of Protestant intolerance, and class antagonism in a situation of prolonged social proximity. Thus, they function as a safety valve by acting as a medium through which strongly registered emotions may find release. While all of these issues are everyday concerns, some of the stories relate events of great significance in the folk memory. By releasing frustrations, they function as a means of coping and maintaining social relationships.

In addition to expressing marginality or to rationalizing the experiences to which they relate, many of these narratives express beliefs and attitudes central to everyday existence. These stories provide a closely constructed framework in which the natural world, an often inimical environment, is related to humanity. By drawing on widely known themes and motifs, this framework illustrates Rathlin's cultural connections with other regions. By permitting the expression of complex relationships of people to one another and to their environment, it illuminates many of the essential characteristics of life on the island. The stories are, therefore, simultaneously universalized and particularized. This corpus of material shows the way in which widely known narrative elements may be shaped to permit both individual expression and the exchange of localized ideas which convey and examine attitudes to fundamental issues of experience and existence. Furthermore, and this is of fundamental importance to an island of which it has been claimed that it will be depopulated by the end of the present century, these stories express a sense of continuity and of empathy with the past.

Notes

1. I should like to thank Mr. and Mrs. T. Cecil, Mrs. P. McFaul and Mr. and Mrs. J. McFaul for all their help and kindness, and for sharing their stories. I also express gratitude to the late Mrs. B. McKenna neé McCurdy and the late Mr. Alec Anderson for their help and generosity. Finally, an appreciation goes to R.D. Ballard and G. McManus for the accompanying map.

2. See J.H. Elwood, "A Demographic Study of Tory Island and Rathlin Island, 1841–1964," *Ulster Folklife* 17(1971).

3. See W. Clark, *Rathlin—Disputed Island* (Waterford: Volturna P, 1978).

4. See L.M. Ballard, "Rathlin: History and Folklore," *A Conservation Guide to Rathlin Island* (provisional title), ed. A. Stott (Belfast: H.M.S.O., forthcoming 1991).

5. The Gage family were resident landlords and the island remained in their possession until early in the present century. Their influence on local affairs was, therefore, strong and direct. The family is Protestant, and for a substantial period in the nineteenth century the Rev. Robert Gage was both landlord and rector. The family dwelt in a substantial Manor House which occupies a position with a commanding view of sea approaches to the island from Ireland. The present generation of the family maintains close links with the island, and are regular visitors from whom I have enjoyed generous hospitality.

6. See N. Holmer, *The Irish Language in Rathlin Island* (Dublin: Hoggis, Figgis, 1942).

7. This is also true of the Tyrone story teller Frank McKenna who not only keeps a notebook, but who in the absence of an audience has made cassette recordings of his own tales. A professionally made recording of Frank McKenna's stories is available from the Ulster Folk and Transport Museum.

8. Although especially in the nineteenth century a high proportion of islanders were Protestant, today the population is almost entirely Roman Catholic.

9. It is worth remembering Jeremiah Curtin's comment, "My host was a man who retained a belief in fairies, though he did not acknowledge it—at least explicitly and in words. 'When I was a boy,' said he, 'nine men in ten believed in fairies, and said so, now only one man in ten will say that he believes in them. If one of the nine believes, he will not tell you; he will keep his mind to himself.'" (*Tales of the Irish Fairies* [London: David Nutt in the Strand, 1895]). Might it be that the idea that fairy belief is fading and belongs to the past is part of this complex?

10. Ulster Folk and Transport Museum cassette sound recording (hereafter UFTM C) 78–55.

11. UFTM C78-55. David Thomson, *The People of the Sea: A Journey in Search of the Seal Legend* (London: Baerie and Rockliff, 1965).

12. Ulster Folk and Transport Museum reel-to-reel sound recording (hereafter UFTM R) 80-14.

13. UFTM C79-29. This story is widely known in Ireland and in other regions of the northwest seaboard. See, for example, Rosemary Power, "'The Midwife to the Fairies' in Ireland," *Sinsear* (1982–83); also see the comparative study, Críostóir Mac Cárthaigh, "Midwife to the Fairies: A Migratory Legend," MA thesis, Department of Irish Folklore, University College, Dublin, 1988.

14. UFTM R80-14.

15. UFTM C79-29.

16. UFTM C79-33.

17. UFTM R80-14.

18. UFTM R90-14. See Patricia Lysaght, *The Banshee: The Irish Supernatural Death Messenger* (Dublin: Glendale P, 1986).

19. UFTM R80-14.

20. This, with other beliefs related to the seals (which form a substantial body of material on the supernatural not addressed here) is discussed by L.M. Ballard in "Seal Stories and Beliefs on Rathlin Island," *Ulster Folklife* 29 (1983). Also see Thomson.

21. UFTM C79-29.

22. UFTM R80-32.

23. This story is cited by L.M. Ballard, "Oral Tradition in the Ards," *Field Excursions in Ulster III, the Ards Peninsula*, eds. J.T. Steele and P.S. Robinson (Ulster Folklife Society, forthcoming 1991).

24. UFTM C79-32.

25. UFTM R80-14.

26. UFTM C79-29.

27. UFTM C79-32.

28. This issue is discussed in Ballard, "Rathlin: History."

29. UFTM C80-14.

30. UFTM C79-33.

31. UFTM C79-33.

32. UFTM C79-33.

33. UFTM C79-33.

34. UFTM R80-16.

35. UFTM R80-29.

36. UFTM R83-112.

37. UFTM C79-29.

38. UFTM R80-16.

39. This story is among those discussed in Ballard, "Seal Stories."

40. UFTM C79-32.

41. "The Children of Lir" is a very well-known literary story, sometimes referred to as one of the "Three Sorrows of Irish Storytelling." Among the many versions is "The Fate of the Children of Lir," in Lady Augusta Gregory, *Gods and Fighting Men* (London: John Murray, 1905) 140–58.

42. UFTM R80-17.

43. UFTM R81-52.

44. UFTM C78-55.

45. UFTM C79-29.

46. UFTM C79-29.

47. UFTM C79-33.

48. UFTM C79-24. Other stories on this theme are included in Linda-May Smith's "A Clerk in Fiend's Clothing," *Ulster Folk and Transport Museum Year Book* (1976–77).
49. UFTM R84-118.
50. UFTM C79-32.
51. UFTM C79-32.
52. UFTM R80-16.
53. UFTM R83-112.
54. UFTM C79-24.
55. UFTM R83-115.
56. UFTM R83-115.
57. UFTM R80-30.
58. UFTM R80-14.
59. UFTM C79-33.
60. UFTM R80-30.
61. UFTM R81-57.
62. UFTM R84-118.
63. UFTM R84-118.
64. Landlord stories are the subject of Seamas MacPhilib's study, "*Jus Primae Noctis* and the Sexual Image of Irish Landlords in Folk Tradition and in Contemporary Accounts," *Béaloideas* (1988).
65. UFTM R84-118.
66. UFTM R80-29.
67. UFTM C79-29.
68. See W.Y. Evans-Wentz, *The Fairy-Faith in Celtic Countries* (1911; Atlantic Highlands, N.J.: Humanities P, 1977).

Balquhidder Revisited: Fairylore in the Scottish Highlands, 1690–1990[1]

Margaret Bennett

As work grinds to a halt each Saturday evening in the Scottish Hebrides and a silent, church-oriented Sunday descends, visitors suddenly become aware of the most visible traits of a strong faith that characterizes the local population. "Sunday is a dead day," they complain. "Can't even buy a pint of milk. Better check the ferry times as the locals have it arranged in the most inconvenient way." And on it goes, year after year. Visitors come and go, and echo their bemused response to this aspect of the local culture, showing minimal understanding and causing occasional irritation to the Highlanders and Islanders who strongly uphold a predominantly Calvinistic faith. The Catholic islands are sometimes regarded as providing welcome relief from these extremes, but are probably no better understood at the end of the day.

The view from the inside offers a much more acceptable set of explanations to the lifestyle and belief system. A Sunday of total tranquillity, for example, comes as no fanatical taboo to the crofter who spends his days working in conditions which can be unbearably hard regardless of the idyllic landscape. The devotion to God on this day reflects the faith of the other six days of the week, while his personal renewal of a day's rest has often been regarded as a welcome respite from the drudgery of crofting.

On a more personal level, the publicly viewed faith of my kinsfolk was characterized in childhood by recurring events in the home of my maternal grandparents on the Isle of Skye: morning and evening Scripture readings; grace before and after meals; Saturday nights spent polishing all the shoes, peeling potatoes and bringing in the peats for Sunday; the regular appearance of "Remember the Sabbath Day . . ." in the classified section of the local newspaper (often, to my amusement, set beside the "Lost and Found Sheep" section with its accurate specifications of the bodily location of blue or red keil [paint] marks, branded horns and the easily identified Gaelic citations of earmarks). And when we moved to the Isle of Lewis, on the *machair* (common grazing land by the sea) near our house was set the rather less common though highly memorable, reminder of the Fourth Commandment in the form of an enormous wooden structure, much taller than a man, in the shape of the figure four: "Remember the Sabbath Day to keep it holy; six days shalt thou labour . . . the Lord blessed the Sabbath Day and hallowed it"[2] written all over it in small letters, constantly and loudly sending us its message. We could see it a mile off, and so we did observe the Sabbath Day, or at least were seen to try. The visitors, however, seldom understood. The Lord's Day Observance was and is, however, only one small part of the whole system.

To be part of a society which is not only monotheistic but predominantly presbyterian seems acceptable enough from the inside and can be easily observed from the outside; the rules have been well rehearsed for several centuries. What is much less visible to the sightseeing visitor is the other faith common to Highlanders and Islanders, as explained by my mother, Peigi Bennett.

> You see, we grew up with stories, well not stories, but the fairies were always sort of in the background—the same as ghosts and the *each uisge* [water horse]. My mother used to frighten us . . . there was a burn, a stream running down not too far from our house. . . . And it ran down to the river. Well, it was very steep going down to the river and of course she would always be busy, you know, there was such a lot to do. And so that we wouldn't go near this river she would say to us (in Gaelic, of course!) "Now if you go near that river the water horse will get you," and we believed every word of it. *"Na teid faisg air an amhuinn no beiridh an t-each uisg' ort."* . . . Oh well, this is what we heard, and we were always scared of the river because we were convinced the *each uisge* would get us. . . . Oh it was huge! Well, we were only tots—it was probably like the unicorn, something like that, with big horns. . . . And you never saw the whole of it, you only saw the head coming out of the water (like the Loch Ness Monster [appears]) the way I imagined it, coming out of the water.[3]

The next generation, however, had no water horse. A "rational discussion" had apparently taken place, and inspired by more sophisticated worldviews that arrived in Skye at the end of the Second World War the family took a definite decision to protect us from the fear of the water horse. It simply wouldn't be mentioned ever again. For a number of years my mother was demented by the fear of our drowning in that same river, and my grandmother showed her frustration by blowing a shrill whistle to command our attention, then shaking a *cromag* (shepherd's crook) wildly in the air to signal to us to get away from the river at once. Our punishment would be her wrath, but it was never enough to keep us away from the riverbank as the *each uisge* had done in my mother's day.

The fairies, however, were quite another matter. Right across the river from my grandparents' home was the Fairy Glen. Everybody knew about it.

> Oh, *Bail' an cnoc*, the Fairy Glen . . . it was such a beautiful glen; there's three hundred and sixty-five hills in it. And we looked over to it from where I was brought up. But in the old days it wasn't called the Fairy Glen.[4]

The glen was, in fact, renamed in the mid-twentieth century because a local man, Donnchadh M., often saw fairies in it. It was well-known that he had second sight, saw visions, and even saw a token of his own death. The villagers were all aware of his gift, and because the glen was so beautiful and already had the magical number of three hundred and sixty-five hillocks, the wife of the local hotelier was said to have given it the present name. Some say that she thought the name would be charmingly attractive for the tourists, who would not know its origin, and its connection to Donnchadh and the fairies.

Closer to home on our side of the river "Great Auntie Katie was always talking about the fairies," and not even her years in Edinburgh as housekeeper to a bishop had managed to alter her views.[5] Born in the late 1870s, she was, in her day, far from unique; her faith was virtually commonplace right through to the first half of the twentieth century and did not seem to be in the least at odds with stalwart presbyterianism from our island or Roman Catholicism from our neighbors' either.

A more widely known example from my childhood on Skye was the late Dame Flora MacLeod of MacLeod of Dunvegan who firmly believed in fairies—we heard her say so. Her faith was not simply based on the wonderful legends pertaining to her clan, such as the Fairy Flag at Dunvegan Castle, or the gift of music to the famous MacCrimmon pipers, or the Fairy Bridge that still stands; it was undoubtedly part of a way of life that characterized many Highlanders and Islanders of that era. A wide-ranging sample of recordings from the archives of the School of Scottish Studies confirms this, and adds to it the fact that the belief in fairies is not confined to Gaelic Scotland in its geographic scope—the Orkneys and Shetlands are well represented in the several hundred examples recorded during the past four decades, and there also is the occasional occurrence in the Lowlands.[6] A survey of the material indicates that the vast majority of these accounts were collected during the 1950s. Many fewer accounts were deposited in the 1960s, and the numbers rapidly declined through the 1980s.

What then of the closing decade of the century? If such beliefs do survive in Scotland and do not appear in recent recordings, it may be the case that fewer collectors are asking specific questions about fairy beliefs— during the past decade there has certainly been a concentrated

Plate 1. The Fairy Glen, Uig, Isle of Skye. John Stewart is making hay on his croft in Glen Conon; behind him, where the craggy rock juts up, is the Fairy Glen with 365 hillocks, ca. 1953. (George Bennett)

effort to obtain more urban material. It is also possible that a folklore fieldworker who can share a background of fairylore is much more likely to turn up such beliefs; or, judging by the trend of the existing archive recordings one could predict a complete disappearance of the fairy faith. Only new interviews and recordings could satisfactorily respond to the question of survival of fairy beliefs in the 1990s.

Since a nationwide survey for the purpose of this paper seemed out of the question, I decided, therefore, to choose one small area well-known for its past associations with fairies, Balquhidder in Perthshire, the original home of the Rev. Robert Kirk (1641?–1692), author of the famous treatise on fairies *The Secret Common-Wealth*.[7] More than three hundred years ago he was the parish minister who preached in the local church (see Plate 2) and lived in the manse nearby. The ruined church can still be seen today close to the present church which was built by David Carnegie of Stronvar, Balquhidder in 1855, while the area of the glebe has virtually remained the same. A considerable number of tourists visit the kirkyard every year, mostly to see the grave of Rob Roy with its simple inscription: "MacGregor despite them." Scotland's Robin Hood figure draws much more public notice than the "man who saw the fairies," and although the visitors' guidechart makes mention of him, this notion from the distant past is largely ignored. Of greater interest to tourists are three material items from Robert Kirk's ministry in Balquhidder: the hand-forged bell bearing his name (see Plate 3), the baptismal font which was in use even before Kirk's time, and the Gaelic Bible, now yellowed with age, in Kirk's careful handwriting. Once in a while a tourist will enquire about the location of his grave, but when told that he moved to Aberfoyle where he was eventually taken away by the fairies, the search in Balquhidder ends.

Virtually all the local people know of Robert Kirk's association with the Balquhidder—he was born about 1640, the seventh son of a minister; he was known to have the second sight, a facility quite common to seventh sons; he became a student of theology and was educated at the universities of St. Andrew's and Edinburgh; he was minister in Balquhidder from 1669 (some say 1664) to 1685, and is well remembered for his scholarly work in the Gaelic language. During the course of his ministry in Balquhidder, he undertook to transcribe the entire Bible from the original Irish script characters into Roman characters so that the Highlanders could read it more easily. He also translated the first hundred psalms into Gaelic metrical verse and published his edition of the Gaelic psalter in 1684.

> He helped . . . to translate the Bible into Gaelic. Quite a job. It's [kept] in the kirk [church] in one of these [glass] boxes.[8]

Plate 2. The ruins of Balquhidder church where Robert Kirk preached. (Tom McKean)

Plate 3. The bell of the old Balquhidder church, now housed in the new church, Balquhidder. (Tom McKean)

And of his personal life, ninety-year-old Mrs. MacGregor, a regular attender and member of that same church, added:

> I'm very interested in Kirk. . . . Oh, I didn't hear an awful lot about him. . . . He was twice married, of course, and his first wife was buried in Balquhidder. And he wrote a poem to her—it was on the gravestone; and he designed the gravestone. It fell, and it was taken over to the ruins [of the old churchyard]. The last I heard of it at one of our meetings it was to be restored. He was quite a lad, Kirk was . . . I think he was a wonderful man!

There are constant reminders of Robert Kirk in the village of Balquhidder, the adjacent hillsides and throughout the glen. He is, however, best remembered as the minister who saw the fairies: "He was going for a walk one day, and he saw some."[9]

> Och yes! It was understood! There was a fairy knowe [hillock] at the manse . . . and all over the place. I mean they took the fairies for granted—took them for granted . . . and *we* take them for granted too. Oh, he [Robert Kirk] saw them during his first marriage, I believe, because it was his first wife that was in Balquhidder, you see. And he met them but he didn't divulge what they, eh . . . and of course he was taken away by the fairies. They say he was buried, but the coffin's empty. It's not here, it's at Aberfoyle. And you see, people [nowadays] don't believe that he was taken away by the fairies, but anyhow they say that this coffin was empty. Well, you see, the people [in those days] would *have* to believe that—he was their minister! They had a funeral and a coffin and they buried it, but Robert Kirk wasn't in it. He was away![10]

Not only did his parishioners believe it, but Kirk's successor, the Rev. Dr. Grahame, gave an account of it in his *Sketches of Picturesque Scenery*, and three centuries later his story is still being told.[11]

> . . . it was Kirk who, after he was taken away by the fairies he appeared to someone and told him at a certain time, at a christening, if he did such and such a thing, he spoke out, that he would appear, that he would be released—he would come back. But this man, he took fright and he didn't do what he was asked. And that was the finish. He never came back.[12]

Sir Walter Scott gives a more detailed version of the same incident in his *Demonology and Witchcraft* (1830).[13]

> After the ceremony of a seeming funeral, the form of the Rev. Robert Kirk appeared to a relation, and commanded him to go to Grahame of Duchray. "Say to Duchray, who is my cousin as well as your own, that I am not dead, but captive in Fairyland; and only one chance remains for my liberation. When the posthumous child, of which my wife has been

delivered since my disappearance, shall be brought to baptism, I will appear in the room, when, if Duchray shall throw over my head the knife or dirk which he holds in his hand, I may be restored to society; but if this is neglected, I am lost forever."

Scott concludes that Kirk was in fact "visibly seen" at the christening, but Duchray was so taken aback by his appearance that he did not fulfil the request to throw the dirk. Consequently Robert Kirk remained captive and was never seen again.

While there is still a mystery surrounding the exact circumstances of his disappearance or death, Kirk's essay, *The Secret Common-Wealth*, expounds the thoughts he had about the fairies during his lifetime. The earliest published edition was said to have been printed from a "manuscript copy preserved in the Advocats' Library" although neither Sir Walter Scott nor later researchers have come across Kirk's original writing from 1691. In Scott's library at Abbotsford is preserved one of the hundred reprints bearing Kirk's name, printed for Longman & Co. in 1815. Subsequent editions are based upon this one, the most well-known including a commentary (longer than the essay itself) by Andrew Lang, published in 1893. Lang's sometimes skeptical remarks, however, have not always been in accord with the feelings of natives to the district. "Lang affixed some of his most characteristic Grass of Parnassus to the edition of 1893," wrote R.B. Cunninghame Graham who sponsored and introduced the 1933 edition, and regardless of what outsiders may think of Robert Kirk, Graham affirmed that

> We the natives of the district are well assured that he was left away, and still lives in the recesses of the Fairy Hill, serving the fairy mass. . . . Could he return, he might expound to us. . . . We know, he once kept a tryst with Grahame of Duchray, but though the fateful dagger was not cast . . . that was to have restored their pastor to the Scottish-Irish congregation, it may be that, like Orpheus, he too looked back to his "owne herde" and so was lost.[14]

Despite the fact that the book has held the interest of folklorists for decades, it features little in Balquhidder. The local school teacher has "heard of it" but hasn't seen a copy as there is no edition of it in the small library of the local village school. Mrs. MacGregor, a keen reader with a substantial home library, seems to pay little attention to it, almost dismissing the existence of a copy she can't locate with "Oh . . . I've got this book, 'Commonwealth of Fairies,' somewhere here. . . ." Local interest in Robert Kirk and the fairies is more from personal experience of Balquhidder and the glen in which it lies.

Three centuries have passed since Robert Kirk walked the same hills the MacGregors have known for generations, and even the age of television does not prevent today's children from following the pattern that was well established among the older folk—that of traipsing here, there, and everywhere. The children who attend the local school have frequently visited and explored the fairy knowe and the entire area which was the focus of Robert Kirk's experiences. Their little school is, after all, situated right next to the church which most of the villagers attend. The parish minister, the Rev. W who "comes from south of the Border," is also a welcome visitor to the school where he is generally invited to "important events" and occasionally addresses the small assembly.

It is also well-known in the village, however, that the Rev. W takes a dim view of "all this talk of fairies" and positively discourages such beliefs as may exist among the locals.

> The minister is very much against it—he thinks it's downright wicked. . . . Of course the Rev. W doesn't believe in fairies at all. . . . So he sort of belittles, well, he'll tell you he doesn't, but he does! He doesn't approve.[15]

The Rev. W's main partner in debate is the lively and outspoken Mrs. MacGregor. One of the oldest residents in the parish, she was born on her father's prosperous sheep farm on the Braes of Balquhidder in May 1900. Although her lifelong home has been in the area, as a child she had to go to boarding school near Stirling: "Oh well, you couldn't go five miles to the village school every day in those winters" when the road was often closed by snows or floods. A well educated woman who has travelled widely, her family ties are firmly in "the Braes."

> Father managed the farm himself—he had seven shepherds, a man for the horses, an odd person . . . oh it was all Gaelic he spoke with them . . . I mean that was the language they used; they told him what was happening on the hill and what not. It was all Gaelic, Father's native language . . . well, before I went to school I could understand it and I could speak . . . then when I went to boarding school, you see, you'd have to learn French and German . . .
>
> . . . Of course a lot of the shepherds and people who came had second sight—they would foresee things that were going to happen . . .
>
> . . . Mother had a girl, she came when she was fourteen, from Skye, from Portree. . . . Oh she could see things . . .

And Mrs. MacGregor went on to relate instances of second sight which she had encountered in or near her own house. "The Glen was full of Highlanders," who have always known that people with second sight (just like Donnchadh M. in Skye) have the ability to see fairies.

As mentioned earlier, however, in recent years there has been a significant influx of newcomers to the area, some to farm on the Braes, some to "get away from it all," and some to provide the basic services of teaching, preaching, and medical care. While Mrs. MacGregor can accept some of the changes that are taking place, it completely baffles her why any outsider would come into the glen and openly question the traditional faith of her people, or why they might be so presumptuous as to dictate that the locals should abandon these age-old beliefs. She views it as a serious matter to which she has given much thought, aired a few opinions. She has no qualms about observing polite silences.

> Oh, I said [to the minister] "I don't know what you came to Balquhidder for, and I don't know how you can be living in Balquhidder and not believe in fairies!"

Thus the discussion warmed up. She could not, however, convince the minister that his pastoral duties were not in conflict with Highland tradition. There had been, after all, many other "men of the cloth" who had lived in the same manse before him *and* believed in the fairies. They blended in with the community and had a true understanding of the Highlanders in their pastoral care.

> Oh, he thought it was sacrilege! He said, "Well I believe in God."
> "Oh well, so do I. What's God like?" I asked him. "How does *He* appear? How does *He* tell you things?"
> And he sort of said "Oh these are ridiculous questions! Well," he said, "have you *seen* a fairy?"
> "No," I said, "but you can be guided. God guides you but you don't see *Him*."
> Oh well, the minister doesn't answer, does he? If he can't answer he doesn't answer.

She acknowledged that the Rev. W is clearly from another culture and simply doesn't understand Highlanders who, within their belief system, accept "God, Christ, the Holy Spirit, ghosts, fairies, water horses— everything all together," and most emphatically stated that they "accepted them *very* sincerely . . . I mean there was no question about it!" As far as faith in the fairies goes Mrs. MacGregor is certain that there is no need to *see* in order to believe; faith is believing without seeing. There are, however, some who are privileged to see: "[Robert Kirk] saw them at the manse. *He* believed in them." Mrs. MacGregor is nevertheless under the impression that he did not "divulge exactly what they were like." (This is not actually the case, as Kirk's manuscript includes details of appearance, habitation, lifestyle, and attitude of the "*Sith*" or "Good People.") Her own impressions of what they look like are partly influenced by her reading of Shakespeare and partly from what she heard in childhood:

> Of course when you read the "Midsummer Night's Dream" and all that you sort of get something. . . . I always imagine that they're flown in from

somewhere . . . that sort of falls in with the fallen down from Heaven
[fallen angels].

Regardless of what they look like, Mrs. MacGregor has a much more
defined opinion of their characteristics.

MM: Oh they [local people] think they're good . . . perhaps they don't
      associate them with any o' the bad things that happened . . . But
      they may influence things for good . . . you often don't know if
      the fairies have worked in your interest, you see, you don't
      know. But I'm quite willing to believe that it's the fairies. I don't
      think we know all the good the fairies do.
MB: Was anybody afraid of them?
MM: Oh they weren't afraid of them, oh no! The fairies were good
      people. Oh, yes!

Surprised at the apparent skepticism of my question, Mrs. MacGregor
was even more surprised to hear my mother ask her about changelings.
"Changelings? What's that?" she asked as if she had never heard of a baby
being stolen by the fairies or a changeling child left in its place. She
enquired of my mother who generally agreed with her statement about
their basic goodness but added that there were some situations in which
you had to be specially careful.

In the olden days if the mother was working in the fields she would take
the baby out with her wrapped up, and it was left wrapped up behind a
stook or a haystack—and I thought that's when the babies were stolen.
They were left outside while the mother was working.[16]

Specific places within the district where Kirk saw the fairies are,
however, much better known.

You know, he would go out there [to the fairy hill near the church in
Balquhidder] of course, and I've no doubt to Stratheyre as well, to the
hill. . . . The fairy places? Well, the manse, opposite the manse across
there, in the glebe it would be, is a knowe and that's one of them. That's
the chief one, I think. In Stratheyre, of course, there's the hill near
Stratheyre, *Beinn an t-Sithein* [Fairy Hill]. It's over behind the other side,
you know. It's all trees now, of course, they planted, *ruined* it! Those
blasted trees! Well they [The Forestry Commission] call them fir. Oh
they're big now . . . it's a beautiful hill, a beautiful shape. But you see,
these people who are keen on trees on hills, they're destroying all the
contours and the light and the shade and everything—hills are wonderful
for that, wonderful! Oh it's famous . . . I don't think I've been to the top,
though I've walked on it long, long, long ago. But no use walking in the
trees, you can't see anything—there's no birds, there's no nothing . . . they
say there are birds, but there aren't![17]

The exact location of fairy encounters is no secret strictly kept by the locals. Mrs. MacGregor pointed out that the Ordinance Survey maps of the area have long since pinpointed them all, and two nineteenth-century ministers of the parish produced a small booklet which has been in her family for many years: "They were wonderful men, wonderful! And this is the booklet," she said, reaching for a well-worn copy of *Gaelic Topography of Balquhidder Parish* (1886).[18] Yet again she acknowledged her admiration of the work of several more recent parish ministers who were key figures in community life. The booklet which was from her parents' era contains the following fairy place-names (with translations): *An Sithean*: the knoll of the men of peace, or the fairies; *Beinn-an-A-Sithean* (sic): the hill of the fairies' knoll; *Cnoc-an-t-Sithean*: the little hill of the fairies, or men of peace; *Creag-nan-Seichean (Shithichean)*: the rock of the fairies; *Glen Shonie (Gleann Shithean)*: the glen of the fairy knolls; *Lon-an-t-Sithean*: the meadow of the fairies' knoll; *Sitheag*: a little fairy knoll; *Sithean-a-Chatha*: the fairy knoll of the battles;[19] and *Sron Shonnie (Sron Shitheachan)*: the promontory of the fairies. Throughout the length and breadth of the parish one is never far away from a fairy place as all the social events in Balquhidder are located very close to the best known fairy knowes, with the church, school, village hall and shop all in its immediate vicinity.

Until she had been asked "all these questions," Mrs. MacGregor had regarded the fairies as an unspoken part of everyday life. As she already said, "I mean there was no question about it!" To which Peigi Bennett replied:

No, that's right, no question about it. And you see if you grow up with that, well, it stays with you all your life, doesn't it?

And becoming almost impatient with the one who had been asking the questions, Mrs. MacGregor turned to Peigi and remarked:

But in the old days they accepted things they were told—they didn't ask all these questions, did they?

Her friend agreed with her and added,

Yes, same as us accepting the *each uisge* .... There's so much in life that you can't explain, and ... to say that you *don't* believe in any of that, I mean it's senseless, really, isn't it, because there are so many things that happen that just make you think.

They were both of the opinion that these old beliefs were becoming a thing of the past. Does anyone today believe in the fairies?

No one that's here today, I don't think ... No one is fairy-minded ...[20]

And apart from a few old people whom Mrs. MacGregor actually named, she could think of no young person today who might hold the same beliefs as she and her forebears held. There was, however, one point she had to consider: after her fruitless discussions with the minister, and apart from the recent exchange of ideas with my mother, she had not enquired of anyone else's beliefs in recent years.

In the entire glen there are only eleven school-age children, and although Mrs. MacGregor sees them at church regularly each Sunday, she has never discussed such things with any of them. (Besides, it didn't seem the appropriate thing to do after listening the Rev. W's morning service!) She doubted very much, however, if any of them would believe in the fairies, especially as she imagined them to be actively discouraged from doing so.

A visit to the school five miles from her house was obviously the simple way to find out. The children were told by their teacher that they were to have a visitor who would tell them a story and maybe sing a song. And as they relaxed on a Friday afternoon with the week's work behind them, I arrived with a tape recorder, set it up, and ignored it. I think I told them a story about a baby who was stolen by the fairies, and sang the Gaelic song about the same event—a song my mother had often sung to me as a lullaby. The rest of the afternoon speaks for itself, just as the children freely spoke for themselves.

MB: Do you know anything about the fairies in Balquhidder?
Grant: Well, the minister was going for a walk one day and he saw
         some . . . ages ago. I can't remember when . . . Another minister.
         Up there [pointing behind the school towards the church].
Mary: I heard that there was a fairy mound up the back behind the
         church . . . It sounds hollow there, like it's empty inside.

The children all agreed. They had been there many times, were convinced that it is "different to other places" which do not have that same hollow sound when you tap, because it is "very special . . . where the fairies live." And realizing the gravity of revealing all this, Evan anxiously cautioned me: "You wouldn't be able to dig in it because it's a graveyard." He had my immediate assurance that I wouldn't even dream of it. I did, however, wonder what the fairies are like?

Grant: Small.
MB: Even smaller than a five-year-old?
All: Yes!
Katy: About the size of your thumb.
Alan: About the size of a finger.
Meg: About the size of my doll. [less than six inches]
Evan: They're like us except smaller . . .

Grant: They look like ordinary people but they wear kilts and
         stuff . . . They'd be in MacLaren tartan because they came round
         here to Balquhidder and they went up to the Manse Rock and
         camped there. [The colors are in the MacLaren tartan are] black,
         blue, green, and yellow and red.

Though I gave no indication of it to the children, I had never heard anyone
else talk of the notion of fairies wearing kilts. It is not an idea which is
well-known in Scotland—for example, among the several hundred tape
references to fairies in the School of Scottish Studies archives it does not
appear at all. Nevertheless Robert Kirk noted that

> Their Apparell and Speech is like that of the people and Countrey under
> which they live; so are they seen to wear Plaids and variegated Garments
> in the Highlands of Scotland. . . . Their Women are said to Spine [spin]
> very fine, to Dy, to Tossue, and Embroyder . . . [21]

Although Kirk did not include specific details of their plaids (or tartans),
young Grant suggested that this had been the case for a very long time.

Grant: Maybe ever since the MacLarens came. Maybe they're the
         spirits of the MacLarens and they turn to fairies.
MB: Spirits of ones who have died, d'you mean?
Grant: Yes . . . And they come back as fairies.

This seemed to me a fairly complex idea for a child who could not
possibly have read Kirk's essay. Even if he *had* obtained a copy, the
language and orthography is well beyond the comprehension of the
brightest eight year old.

MB: Is this something you have thought about yourself, Grant, or is
         it something somebody told you?
Grant: Oh, no, I've thought about it myself.
MB: Is it the sort of thing you talk about at home with your family?
Grant: No.
MB: Nobody does?
Grant: Not really.
MB: Just yourself?
Grant: Yes. I talk to myself.
MB: Out loud?
Grant: No. Inside my head . . .
MB: What gave you this idea—living in Balquhidder?
Grant: Yes.
MB: Is Balquhidder a special place?
Grant: Well to me it is . . . it's the MacLaren's home country.
MB: Have you lived here all your life?

Grant: No, I was born in Germany—Berlin. . . . Then I went to
         Moscow, then I went to London, then I went back to Russia,
         then I went to London again, and then I came up here.
MB: Would you like to stay here forever?
Grant: Yes!

If the village itself is the inspiration of these beliefs which can still be
encountered in the twentieth century, then perhaps revisiting Balquhidder
to look more closely at its characteristics might shed some light on the
matter. The general topography and spectacularly beautiful landscape that
surround it are probably very much as they were three centuries ago
despite today's influx of tourists. There seems no doubt that the children
who live there interpret their own experience of their home surroundings,
and without prompting from text or teacher come up with their own
conclusions.

The fairy knowe behind the church is well loved by all of them, and is
a favorite place to visit during the leisurely lunch break (see Plate 4). They
remind each other of the fact that this was where the minister saw the
fairies, create pictures of it, and imagine the comings and goings of the
fairy world. We might well wonder how the fairies gain entrance to such a
place?

Grant: Maybe they just fly in. Maybe there's a secret hollow in the
         bottom . . . the grass is covering it so they can just push away the
         grass and use it as a door.

Though frequently visited by locals and outsiders, the fairy knowe is, for
all that, a silent, fresh smelling, soft knoll, of very deep vegetations, quite
dramatically different to its surrounding area. Suddenly the flora is lush
and green, even in March when the rest of the landscape is struggling to
leave the winter shades behind. The mosses that grow there are thickly
knitted into the knoll, and in any square foot of it there is captivating
interest and variety. Different to the rest of the surroundings? It would be
very difficult to press a case against that idea.

There have been, as Mrs. MacGregor hinted, some dramatic changes
which have been imposed on the lifestyle of the villagers in recent years. A
considerable number of back-to-the-landers who find it an ideal place to
get away from it all now farm much of the land. They consult each other
in English, and the few Gaelic speakers who remained have long since
been forced to abandon the native language. The village is well and truly
on the tourist map, with road signs on the main highway to indicate the
scenic drive, the auld kirk, and Rob Roy's grave. Aside from the tragic loss
of the language, the effects have not been totally negative. Many of the
local folk now have more time than they did in days gone by to take pride
in keeping the churchyard and the auld kirk in neat order. On any Sunday

Plate 4. The fairy knowe, Balquhidder. (Tom McKean)

Plate 5. "Robert Kirk," cloth collage, student, Balquhidder School. (Joan Mann and Ian MacKenzie)

morning they are heartened to see the local congregation boosted by resident incomers who are dedicated to "fitting in," and in the summer months a number of tourists also fill the pews. At no time is the kirk more full, however, than when the MacGregors and MacLarens hold a clan gathering on their ancestral homeland.

In recent years there has been an enormous surge of national and clan pride. Balquhidder has observed pilgrimages of the MacGregors and MacLarens descending upon it from all over the world—"fae a' the airts and pairts" as the locals say. They have watched (and some have even participated in) several spectacularly colorful events, such as the clan gatherings led by the chief. The children whose school is right next to the kirk have watched in wonder as a busload of Texan MacLarens proudly dressed in all variants of the tartan and costume arrived to visit their hallowed ground. There, along with a good many local MacLarens, they filled the church in a service of dedication and thanksgiving. Afterwards, as they combed the churchyard and fanned out in all directions, all who were able headed for the hillside where they could climb upon the Manse Rock to take in the breathtaking view. From the classroom windows these tartan clad visitors might scarcely appear to be the size of your thumb! Their once in a lifetime visit to the Braes of Balquhidder would leave a lasting impression upon them, but there is no doubt that they in turn left a fair impression upon Balquhidder.

Returning spirits? Who knows? Robert Kirk's ideas about departed souls were put forward three centuries ago and can be consulted in his essay *The Secret Common-Wealth*. He also left comparative comments on the same fairy places that are shown by modern Ordinance Survey maps, how to gain entry to fairy hills or knowes, and numerous other aspects of fairy life which are occasionally discussed in Balquhidder today. For example, the fairy rings (including stone ones) which Kirk described are apparently still encountered in 1990.

MB: Little toadstools? What are they like?
Evan: Some of them grow in circles.
MB: Is there a special name for these circles?
Mary: A fairy ring.
Grant: In the nighttime people say that fairies come out and dance on the mushrooms all round in the fairy rings. And sometimes they jump or dance on top of them or they just sit on these little toadstools and eat off the big ones.
MB: Sort of like a dining room?
Grant: Yes.
MB: Is it like furniture?
Grant: Yup! You could say that . . .
Katy: Once when me and Sally, Mary and Jean, when we went up to the *fank* [community sheep pens] and brought a picnic we saw a fairy ring, and it was made out of stones.

Jean: It was stones in a ring shape. It was about that size [indicates about a meter] . . . Well, we went up and Mary said "There's some fairy rings." I hadn't been [living] there very long and we went along to the fank one day for picnic and we just came across this big circle and she said "That's a fairy ring . . ."

Katy: One time my wee sister ruined a wee fairy house by mistake. She fell . . . and then she put money, about £2 or £1 under her pillow and they took the money, the tooth fairies.

MB: Sally, what happened when you fell?

Sally: Well, the wee house? Well, I fell on this hole when we were out walking and my foot slipped and it went onto . . . and it knocked the wee house down.

MB: What kind of a wee house was it?

Sally: A toadstool.

MB: Oh, I see! And your Mum said?

Sally: "Put money under your pillow."

MB: Why did you put the money under your pillow?

Sally: To say "Sorry."

MB: Then what happened?

Sally: Then they took the money . . .

Jean: They said "Oh, that's OK you've gave us the money, we can go and get a new one."

Grant: Well, I think they said "We can take your money; now that might teach you a lesson to try not to do that again."

MB: And the next time, Sally, when you were out and you saw little toadstools did it make any difference then?

Sally: Yes.

MB: Did you step on them?

All: [laughter]

Sally: [indignantly] No!

MB: Were you more careful then?

Sally: Yes . . . And [later] they gave me the money back.

The well-known tooth fairies (not apparently encountered in Kirk's day) have found their way into Balquhidder beliefs. They are not, however, totally unrelated to the rest of the fairies, as Grant quickly pointed out:

Katy: I was going to say about the tooth fairies . . .

Grant: Maybe it's the fairies in the mound that come down . . .

Katy: Well, if you put the tooth under your pillow they sometimes come and take it and give you money . . .

Grant: Well, in the evening you take your tooth and you put it under your mattress or under your pillow, then you go to sleep. And in the morning you look where you put it and normally there's some money—or your tooth is still there if it's not cleaned properly.

MB: Oh? If it's not cleaned properly they won't take it?

Grant: No.

MB: And what do you do then?
Grant: Well [if there's money there] then you can spend it or save it.
MB: And could you shine the tooth up and put it back?
Grant: OK, well, you could *brush* it and put it under, and if you want
        you can write a letter then, and say like "Please may you put
        money instead of this tooth 'cos I've cleaned it now."
MB: And do you think that's the fairies trying to teach you
        something?
Grant: Yes.

The lives of the fairies are, according to the children, just as busy and
varied as ours, yet their activities seem to be drawn from a wider span of
centuries. For example, they retain ancient practices which have become
obsolete among mere mortals, yet they also embrace the very modern
custom of observing birthdays which had never been heard of in Gaelic
Scotland even in my mother's day:

MB: What sort of things do you think the fairies do . . . how do they
        spend their days?
Grant: Cooking. Seeing how the life in Balquhidder is.
Mary: Making bows and arrows.
MB: What do you think they do with them?
Sally: They maybe kill things . . . wee miniature flies.
Mary: . . . wee miniature arrows for insects.
Grant: And maybe they might shoot at people — they might think of
        Balquhidder as their homeland, or something like that.
MB: Are they looking after Balquhidder?
Grant: Yes . . .
Jean: What about when children wish on their birthday cakes? . . . You
        wish to the fairies and the fairies will maybe bring you what you
        wish for . . . Well, when you've got the birthday cake, when you
        blow out the candles you wish at the same time and sometimes
        your wish comes true.
MB: Are you actually wishing to the fairies?
Jean: Mmmm!
MB: Has your wish come true?
Jean: Well, once when I was on holiday in Skye it came true . . .
Evan: I had a birthday cake and I wished and my wish came true . . . I
        did the wish in my head.
Grant: And if you do it out loud it doesn't come true, or if you tell
        anyone it won't come true.
MB: Oh, I won't ask what it was then! That would spoil it, wouldn't
        it?
All: Yes.
MB: When you wish, are you wishing *to* anyone?
All: To the fairies.
Grant: Well you don't need anyone to wish it to, but you just wish and
        they'll pick it up—everywhere. They're everywhere and they'll

> hear you . . . Well then if it's something like "I'd like to be
> strong" then you can't say. Then, say you told someone, you see,
> then they [the fairies] will know you told . . . And even if it
> doesn't come true, don't tell anyone, for one day it might come
> true!

So ended the recording, but not without leaving me convinced that
belief in the fairies is alive and well in Balquhidder. Most convincing of all
is the children's belief that the fairies teach us lessons—simple respect and
regard for nature, whether it is the perpetual care for plants or fungi that
grow in our vicinity, or the daily attention to our teeth. "The fairies make
you think about these things." Irrespective of pressures from the outside
world of adults with their "green" or ecological advertising, their family
campaigns to establish good habits, their save-your-soul messages from
the pulpit, the children of Balquhidder have established their own
cosmology to which they relate in their everyday lives. And belief in the
fairies is clearly an important part of their world—even in the 1990s.

> There's so much in life that you can't explain and . . . to say that you *don't*
> believe in any of that, I mean it's senseless really, isn't it? Because there
> are so many things that happen that just make you think, and you think
> "Well, there *must* be something . . . like spirits" . . . I don't know.[22]

Notes

1. For the purpose of this article I have decided not to use the real names of
   any of the Balquhidder informants interviewed. My mother's name is the
   only one that remains unchanged. All the tapes cited here were recorded in
   March 1990 and are housed in the archives of the School of Scottish Studies
   at Edinburgh University. Special thanks are due to: all the informants who
   took part in the taped interviews; Joan Mann who arranged my visit to her
   classroom and lent the collages; Tom McKean for taking the Balquhidder
   photos; George Bennett for the 1953 photo; the sound archives of the
   School of Scottish Studies; and to the photographic archivist Ian
   MacKenzie for preparing the photos for publication.
2. The complete text which appeared was the King James version of
   Deuteronomy 5.12. The structure was located on the *machair* on the
   isthmus of the Eye Peninsula on the Isle of Lewis.
3. Mrs. Peigi Bennett, née Stewart, from Uig, Isle of Skye, recorded in 1990;
   hereafter cited PSB.
4. PSB; see Plate 1.
5. PSB.
6. The entire range of tape-recorded examples covers an enormous scope of
   motifs: fairy encounters, fairy lovers, fairy music, fairy gifts, fairy
   dwellings, food for the fairies, fear of the fairies, changelings, love of the

fairies, and so on. Comparatively few of the recordings have been published, though the School of Scottish Studies periodical *Tocher* has occasional citations (see numbers 12, 14, 26, 27, 28).

7. Citations here are to Robert Kirk, *The Secret Common-Wealth of Elves, Fauns, and Fairies* (1893; Stirling, Scotland: Eneas Mackay, 1933); another edition is *The Secret Common-Wealth & A Short Treatise of Charms and Spels*, Mistletoe Series, ed. Stewart Sanderson (Totowa, New Jersey: Rowman and Littlefield for the Folklore Society, 1976). Surprisingly, the archives of the School of Scottish Studies until very recently had no recordings concerning fairies from Perthshire although there are numerous accounts from other parts of the district. During the past ten years I have been "no stranger to the village" mainly because my sister, Mrs. Joan Mann, became schoolmistress of the small Balquhidder school and my mother subsequently moved to a cottage on the opposite side of the glen. My observations of the comings and goings have been based on visits on weekends and occasional holidays—simply being in the village, attending the local church on Sunday, wandering through the kirkyard on fine days (and eavesdropping among tourists), joining in the *ceilidhs* in the village hall, and making the occasional tape recording of local traditions which, until 1990, focused on local reminiscences of the sheep farming community and playground games of the children at the local school.

8. Mrs. MacGregor, Balquhidder, 1990. Hereafter cited as Mrs. M.

9. Grant, age 8, Balquhidder, 1990.

10. Mrs. M.

11. Rev. Dr. Grahame, *Sketches of Picturesque Scenery* (n.p., n.d.).

12. Mrs. M.

13. Sir Walter Scott, *Letters on Demonology and Witchcraft*, 2nd ed. (London: Murray, 1830) 105.

14. Kirk 17–8. The reference to the "Scottish-Irish congregation" has no geographical bearing nor historical implications of immigration, but is, in today's terms, simply synonymous with "Gaelic speaking." Until well into the second half of this century the congregation was entirely Gaelic speaking, and that language in Kirk's day was undoubtedly much closer to what we now refer to as Irish Gaelic—basically the same language, which, in seventeenth-century writings (e.g., Martin Martin's *Description of the Western Islands*, ca. 1695) was generally referred to as "Irish." Regarding "Fairy Hill" the authors note: "This knoll is a very exposed stormy place at the head of the pass between Balquhidder and Loch Lomond. The battles indicated by the name are those of the stormy winds." They do not, however, state whether this comes from oral tradition, or from their own wish that the readers should not think it was the fairies who had the battles.

15. Mrs. M.

16. PSB.

17. Mrs. M.

18. Rev. Alexander M. MacGregor and Rev. David Cameron, *Gaelic Topography of Balquhidder Parish as Given in the Ordinance Survey Maps*, with explanatory notes by the late Rev. Alexander M. MacGregor, Minister of

the Parish, 1868, with additional notes by Rev. David Cameron, the Present Minister, 1886 (n.p.: printed for private circulation, 1886).
19. See Kirk 73.
20. Mrs. M.
21. Kirk 73.
22. PSB.

Trolls, Hillfolk, Finns, and Picts:
The Identity of the Good Neighbors
in Orkney and Shetland

Alan Bruford

The population of the "Otherworld" in the Northern Isles of Scotland, the archipelagoes of Orkney and Shetland, is as obscure in origin as their population in this world and perhaps more diverse. Like most otherworld populations, they share only one feature—they can all be dangerous. The Orcadians and Shetlanders also are not unusual in having romantic illusions about their own origins which can be challenged in the light of archaeological, genealogical and linguistic evidence. The legend is that they are all descended from Vikings who took the islands by force in the Dark Ages and massacred all the inhabitants, and remain closer spiritually as well as geographically to Bergen than to Edinburgh; these are not the Northern Isles of Scotland, but the Southern Isles of Norway. The evidence[1] is that the pre-Norse population owed cultural and probably political allegiance to the Picts who ruled most of Northern Scotland at the time. Some of them probably spoke Pictish, a Celtic language akin to Welsh; a few, perhaps missionaries, may have spoken Gaelic; most may have spoken an older language of which we know next to nothing. In any case, though they have left little trace of any of these languages except on a few placenames like the islands of Unst and Yell, the archaeological record shows too much of their culture surviving the arrival of Norsemen—as settlers rather than raiders—to suggest that they were totally massacred or even driven into the hills and wild places, and a good deal of intermarriage seems likely. Moreover, long before the islands were pledged to Scotland by the King of Denmark in 1468-9 in lieu of his daughter's unpaid dowry (and never redeemed) they had Scottish or half-Scottish earls who brought in followers from the mainland, and more flocked in over the first two centuries of Scottish rule, until most of the landowners and quite a few of the tenants bore Scottish surnames. Today many of the commonest names in the islands—Tulloch, Leask, Fraser, Mackay—are of undoubted mainland Scottish origin, and though the dialects contain a good many words of Norse origin, and more have been lost over the past century, most of their grammar and basic vocabulary is broad Scots. The islanders retain a strong sense of their own identity, talking of going "to Scotland" rather than "South" or "to the mainland," and resisting attempts from either London, Edinburgh, Inverness, or Wick to meddle too much in their affairs, but they have no real desire to be ruled from Oslo or Copenhagen either.

Most islanders more than half-believed in the spirit world a hundred years ago. This may well tell us more about their true nature than the galley-burning rituals of Up-Helly-Aa, deliberately created to emphasize the Viking theory within the past hundred years. Those invented rituals have been acts of public defiance, but the beliefs in the spirit world were private and recently at least, those who admitted to them risked being mocked by their neighbors. The stories of the Otherworld are generally memorates or genuine belief legends, told of real people in real places and in bulk, sufficiently terrifying to make sure that children did not stray away from the house in the dark.[2] They are quite different from traditions of giants, who are either fairytale ogres, made to be defeated, in the rather rare Märchen types of the Northern Isles,[3] or the burlesque monsters who heave standing stones at each other and drop islands out of their baskets in origin legends (though the fairies too take part in one such story).[4] Nobody would be afraid to go out at night for giants. In several places one hears of quite recent characters, apparently self-appointed shamans, who would sense the spirits of evil massing to attack and go out of the house at night.

> He'd suddenly spring up, he'd say, "They're out! That's it!" He'd get dressed . . . maybe a wild night, he'd get dressed, oil coat, sou'wester, and take his—always took his heavy stick and he would set off . . . in the pitch darkness. He'd come home sometime durin' the night, all over covered of mud, all hacked . . . an' blood. He'd say, "It was a tough fight," he says, "but I beat them." Now where he'd been or what happened nobody knows, but he'd be out for hours on end, come back like that.

The beings who made the shaman bleed were definitely specified at the beginning of the account: "He was the man with this fairies or trows—he knew the night they would come out."[5]

Terminology: Land Fairies

Fairies or trows? There may be a difference, but they were both small beings who were more often encountered in crowds than singly— "trooping fairies." We will consider their appearance and nature shortly, but first we must clear up the terminology, which has a bearing on their origins and the roots of those who feared them. There seems no doubt that *trow* is a variant of the Norse *troll*. Trolls are generally imagined as large and ugly, trows as small though often also ugly; but though trolls may function as fairytale ogres in Norse *Märchen* and ballads, or as stone-throwing giants in origin legends (see Christiansen's note under ML 5020ff),[6] they are not necessarily solitary spirits. In the ballads they populate their own Arctic kingdom of Trollebotn;[7] in legends like the one Dasent translated as "The Cat on the Dovrefell" (ML 6015) the beings who take over a house at Christmas may be either fairies (*huldre*) or trolls,[8] and in ML 6045, "Drinking Cup Stolen from the Fairies," it may be a troll who appears at the door of the fairy dwelling.[9] Christiansen himself admits that the same tales may be told of either type of being,[10] but contends that "in the Norwegian tradition a line of distinction is drawn between the trolls and the *huldre*-folk." He feels that "the trolls have long since passed out of actual folk belief," like the giants (*jotuns*) to whom "they are closely related," but admits that the question "whether the trolls and *huldre*-folk came from the same stock or had different origins altogether" is still unanswered.[11] However, the use of "trow" in Orkney and Shetland to mean something very like the "family" of beings covered by *huldre* in Norway suggests that they may come from the same stock. *Huldre* are sometimes the same size as humans and sometimes small,[12] like Gaelic fairies (*sidhichea*),[13] and they are grotesque rather than beautiful, with long noses or cows' tails.[14] The term *huldre*-folk, meaning "hidden people," is associated with their origin as the "hidden children of Eve" (unlike the trows who fell from heaven with Lucifer),[15] and the term does not seem to be known in early Norse sources, though *huldufolk* was a regular alternative to the usual term *álfar* or elves in nineteenth century Icelandic and Faroese legends.[16] It seems possible that "troll" was taken overseas by the early pagan settlers of Orkney and Shetland as a catchall term for supernatural beings who were to be respected and avoided rather than worshipped, before it became specialized as a description of the larger and more menacing ones and *huldre* was developed as the general term for the rest along with their Christian origin legend; but the latter may have reached Orkney only to become corrupted, as we shall see.

The characteristics of trows, or at least the stories told about them, were certainly strongly influenced by Scottish fairylore, and while "trow" remained the usual term in a majority of districts, "fairy" was almost exclusively used in others, though "trow" might be a term that was known. James Henderson in South Ronaldsay said, "in the old days they were trows, sea trows and land trows, but . . . in my people's time . . . the trows . . . were more a memory or a talk of what they had done; they were then fairies." And another time, "The trows was sort o' the right name for them, but they would refer to them as fairags"[17] (using the Gaelic diminutive ending -*ag* borrowed regularly in this part of Orkney nearest to mainland Scotland). Tom Tulloch in North Yell, almost at the opposite end of the two island groups, told several stories about fairies and only one about trows (who lived locally in a "trowie hadd," a word used for a wild beast's den, under a hillock, until they were driven away to the Faeroes by the evangelical activities of a famous minister early last century). He explained that

> as it was telled i' my boyhood days aboot faeries . . . they were supposed to be a more, kind o' a gentle, gossamer being as what the trows wis . . . the faeries wis more or less a hairmless race . . . they were more up fir gaiety and all that . . . The trows wis . . . more closely associated til a earthly being, 'at they could either be good or bad, according to whit way you dealt wi them.[18]

In practice either "trows" or "fairies" (or "fairags") could be named in most recurrent legend types, according to local or individual preference, or a term like "hill-folk," also paralleled in Norway,[19] might be preferred to either. Perhaps, however, "hill-folk," "hillyans," or in a hybrid form "hillitrows," mean more than they seem to; they could be rationalized corruptions of the *huldu* prefix (to use the Icelandic form) which may also appear in "Hildaland" as a name for the usually hidden otherworld island.[20]

"Elf" could derive directly from Old Norse *álfr*, but the form more likely came to the Northern Isles through Scots, where it was a more usual term than "fairy" when the islands were being colonized from Scotland. Apart from its use in the term "elfshot" for cattle, or occasionally people with unexplained illnesses thought to be caused by the fairies—which at least in Shetland was often replaced by "trowshot"[21]—the term was not often heard in the islands, but James Henderson makes an interesting distinction: "An elf was a male fairy . . . an the fairy was the female." He mentioned this to explain a story told to his father as a boy in South Ronaldsay (about the 1840s) by an old neighbor who said she had been out one night and "she set her foot on an elf, an it went away with a grunt!"[22] Such an elf seems to belong with the trows or dark elves, rather than the light elves described by Snorri Sturluson,[23] whose description was probably used by Tolkien in his popular fantasy novels. They are social beings, but there are also a couple of terms for solitary spirits. The "hogboon" or "hugboy," derived from Old Norse *haugbúi(nn)*, "howe-dweller," was only mentioned in Orkney, where ancient burial mounds (mostly pre-Norse) for the spirit to inhabit were plentiful. The character of the very substantial "living corpse" of the Icelandic sagas, like the one whom Grettir fights for his treasure,[24] has changed—as in Norway where *hauge*-folk is another synonym for *huldre*-folk[25]—and the hogboon is usually depicted as a protective or fertility spirit, a natural enough role for the ancestor buried in the local grave mound. He features in the legend of the mischievous domestic spirit which the farmer cannot escape even by moving house, told of the Nordic *nisse* (ML 7020). Ernest Marwick suggests convincingly that the other solitary spirit, the imported Scottish "broonie," may have replaced him in Shetland.[26] The story of Hughbo, the brownie of Copinsay in Orkney,[27] combines both names in the story of the brownie or *nisse* who refuses to help about the house after he is given new clothes (ML 7015), and the offerings of milk poured on burial mounds for the hogboon in Orkney might be poured into a hollow stone for Broonie in Shetland, as they were for the cattle protecting *gruagach* in the Highlands.[28]

Sea Fairies, Seals, and Finns

James Henderson's mention of "land trows and sea trows" is unusually precise. "Sea trows," according to Walter Traill Dennison, are grotesque creatures who steal the fish from fishermen's hooks, but as we shall see, Dennison's definitions are suspect and such a term could well apply to the underwater equivalents of the land trows or fairies, although Henderson's own story about such a being simply calls him a "sea man."[29] It is a rare variant of a Norwegian type (ML 6000) told of a land fairy and in a few cases the native element is not important. The basic belief is that everything on land, including the fairies, has a counterpart in the sea, and these beings can live underwater, or sometimes on an island out to the West which is only rarely visible to humans, as in another of Henderson's stories; this corresponds to the Norse island of Utröst or the Hebridean Rocabarraigh, though the name still remembered in Orkney, "Heather-Blether," sounds deplorably like a comic title for a Brigadoon-style piece of Scotch kitsch.[30] If they do live in the sea itself, the more usual concept is that the sea trows take the form of seals there and are only humanoid on land, though Henderson's cousin John Halcro was quite definite that in South Ronaldsay belief sea men used a "sea skin," *not* a sealskin, to go underwater and apparently kept their human shapes. It was presumably a woman of this species who asked two Stronsay men for a lift home from the Lammas market in Kirkwall and disappeared with her shopping over the side of the boat halfway home, but was back at the market unharmed next year.[31] In most cases, however, the sea trows appear in the sea as seals and are generally simply called "seals" or "selkies," which means the same thing. (I should stress two points I have made elsewhere.[32] "Silkie" in the title of the ballad "The Great Silkie of Sule Skerry" [Child 113] is just an attempt to write "selkie" as pronounced in the dialect of the island of Unst, where the ballad was first recorded, actually with a long "i" as "sealkie"; "selkie" in itself does not imply the ability to take human form any more than "seal" does.) Thus, Brucie Henderson's Shetland account of the angels who fell with "the Son o the Moarnin,"[33] "the ones 'at fell on the ground was supposed to be the trows or ferries and the ones 'at fell into the sea was supposed to be the seals"—though he says nothing at this point about any supernatural quality, merely that (all) seals are "illsanctified" and can look like people swimming if "you just look carelessly at 'm."

The terminology is further confused by a belief brought from Norway, where it is recorded in the sagas, that Finns (that is the Lapps and Finns of northern Norway, or their shamans) had magical powers, including the ability to travel long distances almost instantly and change into seals and other animals.[34] In most Shetland stories it is clear that seals who also appear in human form are such "Norway Finns." For instance, in the common legend of a man who sticks a knife in a seal that escapes and gets the knife back years later from someone who still bears the scar where he was wounded as a seal, the encounter nearly always takes place in Norway, though this is not true of Gaelic variants, where it may simply be in another island, not necessarily an enchanted one.[35] In Orkney, again, the belief is not so clear. Ernest Marwick's statement that "in Shetland, Fin Folk and Seal Folk were frequently confused, but in Orkney they were completely distinguished,"[36] is the opposite of the true situation. In Shetland the nature of the Finns as human magicians and not the sea trows who appear in the seal bride story (ML 4080) is generally quite clear, but in Orkney the term "Finn" may have been applied to sea trows. Marwick's distinctions and possibly the confusion of the mortal and immortal beings, come from the romantic inventions of Dennison, one of those Victorian antiquaries who did not scruple to fill in what he saw as gaps in oral tradition with his own ideas. While the tradition supplied basic details such as the name "Finn" and the people who lived in the sea, the unusually detailed descriptions of the "Fin Folk" and their undersea home sound like something from an early book for children. The Fin Man "had a dark, sad face. Disposed so neatly round his body that they were usually taken for clothing were the fins which gave him his name." He is merman rather than seal, therefore, and the mermaid is the female of the species. "Orkney storytellers used to describe with exquisite imagery the town of Finfolkaheem at the bottom of the sea.... Its gardens were full of coloured seaweeds.... A vast dancing hall, built of pure crystal, was lit most entrancingly by the phosphorus in the sea; it was curtained with the ever changing colours of the Northern Lights."[37]

While both Finns and sea trows could provide occasional help, or mates, for ordinary humans, they were traditionally regarded like all magicians or supernatural beings as dangerous and to be avoided if possible. Dennison was attracted to them at an early age and wrote a poem, "The Finfolk's Foy [festival] Sang," which he found "among my juvenile papers" and could no longer remember which lines he had "added . . . to the oral original"—in other words even he doubted whether it could be accepted as pure oral tradition. I have argued that a poem put into the mouth of alien beings and beginning "O' blithe is de land dat's fae man far awa!" is totally foreign to traditional ways of thinking and must be all Dennison's own,[38] as must be the greater part of "The Play o' de Lathie Odivere," the dialect mini-epic which he built round an Orkney version of the ballad of the Grey Selkie (Child 113) mentioned above.[39] Here the Selkie rules the "selkie folk," not the "Fin Folk," but again the ballad story of the tragic consequences of a broken taboo is given a happy ending when the Selkie rescues Lady Odivere from her Crusader husband, who is about to burn her for adultery, and carries her off to his undersea kingdom. Not only official Christianity, as represented by the sheriff in George Mackay Brown's *An Orkney Tapestry*,[40] but popular belief as exemplified in the ballad of Tam Lin (Child 39) depicts the sort of otherworld she went to as not far short of Hell, and it takes a Romantic eye to see this as a happy ending.

When the superimposed definitions are cleared away the sea trows are still surrounded by confusion, probably because the Northern Isles were the meeting place for so many cultures.[41] The Norse strand consists mainly of the stories of shape-changing Finns. The sea trows, dangerous as they may be, seem nowhere near as malevolent as their modern Norwegian counterparts, the maritime *draugs*, whose name means "living dead," since they are said to be the spirits (or animated corpses) of men lost at sea. The otherworld island, however, is a less fearsome concept shared by Norse and Gaelic tradition. The story of the seal woman captured by stealing her seal's skin—a local variant of a worldwide motif told elsewhere of swan-maidens or heavenly maidens—is given a number by Christiansen, ML 4080, but he can only find one version from all Norway,[42] whereas there are hundreds recorded all along the Atlantic coasts from Ireland to Iceland.[43] This is clearly a different strand, which could as well have its origins in Shetland or anywhere along the route as at the Irish end. Other stories of unions between people and seals, especially between a mortal woman and a seal man as in the ballad, in the story of the "Selkie Boy" of Breckin in North Yell and another match which is held responsible for an actual hereditary disability in Orkney, involving a thickening and hardening of the skin on the palms of the hands until they are as clumsy as the reputed ancestor's flippers[44]—these seem to be unique to the Northern Isles. Taken with the memorates which suggest it may be unlucky to kill or hurt seals, though they were regularly hunted for skins and oil in many places up to this century, they seem to point to the survival of a pre-Christian taboo on harming a sacred, possibly a totem animal in these islands. The mermaid, who tends to replace the seal woman in versions of ML 4080 from the east coasts of Scotland and Ireland, may be a different strand again, an English language one perhaps, or one brought home by deep-sea sailors; but she features little in genuine legend in Orkney and Shetland, though there are several accounts there of mermaids being seen or even caught. One man I have recorded who saw one swimming off Flotta about 1920 was definite that it was not a seal, and the black head and white body he described tally with the published account of one "seen by hundreds of sightseers" off Deerness, fifteen miles away, thirty years earlier.[45]

Picts and Other Euhemerizations

Before we come to similar descriptions and relationships for the land fairies, there is one further name to deal with. There is no time to consider the local versions of the water kelpie ("nyuggle," "tangie," "shoopiltie") which unlike the water horses of the Highlands seem to appear only in horse form, not human, or the quite large number of names recorded for individual trows, which may well have significance for anyone studying the survival of Norse (or Pictish?) elements in the language of the islands.[46] But I have to include the term used by one Shetlander who told me many stories about trows, but hardly ever called them trows, the late James Laurenson of Fetlar. He always referred to them as "Picts." Obviously he was convinced by one of the widespread theories about the origin of fairy beliefs, the euhemerizing idea that they reflect the actual survival of members of a conquered race in the wilderness on the fringes of their conquerors' settlements. This explains why the fairies are smaller, fear iron (which they had not yet developed), live in hillocks (round turf-roofed houses sunk in the ground) and so on. Some notable folklorists like J.F. Campbell of Islay—who compared turf-roofed huts he had seen in Lapland[47]—have been proponents of this theory. In fact the mounds associated with the trows in Orkney are generally chamber tombs or brochs abandoned long before the Norsemen arrived. The Picts certainly had iron and there is no evidence at all that they were smaller than Scots or Norsemen,[48] though popular imagination has long since stereotyped them as little dark haired "Iberian" people as opposed to the tall blond Wagnerian Vikings. The Pict = trow equation was used for instance by the late Andrew Cluness, whose *Told Round the Peat Fire* is a collection of stories published in 1955, mixing retold folktale with historical fiction. In the fourth chapter, "Trouble with the Trolls," the "trolls" who steal Norsemen's livestock by night, until it becomes easier to leave out offerings for them, are revealed to be Pictish guerillas living in sea caves.[49] Jamesie Laurenson, an antiquary as well as a tradition-bearer, had made the same identification years earlier and would make confident statements like "that Picts, they used to steal boats," or even claim the words of a diddled tune, "Dow treedle daddle . . . ," as "proper Pickish."[50]

Other theories about the nature of the fairies—that they represent the spirits of the dead, or pagan gods, or symbolize wild nature; that they function as scapegoats for unexplained troubles and bogeymen to keep children from straying; that they derive from archetypal dreams of little people, or occasional visions of elemental spirits that do exist—all have something to be said in their favor and will be kept in mind along with the geographical origins of the beliefs during the analysis of tale-types and beliefs which follows. One further variety of (purely local) euhemerization, however, may be noted. It depends on one of the main themes of historical legends in the Northern Isles—the press gang. The fishermen of these islands were a main target for this method of forced enlistment in the navy during the Napoleonic Wars because they were experienced seamen who could understand orders in English better than their Gaelic-speaking counterparts on the west coast. Whole families of local legends have grown up about individuals eluding, tricking or even terrifying the sailors of the press gang. According to these accounts the male populations of whole villages in Shetland hid in sea caves. Apart from what fish they could catch, these men were fed by their wives who left food in agreed spots while tending cattle in the hills; this food was then picked up by the men at night.[51] It is quite natural that such literally "hidden people" should be confused with the trows. So Tom Anderson heard one woman in Delting describe what is often remembered in Shetland, the leaving of food in the barn for Broonie, but instead of Broonie she said "Troomie," a name she associated with a song, almost certainly the Scots ballad of "Thrummy Cap,"[52] and explained that this was a code name for the men hiding from the press gang, or according to her, deserters (not only Shetlanders?) who came ashore from naval ships at that time. The food left for "Troomie" included corn, which visiting deserters would grind on the handmill in the barn; "a little would be taken and the rest left for the crofter"—a typical brownie's task. She knew that superstitious people attributed this to the trows, but really it was done by the deserters. The clinching statement was that "Troomie was all right— leave him food, but—on no account leave him clothes." She explained this belief as being because "they were in uniform" (most unlikely for lower ranks in Nelson's navy) and "if they got any civilian clothes at all, they could destroy the uniform" and pass for civilian Shetlanders; apparently it was showing too much sympathy for law-breakers to let them get away with it entirely. But of course this uncharacteristic conclusion is merely a rationalization of the belief derived from ML 7015, the story already mentioned of the brownie who does no more work once he is given clothes as well as food.

I have also recorded in Unst a version of a legend, as far as I know confined to Orkney and Shetland but quite often collected in some islands, where a man working in a little water mill by night, as was traditional, heard two trows coming in to warm themselves at the kiln fire of the mill and hid under a pile of "gloy" or fine straw; but he failed to stay absolutely still, and one trow said to the other, "Gloy gings!" (Straw walks!). The other laughed and said in rhyme something like this (various grotesque names are used in different places):

> Sit thee still, Skeenglo,
> And warm thee weel thee wame, [your belly]
> For weel kens Skeengles
> That gloy canna gang.[53]

The implication seems to be that trow science cannot comprehend the idea of straw "walking" because someone unseen moves it. In the version I recorded it was said by one press gang member to another, so that the man hiding there escaped and the meaning there *may* have been that a sympathetic Shetlander said it to a stupid Englishman to let the man escape. In any case, once again the idea of hiding has been transferred to the better known context. In one story I recorded, the storyteller, though the tale ran in his own family, was confused by the placename "Da Tieves' Knowe" (The Thieves' Knoll) where the fiddler taken to play for the fairies was captured. Instead of letting him be released after the fairy wedding, he borrowed the end of another Shetland legend, where a boy captured by a sheep thief escapes by suggesting a night expedition to his own home to steal other food as a change from mutton and alerting the household, so that the thief—or in this case the whole band of thieving trows!—is captured.[54]

Legend Types and Origin

I propose next to consider the recurrent tale-types about trows in the Northern Isles from the point of view of their affinities. The last two types mentioned illustrate the possibility of stories migrating within one or both of the island groups which are not known outside them, or are legends from elsewhere changed to suit local conditions. The "gloy canna gang" types seems to be unique to Orkney and Shetland; indeed the rhyme seems to be composed in the Norse influenced Scots of the islands rather than translated even from their own dialect of Norse (Norn) and would not be fully understood outside the Norn culture area (which includes eastern Caithness on the mainland). "Gloy" is a word of Anglo-French origin which is now only used in that area.[55] The fiddler asked or forced to play for a fairy wedding or other dance is a theme very popular in Shetland with its strong tradition of fiddle playing. The story just mentioned is one of six on that theme in Nicolson's book, out of a total of twenty-nine tales of the trows.[56] There are occasional mainland Scottish versions, mostly about pipers rather than fiddlers, but if the idea is a mainland one it is certainly one that flourished when transplanted to the soil of Shetland.

Some legend types are known throughout most of western Europe, if not most of the world, like ML 7015, the Brownie "paid off" (*Ausgelohnt*) with a new suit, which has already been mentioned. Another such is ML 5085, "The Changeling." In fact, though the *belief* in changelings was strongly held in the Northern Isles and there are accounts of children narrowly escaping death by burning (to drive out the fairy and bring the natural child back),[57] I know of only one example of the standard international legend of the fairy betrayed by exclaiming at the sight of brewing (in this case carrying away ashes) in eggshells[58] and none of other types common in mainland Scotland (e.g., the "baby" playing an oat straw like bagpipes to a visiting tailor; the lack of pipers is not an insuperable cultural obstacle, because a variant is known where the changeling plays the tongs like a fiddle). ML 5070, "Midwife to the Fairies," is said to be known throughout most of Europe and parts of Asia up to Japan. A recent study from Ireland,[59] after a detailed analysis of Irish versions and a scrutiny of parallels from much of Western Europe, concludes that there are two main redactions, one involving a magic ointment which enables the midwife to see the fairies when others cannot, the other beginning with the midwife offering her help to a pregnant frog or other animal which later proves to be a fairy woman. The first alone is known in England, Wales and France, the second alone in Central Europe, but both are found in Scandinavia and have reached Ireland, perhaps, through Scotland. The story is well-known in Shetland (not Orkney) in the "ointment redaction" alone, but as there are no frogs in the islands the other redaction could hardly take root as a local legend. One of the seven Shetland versions, like some Norse ones, makes the mother whom the midwife attends a stolen mortal rather than a fairy, and several mention people thought to be dead being seen in the fairy dwelling.

A less well represented international type in the islands is ML 5075, "Removing a Building Situated over the House of the Fairies"; I cannot locate a version with the theme in the title (where a drain discharges into the underground dwelling), but I have recorded two Shetland versions of a Gaelic variant where an animal's tether-peg or the like makes a hole in the fairies' roof.[60] The theme of fairy help with the harvest (ML 6036) is found in Gaelic, Norse and Shetland stories, but the details of the story seem to be different in each case; only the Shetland versions have a rash promise of the farmer's best cow as payment.[61] ML 4075, "Visits to the Blessed Islands," is likewise assigned no definite plot by Christiansen, and the versions which unusually can be reported from Orkney and Caithness rather than Shetland, have a different theme from any Gaelic version I know, centering on the discovery (but not rescue) of a woman thought to be dead who has been abducted by a sea man.[62]

Some legends seem to be recorded from Norway, the Northern Isles and Lowland Scotland only, though this may be a false impression because I have not had time to classify all the hundreds of Gaelic fairy legends there are in periodicals and manuscript collections. One is ML 6050, "The Fairy Hat." Here, the islands go with the Lowland version, where the hat is mentioned in the words which allow the mortal to join the fairy ride but not "thrown to him" as in Norse versions. "Up hors, up hedik" is clearly the Lowland cry of "Horse and hattock!,"[63] though the reference to riding on a *bulwand* (mugwort or dock stem[64]) is a local interpretation of the "horse." ML 7020, "Vain Attempt to Escape from the *Nisse*," brownie or hogboon, has already been mentioned. It is known in Orkney, the Borders and Yorkshire, but not the Highlands. Similarly ML 6010, "The Capture of a Fairy"—a child called away by the crying of a strange name—appears in several Border and Shetland versions, but not in Gaelic. Only Shetland, I think, has a variant where it is a dog—or even "an object like a fiddle"!—that is summoned by the strange cry.[65] There is no need to suggest that these stories shared with Norway go back to a common Germanic heritage. "Horse and hattock!" must have gone north with Scots settlers, probably since 1500, and it is by no means impossible that the rather vaguer Norse versions come from a similar source.

I have only identified two Norse fairy legend types which are shared with the Northern Isles and not with other parts of Scotland. One is old enough to have been recorded with the fairy message it contains in almost pure Norn, though more recent versions from Fetlar are more comprehensible.

Thu 'at rides the red [horse] and rins [leads] the grey,
   Tell Tuna Tivla
   'At Funa Fivla
Is faan i [Has fallen in] the fire and brunt her [burned herself].

The message was heard by a man passing the fairy hill of Stackaberg and reported to his family when he got home. A fairy woman milking their cows in the byre overheard this, dropped the copper pan she was milking into and fled for home crying, "That's my bairn!" The "fairy pot of Upper Taft" was kept in the family for generations, reputedly, to testify to the truth of the story, until someone forgot the precaution of leaving it with the Bible in the iron pot-chain overnight and it was repossessed; but the "fairy kit of Gutcher" in Yell, obtained in similar circumstances, may still be extant. Another fairy vessel was found a few miles from the other two in Unst and Jakobsen reports the rhyme from further away, in Foula.[66] This Shetland legend is ML 6070, of which Christiansen lists 69 very similar versions—except that the fairy woman is usually stealing beer—of which 28 are from nearby Western Norway, often with similar -*la* names for the fairies. My one example of ML 6000, "Tricking the Fairy Suitor," comes by contrast from the other end of the island groups, South Ronaldsay in Orkney. It is James Henderson's story already mentioned about the sea man,[67] who tries apparently to court a young woman by coming in (through a locked door) late at night and sitting up with her. Her father takes her place and asks the sea man's advice on how to stop a "sea bull" getting to one of his heifers; he then applies it to his daughter, leaving her hair and nail-parings above the door and the would-be seducer cannot get in and goes away lamenting, "Eh my, there mony a man done themsels ill wi their tongue, and I'm don the sam!" (I've done the same!). In the Norwegian type (34 versions, 10 from Western Norway) the man and the fictitious bull belong to the land fairies and the remedy is usually herbal. Although there are no exact parallels to this plot from Gaelic Scotland, one is reported from Gaelic Ireland, and I have noted elsewhere how many Scottish Gaelic parallels there are for the bovine metaphor: giving love charms to the cow; giving the fairy suitor not a lock of the girl's hair but one from the tail of a cowhide that then runs off to the fairy hill; asking the slighted fairy mistress who is preventing the wife's child being born for advice on a goat in prolonged labor.[68]

A far greater number of fairy legend types from Orkney and Shetland are also well-known in the Highlands, but not mentioned by Christiansen. Here they can only be listed, with minimal descriptions and references to some published examples. The classification numbers beginning with "F" are from a provisional index of fairy and other supernatural legends I devised for the School of Scottish Studies in 1965–6.

F15   The piper vanishes in the fairy cave (usually from shore to shore of an island).[69]

F21   Absence for many years in the fairy hill, which seems only hours or minutes to the victim (often a fiddler in Shetland. Orcadians claim that Rip van Winkle came from Washington Irving's father, who was born and bred in the island of Shapinsay, not from Dutch legends).[70]

F22   The same theme, but the victim has willingly joined a fairy dance, usually carrying a container of drink or a basket of fish on his back, and is generally rescued by a companion who saw him go, a year later.[71] The Gaelic stories of the *sluagh* or fairy host carrying people off and returning them, or chasing them for their lives—which are something like Norwegian tales of the *oskorei*—seem not to be known in the Northern Isles,[72] nor are several types about the abduction of women, or their recapture from the fairy host. The next two types where their capture is prevented have been told there.

F34   A man taken by the host prevents them from taking a bride.[73]

F59   A husband manages to save his wife from abduction and finds the wooden image which the fairies were going to leave in her place.[74] This legend seems to be better known in Lowland than Highland versions, and the same is true of the next type.

F31   The fairies or trows quit the district for good.[75] While this legend is known in many parts of Europe, including *Northern* Ireland, perhaps Gaelic (and Norse?) belief in the fairies remained too strong to countenance it.

F88   Fairies ask for a sieve in obscure or distorted language.[76] This is one for the euhemerists (though I doubt whether the Orkney version, where the fairy wants a sifting sieve and can only say "piftin piv," can be taken as proof that he was a P-Celtic speaking Pict!).

F86   Fairies borrow oatmeal. Like the previous citation, this type shows fairies to be quite human in their needs. In Gaelic versions the loan is repaid with meal from a drying-kiln that went on fire, while in Shetland they simply repay with improbably choice meal from the best part of each ear of corn.[77]

F103   Learning tunes from the fairies is, as noted already, commoner in Shetland than any part of Scotland.[78]

F105   The gift of healing from the fairies. Probably the most widely reported instance is the Shetland story of "Farquhar's pig," a jar of ointment left by some trows exorcised by the name of God, which had such a reputation as a cure-all that several people at the beginning of this century all claimed to have the original.[79]

F143   "Mysel' i' da mill," a version of the international "Myself" or "Noman" motif (K602), but it is used as in a widespread Gaelic legend to prevent fairy vengeance on someone who got rid of an unwanted fairy suitor bothering him at the mill by scalding her with hot food; the trows ask who did it and she says "It was 'Myself-in-the-Mill.'"[80] In the Shetland story "Myself" is a man who scalds a female trow with a hot chicken, whereas in most Gaelic versions a woman gets rid of an amorous male fairy with a potful of hot porridge, but the relationship is clear.

Considering that most Scottish settlers, at least in Shetland, where far more of the legends have been recorded, came from the non-Gaelic east coast, the overlap with the Gaelic tradition is striking. There are dozens of well-known Gaelic types *not* represented, certainly, including perhaps the most popular motif of all, where a changeling or a band of unwanted helpers are got rid of by a cry that the fairy hill is on fire (F142). Another very surprising absentee is ML 5080 (F111), "Food from the Fairies" (two men hear fairies churning underground and wish for the butter on bread in Norway, or a drink of buttermilk in the Highlands; they are offered it and the one who refuses what he wished for has bad luck). This is well-known in Highland and Lowland Scotland as well as Norway, and its absence in the Northern Isles is surprising—but the fact that it has not been recorded (as far as I know) does not mean that it was never told there. The absence of anything like Gaelic fairy lover (*leannan sidhe*) traditions or the Norse ML 5090, "Married to a Fairy Woman" may be made up for by the frequency of seal bride tales. But to return to the Gaelic overlap, the lack of fairy legends from eastern Scotland in modern collections does not rule out the likelihood that most of the Highland types circulated there around the sixteenth century when settlers were leaving for the Northern Isles. Ballads and confessions in witch trials testify to a strong fairy belief in an area which two or three centuries earlier had been almost entirely Gaelic-speaking.

On the other hand, I have argued elsewhere that it is seldom possible to prove that a legend goes back to the Middle Ages, let alone pagan times.[81] An illustration used there shows how speculative deductions from such evidence can be immediately taken up by an archaeologist as proof of a Pictish survival. F22, "Dancing in the Fairy Hill," is recorded as a local legend from many parishes of the mainland Highlands and in the Western and Northern Isles, but seems to have neither Irish, English or Norse parallels. However, a close variant (located at an open-air fairy ring, not a mound) is quite well-known in Wales, and the only likely early contact between the Northern Isles and Wales would be through the Picts and Strathclyde Britons, both P-Celtic speakers;[82] but is it the only possible means of contact, or has the picture been distorted by the disappearance of Lowland and North English versions since the Middle Ages?

If some of the Highland overlaps could go back to Pictish times it would help to explain why such deep rooted traditions outnumber those of the Norse invaders—where these stories did not arrive, as some surely did, through later contact with Christian Norway. In any case here at least the Norse element in the cultural heritage of the Northern Isles can be shown to be smaller than the Scottish contribution. We should not forget the purely local element; the nature of the comparison has meant that stories only found in the Northern Isles may have been left out, certainly if not recorded more than once. As far as I can tell the "Gloy canna gang" type (F16C) is a local invention and in its present form at least dates from after the introduction of Scots. The stories of fiddlers playing for the fairies—again, in their present form—seem to be local creations since the fiddle became popular in Shetland in the eighteenth century. And at least one other type, where fairies borrow a fishing boat and take it out with the owner hiding in it to watch them,[83] with varying sequels but not the disastrous ones of ML 4070, "Sea-Sprite Trying out the Seats of a Boat," which is vaguely similar—is common to Orkney and Shetland alone. Who can tell which other types may have been invented in the Northern Isles and spread south to Scotland, or even north to Norway?

Descriptions, Nature, and Function

Legends are easy to compare from place to place and can be the basis for many of the ideas that are held about the fairies, but they can be amplified from more ephemeral traditions, memorates and personal experiences, and just things people say, to give a clearer picture of these beings and their place in the belief system of the islands. Bearing in mind that all traditions of the Northern Isles can vary from island to island and parish to parish—so for instance Laurence Williamson noted of the water horses, nyuggle and tangie, "not known in Fetlar and Yell"[84]—we can attempt to clarify the total picture at least of the social land fairies or trows in Orkney and Shetland. The evidence here will come often from untranscribed tape recordings and things people have said to me, or refer back to stories already mentioned, so there will be fewer specific sources cited than for the legends.

Generally speaking they are like people and live fairly close to other people; they are "Good Neighbors" and can be explained as Pictish survivors. They eat the staple human foods, oatmeal, milk (and dairy products?) and fish, and keep their own cows as well as stealing and milking other people's, but rely on borrowed boats for fishing. They may not be much good at fishing from the rocks either. A Yell man said a fairy hit him on the ankle with a hammer and demanded some of the water used to boil the fish he had just caught fishing from the rocks.[85] The pain in his ankle left him when he complied with the fairy's request by pouring a quart of it round the boulder the fairy had come out from under—which sounds more like an offering for a divine cure than a transaction with a neighbor! This seems to have been a little man, but the fairy who came from the midwife, and according to Brucie Henderson lived under a boulder in the same part of Yell, looked just like one of the neighbors. The size question as always is insoluble. J.G. Campbell, who summarizes the problem for Highland fairies very well, concludes that they may have been able to vary their size, but no tale says so and "the true belief is that the Fairies are a small race, the men 'about four feet or so' in height, and the women in many cases not taller than a little girl. . . . Being called 'little,' the exaggeration, which popular imagination loves, has diminished them . . ."[86]—but where necessary, for instance when they court humans, they can be bigger. Much the same seems to hold true in the Northern Isles.

Other features are designed, it seems, to show that they are *not* exactly like people: they symbolize the wild, or bear traces of former near divinity (some skill in magic at least), or resemble a vanished race—so they must be different. Apart from being smaller, they have difficulty with our language, have strange names, lack things which they have to steal from us, and come into our mills and houses to warm themselves at a fire (do they have fires?) or to wash their babies—and if they find no clean water indoors overnight, they wash them in buttermilk or swats (a drink made with oat husks) which they put back in the churn for the family to drink.[87] Their belongings also may be miniature, like the "Fairy Pot,"[88] or a shoe which was made into a snuffbox.[89] Rather than a fiddle they play a *poche*, the pocket fiddle used by dancing masters, though by the description it had only one horsehair string.[90] More important, they live underground, under boulders, in knowes (mounds) or "trowie hadds," or under the sand where people stretched new-made Shetland shawls,[91] or in one case in a sea cave below a house on the Out Skerries, where they could lift a flagstone in the floor to steal oatcakes.[92] One extraordinary memorate from Yell tells of a fairy boy who jumped out of a crack in a peat bank and claimed he had a "run" from one end of the island to the other, apparently underground.[93] Similar placenames are mentioned in a strange account noted by Laurence Williamson of a magician in Yell called Rowland who "put people into and took them out again from the fairies" to be cured of illness, and "said that as good a street as any in London ran underground 'from da ha o da reath to trolyagars huls.'"[94]

If the fairy Otherworld is underground and the fairies are magic if not divine, are they the spirits of the dead, or underground deities who guard the dead? Though Ernest Marwick's interpretation of the hogboon as the spirit of the founder of the farm[95] seems convincing, on the whole the more social trows seem to be the keepers of the dead. Various stories mention a midwife or a fiddler[96] seeing people, generally women, who were believed to be dead in a fairy dwelling. Though this may be mainly due to the belief in fairies taking women (who died in childbirth especially) and leaving wooden images in their place—as Rowland did with the people he "put into the fairies"—which would be buried as their corpses, a few stories seem to show the fairies or trows as guardians of all the dead, perhaps a lingering relic of the gods of the pre-Christian paradise. In "The Three Yells" a dead Shetlander summons his neighbor in a dream to meet him at a place called the Hole of Cudda, "famous for trows," at midnight. The dead man tells the other his wife is unfaithful; it has been "a job to him to get back to this world again," and the other must get home before he hears the third of the three loud yells of the title. He manages to be just through the door on horseback when it sounds, but the mare's hindquarters are outside and she drops dead.[97] Here the function of the trows is not very clear. Do they utter the yells, or guard the gate to the otherworld? A story from North Ronaldsay in Orkney is more definite. Here a young man whose wife has died asks a witch how he can see her again and is advised to go to a cave under a stone pillar near the desolate north end of the island on the night of the full moon. He must throw in a black cat (as sacrifice to the Devil?), read a few verses from the Bible (to placate God?) and take a thick oaken staff, because his wife would rise up and "the fairy folk would try to stop her. But . . . when he heard his wife speaking he had to jump in and use the staff, and use it without mercy until he got a hold of his wife." When he did this he was able to speak to his wife all night, every full moon.[98] There seems to be a mixture of beliefs here, but this is surely more than a case of a wife abducted by the fairies and thought dead. The picture is, however, quite akin to the one we opened with of the South Ronaldsay man fighting the fairies all night, apparently as a shaman protecting his community.

The functions of the fairies in the Northern Isles, then, vary from case to case as they do everywhere. They can very often be dangerous beings to be fought off with an oak staff, but they may equally well be placated with offerings of milk or fish broth and provide good luck, if not physical help or cures. They serve a useful purpose as scapegoats, to be blamed for changing sickly or handicapped babies, stealing women who die in childbirth, or shooting cattle with unexplained ailments. In a region where very recently old women were accused of stealing the "profit" of their neighbors' milk, and indeed it was believed they could[99]—possibly because Orcadians and Shetlanders churned whole milk rather than cream and this could quite often mean a lot of hard work and no butter—the community was saved from further feuds over witchcraft if it was believed that the sick cow was trowshot rather than bewitched; and though burning gunpowder-filled straws as firecrackers to frighten off the trows, shouting as one informant heard "Fly, you buggers, fly!" can hardly have helped the cow, it may have helped to relieve the owner's feelings, as did going out at night to fight the fairies. To children, however, fairies might be bogeys to keep them from straying at night; for housewives, a warning to keep fresh water in the house overnight; for fiddlers, an explanation for tunes that suddenly came into their heads, or for anyone an excuse for things inexplicably lost, or found. For some people, they symbolized the spiritual, unseen side of things in a homelier way than official Christianity, and people may have identified with their love of the secular music and dance which the unpopular Scots ministers frowned on. Certainly the superstition that spinning wheels must be put out of commission over the twenty-four nights of Yule, lest the trows interfere with them, was a good excuse for women to enjoy themselves at a festival which the church tried to suppress. But in a general way, they stood for both wild nature and the supernatural and everything inexplicable, good or bad, which modern society feels it can explain in more scientific terms like "greenhouse effect" or "chaos theory."

Much of this is probably true of fairies everywhere, so to preserve the local flavor I would like to finish with some Orkney and Shetland descriptions of what fairies, or trows, or beings people have seen actually looked like. Needless to say they had no wings or antennae and would not have fitted in a cowslip's bell. As with eyewitness accounts of such beings I have heard from much further south, they were mostly seen by children under the age of ten, who said they were smaller than themselves, there were many of them, and they wore comparatively drab colors. Marwick says that trows "usually dressed in grey," and later quotes an anonymous Victorian Shetlander's description of fairies with more colorful faces ("yellow complexion . . . red eyes and green teeth") than clothes: "They dress uniformly in dark grey, and both sexes wear murat [natural brown wool] mittens."[100] The only recent Orkney sighting I can quote contradicts this; it comes from John Mackay's MS. notes.[101] Mackay sent me to see the man who saw the trow, but I was (perhaps unjustifiably) reluctant to question him about the experience. As a young man in Stronsay about 1920, he was coming home from church with three others along a sandy beach when he suddenly "stopped and pointed to a spot just where the grass and the sand on the foreshore met. 'Do you see that little man?' he said. 'He must be a trow.'" In fact only one of the other three could see him. The description is brief: "A small man about a foot high clad in green and red."

The two Shetlanders I have recorded myself gave rather different accounts of crowds of little people in black and white clothes. They both volunteered their accounts, though I suppress the names here just in case surviving relatives might be embarrassed. The later of the two sightings was in 1914 and was interpreted afterwards by some as an omen of the coming World War. My informant, who was ten years old at the time, and her younger friend had been to fetch milk from a farm in the island of Unst and were playing as they often did in a ruined house, climbing on the walls to look for birds' nests.

> Then we sat up on the side of the roof and all at once there was this, white from one side and black from the other side, just wee things about this height [two feet or less], just like men . . . No women, no, they were just like men, little bodies . . . The black came from one side and the white from the other side, and they fought and they fought and they fought, and we sat there spellbound both clutching together, looking at these things . . . And they just fought away, and then the black ones seemed to disappear, and the white ones stayed for a while and then they went, just disappeared like that. We never realized that we'd seen something, you know, that was na really there, it was just something queer. And we took to our heels and we made for home as fast as we could go. I never yet know what happened to the milk . . . [102]

Less than a week before I had recorded an old seaman, born in 1888, on the mainland of Shetland. He had been scornful of the witchcraft beliefs of his elders, but suddenly began to tell me of some women in theneighborhood who had been haunted by something that sounded to me like a poltergeist. When he was "only a little boy" one of the women came to visit his mother, and she and the boy and their dog went part of the way home with her (my impression was that this was in the twilight or after dark on a winter afternoon, but I can find nothing on the tape to say this). He always felt that what he saw "had something to do with that lady" and her haunting.

> When we came so far ... the dog started to make queer noises, and eventually the dog lay across my mother's feet ... [so] that she could hardly get clear. And a little way to one side I saw a multitude of little men and women—this is God's truth, you know ... I'm not exaggerating, I saw this myself, saw this multitude of little men and women ... I've told the same story to many a one—I saw that just as plain as I see you sitting there. ... How were they dressed? Well, it appeared to me that these little men were dressed kind of with dark clothes on them. And it appeared to me that these little women were dressed a kind of dark, but they had something that appeared to me to be white in front of them. (Like an apron?) Yes.[103]

When he told his mother on the way home what he had seen she dismissed it as "a lot of foolishness" but there is no doubt that he was sure he had seen these people. Neither account uses the words "trows" or "fairies," and neither sounds like conventional accounts of them except that they were little people. The picture I get from the second description suggests a crowd of little Puritans or Pilgrim Fathers, but no doubt many such accounts in the past have gone towards the body of belief in the trows. Like all such terms, "trows" is just a peg to hang accounts of the strange and unexpected on, and it means something slightly different to everyone who uses it.

Notes

1. See for instance R.J. Berry and H.N. Firth, eds., *The People of Orkney* (Kirkwall: The Orkney P, 1986), esp. Chapters 7–10 and 13.
2. I have often been told how frightened people were as children to go outside after a storytelling session of fairy or "trowie" tales, and two sisters in the West Side of Shetland told me that their parents deliberately told many such tales because the girls had a habit of going out to the hills at night near dangerous cliffs.

3. See "The Boy and the Brüni," *Tocher* 11 (1973): 96–7, and Laurence G. Johnson, *Laurence Williamson of Mid Yell* (Lerwick: The Shetland Times, 1971) 119–20.

4. (Fairies) "Peerie Merran's Spoon" in Alan Bruford, ed., *The Green Man of Knowledge and Other Scots Traditional Tales* (Aberdeen: Aberdeen UP, 1982) 92, and *Tocher* 28 (1978): 205; (Giants) Ernest W. Marwick, *The Folklore of Orkney and Shetland* (London: B.T. Batsford, 1975) 30–2.

5. *Tocher* 26 (1977): 103, from John G. Halcro, South Ronaldsay. The name of the shaman, who lived under a hundred years ago, is suppressed because his family would not like it known, but it may do no harm here to reveal his nickname, "The Black Doctor."

6. Reidar Th. Christiansen, *The Migratory Legends*, Folklore Fellows' Communications 175 (Helsinki: Suomalainen Tiedeakademia, 1958) 88. Cited hereafter only as ML with type number; "Christiansen" means the next reference.

7. Reidar Th. Christiansen, ed., *Folktales of Norway* (London: Routledge & Kegan Paul, 1964) xxxiv.

8. Christiansen 121–3 (trolls) 123–4 (*huldre*).

9. Christiansen 120. In fact there is no indication that other "fairies" are in the mound, which in the two previous versions is inhabited apparently by a solitary *draug* or "living corpse."

10. Christiansen xxxiii referring to tale on 84–6.

11. Christiansen xxxiv.

12. Christiansen xxxvi.

13. John Gregorson Campbell, *Superstitions of the Highlands & Islands of Scotland* (Glasgow: James MacLehose and Sons, 1900) 9–11.

14. Christiansen xxxvii; ML 5090, 5095.

15. Christiansen xxxviii, 91–2 (AT 758). Johnson 138. See also reference in note 33.

16. E.O.G. Turville-Petre, *Myth and Religion of the North* (London: Weidenfeld and Nicolson, 1964) 232 and source cited there.

17. *Tocher* 26 (1977): 102.

18. *Tocher* 30 (1978–79): 370 (some spellings standardized). E.W. Marwick 33, lists some uses of "troll" and "trow" in old dialect terms, but omits the adjective "trowie," still heard in Orkney, for which Hugh Marwick, *The Orkney Norn* (Oxford: Oxford UP, 1929) 195, gives two main meanings: "1. weakly, ailing; 2. of little account, worthless." I think it might also mean bad-tempered.

19. Christiansen xxxiii (*berg*-folk); E.W. Marwick 33.

20. "Hillyans," a Papa Westray local term: John D. Mackay, manuscript collection of "Miscellaneous Orkney Lore," archives of the School of Scottish Studies, University of Edinburgh (cited as "Mackay MS") 52. "Hildaland," E.W. Marwick 26, following Walter Traill Dennison.

21. E.W. Marwick 42–5.

22. *Tocher* 26 (1977): 102.

23. Turville-Petre 231.

24. G.A. Hight, trans., *The Saga of Grettir the Strong* (London: J.M. Dent, 1913) 42–5; cf. Tolkien again for "barrow-wights."

25. Christiansen xxxii (cf. the *draug* in note 9 for the earlier concept).

26. E.W. Marwick 39–42 (hogboons in general); 40 (broonie); 42 (ML 7020). It is possible that the term *godbonde* for the guardian of the farm (Christiansen xi) may have become confused at some stage with *haugbui*. In one origin legend the Hugboy is a vast giant: Donald A. MacDonald and Alan J. Bruford, eds., *Scottish Traditional Tales* (Edinburgh: School of Scottish Studies, privately printed, 1974) 98.

27. E.W. Marwick 148–50.

28. (Orkney) E.W. Marwick 40–41; (Shetland) G.F. Black, coll., Northcote W. Thomas, ed., *Examples of Printed Folk-Lore Concerning the Orkney and Shetland Islands,* Publications of the Folk-Lore Society XLIX (London: David Nutt, 1903) 20, quoting John Brand (1703), mentions only wort (unfermented beer) poured into "Brounies Stone" for help in brewing, and for help in churning, milk sprinkled round the house, but recent oral evidence is that milk was left in a stone; (Highland) Campbell 185–6, 193.

29. (Sea man) *Tocher* 26 (1977): 100–1; (sea trows) E.W. Marwick 30, summarizing Walter Traill Dennison, *Orkney Folklore and Traditions* (Kirkwall: Herald P, 1961) 14–6. This book (cited as "Dennison") is E.W. Marwick's reprint of articles published by Dennison mainly in *The Scottish Antiquary* volumes V to VIII (1891–4). Brand's account of sea trows two centuries earlier, as "great rolling Creatures" that break fishing-nets (Black 45–6) makes them sound more like whales than sea people.

30. *Tocher* 26 (1977): 95–6, reprinted in Bruford, *Green Man* 93–4; cf. note 62. (Hether Blether) E.W. Marwick 26. (Utröst) Christiansen xxxi, 55–60. Rocabarraigh—recordings from Barra, North and South Uist in School of Scottish Studies archive.

31. *Tocher* 28 (1978): 199–200; (sea skin) *Tocher* 26 (1977): 96–7.

32. Alan Bruford, "The Grey Selkie," *Scottish Studies* 18 (1974): 63–81; also in E.B. Lyle, ed., *Ballad Studies* (The Folklore Society Mistletoe Series, Cambridge & Ipswich: D.S. Brewer, 1976) 41–65. "Child" references, of course, are to Francis James Child, ed., *The English and Scottish Popular Ballads*, 5 vols. (1882–98; New York: Dover, 1965). I only realized that "sealkie" was the pronunciation of "selkie" in Unst (and North Yell) after writing this article.

33. *Tocher* 8 (1972): 256–7.

34. Christiansen xxvii, 39–42 (ML 3080); cf. *Tocher* 34 (1980): 272–3.

35. *Tocher* 34 (1980): 274; D.A. MacDonald, "Some Aspects of Visual and Verbal Memory in Gaelic Storytelling," *ARV* 37 (1981): 120–1 (North Uist man finds seal man he wounded with a club in Harris).

36. E.W. Marwick 25, cf. 48–9, which gives a very useful collection of information about Finns as enchanters on land in Shetland.

37. E.W. Marwick 25–6, summarizing Dennison 17, and details from 34–41.

38. Dennison 43–5; cf. Bruford, "Selkie" 71–2.

39. Bruford, "Selkie" 70–6.

40. George Mackay Brown, *An Orkney Tapestry* (London: Quartet Books, 1973) 173–8.

41. Berry and Firth 7–12.

42. Christiansen xxx–xxxi.

43. Berry and Firth 172 and 206; the Dublin study referred to there is still in progress, but the westerly distribution of the legend is clear.

44. E.W. Marwick 28.

45. (Flotta) SA 1974/70 B5 ("SA" is the classification containing year of recording, of School and Scottish Studies field recordings; informant's name suppressed to avoid embarrassing relatives). (Deerness) E.W. Marwick 24–5.

46. E.W. Marwick 33–4.

47. J.F. Campbell, *Popular Tales of the West Highlands* (new ed., Paisley: Alexander Gardner, 1890) 1: xcv–civ.

48. Berry and Firth 61, shows that Norse pagans in Orkney and Shetland were relatively short, but there are no comparative statistics for Picts.

49. Andrew T. Cluness, *Told Round the Peat Fire* (London: Robert Hale, 1955) 94–133. Cluness in fact makes a Pict talk of "our thralls the little folk," who resisted with them "free Pict and peasant alike" (119–20) and became one element in the belief.

50. *Tocher* 12 (1973): 139 and 19 (1975): 84.

51. *Tocher* 29 (1978): 303–23, (hiding in caves) 307–8.

52. SA 1970/306 A. The ballad "Thrummy Cap" by John Burness (Robert Ford, *Auld Scots Ballants* [Paisley: Alexander Gardner, 1889] 1–14) was well-known from broadsides or garlands in Orkney and Shetland; the ghost defying hero's epithet is usually shortened to "Thrummy" in the ballad, and a refrain something like "Trom, Trom, Tromie" was added when the ballad was sung, according to another friend of Tom Anderson (the well-known fiddler) recorded by Margaret Mackay on the same tape.

53. Mackay MS 21. See also Johnson 119; John Nicolson, *Some Folk-Tales and Legends of Shetland* (Edinburgh: Thomas Allan & Sons, 1920) 32. Nicolson also published much the same collection of tales of the trows in a different order in *Restin' Chair Yarns* (Lerwick: Johnson & Greig, n.d.). The press gang adaptation is SA 1974/210 A4.

54. SA 1974/197 A1. The original story is in Nicolson, *Some Folk-Tales* 18–9— the hero has the same surname, comes from the same township and had the same skill on the fiddle as my informant. The proper end is that he is released by the trows after playing for them and bound to secrecy about his adventure; he has good luck until he tells the story when drunk, and then loses all he had gained and dies poor and blind. One version of the sheep thief legend (migratory within Shetland) which supplied the end is in Nicolson, *Some Folk-Tales* 54–6.

55. Mairi Robinson, ed., *The Concise Scots Dictionary* (Aberdeen: Aberdeen UP, 1985) 238.

56. Nicolson, *Some Folk-Tales* 13–9 (of 13–46).

57. J.T. Smith Leask, *A Peculiar People and Other Orkney Tales* (Kirkwall: W.R. Mackintosh, 1931) 253, gives an example from the last century; cf. *Tocher* 27 (1977–8): 172; cf. Black 36 (searing paralyzed limb as one taken by trows).

58. Nicolson, *Some Folk-Tales* 21–2.

59. Críostóir Mac Cárthaigh, "Midwife to the Fairies: A Migratory Legend," MA thesis, Department of Irish Folklore, U College, Dublin, 1988, Chapter X "The International Context" and Chapter XI "Conclusion."

60. *Tocher* 28 (1978): 197 (pins to stretch Shetland shawl on short grass over sand, Unst); SA 1974/196 A2 (tether-pin, Delting). Cf. J.F. Campbell 2: 49; J.G. Campbell 13, 95–6.

61. Nicolson, *Some Folk-Tales* 37.

62. For James Henderson's Orkney version see *Tocher* 26 (1977): 95–6, reprinted in Bruford, *Green Man* 93–4; Dennison 47–51; The Viking Club, *Old-Lore Miscellany of Orkney, Shetland, Caithness and Sutherland* (cited as *Old-Lore*) 2 (1909): 105 (Orkney), 163–6, 210–2, and 3 (1910): 44–6 (three part version from Caithness, with seal husband in cave); SA 1961/26 B4 (Shetland).

63. Johnson 117–8; *Old-Lore* 5 (1912): 16–7; Black 21. Cf. Sir George Douglas, *Scottish Fairy Tales* (London & Felling-on-Tyne: The Walter Scott Publishing Co., n.d.) 118–20 (after Scott, *Minstrelsy of the Scottish Border*, vol. 2). "Hattock" is a diminutive of "hat" (Robinson 270); for the related story of witches, where headgear rather than broomstick helps them to fly, see Alan Bruford, "Scottish Gaelic Witch Stories: A Provisional Type List," *Scottish Studies* 11 (1967): 27–30 and note 24.

64. E.W. Marwick 35, quoting Johnson, interprets "bulwand" in the Orkney sense of "dock," but the Shetland meaning is "mugwort" according to John J. Graham, *The Shetland Dictionary* (Stornoway: Thule P, 1979) 9.

65. *Tocher* 28 (1978): 225, is typical, with the cry "Hannie, hornie, hi!" Lowland parallels are in Hannah Aitken, *A Forgotten Heritage* (Edinburgh and London: Scottish Academic P, 1973) 17–8 and 123 (different but seemingly related memorate). (Fairy dog) Nicolson, *Some Folk-Tales* 42; *Tocher* 28 (1978): 197. "Object like fiddle," Johnson 118.

66. Jakob Jakobsen, *An Etymological Dictionary of the Norn Language in Shetland*, 2 vols. (London: David Nutt, 1928) 1: xcv–vii (Foula and Fetlar versions of rhyme, with or without story). Other Fetlar versions in Johnson 117 ("People say the pan is still in the house, some say built in the wall") and Black 34 (brass pan "hung on a nail with a piece of flesh or some sort of food inside it" till one night this was forgotten and it vanished) as well as recent oral tradition, especially SA 1970/244B, main source of rhyme and account in text. Yell "kit" (normally a staved wooden vessel, but this is copper): oral tradition, not attached to rhyme. Unst version: Jessie M.E. Saxby, *Shetland Traditional Lore* (Edinburgh: Grant & Murray, 1932) 153 (silver cup, eventually recognized as a chalice and claimed by minister!). Hibbert in 1822 (quoted Black 42) suggests that trows had left "innumerable" such utensils.

67. *Tocher* 26 (1977): 100–1.

68. Alan Bruford, "Problems in Cataloguing Scottish Supernatural and Historical Legends," *Journal of the Folklore Institute* 16 (1979): 156. I found the fairy mistress story (*Tocher* 28 [1978]: 204–7) after writing this. The Irish version of ML 6000 from County Mayo is in Bo Almqvist, ed., *Crossing the Border* (Dublin: Department of Irish Folklore, U College Dublin, privately printed 1988) 43–4; a herbal remedy for a "sick calf" keeps a little girl from being harmed by a fairy man.

69. See *Scottish Studies* 24 (1980): 43–5.

70. Nicolson, *Some Folk-Tales* 14, and *Tocher* 26 (1977): 104–5, are typical examples; compare J.F. Campbell 2: 57–62.

71. *Old-Lore* 2 (1909): 108 and 3 (1910): 30–1 (both Orkney); cf. note 79.

72. J.G. Campbell 69–72; Christiansen xxxii–iii, 75–6. Nicolson, *Some Folk-Tales* 44, where trows carry a man a long way in five minutes, is reminiscent of some *sluagh* tales.

73. The first two "horse and hattock" tales in note 63 end with this motif; cf. J.G. Campbell 88–9, and *Tocher* 39 (1985): 146–9.

74. E.W. Marwick 170–2 (from Douglas); Nicolson, *Some Folk-Tales* 25; Black 32–3. Compare Aitken 16, from Dumfriesshire.

75. *Tocher* 28 (1978): 226 and 30 (1978–9): 370 (reprinted in Bruford, *Green Man* 97). Compare Aitken 122 (from the Scots-speaking East coast of the Highlands).

76. *Journal of the Folklore Institute* 16 (1979): 158; Gaelic tale referred to there published in *Tocher* 28 (1978): 196, and cf. 195.

77. G. Campbell 150–2; *Tocher* 28 (1978): 194; Nicolson, *Some Folk-Tales* 35.

78. Nicolson, *Some Folk-Tales* 13–9 (of 13–46).

79. E.W. Marwick 136; Johnson 119.

80. Nicolson, *Some Folk-Tales* 31; cf. J.F. Campbell vol. 2, 203–7.

81. Alan Bruford, "Legends Long Since Localised or Tales Still Travelling?" *Scottish Studies* 24 (1980): 43–62.

82. Bruford, "Legends Long" 54–5; Berry and Firth 174.

83. Nicolson, *Some Folk-Tales* 33–4 (Shetland); *Tocher* 26 (1977): 103 (Orkney).

84. Johnson 116.

85. *Tocher* 28 (1978): 203–4.

86. J.G. Campbell 10.

87. Johnson 136; Nicolson, *Some Folk-Tales* 39.

88. See note 66.

89. Nicolson, *Some Folk-Tales* 45.

90. *Tocher* 12 (1973): 140.

91. See note 60.

92. Nicolson, *Some Folk-Tales* 43.

93. *Tocher* 28 (1978): 224–5, reprinted in Bruford, *Green Man* 95–6.

94. Johnson 137–8. Compare from the other version "I go frae the Grey Steen o Stourascord to the Knowes o Troilasahoull"; the latter name is probably Trollakeldas Houlla in the north end of the island, a "troll" name—compare the haunted "Trolhouland" on the mainland of Shetland (Black 40, 42)—while Stourascord is in the south.

95. E.W. Marwick 39–40.

96. *Tocher* 28 (1978): 202–3; Johnson 136.

97. *Tocher* 28 (1978): 217, reprinted in Bruford, *Green Man* 72–3.

98. MacDonald and Bruford 124; Mary Scott, *Island Saga, The Story of North Ronaldsay* (Aberdeen: Alex Reid, 1968) 155–6.

99. See for example *Tocher* 34 (1980): 278.

100. E.W. Marwick 33, 42; cf. Saxby 149–50, 157, 161 for trows dressed in grey or even referred to as "Grey folk."

101. Mackay MS vol. 1, 27.

102. SA 1974/209 A4. Spellings normalized to standard English; little need to change vocabulary, though "Aa at eence there wis this . . ." could in Scots mean "All at once there were these . . ."

103. SA 1974/203 B2. Spellings normalized similarly; here "this little men wis dressed . . ." is changed to "these little men were" and "I'm told" (the regular Shetland form) to "I've told."

Ballads of Otherworld Beings

David Buchan

In one important particular the balladries of Northern Europe differ from
those elsewhere on the continent; the ballad traditions of the Nordic
countries and Britain, especially Scotland, are distinguished by the relative
prominence of their supernatural ballads. This prominence generally
declined in the anglophone tradition transplanted to North America,
although certain groups of ballads retained a strength in societies where
they continued to fulfill certain socio-cultural functions for their
audiences, such as the revenant ballads in Newfoundland.[1] In British
balladry the supernatural ballads constitute one of the three major
subgenres, one which itself comprises six minigenres, among them the
ballads of Otherworld beings.[2]

Although some versions have been recorded in North America and
one or two in England, this minigenre, as recorded, is preponderantly
Scottish, which serves to underline the specifically Scottish-Nordic linkage
in supernatural balladry. Two types, in fact (CH 113 "The Great Silkie of
Sule Skerry" and CH 19 "King Orfeo"), have been recorded only in the
Northern Isles, where the culture has a Nordic base. To investigate this
minigenre the method of talerole analysis has been employed. By this
method one distinguishes the concrete fact of character from the abstract
concept of talerole, defined, essentially, as the interactive function served
by a character within the narrative, in order to perceive the essential
patterns of types, subgenres, and genres, and their cultural significance.[3]

The group contains nine ballad-types, in two subgroups, where there
obtain three taleroles: Bespeller, Bespelled, and Unspeller. In the stories of
the group an Otherworld being bespells a mortal and then the spelling is
terminated, either by its uplifting or by its running a fatal course. The
definitions of the taleroles are relatively self-evident: the Bespeller is the
Otherworld being who lays a spell upon the mortal, the Bespelled is the
mortal on whom the Otherworld being lays the spell, and the Unspeller is
the character responsible for the uplifting of the spell. In one subgroup
normally all three taleroles obtain, but in the other only two—Bespeller
and Bespelled. Right away, then, analysis of the taleroles reveals a
classificatory distinction between, on the one hand, those types with three

taleroles which involve land-based Otherworld beings, and on the other, those types with two taleroles which involve water creatures.

As we can see from the schema below, the characters who fill the Bespeller role are all Otherworld beings. In the first group are the King of Elphin (I have regularized the various terms Ferrie, Faerie, Elfland, Elphan, to the old Scots term Elphin), the Queen of Elphin, an Elphin being remarkable for his smallness, and a giant (or "Etin") who lives in a wood but who has hill-folk among his Nordic parallels. In the second group are a mermaid, a Finn (man, seal, and underwater denizen), and a water sprite (also called a "mermaiden" but inhabiting a river or well rather than the sea). The Bespelled figures are all mortals, and of the opposite sex from the Bespeller, except for CH 40, where the Queen of Elphin commissions a nurse. The Unspellers include a husband, a lover, a son of the central pair, and on two occasions the Queen of Elphin figure who also occupies the Bespeller talerole and who relinquishes, or promises to relinquish, her captive after a certain period of time has passed. The types of the second group do not have an Unspeller, but one with a hybrid talerole pattern (CH 42/85) has the standard third talerole of the Romantic and Tragic configuration, the Partner.[4]

Examination of the taleroles, then, underlines that there exist two distinct subgroups, which feature interestingly different patternings. The types of the first subgroup, for instance, all end happily. In "King Orfeo" (CH 19), the King of Elphin abducts the lady of King Orfeo (a manifestation of Orpheus) who gains admittance to the fairy hall and liberates her with his music.[5] Tam Lin (of CH 39) has been abducted by the Queen of Elphin but is liberated on Halloween by his lover who undertakes a complicated ritual of transformation. Thomas in "Thomas Rymer" (CH 37), by failing to observe a taboo is taken by the Queen of Elphin, with whom he journeys through Otherworld territory to the Fairies Court where he serves the Queen seven years and is then liberated, with "the tongue that can never lie" (37D10)—the gift of prophecy. In "The Queen of Elfan's Nourice" (CH 40) a nursing mother is abducted by the Queen of Elphin to act as nurse for her child and is promised liberation, a return to "Christen land," when the child stands at her knee. Hind Etin (of CH 41) abducts a lady who bears him seven sons, the eldest of whom one day liberates her and his brothers by leading them back to this world "for to get christendoun." In "The Wee Wee Man" (CH 38) a lady admires a diminutive Elphin creature with whom she journeys to a bonny hall in Elphin, which suddenly vanishes. This last, rather slight, ballad-type, of which no version is longer than eight stanzas, manifests the basic pattern in weak fashion, with the lady being invited rather than abducted (though there is an element of compulsion in the fourteenth century analogue "Als y yod on ay Mounday"), and with her being not so much liberated as simply released by the abrupt disappearance

Schema
Ballads of Otherworld Beings

	TYPE	TALEROLE CHARACTER	BESPELLER	BESPELLED	UNSPELLER
GROUP I	19	(King Orfeo)	KoE	S	H
	39	(Tam Lin)	QoE	H	S
	37	(Thomas Rymer)	QoE	H	QoE
	40	(The Queen of Elfan's Nourice)	QoE	S	QoE
	41	(Hind Etin)	UG (Guide)	S (Sojourner)	Sn + 1
	38	(The Wee Wee Man)	UE	S	
GROUP II	113	(The Great Silkie of Sule Skerry)	USel	S	
	289	(The Mermaid)	UMer	H^n	
	42/85	(Clerk Colvill/ Lady Alice)	UMer	H	PARTNER S (in A, B versions) HM (in C version)

ABBREVIATIONS

H:	He, leading male character
S:	She, leading female character
Sn:	Son
HM:	H's Mother
KoE:	King of Elphin, Ferrie, etc.
QoE:	Queen of Elphin, etc.
E:	Elphin
U:	Unmortal
G:	Giant
Sel:	Selchie, Finn
Mer:	Mermaid
n:	a no. of (as in H^n)
+1:	an ancillary character also filling the talerole

of the Elphin scene. In other ways it conforms to the basic pattern.[6] It would seem this type either has come down to us in attenuated form, or what is more likely, a story from elsewhere has only partially assimilated to the balladic pattern. To indicate that this type reflects rather than realizes fully the patterning of the group, the relevant talerole terms have been modified to "Guide" and "Sojourner." For the generality, however, an Otherworld being abducts a mortal to Elphin, from which bespelling the mortal is in time liberated.

In contrast, the types of the second subgroup end unhappily. The woman of "The Great Silkie of Sule Skerry" (CH 113), having been bespelled into bearing a child to the Grey Selchie without knowing the father, is confronted by the selchie who acknowledges paternity and prophesies the death of himself and their young son in the sea at the hands of her future husband.[7] In "The Mermaid" (CH 289), which exists in one *ca.* 1765 broadside version of fourteen stanzas and a number of traditional renderings of less than half that length, the ship's crew see the mermaid, lament one by one their impending death, and go down with the ship. The last type, well known by its analogues from Denmark and Brittany, "Elveskud" and "An Aotrou Kont," actually comprehends two numbered types in Child, CH 42 ("Clerk Colvill") and CH 85 ("Lady Alice"), which have been shown by versions recorded in America to belong to the same "supertype."[8] Here a man deserts his water sprite mistress by marrying an earthly wife and the scorned "mermaiden" bespells him fatally, his death being followed by that of his lady.

We are now in a position to refine the basic patterning for the two subgroups: in the first, a land-based Otherworld being abducts (or in CH 38 invites) a mortal to the Otherworld from where he or she is, after a period, liberated; in the second, a water-based Otherworld being has contact with a mortal and the contact ends with the death of one or other of them. A marked feature of the first subgroup is that they all contain a stay in, or visit to the Otherworld, whereas in the second subgroup the interactions take place in this world at (CH 289, 42/85), or presumably near (CH 113) the watery abode of the supernatural creature. In general, however, the dominating distinction is that the first subgroup have romantic endings while the second have tragic endings. The message conveyed is that even if you are "taken" by the "gweed folk" of Elphin you may well, given certain conditions, return to this life but if you have dealings with creatures from a water-Otherworld your relationship will end disastrously. In two types of the second subgroup, the Bespeller causes the death of the mortal through malevolence, but in the third, the Bespeller prophesies the death of himself and their son through a stroke of Fate, which reinforces the apprehension that though one can escape from Elphin, there is no escape from disaster after dealings with the water creatures.

Within the two subgroups recurrent features indicate that a major function of the minigenre is to convey useful cultural knowledge. The ballads portray the Otherworld and the Otherworld folk and in doing so transmit information about the Otherworldly elements of the traditional cosmological picture. They present, for example, the salient characteristics of different kinds of Otherworld beings. Child 113 has the Finn explain his tripartite nature:

> "I am a man, upo the lan
>> An I am a silkie in the sea;
> And when I'm far and far frae lan,
>> My dwelling is in Sule Skerrie." (113:3)

As Finn he inhabits the Otherworld beneath the ocean, but clothed in a sealskin, he can inhabit the sea as a selchie, and without the sealskin, he can behave as a man on land. The other water creatures are both mermaids and dangerous: viewing the sea-mermaid is fatal, as in consorting with the river-mermaid. Among the land creatures the etin, or giant, stands apart, for he exists as a solitary of his kind in a wood, with a somewhat blurred personality in the Scottish versions although his Nordic analogues include a king of the hill-folk.[9] In contrast the Elphin folk exist very much as a social company, whether enjoying music and dancing at the hall, or travelling as "the seely court" (or fairy host). "The Wee Wee Man" highlights in its short compass a number of Elphin features: the magnificence of the Elphin ladies and their dwelling, their propensity for dancing, their ability to disappear in an instant; what seem to be uncharacteristic features are the main character's smallness and, possibly, his strength, for normally the creatures of Elphin have like Revenants the same stature as human beings. The King and Queen of Elphin are distinguished by their willingness to abduct a good-looking mortal. Where, however, the abducted males of "Thomas Rymer" and "Tam Lin" put themselves in the Queen's power by failure to observe a taboo, the abducted female of "King Orfeo"—like the one in "Hind Etin"—is simply stolen by the King of Elphin. The Queen of Elphin will also habitually commission a human mother as a nurse. Though here ascribed for dramatic heightening to King and Queen, these features in legendary belief belong to the fairy folk in general. "The Queen of Elfan's Nourice" and "The Mermaid" are, in fact, simply short dramatizations of a belief. Not only the Otherworld beings but also the Otherworld itself, as place, as environment, is depicted throughout the subgroup, most markedly in "Thomas Rymer," whose versions contain the well known stanzas with the tripartite cosmological picture of Heaven, Hell, and Elphin:

> When he had eaten and drunk his fill,
>> "Lay down your head upon my knee,"

> The lady sayd, 'ere we climb yon hill,
>   And I will show you fairlies three.
>
> "O see not ye yon narrow road,
>   So thick beset wi thorns and briers?
> That is the path of righteousness,
>   Tho after it but few enquires.
>
> "And see not ye that braid braid road,
>   That lies across yon lillie leven?
> That is the path of wickedness,
>   Tho some call it the road to heaven.
>
> "And see not ye that bonny road,
>   Which winds about the fernie brae?
> That is the road to fair Elfland,
>   Whe[re] you and I this night maun gae." (37A 11-14)

The portrayal of both the personnel and the environment of the
Otherworld conveys, then, important cultural information about not only
the world around, but the world around that.

The minigenre also fills out the cosmological picture by indicating the
conceptual relationship between this world and the Otherworld, for many
of the ballad-types have as a pronounced, even governing theme, the
apposition of the natural and the supernatural worlds. In all, of course,
there exists the implicit apposition of the two worlds through the
juxtaposition of the Otherworld being and the central mortal figure, but
even in a slim and somewhat fragmentary ballad like "The Queen of
Elfan's Nourice" that can be made explicit, as in the core stanzas when the
human mother laments her conscripted state as nurse in Elphin:

> "I moan na for my meat,
>   Nor yet for my fee,
> But I mourn for Christen land
>   It's there I fain would be."
>
> "O nurse my bairn, nourice," she says,
>   "Till he stan at your knee,
> An ye's win hame to Christen land,
>   Whar fain it's ye wad be." (40: 7, 8)

This ballad functions like a legend in its dramatization of a belief, but
where a legend would validate the belief through telling a story about a
specific person in a known place the ballad reinforces the belief through
communication of the human poignancy that results from a dramatic
actualization of it. Just as in "The Queen of Elfan's Nourice," the antithesis
of Elphin is "Christen land," so in "Hind Etin" the antithesis stands

between "the guid church" and "guid green wood" (A48-51) and
considerable emphasis is accorded the christening and "gude kirking"
(and to the fact that Hind Etin is someone "wha neer got christendame"
[B15, 19]). In these instances the antithesis to the Otherworld is quite
specifically the Christian world, but such is not always the case. In "Tam
Lin," for example, although some religious motifs appear, the story is
dominated by a distinctly non-Christian ritual of transformation, which
can be undergone only at a very specific time and place: the one time in
the year—All Hallows Eve/Halloween—when for a short period the two
worlds, this one and the Otherworld, actually intersect. In "Clerk Colvill"
the apposition of the two worlds is dramatized through two relationships,
rather than one: one with his mortal lady and one with the mermaiden. In
the C version the water sprite presents him with a choice, similar to those
in Nordic analogues, between this world and death and the Otherworld
and life:

> "Will ye lie there an die, Clerk Colin,
> Will ye lie there an die?
> Or will ye gang to Clyde's Water,
> To fish in flood wi me?" (42C 10)

Many of the appositions would be susceptible to analysis through binary
oppositions. In "The Great Silkie of Sule Skerry" there exists the apparent
mediation of the difficulties of the mortal-Otherworld relationship in the
child, but its foreseen death through blind Fate merely emphasizes that
resolution of the difficulties is impossible.

The minigenre not only presents information about the Otherworld
beings and their environments, and their differences from this mortal
world, but also provides guidance for the behavior of mortals towards the
Otherworld folk. One would learn to have no dealings, if they could be
evaded, with the water creatures, and to avoid Elphin abduction through
the observation of certain taboos. One learns, however, that when one is
taken by the Elphin folk liberation is possible: if one dutifully performs the
required service (as in CH 37 and 40), or if one exercises courage and
initiative and at the same time utilizes the protection of the Church (as in
CH 41) or a special skill such as musicianship (as in CH 19) or a special
knowledge such as that of the transformation ritual of "Tam Lin." That
last example brings to mind the stress in the Wit-combat ballads on the
knowledge necessary for mortals to withstand the attentions of their
Otherworld interlocutors.[10]

An examination of the taleroles of the Otherworld types has led on to
an understanding of the cultural functions of this minigenre. As well as
telling a good story, they convey cultural knowledge through an
exposition within narrative of the Otherworld and the Otherworld beings:
their nature, characteristics, and practices. Complementarily, they are

concerned with furnishing guidance for mortal conduct towards the Otherworld beings. Talerole analysis illuminates not only function and meaning but also a related topic, classification, particularly through the revelation of the two groups of types within the minigenre. Their differentiation gives a sharper perspective to the patternings and thematic emphases and enables one to perceive a central distinction in the cultural messages conveyed: death, though perhaps a threat, does not result from dealings with land-based Otherworld beings, but death, for someone, does inevitably result from dealings with water-based Otherworld beings.[11]

Notes

1. David Buchan, "Taleroles and Revenants: A Morphology of Ghosts," *Western Folklore* 45 (1986): 143–60, and "Sweet William's Questions," forthcoming in *Studies in Newfoundland Folklore*, eds. G. Thomas and J.D.A. Widdowson (St. John's: Breakwater); Isabelle Peere, "'If you kiss my clay-cold lips': An Examination of Revenant Ballads in Newfoundland," *Tod und Jenseits im Europäischen Volkslied*, ed. Walter Puchner (Ioannina: U of Ioannina, 1986 [1989]) 263–82.

2. David Buchan, "Talerole Analysis and Child's Supernatural Ballads," forthcoming in *Ballads and Oral Literature*, ed. Joseph Harris (Cambridge, Mass.: Harvard UP).

3. For other studies of ballads by talerole analysis, see David Buchan, "Propp's Tale Role and a Ballad Repertoire," *Journal of American Folklore* 95 (1982): 159–72; "The Wit-Combat Ballads," *Narrative Folksong: New Directions. Essays in Appreciation of W. Edson Richmond*, eds. Carol L. Edwards and Kathleen E.B. Manley (Boulder, Colo.: Westview, 1985) 380–400; "Traditional Patterns and the Religious Ballads," *The Concept of Tradition in Ballad Research*, eds. Rita Pedersen and Flemming G. Andersen (Odense: Odense UP, 1985) 27–41, 49–52; and "Taleroles and the Witch Ballads," *Ballads and Other Genres, Balladen und andere Gattungen*, ed. Zorica Rajkovic (Zagreb: Zavod za istrazivanje folklora, 1988) 133–40.

4. Buchan, "Propp's Tale Role" 162–5.

5. For a sixteenth-century Scottish romance on the Orpheus story see Marion Stewart, "King Orphius," *Scottish Studies* 17 (1973): 1–16; for an 1894 version of the ballad and references to versions recorded from John Stickle in mid-century see Patrick Shuldham-Shaw, "The Ballad 'King Orfeo,'" *Scottish Studies* 20 (1976): 124–6.

6. For the analogue see E.B. Lyle, "'The Wee Wee Man' and 'Als Y Yod on ay Mounday,'" *Ballad Studies*, ed. E.B. Lyle (Cambridge: Brewer, 1976) 21–8.

7. For a discussion of this ballad, and a number of versions, see Alan Bruford, "The Grey Selkie" in Lyle 41–65.

8. See Tristram Potter Coffin, *The British Traditional Ballad in North America*, rev. ed. Roger deV. Renwick (Austin: U of Texas P, 1977), and Bertrand H. Bronson, *The Traditional Tunes of the Child Ballads*, 4 vols. (Princeton: Princeton UP, 1959–72) 1: 334–5; 2: 392–407. For the analogues see *The Types of the Scandinavian Medieval Ballad*, eds. Bengt R. Jonsson, Svale Solheim, and Eva Danielson (Stockholm and Oslo: Universitetsforlaget, 1978), TSB A64; Donatien Laurent, "Breton Orally Transmitted

Folk Poetry," *The European Medieval Ballad: A Symposium,* ed. Otto Holzapfel (Odense: Odense UP, 1978) 16–25; and Beatriz Mariscal de Rhett, "Notes on the Trans-Cultural Adaption of Traditional Ballads," Puchner 229–45.

    9. See TSB A54, A47.

   10. Buchan, "The Wit-Combat Ballads" 385–7, 391–2.

   11. This is a somewhat revised version of "Taleroles and the Otherworld Ballads" in Puchner 247–61.

Appendix
Thomas Rymer

The following version of "Thomas Rymer" was recorded from Duncan Williamson, a Scottish Traveller, by Dr. Linda Headlee Williamson on 28 July, 1977. It is published by permission of the Williamsons and the copyright holder, the School of Scottish Studies, University of Edinburgh (SA 1977/147/B3), in whose magazine it was first printed: *Tocher* 27 (1977): 175–8. This is the first version of the ballad to be recorded from tradition since the early nineteenth century. A later, 1986, version appears in Duncan and Linda Williamson, *A Thorn in the King's Foot* (Harmondsworth: Penguin, 1987) 252–7.

1   Oh True Thomas he lay on the Huntly bank,
     Beneath an eilton tree,
     Oh when he saw a lady fair
     Comin ridin ower the lea.

2   Her mantle it was of the forest green
     And her tresses oh sae fair,
     And from every tass of her horse's mane
     Hung twenty siller bells an mair.

3   True Thomas he doffed off he's hat;
     He got down upon his knee;
     He said, "Lady, you're the greatest queen
     That ever I did see."

4   "Oh no, oh no, Thomas," she said,
     "That name does not belong to me,
     For I have come from Elfin land;
     I have come to visit thee.

5   "And you maun come, oh Thomas," she said,
     "You maun come along wi me,
     For I am bound for Elfin land;
     It is very far away.

6   "Oh mount up, mount up, oh Thomas," she said,
     "And come along wi me;
     And you will come to Elfin land;
     It is very far away."

7   So they rode, and they rode, and they merrily merrily rode,
     And they merrily rode away,
     Until they came to a great river
     That lay across their way.

8   "Oh what river is that," True Thomas he said,
     "That lies across our way?"
     "Oh that is the river of tears," she said,
     "That is spilled on this earth in one day."

9   So they rode and they rode, and they merrily merrily rode,
     And they rode for a night and a day,
     Until they came to a red river
     That lay across their way.

10 "Oh what river is that," oh Thomas he said,
    "That lies across our way?"
    "Oh that is the river of blood," she said,
    "That is spilled on this earth in one day."

11 So they rode and they rode, and they merrily merrily rode,
    And they merrily rode away,
    Until they came to a thorny road
    That lay across their way.

12 "Oh what road is that?" oh Thomas he said,
    "Oh please to me do tell!"
    "Oh that is the road we must never lead,
    For that road it leads to hell."

13 Then they rode, and they rode, and they merrily merrily rode,
    And they merrily rode away,
    Until they came to a great orchard
    That lay across their way.

14 "Oh light down, light down," oh Thomas he said,
    "For it's hungry that I maun be;
    Light down, light down," oh Thomas he said,
    "For some fine apples that I do see."

15 "Oh touch them not," the Elfin queen said,
    "Please touch them not, I say,
    For they are made from the curses
    That fall on this earth in one day."

16 Then reachin up into a tree,
    Into a tree so high,
    She plucked an apple from a branch
    As she went riding by.

17 "Oh eat you this, oh Thomas," she said,
    "As we go riding by,
    And it will give to you a tongue
    That will never tell a lie."

18 So they rode and they rode, and they merrily merrily rode,
    And they rode for a year and a day,
    Until they came to a great valley
    That lay across their way.

19   "What place is this?" oh Thomas he said,
     "The likes I have never seen,"
     "Oh this is Elfin land,"
     Oh said the Elfin queen.

20   So Thomas got some shoes of lovely brown
     And a coat of elfin green,
     And for seven long years and a day
     On earth he was never seen.

Fairylore: Memorates and Legends from Welsh Oral Tradition[1]

Robin Gwyndaf

Once upon a time there was a boy who lived on a farm, high in the hills of north Wales. Occasionally when he was not needed to help with the housework or on the farm, or when he just felt like wandering over his "country estate," he would leave the farm yard, walk along Cae Bach (the little field) until he came to Y Giat Goch (the red gate). Once through this gate he was right in the center of a circular piece of land about ten yards in diameter. The grass there was always green—unusually green—and always fine and even, like velvet. There the young lad would sit for hours and dream his time away. Nowhere would he be happier than in that green circle of land near the red gate, because there the fairies would come and take him with them on a long, long journey, over the Foel Goch hill, Llangwm village nearby, and the Berwyn mountains, to a wonderful land of beauty and plenty, sweet music and dance.

The author of this essay was that young boy! I mention my childhood recollection not to emphasize the power of imagination, but to point out that the belief in the fairies persisted in Wales into the late forties and early fifties of this century. Eventually I came to know about a little book called *Y Tylwyth Teg* (The Fairies), first published in 1935. It is one of the most charming books about fairies to appear in any language, written with sincerity and a warmth of feeling and beautifully illustrated throughout in green by T.J. Bond, Liverpool. The author, Hugh Evans, was born and bred in my own native parish of Llangwm, Clwyd. After spending over fifty years of his life in Liverpool as a successful and pioneering printer and publisher of Welsh books and periodicals, he wrote this book in which he recalled with sympathy the fairy friends of his childhood days and gave a vivid account of fairy traditions elsewhere in Wales.[2]

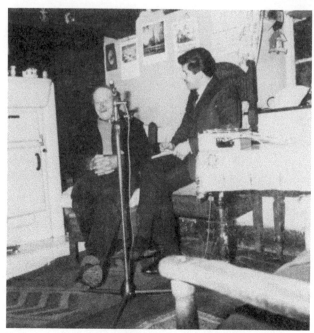

Figure 1. Lewis T. Evans (1882–1975), noted tradition-bearer, with Robin Gwyndaf, April 1966. (National Museum of Wales)

Welsh Tradition-Bearers

Hugh Evans also gave his full support to the work of Dr. Iorwerth C. Peate, Keeper of the Folk Life Collections at the National Museum of Wales and later the founder and first Curator of the Welsh Folk Museum at St. Fagans, near Cardiff, which was opened in 1948. Since joining the staff of the Folk Museum in October 1964 I have undertaken a national survey of Welsh folk narrative tradition. Over 3000 informants have been interviewed and of these some four hundred were recorded on tape, amounting to about six hundred hours of recordings, containing some 18,000 items of narrative, of which roughly six hundred relate to fairylore.

Twenty-one of these fairylore items, along with a traditional narrative of my own retelling, have been selected for this presentation. The texts were translated from the Welsh as literally as possible in order to convey something of the flavor and rhythm of the original recordings. The main fieldwork emphasis during 1966–89 was in the Welsh-speaking areas of north and southwest Wales. The number and distribution of the items selected for translation in this present essay, therefore, reflect this emphasis.

Wales has a very long and rich folk narrative tradition.[3] Although comparatively few heroic tales and tales of magic (*Märchen*) and romance (*novelle*) have survived in current Welsh oral tradition, there is no shortage of brief local legends (*Sagen*) illustrating belief in the supernatural. These belief legends relate, for example, to: the fairies; mine knockers; the Devil; witches; magicians; ghosts; death omens; giants; and mythological animals, such as dragons, winged serpents, black dogs, and water monsters.

Because these legends are based on various folk beliefs, it is important to remember that the content of many of them was once widely believed to be true (and belief, of course, is one of the main differences between a folk legend and a folktale). When a person actually experiences a certain belief we may refer to this experience as a "memorate," a term first coined by the Swedish scholar Carl W. von Sydow.[4] A memorate describes a supra-normal or paranormal experience undergone by the narrator or by an acquaintance or ancestor. Memorates relate mainly to personal narratives and to what we could term the individual or family tradition. With the passage of time many of these empirical narratives have become stereotyped and the content is more schematic and impersonal. They follow a certain plot formula which can travel easily from one district to another. They correspond to the *Sagen* in form and style and are well on the way to developing into local belief legends and becoming part of the collective tradition of the community.[5] In time, more and more motifs relating to the world of fantasy and the fabulous are added to the "true" legend. Often they are told as stories and although the local element is still very obvious, the terms "migratory legends" and "fabulates" used by scholars to refer to such narratives aptly convey their nature.[6]

The selected fairylore texts which follow reflect this development and include memorates, local legends and fabulates. However, one should always be conscious of the danger of categorizing folklore and overemphasizing the importance of classification—as it is not always possible, or desirable, to draw a strict dividing line between one genre and another. Genres, after all, exist mainly in the folklorist's mind. The informant is not interested in classification but in communication.

Neither should one draw a firm dividing line between two other terms coined by von Sydow, namely "active tradition-bearer" and "passive tradition-bearer."[7] Generally, however, those persons who recite memorates and legends today concerning the fairies (as with other aspects of the supernatural) may be described as mainly passive or occasional tradition-bearers. Even so, although belief in the fairies seems to have almost died out by now in Wales, there are still a surprising number of people who can testify to the mysterious dealings of fairies with human beings in various Welsh communities. As the magician Gwydion, "the best storyteller in the world," remarked in the Fourth Branch of the

Mabinogion[8] (a collection of eleven classical Welsh tales), they too, will "tell a tale gladly" when asked and especially to whoever is prepared to listen with sympathy and understanding.

Of the items selected for this essay, only one informant could testify that he had actually seen fairies (text 8). But a number of the informants testified to firsthand knowledge of the belief and experiences of members of their families or close acquaintances. Furthermore, although not all of them actually believed in the paranormal elements inherent in their narratives, they have recited them with sincerity and reverence. Their attitude is typified by the Carmarthenshire man who confessed:

> I cannot tell how the truth may be,
> I tell the tale as 'twas told to me.[9]

Today these passive tradition-bearers who have inherited fairylore are decreasing in number and when they die their legends may die with them. There are and there will be other, more contemporary narratives, of course (the tradition of reciting humorous jokes and anecdotes, for example, is very much alive), but these men and women must be recorded now, for their like will not be heard again. The words of the countryman published in a seventeenth-century English tract are just as relevant today as they were then:

> We old men are old chronicles, and when our tongues go they are not clocks to tell only the time present, but large books unclasped; and our speeches, like leaves turned over and over, discover wonders that are long since past.[10]

Recording the Fairy Tradition

Writers throughout the ages have attested to the firm belief of the Welsh people in the fairies. One of the earliest was Giraldus Cambrensis (Gerallt Gymro, Gerald the Welshman, 1146–1223). In 1188 Gerald accompanied Archbishop Baldwin on a tour of Wales in an attempt to raise an army for the third Crusade. As a result of this journey Gerald wrote two classic books: *Itinerarium Kambriae* (Journey through Wales) and *Descriptio Kambriae* (Description of Wales).[11] In the first of these books Gerald records in detail the experience of the priest Elidyr (Eliodorus) as a boy of about twelve in the vicinity of Swansea, south Wales.

Because of the cruelty of his teacher, Elidyr escaped from school and for two whole days hid in a hole on the river bank. Then, two fairy dwarfs came and led him underground to a most beautiful and wonderful country. He was allowed to play with the king's son and never before had he been so happy. Occasionally he would be allowed to visit his country, but on those occasions he presented himself only to his mother. One day his mother begged him to bring her one gift of gold from amongst the fairies' plentiful treasures and the boy stole the golden ball with which the king's son used to play. Just as Elidyr was about to enter his mother's house, he stumbled over the threshold and fell. But before the ball touched the ground, two fairies came. They saved the ball from breaking, scorned the boy for his dishonesty and left. Elidyr felt full of remorse for his wicked deed and wished to apologize to his fairy friends. But although he searched for a whole year, he never again found the door on the bank of the river which would have led him to that country of wonder and joy.

Later in 1691 Richard Baxter published *The Certainty of the Worlds of Spirits*. From that time onwards valuable accounts of Welsh fairy traditions and legends have been recorded in scores of manuscripts, books, periodicals and local newspapers. Special reference should be made to two classic publications: first, *Celtic Folklore: Welsh and Manx* (1901), by Sir John Rhŷs (1840–1915), Professor of Celtic at Oxford and Principal of Jesus College and second, *Welsh Folklore and Folk-Custom* (1930), by T. Gwynn Jones (1871–1949), Professor of Welsh at University College of Wales, Aberystwyth and a leading Welsh poet.[12]

Welsh Names for the Fairies

The usual Welsh name for the fairies is *Y Tylwyth Teg* (the fair family, or tribe). The name first appeared in a *cywydd* (poem in the strict traditional *cynghanedd* meter), entitled "Y Niwl" (the mist), composed by an anonymous poet probably during the first quarter of the fifteenth century. No doubt, the name was part of the folk speech of the Welsh people much earlier. It seems, however, that the Welsh term *Y Tylwyth Teg* is based on a misconception of the original meaning of the English word *fayries* (fairy-folk, Fairyland) which first appeared at the beginning of the fourteenth century.[13] The term *fayry*, and its various forms, derives from Old French *faerie* in which the first element *fae* comes from Middle Latin *fata* and Classical Latin *fatum* (fate, destiny). *Teg* in the Welsh name *Y Tylwyth Teg*, however, is a literal translation of the English "fair" (beautiful, fine).

The term *fayry* translated as *Tylwyth Teg* (fair family) first appeared in a standard dictionary in 1547, *Dictionary in Englyshe and Welshe* by William Salesbury, and ever since the name *Y Tylwyth Teg* has been in common usage by the Welsh people when referring to the fairies. The name seems also to convey accurately the Welsh people's conception of the fairies. They were usually fair, fine and beautiful. True, there were "good" and "bad" fairies, and the bad, ugly, ones were to be feared. Those, for example, were the culprits responsible for exchanging human babies for their own dwarfish offspring. In general, however (as the translated texts in this essay demonstrate), the Welsh fairies were believed to be benevolent by nature and were to be treated with kindness and respect.

They lived in communities ruled by their king, Gwyn ap Nudd (Gwyn son of Nudd). Nudd conserves the Brythonic or Celtic form of the god Nudons or Nodens. (One of the temples where he was worshipped was at Lydney Park, Gloucestershire.) Indeed, one early name for the Welsh fairies is *Tylwyth Gwyn* (Gwyn's family). That name appears, for example, in another *cywydd* also entitled "Y Niwl" (the mist), composed by the celebrated poet Dafydd ap Gwilym (ca. 1320–70).

Gwyn ap Nudd was King of *Annwfn* (or *Annwn*), the Underworld (the deep). Welsh fairies were, therefore, also occasionally called *Plant Annwfn* (the children of the Underworld) and *Gwragedd Annwfn* (the women of the Underworld). These women were comely figures dressed in green.[14]

In parts of Dyfed, southwest Wales, fairies were sometimes called *Plant Rhys Ddwfn* (the children of Rhys of the deep or Rhys the deep/wise) who lived on islands far out at sea. According to one tradition Rhys was said to be chief of a country lying beneath Cardigan Bay on the west coast of Wales.[15]

In parts of south Wales, Glamorgan in particular, fairies were called *Bendith y Mamau* (mothers' blessing). One theory is that these were the descendants of the Celtic goddesses *Matronae* or *Matres* (mothers). Another theory is that originally the fairies would have been called *Melltith y Mamau* (mothers' curse) and that the phrase *Bendith y Mamau* was used to please them and so avoid their curse.[16]

One other name sometimes used for the fairies, especially in Dyfed, was *Dynon Bach Teg* (little fair folk).

Nature, Complexion, and Size

Welsh fairies are non-ghostly apparitions. Their habits and activities resemble those of men. It was once believed that the taller type were inclined to dishonesty. They stole butter and cheese and milked cows and goats. The smaller race, which figure most prominently in Welsh tradition, on the other hand, were beautiful and gentle folk. They were playful, fond of music and dance, and kind to mortals. Reports of their actual size vary, but generally they were held to be the size of a six-year-old child or, in the words of one informant describing the fairies who accompanied his Grandfather: "They were as high as his knee . . . and he was a short man" (text 7). However, fairy females who took human husbands and had children from them were fully grown. Welsh fairies were usually of light, fair (*teg*) complexion and were often dressed in green and sometimes wore a red cap.

They were believed to be immortal. Certain children and adults considered to be of fairy descent never died (text 2). There were sometimes complications when a fairy maiden married a mortal man. For example, in the "Llyn y Fan Fach" legend (text 20), the fairy wife usually left her husband and returned with her animals to the lake.

The Fairy Realm

Fairyland was a place of plenty and beauty, wonder and joy, full of golden treasures and evergreen grass and trees and its inhabitants were forever young. The various methods of getting in and out of this magical realm, reflected in the texts accompanying this essay, include open caves, magical rocks, and underground passages (texts 1, 5, 10), as well as lakes, pools, river banks, marshy ground (texts 2, 7, 18, 20) and mist. It was also possible to enter the otherworld through fairy circles or rings (see texts 2, 4, 7).

Legends of mortals enticed into the fairy realm, or abducted by fairies, are numerous. A few legends relate the strange experiences of mortal men being enchanted into Fairyland through listening to the sweet song of a bird. One such bird sang to a lad called Siôn ap Siencyn of Pencader, Dyfed. He had been in the woods, so he thought, merely for ten minutes, but when he awoke the tree upon which the bird sang had withered. When he returned to his home an old man informed him of the words of one Cadi Madog of Brechfa: "She used to say that you were with the fairies and would not return until the last drop of sap in the tree had been dried up." This and other similar legends are reminiscent of the well-known tale of Branwen in the Second Branch of the Mabinogion. Only seven men return to the Island of the Mighty from the tragic war in Ireland. The men are grieving, having buried Branwen. They carry with them the head of their beloved Bendigeidfran, Branwen's brother. At Harlech, three birds appear, the Birds of Rhiannon and sing them a most wonderful song for seven years.[17]

A very long time in this world, therefore, seems to have been just an instant in the fairy world. According to the legends included with this essay the times spent in Fairyland are as follows: one year (text 17); a year and a day (text 18); seven years (text 22); fifteen years (text 16); one hundred years (text 12).

By far the most common tradition in current Welsh fairylore is that which refers to green circular patches of land known as *cylch y Tylwyth Teg*, fairy circles or rings. Often these green patches are associated with mushrooms, as in the testimony of Martha Williams.

Figure 2. "Into Fairyland. Siôn ap Siencyn listening to the sweet song of a bird." From a drawing by Ifor Owen. (National Museum of Wales)

> Of course, we thought that the fairies came to places where there were green patches—a green, green patch—and that they would dance on these green patches. We firmly believed that, and we thought that the mushrooms were parasols or umbrellas for the fairies . . . (text 10)

These green fairy patches were regarded as sacred. They were not to be tampered with and farmers who ploughed across them were cursed.

The fairies of Wales were very fond of music and dance. Many a young lad on moonlit nights claimed to have seen them dancing on hill tops or in the fairy ring and was enticed to join in the circular dance. Once a mortal got into the fairy ring, it was believed to be very difficult to free him. One method was to place a stick of rowan tree across the circle. The rowan was considered a sacred tree because its wood had been used to make the Cross and its red berries signified Christ's blood.

Fairy Possessions

Although fairies were small in size, they were said to possess many of the artifacts which belonged to human beings. Tiny white clay pipes found in the soil were believed to be used by the fairies for smoking (see texts 7, 10). Prehistoric circular holed stones, once used for spinning wool, were believed to be the fairies' whetting stones. A certain type of greasy rock petroleum, found especially on limestone, was called *menyn y Tylwyth Teg* (fairy butter).

There were magical fairy harps; fairy ropes, *rhaffau'r Tylwyth Teg,* described by one informant as being your own conscience at work (text 7); and fairy money. Sometimes their money was described as being similar to "silvery dry leaves" and sometimes as real money; for example, half crowns (as in texts 14 and 15). If, however, one was fortunate enough to discover or receive fairy money, there was a certain code of conduct to be respected—that money was not to be disclosed outside the family, or else it would stop.

The most valuable possessions of the fairies were their animals: dogs, horses, sheep, goats and cattle (no mention of pigs or cats). The wonderful fairy cattle, associated with a number of mountain lakes in Wales, were a remarkable source of wealth to any farmer who owned one of them. Such a cow would give a never ending supply of rich, creamy milk and its offspring would be the wonder of the whole locality. But woe to the farmer who ill-treated a fairy cow as in the legend of *Y Fuwch Gyfeiliorn*, the "Stray Cow" of Llyn Barfog (bearded lake), near Aberdyfi, in Gwynedd, north Wales.[18]

There is also a folk tradition which links a certain fish known as *Torgoch* (arctic char) with fairies. Although this fish is found in a few mountain lakes in Snowdonia, north Wales, it is particularly associated

Figure 3. "Twm pulling his friend Iago out of the Fairy Circle." From an illustration by T.H. Thomas in *British Goblins*, 1880. (National Museum of Wales)

with Llyn Bodlyn, Dyffryn Ardudwy, north Wales. Legend tells us that the fairies placed a great supply of this fish in Bodlyn Lake as a token of gratitude to a young local shepherd for helping them.

Fairy Activities

One activity generally disliked by the Welsh people was the fairies' practice of attending fairs and markets. They were blamed for high prices and people were afraid of bidding against them in fear of their revenge. Such reports of people having actually seen the fairies at markets are few.

Much more numerous, however, are the accounts of fairy activity in Welsh homes. It was once a common belief that a sure way of pleasing the "little people" was to set aside some milk and food for them at night and a bowl of clean, warm water for them to wash themselves and especially their children. In return the fairy folk left some money. A miller from north Wales went out to his mill late one night and was surprised to see a fairy woman, completely naked, bathing herself in a vessel of water. There are reports, too, of fairies making use of mills at nights to grind their flour.

They would also occasionally use the spinning wheel for spinning their wool and a round griddle and iron pan for baking their bread. (It was once a custom to place the iron pan across the griddle to form a sort of small oven in the fire.) In these legends the fairies appear as a primitive people who lived in caves and lake dwellings and who made use of the tools of the more technologically advanced human settlers.

Similarly, fairies sometimes needed the services of human midwives (see texts 9, 11). One recurrent motif emphasizes that the human midwife should never touch her own eyes with the ointment used on the fairy infant's eyes.

Christian baptism of children is still a common practice in Wales. It was once believed that the infant should be baptized as soon as possible, otherwise it would be in danger of being exchanged for a fairy changeling—an ugly, screaming, peevish, old-looking fairy offspring. Some parents believed that the child should be baptized within seven days, others within fourteen days.

One belief was that the fairies exchanged babies in order to strengthen their own stock. A common method of protecting an unbaptized baby was to place a poker or fire-tongs across the cradle. Sometimes they were placed against the fire grate in the shape of a cross. One method of retrieving a human baby and getting rid of a fairy urchin was to place salt on a shovel, mark it with the sign of the Cross, open a window, and then place the shovel over fire to bake the salt. Another method was to throw little pieces of iron towards the cradle. In these and other such legends, the fairy fear of iron is, of course, a central motif.

Figure 4. "Fairies spinning." From a drawing by Margaret D. Jones. (National Museum of Wales)

Legends of fairy changelings are commonplace in Welsh folk tradition (see texts 3, 6). So too are legends of fairy women marrying mortal men. These legends are usually associated with Welsh mountain lakes. In some versions the man is not allowed to marry the fairy maiden until he can discover her name (as in the famous tale of Rumpelstiltskin). The main

Figure 5. "Fairy twins" (changelings). From an illustration by John D. Batten in *Celtic Fairy Tales*, 1892. (National Museum of Wales)

Figure 6. "Baking salt on a shovel to get rid of a changeling." From a drawing by Ifor Owen. (National Museum of Wales)

motif here is that knowledge of a person's name gives one power over that person.[19] Some of the Welsh fairy names are: Sili-go-dwt, Jili-ffrwtan, Trwtyn-tratyn and Penelope, the last name associated with Ystrad, Betws Garmon, Gwynedd. A sure way of angering the inhabitants of this district in former times was to call them "Pellings," suggesting, therefore, that they were the descendants of the *Tylwyth Teg.*

Another common motif in the fairy marriage legends is the fairies' fear of iron. The human husband should on no account strike his fairy wife with iron, or else she and all her animals would leave him and return to the lake. In some versions the man should not strike his wife "three causeless blows." The most well-known and best loved of all Welsh legends of fairy marriages is that of "The Fairy Lady of Llyn y Fan Fach and the Famous Physicians of Myddfai" (see text 20).

Use, Function, and Meaning

The Puritan movement of the seventeenth century and the Religious Revivals of the eighteenth and nineteenth centuries contributed much to the gradual disappearance of communal gatherings and of many ancient rites, ceremonies and customs in Wales. Even so, the practice of storytelling in Welsh communities was not suppressed. It has continued ever since with surprising vigor. There was, however, a process of functional adaptation. The emphasis became increasingly moralistic and didactic, and this is clearly reflected in Welsh fairy legends. Entertainment was not, necessarily, the prime function. Whether people actually believed in the fairies or not, a practical use was made of fairy traditions and beliefs for ethical purposes. Many of the legends became sermons and homilies in miniature.

Fairies were otherworld beings to be regarded with fear. Parents warned their children not to be late returning home at night, or not to wander too far from home during the day. They were not to "cross the border" in case they would be enticed and captured by the fairies and taken away to their country for a long time. But the fairies were also to be treated with kindness and respect. Housemaids were told to keep their rooms clean and tidy and before going to bed, to leave food, milk and clean, warm water for the fairies. In the morning the maids would be repaid with shiny silver coins. Fairies also gave money to help the poor, and they could provide fairy ropes to keep people on the "straight and narrow" path.

In many fairy legends the listener is reminded of a certain code of conduct which had to be respected. The person who received fairy money was not to disclose the source of his new wealth. The man who married a fairy wife was not to strike her with iron, or give her three blows "without a cause." The farmer who received a fairy cow was not to ill-treat her. The harpist who misused a fairy harp was forced to play until exhausted. Pride and dishonesty are punished with grief and suffering. Love and kindness are rewarded with joy and wealth.

There is one other consideration which further explains the persistence of belief in fairies and the long and rich tradition of reciting fairy legends. Civilizations may disappear, beliefs may change, but our innermost desires have remained the same through the ages. One of our most constant desires has been to avoid the routine and certainty of this world and escape into the enchanting world of the unknown. Especially when "chance and circumstances [are] not fully controlled by knowledge,"[20] the Welsh, like people everywhere, have resorted to magic and belief in the supernatural world. Since time immemorial humanity has longed for the "lost paradise," the "still center" of the mystics and the land "flowing with milk and honey," as described in the Bible. In mundane daily life on earth we desire to taste the bliss of everlasting life, so that we too can proclaim with Peter in his Second Epistle (3. 8): "One day is with the Lord as a thousand years, and a thousand years is as one day." People desire to be taken to the Island of *Afallon* (*Insula Avallonis*) where King Arthur was gently carried to be healed of his wounds, or to the evergreen, ever-young land of *Tir na n-Og* of Irish and Celtic tradition.

In the midst of grief and suffering, people desire to proclaim with Dylan Thomas: "And Death shall have no dominion." Although aware of mortality, our greatest desire is to experience the wonder and bliss of life, to see as we have never seen before and to hear, even for a short while, the pleasant song of the Birds of Rhiannon. Throughout the ages, magic and belief in the supernatural have delighted and sustained the human spirit, for, to quote Alwyn and Brinley Rees, magic has "the power to breach the constraining boundaries of the finite so that the light of eternity may transubstantiate that which is commonplace and fill it with mystery."[21]

The land of the fairies was full of that mystery. It was a place of joy and beauty, peace and tranquility, love and kindness, and everlasting life. The constant desire for such a heavenly place is well expressed by the many informants whose living traditions are provided in the following texts. Robert Owen Pritchard's query, "if some things give you pleasure, well, why not believe in them?"(text 2) makes good sense, especially when you consider Martha Williams' observation that, after all, "we are the fairies' children!" (text 10).

Texts[22]

1. THE FAIRIES IN PETER GREEN'S CAVE

Did your mother believe in the fairies?
Well, I can't say if she believed or not, but she would give me the impression that she did. And that impression, of course, caused me to believe. Yes, to believe firmly in the fairies and to take a keen interest in them, although I would be afraid of them. And you'd be in trouble if you came across the fairies, or they came across you, in some enclosure or wood where they lived. And they lived in many places. They lived in Coed yr Henblas [Henblas Wood], as we say. And in the cave—Ogof Pitar Graen [Peter Green's Cave] we used to call it. Well, the fairies were there. There was no argument about that. But, of course, they wouldn't be out all the time. Sometimes when it was quiet the fairies would play outside the cave's door, so they said. And the old people used to say that they always had their eye on small children—if they could get hold of them. If they caught a young child, they would take it inside the cave and keep it for one year and a day.

And, of course, because of this we would be afraid of the fairies, although we would take much interest in them. They'd tell us that they were tiny, tiny little people, and so forth. And then I would be warned by my mother always—and many another mother warned her children—not to go near the cave, unless somebody took care of us, because there was a danger that the fairies would get hold of us. And for the life of me I wouldn't cross the boundary which my mother had set. And that boundary was the Church, because the other side of the Church was this cave, you see. It's in the middle of some fields in a very lonely place. It was an ideal place for fairies and the like to settle there, because of the peace and tranquility.[23]

2. FAIRIES NEVER DIE

And what did you call such children?
"Chance-chickens" or "wild-duck chickens." A "wild-duck chicken" was quite a common saying. And some people called them "plant Tylwyth Teg," "fairy children." But there is another story about fairy children. It's a story about a certain old family. Oh dear! I mustn't give too many details, there's so many of them still alive today.

This family went out in the evening on the shortest day and heard a child crying. They didn't have any children themselves and they were too old to have any. They began to search for the baby. And there was heavy mist, as we often have in Betws Garmon and that part of the country, covering the ground like a blanket. And they proceeded underneath a cloud of mist in the direction of the crying. And, by God! What did they find but a young child. They lifted it up and took it to the house. And, as it was in those days, nobody thought of coming to search for it. God! That's some time ago now. Perhaps a girl had been unlucky and had left it there quietly. She may have known about the old people that they perhaps would hear its cry.

However, the two brought him up as their own son. He was to inherit everything. Well now, this son got married and had a family and many of the family are alive today—I could name many of them, though perhaps I better not. But this is what they used to say, "One of those nobody ever saw any of them dying; the fairies would come to take them away before you could see them." And I remember now, my brother and I on our way to work one morning and we met an old character, Twm Jôs, one of our fellow workers, who had been talking to another worker and had enquired about his father.

"Oh, he's been dead since this morning," the man replied.

"Dear me! What time did he die?"

"Well, I can't tell you exactly because there was no one near him. He had died quietly with no one of us present."

"The fairies had come to fetch him!," was Twm Jôs' immediate remark . . .

Was there a belief at all that fairy children were different than other children?

Well, yes, that a certain luck would follow them always, always, always. Just imagine now that you've ventured upon a deal or something. Goodness me! If you were one of the fairy children, you wouldn't fail. There was luck. You would almost say that it had been foreseen— predestined.

Who told you this?

Well, an old character from Aber-soch. In every district there are fairy children. Almost in every district. There was a man in Rhoshirwaun who used to tell me that he had many conversations with some of them. The old man has been dead for some time. He was trying to tell me that "There's an old place on the roadside. You see reeds grow there. It was in the middle of these reeds I talked to them." Well, I wondered whether he was mentally sound, because he experienced such visions. But good God, no! He was regarded as one of the most responsible persons in Rhoshirwaun. Dear me! It was strange to hear this man talking . . . exactly as if he had been conversing with them.

What was his name?

Well, I better not tell you . . . Yes, well, Owen John Roberts . . . his daughter still lives on the same farm.

Are there many people who still know about this belief in the fairies?

Well, they are nearly all old people. Yes, old people. Goodness me! Young people of today just laugh at you if you happen to talk about such things to them. Its nothing but fun for them.

Do you think that there is a possibility that its true?

I don't think that there's any truth in it, as such, but there are certain things—say now heaven and hell—well, I tell myself: "If there is such a place as heaven, I'd rather be there than in the other place!" Similarly, it does no harm, if some things give you pleasure, well, why not believe in them?[24]

3. THE BEAUTIFUL BABY AND THE UGLY SCREECHING FAIRY URCHIN

What is this tale about the fairies of Dyffryn Mymbyr?

Oh! The fairies of Dyffryn Mymbyr. There was a very beautiful baby in his cradle under the care of his grandmother. Dyffryn Mymbyr house is built on some sort of a step, high above and from the house they could see all the land below them. It's that kind of a farm. And now all the family— the men and the women—had gone down to the fields to work in the hay harvest and had left the little baby in the care of his grandmother. And grandmother was kind of dozing by the fire and the baby was asleep.

And, goodness me! The grandmother awoke. There was terrible screaming and she turned towards the cradle. By God! What was in the cradle but the most ugly little thing you have ever seen—a monster-looking little creature, screaming his head off and this beautiful baby had disappeared. The grandmother was terrified. She calls now on the workers to come up from the fields. And they came. And, true enough, someone had exchanged the baby. And they believed that the fairies had been there.

"Well, what can we do to get the baby back?" That was the question. And someone suggested that there was a person living at Trawsfynydd who was quite a magician. He could probably tell them what to do. And they travelled all the way to Trawsfynydd. And this was his advice. Once they had returned home they were to take a spadeful of salt and bake it and then place the baked salt in front of the door to the house and wait. And, indeed, this they did. In a few minutes the baby had been returned and the ugly dwarf had vanished. That is the story of the Dyffryn Mymbyr fairies. And they used to say that the fairies were responsible for the exchange. It is a very well-known story in the area. There are, of course, tens of stories about the fairies of Nant Gwynant and other places . . . [25]

4. *THE FAIRIES SINGING AND DANCING IN THE PEAT BOG*

What have you heard from your ancestors—your family—about the Tylwyth Teg [fairies]?

Well, I'll tell you about the fairies. They would say—my grandmother—and I've heard this more from my aunt, her daughter, my father's sister, and from my father also; they would firmly believe, you see, that the fairies did exist. Now in the old days every house and family and this hotel here on the Lord Penrhyn Estate—Gelli, my home, is on that estate—they had the right to cut peat, to go cut peat as fuel in the winter from the Bwlchgoleuni peat bog and that is about two miles up in the direction of the upper banks of Llyn Ogwen [lake], this side of the river. And each one had some sort of an allotment where they would cut the peat and men would be working there this time of the year for weeks, cutting peat for me, and for you and others. And an old uncle of mine, I believe, was one of them—old "Uncle Dafydd" my father used to call him.

And now the children, the women and all the family would go up to the peat bog on a fine day to help with the peat—to dry it and carry it into ricks. And there on some warm misty day they would hear the fairies—so they said. Tut! They heard some sound—some music, sweet music. Then the mist would open and suddenly they would see a circle of tiny beings dancing and disappearing immediately. That was the story of the fairies and my grandmother conscientiously believed that she had seen such a thing.[26]

5. *THE TWO BROTHERS WHO SAW THE FAIRIES THROUGH A HOLE IN THE WALL*

My brother and I used to go up to the top of a narrow little field where Grandfather told us we had to hide and not to show ourselves. There was a dry stone bank there about six feet high over which we could not see because we were too small. We used to take out stones very quietly from the wall and gaze through the hole we had made in the wall. Within a few yards of us was the old Carreg Lefain which was like a piece of rock and in the center was a stone . . . When we were older we realized that this stone was an "echo stone."

It was in order to see the fairies that we stood staring through the hole in the wall. The wind had turned and was coming from the east by now. It came through the hole in the wall till water filled our eyes. It was beginning to grow dark. After waiting a long time we saw the fairies dancing round the stone—little things dressed in the daintiest many colored clothes you ever saw. They were like a garden of flowers. Then we ran to Grandfather to tell him the story.

I was about eight and a half years old when I saw the fairies and my brother, Harri, was about ten years old. They were not more than two feet tall. They had many colored clothes, like flowers and wore long caps with peaks high up on their heads. They looked like a garden of flowers on the move. They danced around the stone. We saw them simultaneously. We were frightened in the most awful way, afraid to disturb them, so we were as quiet as mice. Grandfather had warned us that if we showed ourselves it would not be well with us and we would vanish. Perhaps we would sin against the fairies, too, because we were watching them, you see. We were about fifty yards from the stone. We had made certain that we would be near enough to see and be able to hide from the fairies at the same time. It was a pleasant time, about the end of August when the days were beginning to draw in. Grandfather used to tell us that it was in the evening that the fairies appeared, when the sun was setting and when we were in the brooding silence.

We had been there several times and had seen nothing. And that was the time we did see them. I cannot say whether we created this picture in our minds or not. That could have been very easy. I cannot tell you whether the story is true or not, or that we had been there such a long time that the imagination was aroused. But we *both* saw them. When we saw them, there were about a dozen or fifteen of them, I should say. We dared not go there at night and seeing them had made us frightened.

Grandfather used to say: "Didn't I tell you that they were there? There you are, you are all right now!"

As I grow older I think a lot about these pleasant things.[27]

6. A FAIRY DWARF: "ELIS BACH Y NANT"

There is a tradition in Nant Gwrtheyrn about "Elis Bach y Nant" [Little Elis of the Nant]. Well, he was some kind of a dwarf, this Elis Bach. There were three farms in the Nant at that time and his family lived in one of them. I don't remember its name. It's too long ago. And they lived on this farm. And there was this Elis, the dwarf and Robin, his brother. And they sold goats. Drovers came there at a certain time of the year to buy. Then Elis would go inside the cupboard—he was as small as that—and he would shout: "Eating this—eating everything!" He didn't want them to eat the food, you see.

Yes! . . . And he was not able to talk properly like us . . . And he wasn't able to walk down the footpath, only backwards. His legs were too short.

When did he die? Was it a long time before you were born?

Dear me! Yes! . . . And that is what they used to say—that he was a fairy changeling . . . The fairies had taken one of the Nant's children and had left this one in the cradle in its place.

Did you hear that the old people used to do something to prevent the fairies from exchanging children?

Didn't they put the poker across something? I remember an old woman in Nant Gwrtheyrn doing that—placing the poker across the fire. "Why do you do that?" I asked her. "To keep the Devil away!" she answered.[28]

7. A GRANDFATHER'S LIFELONG ADVENTURE WITH THE FAIRIES

Nobody today believes in the fairies, I suppose?

No, I don't think there is anyone today. But the old people were firm believers, because they testified, you see, most strongly, that they had met them. My grandfather was one of them. He had met the fairies on more than one occasion. And they were always the ones who were ready to help. There were other types, so they said—bad ones. But there were good ones also and my grandfather never met any but the good ones.

Once, when he was a young lad, he had been driving cattle to Pwllheli. And the fog came. And Pwllheli was very far from Aberdaron in those days, as far as Cardiff is from Aberdaron today. Anyway, he had lost his way. He had been in town all day, at the fair and by the evening his master had sold the animals, and he had to walk home. He was completely lost; he had no idea where he was in the middle of this mist. And the result was, the fairies came to walk by his side. They led him home every step of the way and conversed with him throughout the journey. And nothing but good was discussed during the whole journey from Pwllheli, nothing but the good, according to the old man.

How old was your grandfather then?

He died in 1918 and they had no idea of his age . . . He was bound to be about ninety-two when he died . . .

Did you ever hear him saying anything about what kind of beings were the fairies to look at?

Well, the most beautiful beings anyone ever saw. Very light complexion. Those, he said, were the good fairies, but each bad one was dark and ugly. That is all I can say on the matter, as he described them. And he portrayed the bad ones from what he had heard, only the good ones he had met . . .

Did he tell you anything about the bad ones?

The bad ones were always leading people into trouble . . .

Did he tell you anything about their size?

Well, they were as high as his knee, so he said, and he was a short man.

And what was the nature of their body?

Exactly like a human being, he said, graceful and beautiful.

Did they wear clothes?

Yes, they wore clothes. Knee breeches, he said—always—made of blue velvet, and some kind of white ribbon around its knee. I did not believe him, mind you, but he was quite definite on the matter, you see. There was no purpose in arguing. He had met them. And he was not a dull man, either . . .

That tale about your grandfather having lost his way home from Pwllheli Fair, do you remember him telling you where exactly it happened?

He was in some marshy ground. I believe that it's that bog which is near Pwllheli. He was in water, anyhow, and he didn't know what would have happened to him that night if the fairies had not come to his assistance.

Had he asked for guidance at all? Had he prayed?

Yes, he had prayed. He was a firm believer in prayer . . .

What exactly did these kind little people tell him on his way home?

Well, they talked mostly about singing and dancing. And Taid knew step y glocsen [clog dance]. He was a specialist in clog dancing. I saw my grandfather performing the clog dance. And he said that it was the fairies' dance and dawns y cylch [circle dance]—whatever that was. I didn't know anything about that and I wasn't wise enough to ask him about the circle dance. And that was the great dance of the fairies—the circle dance . . .

They say that the fairies are very fond of marshy ground, don't they?

Yes, they do.

Did you grandfather make any remark?

Yes, he had a definite observation. "Y Gors" [The Bog] was the name of the farm where the fairies' meadow was at Anelog. That is where they performed the circle dance . . .

Did you hear your grandfather telling you how the fairies sustained themselves? Did they eat?

Well, I heard him saying that they would receive butter and milk and eggs from the farms. I heard him saying that . . . that when there was great poverty in a house they would leave a basket at the door, and butter and eggs and a can of milk. I heard him saying that. For the poor if there was an emergency, shortage of food and the children suffering. That is all he told me . . .

Did you hear anything about fairy money?

Yes, he talked about fairy money. They had given many treasures to some people, especially if they had done some good deeds in this world. Then they would be given a prize for those deeds. A widow having lost her husband, she gets up the next day and finds a purse of money on the table. I heard him saying that. But if you ask me to locate the incident, I can't.

Did you hear your grandfather explaining what fairy money was?

Well, gold. That is what he always said. I never heard him mentioning silver. And I never heard either that it had been coined. He only mentioned its value ...

Did you hear about fairy ropes?

Yes, I heard about those also ...

What did your grandfather say about these ropes?

Well, imagine that I've decided to steal from a certain house tonight and in order to keep me on the right path the fairies had set up ropes, and when I would be on the point of completing the act, I would stumble over these ropes and become entangled in one bundle. Then I wouldn't be able to carry on with my proposed plan. That is what he said. Something would come to prevent you. Something would tell you not to ... Those were the terms my grandfather used to describe these ropes ... Perhaps someone has done you a bad deed and you decide: "I'll have my revenge to the full." Perhaps if you had carried out your threat you would have killed that person. Something prevented you from acting. I think it was your conscience ...

Do you remember him telling you a story to convey this?

Yes! I heard him telling a tale about one old sailor who had decided to have revenge on another sailor. Both had been sea pirates. And he had decided to kill him. But he became entangled in fairy ropes on Rhosydd Gwrthrian. I don't know anything about these two pirates or their names. But if that pirate had killed the other, he would have been hanged on Bryn y Grocbren [Gallows Hill], Y Cwrt [The Court]. That is where they used to hang offenders—Bryn y Grocbren. He was prevented by the fairy ropes. His own conscience, I would have thought ...

... can you remember the nature of the conversation between the two of you? How did he talk?

Well, the last thing he would tell me would be: "You remember to keep on the right path. If you keep to the path, nothing but goodness will come to you. And if you lose your way, only the worse will come to you—evil." That is how he would always end every story.[29]

8. THE BOY WHO SAW A LITTLE GREEN AND RED FELLOW IN A CIRCLE OF WOOD

This experience you had, could you describe what happened when you saw that being?

Yes, I will, though I have never talked about it much, really. I'd gone with a little old two-wheeler bicycle I had—"Dandidilwcs" [Dandy deluxe] I used to call it. My father had brought it with him from the sea and had given it to me sometime as a gift. This little bicycle was shining like a shilling with a small cart behind it. I was on my way to Gwynfryn

Orchard to collect firewood. At the opening of the front drive to Gwynfryn there is a little lodge, and nearby there is a circle of black trees. Inside the circle there's moss. It sounds very romantic. There were very old tree stumps. The shape is still there as it was then before they were destroyed.

I had looked forward to having a smoke—as schoolboys do—within this circle, while collecting firewood. I had a two-penny paper packet of Woodbines in my pocket—"two-penny Woodbines," as we used to call them. I took the Woodbine out of my pocket, lighted it, took one whiff and I heard the sound of leaves. Then I saw a little old fellow coming from the direction of some green bushes. Well, it was a little less than a yard tall perhaps, that is how it seemed to me, about a yard in height. The only other thing I remember clearly is that from his waist down it was green and some reddish color around its face. That's it. Green and red and a tiny little man. He didn't say anything. At first I was a little afraid. Then I wasn't afraid at all. Not at all. And I can't remember seeing him leaving. I remember him coming. I have no recollection at all of him leaving. But I remember seeing him, right enough. We didn't say anything to one another, but that's it for you, *it was there.*

And I've only mentioned this to two or three people ever, because I'm afraid. I don't know, but I seem to think the less I say, the more likely I am to see him again. I was also foolish enough to go back there once or twice when I was older. I took one of our children, the eldest daughter. I didn't tell her why. Anyhow, I took her—in hope. But I never saw nothing afterwards.

How old were you when you saw . . . ?

Oh, well, when I had that little old bicycle—about eight or nine, I should think. Mind you, it was something quite positive, because it was moving. I know that it was, there's no doubt about it. It wasn't some twig moving, or my own imagination, or anything of the sort. It was there, sure enough, that little old fellow.[30]

9. THE GIRL FROM HARLECH FAIR WHO BECAME A MIDWIFE TO THE FAIRIES

Long ago there came to Harlech Fair a man on a white horse—terribly grand—to look for a maternity nurse. He wanted a maternity nurse because his wife was expecting a baby. There were no doctors in those days. And he found one in Harlech and she went with him. And they were going along the old Roman road and they had come to Cwm Nancol. And I have a lot to say. I think a lot of Cwm Nancol. I feel myself happy there always. I thought the fairies were there.

And she had gone through a lot of paths—the horse was going—and had come to a big rock, and the rock had split in two, and he had gone into a cave, and he and she were on the back of the white horse. And she was going through darkness, and after going quite a distance through this darkness she came out in a fine city, a grand city, grand houses and the people were grand, and there was plenty of everything there. She had never been as happy anywhere. And the baby arrived in a few days. And she was washing the baby—attending to the baby night and morning—and she was putting oil all over him. And this man had told her to take care that she did not let the oil, if it was on her hands, touch her eyes in case she lost her eyesight. And she had taken care. And he had brought her back to Harlech and had paid her well.

And in two and a half years, he comes again to Harlech to look for her. And she goes. And exactly the same way as before. And she, without remembering at all, after being there a few days had rubbed her eye. And she saw with that eye altogether differently from the other eye. The people were small and everywhere was dark. She tried to put something on the eye and when she saw the man she tells him what had happened, and that she sees the place dark, and that she is worried, that she thinks she is going to lose her eyesight. ˙

"Go to pack your things," said he. And she went. And he brought her home immediately. He paid her well. But she did not lose her eyesight either.

Wasn't it strange, that she saw in the dark and those things were small? And she swore that it was fairyland.[31]

10. *THE FAIRIES: GENTLE FRIENDS OF THE PEOPLE*

Do you know of a place here at Llandanwg, or nearby, where they said the fairies would come?

Well, yes, in the old days. I believe myself. Of course, we thought that the fairies came to places where there were green patches—a green, green patch—and that they would dance on these green patches. We firmly believed that, and we thought that the mushrooms were parasols or umbrellas for the fairies and that they had been left there to keep the ground dry for them to dance. That was the purpose of the mushrooms. *How did you come to believe this?*

Well, I believed because my mother would tell stories and tales about them. I firmly believed because I had heard other people saying . . .
Weren't people in the old days afraid of the fairies coming into the house?

Yes, they were.
Do you remember people placing something somewhere to prevent the fairies from coming?

No, I can't say. I believe that everyone accepted the fairies—that you received nothing but gentleness from them. They were something for you to be glad of, that is what I thought.

So you didn't hear of anyone placing the poker or the fire tongs across a cradle, for example?

Oh! Dear me! No . . .

What size were they?

Oh, they were little things. Not tiny, tiny. But they were little things. They were little people . . .

Did you hear that they had little old pipes for smoking?

Yes, they had pipes for smoking.   '

What kind of things were those, do you know?

Well, I always thought that it was an earthenware pipe . . .

Was there a certain time of the year you would be more likely to see the fairies?

Yes, during the mushroom season.

Oh!

Yes. We felt then that we always had company . . . And I would firmly believe when I was a little girl that they would come to this green place to dance.

Where was this green place?

Well, in a place where there was much water. It was in a hollow, and there would be a tremendous amount of mushrooms growing in those places, until we believed that there was some connection between the fairies and mushrooms. Perhaps it was food for the fairies . . . And we strongly believed that their home was underneath the ground . . . And I don't think anyone saw the fairies during the daylight. I believe that if we had risen early enough in the morning, then we would have seen them dancing. We had come to believe that, of course.

You said just now that they lived underground, was it in some sort of caves?

Yes, most probably, in some kind of caves. You remember that story I had about the white horse—that went underground and she [the midwife] described them going there.

Yes, she did. Did you hear of some cave in this district which is connected with the fairies?

No, I can't say that either. But I always thought that they were in the direction of the river Artro, up in the Nancol valley.

That's it.

And yet, you know, it gives you some kind of joy to think about it, even if there is no truth in it. I've always had a high regard of my life as a child. I've had a very happy life, although I had to start working as a very young child. I've always been happy. Everybody has been very kind to me, even today in my old age.

Perhaps the fairies still exist, but that nobody sees them anymore?

Yes, I'm sure they do! We are the fairies' children![32]

11. *NANSI'R DOLYDD AND THE FAIRY BABY*

An old woman, called locally Nansi'r Dolydd, was a widow and lived in a little house which wasn't a farm or anything. And she would go out to work to try to earn a few pence to help her to get food. One morning she wanted to set out early and had decided to get up and do her housework at the crack of dawn. And it was a fine morning and she opened the door, and what was on the doorstep but a little child, the prettiest she ever saw. And she had no idea at all what to do with it. She took it into the house and if I remember what was said, there was a short note asking would she bring up the child, that she wouldn't go short. And there were tiny clothes and everything for this little child. And the old woman took it, although she realized that really she couldn't do so, because she was working that day on a farm in the very top of the valley. But there was nothing to be done, for she could not go there, and she stayed at home.

She looked after this child afterwards, and every morning there was food. I am not sure what; I can't say what. Milk, probably, at first, and clothes for this little child. There would be a pair of gloves, too, and a box of ointment, and a note instructing her to rub this little child's eyes with the ointment every morning after she had washed it, but she was to remember to wear gloves. And she was not to touch her own eyes with this ointment. She had to be careful to take off the gloves after putting the ointment on the child's eyes. But the child grew, didn't it, and thrived, and the old woman thought the world of it by now. Yes! Oh, it was months old, drawing to one year of age. And one morning as she puts the ointment on the child's eyes, an itching came over one of her own eyes, and without thinking she rubbed her own eye, and she saw what the child was—one of the fairy children.

Well, she had the fright of her life, yes; because this warning that she was not to touch her eyes was because she was not supposed to know that it was a fairy child. But there it is, it happened. She put it in its bed that night and she went to her own bed sometime. The child was sleeping soundly. She woke up in the morning and went to look. By then the child had vanished. They had left her a sum of money for looking after it, but they had taken it away when it became known that it was a fairy child. And the old woman never saw it again.[33]

12. *IN FAIRYLAND FOR A HUNDRED YEARS*

Were there any fairy circles [rings] in the district?
Yes, there were circles here and there in the district.
Where exactly do you remember seeing these rings?

Well, I remember seeing a circle on Ty Du's land [my home] up near Beudy Gwyn [white cowshed], as we used to call it. It was marshland, but round. It was very strange. A round circle.
What was the size of the circle?
Well, I would say about ten yards.
Across?
Yes, across, or more, perhaps.
Was it of a particular color?
It was more green than the rest. No rushes or anything grew on it, only moss or fine grass.
And the name of this field was?
"Gweirglodd Beudy Gwyn" [Beudy Gwyn Meadow] we used to call it . . .
Would you go to this circle to play?
Goodness me! No! We would be too afraid in case the fairies would find us and take us away to their place.
Who would tell you not to go?
Oh! Uncle Thomas. "You better not go there," he'd say, "in case the fairies take you."
He believed in the fairies?
Well, I can't say, but, anyway, he would tell me tales about them in a most interesting manner.
Would he tell you that fairies were fond of going to marshy or rushy places?
I don't know what the reason was. They were in places that not many people travelled through. A more lonely place, perhaps.
You never saw the fairies in the circle?
Well, no, I didn't see them, but I heard about a boy who entered the circle and they say that he never came back . . . There are many stories . . .
Tell me the tale of the young boy who entered the circle.
Oh, well, he was the son of a small farm and was going for a walk one evening. He had gone some distance from the house and he entered into this circle. And, indeed! The fairies came to dance and the boy stood in the center looking at them. He wasn't realizing that time was passing, but one of the fairies came to him.
"Would you like to come with us to our country?"
"Dear me, yes," the boy replied.
"Well, come down these steps here this way."
And he hadn't noticed before that there were any steps there. But he goes down these steps, down and down. After walking for a while he came to a certain country, the most beautiful he had ever seen. All color of flowers in it and birds. Well, he was absolutely fascinated. He was taken to a large room and was given a feast. He had been like that for a while and the boy thought: "I haven't been here long."
And one of them said: "You may sleep here tonight, if you like."

"Oh no, it's no use, my father and mother won't know where I am," remarked the boy.

And he went around again to see the country and the animals they had. Their cattle were very special. And after he had been he felt a little homesick and he said: "I'd like to go home now."

"Oh, we'll escort you," they said, "we'll take you to the top of the steps, you'll be able to find your way then."

And they took him. And after he returned to the circle he makes his way for home. And he goes to the house. Dear me! There were strangers in the house. No one knew him.

"Where are my father and mother?" he asks.

"Your father and mother," they said. "Goodness me! We don't know who you are, tell us your name."

"Robin Jones is my name," he answered.

"Good God! We don't know. We've been living here for nearly fifty years," they said.

"Well, don't talk nonsense," the boy remarked, "it was only last night that I left."

"Oh, there's something wrong with you," said the people, "you didn't leave last night."

Well, the boy looks around and he couldn't see that anything had changed. And he thought, "Well, I'll go and get some sense from somewhere." And he went to see some neighbours. Goodness me! The neighbours weren't there either. Strangers there again.

And they said, "We heard some talk once about a Robin who had gone into the fairy circle but this happened over a hundred years ago."

And the boy had been in Fairyland for over one hundred years and had returned. Then he didn't know anybody.[34]

13. *THE MAN AFFLICTED BY A FAIRY AWL*

Two men had gone for a walk and what did they see but fairies going about their business. Some were dancing, some were singing and some were occupied by different trades—tailors and cobblers and so on. They stayed long to look at them before leaving. They weren't there too long either. And goodness! One of them found that he was terribly lame the next day. He could hardly move. And he was like this for ages. He went to an old magician to find out what was wrong with him. What had happened was that he'd seen the fairies working. "If you climb to the top of a tree after one year and a day," the magician said, "you'll see them again."

And so it was. He went to the top of the tree after a year and a day. And there they were, some tailors, others cobblers, and still others singing and engaged in all sorts of merriment. Well, one of these cobblers had lost an awl. He'd looked everywhere for it and for the life of him couldn't find it. "Well, there it is," said another to him, "in the backside of that man on top of the tree." The fairies climbed up there and pulled it out and went away. The man climbed down and was perfectly well. And that's the story of the fairies under the tree.[35]

14. *A POOR MAN FINDS FAIRY MONEY*

I heard Dafydd Jones saying he'd heard Huw Jones Pentrellyncymer—that's what we called him . . . relating how he'd ventured out into the snow when he was very poor and living in Pentrellyncymer, in The Boot. Anyway, there'd been very heavy snowfalls and he didn't know what to do. He had no money, not a halfpenny, but he ventured out to Llanfihangel Glyn Myfyr one afternoon. Well, it was quite early in the afternoon and he was following the path in the snow and what did he find on the ground but four half crowns. He picked them up. He decided not to advertise his find—to ask around to find out who'd lost them. But he didn't hear that anyone had lost them. And there was no sign that anyone had been there, no footprints. He bought delicacies with some of the money and from then on he was never short of money for as long as he lived—up to the time that he related the story. And he was certain that it was fairy money, that the fairies had come and left the money for him, real half crowns.[36]

15. *"ROBERT THE TAILOR" AND THE FAIRY HALF CROWNS*

"Robert the Tailor" lived in Cefn-brith with his wife. He went to Cerrigydrudion to pay for the repair of his clock. It cost half a crown and that's all he had in his pocket. The next day—it was a Sunday—he went for a walk and when he put his hand in his pocket, well! There was a half a crown there. And he had no money before then. Off he went home to have his tea. His wife went to a drawer to get her cap out and found half a crown in her cap, too. They had no idea what to do.

He went to the village the next morning to ask the watchmaker if he had paid for the repair of the clock. He had, indeed, paid half a crown for the repairs. He went home to tell his wife. She became very tearful and went to tell the story to her neighbours. And the half crowns stopped. He had found a few others in various places, but they stopped after the old woman told the story. And that's what I heard old "Robert the Tailor" reciting.[37]

16. *IN FAIRYLAND FOR FIFTEEN YEARS*

I don't recall a lot about that story. It was about these two men who
went for a stroll and one of them lost the other, I'm pretty certain. And
what one of them saw was fairies dancing and he stopped to look at them
and to listen to them. And that's where he was for a bit, for about two or
three hours, he thought. Then he went home and on the way he met this
man who greeted him:
"Good evening."
"Good evening," he replied.
"Hello," he said, "aren't you Jack my cousin?"
"God, yes," said he.
"How long is it since we lost each other?" said the other man.
"Well, let me think. I've been married for ten years and it was five
years after losing you that I married. That makes fifteen years."
And he'd thought he'd only been in the company of the fairies for a
couple of hours.[38]

17. *THE MAID WHO WENT OUT FOR A PENNY'S WORTH OF YEAST*

Tell me who used to recite to you that tale about the fairies?
Well, I think that it was Edward C. Rees, from Cross, who told me the
story about the fairies. He was very interested in old history. And he
would tell me about a maid living at Rhiwhiraeth Isa, she had been sent to
a nearby farm to fetch a penny's worth of yeast. And, indeed, she came
across the fairies and she became lost. She was away for a whole year, so
he said. And she returned in one year and brought the bottle of yeast with
her. I heard him telling that tale and they used to say that there was a fairy
ring on Cae Ty Ucha [Ty Ucha field] near Rhiwhiraeth Isa.[39]

18. *LISA PEN-SARN'S WARNING*

Who in your district believed in the Tylwyth Teg [fairies]?
Oh, I think that the fairies have some connection with bog land, and
because I lived near Cors Garon [Caron Bog] I remember that story very
well. Really, it wasn't a story at all. Lisa Penn-sarn was the woman. She
would call at our little cottage on her way to Tregaron. She had a small
farm and she would bring a bottle of milk under her shawl to my mother.
Then she would come back to fetch the bottle and Mam used to make her
a cup of tea, and we as a troop of children would listen to her stories.
And amongst other things she would tell us about the fairies, that
they lived near Y Gwndwn Mawr, a small farm by Cors Garon. She told us
about the woman of Pengwndwn, Swyddffynnon—that again was a little

farm—she had sent the servant lad to Swyddffynnon village to fetch yeast for baking bread. And she was saying to the little lad:
"Don't you be very late now, John." She wanted to bake the bread.

But although they waited and waited for the lad, he returned in one year and a day and said to his mistress: "Was I long, mistress?" They [the fairies] had captured him on his way back to the farm from the village and had taken him away. He had been living with them all that time most happily.

And Lisa used to say afterwards to my mother: "You take care of these children, don't let them far out of your sight. There are fairies living out there on the banks of the little river on Waun y Trawsgoed [Trawsgoed Meadow]. I tell you, Catrin, don't you let these children go very far." And, do you know my mother believed her. She would keep an eye on us. If we went that way to play she would call on us to come back. There was a strong belief in the fairies in these districts those days.[40]

19. *THE FAIRY BABY BORN WITH TEETH*

What is this tale now?

Well, this is the story as I heard it. There was a girl—she was maid-servant on the farm—and she gave birth to an illegitimate child. And it was a very special one. Its mouth was full of teeth at birth. And it could talk and answer questions.

A certain person in the district who was reputed to be a witch had heard about this child; people had been talking.

"Oh, it won't be with them for long," she said.

"How's that?"

"Oh, it will return to its own company."

"What do you mean?"

"Oh, it will return to the fairies. That's where it has come from."

What they called *criddyn* [changeling]. What that means, I don't know.

Well, the child was now lost. Every search for it was in vain. They went to see the witch and she told them: "You go now on a certain moonlight night to such and such a field and keep watch. The fairies will come there to dance."

And so it was. The child was seen in the procession with the fairies. And they disappeared and were never seen again. The people were very frightened. That is the story as I heard it.[41]

20. *THE FAIRY LADY OF LLYN Y FAN FACH AND THE FAMOUS PHYSICIANS OF MYDDFAI*

The only son of a widow living at the farm of Blaen Sawdde, near Myddfai in South West Wales, was one day looking after his mother's cattle on the banks of a mountain lake called Llyn y Fan Fach. Sitting on the surface of the water he saw a most beautiful maiden combing her hair. He offered her his barley bread, but she said: "*Cras dy fara* [crimped is thy bread]; *nid hawdd fy nala* ['tis not easy to catch me]." Then she sank into the water.

The love stricken youth returned home and told his mother, who advised him to take moist bread with him the next day. After waiting for many hours the maid appeared. He once more offered her bread and she said: "*Llaith dy fara* [moist is thy bread]; *Ti ni fynna* [I do not want thee]." Smiling, she again vanished.

The mother then suggested slightly baked bread. After another long wait he was astonished to see cattle walking on the surface of the water, followed by the maiden. This time she accepted the bread and consented to be his wife, but on one condition: "If you strike me three causeless blows," she told him, "I will leave you for ever." Suddenly the maiden plunged into the water. After a short while a tall, hoary-headed man came out with two beautiful ladies. "I will give you my daughter in marriage if you can tell which one of these she is," said the hoary-headed man. They were so much alike that the youth was on the point of saying he could not, when the one with a star on her sandal thrust her foot forward just a little and he pointed to the girl he loved. "You have chosen rightly," said the father, "I will give her as dowry as many sheep, cattle, goats and horses as she can count on each with one breath." Then she began counting as rapidly as she could, by fives, and the exact number of animals counted each time came out of the lake.

The young couple were married and lived happily for many years on the farm of Esgair Llaethdy and had three sons. One day they had been invited to a christening in the neighbourhood. The husband told his wife to fetch a pony from the field and he went to the house for her gloves. When he returned she was still standing in the same place and the husband tapped her playfully on the shoulder with one of the gloves and said "Go, go." And it was then she reminded him of the three strokes without a cause and warned him to be careful.

Some time later they were at a wedding, when the wife suddenly burst into tears. Her husband tapped her on the shoulder and asked her why she was weeping and she answered "I weep because the young couple's troubles are now beginning and so are ours, too, for this is the second causeless blow."

Years passed on, but at a funeral one day the wife began to laugh most gaily. Touching her arm the husband urged her to be quiet, but she replied: "When people die their troubles are over and so, dear husband, is our marriage. This is the third causeless blow; farewell for ever." She walked towards Esgair Llaethdy and called her cattle and all the other animals by their Welsh names:

> Hump-brindled, Hornless-brindled,
> Rump-brindled, White-freckled,
> Four meadow-speckled ones,
> Old White-faced,
> And Grey Squint-eye,
> With the white bull from the King's Court,
> And the little black calf which is on the hook,
> You too return home fully recovered.

They all followed her, even the little black calf, though slaughtered and hung upon a hook. Four oxen ploughing in the field on the mountainside were also called and they dragged the plough with them making a deep furrow which remains to this day. Led by the lady, all the animals disappeared into the Fan Fach lake.

One day at a mountain gate near Dôl Hywel, now called Llidiart y Meddygon [Physician's Gate], the mother suddenly appeared to Rhiwallon, her eldest son, and told him that his mission on earth was to heal the sick and she gave him a bag full of medical prescriptions. On several occasions later she met her three sons on the banks of the lake and once she even accompanied them on their return home was far as a place still called Pant y Meddygon [Physician's Dingle], where she revealed to them the medicinal qualities of various plants and herbs.

Rhiwallon and his three sons, Cadwgan, Gruffudd and Einion, became physicians to Prince Rhys Grug, who gave them lands and privileges. They wrote down their knowledge in manuscripts and their fame as physicians was soon established over the whole country, and it continued among their descendants until the nineteenth century.[42]

21. THE WHITE COW

There once was a farmer and his wife who lived in a little farm in the valley, somewhere in Wales. He had six or seven cows and was quite successful. But one winter he was out cutting a ditch, and it was a very wet winter, and he became ill with severe cold and arthritis. And that winter he had to give up farming with the thought that things would become better in the spring. But when spring came, he was no better, although his wife was helping him as much as she could. Then the hay harvest failed and things went from worse to worse. They were in debt and could not pay the rent. In the end the bailiffs were called in and they had to sell everything.

That night he and his wife were sitting around the fire and they were broken-hearted. The sale had taken place and everything had been sold, and the two of them were very depressed.

"Oh, come now," said the wife, "something is bound to come again. Dawn is sure to follow the night. Come, let us go to bed."

The two go to bed. There was not much sleep. They were grief stricken. But at dawn what should they hear but the clear bleating of a cow coming towards them. They couldn't believe it.

"You're imagining it."

"No, no," she says. And she gets up to the window. "Liam *bach* [dear], there is a lovely white cow in the yard. It's a very beautiful cow, I've never seen a better one. And she's waiting to be milked."

"Well, you better get up then," he says.

She got up and milked the cow. And, by God! She gave a bucketful of milk. But she was a very special cow, not like any other. They enquired in the nearby farms whether anyone had lost a cow. Some people suggested that she had come from the fairies, although the farmer and his wife didn't quite know what to think of that suggestion.

They continued to milk the cow and to make cheese and butter. In time the cow gave birth to a little calf. And the family grew, one by one. Eventually, the white cow had given birth to some six or seven calves. But the white cow became old and had no milk. Then they decided to get rid of it. They called for the butcher to come and kill the cow. Its meat would be salted and sold.

The butcher comes. He ties the cow with a rope, takes off his coat and pulls up his sleeves. He lifts up the hatchet to give the cow a blow to kill it. But when the hatchet was up and ready to descend on the cow's head a voice was heard crying: "Come, come. Come home my little maid. Come home to your children." And the cow gave one loud bleat. She pulled and the rope which held her broke. Then she and all her offspring followed one another and went into the lake. They disappeared under the water.

And everybody was certain that the cow and her offspring had been sent by the fairies to help the poor old couple.[43]

22. *INTO THE FAIRY CIRCLE WITH A LOAF OF BREAD*

This little girl lived in a tiny little house and her mother said to her: "Go to the shop to get me a loaf of bread for tea, it's three o'clock, so that we can have a nice little tea at four."

"Alright," she replied.

"And remember not to come back across the field, because there's a fairy circle there and you could well tread on it, and then you wouldn't be able to return, they would take you away."

She goes to the shop. Well, indeed, the temptation was too much for her. She saw the shortcut across the field and she thinks to herself: "Oh, I'll go this way now." And she goes towards the circle—the fairy circle—and she says to herself: "I'll place the loaf down in the center and I'll put one foot on the loaf and I'll jump across over to the other side of the circle, so that I won't have put one foot in the circle." Then she places the loaf in the middle of the circle with her foot on it and jumps across. But, oh dear! Before she completes her jump she has disappeared.

Her mother now is worried that she is so late returning and begins to search for her and naturally, comes to the conclusion that she has gone to the fairies. In about seven years she comes back to the house and the loaf is quite fresh.

"Here it is, mam," she says, "here's the loaf for you to have tea."

"My dear little girl, where have you been?"

"In the shop to get a loaf of bread for you."

"Oh! No, my girl. Seven years have passed since you went to the shop for a loaf. And that's what happens to a child who disobeys its father and mother."[44]

Notes

1. I wish to thank two of my colleagues for their very kind assistance in preparing this essay: Mrs. Sioned Thomas and Mr. John Williams-Davies. All the prints published, unless otherwise noted, are from the Welsh Folk Museum (WFM) Archive, St. Fagan's, Cardiff.

2. Hugh Evans, *Y Tylwyth Teg* [the fairies] (Liverpool: Brython P, 1935). Evans is also the author of *Cwm Eithin* (Liverpool: Gwasg y Brython, 1931), a classic book of reminiscences of his native district. It has been translated into English by E. Morgan Humphreys as *The Gorse Glen* (Liverpool: Brython P, 1948).

3. See Robin Gwyndaf, *The Welsh Folk Narrative Tradition: Adaptation and Continuity* (Cardiff: National Museum of Wales, 1988), *Chwedlau Gwerin Cymru: Welsh Folk Tales* (Cardiff: National Museum of Wales, 1989), and the references quoted in these works.

4. First introduced in his "Kategorien der Prosa-Volksdichtung," in 1934. See C.W. von Sydow's *Selected Papers on Folklore*, ed. Laurits Bødker (1948; New York: Arno P, 1977) 60–88.

5. For recent studies relating to memorates and local folk belief legends, see: Linda Dégh and Andrew Vázsony: "Legend and Belief," *Genre* 4 (1971): 281–304 and "The Memorate and the Proto Memorate," *Journal of American Folklore* 87 (1974): 225–39; Robin Gwyndaf, "Memorates, Chronicates and Anecdotes in Action: Some Remarks Towards a Definition of the Personal Narrative in Context," *Papers of the*

8th Congress for the International Society for Folk Narrative Research, eds. Reimund Kvideland and Torunn Selberg (Bergen: International Society for Folk Narrative Research, 1984) 1: 217–24; Wayland D. Hand, ed., *American Folk Legend* (Berkeley: U of California P, 1971); Lauri Honko, "Memorates and the Study of Folk Beliefs," *Journal of the Folklore Institute* 1 (1964): 5–19; Juha Pentikäinen, "Belief, Memorate and Legend," *Folklore Forum* 6 (1973): 217–41.

6. For a classification of folk legends, see Reidar Th. Christiansen, *The Migratory Legends,* Folklore Fellows' Communications, No. 175 (Helsinki: Suomalainen Tiedeakademia, 1958). For a classification of fairy motifs see Stith Thompson, *Motif-Index of Folk Literature,* 6 vols. (Bloomington: Indiana UP, 1956) motifs F200–399.

7. von Sydow 60–88.

8. The Fourth Branch was composed probably during the second half of the eleventh century. See Gwyn Jones and Thomas Jones, *The Mabinogion* (London: J.M. Dent, 1948).

9. William Howells, *Cambrian Superstitions* (London: Longman, 1831) 144.

10. George Ewart Evans, *Ask the Fellows Who Cut the Hay* (London: Faber and Faber, 1965) 4.

11. For English translations, see *The Journey Through Wales and The Description of Wales,* trans. L. Thorpe (Harmondsworth: Penguin, 1978).

12. Sir John Rhŷs, *Celtic Folklore: Welsh and Manx,* 2 vols. (1901; Aldershot: Wildwood House, 1980); T. Gwynn Jones, *Welsh Folklore and Folk-Custom* (1930; Totowa, N.J.: D.S. Brewer, 1979).

13. See W.J. Gruffydd, *Folklore and Myth in the Mabinogion* (Cardiff: U of Wales P, 1958) and J. Gwynfor Jones, "'Y Tylwyth Teg' yng Nghymru'r Unfed a'r Ail Ganrif ar Bymtheg" (Fairies in the Sixteenth and Seventeenth Century Wales), *Llen Cymru* (Cardiff: U of Wales P, 1964–5) 8: 96–9.

14. See Rhŷs 141–6.

15. Rhŷs 1: 158–62; T. Gwynn Jones 53.

16. See Rhŷs; Gruffydd.

17. Gwyn Jones and Thomas Jones.

18. Rhŷs 1: 141–6; also see text 22.

19. See Rhŷs 2: 583–630.

20. A reference to Bronislaw Malinowski's theory of magic, quoted in Gustav Jahoda, *The Psychology of Superstition* (Harmondsworth: Penguin, 1969) 127–8.

21. Alwyn and Brinley Rees, *Celtic Heritage: Ancient Tradition in Ireland and Wales* (1961; London: Thames and Hudson, 1978) 351.

22. Information provided in notes for the texts include the Welsh Folk Museum (WFM) Archive tape recording number and the date of the recording, the name of the informant, the place of the recording, the informant's date and place of birth (b.), the informant's major occupation(s), and other contextual data.

23. WFM Tape 1635, 14 September 1976; Ifan Gruffydd; Llangristiolus, near Llangefni, Anglesey, Gwynedd, N. Wales; b. 1896, Llangristiolus; farm servant, custodian; author of two classic books of his reminiscences.

24. WFM Tape 4526, 26 February 1975; Robert Owen Pritchard; Llanddaniel, Anglesey, Gwynedd, N. Wales; b. 6 June 1904, Betws Garmon, Gwynedd; member, Milk Marketing Board. His testimony relates to the little village of Betsw Garmon, near Llanberis, in Snowdonia and to two districts, Aber-soch and Rhoshirwaun, near Pwllheli, in the Llyn Peninsula, Gwynedd.

25. WFM Tape 3910, 27 June 1973; Evan Roberts; Capel Curig, Gwynedd, N. Wales; b. 15 September 1906, Capel Curig; quarryman, botanist, Warden for the Nature Conservancy Council, expert on the rare plants of Snowdonia. Numerous fairy legends have been collected in Nant Gwynant and other districts in Snowdonia and these have been discussed in detail by Rhŷs.

26. WFM Tape 3910, 27 June 1973; Evan Roberts; as above.

27. WFM Tape 4367, 16 August 1974; William John Jones; Drws-y-coed, near Beddgelert, Gwynedd, N. Wales; b. 15 October 1905, Ceunant near Caernarfon; farmer and local poet. The informant remarked that he and his brother had been staring through the hole in the wall for about three hours, to say the least. The fairies only danced around the stone, not on it, and the boys heard no sound. It was light enough to see them. They had not seen pictures of fairies nor had they heard more about them than what their grandfather told them. He was very fond of telling stories like this to comfort the two boys after a day spent helping on the little small-holding. Their grandfather never told them that there were fairies anywhere else in the district, and he never said that he himself had seen them, only that they were there near the Garreg Lefain (echo stone). It was a huge rock about twenty yards square, and the stone itself was on top of the rock. If anyone stood on it, it shook.

28. WFM Tape 1973, 22 October 1968; Ellen Evans (1879–1972); Llithfaen, near Pwllheli, Gwynedd, N. Wales; b. Llithfaen; maid, housewife, Sunday school teacher; she published her reminiscences in a local newspaper. Since the early fifties until recently (with the foundation there of the Welsh Language Center) Nant Gwrtheyrn (*nant* = stream), near Llithfaen, has been a deserted village, enclosed between the sea and steep slopes. When she was a young girl the informant used to visit some of the houses to work as a maid and to knit. She heard the tradition about "Elis Bach y Nant" (*bach* = small, dear) from her aunt, Elin Hughes, in particular. But it is also a very well-known tradition.

29. WFM Tapes 1989–90, 28 October 1969; William Jones; Aberdaron, near Pwllheli, Gwynedd, N. Wales; b. ca. 1900, Aberdaron; blacksmith, keen reader.

30. WFM Tape 3543, 18 July 1972; W.S. ("Wil Sam") Jones; Rhos-lan, Cricieth, Gwynedd, N. Wales; b. 28 May 1920, Llanystumdwy, Cricieth; motor garage worker before becoming full-time playwright and comedy scriptwriter. The circle of trees was about five yards in diameter. The little "fellow" or "being" wore a red cap.

31. WFM Tape 1298, 9 March 1966; Martha Williams; Llandanwg, near Harlech, Gwynedd, N. Wales; b. 21 March 1884, Llanfair, near Harlech; housewife. Both the informant and her mother, from whom she heard the story, were strong believers in the fairies. Martha Williams could not say in which rock the cave was, as Cwm Nancol had many rocks.

32. WFM Tape 2002, 1 November 1968; Martha Williams; as above.

33. WFM Tape 2976, 23 September 1970; Gretta Jones; Parc, Y Bala, Gwynedd, N. Wales; b. 16 January 1900, Parc, Y Bala; housewife. The informant heard this story from her uncle, Thomas Jones, her father's brother. He would warn her not to go to certain places because the fairies were there. They were places seldom traversed and out-of-the-way. She had never seen a fairy herself, but had heard of a boy being snatched from a fairy circle and taken to Fairyland. He thought he had been there only one night but when he returned home he had been a hundred years. Her Uncle Thomas told her other stories about the fairies, but his special story is the one about

Nansi's baby. He used to tell her these stories at eventide by the fire, or when the two were walking through the fields. He used to show her an old ruin and say that it was there Nansi lived. She had died long before the informant was born, so the story, she believed, went back to the beginning of the nineteenth century. Nansi's full name, she thought, was Nansi Davies. She was a kind woman, so Gretta Jones thought that the fairies took their child to her for that reason and in order to help her.

34.   WFM Tape 2976, 23 September 1970; Gretta Jones; as above. The informant also heard this story from her uncle, Thomas Jones, at home on the hearth around the fire. Her uncle did not specifically name the farm where the boy lived, but the informant believed it was "somewhere in the district probably." She did, however, remember her uncle calling the boy Robert or Robin Jones.

35.   WFM Tape 2288, 29 April 1969; Lewis T. Evans (1882–1975); Cyffylliog, Clwyd, N. Wales; b. Cerrigydrudion, Clwyd; farmer, craftsman, poet, antiquary. The informant heard this legend from this mother, Catherine Evans, when he was seven or eight years old.

36.   WFM Tape 872, 24 November 1964; Lewis T. Evans; as above. Huw Jones died about 1896. He was a popular local poet and his shop and school in The Boot were important focal points for the Pentrellyncymer area. He was born in Hendre-ddu, Pentrellyncymer. Dafydd Jones, "Dafydd Goes Bren" (David the wooden leg), Tai Ucha, Pentrellyncymer, who told the story to Lewis T. Evans, was a local poet, antiquary and farmer. The informant was familiar with certain natural phenomenon described as "fairy money," although he was unable to offer an explanation for them. He would often come across objects shining like "silver paper" on grazing land which "turned to nothing on being touched." Elsewhere he describes them as "sparkling clusters, just like money" which were often to be seen in certain fields.

37.   WFM Tape 2288, 29 April 1969; Lewis T. Evans; as above. Evans heard "Robert the Tailor" revealing his sudden changes in fortune when he was a young boy in Ty'n-y-gilfach, Cefn-brith about 1890. Robert was convinced of the existence of fairies and believed that they were responsible for leaving the money in "secret little places" in the house. The money was genuine currency and quite a large sum in those days.

38.   WFM Tape 2287, 29 April 1969; Lewis T. Evans; as above. The informant heard the story from his blind uncle, also named Lewis Evans, Pentrellyncymer. He lived with the blind uncle's family and worked on the farm as a servant lad.

39.   WFM Tape 3538, 12 June 1972; Edith M. Ellis; Dolanog, Welshpool, Powys, Mid-Wales; b. 20 April 1902, Llanfair Caereinion, Welshpool; farmer, housewife.

40.   WFM Tape 2581, 19 November 1969; Evan Jones; Llanfarian, near Aberystwyth, Dyfed, W. Wales; b. 7 October 1895, Y Borth, Tregaron, Dyfed; farmer, clerk, shopkeeper, author of books of reminiscences.

41.   WFM Tape 2901, 2 July 1970; Joseph Thomas (1880–1972); Trefdraeth (Newport), Dyfed, S.W. Wales; b. Meline, Dyfed; farmer, craftsman, self-taught veterinarian. The informant heard the legend from Benjamin and Daniel Jenkins, Ffynhonnau, Trefdraeth. The two brothers, and Daniel Jenkins' son, William Daniel Jenkins (also by the Museum), were regarded by Joseph Thomas as the most superstitious family in the district. The informant used to visit them on the occasion of taking the cows to the bull on their farm. The witch mentioned in the narrative would probably have been an old woman, poorly dressed, who lived by begging.

42. This is my narration of one of the most well-known of all Welsh tales. It is based on oral testimonies garnered during one week of fieldwork in the Myddfai district during May 1965 (WFM Tapes 1528–36), and my knowledge of *Meddygon Myddfai, The Physicians of Myddfai,* text edited by John Williams and translated by John Pughe (Llanymddyfri, 1861). This book presents the Physicians of Myddfai's medicinal recipes written down in manuscripts, dating from the Middle Ages and preserved in the National Library of Wales, Aberstwyth. The Llyn y Fan Fach legend (*llyn* = lake) derives from the folk memory of a people who lived in primitive homes and caves on the shores of lakes. It is believed that the description of the cattle is consistent with the type of cattle that were in Britain between the Iron Age and the Dark Ages. The early legend of the fairy "Lady of the Lake" was possibly linked with the much later tradition of the Myddfai Physicians and Rhys Gryg when "the white bull from the King's court" (descendants of the early *urus*) came to be identified with the white cattle of the royal court of Dinefwr in Dyfed, West Wales. Later the lake became associated with a number of beliefs and traditions. It was believed, for example, that there were seven echoes between the banks of Tyle Gwyn and Gwter Goch; that there was an unnatural suction in the surrounding rocks; and that the lake was bottomless. It was also a popular custom in the nineteenth century for people to visit the lake on the first Sunday in August each year to observe the waters "boiling"—a sure sign that the "Lady of the Lake" was about to appear. Indeed, some people to this day believe that the "lovely maidens of Myddfai" (mentioned in a local rhyme) are remote descendants of the beautiful fairy "Lady of the Lake."

43. WFM Tape 6439, 7 April 1979; David H. Culpitt, Cefneithin, near Llanelli, Dyfed, S.W. Wales; b. 1909, Cefneithin; collier. The story was told to him by his father.

44. WFM Tape 6439, 7 April 1979; David H. Culpitt; as above. He heard this story from his father as well.

II. Fairy Belief and Religion

The ties of fairylore and religion have long been apparent. Several well-known fairy origin theories pose religious explanations: fairies are the demoted gods of earlier polytheistic religions; fairies are the descendants of animistic spirits; fairies are the wandering souls of the dead; fairies are heavenly emigrant "fallen angels."[1] Given the religious dimension of fairy belief, there can be little wonder why, as citations in the previous section indicate, a priest or a minister might be summoned to quell fairy activities. Historically, official Christian clergy have often denounced fairies and fairy belief as being evil and satanic. Yet sometimes the relations of folk religion and official religion have been associative rather than antithetical, an established church absorbing and integrating aspects of fairylore rather than eliminating them. Clearly, such cultural contacts have a complex history.

The two essays in this section view sectors of this complicated area through different lenses. Using the theoretical perspective of "hegemony" as refined by Antonio Gramsci, that state domination is a dynamic process involving *cultural* struggle (hegemony, counter-hegemony), Diarmuid Ó Giolláin examines the historical relationship between fairy belief and Christianity in Ireland as an aspect of "struggle between the subordinated cultures of local communities and the hegemonic culture of the state."[2] Today he finds that Irish popular religion has largely lost this battle, its vestiges tied to sacred sites on the landscape—the fairy forts.

The "fairies" that Ann Helene Bolstad Skjelbred investigates are the Norwegian *huldre*-folk (hulders), previously discussed by Alan Bruford. The fairylore-religion case she documents in her article is a marvelous example of syncretism, the merging of similar cultural traits into new forms. Examining the cultural complex of childbirth as rite of passage, she effectively argues that the ceremony of churching, historically maintained by the Lutheran Church in Norway, has been an irrational element in the midst of rationalized Christian orthodoxy, a ritual that actually relates less to Christianity than to the traditional belief that hulders threaten mothers and newborn infants.

Notes

1. See Patrick Logan, *The Old Gods: Facts about Irish Fairies* (Belfast: Appletree P, 1981); Lewis Spence, *British Fairy Origins* (London: Watts and Co., 1946); Stewart Sanderson, "Commentary," *The Secret Common-Wealth & A Short Treatise of Charms and Spels*, Mistletoe Series, ed. Stewart Sanderson (Totowa, New Jersey: Rowan and Littlefield for the Folklore Society, 1976), pp. 1–46.

2. On Gramsci and folklore see Moyra Byrne, "Antonio Gramsci's Contribution to Italian Folklore Studies," *International Folklore Review* 2 (1982): 70–5.

The Fairy Belief and Official Religion in Ireland

Diarmuid Ó Giolláin

The fairy belief is a part of Irish popular religion which has long been of interest as much to romantic writers as to scholars. It has often been referred to as "the fairy faith," but this expression suggests an autonomy which it does not have with respect to popular religion in general. Since 432, when St. Patrick, according to the traditional account, introduced the new religion to Ireland, it has co-existed with Christianity. Both the earlier religious system, of which it was a part, and the new one helped to form the traditional worldview. This essay will examine the relationship between the fairy belief and Christianity as an attribute of the folk tradition itself and as part of a struggle between the subordinated cultures of local communities and the hegemonic culture of the state.

The presence and nature of sacred sites in the countryside gives a good indication of the characteristics of popular religion. Most numerous are the thirty or forty thousand forts or raths, mostly in fact Iron Age ring forts, commonly called "fairy forts," whose strong otherworld associations have helped to preserve them to the present day (see photo).[1] Dolmens, standing stones, stone circles and ancient burial grounds have various supernatural associations—with giants, with the dead, with the fairies or with the mythological figures of the Fianna (who appear in the medieval literature and in the modern oral tradition of Ireland and Gaelic Scotland as a band of warriors who defended Ireland against various supernatural adversaries—Macpherson's Ossian was based on this tradition). The respect given to "lone bushes" or "fairy bushes" has long been attested to; they still often stand unmolested in the middle of a cultivated field. The fairy bush was usually a rowan, holly, elderberry or whitethorn which stood alone in a field rather than in a hedgerow, and thus apparently was not planted by human hand: "the evidence of archaeology and palaeobotany is that these plants first became common in the prehistoric landscape as weeds of cultivation following forest clearances by early cultivators."[2] There are an estimated three thousand holy wells which were formerly resorted to, though few of which still are;[3] most of these are dedicated to Christian saints, representing thus in Christianized form one

Ring Fort, Glenavy, Co. Antrim, Northern Ireland. (Ulster Folk and Transport Museum)

of the most ancient of cults. Finally, there are the churches, graveyards, grottos and other monuments of organized religion, mostly of more recent date, from the Catholic chapels, few of which are older than the last century, to the grottos commemorating the Marian apparitions of Lourdes, which are modern.

The countryside, then, was full of sacred places, both Christian and non-Christian equally integrated into the local culture. But the non-Christian sites were much more numerous, and in greater proximity to man. The non-Christian powers tended to be more obvious and to play a more active role in human life. This appears to have been unequivocally the case at least until the end of the eighteenth century, and it was only from then that the overtly Christian side of religion gradually began to assert itself. Nevertheless folk religion has maintained much of its vitality into the second half of this century, though the more conspicuously non-Christian elements have increasingly been eroded.

The traditional community understood the world in terms of a distinction between itself and that which was outside. Thus it opposed its own inhabited space to the relatively unknown space beyond. The community's own space was the world, the Cosmos, while the rest was a strange, somewhat chaotic region, the abode of all kinds of outsiders. To be a community, a group of people had to be aware of sharing something with each other which they did not share with others. In this way they recognized a boundary between themselves and the outside world. A boundary by its nature orders, and order therefore became the defining criterion of the community. The outside was unbounded and thus lacking in order.[4] It was inhabited by beings—mortal as well as supernatural—whose behavior was at odds with that of the members of the community, which was characterized by order and organization. Anything which upset the natural order of the community tended to be linked to the disorderly world outside. The diagnosis of misfortune identified the culprits as fairies, or evil spirits, or people in league with them, or individuals who occupied ambiguous, "un-ordered" social roles. Various categories of outsiders could be easily confused since the only important distinction was between insiders and outsiders. Thus the Vikings in Irish folklore were often confused with the fairies: "fairy forts" were also known as "Danes' forts," "leprechauns' pipes" as "Danes' pipes" (the remains of the discarded clay pipes of previous generations which were sometimes uncovered while digging or ploughing), while a characteristic of both groups was red hair (which in mortals could indicate, besides Viking descent, the unsociable trait of a bad temper).[5]

The supernatural world was especially the untamed world of mountain, moor and sea, where the fairies lived. But it could also be much closer to man's cultivated space, even having its outposts within it, in the form of fairy forts, bushes and standing stones. In the evening when the order imposed by the sun had dissolved (darkness, in effect, representing a sort of primordial state, a state of pre-order) the otherworld closed in and its dangers waited outside the front door, so that people had to take care not to be out and about without due cause. It could even enter the house unless certain norms, such as throwing out the dirty water (representing disorder), were observed. The fairy world, too, could be above and below the human community. The fairy host travelled through the air and caused "fairy winds." The fairies lived underground, beneath the forts or even under the very houses of mortals. On two festivals, *Bealtaine* or May Day and *Samhain* or Halloween respectively, the boundary days of the summer and winter halves of the year (sharing the symbolic ambiguities of a boundary, which divides without itself belonging to either division), the barrier between the mortal and supernatural worlds came down and otherworld beings moved freely among women and men.

The fairies were a part of life. Tradition told that they called to the door to borrow meal, they enlisted the help of mortal midwives, they lent their cows, they saved people from death and bestowed magical gifts. Due respect was shown to them by speaking of them in a flattering way (the "good people," "the gentry"), thus respecting the taboo known in many societies on mentioning sacred names, as well as by warning them before throwing out the dirty water at night, by making sure not to build over their houses or paths (by using conventional methods such as throwing a hat to the wind to find a site), by not mocking them, by making offerings to them (as of the beestings poured at the roots of fairy thorns or into forts [6]). Their capacity for harm was well-known and feared: they stole food, led people astray, abducted humans and animals and replaced them with changelings, inflicted disabilities and caused sickness and death.

Mircea Eliade has described how in archaic societies the supreme divinities "are constantly pushed to the periphery of religious life where they are almost ignored; other sacred forces, nearer to man, more accessible to his daily experience, more useful to him, fill the leading role."[7] Eliade further observes that misfortune always has a religious meaning:

> Suffering proceeds from the magical action of an enemy, from breaking a taboo, from entering a baneful zone, from the anger of a god, or—when all other hypotheses have proven insufficient—from the will or the wrath of the Supreme Being.[8]

The localism which is so characteristic of popular religion is particularly well-exemplified by the fairies and by the holy wells. The libations of milk or poteen poured on the ground and the food left out for the fairies were examples of the common reverence shown to them. The leaving of offerings at holy wells tended to be tied more to the feast day of the saint to whom the well was dedicated, though of course the waters maintained their powers during the year and the saint's aid could be invoked at any time. The fairies often had their own identified local rulers, such as Áine in Donegal and Clíodhna in Munster, and interprovincial rivalries; these must have helped to articulate local identities in the same way as the holy wells with their cult of the local patron saint. There was no conflict between belief in the fairies and belief in the saints. Both belonged to the same popular religion and inhabited the same mythical universe. When belief in fairies and pilgrimages to holy wells were at their height in the eighteenth and early nineteenth centuries, the presence of official religion was negligible and in no position to greatly interfere with popular religion.[9]

This popular religion clearly had both non-Christian and Christian components, though much of the latter were Christian in form only. According to an eighth-century hymn the Irish worshipped the gods of the *sídh* (the modern "fairy fort") until St. Patrick converted them.[10] Clearly they did not stop worshipping them, but Christianity gave a new frame of reference in which to place them. Thus we have the tradition, well-known in many countries, that the fairies were the Fallen Angels, not good enough for heaven nor bad enough for hell. Likewise the migratory legend of the prospects of salvation of the fairies, who will be saved on the Last Day if they have even one drop of Adam's blood in their veins. Christianity lowered the status of these old gods since it was the victorious religion, and this relationship of power is evident in tradition in the usual superiority of Christian symbols over the fairies—much as it has been suggested that the power of iron over the fairies supposedly reflects the superiority of Iron Age invaders over their Bronze Age predecessors.

Ever since the conversion of Ireland in the fifth century Christianity has been a hegemonic religion and its greater social power and prestige has been manifest in folklore. Many ancient religious phenomena took Christian form in early times—the cult of water by having its wells dedicated to Christian saints, the festival of spring (*Imbolc*) by being dedicated to the Irish St. Brigid (who apparently is a goddess in Christianized form), the excursions to mountain tops which were typical of the harvest festival of *Lughnasa* (which bears the name of the Celtic god Lugh) by becoming Christian pilgrimages (that to Croagh Patrick being the surviving example). Thus we can speak of syncretism from an early period, of pre-Christian phenomena being Christianized and of surviving non-Christian phenomena taking on a Christian frame of reference, as in the story of the origin of the fairies. Worldview came to be composed of different historical religious layers, including a strong Christian element, but since mythical thought is central to all religions this is a question more of form than of content. That Christianity was the sophisticated universal cult of a Supreme Being was, of course, significant, but as Eliade notes, the Supreme Being tended to be remembered and invoked only when all else had failed.

Christian objects or symbols were typically more powerful than fairies or spirits. Holy water, prayers, scapulars, the Sign of the Cross were all effective against the fairies, but so too were salt, spittle, iron or a sprig of rowan—one can separate the Christian from the non-Christian only in a mechanical way. Priests could banish fairies, but so could "wise women" and "fairy doctors." The priest, though obviously part of an official ecclesiastical organization, often played another role in popular religion until well into the nineteenth century, sometimes despite his best efforts to the contrary, and this dual role has not yet been fully lost. He officiated in the sacraments of the Church, but he also could be known to call maledictions from the altar and to believe in supernatural butter-stealing,[11] and the earth from his grave might be used in cures, people believing that his power was not merely *ex officio*.

In legends priests often showed themselves to be wise to the ways of the fairies, as in the Donegal story where a man who lives in dread of them asks the priest if they really exist:

"They do, indeed," said the priest. "There is not a clump of heather from here to Mín na bhFáchrán that has not one of them sheltering under it. But do not have any fear of them: I promise you that you will never see one of them as long as you live."[12]

Sometimes there are limitations to the power of the priest, as in the story, from Donegal too, where he threatens to banish the fairies who are harassing a man who smashed a fairy rock. He decides to desist when the fairies throw a fiery dart at him.[13] In a legend from Waterford a woman named Nóra has the reputation of consorting with the fairies. The enraged parish priest threatens to whip her. She says that she will show the fairies to him and asks him to turn around: "He turned; and whatever he saw, or did not see, he did not make a sound but struck the horse a slash of the whip and away home with him as fast as the horse could strike the road!"[14] Such accounts show an ambivalence towards the idea of Christianity having an absolute superiority of power.

Traditional society in Ireland for a long time was relatively autonomous as far as its dealings with the outside world were concerned. Only in fairly recent times, and particularly in the course of the last century, has that outside world begun to assert itself in the heart of traditional society, as part of the centralizing state. It was then that the traditional society found itself defined in the same way as it had always defined the outside world, as chaotic, un-ordered, savage.

The persecution of Catholics from the 1690s until the Catholic Emancipation Act of 1829 meant that to a significant extent during much of the period the bulk of the population had little clerical guidance and priests kept a low profile. While the influence of the anti-Catholic Penal Laws has been both exaggerated and minimized, it is clear that the attempts of the Catholic hierarchy to come to grips with the "errors" and "superstitions" of their flock were very much hindered by the real limitations imposed on them by a hostile state—the many fruitless clerical condemnations of behavior at wakes from the seventeenth century onwards are, perhaps, evidence of that.[15]

In the first part of the last century Catholic chapels were lacking in many parts of Ireland, Mass being said in private houses or in the open. The pre-Famine chapel, according to Seán Connolly, was often only a Mass-house, used for that purpose only on Sundays and holy days. Confessions were heard and communion administered during the "Stations" (religious services in private houses), and baptisms and marriages took place in the home of the persons concerned or in the parish priest's house. Until the second half of the century the host was not kept permanently in an ordinary chapel, but the "chapel" during weekdays could be used as a schoolhouse or even as a threshing floor.[16]

The lack of a developed official church infrastructure encouraged the maintenance of popular religion and the autonomy of local religious cults.

The strength of popular religion was in inverse proportion to the strength of the official church. Formal religion strengthened its grip as part of the general process of modernization, which encompassed everything from improvements in communications, agriculture, education and in the state infrastructure of administration, revenue and law, to industrialization, urbanization and the growth of political and cultural organizations which transcended merely local loyalties.

The nineteenth century was a time of modernization in Ireland. The Great Famine of the 1840s swept away the rural poor who were most attached to traditional lifestyles, from speaking Irish to believing in the fairies, and made economic improvements, particularly in agriculture, possible. The changes between the beginning and the end of the century were great. Speakers of Irish fell in number from almost half the population to less than a seventh, church attendance among Catholics grew from being the exercise of a minority of perhaps forty percent to being almost universal, and literacy levels increased from less than half of the population to the vast majority.[17] A national system of education, a national paramilitary police force and other innovations meant that the arm of the state came to make its presence felt everywhere. The scope and the pace of social and economic change coupled with the enormous catastrophe of the Famine undoubtedly caused a sort of moral and intellectual breakdown of the old worldview and a spiritual chaos which encouraged people to desperately cling to the new religious truths. In many European countries this period can be seen as a cultural interregnum between the pre-modern and the modern.

The Catholic Church was reformed and modernized. In many ways the local autonomy of religion was ended and subordinated to the newly strengthened central religious institutions. Instead of the local pilgrimages and devotions of popular religion new autonomies were given to the laity through the establishment of lay confraternities and sodalities, of new devotions such as Benediction, the Stations of the Cross, novenas, processions and retreats, and of aids to private devotion such as scapulars, medals and other objects—but under the close supervision of the clergy.[18] Priests, too, were brought into line, many of them before the Famine apparently sharing the mythical worldview of their flocks, as, for example, Bishop Sweetman's regulations from 1771 suggest:

> No pastor, priest or ecclesiastic whatsoever, in the diocese of Ferns, must presume, *sub poena suspensionis et privationis beneficii*, to read exorcisms or gospels over the already too ignorant, and by such ecclesiastics too much deluded people, or act the fairy doctor in any shape, without express leave in writing from the bishop of the diocese.[19]

According to Antonio Gramsci folklore is basically a question of worldview, of a "conception of the world and life" which is "implicit to a

large extent in determinate ... strata of society and in opposition ... to
'official' conceptions of the world."[20] In particular, folklore represents the
subaltern cultures which exist in a state of tension with the hegemonic
culture. Gramsci viewed history as a process whereby a social class attains
a position of dominance economically as well as morally and
intellectually. It acquires the consent of the majority to the general
direction it imposes on society as a result of the self-confidence and
prestige it enjoys through its preeminent role in economic production and
it employs the coercive power of the state to control those who withhold
their consent. Such a dominant class exercises hegemony.[21]

The state has an important role as educator. It has its own worldview
which it considers its duty to impose on all levels of society:

> One of its most important functions is to raise the great mass of the
> population to a particular cultural and moral level, a level (or type) which
> corresponds to the needs of the productive forces for development ...[22]

The dramatic social changes that took place in nineteenth-century
Ireland were conditioned by the same factors which led to the gradual rise
of a Catholic middle class which came to dispute the control of the state
apparatus with the Protestant elite. The Catholic middle class won out
because it managed to rally and mobilize the masses, first on grounds of
religion with the successful campaign for Catholic Emancipation, then on
politico-economic grounds with the campaign for the repeal of the 1801
Act of Union with Great Britain, and later with the movement against the
landlords. "A successful ruling class is one which before actually
obtaining political power has already established its intellectual and moral
leadership."[23] A Catholic nation was consolidated in the process with the
new middle class in the role of its natural leaders. The Famine greatly
eased their task since it got rid of the danger of the landless poor who
threatened class warfare against the Catholic farmers. This large
impoverished rural proletariat was to a considerable extent indifferent to
the Catholic Church whose clergy was mainly drawn from its class
enemies, the farmers, and it had previously shown some interest in
Protestant missionary efforts.

The Catholic middle class which eventually replaced the Protestant
ascendancy over most of Ireland gradually rose to power within the
existing socio-economic and political structures and through assimilating
itself in all but religious denomination and politics to the culture of the
Protestant elite. The Irish Catholicism which developed in the nineteenth
and twentieth centuries was puritanical since its clergy was drawn from a
middle class which consciously modelled itself on the Protestant elite with
its strong Victorian values. Hence, much of the popular religion as
practised by Catholics was felt to be a source of shame and scandal to
them in the eyes of their Protestant neighbors. So wake amusements, the

"patterns" or patron days at the holy wells, and many more activities were roundly condemned.

Sir William Wilde, writing about 1850, quotes a letter written to him by "one of our most learned and observant Roman Catholic friends":

> The tone of society in Ireland is becoming more and more *Protestant* every year; the literature is a Protestant one, and even the priests are becoming more Protestant in their conversation and manners. They have condemned all the holy wells and resorts of pilgrims, with the single exception of Lough Derg, and of this they are ashamed: for, whenever a Protestant goes upon the Island, the ceremonies are stopped![24]

Popular religion declined because the new consciousness which was gradually spreading had no room for it.

In *Irish Popular Superstitions* Wilde wrote with great feeling and sympathy about the devastating changes he witnessed:

> In this state of things, with depopulation the most terrific which any country ever experienced, on the one hand, and the spread of education, and the introduction of railroads, colleges, industrial and other educational schools, on the other—together with the rapid decay of the Irish vernacular, in which most of our legends, romantic tales, ballads, and bardic annals, the vestiges of Pagan rites, and the relics of fairy charms were preserved—can superstition, or if superstitious belief, can superstitious practices continue to exist?[25]

How these changes affected the fairy belief is vividly illustrated by the words of "Darby Doolin, an old Connaughtman of our acquaintance," quoted by Sir William:

> Troth, sir . . . what betune them national boords, and godless colleges, and other sorts of larnin', and the loss of the pratey [potato], and the sickness, and all the people that's goin' to 'Merica, and the crathurs [creatures] that's forced to go into the workhouse, or is dyin' off in the ditches, and the clargy settin' their faces agin them, and tellin' the people not to give in to the likes, sarra wan [none] of the *Gintry* [i.e., the fairies] (cross about us!) 'ill be found in the counthry, nor a word about them or their doin's in no time.[26]

He continues:

> The *good people* are leaving us fast: nobody ever hears now the tic-tac of the *leprechaun* . . . Sure the children wouldn't know anything about the pooca [a mischievous spirit which often took the form of a horse] but for the story of the blackberries after Michaelmas. The warning voice of the *banshee* is mute; for there are but few of the "rale ould stock" [the native aristocracy] to mourn for now; the *sheogue* [fairy] and the *thivish* [ghost]

are every year becoming scarcer; and even the harmless *linane shie* [fairy lover] is not talked about now-a-days, and does not hold discourse with e'er a fairy woman in the whole barony—them that were as plenty as lumpers [a type of potato] afore the yellow male [meal] came amongst us . . .[27]

The belief in fairies declined, along with popular religion generally and other aspects of traditional culture, through the consent of the mass of the people, who accepted the intellectual, moral and political leadership of a class who scorned their culture. The subaltern cultures fell away because the common people came to accept the inferiority of their own culture and the desirability of acquiring high prestige behavioral patterns. The sanctions of the institutions of the civil and political society, which grew greatly in strength and importance, offered a suitable counterweight to any lack of enthusiasm: beatings by the schoolteacher, chastisement by the parish priest, the threat of fines or imprisonment for following traditional customs which could conflict with the law.

Clearly, popular religion did not die out overnight. The more public sources of scandal such as wake amusements and riotous assemblies at holy wells tended to decline more rapidly and more terminally than more private religious practices and a way of thought that can be characterized as mythical. Thus fairy belief declined too, but because of its secretive nature it is more difficult to quantify that decline. The following extracts, all from a collection of Donegal stories collected between 1935 and 1955, emphasize the lessening of belief:

People were afraid of them [the fairies] in bygone times, especially people who were out on the hills late in the evening.[28]

Long ago stones used to fall out of the air, and it was believed that it was the wee folk who threw them down . . . They were called darts, and it was said they were shot at the cattle. . . . There are few of these darts to be seen now since the priests suppressed those of the host who were in the air.[29]

There was much talk about the wee folk long ago, but nowadays there are many young people who do not believe they ever existed.[30]

The women here had a custom long ago if there was a child in the cradle of putting the tongs across the cradle whenever they left the house for fear the wee folk would take the child away.[31]

Long ago when people of this townland went out at night a-visiting they would not leave the house without taking a live ember on a spit. When they had that, there was no danger that the wee folk would make game of them or set them astray as they often did in those days.[32]

It is worth stressing, nevertheless, that the authors of these statements all narrated fairy stories.

What makes the whole question of cultural change more difficult is the fact that an innovation does not necessarily replace another cultural trait. A.M. Cirese has compared the situation of groups who bear popular traditions to bilingualism. Members of such groups participate in the local culture having been socialized into it in the circle of family and friends. But through school, contact with the legal system, membership in churches and so forth they are forced to participate in the official national culture.[33]

The term "diglossia" refers to the phenomenon of a group of people who speak both a local dialect in more intimate and informal situations, and an official national language in more formal and official situations. If diglossia can be part of a community's culture, it stands to reason that a similar dichotomy should be reflected in other cultural spheres, indeed in culture generally, and it is to this that "biculturalism," Cirese's more encompassing term, refers. Thus people can actively participate in the official public life of their church and yet be attached to many forms of popular religion. It is a moot point whether this kind of biculturalism can be long lasting. The evidence of diglossia suggests that the regional dialect will eventually disappear unless it carries some sort of institutionalized national value, as it does, for example, in German-speaking Switzerland or in Luxemburg. As for religious biculturalism it seems clear that it is a transitional phenomenon unless both varieties have high status (as in Japan) or share some other sort of exceptional position (as, for example, the Crypto-Jews of Bukhara). But this is not to award a monopoly of innovation to the high form. Cultural institutions never stand still. There is always a certain tension between the center and the periphery. Some messages may not get through, some may be consciously rejected. Ideas from the periphery may renew, or even destroy, the center.

There is no doubt that the fairy belief survived despite the strengthening of the official church. As late as 1895 the notorious case of Bridget Cleary showed how this belief remained remarkably strong among a Catholic population almost one hundred percent church-going. Bridget Cleary, a twenty-six-year-old woman, lived in Co. Tipperary. In March 1895 she fell ill and was visited by the doctor, who diagnosed bronchial catarrh and nervous excitement. She was also visited by the parish priest, and by the herbalist, who diagnosed her as a changeling and prescribed treatment. Her husband Michael, her father, her aunt, four of her male cousins and two male neighbors tried to force her to drink the cure of milk mixed with herbs. They doused her several times in urine and burned her with a red-hot poker. They asked her if she was Bridget Cleary. She denied that she was a fairy. The following morning the priest said Mass in the house, apparently not noticing that anything was amiss.

Bridget's ordeal continued that evening. This time she was severely burned, and she died from her injuries. They buried her body and spread the story that she had gone away with the fairies. However, two witnesses came forward and gave evidence of what they had seen. The main participants were arrested. One broadside of the period erroneously associated these events with witchcraft.

The Witchcraft Murder,
A Woman Roasted alive in Co. Tipperary.

Composed by Bridget Healy

Within some miles of Clonmel town a horrible deed occurred,
'Twas a murder cruel; and shameful and every heart was stirred,
When the news was spread through the land of the woman's awful fate
She was roasted alive by her nearest friends 'tis awful to relate.

Bridget Cleary was her name her age was 26 years,
She dwelt in a place called Ballyvadeca where she took sick as it appears,
They said she was a fairy a spirit or a witch,
And so they cruelly murdered her and threw her in a ditch.

The night was cold in the month of March she was lying in her bed,
They marked her on the forehead with a poker burning red,
Are you Bridget Cleary they asked her many a time,
She answered yes but they would not stop from doing the awful crime.

They lifted her from off the bed she was in a naked state,
And took her to the kitchen fire and laid her on the grate,
Paraffin oil they threw on her no fear on them, no shame,
And then they burned this poor creature like a Demon in a flame.

They buried her in a lonely place, her husband dug the grave,
And not one there to breathe a prayer for her poor soul to save,
Her grave it was but three feet deep not large enough for a child,
Twas full of water, just near a ditch in a dismal place so wild.

Her father is charged with the crime her husband is also,
Her cousins and also her aunt as the evidence goes to show,
When they finished this cruel murder and thrown her in the grave,
Her husband went distracted this cruel and treacherous knave.

To a fairy fort off he went for he thought his wife was there,
She would be riding a milk white horse guarded by fairies all around,
He was to cut the string that tied her and take her from the ground.

But alas his hopes soon vanished as around him he did stare,
There was the fort but no fairy nor wife was before him there,

Breathe a prayer for her poor soul good christians through the land
An angel bright we hope she is all in that heavenly land.

Some awful torments she did suffer before she met her death,
And her own relations done the deed without the least regret,
The fairy doctor mixed the herbs to be given to a witch,
But they gave them to a christian then roasted her and threw her in a ditch.

May God have mercy on her poor soul every Irish heart will say
And God forgive her murderers all on the Judgement Day.

The participants were tried and sentenced to penal servitude, Michael Cleary to twenty years, the most severe sentence.[34] The background of perceived social values and responsibilities, of marital, sexual and familial conflict, cannot of course be ignored in a case such as this, but it proves the validity of the fairy belief in diagnosing disorder in the individual or in the social body—while at the same time cautioning the romantic against idealizing it; it, too, had its dark side.

Though legends of the fairies can still be heard in Ireland today, few of them are set in very recent times. People do not experience the fairies much any more. What has survived the best is the supernatural aura still held by many to invest the fairy forts, and the belief that damage done to a fort will bring calamity on the perpetrator—which archaeologists acknowledge has preserved so many of the forts for posterity. Nevertheless, increasing numbers of forts are being destroyed by farmers who no longer hold the old beliefs. But the flight from the land, too, as in so many other Western countries, has adversely affected rural values. Rural communities now have little or no cultural or economic autonomy, often providing neither their own food, clothing nor entertainment, and are to an extent merely passive receivers of an international hegemonic or "mass culture," disseminated both from the nearest city and directly through the airwaves. An exaltation of localism, the fairy belief cannot survive in such a climate.

This is not to say that popular religion itself will die out. Modern Marian apparitions show how ancient religious concepts take new forms, and two cases which come to mind, the so-called "moving statues" of Ballinspittle, Co. Cork, in 1985 and the on-going events of Medu Gorje in Yugoslavia, show the same tensions between a skeptical if not downright hostile national Church hierarchy on the one hand and a credulous local clergy close to the people on the other which were already visible in 1771, when Bishop Sweetman announced the regulations quoted above. Many institutions have a similar problem, how to prevent the head from losing contact with the body—the Académie française, for example, trying to expel anglicisms from the spoken language.

But nineteenth and twentieth century Marian apparitions with their apocalyptical messages have tended to take place in more backward and impoverished areas and tend to reflect the uncertainties and stresses of regions whose home grown cultures have been fatally weakened but which have not yet been fully integrated into the life of the modern state. The renewed interest in occultism and the paranormal is of a somewhat different order. It tends to be more of an urban phenomenon and spreads like other elements of modern culture with the help of the media—many bookshops, for example, have sections dealing with astrology, the occult and UFOs. It tends not to be rooted in local conditions, but is rather a facet of a general condition of human alienation in the developed industrial post-Christian world. Astrology "gives meaning to a cosmos regarded by most scientists as the result of blind hazard, and it gives sense to the human existence declared by Sartre to be *de trop.*"[35] UFOs and such parascientific ideas as that of the earth being seeded by extraterrestrial civilizations fulfill the same function of rejecting the arbitrariness of the human condition. In the USSR, the numerous recently reported UFO sightings, the revived interest in all kinds of religion, the renewed appeal of anti-Semitism as a diagnosis for society's ills can be compared to the religious flux of much of nineteenth-century Europe. As Gramsci puts it:

> This means precisely that the great masses have become detached from their traditional ideologies, and no longer believe what they used to believe previously, etc. The crisis consists precisely in the fact that the old is dying and the new cannot be born; in this interregnum a great variety of morbid symptoms appear.[36]

In Ireland, an island on the European periphery, many archaic cultural traits long survived their passing from more central areas. To an extent the country can still be seen as a relic area. The fairy belief has survived for much longer than in most other parts of Western Europe, not because of some sort of "historical viscosity,"[37] but because its function retained its relevance owing to the tardiness of a new consciousness being fully established in Ireland due to the country's peripherality, to the conservatism which was characteristic of post-Famine society (largely peasant proprietors) and to late urbanization and industrialization.

Notes

1. Seán P. Ó Ríordáin, *Antiquities of the Irish Countryside* (London: Methuen, 1965) 1.
2. E. Estyn Evans, *Irish Folk Ways* (London: Routledge and Kegan Paul, 1957) 297.
3. Evans 298.

4. Mircea Eliade, *Lo sagrado y lo profano* (Barcelona: Labor, 1983) 32 and J.M. Lotman, "On the Metalanguage of a Typological Description of Culture," *Semiotica* 14.2 (1975).

5. Diarmuid Ó Giolláin, "Myth and History. Exotic Foreigners in Folk-Belief," *Temenos* 23 (1987).

6. Evans 304.

7. Mircea Eliade, *Patterns in Comparative Religion* (London: Sheed and Ward, 1958) 43.

8. Mircea Eliade, *The Myth of the Eternal Return* (Princeton: Princeton UP, 1971) 97.

9. See S.J. Connolly, *Priests and People in Pre-Famine Ireland 1780–1845* (Dublin and New York: Gill and Macmillan and St. Martin's P, 1982) and Seán Connolly, *Religion and Society in Nineteenth-Century Ireland* (Dundalk: Dundalgan P, 1985).

10. Proinsias Mac Cana, *Celtic Mythology* (London: Hamlyn, 1970) 65.

11. Connolly, *Priests* 112–3.

12. Seán Ó hEochaidh, Máire Mac Néill, Séamus Ó Catháin, *Fairy Legends from Donegal* (Dublin: Comhairle Bhéaloideas Éireann, 1977) 171.

13. Ó hEochaidh, et al. 309–11.

14. Pádraig Ó Milléadha, "Seanchas Sliabh gCua," *Béaloideas* 6.2 (1936): 57–8.

15. Seán Ó Súilleabháin, *Irish Wake Amusements* (Cork: Mercier P, 1967) 146–54.

16. Connolly, *Priests* 94, 96–7.

17. This period is covered in many works. See, for example, Connolly (1982 and 1985), L.M. Cullen, *The Emergence of Modern Ireland 1600–1900* (Dublin: Gill and Macmillan, 1983) and R.F. Foster, *Modern Ireland 1600–1972* (Harmondsworth: Penguin, 1990).

18. Connolly, *Religion* 54.

19. Connolly, *Priests* 112.

20. Antonio Gramsci, *Selections from Cultural Writings*, eds. and trans., David Forgacs and Geoffrey Nowell-Smith (London: Lawrence and Wishart, 1985) 189.

21. Tony Bennett, Graham Martin, Colin Mercer, Janet Woolacott, eds., *Culture, Ideology and Social Process* (London: Batsford, 1981) 197, 199, 213.

22. Gramsci in Bennett et al. 216.

23. James Joll, *Gramsci* (Glasgow: Fontana, 1977) 100.

24. Sir William Wilde, *Irish Popular Superstitions* (Dublin: Irish Academic P, 1979) 17.

25. Wilde 10–1.

26. Wilde 11.

27. Wilde 13.

28. Ó hEochaidh, et al. 37.

29. Ó hEochaidh, et al. 81–3.

30. Ó hEochaidh, et al. 151.

31. Ó hEochaidh, et al. 167.

32. Ó hEochaidh, et al. 325.

33. A.M. Cirese, "Alterità e dislivelli interni di cultural nelle società superiori," *Folklore e antropologia*, ed. A.M. Cirese (Palermo: Palumbo, 1972) 38–9.

34. This infamous case is recounted in Patrick Byrne, *Witchcraft in Ireland* (Cork: Mercier P, 1967) 56–68 and in Richard Jenkins, "Witches and Fairies," *Ulster Folklife* 23 (1977): 46–8 (reprinted in this volume). The text of the entire broadside is quoted from a copy in the Bigger Archive of the Central Reference Library, Belfast.

Special thanks to Colin Neilands, Department of Social Anthropology, The Queen's University of Belfast, for bringing this broadside to my attention. Neilands has examined this and other broadsides in his 1987 thesis, "Irish Broadside Ballads in their Social and Historical Contexts," The Queen's University of Belfast.

35. Mircea Eliade, *Occultism, Witchcraft and Cultural Fashions* (Chicago: U of Chicago P, 1976) 61.

36. Antonio Gramsci, *Selections from Prison Notebooks*, eds. and trans. Quintin Hoare and Geoffrey Nowell-Smith (London: Lawrence and Wishart, 1971) 276.

37. "Les coutumes ne disparaissent ni ne survivent sans raison. Quand elles subsistent, la cause s'en trouve moins dans la viscosité historique que dans la permanence d'une fonction que l'analyse du présent doit permettre de déceler." Claude Lévi-Strauss, quoted in Nicole Belmont, ed., *Arnold van Gennep Textes inédits sur le folklore français contemporain* (Paris: G.P. Maisonneuve et Larose, 1975) 54.

Rites of Passage as Meeting Place: Christianity and Fairylore in Connection with the Unclean Woman and the Unchristened Child

Ann Helene Bolstad Skjelbred

Norwegian fairylore constitutes an important part of the rural oral tradition of pre-industrial Norway. In its way, it mirrors a self-supporting society based on the primary industries of fishing, hunting, farming and animal husbandry. Fairies can be seen as mediators between the powers of nature and humans. Fairylore is based on the principal conception that nature's total resources are limited and that men are entitled to just their share of these resources. Not only did people have to share with each other, but in many cases the resources of nature were understood to belong to other supranormal agents such as the fairies. Humanity, therefore, had to relate to these permanent and omnipresent supranormal agents in all their affairs. The fairy world was believed to be peopled by creatures with many characteristics similar to those of humans, but also some of distinctive difference. Most important was the fairies' inability to obtain salvation (Christiansen ML 5050).

On the whole, the fairies cannot by definition be seen as "good." They acted as good helpers only when people took care to treat them properly. Otherwise, they sought revenge by causing harm mainly to processes of production and reproduction, the areas where people were most vulnerable (on illness see Alver and Selberg). Even without a reason for revenge, the fairies constituted a threat. This we can see for example in connection with critical junctures in the life cycle, among them the "liminal," in-between, transitional periods that occur during an individual's movement from one status to another (van Gennep). As a rule, people were to use protective measures against supranormal agents during such periods. Not to do so was to give the supranormal agents unlimited opportunities to trespass and do harm. It was important to keep up some sort of balance between the fairy world and the world of humans.

The line of balance between humanity and the fairies, also called "the people underground" or "the invisibles," can be interpreted as a culturally defined normative border between the two worlds. To maintain balance was to keep both humans and the supranormal agents on the correct sides of the border. Humans who had achieved this balance controlled their own existence in face of the continuing threats posed by supranormal agents. This balance was achieved through the use of magical rites. By using rites, people communicated with the transcendental world (Honko). Formally, rites are characterized by special words, objects, and prescribed actions, and through the manipulation of these elements people could protect themselves, avert crises, and placate the fairies and other dangerous powers. To do so was of the utmost necessity to secure life and health. In fairylore, rites have been directed toward fairies and have provided visible proof of active fairy belief.

Among the protective, magical elements used in the rites are some derived from Christianity. Elements connected with the church and the servants of the church are incorporated into fairylore. They do not outnumber other elements used in magic, but they can be said to be among the strongest. Their power must be seen in connection with the dominant spiritual role of the church in Norwegian society, where the church, through the sacraments, administers salvation. This is true especially for the sacrament of christening which represents the decisive transition from heathen to Christian. The terms "heathen" and "Christian" also constitute a set of binary oppositions used to characterize two structural categories.

The sacrament of christening, the church's most important rite of passage, plays an important role also in fairylore, especially during the liminal period between separation and incorporation when individuals are temporarily outcast and therefore subject to danger. As an in-between, transitional period, liminality may be considered in terms of "social imbalance." The social imbalance in the case of christening is an imbalance between humanity and the dominating supranormal powers (the fairies), potential harm being directed towards the potential for procreation.

Sometimes a careful analysis of folklore reveals that things are different than they appear on the surface. This may be shown in two examples where a rite of passage and the status "heathen" in some way plays an important part in a complex of tradition. One is the folklore regarding women who have given birth but who have not been through the ceremony of "churching" and therefore, in Norwegian folklore, are characterized as "unclean" or heathen. The other is through the folk tradition concerning the changeling, which in folklore is a fairy child exchanged by the fairies for an unchristened human child. In both cases, the woman and the child are in the liminal period before incorporation. This means that they are without status and therefore in danger. In the case of the woman, she is also considered dangerous to her surroundings. The danger is not, however, represented by the Devil as it is in Christian rites of passage. Instead, the danger in this vulnerable period is posed by the fairies. By this, a stage in a Christian rite of passage is interpreted within the context of a completely different system of belief, namely the belief in the fairies.

The Woman in Confinement

The ceremony of "churching" of women who have given birth has its background in Genesis (3.16) which has been interpreted as meaning that after giving birth a woman is unclean for a certain period and during this period she is prohibited from touching anything holy or from entering the temple. The Christian church, also the State Lutheran Church in the united Denmark-Norway and later in independent Norway, kept up a ceremony of churching by leading the woman who had given birth into church, but with the explanation that it was for praising the Lord and for the sake of virtue. The belief was that during her confinement the woman was not a worthy member of the church, although she was both christened and confirmed. Her status was that of being "outside." In Norway this ceremony was fairly widespread until the end of the nineteenth century and lasted in a few places as long as the 1930s. In the folklore material, the woman is sometimes termed "unclean" or more often "heathen" during the period of "lying in" until she had been churched. The two terms of characterization are not equal or interchangeable and relate to different sets of binary oppositions. This has caused confusion in the understanding of the folklore connected with the custom.

In spite of the fact that the church ceremony has the concept of impurity as its background, the belief that the woman was unclean and therefore dangerous constitutes a small part of the folklore tradition documented in our archives. It is also clear that the belief in sexual impurity has a very weak standing in Norwegian folklore seen totally. Moreover, it has no roots in Norse mythology and life (Steinsland and Vogt).

In most Norwegian folk tradition, the woman in confinement is characterized as heathen. In a Christian frame of reference, the term "heathen" means un-Christian. In Christian faith it follows that to be heathen means to be in danger from the Devil. However, the folk belief has transferred this evil to the fairies, who represent the utmost danger to production and reproduction in cases of imbalance between the fairy world and the world of humans.

The folklore concerning the unchurched woman in memorates and legends describes the danger, the protective means, and the consequences of neglect; it is similar to the folklore concerning the newborn and unchristened child. It was believed that the fairies wanted to harm or to take the woman in the same way they wanted to take the newborn baby.

The means of protection could be bread, light, fire, silver, steel, the Bible, a page from the hymn-book, the sign of the cross and the permanent presence of an adult and confirmed woman. The final and most effective protection, however, was incorporation into the Christian church.

> The woman in confinement was not to be let outside before she had been to church to be christened. Because they believed for sure that she was heathen and prone to be bewitched and harmed by trolls and other such creatures, especially outside the farm. Until she was christened and had given her offerings in church, she had to wear bread, steel and holy words on her as protection. She was also to have an adult person with her as company both indoors and outdoors. (Espeland 9; my translation)

Judging from the frequency of the folklore tradition characterizing the woman in confinement as heathen, one might think this is case of the binary opposition and structural category of heathen versus Christian, and that there is little of importance to conclude from the less frequent usage of "unclean." But the highly valued criterion of frequency can sometimes lead to false conclusions. Because of the weak standing of concepts of impurity within the frames of Norwegian folklore on the whole, the woman's status of being shut out of the Christian community was instead seen as equal to the status of being unchristened, which had a much stronger standing both in Christianity and folklore. In the context of the dominating system of belief, not to be incorporated in the Church meant to be in danger from the fairies.

Within the context of fairylore the expressions of this danger relate to the binary opposition of heathen-Christian which then seems to be the core of the tradition. But there is no sense in characterizing the woman in confinement, already both christened and confirmed, as heathen. In spite of the low frequency of usage, the core of the folk tradition of the unchurched woman must therefore be the binary opposition, unclean versus clean, taken from Judaism and introduced and kept up by the Christian church (Douglas). It is a ritual uncleanness, in folklore expressed as an impurity with consequences for human relations and for the handling of food and livestock. In Norwegian folklore these concepts have made very few impressions and they will not be dealt with here extensively (Skjelbred 1972). But it must be emphasized that the terms "unclean" and "heathen" which we find in folk tradition in connection with the custom of churching of women are concepts belonging to two different sets of binary oppositions and must be judged in their right context.

The Changeling

Oral tradition connected to pregnancy and birth is comprehensive and shows a deep concern for the newborn child and the dangers surrounding it (Skjelbred 1983, 1989; Solheim). The invisible people were believed to want human children and would exchange them for their own offspring. The belief in the changeling is expressed in dites, personal experience narratives (memorates) and legends, including a migratory legend telling of the remarkable age of the changeling (Christiansen ML 5085; see text examples in Kvideland and Sehmsdorf 207–12).

In spite of its dramatic and heartbreaking content, folklore of the changeling has not been subject to extensive analyses. Gisela Piaschewski's study from 1935 is the most extensive on the matter. A rather large chapter on the changeling is included in a Danish folklore study of mother and child (Møller). Likewise, the folklore of the changeling is treated in the monumental five volume study of Norwegian folk medicine (Reichborn-Kjennerud vol. 2; Kvideland and Sehmsdorf 210). Piaschewski's study covers the distribution of the belief in changelings in the northern Germanic area, its names, prohibitive measures to avoid getting one and means to get rid of it. In one chapter Piaschewski looks into connections between folklore and medicine, a line of analysis taken up also by Møller and Reichborn-Kjennerud. While folk belief states how people got a changeling and how they could protect themselves against having their baby exchanged, memorates narrate how a baby was exchanged with a changeling. The migratory legend concentrates on how to reveal the abnormal child as a changeling and thereby get rid of it.

Folklore regarding the changeling is also linked with the church and its rites of passage through the ceremony of christening. Since the newborn child was not yet incorporated into the Christian society, it was considered heathen. This was a consequence of the Christian concept of original sin. During the liminal period before incorporation, the child was a social outcast and as such, unprotected. In folklore, the child was seen as unprotected and in danger from supranormal powers and agents. Once again, these dangers were not represented by the Devil, but the threat was transferred into the context of the belief in the fairies. Accordingly, the newborn child had to be protected against the fairies by, for example, bread, light, fire, silver, steel, and Christian symbols such as the Bible, the hymn-book and the sign of the cross, and by being under constant supervision. The rules of protection were to be observed continually until the baby was christened.

> When a baby was born, a hymn-book and a knife were placed in the cradle until the baby was baptized. If they didn't follow the custom, the

fairies would come and exchange the child. But after the baby was
christened they could remove the hymn-book and the knife. The fairies
could not get to them then. (Langset 127; my translation).

Christening meant incorporation and a termination of the liminal
period. According to folk belief, christening was therefore the most
effective protection against having the baby exchanged with a changeling.
On the surface, the transformation from heathen to Christian seems to be
the core of the folk belief of the changeling, transferred into the context of
fairylore.

Folklore and memorates make it clear that the main causes for an
exchange with a changeling were that people had not been careful enough
in observing the prescribed means to protect the newborn and
unchristened child. The fairies were said to want human children because
they were so much prettier than their own. To be saddled with a
changeling could also be the result of an act of revenge by the fairies, as is
seen in the two migratory legends "Tricking the Fairy Suitor" and "The
Interrupted Fairy Wedding" (Christiansen ML 6000, ML 6005).

The changeling is described as having both abnormal looks and
behavior. It is ugly, black, with an abnormally big head and with a pale,
wrinkled skin as that of an old person. The changeling cries frequently
and is always hungry. It is slow to learn to speak and walk and to keep
itself clean, if it ever reaches such normal stages of development.

Since the fairies had exchanged the human child with a child of their
own, it was up to the fairies to re-exchange the children. To get them to do
that, the changeling was to be treated with such cruelty that the fairies
would take pity on it, retrieve it, and return the human child. Folklore
reveals that the changeling was to be starved, put on the floor to be kicked
and swept off as dirt, beaten (preferably on dung), on three successive
Thursdays, all with the aim of getting the fairies to take their own child
back and give the humans theirs in return.

There are two misleading approaches in analyzing the folklore
tradition concerning the changeling. One is the obvious approach of
looking at this tradition from the angle of medicine. Clearly, there are
traits in our folklore which point to illnesses such as rachitis, mongolism,
malnutrition, chronic diseases, and mental retardation. But when the
folklore on hand is scrutinized in detail (Møller; Reichborn-Kjennerud), it
is extremely difficult to draw conclusions from the singular traits of
description to specific illnesses. It would likewise be wrong to conclude
that the maltreatment of the sick, mentally retarded, and ugly child
springs from a lack of medical knowledge. Moreover, Norwegian folk
medicine tells of no cures against the changeling or that people sought
medical assistance for the changeling. The folklore of the changeling,
therefore, cannot be interpreted within the frame of folk medicine and

definitely not within the frame of scientific medicine. The latter perspective views folk tradition from the angle of natural science and disregards the cultural context of fairylore.

The other misleading approach in analyzing the folklore of the changeling is to connect it with Christian faith and the belief in a protective rite of passage indicating a transmission from the status of heathen to that of Christian, even if folklore itself points in that direction. In a further analysis of the folklore, we find that christening gives no final security against the fairies and their longing for a human child. Numerous personal experience narratives relate how people would find that their child was a changeling long after it was christened. In addition, the ceremony of christening never reverses an exchange.

> Anne was dairymaid at the mountain dairy farm one summer. It so happened that while she was there she gave birth to a boy. One of the servant girls joined her to assist her for a while during the summer. One night the newborn baby just cried and cried. After a while a woman in black entered the cottage carrying a child. Anne was frightened as the woman came over to the bed and touched the child lying there. Then she left. Anne was sure that she still had her own baby, it was so like her own. But after a while the baby became aggressive and difficult to please. They christened the child and took care of it as before. The boy grew up, however, as a fool without learning to speak or anything. He was hunched and ugly and lowed like an ox. (Hermundstad 86–7; my translation).

The human child is beautiful with smooth and light skin. It learns how to walk and eat by itself and at the right stages. Seen in the context of fairylore, the descriptions of the changeling indirectly describe the opposite of a human child. When there seems to be no direct parallel between the details in the descriptions of looks and actions and specific illnesses, mental retardation or illnesses caused by malnutrition, the details per se must be disregarded as less important. Seen totally, however, folklore gives a description of non-humans. In spite of the emphasis laid on the ceremony of the christening and the transmission from heathen to Christian, what we have here is the binary opposition and structural category of non-humans versus humans. The folklore of the changeling is an illustrious example of the social implications of this category—beliefs and actions in connection with what is socially accepted and what is not (Douglas). Since the changeling was not human, but originated from the fairies, it was justified to treat it differently than a human child. Moreover, the ultimate aim was to get rid of the strange child and the desperate hope was to get one's own pretty, normal child back.

Conclusion

Churching of women and christening of the newborn are two different rites of passage administered by the church with incorporation into the Christian society as their goal. In folklore connected with these rites of passage fairylore plays a dominant role in the explanation and legitimation of the ceremonies. Because of its dominance in the folk belief system fairylore may take the focus away from the values presented by the church, as in the case of the churching of women. A rite of passage may obtain a different meaning than the one originally intended by the church. In the case of the changeling and the ceremony of christening, fairylore again shows its dominance over the Christian values presented in the rite of passage. The folklore of the changeling illustrates that it is not the Christian values of heathen versus Christian that are at stake, but a question of being human or not.

Were our forefathers and foremothers of the Norwegian preindustrial society actually Christians? Definitely so, but there has clearly existed two parallel systems of belief. One administered by the church through such sacraments as christening and confirmation and through the teachings in church, home and school. It is a transcendental and vertical system. It makes its imprint on folklore through the use of Christian symbols tied to the faith and to the church and its servants. A close connection between the church and folklore is seen in lore and legends directly derived from Christian faith, for example the belief in the Devil, the Black book and witchcraft. The other belief system is fairylore, a horizontal system of belief for everyday use, closely connected with nature and production and the life cycle's rites of passage and as vital elements. In fairylore, Christianity has a significant role, but it does not constitute the basic motives.

References

Alver, Bente Gullveig, and Torunn Selberg. 1987. "Folk Medicine as Part of a Larger Concept Complex." *ARV* 43: 21–44.

Christiansen, Reidar Th. 1958. *The Migratory Legends. A Proposed List of Types with a Systematic Catalogue of the Norwegian Variants.* Folklore Fellows' Communications 175. Helsinki: Suomalainen Tiedeakatemia.

Douglas, Mary. 1966. *Purity and Danger: An Analysis of the Concepts of Pollution and Taboo.* London: Routledge and Kegan Paul.

Espeland, Anton. 1933. *Segn og soge fraa Hordaland.* Skien: Norli.

Hermundstad, Knut. 1955. *I kveldseta. Gamal Valdreskultur VI.* Norsk Folkeminnelags skrifter 75. Oslo: Norsk Folkeminnelag.

Honko, Lauri. 1976. "Riter: en klassifikation." *Nordisk folktro*. Ed Bengt af Klintberg, et al. Stockholm: Nordiska museet. 71–84.

Kvideland, Reimund, and Henning K. Sehmsdorf, eds. 1987. *Scandinavian Folk Belief and Legend*. Minneapolis: U of Minnesota P.

Langset, Edvard. 1948. *Segner-Gåter-Folketru frå Nordmør*. Norsk Folkeminnelags skrifter 61. Oslo: Norsk Folkeminnelag.

Møller, J.S. 1940. *Moder og Barn i dansk Folkeoverlevering*. Danmarks Folkeminder 48. København: Ejnar Munksgaard.

Piaschewski, Gisela. 1935. *Der Wechselbalg. Ein Beitrag zum Aberglauben der nordeurop ischen Völker*. Deutschkundliche Arbeiten A: 5. Breslau: Maruscke and Berendt.

Reichborn-Kjennerud, Ingjald. 1927–1947. *Vår gamle trolldomsmedisin*. 5 vols. Oslo: I kommission hos Jacob Dybwad.

Skjelbred, Ann Helene Bolstad. 1972. *Uren og hedning. Barselkvinnen i norsk folketradisjon*. Bergen-Oslo-Tromsø: Universitetsforlaget.

———. 1983. *Register til NFL Bind 51-99*. Del 1: Alfabetisk. Norsk Folkeminnelags skrifter. 100 Oslo: Norsk Folkeminnelag/Aschehoug.

———. 1989. *Register til NFL Bind 51-99*. Del 2: Systematisk. Norsk Folkeminnelags skrifter. 100:2. Oslo: Norsk Folkeminnelag/Aschehoug.

Solheim, Svale. 1943. *Register til Norsk Folkeminnelags skrifter Nr.1-49*. Norsk Folkeminnelags skrifter 50. Oslo: Norsk Folkeminnelag.

Steinsland, Gro, and Kari Vogt. 1979. "Den gamle tro." *Norges kulturhistorie*. 1. Ed. Ingrid Semmingsen, et al. Oslo: Aschehoug. 129–62.

van Gennep, Arnold. 1909. *The Rites of Passage*. London: Routledge and Kegan Paul.

III. Physical Disorders:
Changelings and the Blast

Fairy-human encounters often yield bizarre physical consequences, changelings and fairy "blasts" being two of them. And when people communicate, the strange affliction is always grist for the mill of oral tradition. Folklorist Henry Glassie once told me an extraordinary story that he heard from his friend, Peter Flanagan, in Ballymenone, Northern Ireland.

> And Peter described as having seen, not heard about, but having seen a changeling. He described him as strangely and almost impossibly thin, very long feet, very long, thin legs, as though he weighed nothing at all. And he had a very strange appearance of being enormously ancient, despite the fact that he wasn't. That is, it was a man of perhaps thirty years old who would have looked like he was ninety-five. And he sat in the fire, literally in the fire right next to the fire, and played with the stuff in the fire. The fact is, in Peter's lifetime that baby was seen to fly up the chimney and never appear again. So it's the kind of a thing that we'll say well, this is all perfectly silly. But this is a thoroughly intelligent man, grounded in the twentieth century, though a man of very modest economic means, a farm laborer in the north of Ireland. He was not telling of something he'd heard about. He was telling about something he'd seen, and he saw that changeling, and friends of his saw that changeling leave.[1]

In the fall of 1988 a remarkable narrative about the blast was related to me by Patrick Shea of Pouch Cove, Newfoundland.

> This man went over to the post office, using the regular shortcut across the front of our house, but coming back from the post office, he kept down below in this marsh. And halfway across he got a jab in the left leg, in the calf of the left leg, sort of like something jabbed him. Well, he went on home and it felt troublesome and so on and so forth. It felt troublesome, felt troublesome. And 'twas beginning to protrude, expand, turn black up to the knee and down to the ankle, and they got a doctor in. And the doctor cut this open and out comes little bunches of grass and little splinters of wood, out of this man's leg. There was so much damage done, they cut the man's leg off up to the knee. Now, I was fourteen years

of age and never allowed to go down there, and this "blast" thing was
after coming on the marsh.[2]

What is one to make of unsightly, exchanged children who fly up
chimneys? How does one grapple with grass and wood coming out of a
man's leg? Ethnographic, humanistic folklorists such as Glassie, attempt to
put their ethnocentric biases (e.g., "scientific truth") aside, in order to
sympathetically learn from informants and appreciate their culture and
worldview. Given such a posture, the cultural truth of changelings is
inviolable.

There are other perspectives, however. Changeling fairylore also has
much to offer public sector folklorists, medical specialists, social workers
and others who are sensitive to what these folkloric forms reveal about
attitudes towards disability, not only for the sake of understanding
regional tradition, but to meet the *contemporary needs* of parents and
children in similar or analogous circumstances. Susan Schoon Eberly and
Joyce Underwood Munro have written their essays in this spirit. For
Eberly, who is employed in the field of public health, traditional
descriptions of changelings, solitary fairies, and the progeny of human-
fairy unions, "seem to be folk explanations" of disabled children with
"identifiable congenital disorders," and she documents her hypothesis
with striking folkloric evidence. Munro employs Michel Foucault's
concept of the "medical gaze" in tracing the history of the medical idea of
"failure to thrive" in infants and compares that concept with traditional
changeling accounts. She finds that medical discourse and folk tradition
have shared "attribution of the cause of the phenomenon to the invisible."
Folk tradition has designated the supernatural culpable while medical
discourse has assigned such conditions, "with a sense of wonder," to
"maternal deprivation."

In contrast to Eberly and Munro, Barbara Rieti does not believe that
"folk explanation" in the absence of medical diagnosis can account for the
living narrative traditions about fairy "blasts" in Newfoundland,
especially because "medical consultation may figure in the narrative" (as
above). Instead, she convincingly argues that such Newfoundland
narratives respond to a nature (fairies) versus culture problematic.

Notes

1. Peter Narváez, "The Fairy Faith," *Ideas*, CBC Transcripts No. 11-293
(Montreal: Canadian Broadcasting Corporation, June 29, 1989) 4. Also see references
to Peter Flanagan in Henry Glassie, *Passing the Time in Ballymenone* (Philadelphia: U
of Pennsylvania P, 1982).
    2. Narváez 8.

Fairies and the Folklore of Disability: Changelings, Hybrids, and the Solitary Fairy

Susan Schoon Eberly

In attempting to trace the origins of fairy belief, scholars have interpreted the "Good People" as deified ancestors, nature spirits, descriptions of aboriginal races, half-remembered gods, and/or spirits of the dead. Reidar Christiansen, in *Hereditas*, expresses the notion that fairy belief arose in answer to some of the more puzzling of life's mysteries—the questions of the "untimely death of young people, of mysterious epidemics among cattle, of climatic disaster, of both wasting diseases and strokes, of infantile paralysis and of the birth of mongol [Down's syndrome] and otherwise deficient children."[1] Spence echoes this interpretation in his discussion of the fairy changeling: "Whenever a diseased or cretinous child made its appearance in a family, it was usually regarded as a changeling. . . . The individual case was made to fit the superstition and thus we possess no standardized data respecting the appearance of a changeling. . . ."[2]

Various aspects of fairy belief which seem to be folk explanations of the birth of children with disabilities are discussed in this paper. Specific examples of changelings, solitary fairies—both domesticated and reclusive—and of the offspring of fairy-human matings are presented that seem to offer portraits of children who were born, or who became, different as the result of identifiable congenital disorders.

In many cases, Spence's contention that "we possess no data respecting the precise appearance of the changeling" is true, but in other cases—and often, in the general "ethnic" representation of the changeling—the descriptions are somewhat standardized. Indeed, Spence himself presents a bit of standardization when he quotes Campbell's statement that a Highland changeling is recognizable by its "large teeth, inordinate appetite, fondness for music, its powers of dancing, its unnatural precocity. . ." Spence goes on to state that in Germany, the changeling is known by its large, heavy head and its thick neck.[3] In other words, some patterns of appearance, behavior, and character were recognized. We will return to these patterns, after a brief review of the history of human response to congenital disorders.

History

The more visible of these disorders, those birth defects that are immediately apparent when a child is born, have produced feelings of fear and awe since earliest times. Children born with major physical disorders have evoked a religious response since at least as early as 2000 B.C., when some sixty-two birth defects—whose appearance among Assyrian newborns was painstakingly examined and interpreted by professional soothsayers—were described on clay tablets found in the library of Ninevah. For example,

> When a woman gives birth to an infant . . . whose nostrils are absent, the country will be in affliction and the house will be destroyed . . . to an infant who has no fingers, the town will have no births . . . [4]

In Rome, hermaphroditic children were summarily dispatched; other children with visible disorders were particularly valued for sacrifice in times of emergency.[5] Indeed, the old term for children born with marked deformities was *monster*, a word derived from the Latin *monstrum*, something marvelous, originally a divine portent or warning. Monstrous children were sometimes deified, as in the case of the Egyptian god Ptah, an achondroplastic dwarf, or the cyclopic Greek Polyphemus.[6]

This belief in the supernatural nature of the child born with a congenital disorder continued through the Middle Ages and into the Reformation, when Martin Luther himself coauthored, in 1523, a publication that interpreted the political significance "assigned from God" of a malformed fetus found floating in the Tiber.[7]

Congenital disorders that are not immediately visible,[8] but whose effects become apparent over time, often produced individuals who evoked a similar, though more subdued, response of mingled fear and awe. For example, *cretins*—persons born without any visible disorder, but who develop mental retardation and who may become physically deformed due to thyroid deficiency disease (hypothyroidism), may have been given the name cretin—from *Chretien*, Christian—in reference to the belief that they were "God's children."[9] In some parts of Switzerland, where this disorder was once endemic, it was believed that cretins brought luck to the community by serving as scapegoats, drawing God's wrath onto themselves alone.[10] In this context, it is relevant to note that in Berwickshire it was said that the Brownie was the "appointed servant of mankind to ease the weight of Adam's curse."[11] The luck that the Brownie brought to the house or farm it inhabited is well-known.

Other terms for persons who are mentally or physically disabled—the Irish *amadan* (God's fool), the moon-touched *lunatic* and the *mooncalf*, the *oaf* (from ON *elvr* or elf), or the person who has been (divinely or demoniacally) "touched"—reflect this belief in the special nature of such "different" persons.

Psychogenicity and Supernatural Intervention

A very brief look at the reactions, through history, of western Europeans to the birth of individual, atypical children lays the groundwork for the further examination of the relationship between these reactions and certain facets of fairylore. Warkany, in his history of societal response to children who are born different, wrote in 1951:

> The ancient history of teratology does not teach us much about the origin, prevention, or treatment of congenital malformation; but it tells us a great deal about the human mind and its reactions to unexplained phenomena. If an abnormal child is born to a family or a tribe, [a person] insists upon an explanation. . . . Considering the millennia of observations, explanations have been relatively few and most of the theories of the past are now considered superstitions. Knowledge of the old and deep-rooted superstitions is of some practical importance since ancient beliefs often plague parents even today, as they interpret [the births of atypical children] as portents or punishments.[12]

In the case of congenital disorders, the human mind in earlier times reacted by formulating two primary and often overlapping theories of causation. The first focuses on the thoughts, conscious and unconscious, of the mother during pregnancy. Maternal impressions and responses were held to produce certain clearly identifiable, "psychogenic" effects upon the unborn child. For example, the pregnant woman who was impressed or frightened by the gibbons at the zoo might give birth to a child with anencephaly, whose head appeared to be monkey-like.[13]

A variation on this theory of psychogenicity involved the breaking of a taboo by the mother, as in the case of the Scottish woman who refused food to a needy neighbor who had come begging. Six months later, the ungenerous woman gave birth to a child who had no mouth.[14] If this mother realized and felt guilty about her breach of hospitality, a believer in psychogenicity might posit that her conscious or unconscious sense of guilt led to the defect in her child.

If, however, the child's disability is viewed as the result of divine or supernatural vengeance delivered to rebuke the mother's stinginess, then we have entered the realm of the second group of theories about the causation of congenital disorders, which state that these disorders are caused by supernatural intervention of one sort or another. According to one interpretation of this supernatural intervention, a parent's sin, such as that of the ungenerous woman, might result in divine chastisement in the form of an ill or disabled child. This motif of active, supernatural vengeance is, however, surprisingly rare in the literature of the changeling. Perhaps this rationale became more common with the growing influence of the Christian church. As Chamberlain writes in *Old Wive's Tales*, "Under Christianity, sickness now became evidence of the power and justice of a beneficent God . . . Sickness . . . was the result of sin, and healing a matter of forgiveness."[15]

Of course, insofar as changelings are concerned, supernatural intervention could occur in a most obvious and active form, childnapping, with the changeling left to take the place of the child stolen by the fairies. Some of these change-children were active, if unattractive, little beings. Others were "stocks"; immobile, wooden, doll-like beings who soon lost all semblance of life.

Warkany calls another variety of supernatural intervention *hybridity*,[16] the belief that human beings can, and frequently do, have sexual relationships with non-human beings to produce offspring. One form of hybridity involves human pairings with supernatural partners—gods, devils, incubi and succubi, fairies, and so forth. Often the supernatural parent eventually stakes some claim over his or her child, as in the case of the silkie who returned to an earthly *nourrice*[17] to reclaim his son. The children of these unions traditionally bore a special sign of their unusual parentage—webbed fingers or scaly skin, for example. We will return to these unusual children later.

A second variation on the theme of hybridity involves the more mundane pairing of humans with animals (although the animals in question often have supernatural associations), to produce offspring. According to folk belief, children born to these pairings are also often marked in some way. A child born with a cleft lip, for example, might be viewed as the offspring of a human mother and a father who was a cat or a hare (or a "familiar" in the form of one of these animals). The fact that both the cat and the hare have specifically come to be identified as witches' familiars may have some relationship to the frequency with which cleft lip/palate disorders occur.

When the Christian church began to interpret the birth of offspring with congenital disorders as a sign of supernatural—and demonic—intervention, both men and women had reason to fear for their lives if they parented, or were even in the vicinity upon the birth of atypical newborns, human or animal. In Puritan New England in 1642, a young hired man was convicted of consorting with the devil and was executed, when a sow bore a cyclopic—one-eyed—piglet. In Denmark as late as 1683, a young mother was burned at the stake for giving birth to a child who was, in all probability, anencephalic—born with an incomplete brain and a malformed skull.[18]

The child who survived infancy in spite of a severe mental or physical disorder might also be viewed as evil. Martin Luther labeled one child with severe retardation as no more than a *massa carnis*, a soulless mass of flesh and went so far as to recommend that the child be disposed of by drowning.[19] In the lore of the changeling, however, the "inhuman" or "demonic" nature of the child did not call forth a uniformly negative response, although, as we shall see, some of the techniques used to reveal the "true nature" of the change-child were at least as inhumane as Luther's suggested solution.

Components of the Process of Grieving

In the past, as now, the birth of a child was a remarkable event for both the family and the community. The actual time of birthing was seen as fraught with dangers, physical as well as spiritual, no doubt because death in childbed was so common. In medieval days in much of western Europe, women who had just borne a child were not allowed to attend church until a specified amount of time had passed,[20] and

> Lady Wilde remarks that "Until a woman has gone through the ceremony of churching, after the birth of her child, she is the most dangerous being on earth. No one should eat food from her hand, and myriads of demons are always around her trying to do harm, until the priest comes and sprinkles holy water over her."[21]

Placental blood was believed to be unclean and to attract devils. In many places, a woman who died while carrying a child could not be buried in holy ground because of the unchristened soul she carried in her womb.[22] Yeats wrote that in Ireland, very young children were believed to have "weak spirits" that were hard put to defend themselves against the devils that hovered everywhere. To protect the soul of a newborn who had died, the blood of a freshly killed cock was sprinkled on the doorstep to waylay the demons.[23] Other birthing customs further reflect this concern with protecting the fragile soul of the child, fending off the supernatural child stealers who could come down chimneys or through unguarded doorways; and with defending the mother, in her physically weakened and spiritually vulnerable state, from similar dangers.

When, in spite of all precautions, a child was born with a visible difference, or began to sicken and change, the parents met this with a process of grieving that has remained constant over the centuries. Writing of changelings, Briggs speaks of the despair felt when the ". . . coveted human baby was taken."[24] Commenting on the reactions of twentieth-century parents following the birth of a baby with a congenital disorder, a pediatrician says, "After the birth of a defective child, parents mourn the loss of the wished-for child . . ."[25] and another physician, referring to this "wished-for child," says the parents grieve "for a dream."[26]

The components of the grieving process are well-known to clinical practice and are seen as well in many of the changeling tales.[27] First, there is a time of rejection, of denial; the patterns this denial takes are repeated in tale after tale. Evans-Wentz tells of a family near Breage Church in Cornwall, in which there was

> . . . a fine baby girl . . . and the piskies came and took it and put a withered child in its place. The withered child lived to be 20 years old, and was no larger when it died than when the piskies brought it. It was fretful and peevish and frightfully shriveled.[28]

The message of this and other tales like it is clear: this can't be our child—our child was stolen away.

As the grieving process continues, denial phases into guilt, often mingled with anger. In the changeling tales, this anger may be directed at the child in a very physical way. Often it is rationalized into an attempt to either force the changeling to reveal its true nature, or to force its fairy parents to return the stolen human child. Hartland records that a family could recover the human child by making the changeling cry, by dumping it from its cradle and sweeping it out the door, by leaving it on a dung heap or in a newly-dug grave.[29] Briggs notes that the Welsh change-child would reveal its true nature if set on a heated shovel, or bathed in a potentially lethal solution (due to the digitalin) of steeped foxglove leaves.[30] In Caerlaverock:

> A fine child was observed on the second day after its birth, and before it was baptized, to have become quite ill-favored and deformed. Its yelling every night deprived the whole family of rest; it bit and tore at its mother's breasts, and would lie still neither in cradle nor the arms.[31]

Its fairy nature was "revealed" when it was thrown into a bed of glowing coals.

In the Hebrides, the changeling was left below the high water mark on the beach when the tide was out. When the child's crying was no longer heard, one could assume either that the tide had come in, or that the changeling had fled.[32]

Often, these methods of revealing the true nature of the changeling were little more than socially countenanced forms of infanticide. The tale of Yallery Brown may in fact describe a child left to die.

> Yallery Brown was found under the Stranger's Stone by Tom Tiver . . . [he] was no bigger than a year-old baby, with long cotted hair and beard twisted around its body. The hair and beard were gold, and

soft as thistledown, but its face was brown as the earth, and just a heap of wrinkles with two bright eyne in the midst.[33]

This strange little creature offers Tom Tiver a gift, but ultimately gives a curse, which perhaps reflects the harm that can befall someone who responds inappropriately to the different beings among us:

For harm and mischance and Yallery Brown
Thou'st let out for thyself from under the stone.

Finally, there is the third stage in the psychological process of grieving, that of acceptance. There is, in the words of one psychologist, a "re-presentation" of the newborn, in which the "abnormal child [becomes] an acceptable but different substitute for the lost normal baby."[34] Such acceptance is hinted at in the lore of the changelings, though rarely, as in this account of one such "substitute" for the lost normal baby:

Nothing under heaven could have had a more beautiful face . . . [but] he could not move so much as one joint . . . he was seldom seen to smile, but if anyone called him a fairy-elf, he would frown and fix his eyes earnestly on those who said it, as if he would look them through.[35]

Many of these tales deal with the first stage of grief, that of denial. Other tales, with their accounts of heated shovels, dung heaps, deserted beaches and empty graves, take us well into the guilt and anger of the second stage. Only a very few bring us nearer the stage of acceptance that is hinted at above, perhaps because for many of these little change-children, acceptance would be preceded by the child's natural or unnatural death and the parents would comfort themselves by recalling tales of other families who had also lost beloved children to the fairies.

Unbaptized Babes and Flickering Fairies

It is interesting to note that when an infant died before it had gained full entry into the human race through the rituals of naming and baptism,[36] it might in folk belief be transformed into a species of fairy known variously as pixie, Will-O-the-Wisp, Spunky, Taran, or Short Hoggers—little fay folk associated with mysterious, flickering lights and with lonely, out of the way places. For example, Briggs tells us that it was believed "all over the West County [of Britain] that they [pixies] are the souls of unbaptized children."[37]

Both pixies and the Will-O-the-Wisp,[38] another fay creature believed to be the soul of an unchristened babe, are connected with wayward lights that confuse and mislead travelers. In Lowland Scotland, Spunkies[39] are members of the same tribe of fairies and their name, derived as it is from the glowing "punk" used to ignite fires, suggests again the mysterious, flickering lights. The Tarans, of northeastern Scotland, flit through the dark woods, moaning and crying their unbaptized state.[40] Another fairy of this sort, found near Whittinghame and also in search of a name that no christening had provided, was dubbed "Short Hoggers"—dialect for "Baby Booties"—by a passerby with a kind heart.[41]

Characteristics of the Change-Child

Not all changelings died in infancy, however. In a number of tales from Britain and Ireland, the changeling is portrayed as an adult or even elderly character who must be tricked into revealing his age and who gives away his maturity when he plays the pipes or dances to a wild tune, addresses someone with a poem, or exhibits supernatural powers. A prodigious eater, constantly hungry and continuously demanding food— "Johnny was aye greeting and never growing"[42]—the changeling is nonetheless undersized and sickly. He frequently has unusual features— misshapen limbs, an oversize head, slowness in learning to walk. He rarely sings or smiles or—that most human of all behaviors —talks:

> Mentally retarded children were thus clearly taken for changelings, particularly [children] with hydrocephalus and cretinism. What caused special comment was the fact that they did not laugh or talk. This was interpreted, however, in the way of some modern mothers when they say ambiguously: "My child just won't talk." The changeling deliberately refrained from laughing and talking. If it could be tricked into laughing or talking, then the spell was broken and it was changed into the right child. Its non-responsiveness or its inappropriate behavior were taken to be signs of obstinacy and spite. . . . All the time it dissimulated simply to annoy people.[43]

Most often, as Briggs points out, the changeling is substituted for a boy child.[44] In addition to the characteristics of the changeling given above (characteristics taken more or less directly from the index of folk motifs), other common traits can be identified. Changelings often do not walk, run, or dance unless they think they will not be observed. Most are very small for their age; they may have unusual eyes, ears, and/or hands. They are described in many cases as wizened, with dark wrinkled skin. They frequently cry at all hours of the day and night; in some tales, the sound of their cry itself is unusual.

Congenital Disorders and Changeling Traits

An overview of congenital disorders found in newborns will provide some interesting points of comparison and we will come to that later. But how likely is it that the children/changelings presented in these tales could actually have had congenital disorders? How common are such birth defects?

At the present time, more than 2300 human genetic disorders are known to medical science.[45] Add to these the disorders caused by prenatal infection, such as rubella or syphilis; the metabolic dysfunctions such as hypothyroidism; the physically caused disorders, such as those due to maternal hypothermia (prolonged exposure to cold) or uterine malformation; and the disorders caused by unknown factors (by far the largest category); and the result is that today "an anomalous baby is born somewhere in the world every 30 seconds."[46] Put another way, today about one baby in twenty is born with a congenital anomaly;[47] about one in ten is either born with, or will acquire, a physical, mental, or sensory impairment that will interfere with normal development.[48]

Boys are much more likely than girls to be born with a congenital disorder; one authority says that for most developmental disabilities, three to four boys will be affected for each girl with a disorder.[49] This relationship is reflected in the lore of the changeling, the great majority of whom, as Briggs noted, are male.

Included among the traits most commonly found with the various congenital disorders is failure to thrive, which is linked to delayed mental and physical growth and to delayed development in general (slowness to walk, talk, and perform other "milestone" behaviors at an appropriate age). In changeling lore, we see again and again the "little, wizened boy . . . it never grew. . . ."[50]

Mental retardation is found with many congenital disorders; it can result from central nervous system damage (as with spina bifida), or from problems such as hypoxia—lack of oxygen during birth; and it can also be caused by a number of other factors, such as disease, malnutrition, poisoning, suffocation, or near drowning. Severe retardation will often prevent the development of speech.

Central nervous system disorders are among the more common of congenital disorders and spina bifida, the most common of the central nervous system disorders, occurs today in about 1:1000 births in the U.S. and in about 4-5:1000 births in the U.K.[51] Hydrocephaly, or "water on the brain," found in roughly 80% of all cases of spina bifida, is probably the disorder described in changelings with oversized heads. It occurs when a structural malformation causes fluid to be trapped inside the cavities of the brain. The increasing pressure exerted by the trapped fluid causes the skull to enlarge; untreated, the condition can result in retardation, brain damage, and paralysis. Spina bifida, with or without hydrocephalus, also causes varying degrees of paralysis.[52]

Cerebral palsy, which results from damage to the brain, occurred in the U.S. in 1962 at a rate of about 6:1000 live births;[53] because it is sometimes related to problems occurring during childbirth, or from poor prenatal care, it may have been more common before the advent of modern medicine. Cerebral palsy causes the loss of control of various groups of muscles; the degree of muscle involvement will depend upon the location and degree of damage to the brain. In some cases, cerebral palsy leads to slow, sinuous, rhythmic, involuntary movement of the hands, limbs, and/or trunk. In other cases, motion will be jerky or spasmodic. Both types of involuntary movement may be present in one person. It is just possible that the "wild dance" of the changeling may in fact describe the movements of a person with severe cerebral palsy. Because muscular balance is disrupted in cerebral palsy, serious deformity can result due to powerful, uneven muscle contractions that exert uneven pressure on the bones of the torso and limbs.

Unusually shaped limbs are also symptomatic of a variety of other congenital disorders; the dwarfing syndromes are the first that come to mind. Marfan's syndrome is characterized by very long, slender, "arachnoid" digits and limbs; osteogenesis or "brittle bones" syndrome results in bones which break easily and mend poorly.

Large or oddly placed ears are also found in a number of congenital disorders; "oriental" or "Mongolian" eyes (having epicanthic folds) and eyes with an "anti-Mongoloid" or downward tilt, are also syndrome-specific. Sallow skin may result from Rh disease or from jaundice; aged-appearing, wrinkled skin is found with syndromes like progeria that actually lead to premature aging and is also—and this is no doubt more relevant—characteristic of very small, very ill, and premature babies who have little subcutaneous body fat.

The irritability, constant crying, and ravenous appetite of the changeling can be explained by looking at those disorders that prevent the infant from gaining nourishment from the food it eats. Physiological malformation, such as blind esophagus, cleft palate, and blockage of the small intestine can physically inhibit digestion. Metabolic disorders such as homocystinuria and phenylketonuria (PKU) prevent a child from metabolizing essential nutrients. With galactosemia, a child cannot digest milk. Cystic fibrosis, the most common inherited disorder in Caucasians (one person in 2000 carries the gene),[54] inhibits the body's ability to utilize proteins—resulting in ravenous appetite, severely retarded growth, and often death before the age of twenty.

Particularly among those disorders that are genetically based, we find groups of unrelated children who bear a strong resemblance to one another. The best known example is the child born with Down's syndrome, whose round face, flattened occiput, Mongolian eyes, small size, and mental retardation are familiar to most of us. Other syndromes also produce children who often bear a stronger resemblance to one another than to parents, siblings, or kin. Children with William's syndrome (hypercalcemia, or "Elfin facies" syndrome) are unusually pretty children:

> Patients with this syndrome have elfin facies [features]. The face is memorable . . . the forehead is prominent. Hypertelorism [widely spaced eyes] and prominent epicanthal folds are frequently seen . . . The nose is short and upturned . . . the ears often large and low set, and the [jaw] is small. The chin may appear pointed . . . The upper lip may form a bow, especially in infancy. The smile . . . is worth emphasis. We have had the experience of looking at a child but not yet appreciating what syndrome was [involved], when all of a sudden the child smiled, and it hit us that this was the hypercalcemia syndrome.[55]

Also associated with this syndrome is short stature, heart disease, mental retardation, a low, hoarse voice and a friendly, open disposition described in the literature as a "cocktail party manner."[56]

Children born with Hunter's, or the related Hurler's, syndromes, present a marked contrast to the bright-eyed, friendly children described above. Once said to have "gargoylism," these children appear to be normal at birth. Over time they become heavy browed, their jaws become squared and thick and they develop coarse hair over much of their bodies. Their eyes protrude, their hands become clawed, they breathe hoarsely, and they may become humpbacked. Here, again, temperament is affected. Children with Hurler's syndrome are usually pleasant and affectionate; those with Hunter's syndrome are hyperactive, noisy, rough, and aggressive. Mentally, these children develop normally until they are about two years old; then their mental acuity begins to deteriorate steadily.[57]

There is also a marked superficial resemblance among children who have a number of different genetic syndromes, so that children with Hunter's, Hurler's, Sanfillipo's, Morquio's, Ullrich's, and Scheie's syndromes may resemble one another. The dwarfing syndromes, because of the ways they affect bone growth, likewise lead to individuals who often look alike. Perhaps it was in drawing conclusions about the similarities among such "different" children that people arrived at their descriptions of some of the fairy "races."

It is easy to see that the descriptions of dwarves in folklore draw heavily upon the human experience of individuals with congenital dwarfism; it is likely that the descriptions of those fairy races who left changelings for humans to ponder were similarly based upon human observation, for the birth of "different" children, then as now, was an ongoing part of community life. Many of the tales of "midwives to the fairies," when they describe the "reality" seen by the human midwife after rubbing the fairy ointment into her eye, generalize from the infant's appearance to that of other members of the fairy group. In one tale, the handsome fairy family is transformed; the fairy baby "still maintained the elfish cast of the eye, like his father . . ." and the other children became "a couple of little, flat-nosed imps . . . with mops and mows . . . scratching their own polls . . . with their long and hairy paws"; the father is described as a "strange, squint-eyed, little, ugly, old fellow."[58]

A final generalization that can be made about congenital disorders and their relationship to theories about the nature and motivations of the fairy folk relates to sexual development. A number of the genetic syndromes hinder normal sexual development, so that children having these syndromes will never truly mature.[59] In other disorders, sexual development will occur at an abnormally early age. Perhaps these patterns of atypical—and often infertile—development are the basis for the folklore explanations of fairy barrenness as the motivation for stealing human children. If the changelings "substituted" for human children were regularly observed to follow an unusual pattern of sexual development, perhaps this observation was then generalized to include the "parents" of the fairy child as well and from them to fairies in general. As Briggs wrote, "fairies seem to have been shy breeders, in spite of their interest in fertility."[60]

It would seem, then, that many of the traits most generally ascribed to changelings are also traits found in a wide range of birth disorders. A large or unusually shaped head occurs with such relatively common congenital disorders as hydrocephalus, fetal toxoplasmosis, Down's syndrome, and the dwarfing syndromes.

Traits that are linked—ravenous appetite, irritability, failure to thrive, small size—are logically associated with infectious illness (such as the "wasting diseases" most frequently cited in this context, polio and tuberculosis) and with a range of disorders that effect a child's ability to properly digest food.

Unusual, often characteristic vocalization is associated with a number of syndromes, the most obvious being *Cri-du-chat*, or Cat's cry syndrome, in which a very early symptom is the mewing cry of the very young baby.[61] Inability to speak may result from severe brain damage, from deafness, or from mental retardation, whatever the etiology. Paralysis, most clearly a factor when the changeling is a "stock," may result from brain damage or other central nervous system damage.

Music is often associated with the covert activities of the changeling. In this context it is interesting to note that the characteristic skills of the "savant" syndrome, in which a person with severe mental retardation is exceptionally good at a single, highly focused skill, are listed as being music, mathematics, and rote memory.[62] As stated earlier, the "dance" of the changeling may in fact be the involuntary movements found with cerebral palsy. Rhyming, echolalia, stereotypy—patterns of repetitive speech that are symptomatic of autism, DeLange syndrome, hypercalcemia, and PKU—may account for the "poetry" of the change-child who can speak.

Finally, the withered appearance of the changeling so frequently commented upon in these tales may simply be the appearance of a very ill infant, or it may be the result of specific disorders that actually affect the thickness and pigmentation of the skin. We have, then, the change-child: "an ancient, withered fairy ... wawling and crying for food and attention ... in an apparent state of paralysis."[63]

Three Examples

These observations suggest a strong relationship between changeling lore and children born with congenital disorders. In some cases, more specific comparisons are possible and the fairy individuals now to be considered include not only the changeling, but also the offspring of human-fairy parents, solitary fairies of the domestic sort, and their more reclusive kin, the solitary "nature" fairy.

The number of changelings in the stories that can be tenuously linked to specific congenital birth disorders, on the basis of one or two symptoms and a good guess, are many. Fairy tales that seem to describe specific disorders in clear detail are, as one would expect, much less frequent. In my research (which, I should add, has been far from exhaustive), I have found several examples that seem to me to be convincing; examples in which the symptoms described point to specific disorders. The first of these deals with a particular trait found in many different changeling stories. It is for this reason the most general of these comparisons.

PKU is an inherited metabolic disease that is carried by about one person in seventy and occurs today in the U.S. at a ratio of about 1:10,000–20,000.[64] When two parents who carry the disease produce a child with PKU, the child will appear to be normal at birth. A large proportion of the children born with PKU appear to be light-skinned, light-haired, and blue-eyed.

A common early symptom of PKU is vomiting; because the child cannot metabolize certain essential amino acids, malnutrition occurs. By the time the baby is six months old, symptoms may include seizures, tremors, hyperactivity, and extreme irritability. The child will grow very slowly and will, if left untreated, become severely mentally retarded. Its voice will become characteristically whiny; its odor, distinctly mousy. Microcephaly sometimes occurs and cerebral palsy develops in about one-third of all cases. Longevity is, however, normal. Most children who develop PKU are of English or Irish ancestry; today, diet therapy can prevent the disease from progressing if treatment begins early enough.[65] Now consider, for a moment, the preference of certain of the fairy races for the child who is blonde: "the fairies steal nice, blonde babies, they usually place in their stead their own aged-looking brats with short legs, sallow skins, and squeaky voices . . ." says Rhŷs.[66] ". . . [The fairies] all set great store by golden hair in mortals. A golden-haired child was in far more danger of being stolen than a dark-haired one," writes Briggs.[67] Spence reports that "The late Sir John Rhŷs was told that the Welsh fairies had a hankering after 'the sort of children that were unlike their own; that is, bairns whose hair was white, or inclined to yellow, and whose skin was fair.'"[68] Perhaps this tradition of fairy preference for blonde babies is a recognition of the link between fair-haired children and frailty; the sort of recognition that might occur in response to the birth of children with PKU, a disorder often associated with a light complexion and fair hair.

While PKU is relatively common, as congenital errors of the metabolic system go, the syndrome discerned in the tale of "Yallery Brown" is far less frequent. Yallery Brown, "no bigger than a year-old baby," with his long golden hair "soft as thistledown" and his face wrinkled and brown as the earth, presents several symptoms of the syndrome known as progeria.

As with PKU, an infant with progeria appears normal at birth, or may show no more symptoms than a slight thickening of the skin. After a few months, the features of the child will begin to develop an aged look, with a high, prominent forehead, protruding eyes, a small mouth and a receding jaw, and a very small, pinched nose. The skin becomes stiff and dry, losing its elasticity; it hangs loosely on the body, as wrinkled as the skin of a very aged person and it develops a characteristic brown mottling. The hairline is very high and the hair very fine and sparse. The child will remain small and will begin to look gaunt, for little subcutaneous fat is present to soften its appearance. When the child begins to walk, its posture will be stooped, its shoulders narrow. The child's muscles will be wasted, its joints large and stiff. The voice will be high and piping; the name "Yallery," perhaps from the OE *galan*, to sing, may reflect this vocal tone.[69] Speech develops normally, as does intelligence.

Children with progeria, which occurs only in one of every eight million births, will never grow much larger than a five-year-old; though they age rapidly and prematurely, they never become sexually mature. A child with progeria will rarely live beyond adolescence. Death is usually due to the onset, before the age of ten in most cases, of angina pectoris with atherosclerosis—heart disease.[70]

Yallery Brown, tiny and ancient looking with his fine hair and his brown skin, physically resembles a child with progeria. His ability to speak and his intelligence—however malicious—point to no loss of mental acuity. Perhaps, as his health worsened, his parents left him in a sacred place, by the "Stranger's Stone," in the hope that he might be "taken back" by his fairy family and their own "human" child returned.

Evans-Wentz writes of another changeling whose description makes it possible to venture a guess at the disorder involved.

> In place o' her ain bonnie bairn, she found a withered wolron, naething but skin and bane, wi' hands like a moudiwort, and a face like a paddock, a mouth frae lug to lug, and twa great glowerin' een . . . a daft-like bairn . . . it was ay yammerin and greetin, but never mintet to speak a word . . . it couldna stand . . . it lay in its cradle at the fireside like a half-dead hurcheon . . . a whingin screechin skirlin wallidreg. . . . [71]

Here we have a remarkably clear description of a child born with a chromosomal aberration known as "18-q" or "Carp-mouth" syndrome. Such a child will be noticeably different from birth. An infant with this syndrome will have a very small head, with a high bulging forehead. The eyes—"twa great glowerin' een"—will be widely spaced, deep set, and will have epicanthic folds. The child's ears will be large and set low on the head; deafness often accompanies this disorder and may account for this child who "never mintet to speak a word."

As the second or descriptive name of this syndrome implies, the large, fish-like, down-slanting, and usually (due to hypotonic muscles) open mouth is characteristic—"a face like a paddock, a mouth frae lug to lug." Often in this syndrome the child's fingers will be fused and the thumb simian, proximally placed, and rigid—"hands like a moudiwort," a mole. Both mental and physical development will be severely retarded. Because the child's muscles are hypotonic or "floppy," coordination is often severely affected, which may explain why this infant "lay in its cradle . . . like a half-dead hurcheon."[72]

Waldron describes another child, on the Isle of Man, whose symptoms also suggest a similarly specific diagnosis:

> Nothing under heaven could have had a more beautiful face; but though between five and six years old, and seemingly healthy, he was so far from being able to walk or stand, that he could not move so much as one joint; his limbs were very long for his age, but smaller than an infant's of six months; his complexion was perfectly delicate, and he had the finest hair in the world; he never spoke, nor cried, ate scarce anything, and was seldom seen to smile.[73]

The most suggestive clue here is found in the description of this child's limbs, "very long for his age, but smaller than an infant's of six months." This symptom suggests an "inborn error of the metabolism," homocystinuria. Of the congenital metabolic disorders, homocystinuria is second only to PKU in frequency; as with PKU, children with this disorder are often blonde and fair skinned.

A child with homocystinuria will begin to develop symptoms when about two months old. Failure to thrive, osteoporosis or "brittle bones," and—in some but not all cases—mental retardation and cerebral palsy are found. One symptom, arachnodactyly, is common to this syndrome; the term refers to limbs and digits that are extremely long and thin, or "spider-like."

Children with homocystinuria are highly prone to arterial and venous thrombosis—blood clots—that can lead to encephalitis, paralysis ("he could not move so much as one joint"), seizures, and cerebral thrombophlebitis. Other visible traits of these children include rosy cheeks ("his complexion was perfectly delicate") and very fine, sparse hair ("he had the finest hair in the world").[74]

These three examples, in which change-children are described clearly enough in folklore to suggest a specific congenital disorder, give an idea of the points of comparison that first led me to believe that congenital disorders lie at the root of many of the changeling tales that have come down to us. When information about sexual development, general appearance, and symptoms of congenital disorders are examined alongside changeling lore, the relationship seems too strong to ignore.

The Solitary Fairy

What of the changelings who survived infancy? How were they incorporated into the family and the community, these children with varying degrees of physical and mental disability? The answer, I believe, can be found by examining the tales of the solitary fairies, both domestic and reclusive—the Brownie, the Gille Dubh, Meg Moulach, the Brown Man of the Muirs, the Urisk and the Grogan, and the Fenoderree.

Many of these characters seem to me to represent a person who has mental retardation and who is often physically different as well; the different person whose nature was believed to be supernatural, if only in that he or she received unusual respect as a "luck-bringer"—whether to a house, a farm, a particular pool, moor, or orchard.

Two particular sets of congenital disorders come to mind in the specific context of the solitary "nature" fairy who lived, usually, by a well or stream; who hunted, fished, or scavenged for sustenance; and who was a sort of *genius loci* to a particular place. The first of these disorders are the syndromes that cause dwarfing. Achondroplastic or short-limbed dwarfism occurs in about 1:20,000 births; children born with this syndrome will have normally sized trunks, large heads, and very short limbs.[75] Costovertebral dwarfing results in limbs of normal size, a very short trunk, frequent occurrence of clubfoot, and, in some cases, mental retardation.[76] Anterior hypopituitary dwarfing, the most common dwarfing syndrome, leads to normal body proportions but overall small size.[77]

The second set of disorders that comes to mind are the mucopolysaccharidosis syndromes, such as Hunter's and Hurler's syndromes, mentioned earlier. These also affect growth, cause hair to grow over much of the body, and may lead to a darkening of the skin. Children with these syndromes are often mentally retarded.[78]

Now, consider the Highland Grogach or Grogan, a solitary fairy of small stature, covered with dark hair, who had, as Wood-Martin writes, "an unco wee body, terrible strong."[79] In some tales, the Grogach's head is oversized; in some, his body is loose-jointed and amorphous—hypotonic?

Or consider the Wulver. We aren't told what size he was, only that he lived alone in a cave, that he liked to fish, had the head of a wolf, was covered from head to toe with short brown hair, and that he didn't molest folk if they didn't molest him.[80]

The boggart was a "squat, hairy man, strong as a six-year-old horse, with arms as long as tackle poles, and not too bright."[81] Perhaps in the Wulver, we see a person with Hurler's syndrome; in the boggart, a person with costovertebral dwarfing that has resulted in a small trunk and normal limbs.

Another solitary fairy, the Brown Man of the Muir, is described as a "small, hideous dwarf," with eyes "round and fierce as a bull's." Squat and strongly made, he has an intimidating visage and red, frizzy hair. Interestingly, both the "cow's eyes" and the rough hair texture are associated with hypothyroid disease. Perhaps our Brown Man suffers from hypothyroidism—perhaps he is, to use the old label, a *cretin*.

The Gille Dubh, a historical person who lived in the last century on the southern shore of Loch Druing, had black hair, and covered his nakedness with leaves and moss. He was a gentle creature, fond of children. He also could speak, but rarely did so. At one point, a local landowner organized an armed hunting party, with the aim of taking the Gille Dubh as a trophy —here perhaps we have a hint about why such "creatures" chose to live out their lives in seclusion.[82]

The Social Fairy

Bridging the distance between the truly solitary fairy, who avoided human company, and the domestic fairy such as the Brownie, who often lived in close company with humankind, were such fay folk as the goat-footed Urisk. Half-human and half-fairy, the Urisk was good luck to the farm it chose to honor with its presence. It was particularly fond of herding cattle and also helped about the place with other farm labor. But it made its home away from the farm, usually near a haunted pool, and sometimes would seek out the company of lonely travelers.[83]

The "pygmy king" of Walter Map's tale of King Herla is also goat-footed, a trait that turns up in other fairy folk as well.[84] "Goat-footedness" may refer here to the "tiptoe" walking caused by muscular imbalance or spasm that results from central nervous system damage like that found with spina bifida or cerebral palsy. In a condition called *talipes equinus*, horse-foot, the muscles of the leg contract in such a way that the foot is held in an extended, "toe-pointed" position.[85]

Kin to the Urisk is the Manx Fenoderree, who is "large, hairy, and ugly."[86] His name, according to Creegan, means "one who has hair for stockings," or "like a satyr," thus bringing us back again to goat-footedness.[87] The Fenoderree, also a helper to the farmer, herds sheep, gathers hay, moves boulders, and performs other heavy labor:

> ... most of the larger farms were lucky enough to possess one of him ... he was not then too shy to start work at daybreak and let himself be seen in the grey light by the respectful villagers ... he moved, raked, reaped, stacked, herded ... for he was a doer, not a thinker, mightier in thew than in brain.[88]

In his *Daemonologie*, King James of Scotland describes the domestic solitary fairy as " ... doing as it were necessarie turns up and down the house: and this spirit they called *Brownie* in our language, who appeared like a rough man: yea, some ... beleeve that their house was all the sonsier ... that such sprites resorted there."[89]

The Brownie, similar to the *Bwca* of Wales and the *Bodach* of the Highlands, was a small man, about three feet tall, brown faced and shaggy haired. Often he worked at night, in secret. He reaped, served as a herdsman, watched over the hen yard, ran errands, and on occasion provided "good council at need."[90] When treated well and given the ritual evening dish of fresh cream, Brownies often attached themselves as a sort of mascot to a particular house or family.

In addition to their small size, the Brownies of certain regions might have specific physical characteristics. For example, Aberdeenshire Brownies had "no separate fingers, a thumb and the other four fingers joined in one."[91] Kilmoulis, a Brownie or hob who inhabited mills in the north country, had no mouth but an enormous nose. A Welsh story about a Bwca reminds us that Brownies with noses were unusual in that part of the country, for this particular fairy was named Bwca'r Trwyn, the "Brownie with the Nose."[92] These "noseless" Brownies may in fact be persons with severe cleft lip/palate disorders.

While some have interpreted these solitary fairies to be representative of a shaggy aborigine, hanging about the farm, attached to its service by food and kindness,[93] a theory first suggested by MacRitchie, it seems to me that they are more likely to represent persons with mental retardation and often physical disabilities as well; persons who made their living through labor, receiving in payment a cubbyhole, loft, or warm hearth that would shelter them from the weather. Often they were reclusive and shy—perhaps justifiably fearful through rough experience in society. The traditional belief that a resident Brownie made a house "all the sonsier" is then explicable, through comparison with similar beliefs in the especially blessed nature of the atypical human being, be that person called *cretin*, *amadan*, Brownie, or God's fool.

Human-Fairy Children

Finally, a brief look at the special characteristics of one group of offspring of fairy-human pairings, what Warkany calls the fairy "hybrids"—the children of sea fairies and their human lovers.

Merrow and mermaid traditions abound in the islands and coastal areas of Great Britain. Generally, the female sea fairy is very beautiful; the male, very ugly. Both male and female have a human body with a fish tail; in some stories, the tale may be shed at will when the merrow or mermaid wishes to venture onto land. When a child is born with a "fish's tail," i.e., with fused legs, the condition is known as sirenomelos. The birth of such children no doubt added to the folklore description of the sea people, but since such children nearly always die at birth,[94] there are no traditions of families descended from such offspring. Rather, the offspring of human-merrow matings were believed to be born with webbed fingers and/or toes, and with fishscale skin.

When seal people—silkies, roane, or seal maidens—wed humans, they also produce children with webbed fingers and toes, or with horny growths on their hands and feet. R.M. Douglas, in a recent collection of Scottish folklore (1982), writes that "all the MacCodrums [aka, the 'MacCodrums of the seals'], for one clan at least, are descended of a seal,"[95] and in David Thomson's *The People of the Sea*, when a human woman takes a roane as a lover, all their children have webbed fingers and toes at birth. When this webbing is clipped, to allow handwork, a horny growth appears.[96] Marwick tells of other seal-human couplings, one of which produces a child with a seal's face (again, probably anencephaly); another is the forefather of a long line of descendants, all born with horny palms and soles, greenish in color and having a strong, fishy odor.[97]

In reference to the traits of the offspring of human-sea fairy couples, let us first consider simple syndactyly—webbed digits—the most common of all congenital malformations. Webbing may join only two digits, or three, four, or all.

Fishscale skin, or *ichthyosis*, may occur in the newborn (as ichthyosis fetalis), may cover part or all of the body, may be fatal or may be only slightly disfiguring. Exfoliation, resulting in thick, platy masses of keratin in the skin, may be localized, as on the hands and feet, or may be found all over the body.[98]

As noted earlier, other examples of children believed to be the offspring of human-fairy parents were those born with cleft lip or cleft palate.

Summary

Of course, not all descriptions of fairy races reflect folk remembrances of children born with congenital disorders, but there are a number of fairy characters—the changeling, the solitary fairies, and the child of human-fairy parentage—who seem to so clearly represent certain congenital disorders that they are difficult to interpret as purely the products of imagination.

The changeling is often, no doubt, the infant or very young child who is different, whether that difference arises through injury, disease, or congenital disorder and there are times, as shown above, when the record is clear enough to suggest a fairly clear relationship between the child described and a known disorder.

The different child who survives, perhaps with more mental than physical difference, offers a rational explanation for many of the solitary fairies, be they called Brown Man, Brownie, or Urisk. This character, living quietly on the edges of society, may provide a clue to the origin of ancient tales in which a "monster" and his mother play an important role—tales such as *Beowulf*, with the memorable Grendel and his "dame." This central episode may have grown from the remembrance of a woman living in isolation with her child, outcast because of that child's physical and/or mental differences.

Finally, recognized congenital disorders can be cited to explain many traits common to human-fairy children. Syndactyly and exfoliar disorders can account for webbed fingers and fishscale skin. In fact, a number of the "hidden imperfections" of the fairy races may have their origins in congenital disorders.[99] The "trough backs" of the beautiful ellewomen[100] may recall spina bifida or a condition known as craniospinal rachischisis, in which there is an open trough along the spine.[101] An imperforate nostril, characteristic of the Mull fairies, occurs in human births. The single nostril and great front tooth of the *Bean Sidhe* is found with cleft palate.[102] Huldre folk have tails, an anomaly found in some babies. The Glastyn and the Cowlug sprite[103] have unusually large, oddly shaped ears—a marker trait for certain congenital syndromes. Hairy Meg (Meg Moulach) and other Gruagachs and suchlike furry fairy folk exhibit the hirsutism found in a variety of congenital disorders, among them X-linked syndrome, Hunter's and Hurler's syndromes.[104] Melusine was, periodically, sironomelic. The male merrow in some regions had flipper arms, or phocomelia,[105] a trait we have recently become familiar with as a result of the births of the "thalidomide babies" of the 1960s. Dwarfism is recalled in many tales, where the little person may be called pygmy, dwarf, or leprecaun.

The creation of traditions from an amalgamation of myths, religion, and experience continues; all are important sources of imagery and none excludes the others. Observations of atypical newborns and of children who over time became different, provided a rich source of such images to the storyteller; the tales themselves attempted to provide explanations for differences that were otherwise inexplicable and answers for questions that were otherwise unanswerable.

Notes

Reprinted by permission from *Folklore* 99.1 (1988): 58–77, with some revisions.

1. Summarized in Katharine Briggs, *The Vanishing People* (New York: Pantheon, 1978) 28.
2. Lewis Spence, *The Fairy Tradition in Britain* (London: Rider, 1948) 233.
3. Spence 232.
4. Josef Warkany, "Congenital Malformations in the Past," *Problems of Birth Defects*, ed. T.V.N. Persaud (Baltimore: U Park P, 1977) 6.
5. Warkany 7.
6. Mark Barrow, "A Brief History of Teratology to the Early 20th Century," in Persaud 18.
7. Warkany 7.
8. Examples of birth defects not readily apparent at birth include cystic fibrosis, which becomes evident at varying times between birth and the fourth year; Duchene muscular dystrophy, which appears between the second and fourth year; Hunter's and Hurler's syndromes, which are not evident until after the second month.
9. Leo Kanner, *History of the Care and Study of Mental Retardation* (Springfield, Illinois: C.C. Thomas, 1964) 90–1.
10. Kanner 90–1.
11. Briggs, *Vanishing People* 46
12. Warkany 15.
13. Warkany 8–9.
14. Seán Ó Súilleabháin, *Handbook of Irish Folklore*, rev. in *Hereditas*, ed. Bo Almqvist (Dublin: Folklore of Ireland Society, 1975) 251–75.
15. Mary Chamberlain, *Old Wives' Tales* (London: Virago P, 1981) 33.
16. Warkany 11–2.

17. David Thomson, *People of the Sea: A Journey in Search of the Sea Legend* (New York: World, 1965) 206.

18. Warkany 11–2.

19. Kanner 7.

20. Carolly Erickson, *Medieval Vision* (New York: Oxford UP, 1976) 196–7.

21. E.B. Wood-Martin, *Traces of the Elder Faiths in Ireland*, vol. 2 (London: Longmans, 1902) 13.

22. Erickson 197.

23. W.B. Yeats, *The Celtic Twilight* (New York: Collier Books, 1962) 80–1.

24. Katharine Briggs, *An Encyclopedia of Fairies* (New York: Pantheon, 1976) 70.

25. Noreen Quinn-Curran and Stefi Rubin, "Lost, Then Found: Parents' Journey Through the Community Service Maze," *The Family with a Handicapped Child*, ed. Milton Seligman (New York: Grune and Stratton, 1983) ix.

26. Kenneth Moses cited in Eileen Maley, "A Parent's View," *IDD News* 5.4 (Iowa City, 1982): 4.

27. John Fletcher, "Attitudes Toward Defective Newborns," in Persaud 373–81.

28. W.Y. Evans-Wentz, *Fairy Faith in Celtic Countries* (Oxford: Oxford UP, 1911) 171.

29. E.S. Hartland, *The Science of Fairy Tales* (London: Walter Scott, 1891) 118.

30. Briggs, *Encyclopedia of Fairies* 332–3.

31. Thomas Keightley, *The Fairy Mythology, Illustrative of the Romance and Superstition of Various Countries* (London: H.B. Bohn, 1891) 355–6.

32. Spence 248.

33. Fletcher 380.

34. Fletcher 380.

35. G.A. Waldron, "A Description of the Isle of Man," in Hartland 109.

36. Spence 230–1.

37. Briggs, *Encyclopedia of Fairies* 328.

38. Briggs, *Encyclopedia of Fairies* 231, 438.

39. Briggs, *Encyclopedia of Fairies* 381–2.

40. J.M. MacPherson, *Primitive Beliefs in the North East of Scotland* (London: Longmans, 1929) 113–4.

41. MacPherson 363–4.

42. Briggs, *Vanishing People* 101.

43. Carl Haffter, "The Changeling: History and Psychodynamics of Attitudes to Handicapped Children in European Folklore," *Journal of the History of the Behavioral Sciences* 3–4 (1967–8): 56.

44. Briggs, *Encyclopedia of Fairies* 286.

45. R.R. Lebel, "Overview of Issues in the Genetic Counseling Relationship," *Birth Defects Original Article Series* 14.9 (1978): 4. The most common congenital malformations in Great Britain are Down's syndrome (2:1000 live births; a ratio of 1:1, male to female incidence); cleft lip/palate (1:1000; a ratio of 1.8:1, male to female); clubfoot (3:1000; 2:1, male to female); congenital hip dislocation (1:1000; 0.15:1, male to female); spina bifida (2.5 to 4.5:1000; a ratio of 0.8:1, male to female); and congenital heart defects (4:1000; 1:1, male to female).

46. Fletcher 375.

47. Fletcher 374.

48. R.B. and J. Darling, *The Nature and Prevalence of Birth Defects: Children Who Are Different* (St. Louis, Missouri: V. Mosby, 1982) 23.

49. N.M. Robinson, *The Mentally Retarded Child: A Psychological Approach* (New York: McGraw-Hill, 1976) 24.

50. Briggs, *Encyclopedia of Fairies* 21.

51. James A. Blackman, *Medical Aspects of Developmental Disabilities in Children Birth to Three* (Iowa City: U of Iowa, Division of Developmental Disabilities, 1983) 159–65.

52. Blackman 137–41.

53. Blackman 31–7.

54. Blackman 77–9.

55. William L. Nyhan and Nadia O. Sakati, *Genetic Malformation Syndromes in Clinical Medicine* (Chicago: Year Book Medical, 1976) 276.

56. Anonymous, "Case History of a Child with William's Syndrome," *Pediatrics* 75.5 (1985): 962–8.

57. Nyhan 43–52.

58. Keightley 298.

59. For example, the most common chromosomal anomalies, those that occur in more than 1:1000 live births—Down's, Klinefelter, and triple-X syndromes, and sex-chromosome anomalies—all "substantially reduce reproductive fitness." C.O. Carter, "Genetics of Common Disorders," in Persaud 152.

60. Briggs, *Vanishing People* 93.

61. A.P. Norman, *Congenital Abnormalities in Infancy* (Oxford: F.A. Davis, 1971) 411–2.

62. *Dorland's Illustrated Medical Dictionary*, 26th ed. (Philadelphia: W.B. Saunders, 1964) defines "savant" syndrome as "a person who is severely mentally retarded in some aspects, yet has a particular mental faculty that is developed to an unusually high degree, as memory, mathematics, or music" (649).

63. Briggs, *Encyclopedia of Fairies* 93.

64. Blackman 93.

65. Blackman 197–201.

66. John Rhŷs, *Celtic Folk-Lore, Welsh and Manx*, vol. 1 (Oxford: Oxford UP, 1901) 667.

67. Briggs, *Encyclopedia of Fairies* 194–5.

68. Spence 233.

69. *Webster's Ninth New Collegiate Dictionary* (Springfield, Mass.: Merriam-Webster, 1984).

70. Nyhan 197–9.

71. Katharine Briggs, *A Dictionary of British Folk-Tales in the English Language*, vol. 2 (London: Pantheon, 1970–1) 198.

72. Nyhan 136–9.

73. Hartland 109.

74. Nyhan 3–5.

75. Nyhan 231–6.

76. Nyhan 255–8.

77. Nyhan 231–55.

78. Nyhan 39–63.

79. Wood-Martin 3.

80. Briggs, *Encyclopedia of Fairies* 445–6.

81. Briggs, *Encyclopedia of Fairies* 29–30.

82. Osgood MacKenzie, *One Hundred Years in the Highlands* (London: Bles, 1934) 83.

83. D.A. MacKenzie, *Scottish Folk Lore and Folk Life* (London: Blackie, 1935).

84. Briggs, *Encyclopedia of Fairies* 247.

85. E.L. Potter and J.M. Craig, *Pathology of the Fetus and Infant* (Chicago: Year Book Medical P, 1975) 624–5.

86. Briggs, *Encyclopedia of Fairies* 170.

87. Spence 83.

88. Walter Gill, *A Second Manx Scrapbook* (London: Arrowsmith, 1932) 326.

89. Briggs, *Encyclopedia of Fairies* 348.

90. Briggs, *Encyclopedia of Fairies* 38.

91. Briggs, *Encyclopedia of Fairies* 47.

92. Briggs, *Encyclopedia of Fairies* 56–7.

93. Briggs, *Encyclopedia of Fairies* 394.

94. Potter 601–2.

95. R.M. Douglas, *Scottish Lore and Folklore* (New York: Beekman House, 1982) 111.

96. Thomson 154–8.

97. E.W. Marwick, *The Folk-Lore of Orkney and Scotland* (Totowa, N.J.: Rowan and Littlefield, 1975) 28.

98. *Dorland's Illustrated Medical Dictionary* 474, 647.

99. See J.F. Campbell, *Popular Tales of the West Highlands*, vol. 4 (London: Alexander Gardner, 1890–3) 298 and W.P. Kennedy, "Epidemiologic Aspects of the Problem of Congenital Malformation," *Birth Defects Original Article Series* 3.2 (1967): 1–18.

100. Briggs, *Encyclopedia of Fairies* 92–3.

101. Potter 523.

102. Briggs, *Encyclopedia of Fairies* 40; Spence 47.

103. Briggs, *Encyclopedia of Fairies* 80–1, 191–2.

104. Nyhan 43–53.

105. *Dorland's* 1008.

The Invisible Made Visible:
The Fairy Changeling as a Folk Articulation of
Failure to Thrive in Infants and Children

Joyce Underwood Munro

The belief narrative of the fairy changeling (Thompson F321.1) was widespread throughout northern Europe and is even found in Egypt and India (El-Shamy 180) and in China and in the Pacific Northwest (Hartland 93). It is a bizarre tale of a supernatural race exchanging one of their own ill-thriven infants or little wizened old men for a handsome human infant. The human parents are left with an ugly changeling who somewhat resembles their own child but who never stops crying and never grows, no matter how much it eats. In their desperation, they beat, burn, expose, starve, or trick it into leaving, in the hopes that the fairies will bring back their own child. This unpleasant narrative was particularly prevalent in Ireland, Scotland, Wales, Brittany, and parts of England into this century. Walter Y. Evans-Wentz, writing in 1911 about reputed changelings that he had observed, concluded that "in many such cases there is an undoubted belief expressed by the parents and friends that fairy-possession has taken place" (250). Today, we are far more likely to encounter the changeling in written texts, especially in children's books.

The very strangeness of the changeling story prompts collectors to attempt to explain what they "really" are, in an effort to interpret the folk belief. Edwin Sidney Hartland wrote in 1891 that children who were called changelings "were invariably deformed or diseased" (110). He concluded that a reputed changeling in Monmouthshire in the early nineteenth century "was simply an idiot of a forbidding aspect, a dark, tawny complexion, and much addicted to screaming" (111). He noted that the stories he collected represented "a living superstition" (118).

Evans-Wentz believed that some of the changelings he had observed were suffering from "some abnormal physical or mental condition, in the nature of cretinism, atrophy, marasmus, or arrested development" (251). Alwyn Rees and Brinley Rees interpret the changeling symbolically "as the personification of the otherworldly side of the human child's nature" (243). More recent collectors suggest that the changeling story was explanatory, and that changelings were sickly children and mental

251

defectives (Simpson 4). Patrick Logan, himself a physician, wrote "it was almost logical to believe that a baby who was a cretin or a mongol was really a fairy changeling" (111).

These comments from collectors suggest that there might be "logical" or scientific explanations of the changeling stories. If so, then a comparison of such a scientific description of syndromes or conditions analogous to those described in the versions of the changeling narrative would help to interpret the narrative and might even "clarify and support traditionally reported features of a phenomenon" (Hufford xiv). The question then becomes one of the relative legitimizing effects of folk narrative and scientific discourse. Would "scientific" explanations of the changeling allow us, who do not believe in fairies, nevertheless to believe in "changelings?"

Fully mindful of David Hufford's warnings that "the establishment of a correspondence between a tradition(s) and an experience(s) must be approached cautiously, and perfect correspondence will rarely if ever be found" (134), I suggest that the changelings described in these belief narratives bear a close resemblance to the infants and children described in current medical literature as suffering from "failure to thrive." These infants fail to grow as a consequence of the parent's failure to form an adequate emotional bond to them, without any apparent physical cause. Older children whose linear growth, emotional maturity, and intellectual development are significantly stunted as a result of the stress of emotional abuse and neglect are diagnosed, significantly for our purposes, as suffering from psychosocial dwarfism. In addition to these emotionally induced growth failures, there are many chronic diseases and congenital deformities which slow normal growth or interfere with normal development. Finally, medicine has long noted various types of congenital and endocrine disorders resulting in dwarfism and giantism. The question remains as to what the relationship of these disorders is to the figures in the folk literature (Neumann).

This paper will first analyze the features of the changeling narrative as it appears in primarily Celtic sources, exploring the phenomena of which it consists in order to suggest that the changeling is a traditional model of the child who fails to thrive. The changeling embodies the idea of the failure of the parent-infant bond and the physical consequences that flow from that failure. By embodying what is not seen, that unknown which is therefore the invisible, the changeling renders it visible. This visibility allows one *"to see* and *to say"* (Foucault xii), therefore to articulate what was formerly beyond the reach of language. Modern medicine's relatively recent concern with the failure to thrive syndrome suggests that in this case, "folk knowledge is sometimes well in advance of scientific knowledge" (Hufford xiii) in recognizing the subtleties of parent-infant bonding.

The essay will next trace the development of the idea of failure to thrive in modern medicine as a medical model for the phenomena accounted for in traditional narrative by the changeling, using the idea of the "medical gaze" as developed by Michel Foucault in *The Birth of the Clinic*. The dynamics of emotional deprivation and of how they translate into physical and emotional atrophy escaped the scrutiny of the medical gaze, remaining invisible to it, beyond language and therefore unarticulated in medical discourse until the middle of the twentieth century. If indeed there had always been some children who failed to thrive, how do we account for the fact that medicine allowed this phenomena to escape its notice so long?

Finally, the medical discourse on failure to thrive shares with the folk narratives a salient feature: attribution of the cause of the phenomena to the invisible, that which is beyond language, an excess of signified over signifier. While the folk tradition credited the supernatural, until recently medical discourse credited, with a sense of wonder that revealed its failure to explain it, "maternal deprivation" for the "changes" observed in infants failing to thrive. It is this shared wonder at these inexplicable changes that so closely links the folk narrative and the medical discourse.

Recently medicine has been able to "reexamine the original distribution of the visible and the invisible insofar as it is linked with the division between what is stated and what remains unsaid: thus the articulation of medical language and its object will appear as a single figure" (Foucault xi). In so subjecting this unruly concept of "maternal deprivation" to its rigorous gaze, medical discourse has been able to bring more of it into the light, to render more of it visible. It stops speaking "the language of fantasy" as it "directs our gaze into a world of constant visibility" (Foucault x).

First we will examine the features of the changeling narrative in depth. Next we will trace the development of the idea of failure to thrive in medicine. Finally, we will compare these two models of rendering the invisible visible.

I. The Changeling Narratives

To understand all the components of the changeling narrative, a selection of printed texts of Celtic versions published between 1825 and 1981 will be examined. Discussions of context are problematic, as most collectors supply little or no information about the context in which these narratives were related. Belief in changelings persists into the present in some areas, and believed changeling narratives still circulate in oral tradition (El-Shamy 130), but we are most likely to encounter the changeling in printed texts, particularly in children's picture books, popular retellings of "fairy tales," and even in professionalist literature (e.g., Gunter Grass's *The Tin Drum* as an example of a psychosocial dwarf). For this reason, several retellings from children's books and from collections of retellings are included. Obviously texts so far removed from original oral narratives cannot be questioned too closely as to source and context, but they do represent changeling narratives as we now receive them.

The only narrative I have heard that might be a believed changeling narrative was told to me in the early 1980s by a medical social worker assigned to the case of a failure to thrive infant admitted to Children's Hospital of Michigan in Detroit. The child failed to gain weight in the parents' home. With normal care, feeding, and attention it gained weight rapidly while hospitalized. There was no evidence of underlying organic disease. Although there was no proof to substantiate it, the mother insisted that the infant was not hers because her own baby had been switched with another baby in the newborn nursery shortly after birth. Could this be a contemporary version of the changeling?

This narrative did not come to me in the "friend of a friend" manner of urban legend, but in the process of interviewing a witness (the social worker) in preparation for a juvenile court hearing on the issue of whether the mother had neglected the child. The mother's apparently mistaken belief that she had been sent home from the maternity hospital with the wrong infant was used as evidence that she had failed to form a sufficient emotional bond with the baby, and that the baby's failure to grow resulted therefrom.

A remarkable feature of the changeling narrative as it appears in the texts selected is its stability. Much of this can be attributed to the fact that published versions have circulated since the early nineteenth century and have been frequently recopied in books of retellings of fairy tales. Another factor may be the inner coherence of the narrative itself, resisting significant alteration in oral retellings. A third factor, and one this essay suggests, is the possibility that the changeling narrative may be derived from experience—not with fairies per se—but with observations of infants and children who fail to thrive and from the need to explain or otherwise account for something inexplicable, something therefore "invisible."

Changeling narratives can be divided into two basic types: one in which the changeling is tricked into revealing his great age by a bizarre cooking exercise, usually the "Brewery of Eggshells" (Thompson F321.1.1.1), frequently by addressing the human mother in verse (F321.1.1.3) or calculating his age by the age of the forest (F321.1.1.5). A second type of changeling, which I will refer to as the "Young Piper" from the title given to the principal versions, betrays his maturity by playing on the (bag)pipes (F321.1.1.2), dancing wildly to music (F321.1.1.2.1), or showing supernatural capacity for work (F321.1.1.4). An Icelandic variant which I place with the Young Piper is the "Changeling Who Stretched." Scandinavian fairies are human size, and have to be beaten and kneaded into human infant size. They are said to need to stretch from time to time, when they believe they are unobserved (Simpson 26–7; Logan 109). A changeling can also be tricked into betraying itself by a threat of throwing it upon the fire (F321.1.1.6) or of whipping it (F321.1.1.7) to cause it to cry out in speech. Both types of changelings are noted for their lack of normal growth (F321.1.2.1). They are always hungry, they demand food all the time (F321.2.2) and they appear sickly (F321.1.2.3).

Once the changeling has revealed itself, it must be banished. Methods include throwing it into water, into a ravine, or on the fire (F321.1.4.1-3); leaving it on a dunghill or barrow (F321.1.4.4); threatening it with burning (F321.1.4.5); beating it and leaving it outside (F321.1.4.6); paying no attention to it (F321.1.4.7); or even being kind to it (F321.1.4.8). These methods are used not only for banishing the changeling, but in the hope of inducing the fairies to return the human child.

The narratives examined are listed in the Appendix and numbered for ease of reference. Versions 1–7 are of the Brewery of Eggshells variant, 8–10 are of the Young Piper, and 23–25 of the Changeling Who Stretched. The other texts are included because they highlight the motif that the fairies can be foiled in their attempt to make a "change" (11–13), that the change cannot always be undone (19), that one can negotiate with the fairies for return of the human child (15, 16, 18), and that it may be necessary to maltreat, expose, or abuse a changeling in order to banish it (14, 20, 21, 22). References to other variants will also be made.

For purposes of this article, the motifs of the tale have been renumbered and in some cases renamed in order to expand on the various features they contain. Because these texts are being examined as data (Hufford xiii), it is helpful to make a more detailed and specific analysis of their features. The selected texts are not intended to be exhaustive, but among them they do cover most of the motifs listed in Stith Thompson's *Motif-Index of Folk Literature*. Of course, not every motif belongs in a given version. Using the approach of Claude Lévi-Strauss, that a myth consists of all its versions (92), the following fifteen features of the selected texts will be discussed: description(s) of the parent(s); whether infant is baptized or named; whether the parent leaves the child alone; fairies effect the change, or are foiled in attempt; parent notes change; physical description of changeling; behavioral description of changeling; scapegoating of the changeling; changeling does not grow or develop; food issues; consultation with wise woman/man; advice to trick changeling; changeling betrays self; methods of banishing changeling; changeling banished; the human child returned/not returned.

Circumstances of the Parent(s)

Many of the texts point out special circumstances of the parents. A number of them are single parents—widows or widowers (Appendix 5, 7)—or the parents are "newly married" (8) or unmarried (22). In one narrative the mother is ill and the child placed in the care of a girl (18). In another, the child's family is involved with smugglers who find the child on the road, the change having been foiled (13). "As the urgency of their business did not permit them to return [to the parents' home], they took the child with them, and kept it until the next time they had occasion to visit Glen-livat." Meanwhile, the mother is left to deal with a "stock," a wooden effigy of her "real" baby, wasting away and uttering piteous cries, until the smugglers return and produce the "real" child.

The house where a changeling comes is not a happy one. The mother is sometimes described as "unhappy" (3), and the household may be described as "the house of strange strife" (1). Isolation of the parents appears in some of the variants; they may be "two lonely people" (4) or living out on the moor (11), presumably away from others. Their cottage may be "isolated" and the two sons "pledged to secrecy" about the changeling (Quayle 34). Often only one parent figures in the story (2, 3, 9, 16, 17, 19, 24); if she is married, no reference is made to that fact.

Whether Child Baptized or Named

Children are in most danger of being "changed" if they are unbaptized (Croker 61; Briggs 1967, 115; T. Gwyn Jones 69; Logan 106). The unbaptized are in a nameless state, and thus more subject to the depredations of the supernatural. A number of versions simply state that the fairies were able to effect the change because the child had not been baptized in time (4, 9). In most versions, the child is not called by a name. The more literary retellings may name the child (7). Almost always the changeling is referred to as "it."

Whether Parent Leaves Child Alone

There are a number of precautions that parents can take to protect their unbaptized infants from being "changed." These usually involve surrounding the child with iron (sometimes in the shape of a cross), covering him with an article of the father's clothing, or placing a four-leaf clover or common plantain ("St. Patrick's leafeen" 18) over the child. But the best safeguard is constant vigilance. Sometimes the fairies themselves set up a distraction for the parent and effect the change while the parent investigates, for example, why the cattle are lowing (7). But usually the parent has had to leave the child alone to help with the haying (19, 20, 22), or to do the necessary chores (1, 6, 21, 18). Sometimes the parent simply neglects the child, even failing to keep him clean (11). The thought is that the fairies would not be able to change the child if the parents were supervising it properly.

Fairies Effect Change, or Are Foiled in Attempt

If someone blesses the child at the time the change is being made, it will foil the "felonious fairies" (12, 13). In some versions the fairy prefers her own child and will return the human infant or give the parents instructions on how to recover it (15). In others the fairy will surrender the human child if her own is given a drink of "some ennobling human milk" (16). If the fairies try to take a truly dirty child, it may take them so long to clean it that they will be forced to abandon both the task and the human infant at daybreak (11).

It is interesting to note that the word *exchange* is almost never used in these narratives. Rather, the fairies "change" the human child. The *Oxford English Dictionary* defines the transitive verb *change* as "to exchange" or "to make an exchange," and notes that "for this *exchange* is now the ordinary prose word, but *change* is still in dialect, archaic, and poetic use. . . ." Another definition given of the transitive verb *change* is "to make (a thing) other than it was; to render different, alter, modify, transmute." *Change* thus signifies both "to exchange" and "to render different." The ambiguity of the changeling legend is enacted on the very level of language itself.

Parents Note the Change

After the change is made, the parent notes it by saying that it is "not the child I gave birth to" (Evans-Wentz 251), "you are not my Griff" (Gwyn Jones 201), "you are not my child" (7), "they're not ours" (1), and "deep in her heart, she felt quite sure that that the child was not her son" (Eirwin Jones 64). The parent knows there has been a change because "there was my own fine child whipped off me out of his cradle . . . and an ugly bit of a shrivelled up fairy put in his place" (2). Or the changeling was "half the size of her own child" (20), or sick when the mother returns from leaving it alone (21), or "an ugly, wizened, crying brat" (Strindberg 42) in the place of the real child.

Sometimes the parent merely observes that "he was not the same" (19) or that he "appeared changed" (Keightley 473). The changeling usually seems somewhat like the child; for example, it has "a little wizened face as ugly as a walnut, yet bearing some resemblance to their own sweet child" (Quayle 37). Sometimes the parent fails to note the change, and a wise woman has to point out "that's no bairn of your own!

'Tis a changeling that's lying there in that cradle!" (Nic Leodhas 106). Or "the neighbors all suspected that he was something not right" (Croker 48).

Physical Description of the Changeling

These creatures are neither pretty nor welcome. After the change, the child becomes uglier (7), becomes ill-favored and deformed (9), becomes diseased (13), is shrivelled up with withered face and wasted body (2), begins to look like an imbecile (6), and is wrinkled like an old man (Manning-Sanders 120). One changeling is described as a miserable, ugly, ill-conditioned brat with long, shaggy, matted, curled hair, thin crooked legs, and the gut of a cormorant (Croker 48). He might be "not right in the head," and "ugly and loathsome" (23). Sometimes twins have been changed (1).

In addition to being shrivelled up and looking like a little old man, the changeling is ill-thriven (4), "evermore craving food and yet it never grew nor throve" (22), and "ate everything, and nothing showed on him, neither food nor days [age]" (21). He is "always crying and never satisfied" and "aye greeting [wailing], and never growing" (8).

Changelings could also be identified by their big heads, like the two-year-old who was no longer than a shoe, had a mighty big head, and was unable to learn to speak (Hartland 113). But always the changeling bears a physical resemblance to the "real" child. "Although its face was so withered, and its body wasted away to a mere skeleton, it still had a strong resemblance to her own boy" (2).

Behavioral Description of the Changeling

The changeling is seen as always crying and never satisfied (8), greedy with food (23), uttering piteous cries (13), and yelling every night, biting and tearing the mother's breasts, and unable to be still in arms or cradle (9). When dipped into cold water, it screams with laughter, "giggling and chuckling to itself in a manner more like a foolish old man than a baby" (Manning-Sanders 121). The changeling is also described as making strange sounds (23) or as being uncannily watchful, his eyes are "for ever moving in his head, as if they had the perpetual motion" (Croker 48).

Most remarkable is that the changeling will frequently behave differently when the parents are not around. This is true of all the Young Piper stories, where the changeling hops out of the cradle to dance and play the pipes for a visitor or do the chores for a servant girl (8, 9, 10). When the parents come back, it returns, whining, to the cradle. It also "stretches" when the parents are not present (23, 25). When the mother is away, the screaming, unsmiling changeling is observed through the window by neighbors to be "laughing and in great delight, whence they judged that it had agreeable company with it" (17), even though it was alone. "This changeling behaved in a strange and uncommon manner, for when there was no one in the place, he was in great spirits, ran up the wall like a cat, sat under the roof, and shouted and bawled away lustily; but sat dozing at the end of the table when anyone was in the room with him" (4). The changeling might "get out of bed at night and torment the family with loud noises" (Quayle 33). One of the marks of the changeling is that it is very "changeable" in its behavior.

Food Issues

In many of the variants, the changeling's food intake is remarkable enough to be commented upon. One of the signs of a changeling is his "insatiable appetite" (4, 7, 21). He eats enough for four, is never satisfied, and does not care what he eats (Croker 50). "As regards food he was as greedy as could be" (23). Another changeling is seen "dribbling from its mouth" (18). Despite the huge appetite, the changeling fails to grow in all these tales. In fact, it is one of the hallmarks of a changeling that it does not grow.

Perhaps it is not surprising that the tricks used to get the changeling to reveal his age involve weird food items, such as a pudding with hide (4), a cooking pot with an absurdly long stirrer (6), ridiculously small quantities of food, as in the Brewery of Eggshells, or the cooking of a black hen with all its feathers still on it (7). If the changeling has an insatiable appetite, then the way to trick him is through food.

Scapegoating the Changeling

Aside from the fact that no one is happy about having such a miserable and uncanny creature as a changeling around, he is also characterized as a wild creature, devil, or monster. The parents are "sadly plagued" with the changeling (22). He is seen as the cause of unlucky happenings and arouses disgust and loathing (Croker 50). When the husband threatens to leave the wife, it is blamed on the changeling, for there is no peace in the house:

> Poor Janey was beside herself with the plague it was to her. And as to Janey's husband—if he didn't run off and leave her, he came nigh to doing it many a time. There was no peace at all in that little house. Janey was most of the time in tears, and quarrelling with her man, and he with her, both of them on the edge because of the thing in the cradle. (Manning-Sanders 121)

As long as there is a changeling about, there is unrest in the home. "In Treneglwys there is a certain shepherd's cot known by the name of Twt y Cymrws because of the strange strife that occurred there" (1), and the strife ends when the changelings are cast into the lake and the true twins returned to the parents. The changeling is seen as the cause of the marital strife in these variants.

Changeling Does Not Grow or Develop

Along with the insatiable appetite and the old-man appearance, the other necessary characteristic of a changeling is that it does not grow or develop, no matter how much it eats. "He never grew in a year" (7). He is ill-thriven, unable to stand alone or leave the cradle (Croker 50). He stopped growing (6). "The boy's stomach was like an irrigation canal. He ate everything, and nothing showed on him, neither food nor days [age]" (21). He fails to grow (4) and is most commonly described as "ill-thriven" (4, 22):

> And then how it ate! There was no satisfying its appetite, and yet it didn't grow any bigger; and however much it was stuffed with food, it remained thin as a stick. (Manning-Sanders 121)

Consultation with Wise Woman/Man

At some point the hapless parent consults with someone on what he or she should do about the problem. Usually it is a wise woman (2, 6) or a wise man, wizard, or fairy doctor (1, 7, 18, 19). In other variants a neighbor or a "smart girl" (4) or a traveling student (22) advises the parent. Sometimes the mother denies that the child is a changeling and resists the suggestions on how to trick and banish it:

> Mrs. Sullivan of course could not disbelieve what every one told her, but she did not wish to hurt the thing; for although its face was so withered, and its body wasted away to a mere skeleton, it had still a strong resemblance to her own boy: she therefore could not find it in her heart to roast it alive on the griddle, or to burn its nose off with the red hot tongs, or to throw it out in the snow on the road-side, notwithstanding these, and several like proceedings, were strongly recommended to her for the recovery of her child. (2)

Note that in this variant, the word "recovery" carries two meanings; it signifies both recovery from an ill-thriven state and recovery from the custody of the fairies. Again, the ambiguity of the narrative is borne at the level of language itself.

In another version, the elder son returns from the wars and sees his younger brother still in the cradle. He tells his mother that is it not his brother, yet she protests that it is (3).When a traveler calls out to the mother that the child is a "wild creature," the mother replies that "it was her dear child which would not grow or thrive" (22). What is clear to outsiders is not always clear to the parent. Yet in most of the versions, the parent is eager to test the changeling and then take the appropriate action to banish it. In some cases, the mother or wife of the fairy assists the human parents in recovering the child (15).

Advice to Trick Changeling

The most commonly given advice is for the parent to prepare the Brewery of Eggshells, a mess of pottage in a single hen's egg meant to feed all the reapers at harvest time. Or the parents may roast a black hen (or a white hen with three black feathers on its head), usually in the Welsh variants (7). Broom handles fashioned into an incredibly long pot stirrer (6) and the pudding with hide (4) are other common devices.

Other methods are more direct, such as throwing the changeling on the fire (5, 9, 10), suspending him over the fire (13), jamming a red hot poker down its throat (2), burning him with hot tongs (14), whipping him (3, 6, 11, 21), putting him on a red hot griddle (8), and leaving him on the crossroads (11), threatening to burn down the fairy hill (15), withholding food from him (Strindberg 42), pinching and beating him without mercy (20), and throwing him into a stream or lake (1, 22). In contrast to heaping abuse upon the changeling, one version advises being kind to it so that the real child, being captive of the fairies, will be well treated in turn (18, 19; Hartland 126).

Changeling Betrays Self

When the trick or test is put to the changeling, he reveals his great age, sometimes in a rhyme or formula. Several are reproduced here to convey how bizarre and uncanny this precocious speech seems from one believed to be an infant or young child.

> Acorn before oak I knew,
> An egg before hen,
> But I never heard of an eggshell brew
> A dinner for harvest men. (1)

> I'm fifteen hundred years in the world,
> and I never saw a brewery of eggshells before! (2)

> I am old, ever so old,
> but I never saw a soldier brewing beer
> in an eggshell before. (3)

A pudding with hide!
and a pudding with hair!
a pudding with eyes!
and a pudding with legs on it!
Well, three times have I seen a young wood at Tiis Lake,
but never yet did I see such a pudding!
The devil himself may stay here for me now! (4)

I have lived 800 years and I have not seen
the like of that before! (5)

I'm old enough now, as my whiskers show,
and I'm a father with eighteen children in Elfland,
and yet never in my life have I seen
so long a pole in so small a pot! (6)

I am very old this day,
I was living before my birth,
I remember yonder oak
An acorn in the earth,
But I never saw the egg of a hen
Brewing beer for harvest men. (7)

These startling utterances are calculated to demonstrate how unnatural the elderly infant is. The pudding with hide also arouses feelings of disgust.

In the Young Piper variants, the changeling betrays himself to an outsider by performing feats that would seem impossible for a small child. The outsider then tells the parents and together they try to get rid of the changeling. In many variants, there is no attempt to recover the "real" child; it is merely enough to be rid of the changeling.

Methods of Banishing Changeling

In some versions, it is sufficient to cause the changeling to betray himself. He obligingly leaves, usually up the chimney, and somehow the "real" child is returned. In other accounts, positive action must be taken and it is not pleasant. Burning (Hartland 120), going after the changeling with hot tongs (2), throwing the changeling in the lake (1) or river (1), placing him on a hot griddle (8), beating him (6, 20, 21), and even treating him kindly (18) are some of the banishment methods. Other means are reminiscent of medieval torture, such as placing the changeling on a red-hot shovel, branding him on the forehead with the sign of the cross, grabbing his nose in red-hot tongs, throwing him into the fire, exposing him to the elements, and suspending him in a creel over the cook fire, are all popular methods (Hartland 120). According to the rules of the ordeal, if he screamed he was a changeling.

Whippings are advised by the Virgin (Keightley 436) and the village priest (Keightley 471), adding the weight of ecclesiastical authority to the abuse meted out. After the banishing has brought the fairy mother to reclaim her own, she sometimes remarks that she had taken better care of the human infant (Keightley 436).

Changeling Banished, "Real" Child Does/Does Not Return

The banishing of the changeling has one of four results. In many versions the changeling is banished and the "real" child is returned, almost simultaneously (1, 2, 3, 6, 7, 9, 14, 21, 22). In others the only result is getting rid of the changeling; there appears to be no concern about the return of the child (4, 8, 10, 23, 25). Most of the Young Piper variants are concerned with banishing only. In some versions there is either no resolution because none is sought (17, 23, 25) or the banishing fails and the family makes a good adjustment to living with the changeling (19).

In the fourth type, the "real" child is returned but it takes a period of time. A wise woman advised the mother to duck the child in cold water every morning for three months, and "at the end of that time there was no finer infant in the Cwm" (Hartland 123). In another version the fairy doctor recommends laying the changeling on a shovel outside the door from sunset to sunrise, giving the baby foxglove leaves to chew, and pouring cold water over the baby. This advice held that in three days the fairies' power over the child would cease, but the baby died on the third night.

The treatment with cold water and foxglove leaves may not be so farfetched as it seems. Infants with heart disease often fail to grow normally. Foxglove leaves are the source of digitalis, a drug used for treatment of some heart conditions. Digoxin, derived from digitalis, is used for treatment of supraventricular tachycardias in children (Rudolph 1275; Gellis and Kagan 150; Daniel Postellon, M.D., personal communication). Cold water, applied either by a damp cloth to the face or nose or by administering ice water to the stomach with a nasogastric tube, are methods of stimulating the vagus nerve in an attempt to stop an attack of paroxysmal supraventricular tachycardia (Rudolph 1275). Medicine was recognizing the value of digitalis in treatment of heart disorders at least as early as 1785 and 1799 (Goodman and Gilman 677–8).

In Germany the cure for a changeling was to take it to Cyriac's Mead and leave it lying there, giving it water from Cyriac's Well. After nine days it would either die or recover (22). Sometimes the parent has to go to the fairy hill to demand return of the child (5, 15). In one variant the child was returned, but "the fairy spell hung over the boy for a year and a day, but then he was himself again and became the finest smith in the country" (5). Sometimes the parents had only to wait until the next day (18).

As noted above, a number of tale collectors actually saw reputed changelings. Hartland cites the report of another collector, who concluded that the "changeling" that he had seen was suffering mesenteric disease. He describes the changeling as having "[a] wasted frame, with sometimes strumous swelling, and [an] unnatural abdominal enlargement . . . [giving] a very sad, and almost unnatural, appearance to the sufferer" (Hartland 110).

In Cornwall in 1843 a charge of mistreating a child was dismissed for lack of evidence; the household, believing that one of the children was a changeling, treated it harshly (Dean and Shaw 93). Hartland reports a trial in Clonmel in May of 1884:

> Two women were reported in the "Daily Telegraph" as having been arrested at Clonmel on the 17th of the month, charged with cruelly ill-treating a child three years old. The evidence given was to the effect that the neighbors fancied that the child,who did not have the use of its limbs, was a changeling. During the mother's absence the prisoners accordingly entered her house and placed the child naked on a hot shovel, "under the impression that this would break the charm." As might have been expected the poor little thing was severely burnt, and, when the women were apprehended, it was in a precarious condition. (Hartland 121–2)

Even Martin Luther reported changelings, including one who was shaped like a child and would do nothing but feed; it would eat "as much as two clowns or threshers were able to eat" (Hartland 109). Luther attributed this to the devil, "for the devil hath this power, that he changeth children, and instead thereof layeth devils in the cradles, which thrive not, only they feed and suck . . ." (Hartland 109). The test of their true nature was their inordinate appetites (Hartland 124). He advocated throwing changelings into the river.

The notion of throwing sick or ill-thriven infants into the river persists in the folklore of contemporary medical education, in the form of a joke told among medical students.

> There is a foreign medical resident in a neonatal intensive care unit. He is on teaching rounds with his attending physician, and after a long discussion about one sick infant says, "In my country, we call that a reever baby." The rounds proceed, and several more times the resident comments, "In my country, that is what is called a reever baby." After rounds are finished, the attending physician says, "This is very interesting. Can you tell me more about reever babies?" The resident answers, "In my country, you throw such babies in the reever." (Daniel Postellon, M.D., personal communication)

At the beginning of the twentieth century, industrialized Western culture did not advocate throwing infants into the river. Instead, the institution of the foundling hospital was the preferred method of handling abandoned infants and children. In hygienic surroundings, these children were fed, clothed, and given a clean cot in which to sleep. However, most of them became withdrawn and lost weight rapidly, many for no apparent physical reason. Most of the infants placed in these hospitals died before reaching the age of two. In addition, infants hospitalized for the treatment of illness, if kept in the hospital too long after their illnesses began to resolve, would turn apathetic, lose weight at an alarming rate, and many of these would die as well. These infants looked and acted in some respects like the changelings we have been describing. It was here that medicine took its first formal look at failure to thrive, turning its gaze upon infants and children in hospitals and foundling institutions, in an attempt to explain the inexplicable, the invisible threat that felled so many children.

II. Failure to Thrive

The medical concept of "failure to thrive" dates from L.E. Holt's description of the clinical manifestations of failure to thrive in 1899 (Wilcox, Nieberg, and Miller 391). This is not to say that medicine was unaware that infants and children do not thrive in adverse emotional environments, but that "little documentation of these effects on the physiological aspects of physical growth were made" until the 1940s (Gardner 1980, 73). The connection between growth failure and emotional deprivation was first made at the beginning of this century in studies of children living in foundling hospitals or hospitalized for extended periods of time for treatment of illness (Chapin, 1908, 1915). The fact is that of the infants who were placed in foundling hospitals before the age of one year, almost one hundred percent did not live until their second birthday (Chapin, 1915).

Henry Chapin recognized that the atrophic infants derived their "defective vitality from the wretched environment that so often surrounds them when returned to their homes" and he laid the fault to "deficient and inefficient fathers and mothers" (1908, 491) He argued for a "boarding out" (foster care) program in place of the invariably lethal hospitalization.

Chapin supported his argument with statistics showing that the foster care of "infants suffering from chronic malnutrition due to prolonged faulty care and feeding" (1908, 492) dramatically reduced mortality. In addition to numbers, he also related three case studies, two of them illustrated with "before" and "after" foster care photographs. This may have been one of the first uses of photographs to document failure to thrive and the dramatic recovery that is possible in a proper environment.

One case was Esther K. who on May 18, 1905, at age thirteen months, weighed nine pounds, eight ounces and was suffering from extreme atrophy. With her photograph, Chapin turned the medical gaze upon the failure to thrive infant. She is wasted to a skeleton, her head appears too big for her body, and from her posture, it seems clear that she cannot sit up by herself. Adjacent to this photograph, which reminds one of nothing so much as an inmate of Auschwitz, is a photograph of Esther K. taken on September 8, 1905, four months later, when she weighed eighteen pounds, eight ounces, almost double the former weight. She is sitting up, smiling, and appearing like a normal child. The weight gain had all been accomplished in a foster home, where she had been bottle fed and given individual attention (1908, 494).

Chapin's use of these photographs is interesting not because doctors had never seen atrophied infants before; no doubt many had too much experience with them. But Chapin's showing the picture of the same child so quickly improved forced the medical profession to *look* at the effects of emotional deprivation in light of a successful program of treatment. The entire notion of the foundling hospital was called into question. In 1915 Chapin recommended that the treatment of acutely ill infants and of foundlings and abandoned infants be based upon an awareness of "(1) the unusual susceptibility of the infant to its immediate environment, and (2) its great need of individual care" (1).

The light that Chapin had cast on the problems of emotional deprivation of infants and children did not fully illuminate them. Nearly thirty years later, in 1942, Harry Bakwin wrote that "one of the most striking and obscure phenomena in pediatrics is the failure of infants to thrive in hospitals" (30). He recounted that at first the atrophy of "hospitalism" was attributed to a poor understanding of nutrition. Later, when it was noted that hospitalized infants and children were subject to chronic fevers which were promptly reduced when the child returned home, the failure to thrive was put down to repeated infection (31–2).

Bakwin noted that the hospitalized infants were not readily responsive to the attendants, and he concluded that "psychological neglect leads to a dulling of the reactivity of the children to emotional stimuli" (32). He also observed that infants in hospitals did not gain weight when fed diets calorically adequate for other infants (32). Following Chapin's lead he presents before and after photographs of a patient, A. S., who was admitted to the hospital at eight weeks for an upper respiratory infection, diarrhea, and vomiting. His symptoms cleared up quickly, but then he began to lose weight. After eight weeks in the hospital, he weighed six pounds, which was fourteen ounces *less* than his birth weight. "He was sick at this time, emaciated, wizened, pale and so weak that it seemed as if he might stop breathing at any minute" (33). The first photograph shows an emaciated infant whose skin is hanging in folds on his arms and legs and who is arching his back and screaming (34). The child was sent home with the mother. The second photograph shows a dramatically improved-looking infant only five weeks later. Bakwin comments that "the effect of the home environment was well nigh miraculous. The child gained promptly, and he has continued to progress steadily up to the present" (34). Bakwin continued the spatial shift of the medical gaze from the infant to the infant and mother as a unit. "It is not surprising, therefore, that the young infant should suffer when deprived of the warmth and security which he derives from contact with the mother or a substitute. . . . The young infant is dependent on the environment for gratification of his psychological needs just as he is for satisfaction of his nutritional needs" (38). But while the gaze was extending its range, something nevertheless continued to elude it in the study of "one of the most striking and obscure phenomena" where "the effect of the home environment was well nigh miraculous."

Bakwin produced another article in 1949, entitled "Emotional Deprivation in Infants." In it he describes the infant who is hospitalized:

> Infants under 6 months of age who have been in an institution for some time present a well-defined picture.The outstanding features are listlessness, emaciation and pallor, relative immobility, quietness, unresponsiveness to stimuli like a smile or a coo, indifferent appetite, failure to gain weight properly despite the ingestion of diets which, in the home, are entirely adequate, frequent stools, poor sleep, and appearance of unhappiness, proneness to febrile episodes, absence of sucking habits.
>
> The hospitalized infant is thin and pale but the pallor is not always associated with a reduction of the hemoglobin. The facial expression is unhappy and gives the impression of misery . . . The infant shows no interest in his environment, lying quietly in bed, rarely crying and moving very little. . . .
>
> In severe cases the symptoms are intensified and the baby assumes the appearance of a wizened, toothless old man. (512–3).

Bakwin does note, however, that "a certain number of babies, reared in the home, show the pallor, the quietness, and the motor retardation which are associated with maternal deprivation," but he does not elaborate. Instead, he returns to his case, A.S., and remarks about the rapidity with which the symptoms of hospitalism disappear when the baby returns to a good home, terming it "amazing." A.S. was, within twenty-four hours of his return home from the hospital, cooing and smiling. Bakwin concludes that "the failure of infants to thrive in institutions is due to emotional deprivation" (520) and recommends that infants be handled more, and that the mother's access to the hospitalized infant not be so restricted.

In 1957 Rose Coleman and Sally Provence reported a case study of two infants who developed environmental retardation in the home, "the etiology, insufficient stimulation from the mother, is in both cases similar to the etiology of environmental retardation in the institutionalized infant" (285). The results of the "deficient and inefficient mothers and fathers" whom Chapin alluded to in 1908 were finally accorded the full attention of that gaze which had scanned the foundling institutions and hospitals earlier in the century. In part because improved practices for handling infants in the hospital had reduced the risks for infants there, the focus on emotional deprivation shifted to children who were failing to thrive in their own homes.

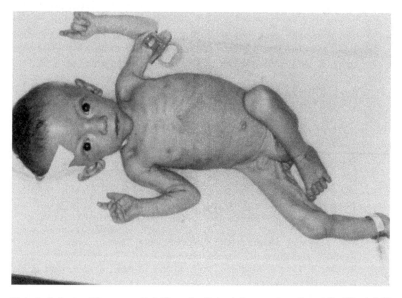

Plate 1. Infant with congenital Grave's disease (overactive thyroid). (Daniel C. Postellon, M.D.)

Once the notion that emotional deprivation could cause failure to thrive became known, medicine began to take care to distinguish children whose failure to thrive was organically based. The growth of infants and children can be compromised by a number of chronic disease conditions, such as congenital heart disease, central nervous system disease, cerebral palsy, coeliac disease, cystic fibrosis, food intolerances, kidney disease, vitamin-resistant rickets, hypothyroidism (see Plate 1), infections, infestations, familial short stature, metabolic disease, and many others (Vines 431; Frasier 67). Care was taken to separate organic from nonorganic failure to thrive. The titles of medical articles reflected this dichotomy of approach, many of them adopting the term "nonorganic failure to thrive" and moving their attention from the physical body of the infant and child to the quality of the parents' emotional bond to the child and the child's attachment to the parent.

Marshall Klaus and John Kennell, active investigators into parent-infant bonding, reported that one-third of the parents who have a child with nonorganic failure to thrive were mourning the recent loss of a close family relative (85). They were consequently unable to care for their infants properly.

R. Kim Oates in 1984 reported that mothers of nonorganic failure to thrive infants were isolated and lonely, and the fathers were often absent or not significantly involved with the family, and they were not supportive of the mothers. The mothers had a history of depression, including suicide attempts.The mothers also had a history of being themselves emotionally and physically deprived during childhood. While most cases came from lower socioeconomic groups, nonorganic failure to thrive does occur at all economic levels (96).

Irene Chatoor and associates studied the disorders of attachment, the infant's ability to form an emotional relationship to the parent or parent substitute. A similar parental profile emerges: marital discord, recent loss or death, social isolation, unmet dependency needs (see Fraiberg), economic hardship, and parent depressed or suffering from character pathology (Chatoor et al. 833). Chatoor looked closely at the interaction between parent and infant and saw "a lack of pleasure by the mother and infant in interactions during feeding," with the mother holding the infant loosely on her lap "without much physical intimacy" (833). This survey of the landscape of nonorganic failure to thrive also includes attributes of the infant which may interfere with attachment, including irritability, difficult temperament, and "hyper-sensitivity to touch, sound, light, or change in position—avoidant behavior that can be interpreted by the mother as rejection" (833). The infant may also be a ruminator, one who willfully regurgitates a feeding, playing with the vomitus in the mouth and as a consequence losing caloric intake from feedings, "as a means of self-stimulation or of relieving tension" (833). Articles like this one, and many others which support similar conclusions, result from the trained medical eye bringing itself into focus on the terrain of the infant-parent interaction. The recognition that characteristics of the infant can contribute to the nonorganic failure to thrive underlines the reciprocal nature of parent-infant interactions and helps to explain why parental perceptions of "fault" may be ascribed to the infant.

This compromised situation holds the potential for active physical abuse. Oates, Peacock and Forrest note that R.G. Patton and L.I. Gardner were the first to point out the relationship between nonorganic failure to thrive and child abuse in 1962 (Oates et al., 1984, 764). Deborah Frank and Steven Zeisel write that "approximately ten percent of children initially hospitalized for failure to thrive will sustain nonaccidental trauma" (1196), and that "fatal outcomes have been noted by multiple investigators among children who suffer both failure to thrive and physical abuse" (1196). Bertram Koel stated the case most dramatically in his review of three cases of failure to thrive which later resulted in fatal trauma to two of the infants:

> Three cases of failure to thrive in infancy were investigated but no pathologic diagnosis was made. Within months after discharge, each was readmitted, critically ill from trauma. Two infants died. Fattening a puny infant is satisfying to the staff, but the child remains at risk of subsequent violence if he is sent home to untreated parents. (567)

The fatalities were due to suffocation and scald burns. An entire new terrain opened up under the new vigilance of the medical gaze.

While many medical articles continued to insist on the strict dichotomy of organic versus nonorganic failure to thrive, some did not. There were articles which pointed out that "maternally deprived infants are underweight because of undereating which is secondary to not being offered adequate food or not accepting it, and not because of some psychologically induced defect in absorption or metabolism" (Fischoff et al. 209). Here the gaze retreats from investigation of the "miracles" and "amazements" which made up the invisible "psychological" components of the failure to thrive. It reminds the profession that it has to search for and to examine what might be interfering with the sufficient feeding of infants.

Norman Ellerstein and Barbara Ostrov note that caloric-deprivation failure to thrive makes up some seventy percent of all cases of failure to thrive, and that failure to thrive is responsible for from one to five percent of all pediatric admissions in the United States (164). Their study "excluded all children for whom organic causes could possibly result in growth failure," still observing the organic/nonorganic division in a situation in which it is clear that inadequate calories results in malnutrition, an organic cause of failure to thrive (164). Of course, this is precisely the point. There is no magic here in the nurturing hospital environment. "Thus, all children with nonorganic failure to thrive suffer from a serious organic insult: primary malnutrition" (Frank and Zeisel 1187). This approach opened up the field of the medical gaze to another finding: "Contrary to the popular belief that weight gain during hospitalization rules out major organic disease, [chronically ill] children often grow in the hospital when many trained personnel are available to share the burden of care" (1195). Findings like these shifted the axis of vision to feeding problems in both chronically ill children and the children who were heretofore seen as "nonorganically" affected.

Charles Homer and Stephen Ludwig had questioned the strict dichotomy made in the literature between organic and nonorganic failure to thrive and created a third category, children whose failure to thrive could be attributable to a combination of organic and nonorganic factors (849). They found that almost half the children with organic disease had psychological problems which interfered with their growth (851).

William Bithoney and associates studied feeding problems and observed that "children with organic failure to thrive are as likely as children with nonorganic failure to thrive to have behavioral-developmental problems associated with feeding" (28). It appears that all children with failure to thrive had either not been given or not taken in or retained adequate calories (30). For whatever reasons, "a number of researchers in the third world have noted that malnutrition per se results in developmental difficulties that are virtually identical to those described in the United States as due to failure to thrive" (30). Therefore, some of the behavioral and developmental problems of so-called nonorganic failure to thrive infants may be attributable to the physical state of malnutrition, itself an organic problem (see Plate 2). Focus on treatment of their "interactive problems and psychologically based feeding disorders" was what enabled both types of failure to thrive children to gain weight and grow (30).

Special cases continued to erode the organic-nonorganic division, arguing for a caloric deprivation model. Even apparently well intentioned and caring parents might find themselves with a failure to thrive infant. Michael Pugliese and associates reported in 1987 that parents who restricted their infants' diets in response to media attention to children who develop obesity, atherosclerosis, or addiction to junk food often induced malnutrition in their children by not feeding them enough or not feeding them the appropriate diet for an infant (175). Prolonged breast feeding of infants in "good" homes with none of the stress factors normally associated with failure to thrive can produce malnutrition (Weston et al. 242–3). The exclusively breast-fed infants and toddlers were simply not getting adequate calories (242).

Studies such as these indicate the complexity of the term" failure to thrive" and some of the problematics associated with it. A move away from a totalizing organic-nonorganic dichotomy has allowed an exploration of the parent-infant relationship as a unit, instead of focusing on what Chapin in 1908 somewhat unsympathetically called the "deficient and inefficient fathers and mothers." As the medical gaze takes in more of the environment, including the stark, blank walls of the foundling hospital and the stark, blank faces of the parent and atrophied infant, more of the problem comes under its control, and less of the mystery escapes its explanatory powers. What had previously been the invisible, the "emotional deprivation" becomes more resolved as "feeding problems," or "maternal non-response to infant cues" as observed by the trained eye. The language stops talking about "miracles" and takes control over the situation. "A new alliance was forged between words and things, enabling one *to see* and *to say*" (Foucault xii).

Nowhere is the use of language about failure to thrive more interesting than in discussions of psychosocial dwarfism, an emotionally induced short stature with developmental and intellectual delays, and of leprechaunism, an apparently genetically caused syndrome in which an infant is hairy, underweight, and has the appearance of an elf.

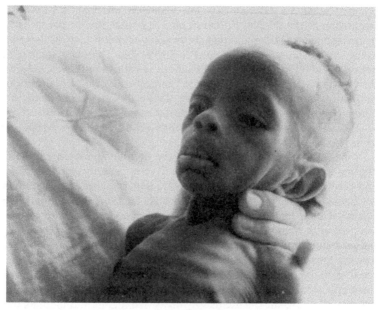

Plate 2. Infant with marasmus, age two months. (Nancy J. Hopwood, M.D.)

In 1947 endocrinological data was used to link maternal deprivation syndrome and children with short stature. Depressed production of human growth hormone was associated with family environments exhibiting parental hostility and maternal rejection (Gardner 1980, 74). Powell, Brasel and Blizzard in 1967 described emotional deprivation and growth retardation in thirteen older children, ages three to eleven, who were referred for short stature. Serious family problems were present, including divorce or separation of the parents, parental alcoholism or psychosis, physical abuse of siblings, with one parent openly saying that she hated her child (1272). Even more remarkable was the behavior of the patients studied. All exhibited a bizarre type of polydipsia, in which "water was drunk from the toilet bowl, glasses filled with dish water, puddles filled with rain water, old beer cans filled with stagnant water [a brewery of eggshells perhaps?] and the hot water faucet" (1272). The parents reported that the children ate:

> ... two or three times as much as their siblings at the same dinner table. Examples of aberration included eating a whole jar of mustard or mayonnaise, a package of lunch meat, a whole loaf of bread, corn flour from a box and seven eggs at one sitting. Two ate food from the cat's dish. (1272)

The patients stole food, some of them hiding it throughout the house. They would stuff themselves with food to the point that their stomachs would swell, then they would vomit (1273). Some got up and roamed the house at night. The children were short for their ages, but only one appeared malnourished. All were withdrawn and socially immature.

When these children were hospitalized for evaluation, "growth began upon or shortly after admission to the hospital" and "during the initial hospital evaluation, polydipsia, polyphagia, and stealing of food either disappeared immediately or persisted for only a few days. A consistent improvement in personality and speech pattern occurred. The children became happier, less withdrawn and far more spontaneous" (1274). And they grew at accelerated rates. In addition, "the growth observed was unusual in that both acceleration and deceleration occurred rapidly with a change in environment" (1277), the deceleration occurring when the children returned to the home environment. The suggested treatment is removal from the home until the pernicious parent-child relationship can be improved, but experience shows environmental improvement to be extremely difficult (1278).

The question was, and to some extent, still is, how does the parental hostility and rejection translate into dramatically stunted growth in these "psychosocial dwarves"? This invisible mechanism is the object of an endocrinological search which must account for the remarkable changes in growth rate that accompany merely a change in environment.

The fact that endocrinologists chose to name the syndrome a type of dwarfism is first of all because those with unusually stunted growth have long been called "dwarves" and the name has been appropriated by medicine. I also suggest that its use is a recognition of the invisible, that which escapes their vigilant gaze as they search for ways to "see" and therefore articulate the mechanism connecting the parental rejection with the bizarre behaviors and the stunted growth.

In the case of leprechaunism, this is perhaps even more obvious. This syndrome was first reported in the medical literature in 1948, and later given this name, to describe an infant who was hirsute, had elfin facies, was emaciated and had other abnormalities. It was an unwanted child, and it died shortly after being hospitalized (Donohue 739). Hirsutism, elfin facies, marked emaciation, and disorders of carbohydrated metabolism are seen in association with starvation (Hopwood and Powell 894). However, the child reported by Hopwood and Powell in 1974 also had a history of bizarre behavior—eating, sometimes to the point of vomiting, polydipsia, and nighttime wakefulness. Within the first few weeks of the thirty-eight day hospitalization, there was a dramatic change in the child's behavior and personality; loss of hirsutism occurred within the first few weeks, and the child gained weight rapidly and showed a gain in psychomotor development. By the twenty-first day, she was behaving like a normal child.This led to the conclusion that the syndrome of leprechaunism might belong in the constellation of emotional deprivation.

But leprechaunism is not as simple as this. It has also been associated with insulin resistance (Kobayashi et al. 1084; Szilagyi et al. 59). Cases have been reported in the United States (Donohue; Donohue and Uchida), in Lebanon (Der Kaloustian et al.), in Eastern Europe (Kallo et al.), and in Japan (Kobayashi et al.). Not all cases exhibit consistent features (Szilagyi et al. 60).

What is intriguing about the syndrome is the name. Changelings in Ireland were often referred to as "'prechauns," short for "leprechaun" (Croker 51). In 1954, Donohue and Uchida credit H.W. Edmunds with suggesting the name "because the patients appeared more to be caricatures than true human beings" (505). They do, however, argue for the usage:

> As no accurate or definitive description of a leprechaun is available, there may be serious and valid objections to the identification of the appearance of these infants with that of a leprechaun. There is agreement, however, that leprechauns were, originally at least, indigenous to Ireland. The consensus is that they are little hairy sprites, although some authorities maintain in addition that they are male and green. Although it may be argued that our cases do not fulfill all the suggested descriptive requirements of a leprechaun, with a little imagination the term can be as

suitably applied to the syndrome encountered in these two infants as the term gargoylism, cretinism (little Christian), and mongolism, which are in common usage. (505)

In this case medicine borrows from folk belief in these sometimes invisible, supernatural beings in order to articulate the unknown that meets its gaze.

The dwarf and the leprechaun are invoked in medical discourse because they provide a shorthand, or a vocabulary, that aids the medical gaze in saying what it sees. The connection may be more than fanciful, as the notion of the changeling may be embedded in our language because it was actually used to articulate this problematic constellation of failure to thrive syndromes. A comparison of the folk discourse to the medical discourse points out how both systems operate to make the invisible (the unknown, that which is beyond language) visible, or known, by subjecting it to the controlling power of the gaze.

III. The Changeling and Failure to Thrive: Making the Invisible Visible

Hufford pointed out that there are three separate subjects at issue in asking whether traditions might be grounded in experience: the traditions themselves, the experiences, and theoretical explanations (Hufford 134). The preceding discussions of the traditional narrative and of the medical explication of a set of experiences revealed a number of similarities between the changeling story and the failure to thrive infant or psychosocial dwarf child. Can we say that the changeling might have been based in the same or similar experiences to those which produce the failure to thrive child? A few specific examples may underline some of the possible connections.

The Relationship of Naming to Parent-Infant Bonding

The tentative nature of parent-infant bonding in the case of a premature or ill newborn is often reflected in the parents' deferral of naming the child. They may delay for days or even weeks, and even when home with the baby, will refer to the child as "it" much more than the parents of a normal healthy infant will (Klaus and Kennell 214). Klaus and Kennell observed hundreds of parents of premature infants saying that "it was *like* their [the parents'] baby," with the implication that somehow it was not really their baby (215).

In the changeling narrative, the giving of a name through baptism is thought to be enough to be a charm against the fairies changing the child.

Hartland cites a story of a mother bringing a child to a minister in the northeast of Scotland saying, "Ye see the craitirs gets their names, an we just think that eneuch, an' we're in nae hurry senning for you" (95). Sometimes nicknames were given until baptism could take place, because of the feeling that "until the initiatory rite has been performed they are looked upon as heathen, and therefore particularly under the dominion of evil spirits" (Hartland 95). This nameless state exposes the baby to danger (Briggs 1967, 100).

Maria W. Piers, a psychologist, studied infanticide and developed the term "basic strangeness" to describe the state of mind of parents who are capable of killing their children: "it is a state in which we 'turn off' toward others and are unable to experience them as fellow human beings" (38). She observes that anything can be perpetrated against a child who is seen by the parent as a mere "thing." She uses Erik Erikson's term "pseudo-speciation," the "phenomenon of being estranged from whole groups that differ from us, in looks, language, occupation, religion, or habitat" (38). She found that pseudo-speciation gives people a rationale for lapsing into "basic strangeness." Being under great pressures can also cause some parents to fall into basic strangeness vis-à-vis a child, and if a mother does so, it can be fatal to the child. The perception of these parents is that they have killed a "thing," not their child (24). "It is precisely this—the acknowledgement that the infant is 'like me . . . my own kind'—that frequently breaks down in infanticidal primates and human beings. They experience their infants as 'things,' not as living creatures" (37).

Hartland observed of the treatment of alleged changelings:

> Frightful as this cruelty would seem to everyone if perpetrated on the mother's own offspring, it was regarded with equanimity as applied to a goblin; and it is not more frightful than what has been actually perpetrated on young children, and that within a very few years, under the belief that they were beings of a different race. (Hartland 121)

According to Hartland, the confession of age of the changeling is proof that "it belongs in fact to a different race, and it has no claim on the mother's care and tenderness" (117). Thus we see that the very ability to give one's child a name is linked with the ability to form a healthy emotional bond to the child. The namelessness of changelings could be seen as a symptom that the parent has been unable to form this bond.

The Changeling as a Failure to Thrive Infant or Child

The changeling appears to be a very accurate description of a failure to thrive infant or child. Review of case narratives of failure to thrive infants and psychosocial dwarves, as we have seen, is like a review of the changeling narratives.

In the case of psychosocial dwarves, the family is disrupted. The parents, particularly the mother, are estranged from the affected child. The child is socially isolated by the family (Patton and Gardner 78). Marital strife is usually marked, and one mother even stated that she hated her child (Powell et al. 1272). Parental hostility and rejection are common, and the syndrome occurs even in families of relatively high economic standing (Gardner 1980, 74). Parental conflict is overt in most cases, and parental communication poor in all cases (Bowden and Hopwood 22). Parental isolation is extreme in some cases (Hopwood and Becker 448). Like the parents of changelings, these parents are living in a house of great strife.

The lack of bonding, of "naming" the child as one's own, is seen to be the primary cause of the developmental failure. "The child's extreme depression, motor retardation, and failure to thrive were related to her mother's inability to establish the usual physical and emotional contacts with her child" (Patton and Gardner 81–2). The mothers of infants who ruminate demonstrate a considerable incapacity to relate adequately to the baby, to want, accept or give to the baby (Richmond et al. 50–1). In short, they are not attached to the child.

Like the mothers of changelings, the parents of psychosocial dwarves or failure to thrive infants may not even perceive that there is something wrong with the child's size or development (Bowden and Hopwood 31). This is another indication of the estrangement from their children.

The behavior of psychosocial dwarves is noteworthy. They usually have a voracious appetite, often eating much more than a normal child their age. They eat and drink bizarre things. In addition they exhibit disturbed interpersonal relationships. The parents frequently try to control the child, either by restricting the food intake, locking them in their rooms at night to prevent night wandering, or restricting them from certain parts of the house. These children are apparently retarded in their speech and intellectual development. Ruminators are described as having alert, radar-like eyes (Richmond et al. 53), like the changeling whose eyes had "the perpetual motion."

The behavior of ruminators and psychosocial dwarves is also very labile. Ruminators will not ruminate if they think that they are being observed. When alone they grunt, groan, and bring up the feeding, playing quite happily with it, like the Changeling Who Stretched (23). Psychosocial dwarves also exhibit labile age-appropriateness, having the ability to appear different ages and to have different developmental abilities at different times. Regression occurs when the parents are present (Bowden and Hopwood 21), just as it does in the Young Piper stories. This lability is the essence of the changeling.

Scapegoating of the child is common, as it was with the changeling. Derogatory epithets, differential treatment of the affected child, and blame ascribed to the child for the problems of the family are all common. "The child becomes the focal point for conflict for diversion of stress within the family" (Bowden and Hopwood 21).

Food issues are central. The deprived child has a strange relationship with food, as can be seen from the above described behaviors. Parents contribute to this by restriction of food or inappropriate feeding (Bowden and Hopwood 21). There seems to be a direct relationship with this response and the Brewery of Eggshells and pudding with hide stories.

Rarely is it the parents who seek help for the deprived child. Usually they are referred by physicians, schools, clinics, and social workers (Hopwood and Becker 439). Although we saw that many of the parents of changelings sought a consultation, many denied problems which were obvious to others.

Children with growth failure due to emotional deprivation are also at risk of physical abuse. Many come from homes where they are overtly physically abused. While there is no data that these parents seek to "banish" the affected child, their abuse is parallel to the treatment meted out to discovered changelings.

As to resolution of emotionally caused growth failure, when the children are removed from the stressful home environment, they exhibit dramatic changes in behavior. The bizarre eating and drinking habits cease. They stop stealing and hoarding food. They no longer eat to the point of vomiting. They become more outgoing and social. Their language and motor skills improve, and they demonstrate a significant improvement in cognitive skills (Bowden and Hopwood 26). They exhibit growth rates of three to six times the normal rate (24). In fact, "the most conclusive evidence for establishment of this diagnosis [psychosocial dwarfism] is the rapid and significant changes in the dynamics of the family relationship and the linear growth upon removal from the stressful home environment" (24). By the same token, if these children are returned to the home environment and there have been no significant changes in the dynamics of the family relationship in the meantime, the children again regress and stop growing, the dwarves again ceasing production of human growth hormone.

The similarity to changeling narratives appears to break down at this point. The "real" child is returned, not removed from the home. There is no instantaneous recovery. However, the fact that the parents in the changeling stories now perceive the infant as "theirs" may be an indication in the successful changeling stories that there has been a change in the parent's ability to bond to the child. As can be seen, not all attempts to get the "real" child back were successful.

What appears to be more pertinent is the dramatic improvement seen in emotionally deprived infants once they are in a supportive atmosphere. In such circumstances changes in affect and behavior occur within a few days, and weight gain and catch up growth is noticeable in a few weeks. It might be this quick recovery that inspired the instantaneous return of the "real" child in the changeling stories. Not all of the returns were instantaneous.

The congruence of the symptoms of failure to thrive and the features of the changeling narrative suggest that the changeling stories may have originated from the same phenomena as failure to thrive. Folk interpretation of the inexplicable, the "invisible," put fairy changelings in the cradle to embody a "change" for which they had no language to express what they saw. With the medical model of failure to thrive, the phenomena embodied in the changeling was rearticulated under the medical gaze, "the relation between the visible and the invisible—which is necessary to all concrete knowledge—changed its structure, revealing through gaze and language what had previously been below and beyond their domain" (Foucault xii). Medicine could now see what had eluded its gaze up until the beginning of this century, but which had not eluded the somewhat differently structured gaze of tradition.

References

Bakwin, Harry. 1942. "Loneliness in Infants." *American Journal of the Diseases of Children* 63: 30–40.

———. 1949. "Emotional Deprivation in Infants." *Journal of Pediatrics* 35: 512–21.

Bithoney, William G., et al. 1989. "Prospective Evaluation of Weight Gain in Both Nonorganic and Organic Failure-to-Thrive Children: An Outpatient Trial of a Multidisciplinary Team Intervention Strategy." *Developmental and Behavioral Pediatrics* 10: 27–31.

Bowden, M. Leora, and Nancy J. Hopwood. 1982. "Psychosocial Dwarfism: Identification, Intervention and Planning." *Social Work in Health Care* 7.3: 15–36.

Briggs, Katharine. 1967. *Fairies in Tradition and Literature.* London: Routledge and Kegan Paul.

———. 1977. *British Folktales.* New York: Pantheon P.

———. 1978. *The Vanishing People.* New York: Pantheon Books.

Chapin, Henry Dwight. 1908. "A Plan of Dealing with Atrophic Infants and Children." *Archives of Pediatrics* 25: 491–6.

———. 1915. "Are Institutions for Infants Necessary?" *The Journal of the American Medical Association* 64: 1–3.

Chatoor, Irene, et al. 1984. "Non-organic Failure to Thrive: A Developmental Perspective." *Pediatric Annals* 13: 829.

Coleman, Rose W., and Sally Provence. 1957. "Environmental Retardation (Hospitalism) in Infants Living in Families." *Pediatrics* 19: 285–92.

Croker, Thomas Crofton. 1983. *Fairy Legends and Traditions of the South of Ireland.* 1825. Delmar: Scholars' Facsimiles & Reprints.

Deane, Tony, and Tony Shaw. 1975. *The Folklore of Cornwall.* London: Batsford.

Donohue, W.L. 1948. "Dysendocrinism." *Journal of Pediatrics* 32: 739–48.

Donohue, W.L., and Irene Uchida. 1954. "Leprechaunism: A Euphemism for a Rare Familial Disorder." *Journal of Pediatrics* 45: 505–19.

Ellerstein, Norman S., and Barbara E. Ostrov. 1985. "Growth Patterns in Children Hospitalized Because of Caloric-Deprivation Failure to Thrive." *American Journal of the Diseases of Children* 139: 164–6.

El-Shamy, Hasan M. 1980. *Folktales of Egypt.* Chicago: U of Chicago P.

Evans-Wentz, W.Y. 1966. *The Fairy Faith in Celtic Countries.* 1911. New York: University Books.

Fischoff, Joseph, Charles F. Whitten, and Marvin G. Pettit. 1971. "A Psychiatric Study of Mothers of Infants with Growth Failure Secondary to Maternal Deprivation." *Journal of Pediatrics* 79: 209–15.

Foucault, Michel. 1975. *The Birth of the Clinic: An Archaeology of Medical Perception.* Trans. A. M. Sheridan Smith. New York: Vintage-Random House.

Fraiberg, Selma. 1975. "Ghosts in the Nursery." *Journal of the American Academy of Child Psychiatry* 14: 387–421.

Frank, Deborah A., and Steven H. Zeisel. 1988. "Failure to Thrive." *The Pediatric Clinics of North America* 35: 1187–206.

Frasier, S. Douglas. 1980. *Pediatric Endocrinology.* New York: Grune & Stratton.

Gardner, Lytt I. 1972. "Deprivation Dwarfism." *Scientific American* 227: 76–82.

———. 1980. "Physiopathology of the Human Growth Hormone with Special Reference to Deprivation Dwarfism." *Problems in Pediatric Endocrinology.* Ed. C. La Cauza and A. W. Root. London: Academic P, 73–81.

Gellis, S.S., and B.M. Kagan. 1973. *Current Pediatric Therapy.* Philadelphia: W.B. Saunders.

Goodman, L.S., and A. Gilman. 1970. *The Pharmacological Basis of Therapeutics.* New York: The Macmillan Company.

Grass, Gunter. 1990. *The Tin Drum.* 1966. Trans. Ralph Manheim. New York: Vintage International-Random House.

Hartland, Edwin Sidney. 1986. *The Science of Fairy Tales—An Inquiry into Fairy Mythology.* 1891. Detroit: Singing Tree P.

Homer, Charles, and Stephen Ludwig. 1981. "Categorization of Etiology of Failure to Thrive." *American Journal of the Diseases of Children* 135: 848–51.

Hopwood, Nancy J., and Dorothy J. Becker. 1979. "Psychosocial Dwarfism: Detection, Evaluation and Management." *Child Abuse and Neglect* 3: 439.

Hopwood, Nancy J., and Gerald F. Powell. 1974. "Emotional Deprivation: Report of a Case with Features of Leprechaunism." *American Journal of the Diseases of Children* 127: 892–4.

Hufford, David J. 1982. *The Terror That Comes in the Night: An Experience-Centered Study of Supernatural Assault Traditions.* Philadelphia: U of Pennsylvania P.

Jacobs, Joseph. 1968. *Celtic Fairy Tales.* 1891. New York: Dover Publications.

Jones, Eirwin. 1978. *Folk Tales of Wales.* Llandysul: Gomer P.

Jones, Gwyn. 1984. *Welsh Legends and Folktales.* London: Oxford UP.

Jones, T. Gwynn. 1930. *Welsh Folklore and Folk-Custom.* London: Methuen & Co., Ltd.

Kallo, A., Irene Lakatos, and L. Szijarto. 1965. "Leprechaunism (Donohue's syndrome)." *Journal of Pediatrics* 66: 372–9.

Der Kaloustian, Vazken M., et al. 1971. "Leprechaunism: A Report of Two New Cases." *American Journal of the Diseases of Children* 122: 442–5.

Keightley, Thomas. 1978. *The Fairy Mythology.* 1878. Rpt. as *The World Guide to Gnomes, Fairies, Elves and Other Little People.* New York: Avenel Books.

Klaus, Marshall H., and John H. Kennell. 1982. *Parent-Infant Bonding.* St. Louis: C. V. Mosby Company.

Kobayashi, Masashi, et al. 1988. "Fluctuation of Insulin Resistance in a Leprechaun with a Primary Defect in Insulin Binding." *Journal of Clinical Endocrinology and Metabolism* 66: 1084–8.

Koel, Bertram S. 1969. "Failure to Thrive and Fatal Injury as a Continuum." *American Journal of the Diseases of Children* 118: 565–7.

Lévi-Strauss, Claude. 1958. "The Structural Study of Myth." *Myth: A Symposium.* Ed. Thomas A. Sebeok. Bloomington: Indiana UP, 81–106.

Logan, Patrick. 1981. *The Old Gods: The Facts About Irish Fairies.* Belfast: Appletree P.

Manning-Sanders, Ruth. 1972. *A Book of Charms and Changelings.* New York: E. P. Dutton.

Munro, Joyce Underwood. 1990. "The Fairy Changeling as a Folk Articulation of Failure to Thrive in Infants and Children: The Invisible Made Visible." MA essay. Wayne State U, Detroit.

Neumann, Von Joseph. 1986. "Der Zwerg in Sage und Märchen—Ursache oder Abbild der Missgestalt des Menschen?" ["The Dwarf in Fable and Story— The Origin or Image of Deformities in Humans?"] *Gesnerus* 43: 223–40.

Nic Leodhas, Sorche. 1965. *Thistle and Thyme: Tales and Legends from Scotland.* London: The Bodley Head.

Oates, R. Kim. 1984. "Child Abuse and Non-organic Failure to Thrive: Similarities and Differences in the Parents." *Australian Paediatric Journal* 20: 177–80.

———. 1984. "Non-organic Failure to Thrive." *Australian Paediatric Journal* 20: 95–100.

Oates, R. Kim, Anthony Peacock, and Douglas Forrest. 1984. "Development in Children Following Abuse and Nonorganic Failure to Thrive." *American Journal of the Diseases of Children* 138: 764–7.

———. 1985. "Long-Term Effects of Nonorganic Failure to Thrive." *Pediatrics* 75: 36–40.

Patton, Robert Gray, and Lytt I. Gardner. 1969. "Short Stature Associated with Maternal Deprivation Syndrome: Disordered Family Environment as Cause of So-Called Idiopathic Hypopituitarism." *Endocrine and Genetic Diseases of Childhood.* Ed. Lytt I. Gardner. Philadelphia: W.B. Saunders, 77–89.

Philological Society. 1971. *The Compact Edition of the Oxford English Dictionary.* New York: Oxford UP.

Piers, Maria W. 1978. *Infanticide—Past and Present.* New York: W.W. Norton.

Powell, G.F., J.A. Brasel, and R.M. Blizzard. 1967. "Emotional Deprivation and Growth Retardation Simulating Idiopathic Hypopituitarism." *The New England Journal of Medicine* 276: 1271–8.

Pugliese, Michael T., et al. 1987. "Parental Beliefs As a Cause of Non-Organic Failure to Thrive." *Pediatrics* 80: 175–82.

Quayle, Eric, and Michael Foreman. 1986. *The Little Peoples' Pageant of Cornish Legends.* New York: Simon & Schuster

Rees, Alwyn, and Brinley Rees. 1961. *Celtic Heritage: Ancient Tradition in Ireland and Wales.* London: Thames and Hudson.

Richmond, Julius B., Evelyn Eddy, and Morris Green. 1958. "Rumination: A Psychosomatic Syndrome of Infancy." *Pediatrics* 55: 49–54.

Rudolph, A.M. 1982. *Pediatrics.* Norwalk: Appleton Century Crofts.

Simpson, Jacqueline. 1979. *Icelandic Folktales and Legends.* Berkeley: U of California P.

Strindberg, Gert. 1959. *Norwegian Fairy Tales*. London: Frederick Muller.

Szilagyi, Peter G., et al. 1987. "Pancreatic Exocrine Aplasia, Clinical Features of Leprechaunism, and Abnormal Gonodotropin Regulation." *Pediatric Pathology* 7: 51–61.

Thomas, W. Jenkyn. 1979. *The Welsh Fairy-Book*. Cardiff: John Jones Publishing.

Thompson, Stith, ed. 1956. *Motif-Index of Folk Literature*. 6 vols. Bloomington: Indiana UP.

Vines, Robert. 1982. "Failure to Thrive." *Australian Family Physician* 11: 430–5.

Weston, Janet, et al. 1987. "Prolonged Breastfeeding and Nonorganic Failure to Thrive." *American Journal of the Diseases of Children* 141: 242–3.

Wilcox, W.D., P. Nieburg, and D.S. Miller. 1989. "Failure to Thrive: A Continuous Problem of Definition." *Clinical Pediatrics* 28: 391–4.

Appendix

1. Jacobs, "Brewery of Eggshells" 223–5   (Wales)
2. Croker, "The Brewery of Eggshells" 65–71   (Ireland)
3. Briggs, *The Fairies in Tradition* 118   (Great Britain)
4. Keightley, "The Changeling" 125–6   (Scandinavia)
5. Briggs, *The Vanishing People* 102–3   (Scotland)
6. Simpson, "Father of the Eighteen Elves" 28–31   (Iceland)
7. Thomas, "The Llanfabon Changeling" 56–64   (Wales)
8. Briggs, *British*, "Johnny in the Cradle" 161–2   (Scotland)
9. Keightley, "The Changeling" 335–6   (Scottish Lowlands)
10. Evans-Wentz, "A Changeling Musician" 128   (Isle of Man)
11. Deane and Shaw, "Betty Stogs" 93–4   (Cornwall)
12. Croker, "The Two Gossips" 81–3   (Ireland)
13. Keightley, "The Strathspey Lads" 393   (Scotland)
14. Logan, "The Father Sees the Change" 106–7   (Ireland)
15. Logan, "The Fairy Wants Her Own" 110–1   (Ireland)
16. Keightley, "Enobling Human Milk" 126   (Hessian)
17. Keightley, "The Dirty Changeling" 398   (Isle of Man)
18. Logan, "Treat the Changeling Kindly" 107–8   (Ireland)
19. Logan, "The Changeling Who Stayed" 108–9   (Ireland)
20. Croker, "The Changeling" 77–8   (Ireland)
21. El-Shamy, "The Changeling" 180   (Egypt)
22. Keightley, "The Changeling" 227–8   (Germany)
23. Simpson, "The Changeling Who Stretched" 25–6   (Iceland)
24. Simpson, "Making a Changeling "27–8   (Iceland)
25. Logan, "The Changeling Who Stretched" 109   (Iceland)

"The Blast" in Newfoundland Fairy Tradition

Barbara Rieti

A middle-aged woman told me about two men who encountered the fairies near her community of Clarke's Beach.[1] One was hunting for cattle in the woods when "something flicked him in the eye, like a bough," and he was permanently blinded: "they think that's what it was, it was a 'blast.'" Another man felt a sharp pain in his face when he drank from a running brook:

> And his face gathered and broke, and everything worked out of it, they said: sticks, stones, feathers, hairs, everything. But his face never went back at all.

("He's still like it," added her husband.) A much older informant in Marysvale told me how her brother got a blast as a young boy, when he thought he saw some other boys coming to meet him at three o'clock after school:

> And that was the good people. The fairies, he called them. And they beat him up, boy. His heart was on the left side; they put it on the right . . . . he was in bed for three years and three months. . . . And his side then broke out, see, in nine holes . . . yes, and everything come out of that. Yes, everything. Hairs, and—everything come out of it that you can mention.

A third informant, in Shoe Cove, told me that "a blast" is when the fairies "shoot something at you"; his father got one in the leg, and although a felt rag was removed, the leg never returned to normal.

Here is the ancient "elf-shot," the *Krankheitsprojektile* envisioned for centuries in far-flung cultures as inflicting illness from malevolent sources.[2] Here also, however, are clear parallels to "modern" legends of contamination and infestation, such as spiders in hairdos and hairballs in lungs.[3] Like most powerful elements in folk narrative, the blast is simultaneously old and modern, expressive both of specific cultural concerns and widespread human tendencies, and amenable to multiple interpretations.

The first, and often only, line of commentary that folklorists usually take on fairy inflicted injury is that the "folk," not "understanding" the biological basis of various afflictions, blame them on a "supernatural" agency. They may elaborate by correlating the symptoms of certain ailments with those found in narrative. The scars on the legs of Mary Hackett (a pseudonym), my only informant who experienced a blast, could have been caused by varicose ulcers which festered for several years, possibly infected (as she suggests) by the various home remedies applied to them. In connection with the blasts from which bizarre items are expelled, teratoma and osteomyelitis are worth particular mention. The first is a congenital tumor composed of tissue foreign to the site, containing one or more of three primary germ layers, so that hair and teeth may indeed be found inside it; although usually found on the ovaries or testes, it may appear elsewhere as a dermoid cyst. The second is a bacterial infection of the bone in which pieces of dead bone may detach from the rest of the bone; these "primary sequestra" may be enveloped by new growth (containing granular material), but characteristically a passage bursts to the exterior where it remains as a constant drain until the necrotic bone is surgically removed. The sequestrectomy is a prominent feature in blast narratives, as in an account given to a Clarke's Beach student about a man who was cutting down an old apple tree when he got a pain in his thumb. The thumb festered until a local healer cut it open,

> . . . and took out rabbits' bones and pieces of rags and felt and you name it, it came out of the hand. He got a blast, yes, really a blast. Because they didn't want the tree cut down—the old people didn't. And they were dead now, oh yes, they were dead for years . . . (74-209/n.p.)

This story is typical of the way in which the onset of an ailment may be linked with the displeasure of some supernatural agency, and the fairies in particular are quick to take offense. One informant said:

> I don't know too many fairy stories but I do know one lady who said she was taken away by the fairies once and they wanted her to drink out of a certain cup, and when she wouldn't drink they threw the cup at her. It struck her in the hip. An apse (boil) broke out and they said that everything came out of that side—moths, hare's teeth—so they said that the fairies did it to her when they threw something at her. (71-44/64)

The cup is a motif in an Irish narrative type in which someone blunders into a nocturnal fairy tea party in a kitchen, and the angry fairies strike her with a teacup or other object; bits of the object later work their way out of the wound (Curtin 179; Jackson 91; Kennedy 1891, 105–9; Kennedy 1870, 140–1). In the only Newfoundland version I know of, which I recorded myself, upon emerging the chip of cup is fitted into a broken cup on the shelf. In any case, there is a widespread prohibition on eating or drinking, or indeed having any interaction with the fairies; so the hapless victims in the account above and below were following—not breaching—traditional wisdom when they were struck. A collector's mother said:

> When I was a little girl our mothers used to always warn us not to talk to fairies, or take anything from them. One day we were playing in the woods when six of them came up to us. They had things in their hands and they used to hold them out to us. But we wouldn't touch it. Then they got angry and threw them at us. One little boy got struck in the hip with something. After this we ran home. His hip got very sore. It "rose and broke," and a piece of comb came out of his hip. He was crippled all his life. (72-104/22)

Although specific provocations may incur otherworlders' wrath, some encounters are entirely accidental. In St. John's, a girl felt something like a hand smack her face, and days later old cloth, rusty nails, needles, and bits of rock and clay came out: "This was the blast and it was believed to have been caused by her walking across the path of ghosts" (FSC74-99). A Clarke's Beach collector recorded that,

> Mrs. Viola Simms . . . recalls an incident when a child became "flicked." A Mrs. Anderson . . . had a son who had been playing outside one evening around dusk. When the boy came in, he complained of a pain in his shoulder that later moved down to his foot. His parents took him to the doctor but nothing could be found wrong. Finally his father said the boy was "flicked" by the dead. The old people often called it "flicked by the good people." This meant that one had been in contact with the dead. Mrs. Anderson decided to poultice the foot, and a couple of days later it broke and they removed two old weatherbeaten bones. These bones in no way belonged to the boy's own body. Mrs. Anderson still has them preserved in alcohol. (FSC76-113)

Part of the folkloristic truism that fairy stories "explain" illness or injury is that the folk diagnosis is made in the absence of official medical models, but as the example above shows, a medical consultation may figure in the narrative, and the diagnosis might be made in preference to a doctor's opinion. John Webster complained in 1673 that when he was a physician in the North of England, "for the most part the common people, if they chance to have any sort of the Epilepsie, Palsie, Convulsions, or the like, do presently perswade themselves that they are bewitched, forespoken, blasted, fairy-taken, or haunted with some evil spirit, and the like" (Latham 33). Some Newfoundland doctors, at least in legend, were more sympathetic than Webster and even made supernatural diagnoses themselves.

A number of children went into Tinkers Marsh, Western Bay, berry-picking. When they came home, they were all full of lumps and bumps. They were taken to the doctor and he said that it was the faries [sic]. He took the children to where they were berrypicking and called out the faries, and when they came out he asked them to touch the children and when they did the lumps and bumps disappeared. (FSC76-38)

Other stories make "doctors baffled" into a motif which reinforces a supernatural interpretation, as does the autopsy which reveals no natural cause of death. A high school teacher told his class about a girl who was taken by the fairies and on her return began to waste away.

Her worried parents sent her to St. John's to the hospital. Here doctors could find nothing wrong with her, but they held her for observation. Several months later she died stark raving mad with hair grown out all over her body. An autopsy revealed nothing. (Q68-44/6–7)

While there can be little doubt that such "fairy" afflictions have their origin in physical and mental disturbances, to say that their main role *is* etiology, that is, to "explain" the disturbances to tradition-bearers, is a limited view which ignores the important contextual fact that the stories are told long after the original event, by people with no particular need to explain anything. Their narrative value, then, must derive from other, or additional, sources. One possible source is the tension between nature and culture which, in a longer study, I have suggested is one of the underlying dynamics of Newfoundland fairy tradition as a whole. In this paradigm (in which the fairies roughly represent "nature"), the blast, with its infusion of noxious organic junk, would represent the threat of intrusive nature in a fundamental and graphic way. Caution must be used in making such culturally specific interpretations, however, for in its broad outlines the Newfoundland blast differs little from its parent stock. Séan Ó Súilleabháin, for example, includes in his questions for fieldworkers, "Were thimbles, pieces of bone, or other objects removed from the wounds of 'elf-shot' people or animals?" (459) and, "Was it believed that some object thrown by the fairies should issue from the sore part of the body before a cure could be effected (e.g., a piece of bone, stone, rag, knife, etc.)?" (479–80). And not only the blast's deep roots in the past but its relatives in modern folk and popular culture demonstrate a powerful cross-cultural appeal. A brief examination of antecedent sources, then, should illuminate not only the Newfoundland blast but its present-day counterparts, such as Margaret Atwood's short story, "Kat," in which a woman saves a teratoma containing hair, teeth, and bones in a jar and names it "Hairball."

Newfoundland fairy tradition comes primarily from southeast Irish and West Country English tradition, and direct parallels can be found in both areas; but of course the whole of fairy tradition is very old, very widespread, and amazingly tenacious. Charles Singer, discussing the "native Teutonic" medical magic of England, delineates two of its four characteristic elements as "the doctrine of nines" and "the doctrine of elf-shot"; he notes that "Anglo-Saxon and even Middle English literature is replete with the notion of disease caused by the arrows of mischievous supernatural beings," and quotes from the *Lay of the Nine Healing Herbs* which herbs work against (among other things) "worm blast, water blast, thorn blast, thistle blast, ice blast, venom blast," and three other "blasts" lost from the manuscript (353–7). Nancy Scheper-Hughes identifies the earliest recorded folk belief about mental illness in Ireland as the Druidic priests' power to inflict madness by casting a "magic wisp of straw," and cites ancient Irish laws on the necessity of "fettering those upon whom the magic wisp has been cast" (78). Straw and grass remain common fairy projectiles in modern Irish and Newfoundland accounts, in which they are often borne on a wind. In St. Brendan's, Newfoundland, for example:

> One woman . . . became a cripple at the age of thirty-five. She explained that it happened one evening when she was weeding a cabbage patch. She was struck in the legs by a straw. The straw was carried by a fairy. Fairies were small creatures wearing full tail dresses, they were found on marshes. Their presence was felt by a strong gust of wind and straw blown around by the wind. People say they went around in a circle making a hissing noise. Today the older people still believe in fairies. (FSC75-262)[4]

Bewitched persons across medieval Europe routinely expelled bizarre items, leading Kittredge to observe that "one of the best-known symptoms of bewitchment was the vomiting of bones, nails, needles, balls of wool, bunches of hair, and other things" (133).[5] Needles were specifically said to have been injected: Reginald Scot, cataloguing witches' supposed crimes in 1584, says, "some write that with wishing they can send needles into the livers of their enemies" (6), and indeed needles were such a popular motif that they were seized upon by pretenders to occult powers: Samuel Rowlands in 1602 knew "persons who pretended to have the art of shooting needles into the flesh," and an Elizabethan "cony-catcher" claimed the ability "to fill a Letter full of Needles, which shall be laide after such a Mathematicall order, that when hee openes it to whom it is sent, they shall all spring up and flye into his body as forceably, as if they had beene blowne up with gunpowder" (Kittredge 133–4). Pins and needles punctuate West Country witchcraft tales: Joseph Glanvil describes a Taunton girl who claimed a witch made her swallow pins which came out of various swellings on her body, and adds that "examples of this sort are infinite" (332); an evil spirit stuck pins into some Bristol girls in 1762 (Kittredge 134).[6]

Although English witch traditions flourished in Newfoundland, I know of only one instance in which a living person (an old man) is held responsible for a blast; the account is from Bishop's Cove, a community of Devon-based settlement, where fishbones and straw were taken from the leg of the informant's friend, who ended up in a mental hospital (FSC70-25/94). Needles, however, became a very popular fairy projectile. According to one collector, "a traditional story in Bay Bulls tells of a lady who often crossed intersecting paths in the woods without bread in her pocket; for not carrying the bread the fairies gave her a 'blast,' i.e. shot needles at her and took away her voice" (70-26/50). "Needles and stuff like that" came out of the arm of one "fairy-struck" man, "and he lost the use of his arm" (64-13/C66/14). Another man was trouting at dusk when he felt "a shower or something" go over him, and went home with a pain in his side. His mother put poultices on it and,

> . . . a darn needle with wistard [darning needle with worsted] came out of it. And they said that's what the good people—fairies threw it at him. Because the fairies didn't want him there that hour in the evening, you know, that's what happened. (76-350/20)

A Bishop's Cove student recalled a story about a local man:

> When he was a little boy about eight years old he got in with the fairies. What they did to him was that they pricked his finger with a small needle. He didn't know for sure if the needle was still in his finger until one year he was down on the Labrador fishing. One day he felt a tingling in his elbow and then a sharp pain. When he rolled up his sleeve, what should he find but a needle sticking out from his elbow. After forty years the needle had worked its way up through his arm to his elbow. (72-262/14)

The blast's long pedigree, by showing its durability in human thought, supports one very twentieth century reading. It has probably struck the modern reader, whether sympathetic to psychoanalytic approaches or not, that there is something rather Freudian about all this "shooting," "pricking" and penetration. Such a reading would suggest that the appeal of "blast" stories comes at least partly from an unconscious use of sexual imagery or symbols. The various projectiles, for example, seem unmistakably phallic. Richard Spears's *Slang and Euphemism* gives "needle" and "pin" for penis (268), and Alan Dundes, in his investigation of couvade, makes a case for a bone as a penis symbol (as in "boner": 1987a, 164).[7] The hair or fur—or the occasional cup—that are also found in the (symbolic?) wound of a blast can also be read as a genital symbol, and since they fill the same narrative slot (that is, the extruded matter) are what Dundes calls "allomotifs" or functionally equivalent units (1987b, 172). In the latter discussion, Dundes mentions the potential of the mouth as a genital symbol (171), which would give an interesting reading to an already startling account of a girl who went for water one night and crossed a "fairy marsh" without bread. She was gone a long time,

> . . . and when she returned she said that she had been on merry-go-rounds with lovely people. Then she giggled and laughed continuously. During her laughing, her mouth kept going up until it reached her ears. The next morning her parents took her to the doctor in Spaniard's Bay and he said it was definitely the fairies who had caused this. He then crossed her mouth. Her parents had to bring her back for this treatment nine days in a row. On the ninth morning her mouth returned to normal and no further treatments were necessary. (FSC74-113)

Here is pleasure run amok, in the ghastly uncontrollable grin. Although there is little overt erotic content in Newfoundland fairylore, there is a direct contextual connection between the fairies and irregular sexual activity which would support the more arbitrary translation of specific motifs. For example, one woman had a mentally and physically disabled "fairy child" because she was taken away by the fairies one night; it is not clear, however, whether she was already pregnant and the experience "marked" the child (a common motif) or whether the fairies were actually considered the progenitors (67-34/C427/23).[8] It might also be significant that the grinning girl lacked bread—a common anti-fairy device and also an explicit symbol of fertility ("bread in the basket," a "bun in the oven" = pregnant). She could also have carried salt, another prophylactic and symbol laden substance.[9]

The number nine pervades blast narratives and folk medicine; in the latter, it is especially prominent in birth related practices, possibly metonymic with the number of months of gestation.[10] Even if one discounts a psychosexual interpretation of individual symbols and elements, there remains in the blast a clear, if grotesque, analogy to impregnation and birth. In a text from North River, the unwholesome issue is even alive, or at least animated by an unnamed force.

> One time there was a dance in the parish hall and during the evening one young man noticed that his hand had become infected and was festering, although he had no recollection of having injured himself. He betook himself to the priest who told him to go home and put a poultice on the infection, and to throw whatever came out of it into the fire. Well, he did this and whatever was inside flew straight across the room. He picked it up and threw it into the fire, whereupon it shot up the chimney like an explosion. (70–20/47)

He was thus delivered from further trouble, but another man with the same complaint failed to follow the priest's instructions, and was harassed by a series of calamities (70-20/47). This account might remind readers of the scene in the 1979 movie *Alien,* in which the implanted creature bursts from the chest of its human host, and along with its siblings creates the series of calamities that make up the rest of the movie. Blastogenesis (reproduction by budding, or asexual reproduction) seems to figure in "space invasion" movies of pods and body snatchers as part of the same antithesis to humanity that characterizes fairy tradition. (Tabloid tales of "alien" infants also abound and bear much resemblance to changeling stories, which I think are about obnoxious ordinary babies as often as abnormal ones—but that is another essay.)

Sometimes a blast extrusion is kept for future inspection; a Bay Roberts man painfully (laboriously?) produced such an artifact:

> One old man told how he went up to the garden at twilight to have a last look at his vegetable garden before retiring. There was a white gull sitting on his prize turnip, the largest one. He started after the bird and kicked at it. When he did the bird vanished and the man took such a pain in the leg that he could hardly get home. The leg got continually worse, swelled up and crippled the man. There was one night it was particularly sore and a huge boil seemed to rise on the leg. The man's daughter [the informant's wife] was there with several neighbors trying to comfort the man, who was in agony. They concluded that the boil should be "let" and proceeded to do so. As soon as the boil was pierced, a long white string came out and continued to fall in a pile to the floor. It fell of its own accord and the swelling abated as the string accumulated on the floor. The string was kept for years after as proof for unbelievers, but the man always had a crippled leg to his dying day. (78-185/24–7)

According to Ernest Jones, birds are a common phallic and birth symbol; in the same discussion he delineates the fertility symbolization of water and wind, both of which are prominent in blast accounts (1974a). Just before she was blasted, Mary Hackett, my informant, had drunk from a pool of extraordinarily "sweet, lovely" water, which her companion could not see. Jones also claims that breath and wind are functionally equivalent, an equation readily apparent in the older records of the blast (1974a). T. Crofton Croker wrote that "the blast is a large round tumor, which is thought to rise suddenly on the part affected, from the baneful breath cast on it by one of the 'good people' in a moment of vindictive or capricious malice" (1: 307). P.W. Joyce defines the Irish term as: "when a child suddenly fades in health and pines away, he has got a blast,—i.e., a puff of evil wind sent by some baleful sprite has struck him" (216), and Ó Conchubhair in "An Offaly Glossary" defines a "blast" as either "a fairy wind" or "an affection of the eye" (188). Cromek speaks of the "pernicious breath" of the Scottish fairies, and gives a cure for a "breath-blasted" child that involved a virgin getting water from a blessed well in a pitcher that had never been wet (246). The virginal Sabrina of Milton's masque *Comus* could cure shepherds of "all urchin-blasts and ill luck signs/that the shrewd meddling elfe delights to make" (34).[11] Jacob Grimm discusses the "blighting breath of the elves": "Blowing puffing beings language itself shewes them to be from of old," he says, since "spirit," "ghost," and related terms are derived from verbs having to do with breath and wind (2: 460–1). Charles Singer, quoted above on the various "blasts," says that the term from which he translated "blast" comes from a common word for a breath or spirit, and points to an "obvious" analogy between wind and disease.

There is perhaps something ludicrous about attributing "symbolic" significance to wind and water in Newfoundland, where the absence of either is more remarkable than their presence (although that in itself may argue for a symbolic interpretation of their importance in narrative); and if wells, chimneys, and needles are the stuff of Freudian analysis, they are also the stuff of everyday life in the outports. On the other hand, it seems only reasonable to suppose that as fairy tradition takes its imagery from human life, it is bound to have sexual underpinnings and overtones. It is worth noting, in closing this line of inquiry, that in the folklore of extraterrestrial beings, the fairies' close kin, an element of sexuality is often explicit, as in their pseudo-medical probes and experiments.[12]

Not all blast stories contain the spewing-forth motif on which I have based the symbolic analyses above, and not all fairy inflicted injuries are called blasts. To round out this discussion, it is useful to consider the common denominator to all the texts, the basic premise that in certain cases disease is caused by the action of some external agent. To say that the fairies or some other supernatural personage are blamed for a disease, however, is still not to say that this "explains" the disease, for as mentioned earlier, the contact is often accidental (summarized by the key phrase "getting in someone's way"). In other words, it is a random unfortunate encounter with malignant but impersonal forces at large in the world, just like viruses and bacteria. As a matter of being in the wrong place at the wrong time, blast stories can actually be seen as a heightened or metaphorical representation of reality, rather than a "prescientific" misapprehension of it. This may be another reason they are found aesthetically and psychologically satisfying, a safe assumption in view of their persistence long after the advent of antibiotics and other adjuncts of modern medicine.

In support of this assumption, I should point out that shaping by tradition can be observed not only in legend but in firsthand accounts, although these are unfortunately rare. Most accounts are told at some remove from the original event, and it might be supposed that elaboration and conventionalization would increase with time and distance, as indeed they often do in fairy narrative; but a valuable set of interviews made in 1972 with three afflicted persons shows that they themselves may do much of the interpretation (72-236). Working in her home community, the collector found a man much persecuted by the fairies, who permanently blinded him in one attack. On another occasion, he heard a voice saying "Hello there," and he answered, "Go to hell, whoever you are." The next day his stomach swelled out and bore a little handprint; his doctor sent him to hospital in St. John's where seventeen stones and a thirty-five pound tumor were removed. "But the thing is," the informant explained, "I never had a stitch up until the fairies gave me that blast" (26). The other two informants were equally adamant, although one had modified her story over the years under pressure from a scoffing family: she still maintained that the fairies had given her a "flick," but she claimed not to remember that fishbones and straw had emerged from her leg, a detail the collector and her mother remembered quite well (65–6). In contrast, the other informant had the support of her family in the diagnosis, and fifty-three years after the event gave a wealth of detail. She was eight years old, walking with her stepsister on a marsh, when a big ball of fire dropped between them (unseen by the sister) and she felt a dart in her leg.[13] The leg swelled until her mother poulticed it and three bones came out; these were put in a butter dish for the doctor but disappeared overnight: "the bad people came and got them," said the informant, who was laid up for nine weeks, ". . . for years and years that spot would break out in May and October when the fairies shift their camps out in the summer and back again in the fall. Even now me leg comes again those months." On further questioning from the collector, she even added that she had in fact seen two fairies that evening; she couldn't see their faces, but they were about two feet tall, and wore turned-up shoes, red suits, and peaked caps (14–8).[14]

Such elaboration occurs when a story is told often, in the context of other stories like it, and the collector observed that the account above was retold "in the manner of someone who has retold something many times" (13). A story does not bear constant repetition merely to explain a particular incident, but because it is found interesting—hence meaningful—at other levels. For this informant, who cleaned houses for a living, the course of a painful injury became a drama in which she was singled out to star: "Judging by her pleased and proud manner in relating this story," the collector wrote, "it is possible that Mrs. Baker has enjoyed the bit of extra attention it has accorded her and may be the bright spot in her hard-working life" (62). A fundamental aspect of fairy stories so obvious that it might be overlooked in the pursuit of more subtle theories is that they are marvellous and mysterious, and whether believed or not, impart an imaginative dimension to everyday life. Fairy tradition posits an otherworld existing alongside the everyday world, with inhabitants who are dangerous, unpredictable, and best left alone. Like fate, the fairies are not to be tempted; but outrageously enough, even the careful and the innocent are not immune to their slings and arrows.

Notes

1. The interviews quoted here were part of the research for a doctoral thesis entitled "Newfoundland Fairy Traditions: A Study in Narrative and Belief" completed at Memorial University of Newfoundland, 1990, and to be published by Memorial University's Institute for Social and Economic Research in 1991 as *Strange Terrain: The Fairy World in Newfoundland*. My field tapes and notes are deposited in the Memorial University of Newfoundland Folklore and Language Archive (MUNFLA) under accession numbers 86-124 and 88-055. I am grateful to MUNFLA for permission to use archive materials for this paper, which was presented in an abbreviated version to the American Folklore Society at Philadelphia in October 1989. (Note: The first number in a MUNFLA accession number gives the approximate year in which an item was recorded, unless otherwise noted; FSC=Folklore Survey Card rather than a manuscript; a "C" number refers to a tape and "Q" a questionnaire.) This essay is respectfully dedicated to my first folklore teacher, Professor Alan Dundes.

2. The standard monograph, *Krankheitsprojektile*, is by Lauri Honko.

3. Shirley Marchalonis discusses medieval analogues for "the fatal hairdo" (267–70); for hairballs in lungs, see Brunvand (1986, 77–8). Brunvand also discusses "bosom serpent" legends, in which ingested insect or reptile eggs hatch and grow into creatures which have to be lured from the stomach (1984, 107–11); Harold Schechter takes up the theme in his book, *The Bosom Serpent* (19–24). Stories of such parasites are known in Newfoundland, but they are quite distinct from "blast" stories, as such "water wolves" are considered a natural or biological phenomenon.

4. For Irish examples, see Wilde (121) and Westropp.

5. He gives copious references to this (453–6) and to the concept of disease as a foreign body (134, 455–6).

6. Bewitched Irish persons also vomited foul matter. Ireland also has a Gaelic "slumber-pin" motif: Ciarán Bairéad summarizes a narrative in which a man has prevented the fairies from abducting a woman upon whom "the fairies take their revenge by putting a slumber-pin into her hair which deprives her of speech" (144–5). Other examples may be found in *Béaloideas* 35–7 (1967–68): two old women (fairies) from a fort put a "slumber-pin" in a girl's ear and substitute a changeling (357); fairies put a "slumber-pin" in another girl's ear and a goose in her place in bed (368).

7. Spears also gives "flicking" for "fucking" (139), and one might also note the phonetic similarity of "flick" to related phallic slang terms like "dick" and "prick." Unlike the term "blast," which is found throughout the province and is well documented in antecedent sources, "flick" seems to be a regional usage in the area of Conception Bay from Clarke's Beach to Carbonear. A likely etymology arises from the conversation of my neighbor, Alexander Parsons, who saw the fairies himself as a boy in Freshwater, Conception Bay, and who knows of an Upper Island Cove woman who was "afflicted" (by the fairies) so that wire and other stuff came out of her hand. This rather formal, almost archaic expression— I do not think he would speak of someone suffering from an ordinary ailment as "afflicted"— elides easily to "flicked," just as the key phrase "in contact" (with the fairies) is often rendered by collectors "in tact" or "in tack." The phonetic conversion would be assisted by the idea of a glancing blow; for instance, a Spaniard's Bay boy who was

"lugged away by the fairies" felt a belt "flick" him on the leg, and when a doctor later removed fish-like bones from the leg he demanded, "Miss, where now has dis boy been flicked with the fairies?" (75-163/18–9). "Afflicted" was the common term for "bewitched" persons in Salem, Massachusetts (see Boyer and Nissenbaum), and in connection with Newfoundland witchcraft, John Widdowson has documented a related usage: an informant told him that in order to break a spell, one had to cause a "body infliction" to the witch by drawing part of her body and attacking it in some way so that the witch was injured in the corresponding place (67-22/23).

8. Sexual suggestiveness is an old strain in fairylore, at least on the part of commentators like Wilhelm Grimm, who wrote of the Brittany fairies, "Woe to the damsels who come near the Courils! Nine months afterwards something new takes place in the house; the birth of a young sorcerer, who is not indeed a dwarf, but to whom the malicious spirits give the feature of a young villager; so great is their power and subtility" (Croker 3: 150). The only fairy lover legend I know of (in Newfoundland) was recorded by Margaret Bennett from Scottish Gaelic tradition on the west coast (180–1).

9. Given a lengthy treatment by Ernest Jones in "The Symbolic Significance of Salt."

10. Women used to stay in bed for nine days after a birth, for example; and one collector observed that miscarriages might occur nine days after a serious fright or injury, and that an infant breast-fed longer than nine months would become frail (75-295/n.p.).

11. Urchin = fairy or evil spirit (Keightley 320).

12. Alien abductors particularly like to poke people with pins, a habit Bill Ellis has noted for its counterpart in Shakespearean fairylore (Narváez 9–10).

13. John Aubrey, describing *ignis fatuus* ("called by the vulgar Kit of the Candlestick") in *The Natural History of Wiltshire*, adds, "it may be this is that which they call a blast or blight in the country." John Britton interpolates an editorial note that as a boy he was "often terrified by stories of their leading travellers astray, and fascinating them" (17–8).

14. The turned-up shoes are the only uncommon detail here, for in general there is little storybook influence on Newfoundland fairy tradition; the small handprint on the first informant's stomach is likewise atypical, as the fairies are only occasionally depicted as being very small. The only instance I know of in which the fairies are tiny *and* winged is hardly Disneyesque, for an informant in Bishop's Cove told me that only a few years ago a swarm of bumblebees surrounded a young man in a boat; as a result of this "blast," the man died in hospital although "there was not a mark on his body."

References

Atwood, Margaret. 1990. "Kat." *The New Yorker* 5 March: 38–44.
Aubrey, John. 1969. *The Natural History of Wiltshire (Written between 1656 and 1691): Edited, and Elucidated by Notes by John Britton*. 1847. Intro. by K.G. Ponting. Newton Abbot, Devon: David and Charles.
Bairéad, Ciarán. 1964. "Scéalta agus Seanchas on Achréidh." *Béaloideas* 32: 99–147.

Bennett, Margaret. 1989. *The Last Stronghold: Scottish Gaelic Traditions in Newfoundland*. Canada's Atlantic Folklore and Folklife Series No. 13. St. John's: Breakwater.

Black's Medical Dictionary. 1985. Ed. C.W.H. Havard. 35th ed. London: A. & C. Black.

Boyer, Paul, and Stephen Nissenbaum. 1978. *Salem Possessed: The Social Origins of Witchcraft*. Cambridge, Mass.: Harvard UP.

Brunvand, Jan Harold. 1984. *The Choking Doberman and Other "New" Urban Legends*. New York and London: W.W. Norton.

———. 1986. *The Mexican Pet: More "New" Urban Legends and Some Old Favorites*. New York: W.W. Norton.

Churchill's Medical Dictionary. 1989. New York: Churchill Livingstone.

Croker, T. Crofton. 1826–8. *Fairy Legends and Traditions of the South of Ireland*. 2nd ed. 3 vols. London: John Murray.

Cromek, R.H. 1880. *Remains of Nithsdale and Galloway Song: With Historical and Traditional Notices Relative to the Manners and Customs of the Peasantry*. 1810. Paisley: Alexander Gardner.

Curtin, Jeremiah. 1895. *Tales of the Fairies and of the Ghost World Collected from Oral Tradition in South-West Munster*. Boston: Little, Brown.

Dundes, Alan. 1987a. "Couvade in Genesis." *Parsing through Customs: Essays by a Freudian Folklorist*. Madison: U of Wisconsin P, 144–66.

———. 1987b. "The Symbolic Equivalence of Allomotifs in The Rabbit-Herd (AT570)." *Parsing through Customs: Essays by a Freudian Folklorist*. Madison: U of Wisconsin P, 167–77.

Glanvil, Joseph. 1726. *Sadducismus Triumphatus: Or, A full and plain Evidence, concerning Witches and Apparitions*. 4th ed. London: A. Bettesworth and J. Batley.

Grimm, Jacob. 1966. *Teutonic Mythology*. 4th ed. 4 vols. Trans. James Steven Stallybrass. 1883–7. New York: Dover.

Honko, Lauri. 1959. *Krankheitsprojektile: Untersuchung über eine Urtümliche Krankheitserklärung*. FF Communications No. 178. Helsinki: Suomalainen Tiedeakatemia Academia Scientiarum Fennica.

Jackson, Kenneth. 1938. "Scéalta on Mblascaod." *Béaloideas* 8: 3–96.

Jones, Ernest. 1974. "The Madonna's Conception through the Ear." *Psychomyth, Psychohistory: Essays in Applied Psychoanalysis*. 2 Vols. New York: Hillstone. 2: 266–357.

———. 1974. "The Symbolic Significance of Salt." *Psychomyth, Psychohistory: Essays in Applied Psychoanalysis*. 2 Vols. New York: Hillstone. 2: 22–109.

Joyce, P.W. 1979. *English as We Speak It in Ireland*. 1910. Intro. Terence Dolan. Portmarnock County Dublin: Wolfhound Press.

Keightley, Thomas. 1968. *The Fairy Mythology: Illustrative of the Romance and Superstition of Various Countries*. New ed. 1850. New York: Haskell House.

Kennedy, Patrick. 1870. *The Fireside Stories of Ireland*. Dublin: M'Glashan and Gill and Patrick Kennedy.

———. 1866. 1891. *Legendary Fictions of the Irish Celts*. 1866. 2nd ed. London: Macmillan.

Kittredge, George Lyman. 1929. *Witchcraft in Old and New England*. New York: Russell and Russell.

Latham, Minor White. 1972. *The Elizabethan Fairies: The Fairies of Folklore and the Fairies of Shakespeare*. 1930. New York: Octagon.

Marchalonis, Shirley. 1979. "Three Medieval Tales and their Modern American Analogues." *Readings in American Folklore*. Ed. Jan Harold Brunvand. New York: W.W. Norton, 267–78.

Milton, John. 1969. *Poetical Works*. Ed. Douglas Bush. London: Oxford UP.

Narváez, Peter. 1989. "The Fairy Faith." *Ideas*. CBC Transcripts No. 11-293. Montreal: Canadian Broadcasting Corporation, June 29.

Ó Conchubhair, Pádraig. 1950. "An Offaly Glossary." *Béaloideas* 20: 188–91.

Ó Súilleabháin, Séan. 1970. *A Handbook of Irish Folklore*. 1942. Detroit: Singing Tree.

Schechter, Harold. 1988. *The Bosom Serpent: Folklore and Popular Art*. Iowa City: U of Iowa P.

Scheper-Hughes, Nancy. 1979. *Saints, Scholars and Schizophrenics: Mental Illness in Rural Ireland*. Berkeley: U of California P.

Scot, Reginald. 1930. *The Discoverie of Witchcraft*. 1584. With an Intro. by Montague Summers. London: J. Rodker.

Singer, Charles. 1919–20. "Early English Magic and Medicine." *Proceedings of the British Academy* 9: 341–74.

Spears, Richard A. 1981. *Slang and Euphemism: A Dictionary of Oaths, Curses, Insults, Sexual Slang and Metaphor, Racial Slurs, Drug Talk, Homosexual Lingo, and Related Matters*. Middle Village, N.Y.: Jonathan David.

Westropp, Thomas Johnson. 1921. "A Study of Folklore on the Coasts of Connacht, Ireland." *Folk-Lore* 32: 101–23.

Wilde, W. R. 1972. *Irish Popular Superstitions*. 1852. Shannon: Irish UP.

IV. The Social Functions of Fairylore

Anthropologist Bronislaw Malinowski first outlined a functional approach to folklore in his essay "Myth in Primitive Psychology." "Myth," he asserted, "fulfills in primitive culture an indispensable function: it expresses, enhances, and codifies belief; it safeguards and enforces morality; it vouches for the efficiency of ritual and contains practical rules for the guidance of man."[1] Like most functionalists after him, Malinowski was concerned with the social consequences of human behaviors as these activities assist in the integration of a society. In terms of the development of the discipline of folkloristics, the functionalist approach has translated into "what folklore does for the folk," that is, what the consequences of folklore are for the people who engage in its enactment and transmission. As in other social sciences, however, most folklorists who have used the functionalist perspective have assumed that folklore, as a component of culture, is a socially cohesive force, tending to integrate the interrelated parts of the social organism. Thus, in a very influential essay, William R. Bascom stressed four functions of folklore—amusement, the validation of culture, education, and maintaining conformity—all of which may be read in terms of maintaining the integrity of the social body.[2]

Conflict within a society and social change in general, however, are not adequately accounted for by strict functionalist interpretations. Some traditional expressive behaviors may serve resistant, aggressive, combative ends that are more socially divisive than cohesive.[3] In the case of the history of fairylore within a nation-state, the usefulness of the Gramscian model of hegemony, a frame that allows for the interpretation of sociocultural struggle, has already been demonstrated in Diarmuid Ó Gilláin's diachronic treatment of fairy belief and official religion in Ireland.[4]

Any kind of social analysis involving fairies is perplexing, however, because fairy belief complicates social consciousness and worldview. As many articles in this anthology indicate, fairies and other extraordinary beings have often been considered in an intergroup, exoteric (what one group thinks of another group) manner, as members of the "Otherworld." On the other hand, the good people have made their presence felt within the community confines of a household or a neighborhood. In this sense they have been thought of as intragroup entities; that is, fairies have been part of an esoteric (what a group thinks of itself and the knowledge that constitutes its collective identity) conception.[5] The entrance of fairies into social consciousness, therefore, yields at least a double image: one being that fairies constitute a foreign, external, challenging, "other" society ("them," "the gentry"); the second image being that of fairies as intimate ("we are the fairies children"), domestic, local ("good neighbors") provocateurs.

Anthropologist Richard P. Jenkins' essay and my own contribution in this section may both be considered functional approaches since they concern the social consequences of fairy belief in community contexts. Like Ó Giolláin's study, these treatments have had to contend with fairylore forms that sometimes appear antithetical to social cohesion. Since they both refer to the integrity of rural societies in the past, however, both analyses ultimately point to integrative functions: "*retaining* control and the myth of social harmony" (Jenkins) and "*maintaining* spatial, temporal and moral boundaries" (my italics). Each study employs different interpretive frames. In probing the history of aggressive witchcraft and fairy behavior in Ireland Jenkins applies a witchcraft/sorcery model refined by Alan Harwood. He argues that "fairies normally attacked within the family," the domestic domain of maternal authority. Specifically with regard to fairy changeling beliefs, he maintains that blame for particularized misfortune has traditionally been attributed to deviant women who exhibited a "background of failed obligations, either within the household or the circle of immediate kin." My essay combines a spatial/temporal media theory of Harold Adams Innis, an interpretation of space from Arnold van Gennep, and Mary Douglas's ideas regarding purity and danger in examining a cluster of legends concerning fairy-human encounters on berry grounds in Newfoundland. Among other things I argue that such narratives reinforce a sense of contractile space and continuous time as well as provide "fairy alibis" within the context of a male dominated moral code.[6]

Notes

1. This essay was published in 1926; it is reprinted in Bronislaw Malinowski, *Magic, Science and Religion* (Garden City: Doubleday Anchor, 1954) 93–148.

2. William R. Bascom, "Four Functions of Folklore," *Journal of American Folklore* 67 (1954): 333–49.

3. See Elliot Oring's critique of functionalist studies in folklore, "Three Functions of Folklore: Traditional Functionalism as Explanation in Folkloristics," *Journal of American Folklore* 89 (1976): 67–80.

4. For a folkloristic review of Gramsci and other western Marxist social critics see José E. Limón, "Western Marxism and Folklore: A Critical Introduction," *Journal of American Folklore* 96 (1983): 34–52.

5. See Wm. Hugh Jansen, "The Esoteric-Exoteric Factor in Folklore" *Fabula* 2 (1959): 43–51.

6. For two studies concerning traditional attitudes toward supernatural aggression that accent the oppressed position of women see John Putnam Demos, *Entertaining Satan: Witchcraft and the Culture of Early New England* (Oxford: Oxford UP, 1982) and Carol F. Karlsen, *The Devil in the Shape of a Woman* (New York: W.W. Norton, 1987).

Witches and Fairies: Supernatural Aggression and Deviance Among the Irish Peasantry[1]

Richard P. Jenkins

The Problem

One of the most common features of so-called "primitive" societies is a belief in categories of supernatural aggression which most anthropologists have dichotomized as "witchcraft" and "sorcery" in the classic mold of the Azande folk model, witchcraft depending on an innate power within the individual's body and sorcery relying for its efficacy on the manipulation of medicines and spells.[2] These beliefs are said to function in similar, not complementary fashions, and the question may then be asked, why do these societies' cosmologies contain both of them? Either set of beliefs may serve as an explanatory framework and a guide to action in the face of misfortune and uncertainty, so why have them both? This question has been raised by Middleton and Winter in the introduction to their symposium on East African witch beliefs, and they conclude that, since neither of the belief-sets is redundant, they must "fit into social systems in different ways."[3] They make the further suggestion that witchcraft beliefs are associated with the interaction of the occupants of ascribed statuses and sorcery beliefs with the interaction of those whose positions are achieved, but do not develop the idea beyond this.[4]

Given this recognition that beliefs in witchcraft and sorcery occupy different niches in particular sociocultural systems, it is all the more disappointing that the problems of precisely *how* this is achieved and *how* the beliefs relate to each other and to the social system, have received so little attention from recent workers. Turner, in the course of a criticism of Middleton and Winter's book, gave the matter little attention except to attack the carefree extension of the Azande folk model to which most anthropologists have committed themselves. He pointed out that a particular society may recognize many different kinds of mystical aggression; to classify witchcraft and sorcery rigidly as the meaningful dichotomy is misleading and can lead to a labelling or pigeonholing approach which diverts investigation away from real social interaction.[5]

The only systematic study that examines in detail the way in which these beliefs in different modes of supernatural aggression "fit into" a particular society is that by Harwood of the Safwa of Tanzania. He relates witch beliefs to a field of social relationships and behavior governed by norms of sharing, unity and rights and obligations: the relations of kinship and "incorporation." Sorcery, on the other hand, is associated with relations of "transaction": behavior governed by norms of recognition, reciprocity and exchange.[6]

Harwood does not say that this correlation between witchcraft and sorcery beliefs and relations of incorporation and transaction is valid cross-culturally, but he does claim that

> Witchcraft and sorcery beliefs may be utilized in a single society to express conflict within any two contrasted social categories ... both witchcraft and sorcery beliefs can exist in the same society because they provide categories for symbolizing deviance from the norms of any two social relationships which are in contrast.[7]

This proposition is open to testing and combining it with Turner's statement that beliefs in mystical power and aggression need not be rigidly dichotomized into categories of witchcraft and sorcery, the following hypothesis arises: in any given social system, different categories of supernatural aggression may be the means of symbolizing deviance from the norms of any categories of social relations and behavior that are in contrast. The categories of opposition may be dyadic or dichotomous but need not necessarily be so. Investigation of this hypothesis follows in this essay.

"Peasantry" is here defined in the widest possible sense: small-scale agriculturalists encapsulated in a wider social system, whose surplus finds its way, usually by the expropriation of rent, to the greater community's marketplace. The peasant economic enterprise is organized on a family basis and usually relies on mixed farming, not just on one crop: the peasant attempts to maximize opportunities for work, not productive capacity and output. The first aim of the peasant farm is thus to provide a livelihood for the family in both social and economic terms.[8] This is not to say that the internal differentiation of the peasantry in terms of class, status, etc. is overlooked, but for present purposes such considerations are not of immediate importance and may therefore be set aside.

Social and Economic Background

Following the Plantations of the sixteenth and seventeenth centuries, the formal social institutions of Gaelic Ireland lay in ruins. Notwithstanding this, and the involvement of a large part of the peasantry in a cash economy, many aspects of day-to-day life remained; either the clachan, a kind of loosely structured hamlet, or the isolated farmstead, remained the residential norm in many areas. The new towns and villages of the ascendancy were expanding, especially in the north and east, but "traditional" settlements remained important until well into the nineteenth century.[9]

Agricultural technology was primitive, spade tillage being the rule rather than the exception, and survival remained dependant on livestock, although cultivation of grain and increasingly the potato, was not insignificant. Sheep, horses, and pigs were kept but cattle were, as they had been for thousands of years, central to the domestic and national economy. This dominance of livestock in Ireland is partly due to its maritime climate; with a high rainfall, low summer and high winter temperatures, the land is eminently suitable for grass and pasturage but not for cereals.[10] Milk cows were of particular importance, "whitemeats," or dairy products, especially butter and buttermilk, forming the bulk of most people's protein intake, meat being rarely eaten.[11]

Ireland was long a land of smallholders, with grazing land held in common. As Crotty has pointed out

> The holding of land jointly greatly facilitated the system, as otherwise the land would have to be divided into individual holdings by stock-proof fences. Further when land was grazed in large units it was possible to shift from one part to another according to season, generally grazing the higher areas and the wetter areas in the summer, and the lower areas and the drier, sounder areas in the winter.[12]

The small plots had ill-defined boundaries and were farmed on the "rundale" system, with an infield under constant cultivation and an outfield used for shifting cultivation and pasturage. In some areas it was the practice for plots to change hands at regular intervals, often by a system of drawing lots.[13]

The rundale system was the economic base of the clachan and although loosely organized, kinship within and between clachans was important.[14] Conflict between groups may have found expression in faction fighting between large opposing extended kin groups at gatherings such as fairs, or in the "no man's land" between rival communities. There was, however, conflict and ill feeling within the group as well and we may speculate that this was less easily given free vent. Evans suggests that conflict was intensified by the co-ownership of land, and sometimes even of individual animals, which was a feature of rundale. He expands on this, pointing out that, as clachans developed and subdivision became more complex "internal rivalries and squabbles were more conspicuous and found more opportunities within overgrown kinship groups which had become too complicated to function smoothly."[15]

An area in which single farmsteads were more common was a different matter, but once again there was cooperation between farmers, dictated by technological limitations and a pastoral economy, with grazing still being communally held in many areas. Cooperation between farms, or "cooring" as it was sometimes called, was probably organized on the basis of extended family kinship ties, if we can safely extrapolate backwards in time from Arensberg and Kimball's material gathered in Co. Clare in the 1930s: the allocation of land was also regulated by kinship. It is obvious from their research that both were sources of tension and we may thus conclude that the social milieu of the clachan and that of the solitary farmstead had much in common: reciprocally organized interfamilial cooperation, often based on ties of extended family kinship, with conflict resulting from these essentially transactional relationships.[16]

The life of the peasant's "basic" family centered on the house and within its walls, upon the fire, "the symbol both of family continuity and of hospitality towards the stranger."[17] There was a fairly rigid sexual division of labour and the woman's work involved the day-to-day maintenance of the family unit—tending the hearth, the care and socialization of the children, milking the cows, churning the butter, and feeding the fowl and young livestock. Her husband was responsible for the heavy work in the fields and with the cattle and he decided on the disposal of the livestock and most of the farm produce. That part of the output which the woman produced, milk, butter, eggs, etc., was disposed of by her and she controlled the income resulting from its sale.[18] Brody has characterized the difference as being between the continuous, all year around labour of the woman, and the seasonal, cyclical and discontinuous labour of the man.[19]

The central importance of the woman, in whose hands rested the safety, continuity and prosperity of the family, both symbolic and actual, must also have been a source of tension, since she was usually an outsider who had married in. In households where the husband's parent remained in the house—and I doubt that this was purely a feature of the post-famine land tenure readjustments—conflict could be extreme, especially between wife and mother-in-law.[20]

There were also other sources of disruption within the family—for example, infidelity, and although there are few data on this in the academic literature, some idea of what went on may be gathered from the oral traditions of the country people themselves.[21] Briefly, too, such things as illegitimacy and premarital sex should be mentioned as potential sources of familial strife; suffice it to say that both appear to have been common and had as their concomitants, infanticide, the abandonment of infants, and on occasion, abortion.[22]

By the end of the eighteenth century the traditional settlement patterns were beginning to break down due to large-scale evictions of small tenants which followed in the wake of an increasing commercialization in farming and the pressure of population growth. Coming into existence, especially in the poorer areas, was a landscape dotted with small plots, each bearing a cabin of sorts, on which families survived by virtue of whatever potatoes or oats they could grow for themselves, and whatever cash crop they could raise to pay the rent. Land, no matter how meagre the plot, became the only thing between the peasant and starvation and subdivision was rampant.

Dairy cattle were especially important as a source of cash since butter was one of Ireland's major exports. There were other supplementary cash sources available, such as linen weaving in the north and east or illicit distillation, but agriculture remained the mainstay. Butter making was at best an uncertain process; for various technical reasons, like the traditional habit of not separating the cream but churning the whole milk, or inadequate sterilization and temperature control, the butter frequently would not come.[23] Given the importance of butter to the domestic economy, a considerable amount of anxiety must have been generated by this unreliability. A further source of extra income for many householders was seasonal migration to work in the harvest fields of England and Scotland.[24] However, even though cattle were no longer the supremely important element in the economic life of the peasantry, they remained crucial to the lives of most smallholders—a barrier between themselves and the bailiff. "A cow's grass," as a unit for measuring land, acquired a new importance.

The famine of the late 1840s was a watershed in Irish history; the rural population declined and the scale and scope of farming became increasingly intensive and market oriented. There developed a new preoccupation with the family land and the desirability of preserving its unity, which led to the fierce determination not to subdivide, documented by Arensberg and Kimball, and by Brody.[25] Despite this radical change much remained that was in existence before the Famine—kinship and the sexual division of labour were essentially unaltered until at least about forty or fifty years ago in some areas.

Within the last few decades there has been a marked change in the lives of the remaining smallholders, particularly in the west. Brody has called this "demoralization," and relates it to a complete change in the social milieu due to depopulation, increased contact with the metropolitan centers, especially via the mass media, and the emergence of a sense of relative deprivation.[26] This marked the beginning of the end for fairies and witches. Collapse of the integrity of rural society is not of direct concern here however, falling outside the scope of this article; but although much changed in Ireland during the last two or three centuries, much that was of great importance for the peasantry retained its vigor until recently: a tradition of pastoral farming, based on kin-organized communities and cooperation, whose major concerns were those of most peasant people—eking a living from an often harsh environment and ensuring the continuity in space and time of the domestic unit. Even under the impact of a cash economy, and later the Famine, much of this and its related value system remained. It may even be that, because of the landlords and a cash economy, "traditional" preoccupations became more important than ever.

Witchcraft and the Evil Eye

Analytically, we may draw a distinction between witches of the evil eye and those believed to use magic and sorcery to achieve their ends but there is no evidence from the material that this distinction was as meaningful to the peasantry as the dichotomy of witchcraft and sorcery is to the anthropologist. Although a distinction may have been made, particularly when taking into account the intent of the witch, there was an apparent confusion between the categories. I propose instead to present my material under three headings: (1) the evil eye; (2) milk and churn blinking; (3) other miscellaneous forms of supernatural aggression. This is not to imply that these categories do not overlap on occasions, but they represent useful analytical categories, based on differences of believed or actual technique and which do not veer away from the folk classifications that seem to have been held.

The Evil Eye

This may be best described as mystical aggression relying on an innate power existing within the body of the witch for its effectiveness. Like many forms of African witchcraft it could be voluntary or involuntary and could be inherited. The power might also be acquired by "black magic."[27] A difference was seen between conscious users of their malign potential and "unlucky folk" who could not control their unfortunate influence, whole families sometimes being regarded as lucky or unlucky.[28] In the west of Ireland at the turn of the century many factors were believed to lead to an individual possessing this unfortunate gift— incorrect baptism, the marriage of an unmarried mother during pregnancy in an effort to secure legitimacy for the infant or the taking of the Devil's name lightly, by saying, "The Devil a-fear of me," or some such phrase, by a pregnant woman. These situations potentially could all result in either mother or infant acquiring an evil eye, although it was often unintentional in such cases.[29] Here is a clear link, recognized by the people themselves, between the evil eye and deviance from the community's moral code, which was important in the attribution of malefic power to particular individuals. There were also general purpose beliefs about the evil eye, for example its attribution to red-headed women[30] or those with dark eyes and swarthy complexions,[31] but these must have been observed in the breach, not in practice. We may imagine that they were used in exceptional circumstances and once again these individuals would probably have been thought to have little control over their powers.

In sensitive areas of social interaction such as those concerning newborn children, pregnant livestock, or churning, it was important to express a positively benevolent interest: this was normally done by uttering a benediction, "God bless the child" or "God bless the work," for example, and lending token assistance to whatever task was in hand. Failure to do this was to invite suspicion and it was considered particularly unlucky to praise anybody or anything without adding a blessing.

Messenger[32] has described recent beliefs about the evil eye on the Aran Islands. The left side is regarded as belonging to Satan and the left eye is the channel through which his power may be channelled into the outside world if he has managed to achieve dominance over the powers of good in the right side of the body. There is however no evidence to suggest that Messenger's dualistic islanders hold a common form of belief and indeed there is no mention of this dichotomization in the earlier folklorists' accounts of the islands.[33]

Belief in the evil eye appears to have existed since antiquity (the evil influence of Balor's eye is described in myth), and it was probably what the sixteenth century skeptic, Reginald Scot, was discussing in this passage:

> The Irishmen addict themselves wonderfullie to the credit and practice hereof; in somuch as they affirme, that not onelie their children, but their cattell, are (as they call it) eybitten, when they fall suddenly sicke, and terme one sort of their witches eybiters; yea and they will not sticke to affirme, that they can rime either man or beast to death.[34]

The belief may persist in some areas even now and it is a case from the 1950s which gives sufficient detail to enable us to understand how discord within a community can lead to an accusation being made.

Mrs. McKinley was a Protestant widow living in "Ballybeg," the Co. Tyrone community studied by Rosemary Harris. She was exceptional inasmuch as she was caretaker of the local Church of Ireland church but never attended divine service; this made her unpopular within the Protestant section of the community. Odd things tended to happen to those who disagreed or argued with her; one man for instance, who had asked her to remove her hens so that he could plough his field, was met with the reply, "Maybe you will and maybe you won't plough the field." That night he forgot to drain his tractor radiator, which froze and burst.

Other misfortunes were attributed to her; a man had a puncture in his bicycle tire three nights in a row after riding past her home.

The crisis came when she opened the church to a number of Roman Catholics in order to let them admire the harvest festival decorations; this was used as an excuse to demand that she be removed from her post. The rector, however, refused to bow to community pressure. It is significant that although not everyone accepted the accusation, Harris is of the opinion that the situation about the church decorations was "set up," across the sectarian divide, in a joint effort by villagers of both persuasions to deal with her malevolence.[35]

One is forcefully reminded here of the villages of Tudor and Stuart Essex, where witchcraft accusations were the result of a person falling under suspicion from a number of families; this MacFarlane has called "the pooling of suspicions."[36] In order for decisive action to have been taken it seems that a number of unfortunate and suspicious circumstances had first to accumulate; one isolated misfortune was not enough. Accusations and counter-accusations might be bandied about in the course of neighborhood disputes, but, unless allegations were consistently made against a suspect, they were probably little regarded.[37]

Many different misfortunes were attributed to the evil eye—malfunctions of agricultural equipment, illness and death in humans and livestock, and other problems. It may be a distortion in the data but it appears that horses fell victim to the evil eye more commonly than to any other form of mystical aggression.[38] What all cases of deliberate use of the evil eye have in common is that they involved aggression between specified people. The point about horses may be explicable in this light since their owners were usually very proud of them; they were a likely focus for jealousy and a consistent feature of evil eye beliefs all over the world is "envy in the eye of the beholder."[39]

The reputation for possessing such powers did not necessarily weaken one's position in the community. Nanny Steer, who lived in Queen's County (Laois) in the early nineteenth century, gained considerable prestige from the fear and respect which she aroused. A young man who neglected to invite her to his wedding suffered the consequences—he went mad on the morning of the ceremony.[40] This is a common theme in European folklore; after all, the wicked fairy in "The Sleeping Beauty" was offended in a like manner. It has also been reported from Tudor England that a reputation for witchcraft was often the last ditch for defenseless old people.[41]

Finally we may perhaps speculate as to which category of person was most often accused of using the evil eye. Quantifiable data are few here, but it seems from the meagre information available that women, and especially elderly women, were most likely to be suspects. Their victims, whenever personal attacks as opposed to attacks on animals were made, were usually adolescent or adult and may have been most commonly male. These conclusions are not, at the moment, readily demonstrable and more concrete evidence will have to be gathered before firm conclusions can be reached.

Milk and Churn Blinking

This seems to be the most important area of witch beliefs and we may discern two main ways the witch was believed to operate: either the cow was deprived of her milk or the churn was "blinked" and the milk would yield no butter. As already noted, the making of butter was an uncertain operation and the latter situation must have been quite frequent. There is a degree of overlap between this category and the evil eye and so it was important to take a few minutes to bless the work at milking or churning whenever such work was encountered or interrupted. Apart from the evil eye there were also recognized methods of committing such crimes, using magical formulae, rituals and medicines. Not only was this believed to be done but there is some evidence that it was in fact practiced.

The most widely accepted technique I shall call "expropriation"; the witch borrowed something from the house or byre of the intended victim: fire, a burning turf or faggott,[42] butter, which to be most effective should be freely given,[43] a churn,[44] or tools and implements of metal.[45] This was not the only *modus operandi*, however; something of the witch's might be hidden about the victim's house and this I call "insinuation." A lump of butter might suffice,[46] or a butter substitute, made from flour or other ingredients, might be used instead.[47]

Sometimes it was enough for the witch to perform just these simple operations in order for the magic to work, but there were times when further conjuration was necessary, for example, when a churn was borrowed and a silver sixpence thrown into it before it was returned[48]— "expropriation" and "insinuation" combined in one rite.

Another apparently popular method of "profit stealing" was by gathering dew from a neighbor's fields or taking water from his well.[49] There is a folktale, told in many parts of Ireland, which bears upon this theme, telling of a farmer (or a priest in some versions) who happens upon a witch at work in the early morning, gathering dew and repeating the spell, "Come all to me, come all to me." Remaining undiscovered the observer adds in jest, "And half to me," with the result that his milk yields are unparalleled during the following year.[50] This belief was strong all over the country and a working-class Protestant poet of the nineteenth century, David Herbison (1800–1880) from Ballymena, referred to it in one of his poems.

And oft ere the sun dried the leaf on the tree
I have found the witch-wife sitting cold by there,
And watched while she cast her old blankets abroad
To sip up the dew from the daisy-clad sod.[51]

A further variation of this technique was to drag a rope through the fields in order to collect the dew.[52] Other methods using rope have also been reported, milking the "tethers," rope used in hay baling, or a rope woven on May Eve from the mane of a stallion without a single white hair.[53] In a village-level informal accusation brought before the convenanting minister of Maghera, Co. Derry, in the early 1800s, animal hair also figures; a woman was successfully accused of stealing milk from one of her kinsmen, using hair from the cow's tail to operate with.[54]

A tradition of shape-changing witches has been connected in places with milk stealing, the witch entering the byre in the guise of a hare or rabbit and sucking directly from the cow. The only remedy was to shoot her with a silver bullet, in the best tradition of European were-animals. There are many tales told and songs sung about injured hares vanishing and the body of an old village woman being discovered in its place.[55]

Finally we come to the most bizarre technique of profit-stealing, the "dead hand," in which milk was churned using the preserved hand of a corpse (we are not told whether it was the left or right hand), thus drawing the victim's butter to the operator's churn. According to some sources this had to be done seven or nine times, accompanied by the appropriate spells.[56] In Co. Longford it was believed that some milk from the intended victim's cows must be mixed with the witch's own cow's milk in the churn: the principle of expropriation once again. This could have unsought side effects, the death of calves or the victimized farmers themselves going mad.[57] There are many descriptions of this in the literature and from many areas.[58] Unlikely as it may seem there were occasions when it was actually used[59] and Croker has described a case he witnessed in which a woman was deliberately falsely accused and the dried hands produced as evidence of her guilt; the plan misfired and her accusers themselves ended up in trouble.[60] The "hand of glory" was also used for other purposes, both legitimate and maleficent; it was preserved by drying or smoking and the hand of an unbaptized infant was believed to be most effective.[61]

A consistent feature of much of the profit-stealing magic was that, in order to be most potent, many of the rituals had to be performed on either May Eve or May Morning. This marked the beginning of the "booleying" season when the cattle were moved from the infield to communally held grazing land; April and May also marked the beginning of the cows' highest milk yielding period when the women would be most busy at the churn. The seasonal difference in milk yields was due to the poor winter feeding available. This was thus the time when profit-stealing would be most profitable. The cows and the milk were also more vulnerable since, in areas where booleying was practiced, they passed out of direct family control and became the responsibility of the community. Butter, too, could be at risk due to purely social factors since churning was often done on a cooperative basis, women with insufficient milk pooling their resources.[62]

Miscellaneous Supernatural Aggression

There were other uses for a "dead hand" apart from profit-stealing; it could be used when committing a crime, to render the criminal invisible or invulnerable to apprehension, or in order to cause those being robbed to fall into a deep sleep. At Loughcrew, Co. Meath, on 3 February, 1831, burglars were surprised with the grisly talisman in their possession.[63] This is a belief well attested for other historical periods and lands, being reported from England as early as 1440.[64] However, the "hand of glory" had beneficent uses as well including curing diseases and skin blemishes by stroking the afflicted person with a corpse's hand before it was buried.[65]

Dead flesh was also used in certain types of love magic, notably *an buarach bháis*, the "spancel of death," a strip of skin removed in one unbroken piece from the top of the corpse's head to its heels. If the loved and desired person was touched by this, their undying devotion would be gained. According to Deeny[66] this was often practiced. Lady Jane Wilde also reported this belief, with the further note that children of a union which had been the result were said to bear a black mark around the wrist, branding them as "sons of the Devil."[67]

It was also possible for a witch to cure illness by transferring the disease to another person, who then died instead. Although this may be regarded as curing, it was essentially malicious magic and was seen as such by the peasantry.[68] Midwives were also believed to be able to "throw" part of the labor pains onto a man.[69]

Much of the magic may be lumped under the rubric "sympathetic magic" and much belongs to the subcategory of "imitative magic": "the magician infers that he can produce any effect he desires merely by imitating it." [70] In the 1890s there was a court case in Co. Louth which illustrates the strength of this type of belief. A woman tried to murder another by "burying the sheaf." She went first to the chapel and prepared herself by saying certain prayers with her back to the altar. Then she made a doll out of wheat straw with a plaited heart and stuck pins in the joints. This she buried near the victim's house, who in theory should have wasted away as the doll decomposed; the effigy should be buried in wet ground for rapid decomposition and a swift death and in dry soil for a lingering and painful death. In this instance, from the Bog of Ardee, the sorceress was discovered one night by relatives of the victim whilst pouring water over the site where the doll was buried to hasten her victim's demise.[71]

To blight the luck of a neighbor's fields one could bury the quarters of a black cow in the corners of one of the fields, and his crops should dwindle as the meat rotted,[72] and similarly, in order to destroy a rival's cows one should stick pins in an effigy of him and throw it in his fields.[73] Eggs could be secreted about his holding with the same intention.[74]

This kind of magic could also be turned against an unfaithful lover; Johann Beer, writing in 1690, says, "When a woman is spurned by her man she consults the sorcerers as to how she may make her successor ill or otherwise bewitch her."[75] Lady Jane Wilde, writing two centuries later, has given us more details. A lighted candle was buried in a churchyard at night and as the candle rotted, the cursed lover faded away. Wilde mentions this in the context of an actual case in which the cursed person died.[76]

In all the descriptions of the sorcery of the peasantry there are frequent references, by the collectors, to the rituals being accompanied by dedications to Satan; however, on evidence from the England of an earlier historical period, it seems unlikely that Devil worship entered into the black magic of the countryside.[77] What may be stated with some certainty is that maleficent sorcery and magic, for a variety of antisocial ends, was definitely practiced. This is in accordance with English and European historical evidence,[78] and with data from many non-European societies.[79] Beliefs and action feed back on each other: "Thus actions can have a feedback effect which makes them logically on a par, and in a certain sense developmentally prior to, values and social arrangements."[80] Concepts and values on the one hand and behavior on the other, must be seen as inextricably linked and they cannot and should not be studied in isolation. It is important to realize that throughout this article not just a system of thought is involved, but also, and just as important, a system of action and social behavior. The two aspects should not be forgotten.

There is one further category of supernatural aggression which deserves brief treatment here—cursing, usually verbal but also possible by means of "cursing stones" or other traditional mechanisms.[81] The use of a curse usually resulted from a genuine or imagined infringement of the communal moral code. One of the most common of these was the "widow's curse," in which an evicted widow laid a curse on the incoming tenant of the house she had been forced to quit following her bereavement. She laid a fire in the hearth made from stones or razor blades.[82]

The ability to curse was often associated with the evil eye. "Rosie" of McAleastown, Co. Down, was believed to be able to inflict a curse lasting seven generations as well as having a malign gaze.[83]

Arensberg's description of "the old man's curse" illustrates graphically the folk view that ill luck followed directly on antisocial behavior. The drama began when two old bachelors who lived together were fired on in the night. Neither of them was injured but local opinion was unanimous in condemning the attack. The old brothers, however, were also regarded as having betrayed their obligation toward their kin by staying on a holding they were not farming. It was also recognized that this situation had arisen from the brothers' devotion to their mother, who had lived long and died intestate. When, a few weeks after the incident, a young man lost an eye working with a scythe, the fact that he was a son of a landless cousin of the old men was enough for the incident to be interpreted as a punishment for his supposed nocturnal crime. As Arensberg points out, there was considerable ambiguity about the respective moral positions of both injured and injuring parties; nevertheless there is a clear indication of the connection between the values of the people and their beliefs in supernatural power and aggression. It is also a good example of the *post facto* reinterpretation of reality which is so common in this area of social life.[84]

The Fairies

The Irish belief in fairies, the "good folk" or the "gentry" is much better documented than their witchcraft beliefs. For this reason most of the beliefs may be passed over, changelings and elf-shot cattle being the two areas of more relevance to this study.

The fairies, as considered here, were conceived of as a "society outside society," with its own leaders, the King and Queen, and its own particular problems—the need for healthy children, women to suckle and raise them, healthy cattle to feed their folk and safe habitations to house them. It is no surprise that these were the same concerns as those of the peasant family. The fairies were in part recruited from the peasantry since they were thought to include dead ancestors.

The fairies lived in raths, the "fairy forts" or "forths," or their equivalents, so many examples of which dotted the landscape, or in "noble places," spectacular or unusual natural topographical features of the countryside. From these the fairies were believed to issue forth, either as individuals, or at certain times of the year, May Eve and Halloween, *en masse* as the fairy host, moving from one dwelling to another, perhaps in reflection of the booleying or transhumance of the human agricultural cycle.[85]

There are many elements of fairy belief which cannot be dealt with here—the *leannán si* or vampiristic fairy lover, the myth of origin which places the fairies in a pseudo-Roman Catholic cosmology as the fallen angels, the leprechaun shoemaker; there is also a coastal and island fairy cosmology, peopled by such beings as the *púca*, the mermaid, and other praeternatural marine life. For brevity's sake these are ignored. One feature of the mythology which is of relevance to this discussion is the believed inability of fairy women either to bear healthy children or to feed them—hence the need to abduct human babies and wet nurses for them. The cattle belonging to the forth were commonly believed to be either of extremely high quality or the very opposite, beasts incapable of providing the inhabitants with adequate subsistence. There is an element of confusion about the cosmology at this point which further research may clarify.

Fairy Changelings

These were children or adult women of childbearing years who were believed to have been spirited away to the fairy dwelling, a sickly or irritable substitute being left in their place. Individuals most commonly diagnosed as being changelings were those who exhibited either some degree of paralysis or a noticeable change in behavior patterns; there seems, however, to have been no hard and fast diagnostic rule. However, adult women were consistently regarded as vulnerable during their childbearing years and particularly in the post-parturient period. Children up to the age of about eight or nine seemed to have been most likely to have been taken. For boys this signified their passing out of the domestic sphere of their mother into the keeping of their father; this was the beginning of their socialization into adulthood.[86] From the small number of reliably witnessed cases, however, there seems to have been no greater likelihood of a male child being diagnosed as "taken."[87] This belief may be related, on the one hand, to post-natal depression and other illnesses of pregnancy and childbirth, and on the other, to the great vulnerability of children of tender years in circumstances of inadequate nutrition, shelter and medical attention. The "mythical charter" of this folk etiology comes from the belief described above: the fairies' need for healthy children and wet nurses. What is not clear is why particular cases of illness were diagnosed as being due to fairy abduction. It may have been enough for the illness to have involved paralysis, loss of speech, and other symptoms, as some writers have asserted,[88] or it may have been enough for the patient simply to have fallen ill. Particularly in the case of women, it seems that family tensions played a major part in many diagnoses—there is perhaps a background of failed obligations, either within the household or the circle of immediate kin, to many of the cases in the literature. For instance, in a case reported by Croker the woman taken had lost her first child, a boy, and became ill while nursing her second; on her return from being "away" several years later, she herself blamed all her misfortunes on her having married someone of whom her father disapproved.[89] Thus we have deliberate deviance from the norm of generational and masculine superordination within the family resulting in unsuccessful child-raising, itself regarded as a moral failing, and fairy abduction.

In the case of Mrs. Hehir, who died in childbirth,[90] there seems also to be a relationship between being taken and deviance. This case is also interesting because, although Lady Gregory collected the material only a week after the woman's burial, there were widely differing explanations of her abduction and death circulating among the neighbors. One was that she was "out walking" with a novitiate priest (possible non-conformity against the norm of priestly virtue), while another was that she had refused to accept an offer of help from a traveling woman whilst churning (and we have seen how important this type of proffered help was). Once again, as in Croker's case above, we seem to have deviance, or apparent deviance, against more than one norm leading to a changeling diagnosis, in this case those of sexual morality, religion, and protection of the family's livelihood.

According to many folk tales men were also taken although I have yet to encounter any concrete examples. Musicians, especially pipers, were favorite targets and a reputation as one who had seen the inside of the fort was guaranteed to enhance a player's local standing. In one tale telling of a man being taken for a long period there is also a link, explicitly recognized in the oral tradition, between deviance and fairy aggression. The man in question had intended to find sponsors for his first male child from outside his kin group, being so proud of a son born after so many little girls. Once again the folk view explicitly recognizes deviance from more than one behavioral or moral norm: the wife's duty to provide male heirs and the husband's obligation to find sponsors for his children at home.[91]

Pipers were not the only ones whose reputations were improved by being "away." Wise women, fairy doctors and other medical or ritual specialists were also commonly regarded as having been away with the gentry. This was not only believed by their clients but was also often a claim of the practitioner concerned.

Other kinds of deviance or misbehavior could lead to being "taken," an incursion onto a rath for example,[92] but this kind of direct flouting of the fairies normally led to correspondingly direct retribution. Thus, such offences as disturbing the fairy host when they were traveling between dwellings, disturbing a fairy tree, building one's house in the wrong place and thereby disturbing a fairy thoroughfare, or even disturbing the rath itself, were more likely to be punished by the "fairy stroke" or the "fairy wind" rather than by being "taken." The "stroke," the "wind," or the "touch" were actual ailments, and it seems that, once again, a degree of paralysis was commonly involved, in these cases more local than general.

In the case of house building, the house and family might be directly attacked. In 1866 at Upper Ballygowan, near Larne, Co. Antrim, two families who had repaired their houses with stones from a ruined house inhabited by the fairies were tormented night and day by volleys of stones and turf. It is interesting that in this case a degree of communally recognized ill-behavior may have been involved. The deserted house was abandoned because the previous owner had been forced to leave by the fairies' ill behavior. Thus those who used its fabric as building material were, in effect, profiting from someone else's misfortune.[93]

The fairies were also liable to wreak revenge on wise-men or wise-women who, by their successful cures, deprived them of their erstwhile victims. This retribution took the form of either a "stroke" or a "touch," or more directly, simple physical assault, a beating.[94] In such cases the connection between public values and fairy aggression may be quite clearly seen, but it was not always so; many wise-men or -women worked their cures with direct connivance from the fairies as we have seen.

It is difficult to know what to make of the numerous cases reported in the oral tradition of people being taken but returning many years later, to the dismay of their families who believed the individual to be dead and buried years before and had restructured their lives accordingly. There are regular references to wives returning only to find their husbands re-married.[95] However, the actual explanation of this phenomenon notwithstanding, it was a belief which had, as we shall see later, great power in the lives and imagination of the peasantry, as had all aspects of fairy belief:

> A firm belief exists in fairies, goblins, ghosts and other extraordinary sights, and many have told and sworn to the writer that not only themselves but everyone in the townland have at the same time seen hundreds of fairies together, some of them mounted.[96]

Elf-Struck Cattle

The symptoms of elf-struck cattle do not seem to have been at all uniform. Sometimes cows had their milk taken,[97] perhaps the symptoms were moaning and a swollen belly, [98] or there might be lumps under the skin and partial paralysis.[99] There may also have been other symptoms. Dairy cattle were most vulnerable and the most dangerous period for them was immediately following calving. This is also the time in a good milk cow's life-cycle when she is prone to succumb to milk fever—the growth of the fetus has drawn heavily on the mother's calcium reserves and, if the calcium falls below the critical amount, because of high milk production following the calf's birth, the animal collapses and may die unless the milk flow is halted.[100]

The folk analysis of the illnesses was that they were caused by a wound, often invisible, inflicted by either a fairy arrowhead or dart (a prehistoric artifact usually),[101] or a fairy bullet (a fossil, often that of a prehistoric sea urchin).[102] The link between moral transgression and supernatural aggression is tenuous in this area of belief, although cows do seem to have been punished for disturbing raths, fairy wells, and other "gentle" places; what does seem clear is the idea that the health of the family's cattle, and hence its survival, was in the custody of the fairies and could be withdrawn at will.

Cows were not the only animals to have been attacked by the fairies. As with the evil eye horses were also potential victims, being ridden during the night, leaving them unfit for work the next day.[103] This belief, though, was not as significant as that in elf-shot cattle.

It must be noted that the fairies were also believed to be responsible for many minor misfortunes about the house. The women had to be careful about throwing rubbish or slops out in case the fairies might be passing by at the time, and a clean house was generally believed to be favorably regarded by its invisible neighbors.[104] This domestic discipline was also an aspect of English fairy beliefs.[105]

Just as witch beliefs clustered around May Day and the beginning of the communally organized agricultural season, those about the fairies and the ancestors came into prominence at Halloween, the end of October, when the cattle return to the farm from the outfield. This is when the raths open and the dead return to their old homes, where food and drink should be left out for them; it is at this time that divination about the future of living members of the family was, and is practiced—who will die, or get married, as in Joyce's short story "Clay."[106] Halloween was also a particularly dangerous time to be outdoors, since the fairies were on the move from one dwelling to another and were particularly likely to abduct people. Rees and Rees have pointed this out in their justly famous study of Celtic cosmologies: "Supernatural power breaks through in a most ominous way on November Eve and May Eve, the joints between the two great seasons of the year,"[107] and they have described the difference between the two festivals as being a distinction between one's luck for the year (May Eve) and one's destiny (Halloween).[108] This is analogous to the distinction between transactional and incorporative social relations discussed earlier. Finally it ought to be noted that a certain amount of fairylore was of importance on May Eve, particularly with respect to the protection of cattle and their milk; this however, does not diminish the significance of Halloween as the fairy festival *par excellence*.

Protection and Cure

Naturally, in a universe bustling with such supernatural dangers there was a need for magical safeguards and remedies. Although, strictly speaking, these lie outside the narrow focus of this article, brief mention of them is made before passing on.[109] This counteraction we may divide into three categories.

General Protection

Some practices were adopted by the folk as all-embracing safeguards against evil. The most important protection was probably the good will of the rest of the community but there were other charms which were popular such as Brigid's crosses, worn horseshoes, and prayers. There do not seem to have been many specific charms against witches or fairies, except in the case of changelings. Male children were often dressed in skirts to fool the fairies and there are numerous charms for newborn infants recorded in the literature.

Semi-Skilled Counteraction

Even with all this protection available there were still occasions on which the supernatural barriers broke down. The results were "blinked" cows or churns and human illness, especially in women and children. When this happened the peasants still had many options open to them. Apart from the divinatory procedures used on the calendar festivals, there were other forms of divination of a more diagnostic nature, such as scapulomancy, consulting animals, and various other oracular rites, which could be used to establish the nature and cause of the complaint.

This done, there were various curative rituals that could be embarked upon, although commonsense remedies, especially of a herbal nature, were widely used. Changelings were normally dosed with medicine (usually one of two things—urine or digitalis derived from the foxglove) and then exposed to the elements, in the belief that this would force the usurper to quit the host body. The most effective cure for the evil eye or witchcraft was to get the attacker to withdraw the malice by spitting on the victim or blessing him. Failing this there were other courses of action available; something belonging to the witch, a piece of thatch or clothing, for example, could be worked upon to force the witch to repent her wickedness.

The situation frequently arose when either the necessary remedies lay beyond the expertise of the average peasant or the readily available protections and cures proved inadequate. It was then deemed necessary to consult a full-fledged ritual specialist.

Specialist Counteraction

There were many names for such specialists: wise-man or -woman,
fairy man or woman, elf doctor, herb doctor, cow doctor or handyman.
For the sake of convenience I shall refer to them in general, as wise-men
and wise-women.

There seems to have been little consistency about the "content" of the
socially accepted role of wise-man or -woman, diversity being the norm:
some were amateur, some full-time; some were general practitioners,
others specialized in particular ailments. There does seem to be a large
degree of consistency, in space and time, in the actual ritual forms they
employed and it seems possible to describe these meaningfully in
generalized terms. These may be best described under four headings.

Oracular and divinatory procedures. The identification of the witch by
the victim or wise-man staring into a bowl of water or a bottle until a
vision of the aggressor appeared; the interpretation of signs in the natural
environment such as plants, or the behavior of animals.

The diagnosis and cure of "blinked" churns or cows. Here there were two
kinds of ritual commonly used; for a churn the basic principle was the
linking of the churn to the central hearth of the house by means of the
coulter and chains of the plough. For the removal of an enchantment
affecting the beasts' milk supply the *modus operandi* was as follows. All the
openings in the house, doors, chimneys, windows, were blocked up. Then,
in a pot hung over the fire were placed new iron needles or pins, the
prescribed herbs and sometimes milk. After a while the house filled up
with fumes. Both courses of action were expected to bring the witch
responsible for the misfortune to the scene in agony, begging for the
counter-spell to be stopped and promising to lift her own enchantment.
This is divination, cure and punishment in one neat package.

The diagnosis and cure of elf-shot cattle. Here again are two distinct ritual
forms, but for the treatment of the same complaint. The basic diagnostic
method in each case is the same: the wise-man measured the cow from the
tip of the tail to the nose, using his forearm as the unit of measurement,
then from nose to tail, and then from tail to nose again. If the cow became
shorter with each measurement then she was "shot" for sure. The first
curative ritual consists of giving the animal a drink of water containing
salt, a silver coin, an arrowhead and sometimes herbs. The second type of
healing rite is characterized by the presence of fire; sometimes the animal
had fire passed under its belly and over its back, sometimes the sign of the
cross burned on it and sometimes small piles of gunpowder ignited on its
back.

The diagnosis and cure of fairy changelings. Several informal means of
dealing with these folk monsters have been mentioned, but there were
other, more drastic, techniques involving fire which seemed to require the

consultation of a wise man or woman for their legitimation. Typically the changeling was held over the fire and this ill treatment was expected to cause it to leap up the chimney and away to its true home, the rath. The stolen human would then be returned. This could on occasion be an ideology of great potency, as the case of Bridget Cleary, described below, and many other tragedies in the literature show.

All the above are stylized ideal-typical descriptions of the rituals employed and it is important to remember that local variations and personal idiosyncrasies combined to make for a rich and varied pattern from place to place and person to person.

Apart from wise-men and wise-women there were other people, priests, blacksmiths and on occasion, albeit rare in Ireland, lawyers and judges, who could be called upon to resolve, in one way or another, cases of witchcraft or fairy aggression.

The Clonmel Tragedy

Before a theoretical summing up, it will assist understanding to adumbrate the real life concomitants of this kind of belief as manifested in the notorious Bridget Cleary case, which occurred near Clonmel, Co. Tipperary in 1895, and which for many years has been wrongly described as a "witch-burning."[110]

Michael Cleary and his wife Bridget lived in Ballyvadlea, Co. Tipperary, where Michael made his living as either a laborer or a cooper (the accounts differ on this point). In the absence of positive evidence to the contrary it is assumed that they were childless. In March 1895, Bridget, then twenty-six years old, fell ill and on 13 March Dr. Crean visited her, diagnosing bronchial catarrh and nervous excitement. The same day Fr. Ryan, the parish priest, also called to see her. At the preliminary proceedings before the magistrate in Clonmel he concluded, with the benefit of hindsight, that she might have been suffering at the time from the beginnings of mental derangement.

Dr. Crean was not the only physician to have been consulted; Denis Ganey, a well-known herb doctor from Kylethlea, over the mountains, had also been consulted on the advice of John Dunne, an elderly neighbor. He decided that Bridget was definitely a changeling, and prescribed the following treatment. At no time does Ganey appear to have supervised the actual cure in person.

On the evening of Thursday, 14 March, there were assembled at the Clearys' house Patrick Boland (Bridget's father), Mary Kennedy (her aunt), James, Patrick, Michael and William Kennedy (her cousins), Dunne and William Aherne (both neighbors). Together they attempted to force Bridget to accept the cure of milk mixed with herbs (probably *lus-mor*, foxglove). That she was an uncooperative patient is demonstrated by the testimony of Johannah Burke, a married sister of the Kennedys, who came in during the proceedings.

Dunne and three of the Kennedys were holding Bridget down on the bed while her husband and father tried to force the drink down her throat, all the time asking, "Are you Bridget Boland, wife of Michael Cleary, in the name of God?" Despite her affirmative answers she was subjected to the further indignity of being several times doused in urine. It was then that Johannah Burke first noticed red weals on Bridget's forehead, the marks of a hot poker which had been used to induce her to take the medicine.

At the instigation of Dunne she was then held over the slow burning turf fire and questioned further, she continued to answer that she was indeed Bridget Boland and not a fairy. It is significant that none of the onlookers appear to have made any serious attempt to call a halt to her suffering even though some of those present later indicated in court that they never had thought she was a fairy. The door was locked apparently, so there was no escape for Bridget or the other participants.

The next morning Fr. Ryan called again and although her condition was serious enough to warrant the celebration of Mass on the premises, he does not seem to have noticed anything untoward going on in the house. When questioned about this in court he defended himself by saying, "The priest is very often the last to hear of things like that."

That night, Friday, Bridget's ordeal continued and came to its tragic conclusion. She was laid on the fire again, this time covered in lamp oil, and as a result died from extensive burns on the abdomen, the lower part of the back and the left hand. Before this final act several things of significance happened. At one point Bridget turned to her husband and said, "Your mother used to go with the fairies, is that why you think I am going with them?" and later on Michael attempted to force her, by way of a test, to eat three pieces of bread, one after another. When she was unable to manage the last one, he forced it, quite literally, into her. One final point is that there does seem to have been some opposition that night to the treatment being meted out to her, especially from the women present.

When it was all over, Patrick Kennedy and Cleary took the body, wrapped it in a sheet and buried it in a bog about a quarter of a mile from the house. The next day, Saturday, a story was circulated by Cleary, Johannah Burke and the others, that Bridget had gone mad and was away with the fairies; Johannah Burke said that she had seen Bridget rushing out of the house and had tried to stop her in vain.

In a small community the truth will out and some days later, on the evidence of Johannah Burke and William Simpson, who had witnessed Thursday night's events with her, all the protagonists were arrested, as was Denis Ganey. Ganey and Mary Kennedy were eventually discharged, the others receiving sentences varying from twenty years penal servitude for Cleary, to six months for Boland and Patrick and Michael Kennedy.

Several conclusions may be drawn from this unhappy case: as has been stressed before, beliefs are not just ideological constructs, but are also plans for action—Michael Cleary and the others did not just believe in fairies in a passive way, they also consummated this belief in action; the action that was taken arose out of a conjunction of events and circumstances—Bridget's illness, perhaps her childlessness, the crucial intervention of John Dunne and Michael's mother's alleged history of involvement with the fairies which may have acted as some sort of precedent (not to mention a case, very nearly as tragic, which had occurred in Clonmel in 1884);[111] and the importance of intra-familial relationships in the case—although the details are unclear, the presence and direct involvement of so many members of Bridget's natal family points to a high level of family concern and interest.

Family and Community: Conclusions

The picture we now have of Irish beliefs in witches and fairies may be concisely summed up. Witches were believed to attack adults, by the evil eye or maleficent magic, stealing butter or milk and "overlooking" animals, especially cows or horses. The characteristic ethos of this sphere of belief was one of interpersonal conflict and envy. Not only was witchcraft believed to be practiced but there is good evidence that it was actually resorted to, to right an imagined or genuine wrong or simply to improve one's own position at the expense of one's neighbors.

Fairies were most active in two other areas of mischief: changelings, usually women or children, and elf-shot cattle. In the latter case it was not the cow's milk which was specifically affected, but her health and general well-being. It is not clear if male animals were also vulnerable.

These beliefs we may call the "moral space" under analysis: moral space consisting of two intermeshed dimensions, first, a system of *action* concepts and action evaluating concepts, and second, a system of *person* categories. These constitute the major structurings of moral space; the behavior and beliefs must be viewed as part of the action of individuals in this "shared conceptual and moral space."[112] "Moral" is used here in a loose sense, all conceptual universes being conceived of as "moral" universes.

The "person" categories in this material are man, woman, child and domestic animal, the victims, on the one hand, and witch and fairy changeling, the aggressors, on the other, with the wise-man or -woman acting as the mediating link between the two. The concepts relating to action and its evaluation have been ethnographically presented above;

these are the behavioral norms attached to various types of interpersonal relationships or brought into play in certain culturally recognized situations. For example, in the case of a woman who became ill shortly after childbirth there was an associated concept of "changeling" available which, depending on the history of the situation and the contingencies with which the interactants were faced, might be mobilized and might not. Given that the situation was thus redefined there were various concomitant action concepts available—for example, call in a wise-man (if this had not already been done), attempt an amateur cure, fetch the priest. However, and equally possibly, the woman's problem might be diagnosed as illness and a doctor or other medical practitioner summoned. An attempt to outline some of the variables which might have led to a particular illness being ascribed to fairy aggression has been made for the case of Bridget Cleary, above. This is the investigation of the actual behavior of real people in a "social field context," that Turner has called for.[113]

Moral space may be, in the Irish material, analytically bisected into two distinct domains: generalized and particularized misfortune,[114] and transactional/communal and incorporative/domestic social relationships.

The Singularity of Misfortune

Given that beliefs in mystic aggression act as an explanation of misfortune, it may be seen that the misfortunes tend to fall into two broad categories: those which are particularized and which lead to action being taken against specific individuals, and those which are generalized, which do not demand the allocation of responsibility to a specific person or persons and which can thus lead to no direct action being taken against the believed aggressor(s).

This dichotomy is of particular significance for fairy beliefs. A changeling is a particularized case of misfortune, but an elf-shot cow a generalized one. In the first case the victim is redefined as an aggressor and treated accordingly; in the second the victim is cured while the aggressor remains semi-anonymous, vague, and unpunished.

Brody's distinction[115] between the continuous labour patterns of the woman and the seasonal or cyclical nature of the man's tasks must be reconsidered. The distinction is directly analogous: particularized misfortunes occur as manifestly unusual interruptions of normality— processes which are normally predictable and repetitive—suddenly go wrong and an explanation must be urgently sought. In activities which are seasonal or cyclical, misfortune tends to be built into the system since the activities are not immediately repetitive and there is an allowance made for the unexpected.

Witchcraft attacks were not always particularized; it was possible for "witches" to be blamed, as opposed to "that witch," but it is my impression that witchcraft was nearly always ascribed to particular persons.[116] It is possible that the not insignificant category of unintentional throwers of the evil eye may have been a form of generalized explanation of misfortune.

The difference is also one of morality, for, as many authors have demonstrated, theories of supernatural aggression and mystic causation are also theories about morality, attempting to clarify the moral ambiguities and perplexities which constantly arise in day-to-day life.[117] However this only applies to particularized misfortune—generalized misfortune does not, in effect, take place in terms of individual wrongness or rightness. There is no pressing need to apportion blame. It is only particular misfortune which leads to action being taken against particular individuals: this I describe as "moral action."

Moral Action

Action dealing with a case of particularized misfortune within a referential framework of mystical aggression may be divided into two categories: attacks by either witches or fairies.

Witches were generally believed to operate in the communal, interfamilial sphere of relationships, Barth's "transactional" sphere, and an attack by a witch was often explicitly believed to follow an infringement of the behavioral norms of this sphere of interaction. When one was attacked the first logical step was to search one's conscience—whom had one offended or otherwise treated uncharitably in the recent past? An examination of one's current social relationships was bound to come up with something.[118] The role of the wise-man in confirming the victim's suspicions here is crucial, providing a recognized way of redefining the aggressor as "witch." As Rosemary Harris's case of Mrs. McKinley shows, an accusation could just as easily stem from the accused's flouting of community norms or mores. It is important to realize that *both* believed attacks and accusations, and the two are by no means coterminous, "provide categories for symbolizing deviance."[119] This gives a new twist to Philip Mayer's insight that witchcraft cosmologies cut both ways—one who can easily accuse others can be readily suspected himself.[120] It is this moral ambiguity that wise-men resolved: by categorizing the suspect as a witch their place in the system was assured and they could be dealt with accordingly.[121]

Fairies, however, normally attacked within the family, the domestic "incorporative" sphere of social interaction.[122] The principal victims were women of childbearing age and children, especially while they were still exclusively within the sphere of the mother's authority.

The moral nature of these attacks, following on a real or imagined failure to discharge domestic or familial responsibilities, is particularly apparent in the case of adult women. By redefining them as nonhuman aggressors it was possible for them to be punished without disturbing the moral equilibrium and external solidarity of the family, the facade of unity and harmony being maintained. This may explain why an open breach of conflict in social relationships, never, or rarely, led to accusations of mystic aggression. The semblance of solidarity had already crumbled.

The question of children who were "taken" poses a problem. What had they done that justified their being thus treated? The answer is, probably nothing. They were punished, we may speculate, for their mothers' crimes—their unsuccessful rearing. By displacing the punishment onto the child (and thus indirectly punishing the mother), the family unit was preserved and the mother lived to breed another day.

Witchcraft beliefs and fairy beliefs are united in at least one major respect. As should be clear from the above discussion, both functioned as a means of displacing or reversing guilt, through a process of redefining other people's social identities, yet at the same time retaining control and a myth of social harmony.[123] This is discussed further below.

The Woman's Position

A second respect in which the belief sets meet is that they both tend to converge on the same focal point, the women. Witches were commonly at their busiest stealing milk or blinking churns, both feminine spheres of responsibility, and witches were believed to be more commonly women than men. The fairies either attacked women directly, or took the children, again a feminine sphere of responsibility. This must be more than coincidence. It must also be more than coincidental that this state of affairs is common, in various cultural trappings, all around the world. Max Gluckman, in a brief examination of the problem,[124] has concluded that "perhaps the basic conflict lies in the fact that women bear the children who are to be competitive heirs for social power, position and property that are formally held by men."[125] Be that as it may, and Fox's speculations on the primacy of the mother-child unit as the essential social grouping are not without their relevance here,[126] there are specific and demonstrable reasons, manifest in the ethnographic material, which account for the woman's position of ambiguity.

In Irish rural society the woman usually married in; marriage was patrilocal. She was, by virtue of her childbearing function, indispensable to the foundation and successful maintenance of the basic unit of production, the family. Nevertheless, she may have remained an outsider to some extent. At the same time she had control, by virtue of the means and relations of production in the Irish peasant economy, of essential agricultural and economic activities such as child-rearing, milking the cows, and butter making. Because of the peasantry's encapsulation in a system of rent-capitalism, milk and butter played a particularly vital role as cash crops in the domestic economy; this must have further underlined their importance and exacerbated the potential for anxiety should their production be interrupted.

The conflicts and ambiguities within the Irish peasant family may be described as follows; first, between the woman's position as outsider and her role as guardian of the family prosperity, and second, between the explicit authority of the husband and the implicit importance of the wife in the economy. Apart from the likelihood that this might precipitate open conflict between husband and wife, it could also have resulted in the wife's position being perpetually ambiguous, and ambiguity is a prime cause of anxiety.

This anxiety, if it became extreme, was capable of resolution within the ideological framework of fairy abduction, enabling the man to reassert his dominance in a socially sanctioned manner without disturbing the family's moral unity by explicitly blaming the woman. Outside the family there was no necessary semblance of unity to maintain and accusations could be directly made—women become potentially culpable, hence witches. It is once again no coincidence that the women apparently most consistently accused were old, widowed, childless or independent; extra categorical in one way or another. Not only this, but they were the most easily victimized members of the community; their very independence was their weakness. Their lack of supportive social ties made them ideal scapegoats.

The role of the wise-men in these situations, is as we have seen, not too difficult to imagine; by redefining people as witches or changelings they clarified ambiguities in the social and moral sphere. This provided the victim/accuser with an unambiguous plan of action for dealing with the situation and was a means of developing a working group consensus.[127] It had as its concomitant the lessening of anxiety and discords in social interaction.

Paradoxically perhaps, in light of the above statement, beliefs in mystic aggression have a decidedly negative aspect. They are part of the price to pay for intense social interaction, a price which was paid by Bridget Cleary and many others whose names have never reached print.

Nadel[128] has recognized that witchcraft fears openly accentuate hostilities and actually add to the stresses of living. This should always be borne in mind as a necessary counterbalance to the crude functionalism implicit in many discussions of the subject. An example of this is provided in Westropp's description of an interfamily feud in Co. Clare which developed out of an accusation of profit-stealing. Following a wise-man's verdict that one family had bewitched the other's milk on May Eve, a showdown took place one night at the well, the opposing factions facing each other armed with pitchforks and guns.[129]

Conclusions

Briefly the conclusions tentatively reached may be summed up as follows. First, witchcraft beliefs served to symbolize deviance from the behavioral norms of communal/transactional social relationships, fairy changeling beliefs from the norms of domestic/incorporative relations.

Second, this deviance could be of two kinds: an individual's own failure to discharge his social responsibilities, leading him to suspect his misfortunes were the result of someone else's dissatisfaction with him; or someone else's persistent deviance. Both could lead, by different routes, to the same conclusion: an accusation, either of witchcraft or of fairy abduction.

Third, such accusations should not be seen, however, as responses to isolated circumstances. Accusations were the end product of an ongoing social process in which circumstances and background information interact and suspicion and conflict accumulate, finally leading to an open accusation.

Finally, the ambiguous position of the woman in peasant society—the tension between the dominant husband-submissive wife ideal and the reality in which the wife was perhaps the more important of the two *within the household*, is central to an understanding both of the content of Irish beliefs in supernatural aggression and the situations in which they were most frequently mobilized. This, I suspect, holds good for many other peasant societies.

On a more general level, it should be stressed that the belief sets outlined above should not be regarded as closed or rigid. That there were times when belief was manipulated is evident from the ethnography and it should be noted that, although the categories were available, whether or not they were used depended upon situational and social factors and/or personal choice. The peasantry should not be seen as dominated by their own beliefs. As time passed, especially towards the end of the nineteenth centuries, an alternative set of etiological categories became available, ones which perhaps held out greater hopes of successful treatment. Hospital, doctors, and veterinary surgeons replaced the wise-men and -women, while a new, and equally mysterious set of casual categories such as "germs" or "infection" replaced the witches and fairies. Only the victims remained.

Old beliefs die hard, however, and there are still many people whose "moral space" is that of a different time than our own. I heard, for instance, of a cow being "blinked" in west Cork in 1975 which was given up by the vet, but cured by a charmer, and seventh sons are in demand as never before. Nevertheless a belief in fairies and witches, of the traditional sort at least, is fast becoming a thing of the past, whether for better or worse is difficult to say.

Postscript, March 1990

In the years since this paper first appeared, my thinking about much of the argument has changed considerably. Were I to start from scratch I would either say something rather different or say something similar rather differently. However, since pressures of time and work preclude me from doing so, I should at least point out that other people—most notably Breen[130] and Glassie[131]—have commented critically upon my original analysis. I recommend them to those who are sufficiently intrigued by the material to consider how my discussion can be developed or an alternative understanding offered.

With respect to Irish folk belief, there are some absences from my citations and some subsequent additions to the literature which are worth mentioning here. Of the "classic" accounts of Irish fairy beliefs, I managed to overlook MacManus's;[132] Evans-Wentz's famous comparative study of Celtic fairylore[133] from 1911 has reappeared. Both are worth a look. There are now two popular books about Biddy Early,[134] and a recent short paper discussing the "witchburning" at Clonmel.[135] Two prolific, although very different authors have also made contributions: Logan's work on folk medicine has been reissued,[136] and Murphy has written on the folklore of Rathlin.[137]

Looking at the broader perspective, there has been a massive upsurge of fine scholarship on European witchcraft and the early-modern witchcraft persecutions. Most of this literature is only tangentially relevant to this paper. Exceptions are two excellent collections of papers about the "evil eye"[138] and a small number of studies of recent or contemporary European witch beliefs.[139] Unfortunately, it remains as much the case today as when I wrote the paper that European fairy beliefs have yet to attract the level of serious scholarly attention which they merit.

Notes

Reprinted with permission from Ulster Folklife 23 (1977): 33–56. A "Postscript" has been added.

1. This article is based on part of a dissertation submitted for the B.A. (Hons.) degree in Social Anthropology at the Queen's University, Belfast. I would like to thank Dr. E.J. Moody for his patient supervision and also Dr. R.A. Gailey, Miss May

McCann and Dr. Milan Stuchlik for their comments. I alone am responsible for the paper's shortcomings. I also owe a debt of gratitude to the library staffs of Queen's University Belfast, University College London, the Linenhall Library, Belfast, and the Folklore Society, London. Finally I thank Shelagh for her secretarial assistance and other help during the research period.

2. E.E. Evans-Pritchard, *Witchcraft, Oracles and Magic among the Azande* (Oxford: Clarendon P, 1937) 21.

3. John Middleton and E.H. Winter eds., *Witchcraft and Sorcery in East Africa* (London: Routledge and Kegan Paul, 1963) 8.

4. Middleton and Winter 12–3.

5. Victor W. Turner, "Witchcraft and Sorcery: Taxonomy versus Dynamics," *Africa* 34 (1964): 323–4.

6. Alan Harwood, *Witchcraft, Sorcery and Social Categories among the Safwa* (London: Oxford UP, 1970) 26, 29. For further discussion of the distinction between transactional and incorporative social relationships see Fredrik Barth, *Models of Social Organisation* (London: Royal Anthropological Institute, 1966) 4, 23–4.

7. Harwood 139.

8. F.G. Bailey, ed., *Gifts and Poisons* (Oxford: Basil Blackwell, 1971) 28–9.

9. E.E. Evans, *The Personality of Ireland* (Cambridge: Cambridge UP, 1973) 55–6.

10. Raymond D. Crotty, *Irish Agricultural Production* (Cork: Cork UP, 1966) 4.

11. E.E. Evans, *Irish Folk Ways* (London: Routledge and Kegan Paul, 1957) 81–4; O'Donovan, John, *The Economic History of Livestock in Ireland* (Cork: Cork UP, 1940) 31.

12. Crotty 5.

13. Evans, *Folk Ways* 21.

14. Evans, *Folk Ways* 9, 31.

15. Evans, *Folk Ways* 31.

16. Conrad M. Arensberg and Solon T. Kimball, *Family and Community in Ireland* (Gloucester, Mass.: Peter Smith, 1961) 62–77.

17. Evans, *Folk Ways* 59.

18. Arensberg and Kimball 33–43, 46–8; Evans, *Folk Ways* (1957) 95; Rosemary Harris, *Prejudice and Tolerance in Ulster* (Manchester: Manchester UP, 1972) 54.

19. Hugh Brody, *Inishkillane* (Harmondsworth: Pelican, 1974) 20.

20. Arensberg and Kimball 126–30.

21. Michael J. Murphy, *Now You're Talking* . . . (Belfast: Blackstaff, 1975) 23–32.

22. K.H. Connell, *Irish Peasant Society* (Oxford: Clarendon P, 1968) 1–50.

23. Conrad M. Arensberg, *The Irish Countryman* (Gloucester, Mass.: Peter Smith, 1959) 191; Evans, *Folk Ways* 97.

24. J.H. Johnson, "The 'Two Irelands' at the Beginning of the Nineteenth Century," in N. Stephens and R.E. Glasscock eds., *Irish Geographical Studies* (Belfast: Queen's U, 1970) 224–43.

25. Arensberg 71–106; Brody 59–60.

26. Brody 16, 70–3.

27. K.M. Harris, "Extracts from the Society's Collection (2)," *Ulster Folklife* 5 (1959): 45.

28. R.H. Buchanan, "The Folklore of an Ulster Townland," *Ulster Folklife* 2 (1956): 50.

29. Lady Augusta Gregory, *Visions and Beliefs of the West of Ireland* (1920; Gerard's Cross: Colin Smythe, 1970) 81–3.

30. Thomas Doherty, "Some Notes on the Physique, Customs and Superstitions of the Peasantry of Inishowen, Co. Donegal," *Folk-Lore* 8 (1897): 12–8.

31. John C. Messenger, *Inis Beag: Isle of Ireland* (New York: Holt, Rinehart and Winston, 1969) 106.

32. Messenger 101–6.

33. Cf. Nathaniel Colgan, "Witchcraft in the Aran Islands," *Journal of the Royal Society of Antiquaries of Ireland* 25 (1895): 84–5; A.C. Haddon and C.R. Browne, "The Ethnography of the Aran Islands," *Proceedings Royal Irish Academy*, 3rd Series, 2 (1891–93) 816 ff; Lady Jane Francesca S. Wilde, *Ancient Legends, Mystic Charms and Superstitions of Ireland* (1887; Galway: O'Gorman, 1971) 70.

34. Reginald Scot, *The Discoverie of Witchcraft* (1584; Amsterdam: De Capo P, 1971) 64.

35. R. Harris 101.

36. Alan MacFarlane, *Witchcraft in Tudor and Stuart England* (London: Routledge and Kegan Paul, 1970) 86, 110.

37. For examples of such "incidental" accusations see: John Stevenson, *Two Centuries of Life in Down, 1600–1800* (Belfast: McCaw, Stevenson and Orr, 1920) 176, which occurred in Carnmoney, Co. Antrim; Thomas J. Westropp, "Witchcraft in Co. Limerick," *Journal of the Royal Society of Antiquaries of Ireland* 21 (1892): 291, from New Pallas, Co. Limerick.

38. Oliver Davies, "Folklore in Maghera Parish," *Ulster Journal of Archaeology* 3rd Series, 8 (1945): 63; Lageniensis, *Irish Folk Lore* (Glasgow: Cameron and Ferguson, 1870) 247; Caoimhín Ó Danachair, "A Record of Some Beliefs and Customs of the Seventeenth Century," *Béaloideas* 14 (1944): 288; Stevenson 22–3; Wilde 72.

39. Brian Spooner, "The Evil Eye in the Middle East," in Mary Douglas, ed., *Witchcraft Confessions and Accusations* (London: Tavistock, 1970) 312.

40. Thomas Crofton Croker, *Researches in the South of Ireland* (1824; Shannon: Irish Universities P, 1969) 93 ff.

41. Keith Thomas, "The Relevance of Social Anthropology in the Historical Study of English Witchcraft," in Douglas, *Witchcraft Confessions* 65–6. For a similar conclusion drawn from American Indian ethnography, see Clyde Kluckholn, "Navaho Witchcraft," in Max Marwick, ed., *Witchcraft and Sorcery* (Harmondsworth: Penguin, 1970) 220; Julian Pitt-Rivers, "Spiritual Power in Central America," in Douglas, *Witchcraft Confessions* 183–4.

42. J. Abercromby, "Irish Stories and Charms," *Folk-Lore Journal* 2 (1884): 32–9; Croker 94; Ó Danachair 288; Gregory 247–9; Messenger 104.

43. Wilde 173.

44. Gregory 247–9.

45. Jeanne Cooper Foster, *Ulster Folk Lore* (Belfast: Carter, 1951) 91–2; K.M. Harris 45.

46. Patrick Kennedy, *Legendary Fictions of the Irish Celts*, 2nd ed. (London: Macmillan, 1891) 135.

47. Thomas J. Westropp, "A Folk-Lore Survey of Co. Clare," *Folk-Lore* 22 (1911): 340; Sir William Wilde, *Irish Popular Superstitions* (1852; Shannon: Irish Universities P, 1972) 54.

48. Leland L. Duncan, "Fairy Beliefs and Other Folklore Notes from County Leitrim," *Folk-Lore* 8 (1897): 161–83.

49. Wilde, *Superstitions* 54–9.

50. Arensberg 192–3; Cooper Foster 90; John Hewitt, *Rhyming Weavers* (Belfast: Blackstaff, 1974) 51–2; Edward O'Toole, "A Miscellany of North Carlow Folklore," *Béaloideas* 1 (1928): 325.

51. Quoted in Hewitt 77.

52. Cáit Ní Bhráidaigh, "Folklore from Co. Longford," *Béaloideas* 6 (1936): 262.

53. Doherty 12–8; K.M. Harris, "The Schools' Collection," *Ulster Folklife* 3 (1957): 12.

54. Davies 65.

55. Mary Campbell, *Sea Wrack: Long-ago Tales of Rathlin Island* (Ballycastle: J.S. Scarlett, 1951) 31; Croker 94; Messenger 101; G.W. Saunderson, "Butterwitches and Cow Doctors," *Ulster Folklife* 7 (1961): 73; W.B. Yeats, ed. *Irish Fairy and Folk Tales* (London: Walter Scott, 1893) 154–5, 163–5.

56. Wilde, *Ancient Legends* 81, 172.

57. Ní Bhráidaigh 262.

58. R. Clark, "Folk Lore Collected in Co. Wexford," *Folk-Lore Record* 5 (1882): 81–3; Michael J. Murphy, "Folktales and Traditions from County Cavan and South Armagh," *Ulster Folklife* 19 (1973): 33–4; Wilde, *Superstitions* 59; Lady Jane Francesca S. Wilde, *Ancient Cures, Charms and Usages of Ireland* (London: Ward and Downey, 1890) 49.

59. Westropp, "Survey" (1911) 332–41; an example from Kilkee, Co. Clare in 1892.

60. Croker 234.

61. Wilde, *Ancient Legends* 81; Wilde, *Ancient Cures* 49.

62. Arensberg and Kimball 71; Evans, *Folk Ways* 27–38.

63. St. John D. Seymour, *Irish Witchcraft and Demonology* (Dublin: Hodges, Figgis, 1913) 232.

64. Keith Thomas, *Religion and the Decline of Magic* (Harmondsworth: Penguin, 1973) 274. A cadaver-hand, associated with this belief, is in the museum collection at Whitby, Yorkshire.

65. Tomás Ó Cleirigh, "Gleanings in Wicklow," *Béaloideas* 1 (1928): 249; Wilde, *Ancient Legends* 81.

66. Daniel Deeney, *Peasant Lore from Gaelic Ireland* (London: Nutt, 1901) 15.

67. Wilde, *Ancient Legends* 83, 100.

68. Colgan 84–5.

69. Gregory, *Visions* 160–1.

70. Sir James Frazer, *The Golden Bough* (1890; London: Macmillan, 1957) 14.

71. Bryan J. Jones, "Correspondence," *Folk-Lore* 6 (1895): 302.

72. Westropp, "Survey" 51.

73. Patrick Logan, *Making the Cure* (Dublin: The Talbot P, 1972) 163.

74. Arensberg 196–8.

75. Translated in Ó Danachair 288.

76. Wilde, *Ancient Cures* 47.

77. Cf. Thomas, "Relevance" 49.

78. Norman Cohn, *Europe's Inner Demons* (London: Heinemann, for Sussex UP, 1975) 152; Thomas, *Religion* 616.

79. Cf. for examples, Scarlett Epstein, "A Sociological Analysis of Witch Beliefs in a Mysore Village," in John Middleton, ed., *Witchcraft Curing and Magic* (New York: Natural History P, 1967) 140; Louis C. Faron, *The Mapuche Indians of Chile* (New York: Holt, Rinehart and Winston, 1968) 82–90; Clifford Geertz, *The Religion of Java* (Glencoe:

Free P, 1964) 106–11; Isaac Schapera, "Sorcery and Witchcraft in Bechuanaland," in Marwick 110.
80. Barth 15.
81. Evans, *Folk Ways* 299–300; Westropp, "Survey" 49–51.
82. Buchanan 49; K.M. Harris, "Extracts" 45.
83. Buchanan 49.
84. Arensberg 28–33.
85. Seán Ó Súilleabháin, *Irish Folk Custom and Belief* (Dublin: Cultural Relations Committee of Ireland, n.d.) 82–6.
86. Arensberg and Kimball 53.
87. Anon., "Collectanea," *Folk-Lore Journal* 2 (1884): 190–1; J. Cooke, "Notes on Irish Folklore from Connaught, collected chiefly in North Donegal," *Folk-Lore* 8 (1897): 299–301; Gregory 42–4; Lageniensis 46; W.R. Le Fanu, *Seventy Years of Irish Life* (London: Edward Arnold, 1896) 39–40; Thomas J. Westropp, "A Folk-Lore Survey of Co. Clare," *Folk-Lore* 21 (1910): 180–99.
88. Croker 85–6; Le Fanu 39.
89. Croker 90–1. The problem of the "runaway match" has been discussed in Arensberg and Kimball 119.
90. Gregory 83–4.
91. Jeremiah Curtin, *Tales of the Fairies and of the Ghost World* (1895; Dublin: The Talbot P, 1974) 6–17.
92. Gregory 42–4.
93. Classon Porter, *Witches, Warlocks and Ghosts* (Belfast: The Northern Whig, 1885) 19–20.
94. Gregory 69–73, 100–2; William Hamilton Maxwell, *Wild Sports of the West of Ireland* (London: Simpkin, Marshall, Hamilton, Kent, 1892) 316–7.
95. Croker 87–91.
96. James Boyle, et al., *Life in the Glens of Antrim in 1830s* (n.p., Glens of Antrim Historical Society, 1968) 29.
97. Boyle 29; James Boyle, et al., *Ordnance Survey Memoir for the Parish of Donegore* (Belfast: Public Record Office, 1974) 39; William Shaw-Mason, ed., *A Statistical Account or Parochial Survey of Ireland* 3 (Dublin, 1814–19) 27.
98. Deeney 3.
99. Doherty 12–8.
100. Logan 166–7.
101. Boyle et al., *Life in the Glens* 29; Boyle et al., *Ordnance Survey* 39; Faulkner C. Mason, "Traditions concerning Domestic Animals," *Béaloideas* 1 (1928): 223–4; Joseph Meehan, "The Cure of Elf-Shooting in the North-West of Ireland," *Folk-Lore* 17 (1906): 202.
102. Boyle et al., *Life in the Glens* 29; Saunderson 73.
103. G.H. Kinahan, "Notes on Irish Folk-Lore," *Folk-Lore Record* 4 (1881): 102.
104. Arensberg 189.
105. Thomas, *Religion* 731.
106. James Joyce, *Dubliners* (Harmondsworth: Penguin, 1956) 97–104; see also Kevin Danaher, *The Year in Ireland* (Cork: Mercier, 1972) 218–27; Ó Súilleabháin 69–70.
107. Alwyn Rees and Brinley Rees, *Celtic Heritage* (London: Thames and Hudson, 1961) 89.
108. Rees 91.

109. Readers requiring more information about these topics should consult my dissertation, "Witchcraft and Fairy Beliefs of the Irish Peasantry," a copy of which is available for consultation in the departmental library, Dept. of Social Anthropology, Queen's University, Belfast. The relevant details are in chapters 5–7, as are the references to the original material on which this summary account is based.

110. My two major sources for this are, Anon., "The 'Witch-Burning' at Clonmel," *Folk-Lore* 6 (1895): 373–84, and Jim McGarry, ed., *Irish Tales of Terror* (London: Fontana, 1971) 54–60. Both agree on the major details and each offers small details not given by the other.

111. Anon., "Collectanea," *Folk-Lore Journal* 2 (1884): 190–1.

112. Malcom Crick, "Two Styles in the Study of Witchcraft," *Journal of the Anthropological Society of Oxford* 4 (1973): 19.

113. Turner 324.

114. Middleton and Winter 10.

115. Brody 20.

116. Cf. Max Gluckman, *Custom and Conflict in Africa* (Oxford: Basil Blackwell, 1956) 82–4; Thomas, *Religion* 668.

117. Mary Douglas, *Purity and Danger* (Harmondsworth: Pelican, 1970) 114–36; Gluckman 86; M.G. Marwick, *Sorcery in its Social Setting* (Manchester: Manchester UP, 1965) 221–46, 281–3.

118. This has also been discussed for the English material; cf. MacFarlane 168–74; Thomas, *Religion* 665–7.

119. Harwood 139.

120. Philip Mayer, "Witches," in Marwick, *Witchcraft* 45–64.

121. Cf. Gluckman 90.

122. Barth's discussion of transactional and incorporative categories has already been referred to; see also Edmund Leach, *Rethinking Anthropology* (London: Athlone P, 1966) 21 for a discussion of the essentially similar categories of incorporation and alliance.

123. MacFarlane 196.

124. Max Gluckman, *Politics, Law and Ritual in Tribal Society* (Oxford: Basil Blackwell, 1965) 223–5, 248–50.

125. Gluckman, *Politics* 225.

126. Robin Fox, *Kinship and Marriage* (Harmondsworth: Pelican, 1967) 37–40.

127. Cf. David K. Jordan, *Gods, Ghosts and Ancestors* (Berkeley: U of California P, 1972) 86; George K. Park, "Divination and its Social Contexts," in Middleton 240.

128. S.F. Nadel, "Witchcraft in Four African Countries," in Marwick, *Witchcraft* 279.

129. Westropp, "Survey" 339.

130. Richard Breen, "The Ritual Expression of Inter-Household Relationships in Ireland," *Cambridge Anthropology* 6.1–2 (1980): 33–59.

131. Henry Glassie, *Passing the Time in Ballymenone: Culture and History in an Ulster Community* (Dublin: O'Brien P, 1982): 780–1.

132. D. MacManus, *The Middle Kingdom: The Faerie World in Ireland* (1959; Gerard's Cross: Colin Smythe, 1973).

133. W.Y. Evans-Wentz, *The Fairy Faith in Celtic Countries* (1911; Gerard's Cross: Colin Smythe, 1981).

134. Meda Ryan, *Biddy Early: The Wise Woman of Clare* (Cork: Mercier, 1978); Edmund Lenihan, *In Search of Biddy Early* (Cork: Mercier, 1987). Lenihan's is the more detailed, better documented and more interesting of the two.

135. Thomas McGrath, "Fairy Faith and Changelings: The Burning of Bridget Cleary in 1895," *Studies* LXXI (1982): 178–84.

136. Patrick Logan, *Irish Country Cures* (Belfast: Appletree P, 1981).

137. Michael J. Murphy, *Rathlin: Island of Blood and Enchantment* (Dundalk: Dundalgen P, 1987).

138. Alan Dundes, ed., *The Evil Eye: A Folklore Casebook* (New York: Garland, 1981); Clarence Maloney, ed., *The Evil Eye* (New York: Columbia UP, 1976).

139. Jeanne Favret-Saada, *Deadly Words: Witchcraft in the Bocage* (Cambridge: Cambridge UP, 1980); Hans Sebald, *Witchcraft: The Heritage of a Heresy* (New York: Elsevier, 1978); Harry A. Senn, *Were-Wolf and Vampire in Romania* (Boulder: East European Monographs, 1982).

Newfoundland Berry Pickers "In the Fairies": Maintaining Spatial, Temporal, and Moral Boundaries Through Legendry[1]

Peter Narváez

> Where dips the rocky highland
> of Sleuth Wood in the lake,
> There lies a leafy island
> Where flapping herons wake
> The drowsy water-rats.
> There we've hid our fairy vats
> Full of berries,
> And of reddest stolen cherries.
> Come away, O, human child!
> To the woods and waters wild,
> With a fairy hand in hand,
> For the world's more full of weeping than
> you can understand.
> W.B. Yeats, from "The Stolen Child"

Contemporary visions of "fairies" invoke images of either quaint folkloric figures, oftentimes associated with a popular children's literature based on folktales, or stereotypes of male homosexuals.[2] In the first instance the figure is regarded as fantastical, while the second "straight" view of "fairy" is deprecatory, connoting malignance and provoking an anxious response to ambiguous identity. The kind of ambiguous identity associated with this latter and more modern usage, one which poses the threat of potential immorality and bodily harm, has made the fairy of tradition a powerful community figure in the folk cultures of Newfoundland's past. As vital aspects of a complex magico-religious belief system, fairies in Newfoundland have affected behavior and worldview.[3] This discussion will focus attention on a cluster of Newfoundland legends and personal experience narratives which, as oral survivals and living, traditional beliefs, reveal how fairies have functioned as folkloric mechanisms for the erection and maintenance of spatial and temporal boundaries.[4] As "survivals" these narratives reflect beliefs and customary practices which continue to be transmitted although their earlier meanings and social functions may have been rejected, altered, or forgotten. As accounts of past family and community incidents these stories relate events which are believed to have actually occurred to the protagonists. Most of the young adult narrators, however, distance themselves from and are skeptical of the traditional supernatural interpretations which they report as integral elements of the narratives.[5]

Time Bias and Discontinuous Space

These tales reflect ideas regarding space and time which are antithetical to those exhibited in a number of emergent "media legends" that I have examined elsewhere.[6] In that study, the media concepts of Harold A. Innis were employed to argue that the "spatial bias" of modern technological media disposed a contemporary generation of Newfoundlanders to view time as being discontinuous and to perceive space as continuous.[7] Accordingly, these ideas were illustrated in a set of Newfoundland legends that humorously condemned spatial incompetence, in depictions of the misuse and misunderstanding of modern media, while revealing a sense of disjunctive time through portrayals of "foolish" elderly protagonists. On the other hand, the fairy legends to be presented here reflect the "time bias" of sensory media, the predominant media of the folk societies of earlier Newfoundland generations, a shaping force which disposes a group to experience time continuously, that is, to expend energies on the conservation and transmission of cultural forms which are previously known and understood as perpetually relevant.[8] In particular, the temporal bias of orality inclines a society to view geographical space as a discontinuous reality, a tendency which fosters a contractionist worldview.[9]

Liminal Space

As orality (language use, dialect formation[10]) nurtured notions of contractile space in the folk communities of Newfoundland's past, specific folkloric mechanisms (e.g., mummering, ghost legends, Jack O'Lantern, mysterious lights, tokens, tragic sea ballads, strangers, fairies[11]) established proxemic boundaries on the cognitive maps of community residents, boundaries which demarcated geographical areas of purity, liminality, and danger. "Liminal" is a term derived from the Latin *limin* meaning "threshold." In the intellectual tradition of Arnold van Gennep, it is usually associated with that period during a rite of passage when a participant experiences the ambivalent realm between one social position and another.[12] This temporal usage of liminality is here transferred to a spatial understanding of areas between known space (purity) and unknown space (danger) where one might experience the benign or the malignant.[13] In commenting on such marginal territories, van Gennep appropriately observed, "whoever passes from one [zone] to the other finds himself physically and magico-religiously in a special situation for a certain length of time: he wavers between two worlds."[14] The fairy narratives under consideration reveal that particularly for women, berry grounds in Newfoundland—zones of muskeg bogs, barrens, and marshlands on the inland geographic fringes of small communities—have constituted liminal spaces, territories on earth's horizontal surface that have been inhabited by fairies who might be regarded as *liminal personae*,[15] creatures of ambivalent status and inclination who, as will be shown, are themselves in the liminal vertical space of "Middle Earth," betwixt Heaven and Hell. Forests, related liminal spaces of particular significance to men, will receive brief mention later in this discussion and have been noted elsewhere.[16] Despite the limitations of a two dimensional medium, the intersection of these horizontal and vertical worlds might be simply diagrammed as follows:

H E A V E N

Fairies

M I D D L E   E A R T H

PURITY	LIMINAL SPACE	DANGER
Known Space	Berry Grounds	Unknown Space
	Forests	

Mortals

H E L L

Fairies in North America

While fairylore has been extensively studied by European folklorists, it is generally assumed that fairies have not existed in North America.[17] Richard M. Dorson maintained that "these beings cavorted and made mischief throughout the isles of Britain, but failed to take passage with the emigrants sailing for America."[18] His rationale for the absence of fairies in the New World was that folk creatures "rooted in the soil" of their homelands could not make the crossing, whereas folk figures who knew no spatial confines such as the Devil, witches and ghosts could. Fairies, like certain other European supernatural figures, were "too closely associated with the culture and the geography of the Old Country to migrate."[19]

The large amount of fairylore apparent in Newfoundland, recently the object of an intensive investigation at Memorial University,[20] appears anomalous, therefore, and may be partially accounted for by the unique history of Newfoundland settlement, environmental factors, and folk theology concerning fairies. As part of the larger question of cultural continuity and the immigrant experience, Newfoundland's peculiar patterns of economic development and settlement are of prime importance for understanding the survival of fairy belief. In Newfoundland, colonizing through chartered companies, the procedure which typified the settlement of other New World British colonies, failed in the seventeenth century largely due to the inadequate development of secondary agricultural resources and because of conflicts with the vested interests of an established seasonal West Country fishing economy.[21] From the late sixteenth century through the 1790s, English and Irish migrated through this West Country fishery, as official winter work crews, illegal migrants, and as indentured fishing servants. The decline of the migratory fishery and the emergence of the inshore family fishery, the development of a town and urban center, St. John's, the granting of official status to Newfoundland as a British colony in 1824, and economic depressions and agricultural failures in Ireland, all contributed toward attracting increasing numbers of immigrants during the late eighteenth century and first half of the nineteenth century.[22] These immigrants only slowly and painfully melded into the merchant fishery economy but Newfoundland's economic conditions were not altogether new to them, for as John J. Mannion has observed, "in southeast Ireland, and to a much greater extent in southwest England, the transatlantic cod fishery and concomitant supply trade ranked as the leading commercial ventures over a considerable period of time, employing great numbers of people in related activities in the ports, in the inland towns and villages, and on the farms."[23] Unlike their migrant counterparts in other areas of North America who journeyed from their homelands as part of a socioeconomic experiment, for religious reasons, or to join an emergent industrial work force, thereby encountering radically different cultural scenes, Irish and English settlers in Newfoundland often immigrated as an extension of their primary occupational pursuits connected with the fishery. On arrival, they encountered a cultural environment and economy that approximated previously known conditions. This pattern of development resulted in a multitude of small isolated fishing "outports," closely resembling the classic "folk society" model,[24] which, not unlike their village counterparts in England and Ireland, served mercantile interests. Until the mid-twentieth century these economically undiversified communities could certainly sustain traditional fairy faith, for as George Story has observed, such "undisturbed" outports long remained "a rich repository of European customs and folkways on the very threshold of the New World."[25]

The environmental conditions of Newfoundland experienced by immigrant populations may also have been conducive to continued fairy belief because they appeared similar to Old World fairy surroundings. Walter Yeeling Evans-Wentz has stressed the significance of weather and scenery in "shaping" the Celtic fairy faith of Ireland and Scotland.[26] His description of the "rock-bound" and "storm swept" shores of the Outer Hebrides certainly portrays Newfoundland coastal conditions as well:

> Commonly there is the thickest day-darkness when the driving storms come in from the Atlantic, or when dense fog covers sea and land; and, again, there are melancholy sea-winds moaning across from shore to shore. . . . At other times there is a sparkle of the brightest sunshine on the waves . . . and then again a dead silence prevails. . . . All these contrasted conditions may be seen in one day. . . .[27]

In addition to similar coastline environs, European associations of inland berry grounds and fairy habitations, particularly well documented for Ireland in connection with the ancient Celtic harvest festival of Lughnasa,[28] were well suited to Newfoundland and Labrador which abound with areas of blueberries and bilberries (also known in Newfoundland as "hurts"), partridge berries, bakeapples (cloudberries), raspberries, squashberries, and marshberries.[29]

Despite unique historical patterns of migration and the presence of environments which appeared hospitable to fairies, the survival of fairy faith amongst European immigrants in North America required an interpretive frame that allowed for one or more of the following possibilities: 1. fairy emigration; 2. fairy propagation in conjunction with mortals; 3. native fairy inhabitants in the new land. In the first regard, Dorson's view that Old World fairies are "rooted in the soil" is correct— theories of fairy origin generally do not allow for fairy transplantation. Secondly, if theories of fairy origin were entertained that emphasized genealogical links with mortals, such as the idea that fairies are unbaptized children or spirits of the dead, the development of a fairy population would have required settlement of considerable duration.[30] In contrast, the predominance in Newfoundland of belief in the "fallen angel" theory accounts for *indigenous* fairy inhabitants.[31] This etiological mythic narrative begins by recounting the casting out of Satan and his angels from Heaven as biblically portrayed in Revelation (12.7–9). The "folk Bible"[32] oral traditions which derive from and expand upon Biblical texts, then maintains that St. Michael appealed to the Almighty to stem the exodus of angels. God rescinded his previous order, and as Katharine Briggs has summarized, descending angels "were arrested on their fall through the universe towards Hell, and stayed where they fell, some in the air, some in the rivers, the sea or lakes, some on earth, and some under the earth."[33] Given adherence to fallen angel folk theology, therefore, we can surmise that until fairies experience their fate on the Day of Judgment they might be encountered anywhere on Middle Earth. In Newfoundland, this folk theology has been so taken for granted that on one occasion, during an interview, a Newfoundland informant voiced surprise when an "educated" folklorist appeared to be ignorant of such well acknowledged "fact."[34] As with Irish and West Country usage, fairies in Newfoundland are often referred to as the "little people" or the "good people," phrases which convey both fear, the taboo of calling fairies by name, and in the latter case, respect for beings who are believed to derive their powers for detriment or benefit from both satanic associations and former angelic status.[35]

Berry Picking

While berry picking as a supplemental food source probably commenced with settlement, patterns of picking berries assumed customary form with the advent of the family fishery in the nineteenth century.[36] Depending on seasonal weather conditions, the region, and the particular kind of berry to be picked, berry picking has usually taken place from late July to mid-October. Whether a day's outing or a week in the bush, traditionally women have been the predominant pickers.

Women usually went in groups of two or three for blueberries, sometimes taking along smaller children who picked berries as well. Rarely did family groups go blueberry picking.[37]

A way back in the twenties and thirties the wife and children usually went berry picking while the husband went fishing.[38]

> About four or five women and their children went and we camped out
> for a week. Sometimes there would be a couple of elderly men among us
> to help to haul up the boats in stormy weather.[39]

Although traditional berry picking has most often involved women and
children obtaining berries for such domestic uses as preserves, jellies,
jams, baked goods, and wine, the significance of blueberries, bilberries,
and partridge berries for income supplement, as some of the narratives
will indicate (10, 19, 21), should not be minimized. From at least the
second decade of the nineteenth century some berries were occasionally
commercially traded for merchants' goods, but it was when the
development of freezer facilities by the fishing industry (1927) coincided
with the unemployment of the 1930s that the Newfoundland blueberry
industry commenced.[40] The ensuing development exploited the
availability of inexpensive laborers, both men and women, who either
received cash—ten cents per gallon of blueberries—or more often,
obtained credit.[41] During periods of intensive effort, Hilda Murray recalls
that men picked with large wooden "berry boxes" and tended to go
"farther away from the community and [travel] over more difficult terrain,
where the women with their buckets and hoops [yokes] would find it
difficult to go."[42] She has also described the typical credit procedure:

> Berries were "shipped" or sold to the local merchants or merchants who
> were agents for St. John's-based firms. No money changed hands at least
> until the 1950s. Those who sold berries were given a "berry note"
> indicating the amount of berries shipped and the price per gallon. The
> value of the note had to be "taken up" in goods in the store where the
> berries were shipped. A family of five or six good berry pickers could, in
> a good season, provide the family with some necessary food items
> purchased from the store—flour, margarine, sugar, molasses, beef, pork,
> etc.—and get winter clothing as well.[43]

Material inducements during hard times often drove berry pickers into
realms of danger. Hegemonic mercantile pressures and traditional
worldview sometimes clashed. The resulting anxieties are captured in the
recollections of a participant, Hubert Brown Abbot of Newman's Cove:

> Back in the thirties there were many people who got lost in the woods.
> They claimed that the reason they got lost was because the fairies led
> them away. There were search parties sent out with lanterns to look for
> the lost person. They would probably spend most of the night in the
> woods searching before they would find the person they were looking
> for. They would find them sitting by a fire which they would make once
> they knew for sure they were lost. In most cases we would find them
> with their caps turned inside out because it was said if you were led

away by fairies, turn your cap inside out and the fairies would go away.[44]

For both mortals and fairies berry grounds were cultural scenes in liminal space involving varying degrees of group participation and solitude. The most common forms of preventive magic used by berry pickers to protect themselves from fairy encounters were to turn articles of clothing inside out[45] or to carry pieces of bread,[46] breadcrumbs, or "fairy buns."[47]

My grandmother told us, "when you go berry picking or any other time in the woods, wear some kind of bandana on your head, because if you get lost the fairies will lead you astray, but they can't get you if you turn your bandana, or any article of clothes, inside out."[48]

[My grandmother] used to warn us that when we went out, going in the woods somewhere, to have a bit of bread in our pockets. And the custom was when the woman was baking bread she always made the sign of the cross on the bread to give God thanks for having flour to make bread, and she always called it the "blessed bread." And the fairies couldn't touch you if you had a bit of bread in your pocket because they couldn't come near that. So we always made sure before we went berry picking or wandering through the woods, that we had little crusts of bread somewhere in our pocket.[49]

Well when I was growing up that's all we used to hear about—the fairies. If you was going berry picking over in the woods the old people would tell you to put bread in your pocket so the fairies wouldn't take you. . . . Or, if you never had bread to put in your pocket, you put silver in your pocket and that used to keep the fairies away. The fairies are little people. They are only about two foot high, two foot tall.[50]

Encounters were sometimes characterized by mortal perceptions of the actual physical presence of fairies, but more often by an awareness of a dreamlike, psychic presence which caused pickers to lose their sense of time and get lost by being "taken astray" or "led astray," "fairy-led,"[51] or by being "in the fairies."[52] The psychic nature of this type of encounter is explained by a resident of Upper Island Cove:

Although berry picking sounds safe enough, it does have its hazards. There were cliffs, foxholes, upturned roots, but by far the most dangerous were the "fairies." . . . Once they had you in their powers they could keep you in a trance for days. Sometimes you would wander around aimlessly or sit on a rock by the stream. . . . Even though no one can remember "being in the fairies," many can remember being one place one minute then someplace else the next and never being the wiser of how they got there. There were many instances of "fairy-taking" in my town and when

I was a youngster my parents were always worried this could happen to me.[53]

Once "in the fairies," the victim might sometimes successfully take protective measures during the ordeal, as previously cited in Abbot's account, but on other occasions mortals might be captured, experience fairy scenes, suffer mental and physical injury ("fairy-struck"[54]), or obtain artistic gifts. For any of these states time was a variable and often imperceptible dimension.

Legends and Personal Experience Narratives

The following legends and personal experience narratives are broadly arranged in terms of the nature of the encounters.[55] The majority have been reported from notes and tape recordings by student interviewers, seventeen to twenty-two years of age, as collected from elderly family members and friends of Roman Catholic and Protestant faiths.[56] In some cases the interviewers have recalled narratives from their own experiences or collected from younger informants who in turn have recalled them from the performances of family elders. One legend, 20, is presented in five variant forms.

Benign Encounters

Narrative 1

This little story concerns a woman from Carbonear, M who is about sixty-five. M belonged to North River. She and her sister and father would go in the boat to get to the place where they were going to pick berries. The woman heard talking going on behind her. So she said she was picking away at the berries. She said she heard a lot of talking and she thought it was her sister who was talking to her and when she turned around she saw six little people and they all had little dippers, each picking berries. Apparently she got scared and ran away to her father. She said it was really true that she did see them. They say they are called "good people" and that they were fallen angels whom God cast out of heaven and they had to spend a certain amount of time on earth.[57]

Narrative 2

One day me, Charlie [brother], and a few friends were up on the hill picking blueberries . . . when Charlie seen a load of people in the distance and he called me over to see if we could recognize them. We couldn't believe our eyes. There was about ten or so, about four feet tall with no faces. We all tried to catch them but we couldn't get any closer to them. Every time we moved, they moved.[58]

Lost Mortal Sustained by Fairies

Narrative 3

This is a story which was told to me by my mother many a year ago [forty-five years]. It's about a little girl that was lost in the woods in the middle of the winter. She wandered off and she was gone for many a day and her parents and her friends they sent out a search party to search for her. She was gone around two weeks. When they finally found her they found her up in a tree and she was partly frostbitten. Well, they took her to hospital and a couple of days after she had both of her legs removed. And a couple of days after she told a story about the fairies how they saved her and they fed her berries and many a piece of food that they could get their hands on and that's what kept the little girl alive.[59]

Mortal Temporarily Lost by Being Psychically Led Astray

Narrative 4

There was a woman from Carbonear who went up over the hills by the Battery Rock to look for her cow. The hills were on the north side of Carbonear. She was taken astray and was gone fourteen days and fourteen nights and your great-grandmother dreamt where the woman was. Meanwhile the priests and the townspeople were having masses said in hopes of her safe return. So they went down and got Patty Hogan who went in with the horse and carriage and he took another woman with him and he told her to take extra clothing in case they found her and her clothes were torn. They went to the spot great-grandmother had dreamt of and the woman was there. They found her and threw clothes to the woman. They asked her how she survived and she told them she had a small piece of bread with her and she would have a small crumb of it everyday and pick berries. She said she was taken astray by the fairies. She was surrounded by the forest and couldn't find her way out. She was alright when she came out. She went to Boston after that and lived to be about eighty-five.[60]

Narrative 5

In 1940 at Cupids, ___, who was deaf and mute all his life went blueberry picking with his family. During this time, ___ got lost from the rest of the family. Suddenly my uncle heard throaty squawks and he went to find ___. When he got to him he was out of his mind and very distraught. When they got him home and had calmed him down they gave him a paper and pen to draw what had happened. On the paper the boy drew a picture of a very short man with a red pointed hat and a long beard. He resembled a dwarf.[61]

Narrative 6

About fifty years ago in Clarke's Beach Mrs. Mildred Parsons' mother went berry picking (bakeapples) in the marsh in Clarke's Beach along with her friends. When it was time to come home her two friends were leading the way and Mrs. Parsons' mother said that they were going the wrong way. She looked down to the end of the marsh and saw a herd of red horses. Her friends knew then that the fairies were leading her so they took her home. It wasn't until they got out over the hill that she knew where she was because the fairies chased her all the way out. If her two friends weren't there she would have gone in the woods.[62]

Narrative 7

A common belief of older members of Fox Harbour is the belief in small "shrunk" people no more than two feet high in stature called fairies. They are denoted by their frequent repetitive laughter and their ability to "take you away." No one seemed more obsessed with this concept than Mary King, commonly called "Mary Charlie" (Charlie is her husband's name given to her to distinguish her from the ten other Mary Kings in Harbour). One year in August when the bakeapples were ripe, she set out to go berry picking alone. When she failed to show up that evening they became worried and by nightfall a full search was carried out in the worst weather. It was raining torrents and the thunder and lightning persisted throughout the night. She was found in the morning in an area called the "Sound" in a condition, as Jim Spurvey describes as "only in her bloomers." Her clothes were nowhere in sight. She was obviously in a frightened state and ran from the ones that found her. They gave her a sweater and a pair of pants. After being taken home and treated for broken ribs, she claimed the fairies had beckoned to her, "Come here! come here!" She remained in bed for months and wouldn't dare move outside the confines of her home.[63]

Narrative 8

One day Nan was berry picking by herself far up in the woods. She started to go astray. Nan knew she was going astray but couldn't turn around. "The fairies had me my dear," she said. Nan noticed it was getting duckish [twilight] and she was getting scared and began to cry. Then she remembered something told to her by her grandfather. He told her to take off her coat and turn it inside out if anything like this ever happened. When she did, the next thing she knew she saw her house. "I had no blueberries," Nan said, "but at least I was home!"[64]

Narrative 9

A woman was once taken by the fairies and when they found her a week later, she was badly bruised but still alive. They saw that the fairies had taken her into the woods and kept her alive on berries. She couldn't remember anything that had happened to her.[65]

Narrative 10

When I was just five or six years old, I was allowed to go berry picking with the family. This was a necessity for our family. It meant money for school supplies, shoes, church dues, hospital fees and other necessities. I wasn't expected to pick many berries, just to help everyone. Come "boil up" time, Pop gave me the kettle to fetch a kettle of water at the pond, which was only a stone's throw away, while he lit the fire to prepare the tea for lunch. This should have taken me about three or four minutes. When I did not return after ten or fifteen minutes, he shouted out to me— no answer. He then went looking and couldn't find me. Soon, all the other members of the family were looking for me. They knew I couldn't have drowned because I had gone to the brook down from the pond. Lunch forgotten, they left berries and buckets and went looking for me. Soon, other pickers had joined the search. They looked, shouted, followed tracks and finally, late in the evening, I was found with the kettle, my cap and apron full of berries, just sitting down about seven or eight miles from where I had left, over bogs, ponds and rivers. I was none the worse for my trek—not tired but I did not know how I had gotten where I was. My parents thought that the good fairies had taken me. No harm was done. All I could remember was getting water and seeing my reflection in the water and then someone calling my name. It was like a dream. This story has been told to me quite often by my family.[66]

Narrative 11

Aunt Gracie Puddester, as she was fondly known, went across the brook to pick a dipper of berries to make a pudding for supper. This was around two p.m. When her husband and two sons came in from fishing, the pot was on the stove cooking for supper but no sign of "Mother." They asked neighbors and someone had seen her going with her dipper. By dark, when she hadn't returned, a search party of neighbors went looking for her. They found her about two o'clock in the morning on a big rock, five miles away, singing "Jackie Walsh's songs."[67] She had never sang in her life and she couldn't remember anything after she crossed the brook, although her dipper was full of berries. It's claimed that the fairies took her. She was none the worse for her ordeal.[68]

Narrative 12

That's around thirty-five [1935] . . . and he went in picking raspberries and didn't come home. So, all hands went looking for him that night yelling out in the woods, so on and so forth—no sign of him. So that created quite a stir the next day. It was quite a crowd the next day. I'll never forget it because when I was leaving to go me father said, "Pat, down in the cupboard now there's a drop of rum; take it because you might come across him you know in the woods and you know you'll have something to give him." So I got with a bunch from this part of the cove and went in over the hills here in this direction. . . . There was people going in from all directions. People gone in very very early that morning. . . . It was coming around half past nine or ten o'clock when we saw the old gentleman walking in . . . up through the country, a little bit past where he should be picking berries because he was out of the berry picking area. Now 'twas no trouble to know this man. He was a noticeable man anyhow—his stature. . . . Now this is very hilly country sometimes he'd be in view sometimes he wouldn't be in view. When we'd be in a hollow, he'd be on a hill. And we started singing out "Skipper! . . . hey! hey! hey!" like you would. But he kept dodging on, dodging on. Now it wasn't till about probably twenty minutes before we found out that we should be catching up on him. . . . But we weren't catching up on him! . . . We suddenly realized that there was something astray there. Every time that he'd come in view he'd be just dodging slowly with this tub in his hand and we're running like blazes! 'Twas nine or ten of us. We're all around yet. . . . By and by two or three men who had gone in earlier coming out. . . . We slowed up then because . . . he was going to be met by those characters coming out. Now here's where it gets tricky. . . . They passed each other. The boys coming out . . . didn't see him! . . . "Didn't you see [him]?!" "What in the name are you talkin' about?" . . . Well there it was. . . . Petten's Pond, now that's where they found the skipper at the foot of Petten's Pond. . . . So here he was with a full tub of berries. . . . This old gentleman did experience, he experienced music he said . . . and the music used to entice him this way and that way and the other but that's all he could explain. . . . He wasn't conscious of any time.[69]

Narrative 13

Years ago when Mom N was young, her mother [W] and G went in over the hill berry picking. Her mother got separated from G and did not know what was happening when she woke up by the side of a stream. She was really tired, her clothes were torn, and her shoes were missing. Her mother had no idea where she was and could only assume that the fairies had carried her away. After all, she was by a brook and it was said that fairies would bring you no further when they came to a brook. G, after an unsuccessful search for W, gave up and began her journey home. When G arrived and told them what had happened Mom N's father and some other men went to look for W. However, they were also unsuccessful. Meanwhile after W had awakened she started walking to try and find home. She came upon some children on a beach and with their assistance realized she was in Bison Cove, a part of Old Perlican. When she first approached these children, they were afraid of her because her features had changed so much. She looked really old and tired. The children shared some food with her and then she left for home. On her way home W saw Captain P coming along in his car. Captain P was a merchant who often visited Bay de Verde. He knew Mom N's parents really well and visited their home regularly. He stopped but would not pick W up because he did not recognize her. Mom N stated that when her mother got home that night, "I could not believe my eyes. She looked like a different person." This event had great impact on Mom N. She was frightened the night her mother walked in the door. It stands out in Mom N's mind because her mother changed so much physically as a result of this ordeal.[70]

Narrative 14

One day D, who was about ten at the time, went berry picking with some family members and all of a sudden she found herself in the deep woods. . . . She claimed she didn't have any knowledge of how she got there and she assumed that the fairies took her there and she felt the presence of the fairies. She heard them talk with her and calling her in low voices and luring her into the woods. And so she was so scared all she could think about was her mother . . . who happened to be dead at the time. So she claims that all of a sudden, her mother held her hand, not as a physical being but as a spiritual being, . . . [and] led her to the rest of her family. But before her mother came to her rescue, whenever she would try to leave . . . the path would close in. And she knew that she would never get out of there because the fairies had her trapped, but . . . she believed her mother . . . got her back to her family.[71]

Mortal Led Astray, Returns and Transforms into Fairy

Narrative 15

K . . . she used to go berry picking often. She was only a young girl. . . . About eighteen, nineteen. Well, she could have been older than that. I don't know. She wasn't married, and her parents used to always try to . . . keep her from like going out around anywhere. They let her go berry picking because a gallon of berries then was five cents, so that's all she was allowed to do. And she went berry picking one time. . . . They were picking blueberries, and there was a lot of blueberries and K was the kind of person, she'd roam off by herself. . . . She used to go—there was a place we used to call "Gallus Wood Ridge" and not too many people would go there alone. . . . There was a lot of stories told about ghosts. There was people, they walked on Gallus Wood Ridge in the fog. They would never return. . . . And K, well you know, "I gotta go try it," right? She did. . . . She left on a Monday . . . morning. She went berry picking because they used to pick berries down there for the minister. . . . The minister used to let them take a day off to go berry picking and whatever money you got when you sold your berries you come back and give it to the church. . . . So K did that and she went in and she was berry picking for at least . . . an hour and a half and nobody could find her. They said, "K's gone again. She's gone off by herself." . . . She was missing for about two days. . . . And they said, "Well Jesus," you know, "where's she gone?" So they called in the RCMP from Harbour Grace and they had dogs out from St. John's and everything like that and "God! Where's K gone?" Well . . . K was a pretty little girl, really pretty and she was about nineteen, twenty years old. . . . You may not believe this but if you ever go to Burnt Point . . . look at her picture. . . . You'll see that . . . within four days after they found her, she turned into a fairy . . . really a fairy too because her face and everything where she was lost . . . she looked like she was about eighty years old. . . . She was found in . . . Little Gull Pond down behind Gull Island . . . laid down . . . in the grass under a spruce tree. . . . It was about . . . four miles from where she was berry picking to. And she had a little bucket of blueberries and she had . . . a small bucket of partridge berries. . . . She told everybody . . . she was walking along and . . . like she fell asleep. She said that the only thing that she remembers . . . was when someone woke her up when they found her under the tree. . . . And the little girl had to go for fifty years, live like an eighty year old woman.[72]

Attempted Abduction of Mortal by Fairy

Narrative 16

[Mrs. Spurrell] said that even though a lot of people didn't believe in fairies, they were real. "They are fallen angels and live underground and are called 'good people.'" She told me this story about a group of people who had seen a fairy. She said they were going berry picking. There were two groups. She was in the last group to leave. The first group were far ahead so she yelled for them to stop. The group had already stopped by a little pond. [She said,] "when they heard us yelling to them, they turned around." When she caught up to them they told her what they saw. They said they had seen a fairy. They said it was a little boy without hair. He had been standing there by the edge of the pond. They said they had never seen him before. He had offered them a mug but no one would take it. If they had taken the mug, the fairy would have taken them away. If he didn't take them away there would be something wrong with them for the rest of their lives.[73]

Abduction, Captivity, and Release/Escape of Mortal

Narrative 17

About twenty-five years ago a woman from Clarke's Beach went in over the "Earth Hill" as it was called to pick blueberries and when six o'clock came she wasn't home. It was dark by this time so a group of men went to look for her. It rained in torrents that night so the men returned without the missing woman. In the morning the search continued and this time they were successful in finding her. She was across a big river which would have to be crossed by a boat and there was no boat in sight. They found her between two rocks. She was not wet and she said she was in a beautiful house all night with lots of food and lots of company. She said she was in a beautiful house all night with the fairies in the heart of the woods and had no explanation of how she got across the river.[74]

Narrative 18

When Mrs. Kennedy was still only a child, there was a young boy in Trepassey by the name of Tommy. When Tommy was still a baby, his parents took him out to the marsh while they went to pick bakeapples. They left the child alone on the marsh. When the child grew up he never developed. He lived until he was ten. It was said that the child never grew because when he was left on the marsh the fairies got him.[75]

Narrative 19

One little boy was picking berries down to the marsh and he was gone an awful long time. They looked for him but couldn't find him. He was discovered hours later in the same place they had searched before. He couldn't remember anything and his berries . . . were all gone. They believe that the fairies had taken him.[76]

Narrative 20a

About forty years ago D . . . went into the woods on Middleton Avenue, Bell Island, to go berry picking. At this time the people believed that if you went into the woods you had to bring some bread with you to feed the fairies so they wouldn't bother you. Well, D forgot the bread. One night some time later some friends of his asked him where he was going and he told them about the time he went into the woods without the bread and the fairies took him. He told them the fairies said he had to come back in the woods every night at twelve o'clock. Well this night his friends held him and wouldn't let him go. The next night he went and never came back for three days and three nights. After he returned he could only say a few words and appeared to have gone "silly." People then believed that the fairies had really taken him and up to the time he died a few years back they always said that this was the reason for his changed appearance after he came out of the woods.[77]

Narrative 20b

The fairies took [D] and kept him for a couple of days. After he got back home they took ribbons of green grass out of his leg.[78]

Narrative 20c

D from Bell Island as a young man got lost in the woods. When he was found he was all disfigured and scarred and simple-minded. While he was with the fairies he learned how to carve figures from wood. That's what he began to do for a living afterwards until he died a few years ago. He carved a church about two feet high which stands in his garden and can be seen today.[79]

Narrative 20d

D was supposed to have been captured by the fairies while walking in the woods one day. He was mentally a normal person. He sold portraits for some company and took pictures as well. His physical characteristics were changed remarkably. One leg had a malformity; his face was acned and he had a strange "fairy-like" voice. He could carry on a fairly good conversation but the cause of his changes are not really known. He was apparently born normal.[80]

Narrative 20e

When going in the woods berry picking you should turn some article of your clothes inside out or else the fairies will take you away. A young boy [D] was taken by the fairies and when he came back he had a limp and his face was pulled to one side. He is now a grown man and he still has the limp, the disfigured face and his speech is queer.[81]

Permanent Captivity of Mortal

Narrative 21

When I was growing up in Seldom, I was really scared of the fairies. My grandmother always told me that if I wasn't careful, the fairies would take me away. The only way to keep me from being led away was to turn my coat or sweater inside out. I believed that the fairies could take me away because Grandmother said that one of her sisters was taken away by fairies. Her sister went berry picking and was never found. When she was gone for a while, some people went to look for her. All they could find was one of her red socks up in a tree and a dipper of blueberries on the ground. Sometimes when Grandmother told the story she said that it was a sweater that was found. When asked how she knew that her sister was led away by the fairies she would say, "Fairies always put a piece of clothing up in a tree to let people know that they had taken the child who was lost."[82]

Narrative 22

This was back in the 1930s. It seemed like fairies were kind of a common thing around our community. And we used to be always told that there were such things as fairies and if children went on the barrens or anywhere alone they should always carry breadcrumbs in their pockets or something to protect them from the fairies. This little boy was seven years old and he went up picking berries one day in the summertime, about early July, bakeapple time I think, and anyway, he didn't have any breadcrumbs. And he didn't return home at night when he was supposed to. People went looking for him the next day and no sign of him anywhere. So they just figured that he was lost. He fell over a cliff or something. Anyway about a month and a half later, sometime in August, some people went up near the graveyard one night. . . . And they saw a little boy about seven years of age and it was like he was really enjoying himself. It was like he was out in the middle of a group of people and they could hear singing and dancing and accordion playing and everything. And he was out there like he was holding hands with all these people. And a couple of the people said that it was the same little boy that got lost. So anyway, everybody in the community then believed that he was captured by the fairies because they never did find any body or anything. They had police looking for him. He just disappeared. . . . There were lots of cases like that. He wasn't the only one people thought was captured by the fairies. . . . It [this incident] taught me not to go around without breadcrumbs. I used to have to go looking for the cows in the evening about three or four o'clock and I always made sure that my pockets were loaded with bread or breadcrumbs so that if anything happened that I was always protected.... I really did believe ... I always believed in that I suppose until I was about sixteen or seventeen. There were lots of fairies where I lived.[83]

Mistaken Captivity

Narrative 23

Back about eighty years ago my grandmother and two of her best friends, Mary and Jean, had planned to go berry picking. It was a beautiful sunny day and they had prepared a picnic lunch. The three of them headed in over the marsh and were talking, laughing, and enjoying the warmth of the sun. They stopped talking when they came across a blueberry patch about two miles from the road. Here they began picking and soon filled up their buckets. My grandmother said to me, "Berries were plentiful back then and now you can't get ne'er one to sell." They sat down and began eating their lunch. It was so hot that Mary took off her new hat. After they had finished eating, the fog ... had crept in over the marsh. The girls felt the fog's cold chill and all agreed to head home. Just as they walked about a half mile Mary remembered that she had taken her hat off. Granny and Jean refused to go back to get the hat so Mary went back herself. The girls waited while Mary ran back to get her hat. An hour passed before Jean and my grandmother decided to go back to the community and get some help, as the fog had become very thick. Granny and Jean were almost in tears and were afraid to go into the house. When they went into the house Mary's mother was standing in the hallway. My grandmother and Jean were crying by now and all they were saying is that the fairies had taken Mary and they wouldn't see her anymore. Suddenly, Mary walked out of a room and started laughing. My grandmother said, "I was so embarrassed, I went home and never left the house for a full week." [84]

Narrative 24

It was a real foggy day and I was about eight or nine years old and I used to have me brother in the woods when we caught so many rabbits and I would bring them home. One day I took the wrong path and ended up getting lost. I was gone for a few hours and the only company I had was me dog Tip. I was sitting down eating a few blueberries when I thought I heard me brother Dave calling out to me. At first I thought it was the fairies trying to get me but when I looked up who should be walking up the path but Dave! [laughter] ... Anyway, we both got a good laugh out of it and went home with our rabbits.[85]

Continuous Time and Absolute Morality

As the foregoing narratives reveal, berry grounds as liminal zones have presented the ever-present possibility of magico-religious danger and tragedy. These orally circulated stories undoubtedly have served as geographical markers on the cognitive maps of community residents and therefore demonstrated segmented, discontinuous space. But such narratives also left moral imprints as cautionary tales and agents of social control. As such, these tales reflect a sense of continuous time through the maintenance of tried and true traditional values which stress the importance of subordinating individual achievement to collective needs (obedience), and the necessity of yielding to the wisdom of generational pressures (the guidance of one's elders). Since temporal continuity and a sense of absolute morality are one and the same, threats to the moral order were ruptures in time, and this danger was an essential element in the "threatening figure" role of fairies in the berry grounds. In addition, however, it is important to consider that these stories may also have expressed youthful anxieties regarding courtship and illicit sexual relations. Lastly, they may have provided culturally acceptable justifications for deviance, thereby extricating participants from embarrassing situations and potential shame.

The Danger of Not Subordinating Individual Effort to Collective Good

The longer the season is, and the more domestic and economic pressures there are to acquire berries, the farther from the community the pickers move, and the greater the likelihood of encountering fairies. The expansionary tendencies of this effort are at odds with the cultural imperatives of contractile space. But more than this, there is the danger of excessive individualism. Pickers go to the berry grounds together but once they get there they scatter. The berry grounds become arenas for the demonstration of individual competence in manual skills and competitive pressures tempt good pickers to roam from liminality into dangerous zones. The more successful picker fills her containers and then further demonstrates her skills and sensitivity to collective obligation by assisting others to fill their containers. A sense of limited good is apparent, however, for if a good picker does *too well* she risks all. If led astray by the fairies she, at worst, may be permanently lost to them, and at least, she may suffer the sanction of community scrutiny. Hence, one of the morals of these stories is that one must subordinate individual initiative to community good, for an individual who becomes excessively involved in advancing her personal prestige may overachieve, get carried away and come to ruin.

The Dangers of Solitude, Men, and Illicit Sex

In keeping with the traditional gender alignment of berry pickers, over two-thirds of the protagonists in these stories are women and only four of the narrators are men. When age is mentioned or alluded to, it is clear that most of these women are young and subject to parental authority and community norms regarding sexual morality. Thus, there are interdictions about the dangers of going out alone without taking the proper precautionary measures (7, 10, 15, 21).[86] But temptations to deviate from these norms are strong and sometimes take the form of seductive voices (14 "calling her in low voices . . . luring her into the woods") calling the woman's name (10) or imploring "come here!" (7). Admonitions not heeded, the temptations of solitude prove irresistible and the interdiction is violated (8 "Nan knew she was going astray but couldn't turn around. 'The fairies had me my dear'"). Without the assistance of women friends (6) the young woman is led "astray," a term which commonly signifies either wandering off or committing moral error. Guilt may be experienced through the image of a parent (14 "she was so scared all she could think about was her mother"). The psychic terror of engulfment in evil is personified by the figure of the "fairy," usually a male and often remarkably phallic (7 "shrunk," 16 "little boy without hair," 2 "no face," 5 "red pointed hat and long beard"). The initial results of this encounter fulfill the worst nightmares of illicit sexual experience—physical punishments and humiliations to be suffered at the hands of a seductive male (4, 13 "her clothes were torn," 7 "only in her bloomers," "broken ribs," 9 "badly bruised"). But perhaps even more devastating are the possibilities of permanent stigmas, marks of spoiled identity (16 "there would be something wrong with them for the rest of their lives") which might take the form of physical or mental impairment (20), or perhaps more appropriately for young women, aging prematurely (13, 15). Obeying parental advice before tragedy strikes, of course, is offered as the best solution (8). In this regard, it is interesting that in one narrative a *deceased* parent saves a victim by leading her to safety (14), the implication being that this intercession is necessary because of the victim's apparent lack of parental guidance in ordinary life.

Fairies as Agents of Embarrassment and Threatening Disrupters of Continuous Time

As is clearly evident from the foregoing narratives, the advent of an individual being fairy-led is a serious temporal disruption to the routine of community affairs and the berry picking effort itself. While the search and subsequent finding of the lost picker may be viewed as a solidarity ritual in which community residents unify in face of crisis, from the lost person's point of view, terror transforms into the ecstasy of relief but then into embarrassment and the need to exculpate oneself from possible censure and permanent stigma (15 "she was the type of person, she'd roam off by herself"). These narratives, therefore, appear to represent the possibility of entering into a coalition with fairies in order to avoid embarrassment and shame. The nature of this traditional mode of personal accountability might be better understood through the following citation of a recent news item.

Woman fined on charge of mischief[87]

Sudbury, Ont. (CP)—A woman who admitted concocting a story about being kidnapped to avoid the embarrassment of getting lost and driving hundreds of kilometers in the wrong direction has been fined $1,500 for public mischief.

Elsa Boecker, 45, of Toronto pleaded guilty Tuesday after telling police she had been abducted in Detroit at a gas station by a man who forced her to drive him to Sault Ste. Marie, Ont., on July 14.

Boecker was heading back to Toronto after visiting her daughter in Detroit when she missed her exit on a U.S. freeway.

In the contemporary spatially continuous world, spatial incompetence of the above variety is especially culpable. The self-conscious distress of embarrassment, an individual emotional reaction to critical group scrutiny, can be escaped by: (1) trivializing the matter and dismissing its significance, often through laughter; (2) transforming the group's perceptions of one's incompetence into an understanding that one's actions have been meaningful after all; (3) achieving cognitive assonance by introducing the idea that accidental incompetence has resulted in serendipitous good fortune; (4) evading one's personal responsibility for the occasion by revealing that one was victimized and could not exert any free will in the matter. Ergo, Ms. Boecker could have: (1) truthfully explained her mistake in a hilarious fashion and belittled it as "no big deal"; (2) indicated that in fact she had planned the extended excursion all along; (3) revealed that the sidetrip was an error, but because of it she discovered a lovely area which she plans to revisit. The excuse which the unfortunate Ms. Boecker opted for, however, was that she was victimized, an idea which took the form, in this age of terrorism, of armed abduction by unscrupulous kidnappers. She formed a "coalition with kidnappers."

Likewise, and as aforementioned, the protagonists of these narratives of berry pickers and fairies might have chosen to coalesce with the psychic powers of fairies so that it might be understood that lost community time was the result of concomitant lost protagonist time as well (9 "she couldn't remember anything that had happened to her"; 10 "I did not know how I had gotten where I was," "it was like a dream"; 13 "[she] did not know what was happening"; 14 "she didn't have any knowledge of how she got there"; 15 "she was walking along and ... like she fell asleep"). Clearly, such a dramaturgic perspective of actors *making choices* is only one interpretive possibility, but the full implications of that possibility should be understood—fairy explanations could be used by participants to mask actual deviant behaviors such as extreme tardiness, premarital sexual relations, infidelity, incest, child molestation, wife battering, and sexual assault. The possibility of concealing scandal through fairy alibis must be considered when approaching enigmatic narratives such as the following:

> I have been told, when I was a little child, [that my aunt was] taken by the fairies. The story that my father told me was that she was sliding one day—well, actually my father was with her, as well, and my uncle, who was older than my aunt. And my uncle returned, but my aunt didn't, and my uncle said, "She won't come down off the hill. She's calling out that she's taken by the fairies." My father ran to the hill, found her. The snow was coming down on her face and she was rolling around in a bit of a trance and kept repeating, "No, let me stay, I don't want to go." And he had to carry her body and bones down off the hill. When they got her home, she was still in a trance and would not come out of it, would not eat, and they put her to bed and ... they had to go for the doctor in a neighboring community. When the doctor examined her, he said that she was pregnant. My aunt didn't have a child. As a teenager she certainly didn't. My father just said, "I knew that was not the case when I came downstairs and he [the doctor] said she's pregnant." He [my father] said, "No she isn't. She was taken by the fairies."[88]

On the other hand, undoubtedly it has been normative in the not-so-distant past for narrators, protagonists, and community residents to *totally believe* that fairies were directly responsible for the common occurrence of people getting lost in unknown space. In such instances fairies did not provide an alibi so much as a reasonable, comprehensible cause. Given either possibility, fairies have furnished one of the few *culturally sanctioned explanations* available for temporal disjuncture and embarrassment, an acceptable rationale everyone has been familiar with.

It is important to stress that although berry grounds have largely been the domain of women, men have also coalesced with fairies in accounting for temporal disruptions that they have experienced in other liminal spatial domains, particularly the woods. The following striking narrative, from the fairy-ridden iron mining area of Bell Island, similarly accounts for discontinuous time by citing travel to fairyland.[89]

> Myself and me buddy were working on the buckets one day, you know. We had to wait for the ore to come up and dump it. It's getting on in the morning and he says to me at about eleven o'clock, "Tom, will you cover

for me for ten minutes. I gotta go down in the woods for a while." I said, "Okay, Jim." So he goes on down in the woods. Time goes by. Half an hour, hour. Still no Jim. I says to meself, "That son-of-a-bitch is down there sleeping." So I rounded up a couple of me buddies and we went down for him, but we couldn't find him. So we came back and told the foreman on the job and he goes and tells the big boss. I can't remember his name now. Anyway, this is something big now, you know, cause Jim was never one to run away from work. The boss comes and forms a search party of about fifty men and we still couldn't find him. Then he sent someone to get the police. It wasn't the RCMP then. It was the local fellows. My son, we searched high and low. Had people come from town and everything but, you know, we couldn't find Jim. This kept up for two or three days. Then one day when I was back to work, up walked Jim out of the woods, a-beaming like an electric bulb. I says, "Where have you been?" He says, "Where have I been? I been down in the woods. That's where I been. Sorry to be so long, but Jesus, no need to be mad. I was only gone an hour. I just met the nicest little people. You go on to lunch now and I'll take over." "Take over," says I. "You son-of-a, where have you been this past three days? We was all worried to death over you." "What are you talking about?" says Jim. "'Tis only twelve o'clock. Listen. There goes the whistle." And so it was twelve o'clock but three days later. Jim was telling me later that he met a whole pile of little people and they had food and beer, and danced and played the accordion. Real friendly, he said. Well, it was some going on when everyone found out he was back 'cause we all thought he was dead, you see. After falling off the back of the Island or something. Yes sir, he was the only one that was ever treated that good by the fairies. But people always thought him a little queer after that. And you know, he swore that was the truth right up until he died. And you know something else, I believe him.[90]

New Media and the Domestication of Liminal Space

Unlike the traditional narrative forms just considered, cultural conceptions of continuous space are often apparent in contemporary Newfoundland narratives. Some comments regarding a joke of recent vintage in Newfoundland, will serve to illustrate this final point. The recurring motifs of several versions which I have heard, and simply jotted down without recording in detail, are incorporated in the following reconstruction which reflects the gist of these variants:

These three fellas were sitting in science class in university. There was a German, an American, and a Newfoundlander. The professor asked them, "What's mankind's greatest achievement?" The German said it was flying—to make man able to cross huge distances in just a matter of hours. That just had to be the greatest achievement ever. The professor mulled that over a bit and said, "Yes, I suppose that is an important achievement." Next he turned to the American, "What do you think was mankind's greatest achievement?" "Space flight. Imagine, being able to send men into space, and then bring them back to earth; that's the greatest achievement ever." And the professor said, "Yes, that was pretty important, too." Then he asked the Newfoundlander, "What do *you* think was mankind's greatest achievement?" And the Newfoundlander said, without batting an eye, "The t'ermos." The professor said, "What?! The thermos?" "Yep." "Why do you think the thermos is mankind's greatest achievement?" "Well in the summertime if you're out in the woods cuttin' a few sticks and it's really hot, you opens 'er up and the freshie[91] is in there just as cold as when you put it in." And the professor said, "Yes?!" "And if you goes ice fishin' in the winter, freezing your arse off, you opens 'er up and the tea in there is still steamin'!" And the professor said, "Yes. But why is the thermos mankind's greatest achievement." And the Newfoundlander says, "Well, *how do it know?!!!*"[92]

While the potential esoteric-exoteric social meanings of this narrative in varying performance contexts are complex, the humor overtly pivots on a popular contemporary theme in Canadian folklore: the depiction of the Newfoundlander as a foolish, old-fashioned, rural bumpkin in competition with the sophisticated, modern mainlander, most often a Torontonian urbanite.[93] The language (usage, grammar, pronunciation), described activities (cutting sticks, ice fishing), and iconic preference ("t'ermos") of the Newfoundlander all assist in achieving this impression. In addition, however, differing spatial attitudes collide. The sophistication of the German and the American who assert the importance of media which provide spatial continuity (flying, space travel) is pitted against the seemingly backward, contractionist worldview of the Newfoundlander who lauds a humble medium which simply provides gustatory comfort while cutting sticks in the woods and fishing on a pond. From a structural point of view, laughter is prompted in the punchline through the cognitive dissonance achieved in the surprise reference to the thermos as a thoughtful entity. It should be noted, however, that within an all-Newfoundland performance context this "bisociation" of two self-consistent but incompatible cognitive frames, inanimate technological (vacuum flask) and animate intellectual (thinking vacuum flask), is propelled by a sense of *truth*.[94] In a laboring environment without kitchen facilities on the geographic periphery of one's experienced world, the vacuum flask not only symbolizes but tangibly transfers the niceties of known domestic space. To an individual well used to a reality of harsh outdoor working conditions the thermos *is* of greater significance than flight or space travel. A final paradox which makes the joke humorous to most contemporary audiences is that the Newfoundlander uses the vacuum flask to domesticate his relatively small spatial reality in the same manner that the German and the American use air- and space-craft: faithful of technological function in extending our sense of space but ignorant of technological workings. The final, ingenuous, awesome question of the Newfoundlander is one which so perplexes the members of an advanced technological society that it is generally avoided as a matter of course.

The matter-of-fact acceptance and faith in the mechanisms which shape our sense of space and time has been of concern in the preceding discussion of how fairies in the berry grounds of Newfoundland have played a spatial and temporal role in the remembered past. The greatest threat posed by fairies to the folk cultures of Newfoundland was that in a cultural world of contractile space where the absolute morality of continuous time was revered, the appearance of a fairy might rupture and invalidate it. As boundary marker and bogey, therefore, the fairy played positive roles in spatially and morally integrating a society against pernicious external forces. While such popular beliefs of past generations may appear preposterous or "quaint" today, it is well to remember that our attitude toward the technological media which foster our sense of space and time continues to be one of faithful acceptance. Indeed, if any group dares to question an accepted "fact," such as man's landing on the moon, they are quickly relegated to the "lunatic fringe."[95] As a popular song lyric summarizes our contemporary posture, "I know it's true . . . 'cause I saw it on TV."[96] Until relatively recently, fairies in Newfoundland have been realities because news of them circulated in a vigorous oral tradition and firsthand evidence of their activities was readily available. Now that we have domesticated space and dismissed fairies from our view we are left alone to ponder our own technological devices. Truly, it is a time to ask, "How do it know?"

Notes

Reprinted by permission from *Lore and Language* 6.1 (1987): 15–49, with revisions. The original title was "Newfoundland Berry Pickers 'In the Fairies': The Maintenance of Spatial and Temporal Boundaries through Legendry."

1. Portions of this article were first presented as a paper at the Popular Culture Association, Seventeenth Annual Meeting, March 24, 1987, "Studies in Folklore Panel," Montreal, Canada.
2. The most thorough semantic inquiry of "fairy" is Noel Williams, "The Semantics of the Word 'Fairy' in English between 1320 and 1829," PhD diss., Sheffield U, 1983; also see his essay "The Semantics of the Word 'Fairy': Making Meaning Out of Thin Air," in this volume. Williams believes that "fairy" meaning male homosexual may have been a usage as early as the sixteenth century (Peter Narváez, "The Fairy Faith," *Ideas*, CBC Transcripts No. 11-293 [Montreal: Canadian Broadcasting Corporation, June 29, 1989]) 2; Hugh Rawson, *Wicked Words* (New York: Crown, 1989), cites a publication from 1896 and argues that the homosexual

meaning of the term "seems to be an American contribution to the language" (141). Whatever its origins, the usage is widespread and has even been accepted by some advocates of gay spirituality; see discussion of the "Radical Faeries," Margot Adler, *Drawing Down the Moon*, rev. ed. (Boston: Beacon P, 1986) 341–8.

3. Although the fairy legends for this paper derive from communities on the island portion of the province of Newfoundland and Labrador, i.e., Newfoundland, it is clear from the observation of Sir Wilfred Grenfell that there has been "a great belief in fairies" on the Labrador coast. See his *A Labrador Doctor: The Autobiography of Wilfred Thomason Grenfell* (Boston: Houghton Mifflin, 1919) 143.

4. I would like to acknowledge the interest of colleagues, students, and friends who have provided me with data and suggestions for this paper. These helpful people include: Bruce Bourque, David Buchan, Roberta Buchanan, Anne Budgell, George Budgell, Ann Hart (Centre for Newfoundland Studies), Philip Hiscock (Memorial U of Newfoundland Folklore and Language Archive), Bryan Hennessey, David Kennedy, W.K. Kirwin, Janet McNaughton, Beni Malone, John Mannion, Elizabeth Russell Miller, Michael O'Dea, Barbara Rieti, Neil Rosenberg, Larry Small, Gail Weir, Marion White, J.D.A. Widdowson, Bob Woolridge. Special thanks go to the student collectors and informants who are cited throughout.

5. This skeptical, though nostalgic attitude is echoed by young Newfoundland author Robert Burt, in his recent children's book about fairies, *Notsomuch a Rainbow* (St. John's: Creative Publishers, 1989), a narrative which he characterizes as "a tale of celebration and of loss." At one point one of his fairy characters, Tir, laments that fifty years ago were "the good old days when fairy raids were carried out on unsuspecting berry pickers" (6).

6. Peter Narváez, "The Folklore of 'Old Foolishness': Newfoundland Media Legends," *Canadian Literature* 108 (1986): 125–43.

7. Harold Adams Innis, *Empire and Communications* (1950; rpt. Toronto: U of Toronto P, 1973) and *The Bias of Communication* (1951; rpt. Toronto: U of Toronto P, 1973). For a stimulating update on the spatial implications of modern electronic media see Joshua Meyrowitz, *No Sense of Place: The Impact of Electronic Media on Social Behavior* (New York: Oxford UP, 1985).

8. For a contrasting portrayal of the weakness of local folk forms in highly literate colonial New England see Richard L. Bushman, "American High-Style and Vernacular Cultures," *Colonial British America*, ed. Jack P. Greene and J.R. Pole (Baltimore: John Hopkins UP, 1984) 345–72. On the relation of sensory media to tradition see Paul Smith "Communicating Culture; or, Can We Really Vocalize a Brownie?" in Peter Narváez and Martin Laba eds., *Media Sense: The Folklore—Popular Culture Continuum* (Bowling Green, Ohio: Bowling Green State UP, 1986) 31–46.

9. Innis, *Empire* 7.

10. James G. Calder, "Humour and Misunderstanding in Newfoundland Culture," *Culture and Tradition* 4 (1979): 49–66; Harold Paddock, ed. *Languages in Newfoundland and Labrador: A Preliminary Version* (St. John's: Department of Linguistics, Memorial U of Newfoundland, 1977).

11. On spatial implications of mummering in Newfoundland see essays by Louis J. Chiaramonte and Melvin M. Firestone in Herbert Halpert and G.M. Story, eds. *Christmas Mumming in Newfoundland* (Toronto: U of Toronto P, 1969); many of these entities are discussed in John Widdowson, *If You Don't Be Good: Verbal Social Control in Newfoundland*, Social and Economic Studies No. 21 (St. John's: Institute of Social

and Economic Research, Memorial U of Newfoundland, 1977); the cognitive maps of fishermen are dealt with by Gary R. Butler, "Culture, Cognition, and Communication: Fishermens' Location-Finding in L'Anse-à-Canards, Newfoundland," *Canadian Folklore canadien* 5.1-2 (1983): 7–21; the supernatural import of tragic sea ballads is treated in Kenneth S. Goldstein, "Faith and Fate in Sea Disaster Ballads of Newfoundland Fishermen," in Roger D. Abrahams, Kenneth S. Goldstein, and Wayland Hand, eds. *By Land and By Sea: Studies in the Folklore of Work and Leisure* (Hatboro, Pa.: Legacy Books, 1985) 84–94.

12. Arnold van Gennep, *The Rites of Passage* (Chicago: U of Chicago P, 1960) 1–14.

13. See Mary Douglas, *Purity and Danger: An Analysis of Concepts of Pollution and Taboo* (Harmondsworth: Penguin, 1970).

14. van Gennep 18.

15. Victor Turner, *The Ritual Process: Structure and Anti-Structure* (Ithaca: Cornell UP, 1977) 95. Writing in ca. 1690 Robert Kirk described fairies as being "of a midle nature betwixt man and Angell," *The Secret Common-Wealth and A Short Treatise of Charms and Spels*, Mistletoe Series (1893; Totowa, N.J.: Rowan and Littlefield for the Folklore Society, 1976) 49.

16. James C. Faris, *Cat Harbour: A Newfoundland Fishing Settlement*, Newfoundland Social and Economic Studies No. 3 (St. John's: Institute of Social and Economic Research, Memorial U of Newfoundland, 1972) 32.

17. See MacEdward Leach, "fairy" in Maria Leach, ed. *Standard Dictionary of Folklore, Mythology and Legend* (New York: Funk and Wagnalls, 1972) 363–5. A few "American fairy immigrants" are discussed by Katharine Briggs, *A Dictionary of Fairies* (Harmondsworth: Penguin, 1977) 6–8. For fairies in Nova Scotia, see Elizabeth Beaton-Planetta, "Influence Upon the Fairy Lore of Scottish Descendants in Nova Scotia," Beaton Institute Eachdraidh Archives, U of Cape Breton, Sydney, Nova Scotia, Ms., MG12, 198. An interesting fairy narrative from Prince Edward Island is presented in Sterling Ramsey, *Folklore* (Charlottetown: Square Deal Publications, 1973) 103–5.

18. Richard M. Dorson, *America in Legend: Folklore from the Colonial Period to the Present* (New York: Pantheon, 1973) 14–5.

19. Richard M. Dorson, *American Folklore and the Historian* (Chicago: U of Chicago P, 1971) 36.

20. See Barbara Rieti, "Newfoundland Fairy Traditions: A Study in Narrative and Belief," PhD thesis, Memorial U of Newfoundland, 1990; this thesis will be published in 1991 by the Institute for Social and Economic Research, Memorial University of Newfoundland as *Strange Terrain: The Fairy World in Newfoundland*.

21. Grant Head, *Eighteenth Century Newfoundland: A Geographer's Perspective* (Toronto: McClelland and Stewart, 1976) 3–51; Raymond J. Lahey, "Avalon: Lord Baltimore's Colony in Newfoundland," in G.M. Story, ed., *Early European Settlement and Exploitation in Atlantic Canada* (St. John's: Memorial U of Newfoundland, 1982) 115–37.

22. Story, "Newfoundland: Fishermen, Hunters, Planters, and Merchants," Halpet and Story 7–33; John J. Mannion, "Introduction," *The Peopling of Newfoundland: Essays in Historical Geography*, Social and Economic Papers No. 8, ed. John J. Mannion (St. John's: Institute of Social and Economic Research, Memorial U of Newfoundland, 1977) 1–13.

23. Mannion 10.

24. See Robert Redfield, "The Folk Society," *American Journal of Sociology* 52 (1947): 293–308; John Szwed, *Private Cultures and Public Imagery: Interpersonal Relations in a Newfoundland Peasant Society*, Newfoundland Social and Economic Studies No. 2 (St. John's: Institute of Social and Economic Research, Memorial U of Newfoundland, 1966); Gerald M. Sider, *Culture and Class in Anthropology and History: A Newfoundland Illustration* (New York: Cambridge UP, 1986).

25. Story 12.

26. Walter Yeeling Evans-Wentz, *The Fairy-Faith in Celtic Countries* (1911; Atlantic Highlands, N.Y.: Humanities P, 1977) 3.

27. Evans-Wentz 5; also see 41, 77 for references to fairies living amongst rocks.

28. Máire MacNeill, *The Festival of Lughnasa: A Study of the Survival of the Celtic Festival of the Beginning of Harvest* (London: Oxford UP, 1962) 20, 177–8, 184, 186–7, 210, 216, 222; Sean Ó Súilleabháin, *Irish Folk Custom and Belief* (Dublin: Cultural Relations Committee of Ireland, 1967) 68–9; Thomas Keightley, *The Fairy Mythology* (London: George Bell and Sons, 1889) 371; Wentz 71–3.

29. Vincent Horatio Abbot, "The Berry Picking Tradition in Newman's Cove, Bonavista Bay, Past to Present" (St. John's: Memorial U of Newfoundland Folklore and Language Archive [hereafter MUNFLA], Manuscript, 77–165); Elizabeth Goudie, *Woman of Labrador* (Toronto: Peter Martin Associates, 1973) 61–2; Hilda Chaulk Murray, *More Than Fifty Percent: Women's Life in a Newfoundland Outport 1900—1950* (St. John's: Breakwater Books, 1979) 21–3. Citations of "hurt" and variations are in G.M. Story, W.J. Kirwin and J.D.A. Widdowson, eds., *Dictionary of Newfoundland English* (Toronto: U of Toronto P, 1982) 262, hereafter *DNE*. Several berry grounds and one pond in Newfoundland have placenames that reflect fairy habitation—"Brownies Flat," Newman's Cove (Abbot 9), "Fairys Pond," Holyrood, "Fairy Meadow," St. John's, "Fairy Knap," Flatrock. My colleague John Mannion has learned from Ally O'Brien, St. John's, that "'Fairy Meadow' by O'Leary's Brook, where the Health Sciences Complex now stands" used to be a place known for "fairies dancing at night to sweet music, and playing hurling!" (written communication, January 1991). Ronald J. Maher, Flatrock, reports the following legend regarding Fairy Knap, as heard from Captain John Grace, former resident: "The story goes that on certain nights when the wind blew in a certain direction, music and happy laughter would be heard coming from a grassy hill overlooking the harbor of Flatrock. From the year 1818 it was generally acknowledged that the fairies were dancing there. The local citizens listened and did not interfere with the merriment. All were very cautious when going out at night to carry a piece of bread along in their pocket to give to the fairies to eat so as they would not be stolen by the fairies. One morning just after 1818, Denis Maher, the local school teacher, was on his way with his men to haul his trap or fish lines. On the shore a man was standing and he asked if he may come along and help his men. Mr. Maher needed more help and he agreed. The man worked very well and soon they had the boat loaded with fish. They were in the process of rowing home just passing Fairy Knap, when the new man looked at the hill and remarked, "Many, many nights I danced there." Maher immediately guessed his identity. He was a fairy. The minute the boat touched land Mr. Maher ordered him from the boat. He jumped on the landing rock and disappeared completely from view. He was never seen again" (written communication, February 1987). Despite E.R. Seary's convincing argument that "Ferryland," a community on the Avalon Peninsula, derives its place name from the Portuguese place name *Farilham* (steep rock), the common usage of "fairyland"

in the sixteenth century, the occasional spelling of "fairy" as "ferrie" or "ferry," especially in adjectival forms (see Williams in this volume), seventeenth-century spellings of the Ferryland area as "Feriland" and "Ferriland," the orality of working–class British culture at the time, the irrationality of "ferryland" as a land of ferryboats, and the vigor of fairy belief, tempt this author to speculate that "Ferryland" might well have been understood as "Fairyland" in the seventeenth century, regardless of its provenance. See E.R. Seary, *Place Names of the Island of Newfoundland* (Toronto: U of Toronto P, 1971) 27–8, 210–1; Briggs 173. Popular understandings of fairy and fairyland are reflected in some of the English and Scottish ballads compiled by Francis James Child. One useful discussion is Lowry Charles Wimberly, "The Ballad Fairy," *Folklore in the English and Scottish Ballads* (1928; New York: Dover, 1965) 167–202. The phonemic similarities of "fairy" and "ferry" are played upon in a recent riddle-jest circulating in Newfoundland which stereotypically links acquired immune deficiency syndrome (AIDS) with homosexuality—*question*: what is the difference between Port-aux-Basques and someone with AIDS? *answer*: one is a ferry terminal and the other is a terminal fairy.

30. Lewis Spence, *British Fairy Origins* (London: Watts, 1946) 65–95; Katharine M. Briggs, *The Fairies in Tradition and Literature* (London: Routledge and Kegan Paul, 1967) 115–22, 141–3.

31. Ó Súilleabháin 82–3; Evans-Wentz 85–6; Briggs, *Tradition* 143; MacNeill 397; Henry Glassie, *Passing the Time in Ballymenone: Culture and History of an Ulster Community* (Philadelphia: U of Pennsylvania P, 1982) 547.

32. F.L. Utley, "The Bible of the Folk," *California Folklore Quarterly* 1 (1942):1–17.

33. Katharine Briggs, *The Vanishing People: Fairy Lore and Legends* (New York: Pantheon, 1978) 81–2.

34. Thanks to J.D.A. Widdowson for this observation.

35. Conrad Arensberg, *The Irish Countryman* (1937; rpt. Garden City, N.Y.: Natural History P, 1968) 163–91; Christina Hole, *English Folklore* (London: B.T. Batsford, 1940) 132–3; Kirk 49 and Stewart Sanderson's introductory commentary to Kirk regarding "euphemistic periphrasis" 45; Heinrich Kramer and James Sprenger, *Malleus Maleficarum*, trans. Montague Summers (orig. 1490?; 1928; London: Arrow Books, 1971) 407; John C. Messenger, *Inis Beag: Isle of Ireland* (New York: Holt, Rinehart and Winston, 1969) 98–9; Evans-Wentz 22, 76–7; Widdowson 123–9.

36. Catherine F. Horan, "Blueberries," in Joseph R. Smallwood, ed., *Encyclopedia of Newfoundland*, vol. 1 (St. John's: Newfoundland Book Publishers, 1981) 209–11

37. Murray 22.

38. Abbot 13.

39. Goudie 90.

40. Horan 210.

41. Abbot 14; Albert C. Badcock, *The Blueberry Industry in Newfoundland* (St. John's: Newfoundland and Labrador Department of Mines, Agriculture, and Resources, 1965) 6. Economic alternatives appear to have played a major role in the decline of male participation in commercial picking after Confederation. See Badcock 6–8.

42. Murray 22.

43. Murray 23.

44. Abbot 33–4.

45. Briggs, *Dictionary* 419; Keightley 300–1. An internationally well-known form of preventive magic (see "Folk Motifs" appended to this essay), the article of

clothing that is reversed in Newfoundland is usually a cap. Author and performer Ted Russell used being led astray while berry picking and the inside-out cap remedy as focal points for his "Uncle Mose" monologue, "The Big Brown Bog," *A Fresh Breeze from Pigeon Inlet*, The Best of Ted Russell, No. 3, ed. Elizabeth Russell Miller (St. John's: Harry Cuff Publications, 1988) 504; on Russell's work and its folkloric significance see Peter Narváez, "Folk Talk and Hard Facts: The Role of Ted Russell's 'Uncle Mose' on CBC's 'Fishermen's Broadcast,'" forthcoming in *Studies in Newfoundland Folklore*, ed. G. Thomas and J.D.A. Widdowson (St. John's: Breakwater, 1991).

46. Briggs, *Dictionary* 41; Kirk 54.
47. *DNE* 167.
48. Gail Ryan, Mt. Pearl, 1985.
49. Sean Lannon from Alice Lannon, St. Jacques, 1990.
50. Jean Smith from Howard Smith, Spaniards Bay, 1986.
51. *DNE* 167; also see "Pixie-led" in Keightley 300–1.
52. Ó Súilleabháin 85.
53. Robert Lynch, Upper Island Cove, written communication, 1985.
54. *DNE* 168; Ó Súilleabháin 47.
55. Notes to narratives indicate collectors, informants, ages of senior informants, principal residences of informants, and appropriate accession information for MUNFLA materials. In a few cases anonymity of informants and narrative protagonists has been provided through the use of fictitious initials.
56. Approximately two-thirds of the informants are Roman Catholic. Religious affiliation might play a role in fairy belief but official church doctrines have not supported fairy faith. The role of the priest in the outport community as portrayed by Newfoundland novelist Margaret Duley in *Cold Pastoral*, a work which is predicated on the berry picker-led-astray-by-the-fairies theme, was one of attempting to discourage such "superstition," for "he had never been able to eradicate the Celtic folk-lore [his people] mixed so strangely with religion" (Margaret Duley, *Cold Pastoral* [Toronto: Griffin House, 1977] 21); see Clara J. Murphy, "The Use of Fairylore in Margaret Duley's *Cold Pastoral*," *Culture and Tradition* 7 (1983): 106–19. On the other hand, the folk memory maintains that sometimes the priesthood disseminated and reinforced fairy belief. Consider the following narrative: "One August night my mother and her niece were travelling home from a garden party bingo with my grandparents. As they were coming down the lane, my mother who was eight, happened to turn around and there in the moonlight two little girls dressed in white were strolling behind. With great surprise my mother said to her parents, 'Two children dressed in white are following us!' My grandmother who is very superstitious reached into her pocket and took out some bread for my mother and her niece. This was believed to be a protection from the fairies or evil spirits. As my grandfather turned around there was nothing in sight. The very next day my grandmother told this story to the parish priest. He said they were lucky not to be travelling alone at night because if they were ever alone they would be taken by the 'good people' called the fairies" (Annette Roche from Rosella Roche, Branch).
57. Clare McGinty from Mrs. Frances Furey, 80s, Avondale.
58. Sharon Murphy from Mary Ellen Murphy, 72, Merasheen.

59. Rick Carey from Bridget Carey, St. John's. This occurred in 1936 to Lucy Harris and was extensively covered in the Newfoundland media. For an full examination of this event see Rieti.

60. Clare McGinty from Mrs. Frances Furey, 80s, Avondale.

61. Doreen Nardini from Heather May, Cupids.

62. Kim French from Mildred Parsons, 73, Clarke's Beach.

63. Debbie Allen from James Spurvey, 75, Fox Harbour.

64. Alvina Drover re grandmother, Minnie Parsons, Bishops Cove.

65. Francis Murley from Mrs. Pearl Penny, Tilt Cove, MUNFLA 72–117, Ms. 14.

66. Ursula Marie Wall, personal experience, fifty years ago, Northern Bay, MUNFLA 83-309, Ms. 8.

67. Sometimes referred to as the "father of Newfoundland country and western music," Walsh had a popular radio show during the mid-1930s on VONF.

68. Ursula Marie Wall from Elizabeth Mullaly, 93, Conception Bay, MUNFLA 83-309, Ms. 9.

69. Ronald J. Maher from Patrick Shea, 60s, Pouch Cove.

70. Denise Riggs from Maria N, 73, Bay de Verde.

71. Shelly Smallwood from Violet Smallwood, Topsail.

72. Nicolette Willcott from Paul Delaney, Harbour Breton regarding local legend told by his father who was from Gull Island.

73. Evelyn Spurrell from Effie Spurrell, 84, Bryant's Cove.

74. Kim French from Mildred Parsons, 73, Clarke's Beach.

75. Margaret Keiley from Josephine Kennedy, 87, Trepassey.

76. Francis Murley, from Mrs. Pearl Penny, Tilt Cove, MUNFLA 72–117, Ms. 11–2.

77. Anon., MUNFLA, 71–22, Card 30.

78. Anon., MUNFLA, 72–95, Ms. 11. This ailment which might be described as "limb struck by fairy contains foreign objects" is a New World manifestation of the European "elf-shot." In Newfoundland it is usually referred to as a "blast" (see Carolyn White, *A History of Irish Fairies*, 3rd ed. [Cork: Mercier P,1985] 40–2 for a different but obviously related form of blast) and sometimes a "fairy blight" (see Briggs, *Dictionary* 25–7). The testimony of Will Quirk, Fortune Harbour, as elicited by John Widdowson, MUNFLA 64-13, Tape C66, reveals that "all kinds of stuff came out" of a crippled arm—"needles and stuff like that." The testimony of Howard Smith, 59, Spaniards Bay, as collected by Jean Smith exhibits the motif as well. A young girl "was going to school, see, with a crowd of other children in the winter. And there's an old house boarded up, no one lived in it. So one of the other children hove her mitten in the house . . . and when she [the young girl] went in to get it a little man cut her across the legs with a whip and she, she took sick. They took her . . . to the doctor and her leg got sore and they took bones and rag and everything out of her leg. . . . And she was crippled for the rest of her life." Bryan Hennessey of St. John's reports that "more than thirty years ago" the mother of an acquaintance from Mahers "for a joke" threw dishwater at what she believed was the lantern of someone she knew who was coming up the path by her house. The light promptly struck her hand and within days her hand became swollen with the "fairy blight." When she had it lanced by a doctor in Cupids "feathers, twigs, and dirt came out of her hand." See the essay by Barbara Rieti in this volume for an extensive examination of this subject.

79. Anon., MUNFLA 71-75, Ms. 21–2.

80. Anon., MUNFLA 71-109, Ms. 42–3.

81. Anon., MUNFLA 72-117, Ms. 8–9.

82. Olive Troake, Cobb's Arm, MUNFLA 84-377, Card and Ms., no number.

83. Jeanette Houston from Virginia Houston, St. Vincents.

84. Peter Kelly from Mrs. Jane Kelly, 95, Long Harbour / Fox Harbour.

85. Margaret Singleton from Selby Singleton, 60s, Tilton.

86. Two of the structural categories of this interpretation are based on the functions of V. Propp, *Morphology of the Folktale*, trans. Laurence Scott, ed. Louis A. Wagner, 2nd rev. ed. (Austin: U of Texas P, 1968).

87. [St. John's] *Evening Telegram* 23 August 1987: 54.

88. Narváez, "Fairy Faith" 5.

89. On iron mines as fairy habitations see Briggs, *Vanishing* 82. Also see Briggs' excellent entry, "Time in Fairyland," *Dictionary* 398–400.

90. MUNFLA 81-55, Ms. 3–5; quoted in Gail Weir, "The Wabana Iron Ore Miners of Bell Island, Conception Bay Newfoundland: Their Occupational Folklife and Oral Folk History," MA thesis, Department of Folklore, Memorial U of Newfoundland, 163–4; also cited in Weir's *The Miners of Wabana: The Story of the Iron Ore Miners of Bell Island* (St. John's: Breakwater Books, 1989) 123–4; fairy traditions on Bell Island were recently a lengthy topic of discussion on Ron Pumphrey's open-line radio program, *Nightline*, VOCM, January 14, 1990.

91. Soft drink made with flavored powder, sugar and water.

92. Special thanks to George Budgell, Bruce Bourque, and Bob Woolridge for this narrative.

93. For "Newfie jokes" see Gerald Thomas, "Newfie Jokes," in Edith Fowke, *Folklore of Canada* (Toronto: McClelland and Stewart, 1976) 142–53.

94. On the mechanisms of humor see "The Jester" in Arthur Koestler, *The Act of Creation* (London: Picador, 1975) 25–97.

95. Hal Morgan and Kerry Tucker, *Rumor* (Harmondsworth: Penguin, 1984),pp. 120–1.

96. John Fogerty, "I Saw it on TV," from Warner Bros. cassette *Centerfield* (92–52034), 1984.

Folk Motifs

The following list of traditional folk motifs discussed in this article derives from Stith Thompson, *Motif-Index of Folk Literature,* 6 vols. (Bloomington: Indiana UP, 1955) and Ernest W. Baughman, *Type and Motif-Index of the Folktale of England and North America* (The Hague: Mouton, 1966):

C211.1	Taboo: eating in fairyland.
D1896	Magic aging after years in fairyland.
D1960	Magic sleep.
D2066	Elf-shot.
F230	Appearance of fairies.
F235.1	Fairies invisible.
F236.3.2	Fairies with red caps.
F239.4.2	Fairies are the size of small children.
F251.6	Fairies are fallen angels.
F261	Fairies dance.
F262	Fairies make music.
F316	Fairies lay curse on child.
F328	Fairies entice people to their domains.
F340	Gifts from fairies.
F343.21	Fairies give mortal skill in music.
F362	Fairies cause disease.
F369.7	Fairies lead travelers astray.
F369.7(a)	Persons who are led astray by fairies break spell by reversing an article of clothing: coat, glove, etc.
F370	Visit to fairyland.
F377	Supernatural lapse of time in fairyland.
F377(c)	Person joins dance of fairies, is in fairyland for duration of dance. Dance seems to last a few minutes, actually lasts weeks, months, or years.
F385.1	Fairy spell averted by turning coat.

V. Fairylore and Popular Culture

Today, most students of culture view the relations of popular culture and folklore in terms of continuum and symbiosis rather than antithesis.[1] The two major interests of folklorists in contemporary popular culture are first, local and small group uses of artistic communications in mass society, and second, the mass mediation of folkloric materials as employed by the creators, performers, and producers of popular culture. To the extent that folklorists focus on how audiences actively participate in and appropriate the codes of popular culture for their own purposes, their primary concern parallels the "active audience" analyses of cultural studies.[2] Based on a variety of primary and secondary sources, the investigations of modern legend and ritual in this section well exemplify the cultural interface of mass society and folk group.

Paul Smith's essay on the Cottingley Fairies is a folkloristic examination of the most popular twentieth century legend concerning fairies—the story of how two young English girls played with fairies and photographed them. Besides recounting the remarkable public controversy surrounding these events he pays particular attention to the pivotal role of visual transmission and personal testimony in maintaining traditional belief and generating new folkloric forms.[3]

Tad Tuleja and Rosemary Wells both offer detailed perusals of the elusive Tooth Fairy, but from very different perspectives. While the Tooth Fairy is now an international phenomenon, both authors agree that in form and usage this fairy complex derives from the United States. In terms of what the ritual means, Tuleja argues that it is an agent of socialization ushering the young child into the world of consumer capitalism.[4] In contrast, for Wells it is a significant rite of passage pertaining to physical, social and psychological change. She also interprets the Tooth Fairy as an icon that incorporates the wonder and fantasy of childhood and the affectionate emotions of parenthood.

Notes

1. See Peter Narváez and Martin Laba, eds., *Media Sense: The Folklore-Popular Culture Continuum* (Bowling Green, Ohio: Bowling Green State U Popular P, 1986);

Harold Schechter, *The Bosom Serpent: Folklore and Popular Art* (Iowa City: U of Iowa P, 1988).

2. For example Dick Hebdige, *Subculture: The Meaning of Style* (London: Methuen, 1979); Angela McRobbie, ed., *Zoot Suits and Second-Hand Dresses: An Anthology of Fashion and Music* (Boston: Unwin Hyman, 1989).

3. See Paul Smith, "Communicating Culture; or, Can We Really Vocalize a Brownie?" in Narváez 31–46.

4. See Gregory P. Stone, "Halloween and the Mass Child," *American Quarterly* 11.3 (1959): 372–79.

The Cottingley Fairies: The End of a Legend

Paul Smith

Residents of a Yorkshire village famous for fairies which two young cousins claimed to have photographed more than 60 years ago were today mourning the death of a legend.

The tale of the fairies of Cottingley Dell near Bingley, was cherished by villagers—particularly the older generation who remember Miss Elsie Wright and her cousin Frances, who took the photographs.

But now the fairy-tale has been exposed by the former Miss Wright.

Miss Wright, now Mrs Hill, 82, and living in the village of Bunny, Nottinghamshire, said: "The photographs were a fake—I admit it at last."

The postmistress told the YEP [*Yorkshire Evening Post*]: "A lot of the older people in the village knew the two ladies and were quite taken up with the story.

"I think that some of them will be a little upset that the story of the Cottingley fairies is finally shown up as a fake," she said.

Yorkshire Evening Post
March 19, 1983

And so closed a chapter of fairylore which had begun in July 1917 when two young girls, Frances Griffiths and Elsie Wright, then aged ten and fifteen respectively, supposedly photographed a group of fairies dancing in a wooded glen in Cottingley near Bradford, England.

In addition to the two photographs taken in 1917, at the instigation of Edward Gardner and Sir Arthur Conan Doyle, the girls took three more photographs in 1920—again purporting to be of the fairies at Cottingley. On and off, over the next sixty-six years, the debate over the authenticity of these five pictures continued. Did the girls actually photograph fairies or were the photographs fakes? Was it all a practical joke? Were the girls awestruck by all the attention focused on them and therefore trapped and unable to tell the truth? These are just some of the many questions which have been persistently discussed over the years by a wide range of interested individuals.

In coming to write this essay, it was not just the question of the "authenticity" of the photographs and the reality of what took place at Cottingley that interested me. Instead, I was also concerned with exploring the Cottingley fairy photographs from the point of view of a folklorist—an approach which has had little attention over the years, and

371

which has even attracted criticism (L. Gardner), if not undue ridicule (Cooper 1990, 79–87).

From the point of view of the folklorist then, just where do the Cottingley fairy photographs fit into the scheme of things? Perhaps ironically, the journalist writing the above piece in the *Yorkshire Evening Post* proffered one possible solution to that question when he described the exposure of the photographs as fakes as being "the death of a legend."

William Bascom defined legend as "prose narratives which . . . are regarded as true by the narrator and his audience . . . set in a period . . . when the world was much as it is today" (Bascom 4). For Bascom, the principle characters of the legend were human "but they also include local tales of . . . ghosts, fairies and Saints" (Bascom 5). However, more recently the narrative status of legend, like the "truth component," has become an issue for debate.

> Perhaps what is needed as a first step towards clearing up the difficulties of definition is to de-classify [legend] as narrative, recognizing that, though it overlaps with narrative, it is not entirely contained within this category. This would have the advantage of bringing definition into line with practice rather than trying to squeeze practice into the ideal corsets of definition. (Bennett 1989, 11)

However, underlying these definitional wrangles, the presence of some "statement" of belief appears to be a feature persistently found in the legend.

> The statement, as we recognized, might contain a second thought, it might display strong doubt, but nevertheless it remains a *statement*, whether negative or positive. This is distinctive in comparison with tale categories. Although objective truth and the presence, quality and quantity of subjective belief are irrelevant, it is all the more relevant that any legend, no matter how fragmentary or corrupt, makes its case. It takes a stand and calls for the expression of opinion on the question of truth and belief. (Dégh and Vázsonyi 119)

With the Cottingley fairies, we find a classic case of a debate between believers and disbelievers (Bennett 1987; Goldstein; Hufford 1982; Hufford 1990; Simpson)—an exchange of statements which, in this instance, focuses upon the "unexplained" and what would be considered by many to be the "anomalous." To that extent, we are dealing with statements and discussions about beliefs which focus on "extraordinary events" in the lives of ordinary people (George 11) and which, for those entering the debate, are germane to what they consider important concerns and issues. As such, the case of the Cottingley fairies, if not legend per se, hovers in that interface between legend and belief.

For the purpose of this study, consideration also needs to be given to the role of the photographs themselves. I would suggest that their existence does not detract from the legendary status of the Cottingley fairies, but rather, for a number of reasons, the photographs form an integral, if not key, part of that legend/belief complex.

Of related interest to the folklorist is the question of the interface between folklore and popular culture—in this instance the role played by the media. The debate about the Cottingley fairies, as appears to be common with many contemporary legends, was not just conducted amongst those individuals immediately involved, or even in everyday conversation amongst the population at large. Instead, the events and the photographs were extensively discussed in the media—primarily through newspapers, magazines and books (Baker; Bird; Klintberg; Mitchell; Oring). Such a public debate propagated two interesting situations. Firstly, it spread details of the Cottingley fairy photographs to a far wider audience than perhaps the two girl photographers ever imagined. Secondly, it has left a record of the beliefs, attitudes and perceptions held by the principle participants in the debate.

By necessity, such a "mediated" record of this debate, as an accurate account of what took place, must be jaundiced. For example, for the purposes of this essay, it would have been extremely tidy to identify the individuals involved, and to describe and contrast the views of the believers with those of the disbelievers. Unfortunately, this is a difficult, if not impossible task to do. Take the case of the two key figures in the story, Frances Griffiths and Elsie Wright. For almost fifty years, between 1917 and 1965, the girls remained very much in the background, and we are not directly privy to any of their testimony. Instead, what we learn about the girls, their beliefs and thoughts about the affair comes to us third, or at the best, second-hand—everything being mediated through other family members via researchers and writers, all of whom have some vested interest in the authenticity of the Cottingley photographs or the existence of fairies.

To that end, this paper is concerned with identifying the principle characters in the Cottingley fairies affair, and with exploring how, why, and to what extent they became involved in the debate. For instance:

> Why did Sir Arthur Conan Doyle, who made it very clear that his interest in the pictures had nothing to do with the to him much more vital subject of spiritualism, fasten on to them with such eagerness? What made Edward Gardner, an eminent thinker in his own field and a busy man, consider the matter of such profound importance to devote some years of his life to their promotion? (Crawley 1983c, 94).

Consequently, I shall not just be looking at the relationship of the participants to the Cottingley fairy photographs and the events which surrounded them, but also at the way in which the participants used the photographs to validate their existing beliefs. Of course, as all forms of folklore are subject to constant change, we will also see that the attitudes and beliefs of a number of the individuals involved similarly become modified as time passes.

And so, as all good stories start, "Let us begin at the beginning." Elsie Wright had left school at the age of thirteen. She had an artistic bent and after a very short spell at Bradford College of Art, obtained a job spotting black and white prints at Gunstons's Photographers in Bradford. Her dissatisfaction with the work and the potential for advancement caused her to leave and take a job elsewhere coloring photographic portraits (Crawley 1982a, 332–3). Sometime between these two jobs, in the summer of 1917, Frances Griffiths and her mother, Annie Griffiths, came over from South Africa, where Frances had been brought up, to stay with her Aunt Polly Wright. There, for the first time, Frances met her cousin, Elsie.

Both girls had a sense of humor (Cooper 1981c, 434) and in different ways could be considered intelligent and industrious. The girls' friendship grew, and they spent much of that summer playing by the beck in the wooded glen at the back of the house (E. Gardner 14). In spite of persistently being scolded for coming home soaking wet after falling in the water, Frances continued to go back there to play. When once questioned why she kept going back so often, "she burst into a flood of hot tears and blurted out, 'I go to see the fairies! That's why—to see the *fairies*'" (Cooper 1990, 20)—a "secret" which, up until then the two girls had apparently only shared with one another (Cooper 1990, 2; Crawley 1983g, 334). Regardless of Elsie's saying that she also had seen the fairies in the glen, the girls were ignored by the adults, who perhaps considered that the report of fairies was little more than an excuse to get them out of trouble.

For Frances, perhaps more so than Elsie, not only did fairies exist, but some lived in the glen, and she could see them (Cooper 1990, 12–9).

> The first time I ever saw anything was when a willow leaf started shaking violently, even though there was no wind, I saw a small man standing on a branch, with the stem of the leaf in his hand, which he seemed to be shaking at something. He was dressed all in green. (Cooper 1983, 2328)

Notwithstanding the scolding they had received for their "adventures" in the glen, "Elsie hit on a way they might justify their story" (Crawley 1982a, 1376). As she was later to recall:

> She [Frances] cried bitterly I know. I said, "Let's go up the beck." I was trying to think of something to get her mind off the troubles. And then I said: "Well, these fairies we see. Well, let's take a picture." I didn't think we'd go on with it. It was just to take her mind off things. But she got this

into her mind. She kept on about it. She livened up and said: "Oh yes, let's try and take one." And so after being nattered a bit I said we'd do it. (Cooper 1990, 21)

And so, early in July 1917, Elsie persuaded her father to lend her his recently acquired quarter-plate box camera and to show her how it worked so that she could photograph the fairies (Crawley 1983g, 332).

> It was on a Saturday at the midday meal that there had been some bantering about "the fairies" and Elsie retorted: "Look here, Father, if you'll let me have your camera and tell me how it works I'll get a photo of the fairies. We've been playing with them this morning." Mr Wright laughed at them, and said he wasn't going to have his plates spoilt, and put them off. But the girls persisted and worried him, and at last he gave way. (E. Gardner 14)

Armed with the camera and just one photographic plate, the girls set off for the beck. They returned in less than an hour—Elsie exclaiming, "We've got the photo, I believe. Will you look?" (E. Gardner 14–5). However, it wasn't until after dinner that evening that Arthur Wright found time to develop the photographs.

> With Elsie wedged in beside him in the small cupboard he put the plate in the dish, fully expecting only a blur, and was startled to see flash up, almost at once, the dark figures which he took to be some white swans. Elsie saw them too, and hearing her father's exclamation shouted to Frances outside, "We've got them; you'll see." When the plate was finished Mr Wright put it aside, saying they'd get a print in the morning and see what the swans looked like! Really uncertain as to what the children could have got hold of, as he told me, he took a sun-print in the morning with some curiosity, and was amazed at what he saw. (E. Gardner 15; see Plate 1)

In spite of having the print before him, Arthur Wright's skepticism of the girls' talk of fairies in the glen was not diminished. Nor was his disbelief shaken when in September 1917, the girls again borrowed the camera and took a second photograph of the fairies (E. Gardner 15).

> His questioning of the girls did not satisfy him, though they insisted that the figures in the photograph were the fairies they had so often described. Nothing would induce the children to give any other explanation, though the parents felt convinced that somehow they were being deceived. Mr Wright told me at this point that neither he nor his wife had ever accepted the story given by the girls, notwithstanding that a month later they got the second photograph. So convinced, however, did Mr Wright feel that the figures must be made of paper or the like that he went up the glen to the waterfall, which he recognized, and searched all about for

scraps of paper cuttings. While the children were away he and his wife searched the girls' bedroom, too, for some sign as to the way it has been managed, but neither in the glen nor in the cottage could they discover anything. Not having found either of the girls untruthful, both were really concerned at the persistence with which they maintained their explanation—so the parents decided to let the matter alone. (E. Gardner 15)

The girls did not borrow the camera again—perhaps they considered that they had the proof that they required. They had told their parents that they played with the fairies in the glen, and here was validation.

In fact, Frances seemed to have been almost "matter of fact" about the whole affair. For example, when on November 9, 1918, she wrote to a friend of hers in South Africa enclosing a print of the first photograph they had taken of the fairies, she certainly did not give it any prominence it in the letter.

Dear Joe [Johanna],

I hope you are quite well. I wrote a letter before, only I lost it or it got mislaid. Do you play with Elsie and Nora Biddles? I am learning French, Geometry, Cookery and Algebra at school now. Dad came home from France the other week after being there ten months, and we all think the war will be over in a few days. We are going to get our flags to hang upstairs in our bedroom. I am sending two photos, both of me. One is in a bathing costume in our back yard, uncle Arthur took it, *while the other is me with some fairies up the beck, Elsie took that one.* Rosebud is as fat as ever and I have made her some new clothes. How are Teddy and Dolly are they well? Teddy and Tibby are well . . . Last summer Elsie (my cousin) and I took a lot of photographs up the beck by our twoselves. I wish you a merry Christmas and a happy new year to you all; be careful not to catch cold sweeping off the snow; doesn't the frost make pretty patterns on the windows? How are you getting on about the 'flue'? We have kept off it so far, nearly all the schools have closed up. Give my love to Edith and your mother and your father. How are you getting on at school? Answer this letter won't you please? I have just been pinning Rosebud her dummey on, so I thought perhaps Dolly would like one so I will send her one.
                    With Love From FRANCES ("Cape Town" 5; my emphasis)

On the back of the photograph she also added, "Elsie and I are very friendly with the beck fairies. It is funny I never used to see them in Africa. It must be too hot for them there" ("Cape Town," 5).

Frances' "matter of factness" about the existence of fairies and the photographs contrasts sharply with that of Elsie's parents. Although the actions the Wrights had taken to disprove the authenticity of the photographs appears to clearly demonstrate the extent of their disbelief in

Plate 1. "Frances and the Fairies." (Brotherton Library, University of Leeds)

Plate 2. "Fairies and Their Sun-Bath." (Brotherton Library, University of Leeds)

both the existence of the fairies and the photographs, the matter is not altogether that clear cut. Without a doubt, Arthur Wright could be described as disbelieving that the girls had photographed fairies, or in fairies per se (Crawley 1983e, 153, 159). Polly Wright, on the other hand, while to a greater or lesser extent agreeing with Arthur in the early days, appears to have changed her stance as matters progressed.

In fact, the photographs would have been forgotten and the matter would have ended there had not their respective mothers' (Polly Wright and Annie Griffiths) developing interest in Theosophy drawn the two women to attend a meeting on "Fairy Life" at the Bradford Theosophical Society in the summer of 1919 (Cooper 1981a, 382; Crawley 1983f, 170). Towards the end of the meeting, Polly Wright mentioned that Elsie and Frances had taken two photographs which might possibly be of fairies. As a result of this remark, the Cottingley fairy photographs were brought to the attention of the Theosophist Edward Gardner—and so eventually to a wider, international audience.

Originally founded in 1875 in New York, with Helena Pretrovna Blavatsky as its corresponding secretary and leading light (Ryan 54–5), the first European headquarters of the Society was established in London in 1890, from whence it steadily expanded as lodges were opened in many major British cities. Members of the Theosophical Society considered themselves to be involved in "a scientific religion and a religious science" (Judge 1).

> . . . this philosophy believes in a hierarchy of administrating, controlling and matter-creating entities, existing as high level vibrations not normally appreciable by human beings. In due course, it suggests, as humanity evolves to become more in turn with the deity, so we will be able to perceive at first the lower orders of the hierarchy and then, as evolution progresses, successively higher ones will be perceived until the cycle is completed and identity with the deity achieved. Humanity, as a whole, the myth runs, has not yet reached the stage when even the lowest order, the nature spirits, can be seen, except very rarely by specially gifted people, having a quality possibly a little ahead on the evolutionary scale. (Crawley 1983d, 121)

In 1920 Edward L. Gardner, then aged fifty, was the president of the Blavatsky Lodge of the Theosophical Society in London. Regarded by many as one of the Society's most eminent teachers and thinkers, he is still held in much esteem today (Crawley 1983d, 120). Gardner had a particular interest in abnormal, spirit photography (E. Gardner 11; Sanderson 91), and he held strong beliefs in the existence of fairies (E. Gardner 39–47).

> First, it must be clearly understood that all that *can* be photographed must of necessity be physical. Nothing of a subtler order could in the nature of things affect the sensitive plate. So-called spirit photographs, for

instance, imply necessarily a certain degree of materialization before the "form" could come within the range even of the most sensitive of films. But well within our physical octave there are degrees of density that elude ordinary vision. Just as there are many stars in the heavens recorded by the camera that no human eye has ever seen directly, so there is a vast array of living creatures whose bodies are of that rare tenuity and subtlety from our point of view that they lie beyond the range of our normal senses. Many children and sensitives see them, and hence our fairylore—all founded on actual and now demonstrable fact!

Fairies use bodies of a density that we should describe, in non-technical language, as of a lighter than gaseous nature, but we should be entirely wrong if we thought them in consequence unsubstantial. In their own way they are as real as we are, and perform functions in connection with plant life of an important and most fascinating character. To hint at one phase—many a reader will have remarked on the lasting freshness and beauty of flowers cut and tended by one person, and on the other hand, their comparatively short life when in the care of another. The explanation is to be found in the kindly devotion of the one person and the comparative indifference of the other, which emotions affect keenly the nature spirits in whose immediate care the flowers are. Their response to love and tenderness is quickly evidenced in their charges.

Fairies are not born and do not die as we do, though they have their periods of outer activity and retirement. Allied to the *lepidoptera*, or butterfly genus, of our familiar acquaintance rather than to the mammalian line, they partake of certain characteristics that are obvious. There is little or no mentality awake—simply a gladsome, irresponsible joyousness of life that is abundantly in evidence in their enchanting abandon. The diminutive human form, so widely assumed, is doubtless due, at least in a great measure, to the powerful influence of human thought, the strongest creative power in our cycle. (Doyle 1922a, 172–4)

For Gardner then, the way fairies look to us was determined by the way our collective unconscious shapes them, in that it may "select archetypal images and project them on to the raw elemental force, producing the materialization of our choice" (Picknett 159).

Sometime early in 1920, a member of the Bradford Lodge of the Theosophical Society forwarded to Gardner prints of the two photographs, supposedly taken of fairies at Cottingley. At first, he appeared skeptical as to their authenticity. "Gardner thought the prints looked like studio fakes, or photographs of a picture, or prints from a doctored plate, of which he had seen many" (Sanderson 91). Regardless, his curiosity aroused, on February 23, 1920, he duly wrote to the Wrights and asked if the original negatives could be sent to him for examination. At the same time he took the opportunity to explain his position.

I am keenly interested in this side of our wonderful world life and am urging a better understanding of nature spirits and fairies. It will assist greatly if I was able to show actual photographs of some of the orders [of fairies]. Of course I know this can only be done by the help of children at present and am delighted to get into touch with such promising assistance as it seems your little girl can render. (Cooper 1990, 27)

The negatives soon arrived, and Gardner took them to be examined by Harold Snelling—a purported expert in fake photography, who certainly had the skill to detect if the photographs were authentic or not (Crawley 1983e, 144).

To Harrow, then, I took the two quarter-plates, saw Mr Snelling and without preliminaries, asked him to make a few prints of both, with a hope that he could strengthen the under-exposed plate. He took the negatives, smiled a little as he glanced at them, and started to ask a question, but stopped. "Wait a moment," he said, and went over to a glass-topped desk, switched on a light underneath, placed the first negative on the top and began examining it with sundry lenses. He spent so long over it that I broke in with the question as to what interested him. The reply was something of a shock. "Several things," said Snelling. "This plate is a single-exposure; these dancing figures are not made of paper nor of any fabric; they are not painted on a photographed background—but what gets me most is that all these figures have *moved* during exposure." This was astonishing enough, but however skilled Mr Snelling might be, I felt that the brief examination was insufficient; it must be as searching as it was possible to apply. So I talked the problem presented with him, told him what I knew of the photographs, which was little enough then, and asked him to analyze the two negatives exhaustively at his leisure, to enlarge them so that any irregularities might be shown up and in short, to break them down as faked work if it was possible to do so. (E. Gardner 11)

Snelling, as far as we can tell, had no interest or knowledge of fairies or Theosophy (Crawley 1983e, 153), and so his independent analysis, we should hope, was based on technical considerations rather than whether or not fairies existed. Perhaps then, to Gardner, Snelling's initial report came as something of a shock.

On calling a week later, as arranged, Snelling told me of his analysis and results. These can be summed up in the statement, which he made with emphasis, that both negatives were straight out-door shots and showed no trace of any faking process with which he was familiar. His first examination had been confirmed in all particulars and on my pressing him further still, he declared that he would stake his reputation on the plates being unfaked, though, he added, they were not good ones, the first being a little over-exposed and the second badly under-exposed. "*I don't know anything about fairies*," Snelling concluded, "*but these photographs are straight, open-air, single-exposure shots*." (E. Gardner 11–2)

For Gardner, the photographs validated his belief in the existence of fairies, and also his view that photographs could be taken of non-material spirits. Perhaps more importantly, however, Snelling's declaration that the photographs were not fakes, Gardner recognized as having major ramifications for the Theosophical movement.

> . . . the fact that two young girls had not only been able to see fairies, which others had done, but had actually for the first time ever been able to materialise them at a density sufficient for their images to be recorded on a photographic plate, meant that it was possible that the next cycle of evolution might now be under way. (Crawley 1983d, 121)

Enthused by the report, Gardner commissioned Snelling to produce negatives, prints and slides of a quality he could use in the illustrated lectures he gave at Theosophical Society meetings up and down the country (E. Gardner 23).

> The instructions I then left with him were that the originals must be absolutely untouched; contact positives were to be made from them, *and the negatives from these could be modified or strengthened to get good-class prints*, but nothing more, no re-touching or treatments, and that two glass lantern-slides be made. (E. Gardner 12; my emphasis)

Consequently, Snelling "improved" the photographs, cleaning up the tonal balance and giving prominence to the fairies. (Crawley 1982b; 1983a; 1983e, 144–5, 153). Such a request by Gardner was not in any way intended to create a deception. All he thought he was doing was cleaning up the evidence for the Theosophical Society members to inspect.

At some point in time, between Snelling's presenting his verbal report and delivering the written version to Gardner at the end of July 1920, Gardner had begun to exhibit slides of the two Cottingley fairy photographs at his public lectures. And it was probably as a result of this exposure to a wider audience that Sir Arthur Conan Doyle, writer and creator of Sherlock Holmes, was to enter the picture.

Like Gardner, Conan Doyle also believed in the existence of fairies (Cooper 1990, 31–2; Higham 263). His initial fascination appears to have been fostered by his uncle, Richard Doyle, the illustrator. However, his continuing interest may have, in part, been in support of his father, Charles Doyle, who had spent much of his life in mental institutions. Charles had kept an illustrated diary which was full of drawings of fairies (Baker; Crawley 1983d, 118; Gettings 2319). Conan Doyle was also interested in photography (Crawley 1983d, 117–8), and particularly spirit photography—a subject about which he was eventually to write a book (Doyle 1922b).

Unlike Gardner, however, Conan Doyle was by this time heavily involved in Spiritualism (Doyle 1924, 395–403):

> Spiritualism. . . is based on two basic propositions: first, that upon death, the soul departs for various spheres or planes of nonmaterial existence beyond the so-called earthplane; and second, that a certain degree of communication between the living and the dead, among the various planes, is possible. (Lellenberg 92)

Some considered his approach to Spiritualism uncritical (Cox 14–5; Lellenberg 15), and his espousing of Spiritualist philosophies lost Conan Doyle many of his friends (Pearsall 167). Regardless, he went on to write what was then considered by many as the authoritative history of the Spiritualist movement (Doyle 1926).

Conan Doyle first heard of the photographs of the Cottingley fairies from the editor of the Spiritualists' publication *Light*, who suggested he contact Felicia Scatcherd (Pearsall 168). She in turn referred Doyle to a cousin of Gardner's, Miss E.M. Bloomfield, who in response to his enquiries forwarded copies of the two photographs taken in 1917 (Doyle 1922a, 20–1). As he had already been commissioned by *The Strand Magazine: An Illustrated Monthly* to write an article on "fairy-lore" for their 1920 Christmas issue, Conan Doyle was obviously interested in following up this lead—if for no other reason than obtaining photographs to illustrate his article. Accordingly, he wrote to Gardner:

> I am greatly interested in the "fairy" photographs which really should be epoch-making if we can entirely clear up the circumstances. . . . It so happens that I am writing an article on Fairies at present, and have accumulated quite a mass of evidence. It will appear, I think, as one of the 'The Uncharted Coast' series in the *Strand*. I would willingly pay any reasonable sum, say £5, to reproduce the pictures and this would be a good way to getting them formally copy-righted both in England and America, which I certainly think the father of the girls should do.
>
> If I might have one or two notes as to who he is, where he dwells, the age of the girls, whether they are in other ways psychic and so forth, it will greatly help me in my description.
>
> We are all indebted to you as the channel by which this has come to the world. (Cooper 1990, 32)

He immediately received the following reply from Gardner:

> Your interesting letter of the 22nd has just reached me, and very willingly I will assist you in any way that may be possible.
>
> With regard to the photographs, the story is rather a long one and I have only gathered it by going very carefully. The children who were concerned are very shy and reserved indeed. . . . They are of a mechanic's

family of Yorkshire, and the children are said to have played with fairies and elves in the woods near their village since babyhood. I will not attempt to narrate the story here, however—perhaps we may meet for that . . .

I am hopeful of getting more photographs, but the immediate difficulty is to arrange for the two girls to be together. They are 16 or 17 years old and beginning to work and are separated by a few miles. It may be we can manage it and thus secure photographs of the other varieties [of fairies] besides those obtained. These nature spirits are of the non-individualized order and I should greatly like to secure some of the higher. But two children such as these are, are rare, and I fear now that we are late because almost certainly the inevitable will shortly happen, one of them will "fall in love" and then—hey presto!!

By the way, I am anxious to avoid the money consideration. I may not succeed, but would far rather not introduce it. We are out for Truth, and nothing soils the way so quickly. So far as I am concerned you shall have everything I can properly give you. (Doyle 1922a, 23–5)

Conan Doyle, although busily preparing to depart for Australia, obviously thought the matter important because he found time to meet with Gardner in London. Conan Doyle had already asked various friends and colleagues for their views on the authenticity of the photographs. Possibly prompted by a variety of skeptical responses (Pearsall 169), the two men decided to submit the prints to Kodak for further expert examination (Doyle 1922a, 29–30), deciding that if the pictures "survived a second expert's judgement. . . . then we should join forces and make the photographs a leading feature in *The Strand Magazine* article" (E. Gardner 13). It was also agreed at this initial meeting that, in order to learn more of what had actually taken place three years earlier in Cottingley, Gardner should travel north to conduct further investigations. For his part, it was decided that Conan Doyle "should examine the results and throw them into literary shape" (Doyle 1921, 25).

Accordingly, the negatives and photographs were examined at some length by the studio chief and two other expert photographers at Kodak. However, it appears that what the experts were shown at this stage were not the original negatives and prints which Snelling had examined, but copies of Snelling's "improved" negatives and prints (Crawley 1983e, 144–5). Not surprisingly under the circumstances, the subsequent report from Kodak, although agreeing with Snelling "that the negatives were a single exposure and that the plates showed no signs of being faked," they did add that ". . . this could not be taken as conclusive evidence . . . that they were authentic photographs of fairies" (E. Gardner 13).

The studio chief added that he thought the photographs might have been made by using the glen features and the girl as a background; then enlarging prints from these and painting in the figures; then taking half-plate and finally quarter-plate snaps, suitably lighted. All this, he agreed, would be clever work and take time. (E. Gardner 13).

Consequently, Kodak's experts were not prepared to certify the genuineness of the photographs "as some operator *might* have made them artificially" (E. Gardner 13).

For the record, Gardner noted that the Kodak technicians were not without bias. "A remark made by one, as we were thanking them and bidding goodbye, was that 'after all, as fairies couldn't be true, the photographs must have been faked somehow'" (E. Gardner 13). It was possibly this expression of disbelief which caused Gardner and Conan Doyle to selectively focus on the statement that "the plates showed no signs of being faked. . ." and to ignore the qualification of "inconclusive evidence" and the lack of willingness to produce a certificate. Instead, they chose to look for validation of authenticity in the "unbiased" positive personal testimonies gathered from Frances, Elsie, and their respective families (E. Gardner 13).

At the same time, another photographic company was consulted, which Conan Doyle later declared, ". . . it would be cruel to name" (Doyle 1920, 464). The subsequent report prepared by F.F. Renwick, one of three Ilford Company experts who critically examined the negatives and photographs, clearly stated that, ". . . I think and believe Storr and Bloch agree there is some evidence of faking" (Crawley 1983f, 171). This was not good news for Gardner and Conan Doyle, for unlike the Kodak report, there was no positive statement which could be used, in or out of context, to support the authenticity of the photographs. Under the circumstances, they chose to dismiss this report. Instead, they calculated that two out of three reports *had* endorsed the authenticity of the photographs—when, in fact, the reverse was true.

It was towards the end of July 1920 that Gardner made his first visit to Cottingley to meet the Wright family and Elsie. Frances, by this time, had left Cottingley and was living with her father in North Yorkshire (Cooper 1990, 35).

> Elsie and I then walked up the glen that I might see the actual sites of the photographs and verify them, and I was glad of the opportunity of questioning the elder girl quietly by herself and of talking things over. We soon found the spots, and the surroundings were unmistakably the same as photographed. . . . Elsie explained where she knelt when taking Frances and the group of dancing fairies and while we were there, I asked why Frances was not looking at the fairies instead of gazing at the camera. The reply was: "Why, Frances wanted me to take her photograph directly we got out of the garden, she was crazy for it; I said we might just as well take her with the fairies—so she had to wait!" A curious explanation this will appear to most, as it did to me, but there it was. Frances, apparently, was much more interested in the camera that they

had for the first time than she was in dancing fairies she could see any day, and from her point of view I suppose it was understandable. This answer of Elsie's is typical of the simplicity I met with throughout the investigation. Indeed, that which impressed me most in our conversation was the utter unconcernedness of Elsie at the affair being anything special. She had seen and played with fairy creatures since she could remember anything, and actually to photograph them did not appeal to her as being very extraordinary. . . . I might mention here, though I will deal with it more adequately later, that both the girls were good simple clairvoyants, quite unspoilt because unaware of it. They had the advantage, also, of being able to see only the subtler physical region and not anything beyond, their extra-sensory perception being strictly limited; hence there was very little confusion or distortion in the focus of their clairvoyance. (E. Gardner 15–7)

It was during this visit that Gardner told the Wrights of the reports on the photographs and broached the subject of including them in the proposed article for *The Strand Magazine*. The Wrights took considerable persuading before they agreed to allow the photographs to be used. Even then, they only did so on condition that neither their actual names, nor that of the village, be used in the article. Returning to London, Gardner met with Conan Doyle, and the two agreed that ". . . the analysis of the photographs, coupled as it now was, with satisfactory testimony on the personal side, justified publishing the pictures in the *Strand*" (E. Gardner 18).

Also in August 1920, Gardner travelled to Scarborough to interview Mrs Griffiths and Frances.

The trip to Scarborough proved satisfactory. I interviewed Mrs Griffiths and Frances, both then seen for the first time, and a half-hour's talk with Frances explained a good deal. The girl, at that time thirteen years old, was mediumistic, which merely means that she had loosely knit ectoplasmic material in her body. The subtle ectoplasmic or etheric material of the body, which with most people is very closely interwoven with the denser frame, was in her case unlocked or, rather, loosened, and on seeing her I had the first glimpse of how the nature sprites had densified their own normal bodies sufficiently to come into the field of the camera's range. This explanation emerged more fully later, however. For the moment I was concerned wholly with the practical arrangements which would enable us to get, if possible, that further evidence which would, this time, be unassailable. Frances was delighted with the invitation she had received from her aunt, Mrs Wright, and in the middle of August she went off to Cottingley to spend the second fortnight of her school holidays there with Elsie. (E. Gardner 19)

As can be seen in the reporting of his meetings with the girls, Gardner persistently attempted to add an interpretation as to their clairvoyant and mediumistic abilities—an interpretation which appears to have been based solely on his intuition and not on any testing or questioning of the girls. Frances later remembered Gardner's visit to Scarborough—although she had no recollection of his discussing her psychic powers and experiences. On the contrary, she found him to be an "uninteresting person . . . who had nothing much to say. . . . It was very difficult with him. They left me alone with him for about ten minutes, and then came and rescued me—he was just scrambling a few notes together . . . he wasn't scientific at all" (Cooper 1990, 39).

Following Gardner's visits to Cottingley and Scarborough and discussions between the two investigators, it was decided that additional evidence should be sought which would dispel any accusation of fraud or that ". . . the children had been the tool of someone skilled in photographic work" (E. Gardner 18). Consequently, Gardner arranged to provide Elsie and Frances with two cameras, and twenty-four photographic plates which had been secretly marked by the manager of Illingworth's photographic factory. Gardner hoped that when Frances returned to Cottingley, the girls would be able to take more photographs of the fairies (E. Gardner 19–20).

The plates were eventually returned and after verification that these were the marked ones, on September 6, 1920, Gardner wrote to Conan Doyle in Australia:

> I have received from Elsie three more negatives taken a few days back [August 26 and August 28]. I need not describe them, for enclosed are the three prints in a separate envelope. The "Flying Fairy" and the "Fairies' Bower" are the most amazing that any modern eye has ever seen surely! I received these plates on Friday morning last and have since been thinking furiously.
>
> A nice little letter came with them saying how sorry they were (!) that they couldn't send more, but the weather had been bad (it has been abominably cold), and on only two afternoons had Elsie and Frances been able to visit the glen. . . .
>
> I went over to Harrow at once, and Snelling without hesitation pronounced the three as bearing the same proofs of genuineness as the first two, declaring further that at any rate the "bower" one was utterly beyond any possibility of faking! While on this point I might add that today I have interviewed Illingworth's people and somewhat to my surprise they endorsed this view. . .
>
> I am going to Yorkshire on the 23rd inst. to fill some lecture engagements and shall spend a day at C., and of course take photos of these spots and examine and take away any "spoilt" negatives that will serve as useful accompaniments. The bower negative, by the way, the girls simply could not understand at all. They saw the sedate-looking

fairy to the right, and without waiting to get in the picture Elsie pushed
the camera close up to the tall grasses and took the snap. . . . (Doyle
1922a, 95–7)

It appears the two investigators now considered that they had obtained
the confirmation they desired as to the authenticity of the Cottingley fairy
photographs, and consequently, they decided to go ahead with
publication.

The two 1917 photographs of the fairies were first published as part of
an article prepared by Conan Doyle for the December 1920 issue of *The
Strand Magazine* (Doyle 1920), which, it appears, sold out in a few days
(Cooper 1990, 45). Under the banner headline "Fairies Photographed: An
Epoch-Making Event Described by A. Conan Doyle" the first part of the
article set out how Doyle came to hear of the photographs, introduced
Gardner's involvement, and discussed the various pieces of evidence
which supported the authenticity of the photographs. The second part of
the article comprised a report by Gardner on how he came to obtain the
photographs, came into contact with Conan Doyle, and perhaps more
interesting, a summary of his findings and feelings after his first visit to
meet the Wrights and Elsie—who, for the sake of anonymity, were being
referred to as "The Carpenters and Iris." The final part of the article
consisted of a note by Doyle making further observations on the
"supporting evidence," Gardner's interview with "The Carpenters" and a
commentary on the fairies seen in the photographs.

Doyle had written the article prior to his departure for Australia, and
he was not to know that Gardner would be successful in obtaining further
pictures. Possibly, because his comments were based solely on the two
1917 photographs, in his introduction, Conan Doyle appears quite
deliberately to distance himself from the affair—never totally
acknowledging his personal feelings on the matter.

If I am myself asked whether I consider the case to be absolutely and
finally proved, I should answer that in order to remove the last faint
shadow of doubt I should wish to see the result repeated before a
disinterested witness. (Doyle 1920, 463)

In spite of his apparent reticence to commit himself, in his final
commentary on the pictures, Conan Doyle, quite matter of factly,
discusses the images as if fairies exist and that these are photographs of
them.

There is an ornamental rim to the pipe of the elves which shows that the
graces of art are not unknown among them. And what joy is in the
complete abandon of their little graceful figures as they let themselves go
in the dance! They may have their shadows and trials as we have, but at

least there is a great gladness manifest in this demonstration of their life. (Doyle 1920, 468)

Not surprisingly, the investigators strove to present the material in a rigorously scientific and fully authenticated manner. To that end, they provided details of the camera and type of plates used, as well as details of the distance of the camera to the subject and the length of exposure. While such an approach must be applauded, there are also some flaws in their documentation. For example, while they report the time of day, month and year the photographs were taken, they failed to record the day of the month.

They also sought from Snelling, specifically for publication, a second endorsement of authenticity which was duly incorporated into the article (Doyle 1920, 467). This endorsement, which in the 1970s caused a paranormal debunker, the "Amazing Randi," to declare Snelling to be ". . . a total incompetent . . . as the evidence proves beyond a doubt" (Randi 33), appears, in fact, to have been very carefully worded, in that Snelling never categorically stated that these were photographs of fairies. Instead he quite correctly observed that they were ". . . entirely genuine, unfaked photographs. . ." (Doyle 1920, 467). This does not mean photographs of paranormal phenomena, as Gardner and Conan Doyle would wish us to believe, but merely that "these are straight forward photographs of whatever was in front of the camera at the time" (Crawley 1983e, 145).

Two further photographs, from the three taken in the summer of 1920, accompanied a second, more general, article by Conan Doyle on "The Evidence for Fairies" which appeared in *The Strand Magazine* for March 1921 (Doyle 1921). This may actually have been written before the December piece (Crawley 1983c, 96), for in it, Conan Doyle makes no reference at all to the photograph of the Cottingley fairies—the only information about them being contained in the captions to the two pictures. This anomalous situation was explained in a note to the effect that

> This article was written by Sir A. Conan Doyle before actual photographs of fairies were known to exist. His departure for Australia prevented him from revising the article in the new light which has so strikingly strengthened his case. We are glad to be able to set before our readers two new fairy photographs, taken by the same girls, but of more recent date than those which created so much discussion when they were published in our Christmas number, and of even greater interest and importance. They speak for themselves. (Doyle 1921, 199)

By publishing this general essay on fairylore, the plan to arrange for "the corroborative evidence, with copies of the new photographs to be published in *The Strand Magazine* for March 1921" had collapsed (E.

Gardner 21). Perhaps this idea had, in fact, been overridden by the dominant Conan Doyle, when he saw the potential of producing his own book on the subject (Doyle 1922a).

In August 1921 Gardner again went back to Cottingley to visit Elsie and Frances. He hoped this time that, in addition to photographs, the girls might manage to capture the fairies on cine film. In fact, things did not work out as planned, and in the end, Gardner only provided the girls with still cameras and plates. Regardless, no photographs were forthcoming (Cooper 1990, 62–3; Crawley 1983a, 13).

Gardner was also accompanied on this visit by a clairvoyant and believer in fairies, whom Doyle mysteriously referred to by the pseudonym of "Mr Sergeant" (Doyle 1922a). Gardner correctly identified him as Geoffrey Hodson (E. Gardner 27), author of *Fairies at Work and Play*, a volume to which Gardner had contributed a lengthy introduction (Hodson 11–24). In spite of the fact that, as Elsie and Francis were later to disclose, they saw no fairies in the glen while Hodson was present, on the contrary, he saw them everywhere (Cooper 1990, 65).

Unbeknown that he was being tricked, Hodson wrote copious notes on the fairies he "saw" and incorporates several descriptions of them in his book (Hodson 32–3, 79, 80). Furthermore, Hodson's notes were to become crucial "evidence" in support of the case, and as a consequence, were featured by both Conan Doyle and Gardner in their respective books (Doyle 1922a, 108–22; E. Gardner 27–35).

Whether Hodson was a fraud, or whether he did believe he saw a rich and varied population of fairy life in the glen at Cottingley is open for debate. Regardless, Elsie and Frances "both refused to read any of his books and considered him a fake" (Cooper 1990, 67).

The initial response in the press to the publication of the photographs was mixed (Doyle 1922a, 59–92). There were those, such as the reformer Margaret McMillan, who declared, "How wonderful that to these dear children such a wonderful gift has been given" (Cooper 1981b, 416). On the other hand, a damning critique was published in *The Birmingham Weekly Post* (Doyle 1922a, 77–81), and in a series of pieces in the literary journal *John O' London's Weekly* (Hewlett; "Shooting"; Wallace; Wheelwright) Maurice Hewlett, the novelist, concluded, "And knowing children, and knowing that Sir Arthur Conan Doyle has legs, I decide that the Miss Carpenters have pulled one of them" (Hewlett 359).

The *Westminster Gazette* was the first newspaper to publish details of the actual identities of the girls and the place where the photographs had been taken. They had sent out a reporter to do an investigative piece, and after much perseverance, he had located and interviewed separately, Arthur Wright, Polly Wright and Elsie (E. Gardner 21). In the subsequent story, although the reporter could find no proof that anything amiss had taken place, he preferred to sit on the fence and so concluded:

> We must, therefore, accept the evidence of the people who declare they
> have seen fairies, and the two Yorkshire girls who claim to have taken
> photographs of them, or agree with the definition given by the compiler
> of a standard dictionary, who says fairies are "imaginary beings, or
> spirits, having a human form, though much below human, and with
> sundry human attributes." In the absence of further material proof the
> majority of people will doubtless take the latter course. ("Fairy Sun-
> Bath")

In reply to his critics, Conan Doyle embarked on a letter writing
campaign (Gibson and Green 291, 294–5). However, the *Strand* articles did
not create the interest and support which Doyle had hoped for. Instead,
the response was one of embarrassment and puzzlement (Pearsall 171).

In January 1921 Conan Doyle wrote to Gardner from Australia, and
while expressing his appreciation for Gardner's efforts, also hinted that
". . . there would be a book out on it all before long, to be written by
himself and E.L.G. . . . and Gardner was to be given an opportunity to
express his Theosophical views" (Cooper 1990, 62). For some reason or
other, this was not to be. Conan Doyle's agent appears to have been
against co-authorship of the book and its possible effect on sales. And so
yet again, Gardner had to take a back seat while Doyle held center stage.
By April 1921, it must have been apparent to Gardner that not only was
there to be no joint book, but as Conan Doyle apparently could not even
find the time to meet with him to plan the next place of their research, the
investigative partnership was coming to an end (Cooper 1990, 63).

The first English edition of Conan Doyle's book on the Cottingley
fairy photographs, *The Coming of the Fairies*, was published on September
1, 1922 (Doyle 1922a). The one thousand copies sold out almost
immediately and the book was promptly reprinted (Green and Gibson
309–10). Although on the surface Doyle's study appears to be a coherent
account of the investigation, in fact, it had been crudely constructed by
simply reprinting the two articles from *The Strand Magazine* (Doyle 1920;
1921), the two-part investigative article which appeared in the *Westminster
Gazette* ("Do Fairies"; "A Fairy Sun-Bath"), and two lengthy examples of
attacks made on their research—one by Major Hall-Edwards in *The
Birmingham Weekly Post* (Doyle 1922a, 81) and another by Maurice Hewlett
in *John O' London's Weekly* (Doyle 1922a, 83–8). While only a cursory
response was made by the investigators to the *Westminster Gazette* piece,
reprinting the two highly critical articles provided the opportunity for
Gardner, via Doyle, to comment at great length and refute the allegations.

In addition, Doyle liberally used transcripts of notes supplied by
Gardner of Hodson's clairvoyant investigations at Cottingley (E. Gardner
30), lengthy extracts from Gardner's notes (probably his lecture notes),
and Gardner's letters to Doyle. Furthermore, we are presented with
various personal communications Doyle had received from readers of *The*

Strand Magazine articles, which discuss beliefs and personal experience narratives about fairies. The whole is concluded with a fifteen-page quotation from Gardner presenting his "Theosophic View of Fairies" (Doyle 1922a, 171–86), and lengthy extracts from Charles Leadbeater's book, *The Hidden Side of Things*.

All in all, Doyle's *The Coming of the Fairies* could not be described as an original work. In fact, there is probably more of Gardner in the book than Doyle. Consequently, it does seem surprising to find that, although Doyle reports Gardner's involvement in the investigation and even includes a photograph of him as the frontispiece to the book, he appears not to have seen his way to share the authorship with Gardner. In part, this follows a pattern, in that throughout, Gardner was treated as the legman and supplier of information to the established "investigator" and writer—Gardner playing Watson to Doyle's Sherlock Holmes.

The affair of the Cottingley fairies was not to end with the publication of *The Coming of the Fairies* in 1922. Conan Doyle, in spite of his earlier reticence, was now committed, and in order to strengthen his case, he went on to produce in 1928 a revised edition of the book in which he included additional photographs of fairies from Devonshire and Germany, and an essay on "Nature Spirits" by Florizel von Reuter (Doyle 1928, 156–7). Similarly, in 1929 Conan Doyle returned yet again to the topic when he reassessed the objections raised as to the authenticity of the photographs (Doyle 1929, 119). Furthermore, the original *Strand* article was reprinted in 1930 in his collection of essays on psychic phenomena, *The Edge of the Unknown*.

It was not until 1945 that Gardner was to "set down . . . in careful sequence a plain and straight forward account of the way our investigations opened, and of the course we took to disprove or establish the genuineness of the photographs" (E. Gardner 9). This slim, but fact-filled volume had, in a sense, been pre-empted by Doyle, in that it covers much the same ground as *The Strand Magazine* articles and *The Coming of the Fairies*. Here, however, we are treated to what in effect is a personal experience narrative by Gardner, which includes commentary on not just what took place during the investigation, but how he views the world of fairies, and how he feels about the events he describes, and the evidence he examined.

> It is not easy to convey the sense of integrity I felt at the end of the investigation; to share it properly one would have to meet the parents and the children as I did. Here I can only register my own personal conversion to the acceptance of the five photographs as genuine in every sense of the word. It took a great deal of time and concentrated attention to convince me, but I can claim that the inquiry was thorough. . . . (E. Gardner 21)

> In many cases, when seeking information, I was interested to note that
> my share in making public the photographs taken in the Cottingley glen
> was a troublesome sort of introduction. Few fairy lovers look with favour
> on anything that gives publicity to the subject. Indeed, reproaches have
> been couched occasionally in no measured terms for what was regarded
> as an unwarranted intrusion and desecration on my part. Only after
> earnest assurances as to my own attitude could I get further and obtain
> those particulars which I have compared, checked and pieced together
> and can therefore set out here. (E. Gardner 40)

Although Gardner's book received a similar critical reception to Conan
Doyle's (Barlow), it is perhaps a measure of the perceived worth of the
volume, and the level of interest in the affair, that it has been reprinted
some six times.

The attention given to the photographs of the Cottingley fairies was to
gradually decline. Gardner never made another visit to Cottingley after
1921, and eventually the girls married and moved away—both going
overseas for varying periods of time. To that extent, they became
inaccessible to the majority of people who may have been "professionally"
interested in their experiences. However, in 1965, a reporter from the *Daily
Express* newspaper traced Elsie, who was living back in England, and
interviewed her in order to update the now almost fifty year-old story. In
spite of the reporter's obvious skeptical stance, Elsie skillfully rebutted his
assertions by commenting, "as for the photographs, let's say they are
pictures of figments of our imagination, Frances and mine, and leave it at
that" (Cooper 1990, 76).

And so was established a pattern which was to persist for the next
seventeen years—a battle of words between believers and disbelievers.
And in the middle, Elsie and Frances, now in their sixties, answering
questions from both sides, but in such a way as to neither confirm nor
deny that they ever actually photographed fairies at Cottingley.

After the *Daily Express* article, the two women managed to avoid any
further publicity for almost five years. However, in 1970 Gardner died at
the age of one hundred, and the BBC Television program, *Nationwide*,
decided to revive the story. Broadcast in 1971, the program included
comments from various technical experts, all of whom doubted the
authenticity of the photographs, and interviews with both Elsie and
Frances. When asked if her father had been involved, Elsie replied:

ELSIE: I would swear on the Bible Father didn't know what was going
on.

LEWIS: Could you equally swear on the Bible that you didn't play any
tricks?

ELSIE: (after a pause) I took the photographs . . . I took two of them . . .
no, three . . . Frances took two . . .

LEWIS: Are they trick photographs? Could you swear on the Bible
         about that?
ELSIE: (after a pause) I'd rather leave that open if you don't
         mind . . . but my father had nothing to do with it, I can promise
         you that . . .
LEWIS: Have you had your fun with the world for forty years? Have
         you been kidding us for ten days?
ELSIE: (laughs)
ELSIE: (gently) I think we'll close it on that if you don't mind. (Cooper
         1990, 77–8)

It was possibly as a result of viewing the *Nationwide* program that in
March 1973, Stewart Sanderson chose to make the Cottingley fairy
photographs the subject of his presidential address to the Folklore Society
in London (Sanderson). After declaring himself a skeptic, he examined the
linguistic ambiguities and the structure of the arguments in Gardner's
accounts, the reports on the photographs by the various "experts," and the
text of the *Nationwide* interviews with Elsie and Frances. Although he
concluded that the photographs were fakes, he did not offer any evidence
as to how this had been achieved—although, as others had done before, he
pointed to the fact that Elsie's artistic abilities possibly provided her with
the capabilities to perpetuate the fraud (Sanderson 101).

Sanderson was immediately brought to task by Gardner's surviving
son, Leslie, who suggested that people should keep an open mind and not
dismiss Edward Gardner as a crank, or the photographs as fakes (L.
Gardner 190–4). Leslie Gardner was well conversant with the events of
1920–21, because he had helped his father on several occasions (Crawley
1983f, 170–1). Not surprisingly, he had always accepted the photographs
as authentic and when interest in the case was revived in the 1960s, he
championed his father's cause.

It was not until 1976 that Elsie and Frances were again cornered by
the media, this time for a fifteen-minute piece for *Calendar*, produced by
Yorkshire Television. The program took Elsie and Frances back to
Cottingley, where, even in the face of tabloid-style television reporting
and a skeptical interviewer, when asked, "Did you fabricate those
photographs?" Frances categorically replied, "Of course not" (Cooper
1981c, 436).

Again the debate faded. That is until 1978, when the Cottingley fairy
photographs were to become a focus of attention for James "The
Amazing" Randi—a magician and professional debunker of paranormal
phenomena. Randi and a team from the Center for Scientific Investigation
of Claims of the Paranormal (CSICP), analyzed the photographs using a
computer image enhancement process.

Image enhancement can show up details that are captured on the photographic image but which, because they are blurred, are not visible to the eye. When CSICP member Robert Sheaffer and colleague William Spaulding applied the technique to the fairy photos, lo and behold, they found, among other evidence of fakery, the strings holding up the fairies. ("Fairy Story" 427)

Randi, whose fostered image is that of a man who has little patience with trickery and deception, when later writing up the investigation, was typically aggressive:

This case features all the classic faults of such investigations. Gullibility, half-truths, hyperbole, outright lies, selective reporting, the need to believe, and generous amounts of plain stupidity are mixed with the most outrageous logic and false expertise to be found anywhere in the field.

I will outline first the case for the defense. Since such claims immediately meet with disbelief, the proponents of this tale were and are on the defensive as soon as their case is stated, and any statements they make are necessarily defenses of their position. (Randi 12)

. . . Such a special world was entirely fictional, for as we shall see, little girls are not always truthful, experts are not always right, and authorities do not always see with unclouded vision. (Randi 21)

When presenting his "damning" evidence, he introduces a hypothesis, which he derived from Fred Gettings (Gettings 2319; Cooper 1990, 114–5), that the source for what he considers to be cardboard cutouts of fairies was the illustrations by Claude A. Shepperton (see Plate 3), to accompany the poem by Alfred Noyes, "A Spell for a Fairy," which was published in *Princess Mary's Gift Book* around 1914 (Noyes 101–4). Ironically, Conan Doyle also had a short story, "Bimbasi Joyce," reprinted in the same volume (Doyle 1914, 23–30).

The results of a second major scientific investigation of the photographs and the events surrounding them was published in 1982–83 by Geoffrey Crawley, editor of the *British Journal of Photography*. Outside the studies by Doyle and Gardner, this almost book-length series of articles stands as the first major postwar analysis of the affair. Acknowledging that the "internal evidence in the prints was insufficient for conclusive proof of fabrication" (Crawley 1983h, 365), in an analysis which is sensitive to the feelings of Elsie and Frances, Crawley looks at all the people involved, the equipment used—in fact, practically every element of the affair we would like to consider—and concludes that the photographs are fakes. Regrettably, however, the one aspect which he does not present in great detail is direct testimony from Elsie and Frances—both of whom were still alive at the time.

Plate 3. "Dancing Fairies" by Claude A. Shepperson; used to illustrate Alfred Noyes' poem "A Spell for a Fairy," *Princess Mary's Gift Book*, 1914. (Brotherton Library, University of Leeds)

Early in January 1983, events were to take a new turn when, before even part four of Crawley's series of articles had appeared, Joe Cooper published a follow-up piece to his three previous articles which were both sympathetic to Elsie and Frances and supported the authenticity of the photographs (Cooper 1981a, 1982b, 1982c). Cooper, who has a background in the social sciences and education, believes in the existence of fairies (Cooper 1990, 75–6; Picknett 156–8) and the paranormal in general (Cooper 1990, 145–7), and had spent a number of years researching the Cottingley fairies. For almost seven years he had regularly talked with and interviewed both Elsie and Frances. This time, however, Cooper was to report that in conversations with the two women during 1981 and 1982, both had admitted that the Cottingley fairy photographs were a hoax.

> My heart always sinks when I look at it. When I think of how it's gone all round the world—I don't see how people could believe they're real fairies. I could see the backs of them and the hatpins when the photo was being taken. . . .
>
> It started, as both ladies agree, with the best of intentions. Frances, she says, was able to perceive many forms of fairy life at the beck at the bottom of the garden of the Wright household and was, understandably, continually drawn back to the stream. Occasionally she fell in and wet her clothes, and was severely told off. . . . Partly to take Frances's mind

off her troubles, and partly to play a prank on grown-ups who sneered at the idea that fairies could be seen, but who cheerfully perpetuated the myth of Santa Claus, they conspired to produce fairy figures that they could photograph convincingly. . . . The attitude of Elsie and Frances to the whole question of the fairy photographs is a typical Yorkshire one— to tell a tall story with a deadpan delivery and let those who will believe it do so. Indeed, Elsie has often said as much: "I would rather we were thought of as solemn faced comediennes." (Cooper 1983, 2338)

This revelation in *The Unexplained* prompted Frances to "go public," and she contacted *The Times*, which published a factual report of her "confession." Shortly afterwards, Elsie added her version of the events, and both exposés have since been examined and remarked upon in detail (Cooper 1990, 121–9, 139–45; Crawley 1983b, 66; 1983g, 335–8; 1983h, 362, 364).

In the introduction to this paper I suggested that, in the case of the Cottingley fairies, ". . . we are dealing with statements and discussions about beliefs which focus on 'extraordinary events' in the lives of ordinary people and which, for those entering the debate, are germane to what they consider important concerns and issues." In looking back over the sixty-six years of debate which has surrounded the photographs, we can identify a whole range of individuals who, for one reason or another, were interested in the affair. There were those who believed in the existence of fairies, and those who did not. Likewise, there were those who believed the photographs were of fairies, and those who did not. Given such a situation, we find that the individuals involved in the debate fall into one of three broad groups:

1. People who *believed* in fairies and also *believed* in the authenticity of the photographs.
2. People who *believed* in fairies but *did not believe* in the authenticity of the photographs.
3. People who *did not believe* in fairies, therefore, *did not believe* in the authenticity of the photographs.

From this, we can see that we are not, in fact, dealing with an either/or situation—believers versus disbelievers. Instead, peoples' individual beliefs place them *somewhere* on a continuum between absolute belief and absolute disbelief—with those who believe in the existence of fairies, but not in the authenticity of the photographs, falling somewhere in the middle.

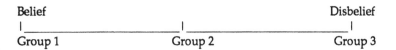

Belief		Disbelief
Group 1	Group 2	Group 3

This situation becomes further reinforced if we examine the roles and beliefs of the individuals involved. Here we find that not everyone fits exactly into one of the three categories. Rather, certain individuals fall in between categories, while others move from one to another.

Perhaps the key factor which determines the position of any one individual on this continuum is the photographs themselves, in that for a number of reasons they play a central role in this legend/belief complex. Firstly, based on a lack of knowledge, people tend to endow technical processes, such as photography, with capabilities they do not possess. Such a situation consequently provides a breeding ground for the emergence of legends and beliefs (Allen 95). Secondly, the photographs have acted as a medium of communication not only for legends and beliefs about the Cottingley fairies, but also for general and specific, positive and negative, stereotypes of fairies (Smith 1975). Thirdly, and perhaps more importantly, the photographs have been persistently used by both individuals and groups of individuals as "reinforcement" for established beliefs—in that they have provided "validation" for the existence, or not, of fairies per se, as well as a multitude of other related issues, views and philosophies (Smith 1987, 190–3).

Irrespective of her earlier assertions, Elsie later admitted that she never ever did believe that fairies existed (Cooper 1990, 139–40). Conversely, it appears that Frances always did believe in fairies, and she persisted in maintaining that she had seen them on numerous occasions (Cooper 1990, 144–5). Regardless of whether one, or both, of the girls believed in fairies, if their parents had initially accepted at face value that the girls had photographed fairies, this would have validated their excuse that they had been playing with fairies in the glen. On a different level, as a practical joke, the photographs provided the girls with a way of obtaining revenge for what they considered to be unfair treatment by their parents (Crawley 1983g, 337). However, their parents apparently did not believe that the photographs were of fairies. To own up to the practical joke would have brought them yet another scolding, and so they stuck to their story—probably thinking matters would be forgotten. As history was to show, this was not to be the case.

> But their prank or joke turned into a sort of monster for them, and the snapping of that camera shutter in 1917 was for them rather like the opening of Pandora's box. Shortly an enormous weight of publicity was brought to bear upon these photographs, supported by the fluent pen of Conan Doyle—who had his own reasons for wanting to believe that fairies were real. (Gettings 2319)

The girls were trapped, and to own up would have resulted in even more trouble. And so, they went along with Gardner and fulfilled his request for more photographs.

One intriguing fact to come out of the eventual confessions was that, while Elsie states that the images of fairies in all five photographs were produced by them, Frances maintained that the final photograph, "Fairies and Their Sun-Bath" (see Plate 2), was actually of fairies (Crawley 1983g, 338). As such, this single photograph remains as validation of her personal belief in the existence of fairies.

But what of the girls' parents? Arthur Wright remained skeptical throughout. He did not believe in fairies, and consequently, he did not believe that the photographs were genuine. In the long term, it was possibly the involvement of Gardner, and more particularly Conan Doyle (who prior to the affair Arthur had admired) (Crawley 1983e, 159), which prompted him not to voice his skepticism. Alternatively, it may have been the possibility of being accused of involvement in a fraud which influenced him. Regardless, he chose not to speak out.

Polly Wright, on the other hand, while she initially seemed to share her husband's skepticism, had a growing interest in Theosophy. Consequently, she would have been exposed to the possibility of the existence of fairies. However, her level-headed correspondence with Gardner indicates that, while she may once have agreed with Arthur, she became a "confirmed agnostic about the photographs" (Crawley 1983f, 170).

Gardner, as we have seen, because of his involvement in Theosophy, subscribed to the view that fairies existed. This, coupled with his interest in photographs of what today we would call the paranormal, led him to the view that, under the right circumstances, certain individuals may be able to photograph fairies. For Gardner then, the Cottingley fairy photographs validated his beliefs at a number of levels. At the same time, if the authenticity of the photographs was proved, the implications for the Theosophical movement would have been enormous. To that end, personal prestige must have played a part in how he decided to handle the matter. However, there is also an undertone of financial gain—though for Gardner, like the girls, this was not great (Crawley 1983c, 91–3). However, while playing down the financial potential of the photographs, being out for ". . . truth, and nothing soils the way so quickly" (Doyle 1922a, 25), on the other hand, he was touring the country and selling copies of the fairy photographs at his illustrated lectures (Crawley 1982a, 1378).

Quite what motivated Conan Doyle to champion the cause of the Cottingley fairy photographs is not easy to assess. He was ridiculed in the press, and his biographers agree that his involvement in the affair "destroyed the notion that he was a man to be taken seriously" (Cox 225). In spite of this, he was a committed supporter of the photographs, and they probably served his purposes in a number of ways. Firstly, the photographs validated his belief in the existence of fairies. Secondly, the photographs validated his belief that spirit photography was plausible.

Thirdly, although the existence of the photographs did not support in any direct way his views on Spiritualism, in presenting them to a wider public, he was asking that people take a fresh look at the way they view the world. In essence, he was saying to people, "so having proved to you that fairies exist, perhaps you should now take a second look at other beliefs, religions and philosophies about which you are skeptical."

> Nevertheless, there can be little doubt that Doyle believed that if the Cottingley pictures caused people to stop and consider the possibility of the paranormal, then their minds might become just that little more open to the doctrine of spiritualism. (Crawley 1983c, 96)

Fourthly, on a more mundane level, there was the financial aspect, in that regardless of his personal beliefs in the affair, the Cottingley fairy photographs became a part of the mechanics of his business. To write about them was not just to spread the word, but also to make money. To that end, it was Conan Doyle who led the way with the publication of the photographs—even when he appears skeptical as to their authenticity. And it was possibly a similar motivation which excluded Gardner from the possibility of being joint-author of *The Coming of the Fairies* (Doyle 1922a).

Hodson's clairvoyant investigations of the affair and his subsequent "extensive sightings" of fairies at Cottingley demonstrates that, for him, the photographs validate the existence of fairies. Furthermore, if fairies could only be seen by "special people," then they could probably also be photographed by them. For Hodson, as the photographs the girls had taken validated that they were "special people," and as he was also supposedly in the same class (after all, he "saw" fairies all the time), if he saw what the girls saw, then the photographs indirectly validated his status also.

In contrast to the blind faith shown by Gardner and Conan Doyle, the group of individuals concerned with various forms of "rational scientific analysis" used the photographs to validate their beliefs that, when attempting to identify fraud of any kind, scientific methods will always prevail. In essence, this is an extension of the "science versus superstition" debate, and we must presume that these people did not believe in the existence of fairies. Into this category we must place the Kodak and Ilford technicians, Geoffrey Crawley and James "The Amazing" Randi— although the latter also uses the photographs, as he does other "paranormal events," to validate his skepticism of the paranormal as well as his position as a professional debunker.

The odd person out in this group of "rational scientists" appears to be Snelling, who Gardner and Conan Doyle maintained supported their views as to the authenticity of the photographs. That does not mean to say that Snelling believed in fairies, or, for that matter, that he believed that these were pictures of fairies. Rather, he appears to have steered away from the issue—confining his comments to an analysis of the negative and prints, and to what he calls the "fairy figures"—a term which did not commit him to speculating if they were actual fairies or not. It must also be acknowledged that Snelling had a financial interest in the affair, in that it was he who provided photographs for Gardner to sell at his lectures (Crawley 1983e, 153). Perhaps Snelling considered that it may not have been good policy to "bite the hand that feeds" by categorically rejecting the authenticity of the photographs. Consequently, he chose his words carefully and reaped the rewards.

In Stewart Sanderson we see an individual who believes that fairies are part of folklore, and therefore do not exist. To that end, he is a confirmed skeptic who uses his arguments against the authenticity of the photographs in order to validate that fairylore is part of folklore. As such, he confirms what he already purports to know. This approach contrasts sharply with that of Joe Cooper who believes in fairies and the paranormal and who saw the Cottingley fairy photographs as validating his position. The subsequent confessions to him by Elsie and Frances, while removing his proof, appear not to have destroyed his belief in the existence of fairies (Cooper 1990, 139–51). Similarly, other observers were not shaken when the photographs turned out to be a hoax. As Leslie Shepard commented:

> Although the famous Cottingley fairy photographs are now known to be fakes, it would be premature to write off the fairies themselves as fraudulent (Shepard 61). . . .
>
> In the Cottingley case, the belief of Frances that she *did see* fairies as a child is obscured by the long drawn out controversy over the faked photographs and the complex motives and attitudes involved. Of course, the belief may be an honest fantasy of childhood, but her clear distinction between the real fairies and the faked photographs argues for genuineness. . . . For myself, I think the balance of evidence is that the fairies were real, even though the photographs were fakes. (Shepard 62)

Ever since the first publication of the photographs, the media has, in a sporadic way, followed every twist and turn of the Cottingley affair. As such, ". . . the story of the Cottingley fairies was only partly created by Elsie and Frances. It was much more the creation of the media" (Gettings 116). In addition, the media has functioned throughout as the equivalent of a tradition-bearer (Bird 289)—communicating beliefs, images and interpretations about both the existence of fairies, and the Cottingley fairy photographs per se, to an ever widening audience.

What would their reaction have been had they been told that the results of Elsie's first attempt would be shown in national newspapers around the world, that the echoes would reverberate down the years until, over a half century later, Elsie would been seen in three million homes around the country in two *Nationwide* interviews? That in 1979 it would be the subject of a 90-minute *Play for Today*—all on a yet uninvented medium called television? (Crawley 1982a, 1376).

In terms of individual involvements, it is difficult to say what motivated the editors of *The Strand Magazine* to originally publish these contributions. Possibly it was the financial incentive to be reaped by using Conan Doyle's name and reputation. Regardless, *The Strand Magazine* provided Conan Doyle with the opportunity to "report" on the Cottingley fairy photographs as if it was "factual" news. Upon publication, the media picked up and reported the story. While some of the coverage agreed with Conan Doyle that these were photographs of fairies, others, such as the *Westminster Gazette*, and more lately the *Nationwide* and *Calendar* television programs, chose to "expose" the affair through investigative reporting. On the other hand, some writers, for example, Maurice Hewlett, chose to "denounce" the photographs as obvious fakes, simply because they did not fit into their existing pattern of beliefs. Regardless of how the story was done, whether as the exposure of a fraud, or a simple pronouncement that the photographs were not genuine, the denigration of the authenticity of the photographs was used as an argument to validate the belief that fairies do not exist, and that the rationality of the press will always prevail.

Irrespective of the way in which the Cottingley fairy photographs have been used as a form of validation of individual beliefs over the years, here we can see elements of folklore, in terms of narratives, beliefs and even practical jokes, interfacing with technology—as exemplified by the photographs and the mass media coverage. This is a situation which is mirrored many times every day. To that extent, what took place at Cottingley in 1917, and the events which have followed, should not surprise us. The fact that the photographs are not genuine is of no great concern to us as folklorists. Instead, what is important is that the photographs became an "extraordinary event" in the lives of ordinary people, and as a consequence, the focus of much attention. In this manner, the photographs have provided countless people with an opportunity to discuss their beliefs about such matters as the existence of fairies, and paranormal photography (Permutt). To that end, the photographs, while drawing on folklore for inspiration, have subsequently created their own lore, and in turn, the debate has contributed in numerous ways to the fairylore tradition.

The funny thing is, none of this was ever supposed to happen. What began as a practical joke, got out of hand, and no one person is to blame. As Geoffrey Crawley put it:

> It is a tale of genuine persons of integrity across a wide band of the social structure of sixty and more years ago, who, by reason of their human

strengths, frailties and genuinely held beliefs, were inevitably drawn into a sequence of events whose chain reaction, once set in motion, could not be reversed. (Crawley 1982a, 1375).

References

Allen, Barbara. 1982. "The 'Image on Glass': Technology, Tradition, and the Emergence of Folklore." *Western Folklore* 41: 85–103.

Baker, Michael. 1978. *The* [Charles] *Doyle* [Pictorial] *Diary: The Last Great Conan Doyle Mystery.* London: Paddington P.

Baker, Ronald L. 1976. "The Influence of Mass Culture on Modern Legends." *Southern Folklore Quarterly* 40: 367–76.

Barlow, Fred. 1946. Review of *Fairies*, by E. Gardner. *Journal of the Society for Physical Research* 33: 203–4.

Bascom, William. 1965. "The Forms of Folklore: Prose Narratives." *Journal of American Folklore* 78: 3–20.

Bennett, Gillian. 1987. "The Rhetoric of Tradition." *Talking Folklore* 1.3 (1987): 32–46.

———. 1989. "Are Legends Narratives?" *Talking Folklore* 6: 1–13.

Bird, Donald Allport. 1976. "A Theory for Folklore in Mass Media: Traditional Patterns in the Mass Media." *Southern Folklore Quarterly* 40: 285–305.

Bord, Janet. 1985. "Cottingley Unmasked." *Fortean Times* 43: 48–53.

"Cape Town Link in a World Controversy: Startling Sequel to an *Argus* Article." 1922. *Cape Argus*, Magazine Section (25 November): 3.

Case, Geoffrey. 1978. "Play of the Week: 'Fairies'." *BBC Radio Times* (27 September): 57.

Cooper, Joe. 1981a. "The Case of the Cottingley Fairies." *The Unexplained* 20: 381–3.

———. 1981b. "The Reappearance of the Fairies." *The Unexplained* 21: 414–7.

———. 1981c. "The Cottingley Fairies Revisited." *The Unexplained* 21: 434–7.

———. 1983. "Cottingley: At Last the Truth." *The Unexplained* 117: 2338–40.

———. 1990. *The Case of the Cottingley Fairies.* London: Robert Hale.

Cox, Don Richard. 1985. *Arthur Conan Doyle.* New York: Frederick Ungar.

Crawley, Geoffrey. 1982a. "That Astonishing Affair of the Cottingley Fairies: Part One." *British Journal of Photography* 129 (24 December): 1375–80.

———. 1982b. "That Astonishing Affair of the Cottingley Fairies: Part Two." *British Journal of Photography* 129 (31 December): 1406–14.

———. 1983a. "That Astonishing Affair of the Cottingley Fairies: Part Three." *British Journal of Photography* 130 (7 January): 9–15.

———. 1983b. "That Astonishing Affair of the Cottingley Fairies: Part Four." *British Journal of Photography* 130 (21 January): 66–71.

———. 1983c. "That Astonishing Affair of the Cottingley Fairies: Part Five." *British Journal of Photography* 130 (28 January): 91–6.

———. 1983d. "That Astonishing Affair of the Cottingley Fairies: Part Six." *British Journal of Photography* 130 (4 February): 117–21.

———. 1983e. "That Astonishing Affair of the Cottingley Fairies: Part Seven." *British Journal of Photography* 130 (11 February): 142–5, 153, 159.

———. 1983f. "That Astonishing Affair of the Cottingley Fairies: Part Eight." *British Journal of Photography* 130 (18 February): 170–1.

——. 1983g. "That Astonishing Affair of the Cottingley Fairies: Part Nine." *British Journal of Photography* 130 (1 April): 332–8.

——. 1983h. "That Astonishing Affair of the Cottingley Fairies: Part 10—Conclusion(?)." *British Journal of Photography* 130 (8 April): 362–7.

Dégh, Linda, and Andrew Vázsonyi. 1971. "Legend and Belief." *Genre* 4.3: 281–304. Rpt. in *Folklore Genres*. Ed. Dan Ben-Amos. Austin: U of Texas P, 1976. 93–123.

"Do Fairies Exist? Investigation in a Yorkshire Valley." 1921. *Westminster Gazette* (12 January): 5.

Doyle, Arthur Conan. 1914. "Bimbashi Joyce." *Princess Mary's Gift Book*. London: Hodder and Stoughton. 23–30.

——. 1920. "Fairies Photographed: An Epoch-Making Event . . . " *Strand Magazine: An Illustrated Monthly* (December): 463–8.

——. 1921. "The Evidence for Fairies . . . With More Fairy Photographs." *Strand Magazine: An Illustrated Monthly* (March): 199–206.

——. 1922a. *The Coming of the Fairies*. London: Hodder and Stoughton.

——. 1922b. *The Case for Spirit Photography*. London: Hutchinson.

——. 1924. *Memories and Adventures*. London: Hodder and Stoughton.

——. 1926. *The History of Spiritualism*. 2 vols. London: Cassell and Co.

——. 1928. *The Coming of the Fairies*. London: The Psychic P.

——. 1929. *Our African Winter*. London: John Murray.

——. 1930. *The Edge of the Unknown*. London: John Murray.

"Fairy Story." 1978. *New Scientist* 79 (10 August): 427.

"A Fairy Sun-Bath: More Remarkable Photographs of Spirit Forms." 1921. *Westminster Gazette* (21 January): 5.

Gardner, Edward L. 1945. *Fairies: A Book of Real Fairies*. London: Theosophical Publishing House. Reprinted as *Fairies: The Cottingley Photographs and Their Sequel*. 2nd ed. London: Theosophical Publishing House, 1951; 3rd ed., 1957; 4th rev. ed. Introduction, Phoebe D. Bendit, 1966; rpt. 1972; rpt. 1974.

Gardner, Leslie. 1975. "Notes on Mr. S.F. Sanderson's Presidential Address, 21 March 1973, on 'The Cottingley Fairy Photographs.'" *Folklore* 86: 190–4.

Gelder, Dora van. 1977. *The Real World of Fairies*. Wheaton, Ill.: Theosophical Publishing House.

George, Philip Brandt. 1973. "The Folk Legend." *Introduction to Folklore*. Preliminary ed. Ed. Robert G. Adams. Columbus, Ohio: Collegiate Publishing. 11–8.

Gettings, Fred. 1982. "Once upon a Time. . . . " *The Unexplained* 116: 2318–20.

Gibson, John Michael and Richard Lancelyn Green, comps. 1986. *The Unknown Conan Doyle: Letters to the Press*. London: Secker and Warburg.

Goldstein, Diane. 1989. "Belief and Disbelief: Is Neutralism Really the Issue?: A Response." *Talking Folklore* 6: 64–6.

Hewlett, Maurice. 1920. "Fairies in Photographs." *John O' London's Weekly* 4 (18 December): 359.

Higham, Charles. 1976. *The Adventures of Conan Doyle: The Life of the Creator of Sherlock Holmes*. New York: W.W. Norton.

Hodson, Geoffrey. 1925. *Fairies at Work and Play*. London: Theosophical Publishing House.

Hufford, David. 1982. "Traditions of Disbelief." *New York Folklore* 8.3–4: 47–55. Rpt. in *Talking Folklore* 1.3 (1987): 19–31 with an "Author's Afterword."

———. 1990. "Rational Scepticism and the Possibility of Unbiased Folk Belief Scholarship." *Talking Folklore* 9: 19–33.

Inglis, Brian. 1985. "Fairies." *Fortean Times* 44: 3.

Judge, William Q. 1893. *The Ocean of Theosophy.* London: Theosophical Publishing.

Klintberg, Bengt Af. 1981. "Modern Migratory Legends in Oral Tradition and Daily Papers." *ARV* 37: 153–60.

Lamond, John. 1931. *Arthur Conan Doyle: A Memoir.* Port Washington, NY: Kennikat P.

Leadbeater, Charles. 1913. *The Hidden Side of Things.* 2 vols. Adyar, Madras and Benares: Theosophical Publishing House.

Lellenberg, Jon L., ed. 1987. *The Quest for Sir Arthur Conan Doyle.* Carbondale, Ill.: Southern Illinois UP.

Mitchell, Roger. 1979. "The Press, Rumor, and Legend Formation." *Midwestern Journal of Language and Folklore* 5: 5–61.

Noyes, Alfred. 1914. "A Spell for a Fairy." *Princess Mary's Gift Book.* London: Hodder and Stoughton. 101–4.

Oring, Elliott. 1990. "Legend, Truth, and News." *Southern Folklore* 47.2: 163–77.

Pearsall, Ronald. 1977. *Conan Doyle: A Biographical Solution.* New York: St. Martin's P.

Permutt, Cyril. 1988. *Photographing the Spirit World: Images from Beyond the Spectrum.* Wellingborough: Aquarian P.

"Photographs Confounded Conan Doyle: Cottingley Fairies a Fake, Woman Says." 1983. *The Times* (9 April).

Picknett, Lynn. 1987. *Flights of Fancy?: 100 Years of Paranormal Experiences.* New York, Ballantine Books.

Randi, James. 1980. *Flim-Flam!: Psychics, ESP, Unicorns and other Delusions.* New York: Lippincott and Crowell.

Ryan, Charles. 1975. *H. P. Blavatsky and the Theosophical Movement: A Brief Historical Sketch.* 2nd ed. 1937. Pasadena, Ca.: Theosophical U P.

"Sad Ending to Fairy Tale." 1983. *Yorkshire Evening Post* (March 19).

Sanderson, S.F. 1973. "The Cottingley Fairy Photographs: A Re-Appraisal of the Evidence." *Folklore* 84: 89–103.

Shepard, Leslie. 1985. "The Fairies Were Real." *Fortean Times* 44: 61–2.

Shiels, Doc. 1985. "Elsie and The Liddell People." *Fortean Times* 44: 60–1.

" Shooting Fairies." 1920. *John O' London's Weekly* 4 (25 December): 383.

Simpson, Jacqueline. 1988. "Belief and Disbelief: Is Neutralism Possible?" *Talking Folklore* 1.4: 12–6.

Smith, Paul S. 1975. "Tradition—A Perspective: Part 2—Transmission." *Lore and Language* 2.2: 5–14.

———. 1987. "Contemporary Legend and the Photocopy Revolution." *Perspectives on Contemporary Legend Volume II.* Eds. Gillian Bennett, Paul Smith, and J.D.A. Widdowson. Sheffield: Sheffield Academic P for the Centre for English Cultural Tradition and Language. 177–202.

Wallace, Edgar. 1921. "Fairies (by Clarkson)." *John O' London's Weekly* 4 (15 January): 483.

Wheelwright, J.E. 1921. "Fairies." *John O' London's Weekly* 4 (5 February): 567.

The Tooth Fairy:
Perspectives on Money and Magic[1]

Tad Tuleja

The loss of a milk or "baby" tooth evokes culturally stereotyped responses around the world, most of them involving ritualized disposal. In some areas the tooth is thrown toward the sun or onto a roof; in others it is buried, dropped into a crack, or eaten; not infrequently it is burned. Among the most common methods of disposal is for the tooth to be offered to an animal in the hopes of receiving a stronger tooth in return. In a contemporary North American variant of this exchange custom, children offer their shed teeth to the "Tooth Fairy."[2]

In the normative Tooth Fairy ritual, the child, following parental instructions, places the lost tooth under his pillow at night. Some children leave notes with the tooth, explaining the loss and requesting payment; others rely on the tooth alone to make the plea. Once the child is asleep, the parents replace the tooth with a gift or, more commonly, money. The child understands upon awakening that the Tooth Fairy has made the exchange. Variants of the custom stipulate that the tooth shall be placed in a glass of water or on a plate and that the child shall be rewarded only if he or she has been "good." This last variant suggests a parallel to the Santa Claus custom—as does the belief that the fairy will not come if the child stays awake in the hope of seeing her.[3]

As an embodiment of magical munificence, the Tooth Fairy is second only to the Christmas benefactor in the folklore of American childhood. Juvenile belief in the figure is as widespread and durable as belief in Saint Nick and the iconic elements of the accompanying ritual—the pillow, the unseen visitor, the transformation of the tooth into money—are as stereotyped in popular culture as the stocking by the chimney or flying reindeer.[4] So firmly entrenched has the Tooth Fairy become in juvenile fantasy life that discovering the "truth" about this shadowy benefactor constitutes a rite of passage out of innocence: to say that someone "still believes in the Tooth Fairy" metaphorically defines him as naive.

Yet while Santa Claus has not wanted for scholarly attention, the Tooth Fairy has been relatively neglected.[5] Psychologists have provided useful data on her place in children's cognitive development.[6] "Tooth

Figure 1. "Ms. America Tooth Fairy" by Sonja Carlborg, a tooth fairy 'beauty queen' whose American Dental Association banner and dental mirror suggest her association with modern dental practice. (Rosemary Wells)

Fairy consultant" Rosemary Wells has investigated popular representations and conducted pioneering surveys on custom details.[7] "Ethnodentist" William Carter and his colleagues have produced an extremely useful catalogue of dental folklore.[8] The contributions of folklorists however, have been scant. Leo Kanner's classic monograph on tooth lore does not mention the custom at all, while more recent studies by Granger and Tanner and later American researchers do so only in passing.[9] Although citations in American archives mention elements of the custom dating from early in this century,[10] the Tooth Fairy's genealogy, her development from folk belief to national custom and her contemporary social function all remain obscure. These three topics are the concern of this paper.

I. An Uncertain Genealogy

Relying on Katharine Brigg's standard work, Rosemary Wells concludes that the dental sprite is "America's only fairy"—a creature "never referred to in European literature," and equally absent from Old World folklore.[11] This is true if you are looking for her by name. Seek a "tooth fairy" in European indexes of folklore motifs and you will come away disappointed.[12] Nor are most Europeans familiar with the figure or the custom (Americanized Britain is an exception). The stylized ritual of pillow, tooth, and money seems not only American in origin, but of fairly recent vintage; archival evidence supports Wells's reasonable guess of about 1900 as a starting point.[13]

The spoor of the Tooth Fairy is weak, but European precursors, if not prototypes, do exist. In the absence of a clear line of descent, let me itemize those European beliefs and practices that invite comparison with the North American custom.

The Tooth Coin as "Fairy Gold"

Among the commonly cited attributes of fairies are their affluence and accompanying generosity; the pot at the end of the leprechauns' rainbow and the fairies' double payment of a debt to humans suggest a broad tradition of philanthropic pixies.[14] With this tradition in mind, Jacqueline Simpson once suggested that the Tooth Fairy exchange may derive from an Old British custom of rewarding industrious servant girls with "fairy" coins, left surreptitiously in their shoes as they slept.[15]

The structural similarities are clear enough—domestic hygiene is rewarded by a *mater familias* acting on behalf of a phantom donor—but one critical element, the lost tooth, is conspicuously absent. In addition, no evidence suggests a transition from shoe to pillow and the Tooth Fairy did not become widely known in England until the 1960s. This first candidate thus seems more a parallel than a precursor.

The Tooth as Propitiation or Self-Defense

Both Irish and British folk traditions are rich in stories of doleful pixie changelings: healthy infants who are exchanged in their cradles for sickly, inconsolable fairy look-alikes.[16] There are structural links between Tooth Fairy customs and folk practices designed to foil such kidnappers. Since teeth have long symbolized imperishability, they function worldwide as talismans against evil.[17] The tooth of a child, set near it as it sleeps, might be viewed, therefore, both as a form of preventive magic and more complexly, as a surrogate sacrifice—a *pars pro toto* offering for spirits who seek to snatch the child itself.

Two peculiarities of the Tooth Fairy ritual lend credence to this idea. One appears in the most common variant of the custom, in which the tooth is sprinkled with salt and placed near the bed, in a glass or on a plate. Salt—probably because of its "magical" preservative properties—has since antiquity symbolized purity, protection, and eternal life. Thus a salted tooth might serve, better than either an unsalted one or salt alone, as a bane against malevolent pixies.[18]

The second peculiarity is that other traditional forms of aversive magic also suggest the pillowed tooth. Iron has been used for centuries as a magical means of protection against evil—most commonly in the form of horseshoes, crucifixes, and knives. To guard sleeping children against evil fairies, one source suggests placing a knife under the pillow; Briggs implicitly links this custom to the Tooth Fairy when she cites a knife held in the mouth![19]

With regard to surrogate offerings, it may be noted that since at least the thirteenth century, Europeans have placated water spirits by sacrificing material goods in place of the children whom the spirits sought, often yearly, as their due; German custom recognized in particular the propitiatory value of coins and the children's own clothing.[20]

Since water spirits are seen as especially hazardous to children, it is interesting to observe that between one such spirit and the Tooth Fairy there is a suggestive linguistic connection. Lancashire's famous "nursery bogey," the "cannibal witch" Jenny Greenteeth, typically lurks in ponds, awaiting children, but in spite of—or perhaps because of—her gruesome nature, she is also sometimes used to elicit obedience ("Go to sleep now or Jenny Greenteeth will get you").[21] Vickery cites the practice in Lancashire families of encouraging toothbrushing by threatening children with Jenny Greenteeth. There is an aesthetic component to such threats, because the pond scum known as Lesser Duckweed (*Lemna minor*) is conventionally said to resemble green teeth.[22] As Wells has pointed out, modern dentists also enlist the Tooth Fairy for hygienic purposes and in some families the standard payment for a baby tooth is reduced by degrees for each cavity the tooth contains.[23]

The Italian "Tooth Fairy": Marantega

Throughout most of Italy, the Christmas season benefactor, corresponding to northern Europe's Saint Nicholas, goes by the name of Befana. Gaunt and toothless, she resembles the stock crone figure of popular legends, yet unlike other witches, she can be kindly to children; it is Befana, the Old One (*la Vecchia*) or the Witch (*la Strega*), who dispenses presents to the deserving at Epiphany.

The Venetian version of this witch, called Marantega, displays generosity not only at the Christmas season, but also when children lose teeth. A shed tooth is placed under the child's bed or under its pillow, and in the night Marantega—thinking perhaps, of her own toothlessness—exchanges it for a coin. Although there is no clear link between this Italian *strega* and the American fairy, on occasion the latter does appear as a witch. In a fearsome illustration for Joan Aiken's story "Clem's Dream," for example, she is the conventionally evil, scraggly-haired crone; here she takes not only children's teeth but their dreams. In a story by Nurit Karlin, the tooth collector is even called the Tooth Witch—complete with black robe, cone hat, and broomstick—until the job is taken over by her fairy apprentice.[24]

French Connections

Similarly isolated and similarly provocative parallels appear in French archival material. Recall that Wells has traced the American custom to about the turn of this century; there are accounts of at least two Gallic tooth rituals that are roughly contemporary. In the first, from 1887, the child puts the tooth beneath its pillow and the Virgin Mary exchanges it for money or a toy.[25] The second account, from 1902, cites a "good fairy" as the benevolent dental agent and the reward is candy, not money.[26]

Chronology favors these French connections, although the genealogy is hazy. In contemporary French tooth exchanges, it is a mouse, not a fairy, who takes the tooth; in a recent dictionary of French superstitions, the fairy agent is banished to uncivilized "Anglo-Saxon" countries.[27] Arguing for the link, perhaps, is the fact that French Canadian children today do offer their teeth to a *fée*.[28] Whether they adopted this custom from French relatives or English neighbors is not clear.

It is tempting to suggest one further French link. The Catholic patroness of toothache, Saint Apollonia, appears in conventional hagiography holding pincers—in martyring her, the Romans first pulled her teeth—and the universal saintly icon, palm fronds. In François Loux's stimulating volume *L'Ogre et la Dent*, a painting of the young woman holding these feathery boughs suggests a comparison to angelic (or fairy) wings.[29] Further research might determine whether this visual resemblance is mentioned elsewhere in the literature.

The Tooth Fairy and the "Tooth Mouse"

Finally, the folklore figure that I consider, in spite of surface dissimilarities, to be the best candidate for the title of tooth *Urfée*: the ubiquitous European "tooth mouse."

Shed teeth are offered to animals throughout Europe, with the commonest recipients being crows, other birds, and rodents. In the most widespread version of hole, behind furniture, or near the hearth or oven—and with a doggerel formula, asks the mouse to exchange it for a better one.[30]

Disciples of Max Müller in the 1920s saw this ritual as a survival of ancient offerings to fire gods. Imaginatively linking the mouse to the sun, they attempted to explain at one stroke the three commonest methods of tooth disposal: whether the child hurled the tooth into the air, threw it into the fire, or offered it to a mouse, the common element was sun worship.[31] In more recent, psychoanalytical interpretations, the mouse becomes a phallic symbol and the surrender ritual an act of compensation, both mirroring and dramatically resolving the Oedipal fantasy.[32]

Figure 2. A possible transition from tooth mouse to tooth fairy. From Mme. D'Aulnoy's eighteenth century tale "La Bonne Petite Souris," *The White Cat and Other Old French Fairy Tales*, ed. Rachel Field and illustrated by Elizabeth MacKinstry (New York: Macmillan, 1928).

As charmingly provocative as such readings may be, I would suggest, with a nod toward William of Occam, that the obvious reason for choosing a mouse is homeopathic. Whatever they may signify metaphorically, mice are undeniably small rodents with great incisors and the good sense to nest in warm, dark places. With magical logic, one surrenders teeth to these rodents in the hopes of getting better, that is rodentlike, teeth in return. The logic is preserved in the offering of teeth to hard beaked crows and in the belief (cited in both Europe and America) that you should never shed teeth where a dog, or a pig, might come upon them—unless you want dogs' or pigs' teeth in return.[33]

At first glance, the candidacy of the tooth mouse seems less probable than that of Jenny Greenteeth, the Virgin Mary or Marantega, but three factors bolster the mouse's case.

First, there is the range of the custom. The shilling in the shoe, Jenny Greenteeth, Marantega, even the visit from the Virgin, represent—to judge from the evidence—quite localized beliefs and family practices. The tooth mouse, on the other hand, ranges from the Baltic to the Mediterranean and also makes frequent appearances not only in North America, but also in Latin America, where it is widely known as "mouse Perez."[34] The sheer body of evidence allows for many intersections, on both sides of the Atlantic, where the mouse could, in effect, have sprouted wings.

Second, there are hints in exchange formulas that hard molars and hard cash can be confused. In most formulas, the child asks the mouse for a "better" tooth and sometimes for a "tooth of iron." Occasionally, however, the child demands a more *valuable* tooth—one made of silver or gold.[35] From iron tooth to gold tooth to gold itself requires only a modest leap of logic.

Third, not only is there evidence, as we have seen, of the switch from mouse to fairy in nineteenth-century France, but there is also what Carter lucidly calls a "credible mechanism" for explaining the shift.[36] That mechanism, first identified by Loux, is a popular fairy tale, "La Bonne Petite Souris," by Madame D'Aulnoy at the beginning of the eighteenth century and reprinted in 1837. In this tale, a nameless "good queen," imprisoned by a nameless "bad king," befriends a mouse that is impressed with her kindness. The creature turns out to be a fairy and she not only frees the queen from her imprisonment, but also knocks out the wicked king's teeth, hides under his pillow to torment him and eventually has him assassinated by his palace guard. A 1928 translation of the D'Aulnoy story depicts the fairy quite explicitly as a smiling rodent—with wings.[37]

Does this prove that the Tooth Fairy was once a mouse? No, but with range, chronology and that "credible mechanism" on its side, it is the most "qualified" of the various candidates. Interestingly, three modern children's authors seem to agree. Fran and Frank McAllister's 1976 "history" of the Tooth Fairy uses the same mouse-to-fairy plot element as

D'Aulnoy; in Lucy Bate's popular *Little Rabbit's Loose Tooth*, the fairy is a rabbit with wings; and in Stephen Kroll's *Loose Tooth*, the children and the fairy (that is, their parents) are bats—like the conventional Tooth Fairy, winged and nocturnal.[38]

II. From Folk Belief to National Custom

Tooth fairies made appearances in the United States as early as the turn of this century and the archival evidence shows that informants who had grown up in the 1920s and 1930s were familiar with the pillow ritual, but the agent of exchange in this period was not commonly known as "the Tooth Fairy," or even as *a* tooth fairy. The reward for shed teeth came from such nonspecializing benefactors as "the fairy," "the fairies," "the good fairy," "the fairy princess," and "the fairy queen."[39] The national stereotype of a single dental fairy only became established after the Second World War.

The term "tooth fairy" is first indexed in popular literature in 1949, when a Lee Rogow story by that title appeared in *Collier's* magazine. Wells takes this as evidence that the custom was by then well established; an alternate explanation would be that the story spurred, rather than merely registered, a developing tradition. In both North America and Great Britain, the stereotype did not achieve popularity until the 1950s; Wells observes that not until 1979 did the custom find its way into "general interest" scholarship.[40]

Why mid-century? Why this sudden spurt to prominence of a long practiced but by no means "codified" folk tradition? Or, to phrase it as a query about genre, What transforms the Tooth Fairy ritual, in the decade or so just after World War II, from a relatively obscure folk belief into a national custom? I would suggest that three significant factors were postwar affluence, a child-directed family culture, and media encouragement.

Postwar Affluence

While researching this paper, I asked my father-in-law, who grew up in rural Arkansas in the 1920s and 1930s, whether his family had practiced the Tooth Fairy custom. "We were too poor," he told me. "Nickels were hard to come by. You certainly wouldn't waste one on a tooth."

This telling comment may be representative. Jacqueline Simpson once surmised that before the 1960s in Great Britain, wealthy households may have observed the tooth exchange custom, but that poorer ones could not afford to.[41] That is a useful speculation about America too. It seems likely that the greater availability of discretionary income during the postwar boom may have facilitated the spread of the custom.

The Cult of the Child

Childhood understood as a distinct and distinctly honored phase of life is a fairly recent development.[42] The idea of catering to one's child, as the *raison d'être* of the family unit, is newer still. It enjoyed a heyday in the 1950s, when the public canonized James Dean for being misunderstood and all "good" parents knew—because Dr. Spock told them so—that their proper role was to serve their children's needs, among them the need to fantasize and to feel loved. The dominance of this new, child-centered view of the family made the 1950s fertile ground for what Wells calls "a symbolic ritual of replacement, born in sympathy, propelled in love and sustained in warmth and care."[43]

Media Encouragement

In his survey of European fairy traces in the New World, Wayland Hand identified publication as a significant factor in the consolidation of folk traditions.[44] The history of the Grimm brothers' tales, the dime novelists' Billy the Kid, and the stock Santa Claus created by Clement Moore and Thomas Nast, bear out his observation. Popular literature—including Rogow's 1949 story and juvenile treatments of the belief appearing from the 1960s on—may have helped to standardize and spread the Tooth Fairy custom.[45]

An even more likely standardizing factor than print, however, was film. Probably it is not mere coincidence that the decade immediately preceding the proliferation of the Tooth Fairy custom saw the release of four feature films in which female "good people" played central roles. In 1939, there was Billie Barnes, as a shimmering Glinda, the Good Witch of the North, in a modern fairy tale, *The Wizard of Oz*. A year later saw the Walt Disney version of Carlo Collodi's *Pinocchio*, in which "The Blue Fairy" served as *dea ex machina*. In Disney's 1950 *Cinderella*, the ash girl was rewarded for her selflessness by a "fairy godmother" who, like D'Aulnoy's character, worked magic with mice. And in 1953, the most diminutive and stereotypical of media fairies, Tinkerbell, was saved from death by the eternal boy in *Peter Pan*. All of these films reached massive audiences, not only upon general release, but also in television presentations; it is likely that they helped to "nationalize" the folk custom.[46] Archival evidence supports the conjecture, for beginning in the 1950s, informants confuse and in some cases consciously identify, the

Figure 3. "The Tooth Fairy" by **Ann Tegen Hill**, is an excellent example of the conventionally pretty, winged, female fairy as codified by postwar Disney films. (Rosemary Wells)

Tooth Fairy with "the blue fairy," "the fairy godmother," "a small tinkerbell," "a Peter Pan with wings," and "the good witch from the Wizard of Oz."[47]

The films may also have helped to establish the Tooth Fairy's gender—a feature that remains highly stereotyped in popular understanding. Wells has collected several examples of male, non-gendered and even non-anthropomorphic tooth fairies, but the Hollywood image still predominates: seventy-four percent of Wells's tally considered the figure to be female.[48]

III. From Magic to Money

Functional analyses of the Tooth Fairy custom, thus far, have been provided only by developmental psychologists. Typically, they have interpreted the domestic ritual as a psychodrama of fantasy management or of condolence.[49] Parental attitudes toward the custom are consistent with this domicentric approach. In Wells's Tooth Fairy survey of over 2000 participants, the principal reasons given for continuing the practice were that it gave the parents pleasure, gave the child pleasure, or made the loss of the tooth less painful. Other respondents cited the child's own expectations or the model established by "other parents."[50] Such perspectives illuminate the ritual from the inside; they do not explain its social utility or the manner in which the transformation of tooth into money validates specific economic behavior.

That behavior, clearly, is open market exchange; the unstated subtext of the Tooth Fairy ritual is "produce and sell." This message stands in sharp, and one might say progressive, contrast to the "anal" message of non-exchange economies—"produce and hoard." The more static formula was evident in those Nordic societies that presented "tooth fees" to children for *cutting* teeth.[51] This is an appropriate reward in a hoarding economy, where the mere possession of goods is a sign of worth.

Not so in more fluid economies, where it is the surrender of goods that drives the system—first according to the principle of reciprocity, then according to the more rationalized homeostasis of monetization.[52] What begins as barter or gift exchange becomes, with the introduction of money, the more organized system of "standard value." So the *quid pro quo* of a tooth for a tooth (even a gold or iron tooth for a bone one) ultimately gives way to cash payment. That is marketplace logic and it is the social lesson that parents teach their children when they direct them to place teeth under a pillow.

Three peculiarities of the custom underscore this observation. First, the Tooth Fairy custom, like any other free market ritual, is affected by broad market forces. Nothing better shows how the ritual reflects economic trends than tooth exchange inflation. Between 1900 and 1975, Wells has estimated, the average amount of money paid for a lost tooth rose from twelve to eighty-five cents.[53] That is still a relatively modest sum, but if the ritual were as innocent of commercial ramifications as is often supposed, one might expect less inflationary impact. That the fairy's payment rises consistently with wages and prices suggests how clearly the custom replicates the macro-economy.

Second, the inflationary spiral is also "micro-determined," by competition among children for greater rewards. As the Lee Rogow story suggested as early as 1949, one factor in the pricing of children's teeth is "wage pressure" from the young "suppliers" of teeth. A recent cartoon by Lynn Johnston makes the point clearly. A little girl, showing her mother a quarter, hopes for a different "toof fairy" next time. Why? "'Cause the one that went to Melody's house gave her fifty cents." Dismay on the mother's face betokens a promise that future payments will be up to market levels.[54]

Third, the tooth rite is by all evidence an adult creation. Surveys agree that supervising parents, not siblings or peers, typically tell their children about the fairy; furthermore, only one in five parents continues the practice because children expect or demand it.[55] Little wonder. The exchange principle is not inherent; it must be learned. The appropriate teachers are caring parents, who understand the economy and can introduce, in a pleasant fiction, its basic rules.

To be sure, parents do not teach the economic model in a calculating, or even conscious fashion. On the contrary, they may take considerable care to disguise the monetary nature of the transaction. The most common amounts left by the fairy, even in 1983, were still the nominal quarter and dime. Children are commonly given to understand that the fairy magically "changes" their teeth into money rather than "exchanging" or "buying" them. She uses the teeth not as commodities but in equally magical or philanthropic ways; they are given to toothless old people or to newborns; they become the wall of her castle, or scattered stars. One ingenious mother from San Antonio leaves her child not "ordinary" exchangeable coins, but glitter decorated ones. Other parents rent the services of Tooth Fairy impersonators, bringing the "magic" of the custom to life in children's bedrooms.[56]

These attempts to purge the fairy custom of monetary implications recall a similar "decontamination" of Christmas customs. In his survey of theories regarding the meaning of Santa Claus, Hagstrom notes that the use of the Christmas elf as surrogate gift bringer allows parents to express "morally uncontaminated sentiments toward children"—that is, to give without the implied "threat" of reciprocity. Waits, in a fine dissertation on Christmas gifts, shows how gift wrapping offsets the "taint" of store bought-goods. And Caplow, studying Christmas gifts and kin networks, suggests that the commercial efflorescence of the American Christmas serves to bolster "important but insecure" relationships.[57] In all of these studies, one sees the parental need to divest a "magical money" event of its economic features.

Zelizer has portrayed the lesson in a broader context. Toward the end of the nineteenth century, she writes, American children began to undergo a process of "sacralization," and to occupy "a separate noncommercial place, *extra-commercium*," in which their economic and sentimental values were "declared to be radically incompatible." But the transformation of the child from a "useful" into a "priceless" family member did not come easily. Sentiment and economics would not stay neatly asunder and so parents had continually to be on guard against a fearful "monetization of the home." The "culturally invented boundary between wage and allowance" proved particularly difficult to maintain, as it was threatened on the one hand by payment for chores and on the other by the tendency to use allowance as a reward for good behavior.[58]

Zelizer's sophisticated analysis helps to illuminate the relationship between the "caring" and the "counting" aspects not only of allowance, but of the Tooth Fairy ritual as well. Just as the family treatment of "priceless" children reflected a tension between sentiment and necessity, so contemporary tooth exchanges reflect an uneasy amalgam of parental affection, parental control, and ubiquitous (if invisible) market pressures. In an economy where the ultimate magic is the power of money, the responsible parent ironically prepares the child for reality by encouraging a fantasy that Wells appropriately calls "a reassuring image of good capitalist values."[59]

Thus magic, whose essence is transformation, is itself transformed. We move from an image of the generic "good" fairy, turning bone teeth into nominal nickels, toward a specialist "tooth" fairy, predictably exchanging molars at the market rate. With the encouragement of mortgage-carrying parents, children now grow more than mere teeth; they "grow" the system by putting their own "products" on the market. That professional impersonators and "Tooth Fairy pillow" manufacturers have turned the ritual into personal profit only underlines the system's genius at turning wishes into coin of the realm.

The process of market cooption has long been understood with regard to the internationally successful figure of Santa Claus. Erich Wolf has aptly, if somewhat cynically, described him as the embodiment of the free market paradigm: "If you are good, you will receive goods."[60] The Tooth Fairy holds a shorter and less visible pedigree but her macroeconomic function, in today's society, differs only in degree. The Tooth Fairy is commonly seen as more personal and surely less commercialized than the American Santa. As the economic subtext of her ritual suggests, however, she can also be viewed as more rationalized. Santa, after all, still brings presents, while the Tooth Fairy translates everything into cash. Santa Claus's promise is pre-monetary; goodness gets you Barbies or a Rambo doll. The Tooth Fairy's promise is more modern; anything, even your own body, can be turned into gold. That, in its final reductive wisdom, is precisely the vaunted magic of free enterprise.

Notes

1. An earlier version of this essay was delivered at the centennial meeting of the American Folklore Society in Philadelphia, October 18, 1989. I am thankful to all those who commented on my presentation, and especially to York University's Carole Carpenter, who sent me information on Canadian tooth fairy beliefs from the Ontario Folklore-Folklife Archive (Carpenter). Thanks also to Karen Pouliot of the Northwestern University Dental School Library for information on Rosemary Wells's work; and to Dr. Wells herself, not only for her pioneering research, but also for sharing stories and illustrations from her collection of "tooth fairiana." Finally, my appreciation to George Carey, for encouraging my interest in folklore and for introducing me to the University of Massachusetts Folklore Archive.

2. For surveys of tooth disposal customs, see Carter et al.; Granger; Kanner; Rooth; Svanberg.

3. Wells (1983b) found that five percent of her respondents practiced the "pillow burial" variant; recollections of my New Jersey childhood and materials from Ontario (Carpenter) and Massachusetts (Krantz) confirm its general popularity. Use of the tooth fairy as an incentive to sleep and to "be good" is also cited in the Ontario and Massachusetts archives; cf. Widdowson 129–30.

4. Prentice et al. discovered in a 1978 survey of sixty young children that only two had *not* been left money by the tooth fairy. Of the over 2000 respondents in one survey (Wells 1983b), eighty-eight percent favored continuing the custom.

5. The reason is obvious enough. Unlike the tooth fairy, Santa Claus has been stereotyped for a century and a half thanks to Clement Moore's 1822 poem and Thomas Nast's later illustrations. For discussions of the Santa Claus custom, see Barnett (especially chapter 2); Hagstrom; Coffin (chapter 4); Sansom; Sereno; Wolf.

6. See Blair et al.; Prentice et al.; Scheibe and Condry.

7. See Wells. The results of her most exhaustive survey appear in her July 1983 *cal* report.

8. The work by Carter et al. is a comprehensive and intelligently annotated compendium; tooth fairies are discussed on 77–82.

9. See Kanner; Granger; Tanner.

10. Tooth fairies are mentioned, by function if not by name, in Brown; Cannon; Hyatt; Puckett 1981. The earliest citation is 1900 (Cannon no. 701).

11. Wells 1980. Rooth, in an interesting analysis of Cleveland practices, concurs that the tooth fairy is "American." It would be more accurate to say "North American," for—as Carpenter's Ontario material shows—the fairy is widely popular with Canadian as well as United States children.

12. Stith Thompson does not mention a tooth fairy, nor do Leach, MacCulloch, or the standard French, German, and Italian superstition collections.

13. Wells 1980.

14. See Stith Thompson, F342; Froud and Lee; Hand, 143.

15. Simpson is cited in Hand. Creighton and Wright also mention the custom as British; Svanberg located it in Mexico.

16. On changelings, see Stith Thompson, F321 and Briggs 1980, 1981, and the essays in this volume by Susan Schoon Eberly and Joyce Munro.

17. The indestructibility of the teeth is mentioned as far back as Pliny. See also Frazer; Kanner; Hoffmann-Krayer and Bachtold-Stäubli; Lindsay; Samson.

19. On salt as a prophylactic against evil see Frazer; Jones; Thompson F384.1; Briggs 1981; Harland; Henderson; Puckett 1926; Coffin and Cohen. The salted tooth left next to the bed is mentioned by Opie and Opie; Radford and Radford; Granger; Waring. When teeth are burned, they are also salted first, to guard their owner against "witches" (Radford and Radford) or "unfriendly persons" (Randolph).

19. On horseshoes, see Lawrence. Froud and Lee mention the knife under the pillow; Briggs 1981, the knife held in the mouth; Puckett 1926 (159) notes the black American belief that a fork under the pillow will protect the sleeper from being ridden by nightmares.

20. For dangerous *Wassergeister*, see Hoffmann-Krayer and Bachtold-Stäubli 9: 166 ff.; and the Grimms, legend nos. 49, 75, and 60–7. Donald Ward's instructive commentary to the Grimms discusses surrogate offerings; cf. Hoffmann-Krayer and Bachtold Stäubli 9: 179. For British water sprites, see Rabuzzi. For similarly dangerous fairies in Newfoundland see Widdowson 124 ff.

21. The concept of "nursery bogey" or "warning fiction" is discussed by Briggs (1980, 1981).

22. For the *Lemna minor* connection, and the use of Jenny Greenteeth as a spur to hygiene, see Vickery. Simpson 1987 (65) cites the conventional warning: "If you don't go to sleep, Jenny Greenteeth will get you."

23. Cited in Munro 46. See also Krantz; Wells 1983c. A modern "tooth fairy" entrepreneur also encourage"s dental hygiene, even carrying a giant toothbrush as a "sceptre." See "Brushing Up."

24. For Marantega: see Riegler 1920 and 1923–24; Negelein; Pitrè. See also Aiken; Karlin.

25. Daleau 35.

26. The 1902 "candy fairy" is cited by Carter et al. 78.

27. See Lasne and Gaultier.

28. See Des Ruisseaux 15.

29. The painting in Loux is by the seventeenth century artist Francisco Zurbarán.

30. Cross-cultural examples of tooth offerings to animals appear in Carter; Rooth; Svanberg; Lewis. For German variants of the *Zahnmaus* custom, see Kanner 50. Carter et al. conflate the hearth or stove mouse with the German "oven man," suggesting the latter as a "folkloristic predecessor of tooth fairy rituals." The conflation is not unreasonable, since a German tradition does anthropomorphize the tooth mouse as *Ofenmann* (Hoffmann-Krayer and Bachtold-Staübli 6: 1194). Cf. Cannon no. 701, where teeth are placed in the oven so the fairies can exchange them for money; and Krantz, who found evidence of teeth being placed on thermostats and radiators.

31. The most elaborate presentation of the sun worship reading is by Lindsay. For European examples, see also Frazer; Negelein; Riegler; Lewis; Samson; Kanner.

For Mesoamerican examples, see Tibon. Dorson's 1955 essay remains the definitive critique of the Müller hypothesis.

32. See Lewis; Russell.

33. The fear of acquiring animal teeth through carelessness is mentioned by Henderson; Randolph; Johnson and Withers; Radford and Radford. It also appears in the European and American archives. The homeopathic explanation was first popularized by Frazer.

34. Examples appear in all archives and are placed in context in Svanberg; Rooth.

35. The best discussions of formulas are Svanberg's and Rooth's. MacCulloch (149) cites an unusual inversion in which the child requests a bone tooth in exchange for gold.

36. Carter et al. 78.

37. The illustration is the endpiece to the 1928 Planche translation.

38. See McAllister and McAllister; Bate; Kroll.

39. See Cannon; Puckett 1981.

40. Wells 1980 identifies Alan Dundes's article on "Fairy" in the 1979 *World Book* as giving the first "general interest" notice of the tooth fairy.

41. Cited in Hand 148. Wells 1980 also lists financial status as an influence on the adoption of the custom.

42. See Aries and for a treatment of nineteenth-century developments, Zelizer.

43. Cited in Dent.

44. Hand 141.

45. For surveys of the juvenile literature see Wells 1980 and 1983a.

46. Carter et al. also cite the possible influence of film.

47. The tooth agent as fairy godmother appears in Ontario (Carpenter); Puckett 1981, nos. 1468 and 1472; Cannon no. 704. As the blue fairy, she appears in Cannon no. 703; Rooth 67. Krantz's sources cited Tinkerbell and Peter Pan.

48. Wells 1983b.

49. See Blair et al.; Prentice et al.; Scheibe and Condry; Wells 1980.

50. Wells 1983b.

51. The Nordic *tann-fé* (tooth fee) is mentioned in the *Oxford English Dictionary*, MacCulloch; Kanner 45.

52. The classic statement of "reciprocity" is given by Mauss.

53. Wells 1983b.

54. The Johnston cartoon appeared as a United Press Syndicate feature on March 4, 1988.

55. Wells 1983b. Blair et al. say that the tooth fairy custom needs "more parental involvement to support than belief in the Easter Bunny or Santa Claus" (694). Prentice et al. reported that ninety-seven percent of their sample of parents actively encouraged their children's belief, even when they were convinced that the child already knew the truth. For a pathological example of parental concern over children's teeth, see Russell.

56. Figures on the "nominal quarter and dime," as well as the distinction between "changing" and "exchanging," are in Wells 1983b. Theories on the fairy's use of the teeth appear throughout the literature; see especially Cannon no. 703; Carpenter; Krantz; McAllister and McAllister. I am indebted to Jan Harold Brunvand for sending me a "Heloise" newspaper column on the Texas mother's "glittered" coins. For an example of tooth fairy impersonation, see "Brushing Up."

57. Hagstrom; Waits; Caplow.

58.   Zelizer; on allowance see 97–112.
59.   Cited in Munro 45.
60.   Wolf 153.

References

Aiken, Joan. 1988. *The Last Slice of Rainbow and Other Stories*. New York: Harper and
    Row.
Aries, Philippe. 1965. *Centuries of Childhood. A Social History of Family Life*. New
    York: Random House.
Barnett, James H. 1954. *The American Christmas*. New York: Macmillan.
Bate, Lucy. 1975. *Little Rabbit's Loose Tooth*. New York: Crown.
Blair, J.R., J.S. McKee and L.F. Jernigan. 1980. "Children's Belief in Santa Claus,
    Easter Bunny, and Tooth Fairy." *Psychological Reports* 46: 691–4.
Briggs, Katharine. 1980. "Some Unpleasant Characters among British Fairies."
    Folklore Studies in the Twentieth Century. Ed. Venetia Newall. Woodbridge,
    Suffolk: Brewer.
———. 1981. *An Encyclopedia of Fairies*. New York: Pantheon.
Brown, Frank C. 1961. *The Frank C. Brown Collection of North Carolina Folklore*, vol. 6,
    "Popular Beliefs and Superstitions." Ed. Wayland Hand. Durham, NC:
    Duke UP.
"Brushing Up on her Bedside Manner, a California Woman Takes the Bite out of
    Losing a Tooth." 1984. *People* 21 (March 21): 101.
Cannon, Anthon S. 1984. *Popular Beliefs and Superstitions from Utah*. Ed. Wayland
    Hand and Jeannine Talley. Salt Lake City: U of Utah P.
Caplow, T. 1982. "Christmas Gifts and Kin Networks." *American Sociological Review*
    47.3: 383–92.
Carpenter, Carole H., comp. 1990. "A Selection of Tooth Fairy Beliefs from the
    Ontario Folklore-Folklife Archive." Correspondence (March 18).
Carter, William, Bernard Butterworth and Joseph Carter. 1987. *Ethnodentistry and
    Dental Folklore*. Overland Park, Kansas: Dental Folklore Books of Kansas
    City.
Coffin, Tristram P. 1973. *The Book of Christmas Folklore*. New York: Seabury.
Coffin, Tristram P. and Hennig Cohen, eds. 1966. *Folklore in America*. Garden City:
    Doubleday.
Creighton, Helen. 1968. *Bluenose Magic: Popular Beliefs and Superstitions in Nova
    Scotia*. Toronto: Ryerson P.
Daleau, François. 1889. *Notes pour servir l'étude des traditions, croyances, et
    superstitions de la Gironde*. Bordeaux: A. Bellier.
D'Aulnoy, Mme. la Contesse. 1928. *The White Cat and Other Old French Fairy Tales*.
    Trans. M. Planche. New York: Macmillan.
Dent, Penelope. 1981. "In Search of the Elusive Tooth Fairy." *Woman's Day*
    (December 16).
Des Ruisseaux, Pierre. 1973. *Croyances et pratiques populaires au Canada français*.
    Montréal: Editions du Jour.
Dorson, Richard M. 1955. "The Eclipse of Solar Mythology." *Journal of American
    Folklore* 68: 394–416.

Frazer, Sir James. 1951. *The Golden Bough*. New York: Macmillan.

Froud, Brian, and Alan Lee. 1978. *Fairies*. New York: Abrams.

Granger, Byrd H. 1961. "Of the Teeth." *Journal of American Folklore* 74: 47–56.

Grimm, Jacob and Wilhelm. 1981. *The German Legends of the Brothers Grimm*. Ed. and trans. Donald Ward. Philadelphia: Institute for the Study of Human Issues.

Hagstrom, Warren O. 1966. "What Is the Meaning of Santa Claus?" *American Sociologist* 1.5: 248–52.

Hand, Wayland D. 1981. "European Fairy Lore in the New World." *Folklore* 92.2: 141–8.

Harland, John. 1873. *Lancashire Legends*. London: George Routledge.

Henderson, William. 1879. *Notes on the Folklore of the Northern Counties of England and the Borders*. London.

Hoffmann-Krayer, E., and Hanns Bachtold-Staübli, eds. 1934–35. *Handwörterbuch des deutschen Aberglaubens*. Berlin and Leipzig: de Gruyter.

Hyatt, Harry M. 1965. *Folklore from Adams County, Illinois*. 2nd rev. ed. New York: Alma Egan Hyatt Foundation.

Johnson, Clifton, and Carl Withers, eds. 1963. *What They Say in New England*. New York: Columbia UP.

Jones, Ernest. 1964 (1912). "The Symbolic Significance of Salt in Folklore and Superstition." *Essays in Applied Psychoanalysis*. New York: International Universities.

Kanner, Leo. 1928. *Folklore of the Teeth*. New York: Macmillan.

Karlin, Nurit. 1985. *The Tooth Witch*. New York: Lippincott.

Krantz, Stephanie L. 1988. "The Toothfairy: From Superstition to Modern Custom." Unpublished paper. University of Massachusetts Folklore Archives.

Kroll, Steven. 1984. *Loose Tooth*. New York: Holiday House.

Lasne, Sophie, and Andre Gaultier. 1984. *A Dictionary of Superstitions*. Trans. Amy Reynolds. Englewood Cliffs: Prentice-Hall.

Lawrence, Robert Means. 1968 (1898). *The Magic of the Horseshoe*. Detroit: Singing Tree P.

Leach, Maria. 1984. *Standard Dictionary of Folklore, Mythology, and Legend*. New York: Harper and Row.

Lewis, Harvey. 1958. "The Effect of Shedding the First Deciduous Tooth upon the Passing of the Oedipus Complex of the Male." *Journal of the American Psychoanalytical Association* 6.1: 5–37.

Lindsay, Lillian. 1933. "The Sun, the Saint, and the Toothdrawer." *British Dental Journal* 5: 453–65.

———. 1934. "Influence of the Sun on the Teeth." *Journal of the American Dental Association* 21: 616–22.

Loux, François. 1981. *L'ogre et la dent*. Paris: Berger-Levrault.

McAllister, Fran and Frank McAllister. 1976. *The Tooth Fairy Legend*. Dallas: Taylor.

MacCulloch, John, ed. 1964 (1930). *The Mythology of All Races*. New York: Cooper Square.

Mauss, Marcel. 1967. *The Gift*. New York: Norton.

Munro, Mark. 1981. "They Believe in the Tooth Fairy." *Boston Globe* (July 15).

Negelein, Julius v. 1923/24. "Zahnwechsel und Mythus." *Archiv für Religionswissenschaft* 23: 357.

Opie, Peter, and Iona Opie. 1959. *The Lore and Language of Schoolchildren*. Oxford UP.

424   *Tad Tuleja*

Pitrè, Giuseppe. 1893. "La Befana in Italia." *Archivo per lo studio delle tradizioni popolari* 12.
Prentice, Norman M., Martin Manosevitz, and Laura Hubbs. 1978. "Imaginary Figures of Early Childhood: Santa Claus, Easter Bunny, and the Tooth Fairy." *American Journal of Orthopsychiatry* 48.4: 618–28.
Puckett, Newbell Niles. 1926. *Folk Beliefs of the Southern Negro*. Chapel Hill: U of North Carolina P.
———. 1981. *Popular Beliefs and Superstitions*. Ed. Wayland Hand, Anna Casetta, and Sondra Thiederman. Boston: G.K. Hall.
Rabuzzi, Daniel Allen. 1984. "In Pursuit of Norfolk's Hyter Sprites." *Folklore* 95.1: 74–89.
Radford, Edwin, and Mona Radford. 1949. *Encyclopedia of Superstitions*. New York: Philosophical Library.
Randolph, Vance. 1947. *Ozark Superstitions*. New York: Columbia UP.
Riegler, Richard. 1920. "Venezianische 'Marantega' und Verwandtes." *Archivum Romanicum* 4.4: 490–2.
———. 1923–24. "Zahnwechsel und Mythus." *Archiv für Religionswissenschaft* 23: 162–3.
Rogow, Lee. 1949. "The Tooth Fairy." *Colliers* 124: 26.
Rooth, Anna. 1982. *Offering of the First Tooth*. Uppsala: Ethnological Institute.
Russell, Claire. 1980. "A Study in the Folk Symbolism of Kinship: the Tooth Image." *Folklore Studies in the Twentieth Century*. Ed. Venetia Newall. Woodbridge, Suffolk: Brewer.
Samson, Edward. 1939. *The Immortal Tooth*. London: John Lane.
Sansom. William. 1968. *A Book of Christmas*. New York: McGraw-Hill.
Scheibe, Cyndy, and John Condry. 1987. "Developmental Differences in Children's Reasoning about Santa Claus and Other Fantasy Characters." Paper presented to the Biennial Conference of the Society for Research in Child Development, Baltimore, April 23–27.
Simpson, Jacqueline. 1973. *The Folklore of Sussex*. London: Batsford.
———. 1987. *European Mythology*. New York: Peter Bedrick.
Svanberg, Ingvar. 1987. "The Folklore of Teeth Among Turkic and Adjacent Peoples." *Central Asiatic Journal* 321.1–2: 111–37.
Tanner, Jeri. 1968. "The Teeth in Folklore." *Western Folklore* 27.2: 97–105.
Tibon, Gutierre. 1972. *El mundo secreto de los dientes*. Mexico: Editoria Tajin.
Vickery, Roy. 1983. "*Lemna minor* and Jenny Greenteeth." *Folklore* 94.2: 247–50.
Waits, William. "The Many-Faceted Custom: Christmas Gift-Giving in America." Unpublished dissertation, Rutgers University.
Waring, Philippa. 1978. *A Dictionary of Omens and Superstitions*. London: Souvenir P.
Wells, Rosemary. 1980. *The Tooth Fairy*. Ed. Susan Bohn. Stevens Point, Wisconsin: private printing.
———. 1982. "Tooth Fairy Update." *cal* 45.12 (June): 6–9.
———. 1983 (a,b,c,). "Tracking the Tooth Fairy." A three-part report. *cal* 46.12 (June): 1–8; *cal* 47.1 (July): 18–26; *cal* 47.2 (August): 25–31.
Widdowson, J.D.A. 1977. *If You Don't Be Good: Verbal Social Control in Newfoundland*. Institute of Social and Economic Research. Social and Economic Studies No. 21. St. John's: Memorial U of Newfoundland.
Wolf, Eric. 1964. "Santa Claus: Notes on a Collective Representation." *Process and Pattern in Culture*. Ed. Robert Manners. Chicago: Aldine.

Wright, Elizabeth Mary. 1913. *Rustic Speech and Folklore*. London: Oxford.
Zelizer, Viviana A. 1985. *Pricing the Priceless Child: The Changing Social Value of Children*. New York: Basic Books.

The Making of an Icon:
The Tooth Fairy in North American Folklore and Popular Culture

Rosemary Wells

How does it happen that belief in a recognized fantasy figure in American life can be viewed, on one hand, as muddled thinking, and on the other hand be considered "a valuable myth"?

Such was the case when William Melton, in the newsletter *West of Wall Street*, said of some spurious thinking in the book he was reviewing, that "if you believe that, you probably believe in the tooth fairy too." And psychologist Julius Segal, addressing adult readers in the national magazine *Parents*, maintained that the Tooth Fairy, along with Santa Claus and the Easter Bunny, are all "important symbols to children . . . magic myths [which] have a very important place in the early years of childhood" (Davidowitz).

The operative words here are "childhood," "magic myths," and "Tooth Fairy." Even though Santa Claus and the Easter Bunny are also important to American culture, they will not be discussed here. First, they have been quite thoroughly researched elsewhere; second, they have become more or less stereotyped and therefore less challenging; and third, and most importantly, they are not associated with fairylore. They also do not carry the same remarkable association with ancient rituals as does the Tooth Fairy, for the Tooth Fairy is just one very viable and influential member of an ancient and recognized "tribe" of representatives including the mouse, rat, and spider which are tied to rituals used to mark a significant period in human life. These "rites of passage," as they are known, take on added significance when their universality is taken into account. Just how a rite of passage relates to new fairylore, what this fairy means to parents and children, how it is portrayed by writers, artists and children themselves, and why a fairy is fast becoming an American "icon" (not a stereotyped one, but a fresh and ever-changing symbol in the American family), are the subjects of this essay.

Background of a Ritual

It has been well documented elsewhere (Kanner; Radbill; Creighton; Rooth; Carter; Butterworth et al.) that all cultures have some method of disposing of shed baby teeth, usually only the first tooth being part of a ritual. One of the best overviews on the subject appeared in the *British Dental Journal* (Townend). Although Townend's purpose was to analyze why some primitive cultures violently extracted permanent teeth, he also analyzed known rituals of disposal of shed deciduous teeth in an attempt to show that both were related.

The disposal of the baby tooth in primitive cultures, he wrote, took one of nine forms: (1) the tooth was thrown to the sun; (2) thrown into the fire; (3) thrown between the legs; (4) thrown onto or over the roof of the house, often with an invocation to some animal or individual; (5) placed in a mouse hole near the stove or hearth or offered to some other animal; (6) buried; (7) hidden where animals could not get it; (8) placed in a tree or on a wall; and (9) swallowed by the mother, child or animal. He did not indicate putting the tooth under a pillow for a "fairy," since that could not be considered a primitive ritual but is a recent development with, we will see, a modified purpose. By linking the disposal of the teeth to burial customs, to indications that teeth were considered a visible sign of strength and power, and to evidence that the sun, fire, hearth, mice and even trees were linked to birth, life and ancestors, Townend concludes that "the worldwide care which has been taken in the disposal of shed deciduous teeth seems to indicate that these teeth have been regarded as having some magical importance to the primitive mind" and the ritual "is an extension of the drama of rebirth" (395).

The value and magic associated with teeth, and the basis for the ancient rituals is evident in a quotation from a brilliant analysis, "The Telltale Teeth: Psychodontia to Sociodontia":

> Because of their symbolic potency it is imperative to guard against the loss of teeth. In the Old Testament one of the most terrible curses involves the appeal to God to break the teeth of the enemy (Job 4.10; Psalms 3.7; Psalms 58.6). Sir James Frazer tells of African tribes in which the king cannot be crowned if he is symbolically emasculated by having a broken tooth; and in another tribe, the ruler is put to death if he loses a tooth. Because of the virtue inherent in teeth, they must not be allowed to fall into the hands of one's enemies; extracted teeth should be buried or hidden, a superstition still evident in the practice of mothers who carefully save their children's baby teeth. Another popular belief has it that teeth should be salted and burned in order to keep them away from witches. Of course, the sexual implications of teeth are familiar to Freud, who interprets the pulling of teeth in dreams as castration. (Ziolkowski)

Many of the ritual disposals of teeth were accompanied by a verbal charm, or saying. The importance of verbal charms and the varieties used in British folk culture are analyzed elsewhere (Forbes). Charms frequently were used to complete an action which was supposed to be medically helpful, or to appeal to someone or something for help. In most tooth rituals both the action and the verbal incantation were used. The action could take the form of one of the nine listed above, and the charm accompanying it would be an audible plea for help to get a new and better tooth to replace the lost one, or be a wish. As an example, take the African Bemba.

The Bemba child matches the lost tooth with a piece of charcoal and throws the tooth to the east and the charcoal to the west with the words: "We mufito ulewa nakasuba, We lino uletula nakasuba," which means, "As the piece of charcoal sinks with the setting sun, a new tooth will rise with the sun at dawn" ("Teeth and African"). The action was the first method of ritual disposal listed by Townend, and the incantation takes the form of a wish.

The charm frequently directly invoked an animal such as the mouse or rat to help the owner get a new and better tooth. While calling on rodents is still current in many parts of Europe and Africa, Mexico and South America, the crow is cited by Rooth in a fine analysis of the European ritual, including maps where the variations predominate. She quotes several Greek areas with saying, "Crow, crow take my old tooth and bring me a new and fine tooth."

The point made here is not that different cultures evoke different animals or objects in their rituals (see Radbill; Carter et al.) but that they felt strongly enough about the loss of the tooth *to do something*, and in so doing, have passed the custom down from one generation to another. The need to call upon something or someone to help the new tooth grow will be referred to later, especially since that part of the ritual is almost always missing in the Tooth Fairy custom.

In all cases, however, it has been through *folklore* and because of *popular culture* and oral communication that these rituals have survived. Only recently have scholars seriously attempted to analyze the basis for some of our strange customs. The fact that these rituals have continued through the ages is due to their relationship to human life and the "rites of passage," a phrase made popular by Arnold van Gennep.

Rites of Passage

When van Gennep published his seminal work in 1908 on *Les Rites de Passage*, later translated into English, social scientists were quick to laud his threefold progression of successive ritual stages and show how they related to transitional life events such as birth, puberty, marriage and death.

The period of time in a child's life during which the Tooth Fairy becomes a viable entity fits very well into van Gennep's three stages of (1) separation, (2) transition (also called margin or limen), and (3) incorporation (or aggregation). In simple terms, and taken only on its lowest level, the *separation* is the loss of the baby tooth; the *transition* is the period when only a gap is evident; the *incorporation* is the appearance of the replacement tooth. However, the end result, either knowingly or unknowingly, is the acceptance of the child as having passed from infantism to childhood, a stage usually accompanied by breaking away from the home environment and the typical influence of the mother, and moving toward a broader worldview through education and socialization.

Thus, on a higher level, the three stages are again fulfilled—the child separates from his home, enters a transition period at school and finally is incorporated into the classroom as a full fledged member. This is the basis for one of the many children's books about this transition—*Molly and the Slow Teeth* (Ross). Molly is the only second grader in her class not to have lost a tooth. When she finally does, the Tooth Fairy visits her, as she has visited all the other members of the class, and Molly writes her name on the board and is finally recognized as being "one of the gang."

This transition time is also the basis for one psychologist's conclusion that the loss of the first baby tooth is the beginning of the male child's breaking with his Oedipus complex (Lewis). And at least one scientist has concluded that the loss of the first deciduous tooth can serve as a definite indicator of a male child's readiness for reading and schoolwork (Silvestro).

However, in the American culture and contrary to many other cultures, the ritual is not reserved only for the first tooth, but for the loss of any of the baby teeth or milk teeth. Since there are twenty such teeth, the Tooth Fairy could appear twenty times, extending van Gennep's transition or liminal period by months, if not years, from age four to about ten. In this case, the final stage, incorporation, does not start until the child disbelieves in the Tooth Fairy, which psychologists have indicated typically to be anywhere from eight to ten years (Blair et al.; Prentice et al.; Prentice and Gordon; Scheibe).

The loss of a baby tooth and the accompanying appearance of the Tooth Fairy can thus be seen as a complex issue, at least in the United States, and possibly in other countries in which the Tooth Fairy is gaining ascendancy. It marks the *physiological* change in the child, the *sociological* one when child shifts from home to school, and a *psychological* one when the child feels ready to accept a different, or adult, worldview when (s)he disbelieves in the existence of the Tooth Fairy. The entire procedure is recognized and applauded as a *cultural* event as well.

In an excellent unpublished paper, Clark visited thirty-two families in the Chicago, Illinois area and conducted in-depth informant interviews with fifteen boys and seventeen girls, aged five to eight and with their respective mothers. She attempted to determine what the children felt was important about the Tooth Fairy, how the parents looked upon the ritual and how these two viewpoints agreed or differed. Her paper, plus my research on the place of the Tooth Fairy in American culture (Wells 1980a,b,c), and some observations on the Tooth Fairy in the popular media (newspapers, cartoons and pulp magazines) are the basis for the next sections.

The Tooth Fairy and Parents

How do parents view their part in the "Ritual of Replacement"? Do they feel uncomfortable masquerading as an imaginary figure? Do they feel pressured by their children to produce a Tooth Fairy, as was indicated by the first published story found in which the Tooth Fairy ritual was central to the plot (Rogow)? Or do they willingly promote it? When young people find out the truth about the Tooth Fairy, are they disillusioned and "turned off," or will they participate in the ritual themselves when they are old enough to do so?

It would seem that if the results of my survey hold true, and from the more than five hundred letters and drawings I have received from children, the custom will definitely be continued by those who were participants as children. Of the 2,324 surveyed, 75% said they favored the Tooth Fairy concept, 20% were neutral and only 3% were not in favor and planned not to be part of it when they were parents.

More telling, it was the *parents* who were the major proponents of the practice, who told the children about the Tooth Fairy, not siblings or peers or books. Thus, 80% of those surveyed said they heard about the Tooth Fairy from their parents, and that they did or will use the concept because it gave (or will give) them pleasure (37%), it gave (or will give) the child pleasure (46%) or it made (or will make) the loss better (38%).

More seems to be at work here, however, than just pleasure or a culturally derived therapy. While parents may feel they are continuing the Tooth Fairy ritual as an emotional help to their child, other factors may be coloring their actions. The mother, for instance, may not want her child to "grow up too soon," to enter the world where there are no magical creatures answering calls or leaving gifts.

Witness the syndicated cartoon strip "Rose Is Rose" by Pat Brady which appeared October 12, 1989. Rose is speaking to her son's friend, Aloysius, and saying how wonderful that he has lost a tooth because he can put it under his pillow that night. Aloysius, however, says he doesn't know why he bothers since the Tooth Fairy forgets all about his house. That night the neighborhood policeman stops Rose from climbing into Aloysius' window, and Rose pleads, "Please, I just want to leave a quarter."

Rose can't stand having a little child's heart break because he is being forgotten. Nor does she want to see Aloysius lose faith in the Fairy. Rose is not the only one feeling this way. Many answering my survey felt that belief in mythical creatures was absolutely necessary for the development of imagination in children, and that adults should do everything in their power to encourage belief. In that regard they would agree with a reporter for *Better Homes and Gardens* who maintained, "Santa is just one of the myths of early childhood, along with the Tooth Fairy, the Easter Bunny, and a score of other bigger-than-life characters. Such myths are basic to a child's development. Small children's lives are filled with vivid images of heroes and friends who help them cope with life at the bottom of the family totem pole" (Kaercher).

Abruptly ending the Tooth Fairy tradition can be a shock as much to the mother as to the child, but for different reasons. Thus, a mother, in a telling article in *Ladies Home Journal,* is enraged when she discovers that someone has disillusioned her daughter. She writes:

> Tonight, Zoe, sometime between your bedtime and mine, I have a special mission to fly. Tonight I will be the Tooth Fairy. The problem is, you have already guessed the Tooth Fairy's real identity. " Mommy," you said as you got undressed to take a bath, " Sarah says there is *no* Tooth Fairy and that it's really you putting the dollar under my pillow. Is that true?"
>
> I felt my throat fill with rage at the worldly eight-year-old up the block who made you question the power of magic. I will deal with her later. Now all I want is to freeze this moment—and you—in my heart before you grow any further away from me. . . . You have only just turned six, the tooth in your hand but the third to come out, and already it seems my little game is up. I feel sorry for myself, because I don't want it to be over. . . . We call Daddy into the crisis. . . . We would both like you to join a little longer in the fantasy that beings can steal into one's house at night to leave presents and not to rob, kidnap or worse. In kindergarten you learned to "stop, drop and roll," if your clothes catch fire, to retreat immediately from any stranger who says hello to you and also to suspect poison or razor blades in every piece of candy you collect at Halloween. Isn't that enough reality for now? (Sobel)

The mother was temporarily satisfied when her child decided not to believe her friend Sarah, but to have faith that there really was a Tooth Fairy.

Older children bursting the bubble of young children's beliefs was the heart of J.B. Park's story, *Jonathan's Friends* where Jonathan's older brother tried to convince Jonathan that all he believed, including the Tooth Fairy, was false. Jonathan preferred his own world of magic and merely felt sorry for his brother. Evidently the author/artist thought Jonathan was right, for the final scene shows Jonathan in Santa's sleigh with all his friends riding happily through the night.

Not only are children reluctant to let go of the Tooth Fairy, but several mothers Clark interviewed also expressed a desire not to see the Tooth Fairy challenged. Said Clark: "In essence, the tooth fairy ritual provides the American mother with symbolic "reverse gears" that decelerates the process of recognizing their son's or daughter's new age status." The Tooth Fairy ritual gave them a form of control over the child, of protecting and extending childhood.

As a corollary, of the thirty-two mothers Clark interviewed, twenty-two had kept their child's shed primary teeth after collecting them. They instinctively felt the teeth must not be discarded, but could not explain why.

Actually, the long-forgotten reason is an ancient and persistent superstition, tied to witchcraft and religion, but still prevalent in some parts of today's world. Before a person can find a final resting place, he or she must have all parts of the body in hand for burial. This means teeth, as well. If teeth were missing, before the party could "go to heaven," he or she must search for them on Judgment Day in a bucket of blood in hell (Radford and Radford; Opie and Tatem).

This ancient injunction was obviously frightening, and since collecting and keeping all milk teeth was nigh unto impossible, the superstition was modified somewhere along the way. If the lost tooth were salted and thrown into a fire with the verbal incantation, "Good tooth, bad tooth, Pray God, send me a good tooth," (note that God and religion have entered the incantation), no witches could take the tooth, no harm would come to the owner, and he or she would not need to account for the lost teeth on Judgment Day. This "burning" ritual also relates to some of the fire disposal methods referred to earlier.

At least one company in Britain (Irving correspondence) has made good use of mothers' reluctance to throw away baby teeth, and offers to treat the tooth and mount it, for a fee, in a Tooth Fairy charm to be worn on a necklace or bracelet. The offer is obviously tempting (the little winged fairy clutching the baby tooth *is* cute), because even without national advertising, The Original Tooth Fairy Ltd. has made over a thousand such charms. The saving of the tooth has changed from fear to nostalgia—the saved tooth being a visible sign of the child's infant period, and mothers have gladly worn these little fairies on chains or bracelets as a symbol of love or as a talisman (ironically, another superstition, like the rabbit's foot, that the strength in the tooth will protect the wearer from evil).

In summary, for the parents, the Tooth Fairy ritual, on the surface at least, is one offered in love to provide sympathy for the child. At a deeper level, however, it encourages imagination but holds the child back from entering an adult world of too harsh reality, of being "too grown up," of losing the distinction of being "my baby."

The Tooth Fairy and the Child

Cartoons have frequently shown children challenging their parents about the "stinginess" of the Tooth Fairy for leaving only a dime or less than some other little pal has received, or has shown children comparing the amount of money left them. Is money the only reason why children believe in the Tooth Fairy?

No doubt the gift of money does have a significant bearing on the popularity of the ritual. It gives the child a sense of independence, a glimpse of what it will be like to be fully grown. It serves as a socially accelerating symbol, not always for selfish reasons. In a few documented instances the child has altruistic feelings in mind when he jots a note to the Tooth Fairy and mentions the economic facet of the transaction. Clark mentions one eight year old who saved her Tooth Fairy money to take her mother and sister to McDonald's, "a gesture which led her to observe: 'I like carrying around my own money. I feel more grown up and more special.'" Or witness the thoughts in a letter written to the Tooth Fairy:

> Dear Tooth Fairy: My tooth came out at school and my teacher gave me a small envelope for it. But I lost it at recess. Then my friend helped me find it at lunch and I put it in my lunch box. But my mother threw it out when I came home. Then my older sister helped me find it. Can I have extra money for this tooth since it caused so much trouble and I want to share with my sister and friend? Thank you very much. (Gabriel)

While I would not go so far as to maintain that the Tooth Fairy is a major factor in instilling some of the cultural norms of sharing, I still would not say that parents are deliberately or knowingly instilling the capitalistic view of "Produce and Sell," which has been expounded by another researcher (Tuleja), although that element is certainly present.

More likely, the Tooth Fairy's appearance visibly marks the child's step into a more adult world, and the coin becomes a magic piece to be kept and not spent. And "coin" seems to be an operative word, at least in many cases. Silver has always had magic connotations, and many a child has preferred a silver coin under the pillow to a paper bill. Such is the case of my own seven year old granddaughter who was thrilled to receive a silver dollar from the Tooth Fairy for each lost tooth and has kept them as good luck pieces.

The children in Clark's study voiced their looking forward to the loss of a baby tooth because "no one can call you a baby," or then you would be a "big kid" with "grown up teeth." The tooth, then, and the associated visit from the Tooth Fairy, represents a "natural symbol" of bodily change, one which finds acceptance with children, and is used as a sure sign they are growing up.

A corollary to this is the practice of writing to the Tooth Fairy. Children find it satisfying to try their newly acquired writing skills to tell their woes about their teeth to someone who will listen and be as concerned about them as they are. These notes serve two purposes. For the mother or father, if the Tooth Fairy writes back, childhood is being extended and the notes become another way of developing imagination and tying the child to the parents. For the child, his adult writing skills are being practiced while at the same time he is getting exclusive attention from a friend. Such a two-way transaction in shown in *Molly and the Slow Teeth* referred to earlier.

Some families have developed the Tooth Fairy messages so they encompass more than just the occasional note when a loose tooth finds its way under the pillow. A letter from a Massachusetts cardiologist is a good example:

> Our local Tooth Fairy takes a very active role in the raising and tutoring of our two daughters, not only carrying out the traditional Tooth Fairy obligation of ransoming lost teeth, but also writing letters to the children, leaving notes for them, and making notations on their blackboards. These messages tend to be notes of encouragement, inspiration, or friendly reminders of things that should be done. Of course, proper dental care is stressed in these communications, but they are not restricted in scope. . . . In fact, the Tooth Fairy plays such a significant role in our family that a small boat we recently purchased has been given that name. (Ockene)

Clark also found that children were afraid of losing what had seemed to be a permanent part of themselves and looked at the Tooth Fairy as someone who not only brought an exchange gift but also assured the child that he would not remain toothless. Only someone with great magic and influence could be so powerful, and children frequently tie the Tooth Fairy in with God. In one interview, Clark asked a seven-and-a-half year old middle-class boy of Italian-Irish descent, "How did the Tooth Fairy get started doing this?" To which the boy replied:

> Probably God made them. . . . One day maybe Adam or Eve, either one, lost their tooth, and didn't know what to do with it. So God spoke to them, and she told them, "Put your tooth under your pillow when you're sleeping and it'll go away and you'll get something for it." [The Tooth Fairy] felt happy because not too many people get to see God while they're living, and then the tooth fairy got to see him any time that she

wanted to. If she had any questions or anything. And she was a very special person because people wouldn't want to be toothless.

To this child, not only was the Tooth Fairy magic and special, but she had the ear of God (variously referred to as female and male). When this boy puts his lost tooth under the pillow, he wouldn't pray to God or even the Tooth Fairy (obviously feminine) to bring him a new tooth. The intent may be the same as the missing verbal charm, but it isn't needed. The Tooth Fairy will help; she doesn't need to be asked.

A 1989 children's book makes this same point when a little bear loses her one and only tooth (Nerlove). The Tooth Fairy promises her a new one will come soon. This is the only function of the Fairy. No exchange takes place, just a promise, echoing some of the primitive chants when a mouse, rat or other animal would be implored to help provide a new and better tooth for the lost one.

Not only does the Tooth Fairy become the lesson bearer for approved social action and a panacea for pain and fear, but as a messenger from God, she functions in a ministerial fashion. Clark states, "children feel that their teeth are put to rest by the tooth fairy in a suitably reverent manner . . . in her ethereal home, or to make necklaces or other valued articles out of them. . . . The ritual provides a funeral-like rite of passage for their teeth in symbolic terms to some worthy "afterlife," aiding the emotional process of losing the tooth."

A symbol of bodily change and passage into adulthood, a friend who will listen exclusively to the child, a magic entity who will ensure the child will not remain toothless, a god or agent of god who will take good care of the precious lost tooth and provide a good afterlife for it—the Tooth Fairy is all of this to the child, facts which children's authors have capitalized on in their various stories about the loosening of a tooth and what happens to it after it falls out.

The Tooth Fairy in Children's Literature

The loose tooth, the pillow, the fairy and the magic disappearance of the tooth with the subsequent reappearance of an exchange has found its way into children's literature more than most people are aware (Wells 1979, 1980, 1983). Since 1952 when McCloskey wrote of Sal's loosening tooth and her frustrated desire to put it under her pillow and wish on it, twenty-nine known books or stories have been published for children relating to the ritual and/or the fairy (see Table), not counting stories written for adults with the Tooth Fairy as a major character or the hundreds of one line references in popular magazines like *People, Better Homes and Gardens, Reader's Digest* and *Parents Magazine*.

Shed Deciduous Teeth and the Tooth Fairy in Children's Literature

Year	Title	Author	Tooth Fairy							Major Action
			Mentioned	Shown	Female	Male	Animal	Adult	Child	
1952	One Morning in Maine	McCloskey								Sal loses shed tooth but gets wish anyway. No fairy. Only pillow and wish.
1962	The Tooth Fairy	Feagles	X	X	X				X	Tells why TF wants teeth, what she does with them.
1963	Tu-Tu and the Joy Bell	Dodge	X	X	X				X	Tells how and why Tu-Tu became TF.
1965	What Happened When Jack and Daisy Tried to Fool the Tooth Fairies	Hoban	X	X		X(2)		X		Adventure. Daisy and Jack try to fool TFs with fake tooth. Search for real one ends in escape from cat.
1968	The True Story of the Tooth Fairy and Why Brides Wear Engagement Rings	Whittaker	X	X	X			X		Glitter and Glisten, twins, become TF and assistant in fairy tale story with magic and Biblical overtones.
1972	Bear's Toothache	McPhail	X	X						Boy puts bear's tooth under pillow.
1974	The Tooth and My Father	Saroyan	X	X		X			X	Small boy explains how shed tooth changes into money by TF.
1975	Little Rabbit's Loose Tooth	Bate	X	X	X		X	X		Little Rabbit, although doubting, decides to leave shed tooth for TF.
1976	Tooth Fairy Legend	McAllister	X	X	X			X		History before TF, discussion of how TF came to be, where teeth kept.
1976	Heather's Feathers	Weiss	X							First grade bird doesn't have TF visit her like other animals, but Feather Fairy does.

Year	Title	Author	Tooth Fairy							Major Action
			Mentioned	Shown	Female	Male	Animal	Adult	Child	
1977	*The Mango Tooth*	Pomerantz								Discusses shed teeth of girl Rosy and what she was eating when they came out. No fairy, but teeth put under pillow.
1977	*Jonathan's Friends*	Park	X	X	X			X		Older brother tries to convince Jonathan imaginary creatures are not real.
1978	"A Tooth Tale" in *Avon's Sweet Pickles Book*	Perle	X							Octopus puts money under pillow, asks TF for teeth.
1978	*A Tooth for the Tooth Fairy*	Gunther	X	X	X			X		Rose loses shed tooth and is worried TF won't come without tooth.
1979	*Lizzie and the Tooth Fairy*	Wolman	X	X	X			X		Tiny TF takes Lizzie on trip to her castle and shows her how and why teeth are kept. Hygiene lesson.
1980	*Molly and the Slow Teeth*	Ross	X							Second grader's teeth are the last in her class to loosen. Writes to TF who writes back.
1981	*Out of the Bug Jar*	Thomas	X	X		X		X		Tom catches the TF and then can't get rid of him. Hygiene and social lessons.
1981	*The Tooth Fairy*	Peters	X	X	X				X	Speculates on what is and is not known about the TF. Affirms she comes at night. Story also on tape.
1981	*The Berenstain Bears Go to the Dentist*	Berenstain	X					X		Sister Bear has loose tooth. Goes to dentist to get help. Puts tooth under pillow. TF comes. Hygiene lesson.
1982	*Zub, the Tooth Fairy*	Schulte-DeWitt	X	X	X				X	Child-like dancing fairy becomes the TF when children help her find a tooth to fit her mouth after she accidentally knocks her own out.

Year	Title	Author	Tooth Fairy							Major Action
			Mentioned	Shown	Female	Male	Animal	Adult	Child	
1984	*Loose Tooth*	Kroll	X				X			One bat loses a tooth before his twin does, which causes problems. TF evidently comes and can't find tooth because it has been stolen.
1985	"Clem's Dream" in *Last Slice of Rainbow*	Aiken	X	X	X			X		TF witch steals Clem's dream along with his tooth and leaves coin. Clem wants dream back and searches for it.
1985	*Tooth Fairy*	Wood	X	X	X			X		Adventure. TF takes Jessica and Matthew to TF-land and shows them what happens to teeth. Hygiene lesson.
1985	*The Tooth Trip*	Eriksson	X							Swedish tale translated. Rosalie, instead of leaving tooth for TF, uses it as bus fare to visit grandmother.
1988	*Airmail to the Moon*	*Birdseye*	X	X						Ora Mae sets out to find who stole her shed tooth she was planning to give the TF. Lists reasons why TF collects teeth.
1988	*Jenny and the Tooth Fairy*	Richardson	X	X		X			X	Adventure. Tells what TF does with teeth and where he gets money.
1988	*The Missing Tooth*	Cole	X							Two boys, best friends, almost become enemies over who will lose a tooth next and get money from TF. Social message.
1989	*Just One Tooth*	Nerlove	X	X	X		X		X	Little bear asks the TF for a new tooth in place of the one she lost.
1989	*No Tooth, No Quarter*	Buller, Schade	X	X	X	X			X	Tooth Fairies, boys and girls, must get good teeth to get good grades on their report cards. Boy Walter helps female TF and has adventure in the Tooth Kingdom. Indirect hygiene lesson.

Four known tales appeared in the 1960s, ten in the 1970s and fifteen in the 1980s, a significant increase and evidence that the Tooth Fairy is a viable subject for authors. And at this time there are two known children's stories currently being written or awaiting publication.

In twenty-six of the tales relating to a shed deciduous tooth, a fairy is mentioned. In eight, the major action tells why he or she collects teeth and what is done with them. Five discuss how the Tooth Fairy got the name or occupation; six are adventures with the Tooth Fairy in which the child learns some valuable lesson, usually a dental one, but sometimes a social one; and in six the action focuses on the child's problem—the tooth won't come out or the tooth is lost.

Images of the Tooth Fairy vary. In the books cited in the Table, there are: a little girl (Feagles, Dodge, Whittaker, Peters, Cole); a full-sized princess-type fairy (Gunther, Park); a typical small flower fairy (Schulte-DeWitt); a witch (Aiken and Karlin); two little old men (Hoban); a ragged boy (Saroyan); a frizzy headed adult blonde (Wood); children, boys and girls, with wings (Buller); a human, dental hygienist type (McAllister); a potbellied, cigar smoking, jeans clad tiny flying male (Thomas); and a fierce warrior boy (Richardson). In the animal realm are a rabbit (Bate), a bat (not shown) (Kroll), a bear (Nerlove) and in place of a Tooth Fairy, a bird Feather Fairy (Weiss).

All of the artists have individual images of the Tooth Fairy, one of the best and most significant differences between Santa Claus, Easter Bunny and the Tooth Fairy. Only the Tooth Fairy can appear in a variety of ways without the child becoming suspicious. A black Santa Claus or one without a white beard would upset most children and make them doubt whether the artist knew what he was doing. But a black Tooth Fairy, a skinny or fat one, a female or male, would make no difference to the ordinary child.

Thus the Tooth Fairy can be pictured as a little child with wings as in Tu-Tu, one of the earliest Tooth Fairies (Dodge); as a humorous, preposterous pixie by a California artist (Figure 1); a dragon running off with an oversized tooth (Figure 2); as a maternal, Blue Fairy type balancing on the bed post (Figure 3); or a beautiful ballerina flying through the air (Figure 4); these latter two having been painted by well-known artists and currently appearing on oversized posters in dentists' offices (Whittle). No child is offended.

Since the Tooth Fairy is thought to be a special fairy interested in the child as an individual, the child also believes the fairy can take on any appearance and be just like they picture her or him and still be just like someone else's image, as well. Changing shapes and appearances are nothing to a magic creature such as the Tooth Fairy. The Tooth Fairy can do anything. And children let their imaginations loose when describing her. A nine year old boy in Massachusetts said:

Figure 1. "The Tooth Fairy" by Rob Browne. From a 17" x 23" hand-painted 1979 lithograph. (Rob Browne)

Figure 2. "The Tooth Fairy Dragon." An original drawing owned by the author. (Rosemary Wells)

Figure 3. A whimsical fat fairy reminiscent of Walt Disney's Blue Fairy, by artist Brian Ajhar of New York. Originally drawn for Whittle Communications' 1990 "Word of Mouth" poster. (Brian Ajhar)

Figure 4. In direct contrast with the other fairies by professional artists, New York artist Vivienne Flesher sees the Tooth Fairy flying gracefully through the air in ballerina style, a fairy type favored by children as well. From the "Word of Mouth" poster published by Whittle Communications. (Vivienne Flesher)

I think there is [a tooth fairy]. I'm not sure. But more likely there is. I think that she looks like an angel with a little wand with a tooth at the end. I think she has dust and she throws it on herself and goes through the pillow, or something. Maybe she trades teeth for money . . . no she wouldn't do that . . . she probably gets the money from saving it up from her allowance. She wouldn't steal it. No, she probably has people who work for her and bring it to her. You'd need a good job to get all that money. When you're younger you get less money and when you're older you get more money. She takes the teeth and throws them at the ground and they turn into flowers or bushes or grass or trees. I think she has a big, huge telescope and a big, huge model of the earth and whenever a kid loses a tooth a light blinks in the house where it's lost. Then she flies down and does her stuff. (Snyder)

Children's Images of the Tooth Fairy

Most of the children's drawings I have received as a result of an article in a health magazine for school children (Haden), show the fairy as feminine, just as do the majority of the artists in the children's books — fifteen females to six males (if you count both male figures in Hoban's book). Although it's not always easy to tell whether a young child has drawn a child or an adult, a male or a female (Figure 5), those which are discernible seem to show an adult female form, frequently with wings, often with a long dress and usually carrying a wand or bag for the teeth and money. The World-Wide Tooth Fairy, by a nine-year-old girl from New York (Figure 6), is obviously feminine, with long hair, wings, and wand and possessing two large bags, one for teeth and one with money. The original colors were blonde hair, purple wings, blue dress and red shoes (influenced, no doubt, by the Wizard of Oz).

The feminine form seems to follow naturally from the child's early conception of the family when the mother is the warm, nurturing party and the father most often associated with the working world. While male Tooth Fairies have appeared, most of them were used for humorous contrast, a twist from the expected. What will happen to the image of the Tooth Fairy in the future, now that the father has a much more visible role in the home, will be worth noting. The trend may already be reversing. Two of the last four published books have male Tooth Fairies!

More illustrations and letters written to the Tooth Fairy can be found in a book, *Letters to the Tooth Fairy*, published by a dental society in Kansas (Wichita). As might be expected since the project was in conjunction with a dental health project, most of the letters assure the Tooth Fairy that the child writers and illustrators have been taking good care of their teeth so the Tooth Fairy would be proud of them.

Figure 5. A second-grade girl draws her vision of a fairy and says: "I like the tooth fairy because she's funny. People say she's not real, but I still believe in her. She leaves me $1.00 a tooth. Does that mean I take good care of my teeth? I hope it does. The end."

Figure 6. This typical Tooth Fairy has long hair, long dress, wings, and a wand. The nine-
year-old artist is probably close to the truth when she labels her figure the "World Wide
Tooth Fairy."

Such solicitude about the condition of the tooth is a modern corollary to the Tooth Fairy myth. The generalized "Good Fairy" of the early 1900s became the singular Tooth Fairy in the 1950s and 1960s and evolved into the "Expanded Duty Tooth Fairy" of the 1980s and 1990s, interested in the hygienic preservation of good teeth and even the advocate of good school and social habits.

Some letters I have received tell of family Tooth Fairies who deduct from the usual exchange rate if the tooth is not clean or if a filling indicates the child has been less than careful about preserving it. Children have also indicated they feel the Tooth Fairy has been collecting teeth for so long that she or he is interested only in the very best teeth for the collection, and they must be very careful of their teeth or the Tooth Fairy won't visit.

Some of the recent children's books also have been accompanied by a text which admonishes children to brush their teeth well, eat good foods, see the dentist regularly, and behave in a manner destined to win the Tooth Fairy's approval (see Table). Popular cartoon strips have picked up this changing facet of the Tooth Fairy's personality. In the syndicated "Dennis the Menace" strip on August 2, 1981, for example, Mother tells Dennis that the Tooth Fairy will not pay for a tooth that didn't belong to him (a warning against stealing and not telling the truth) especially since Dennis had knocked the friend's tooth out in a fight. "The Tooth Fairy hates fighting," she admonished.

The Tooth Fairy Today

There can be little doubt that the Tooth Fairy is an influential fairy in American culture, perhaps the only one with national press recognition (Wells 1982). That this fairy is also important in other cultures is only now becoming evident. Canada, for instance, has had a "superman" type Tooth Fairy originating from the City of Etobicoke Department of Health for many years. He represents the Tooth Fairy Society which any child can join by sending a lost tooth. In return the child will get a membership card, tooth brush, button and certificate.

The ritual has obviously been changed. The tooth is mailed to the society, not put under the pillow, and the Tooth Fairy no longer makes house calls. The Department mails about thirty-five congratulatory letters weekly with accompanying membership privileges. There is something wistful, however, about a recent letter they received and sent to me from a correspondent in Meaford, Ontario. She wrote:

> Dear Tooth Fairy: I have lost another tooth, but a new one is coming. I brush my teeth every day and before I go to bed. My mom said that you don't come to our house any more because the gas for your car costs too

much. She said if I write to you you would send me a sticker. I am only 5
and I can't write yet. My brother is helping me. Thank you for the sticker.

Correspondence from England, Ireland, Tunisia and Spain has also
indicated that the entity titled the Tooth Fairy is gaining recognition over
fairies in general as the collector of shed teeth, and is more than holding its
own against the older tooth mouse and other methods of recognizing the
loss of a deciduous tooth.

Whether the tooth mouse will ever die out and the Tooth Fairy
supersede it is a matter of conjecture. Certainly the spread of English as a
first language, the importance of radio (including a series called "The
Tooth Fairy" in the 1970s [Peterson]) and television in disseminating
references to the entity, and the continued publication of books and
articles relating to the Tooth Fairy will have a telling effect. In addition,
there are growing numbers of commercial ventures, such as Tooth Fairy
pillows, boxes and other artwork to keep the Tooth Fairy constantly before
the public eye (Wells).

The popularity of the Tooth Fairy as a sympathetic figure is the basis
for a suggestion which appeared in *Parents* magazine of June 1990. As a
pediatric "trick," the magazine suggests that when a child has stitches
taken out, the "Stitch Fairy" can help.

> Tell your child that she can put the removed stitches under her pillow.
> (Ask the doctor to put them in an envelope.) The Stitch Fairy, like that old
> favorite the Tooth Fairy, will leave a shiny new quarter in place of the
> stitches. Going through this kind of procedure is difficult; however, the
> idea of a reward may make it easier for some children.

The Tooth Fairy and the Stitch Fairy are really not as closely related as
the writer thinks. The money as a palliative for the child and the
promptings to "make it all feel better" are the main connecting features.
The writer obviously does not know the ritualistic nature of the Tooth
Fairy or its connection to the rites of passage. Such, however, is the case
with any popular custom. It broadens, changes, influences and, in this
case, perhaps even starts a new pop trend. While distinctly different in
historical development and cultural influence, the two fairies do have one
other thing in common—their mythological status.

The Tooth Fairy as Myth

There is no doubt that the Tooth Fairy *is* a mythological creature. The
actual "realness" of the fairy as a supernatural cannot be debated as the
existence of other fairies might be, even though the Tooth Fairy has a
realness of its own to the young children who believe in it. Myths,

however, are not lies, although they are not exactly truths, either, and defining a myth or determining its value to a culture is not easy.

O'Flaherty, in *Other People's Myths,* begins her second chapter with "It is impossible to define a myth, but it is cowardly not to try," and continues for several pages defining what a myth is by telling what it is not. Then she continues:

> A myth is a story that is sacred to and shared by a group of people who find their most important meanings in it; it is a story believed to have been composed in the past about an event in the past, or, more rarely, in the future, an event that continues to have meaning in the present because it is remembered; it is a story that is part of a larger group of stories. . . . their content deals with human questions of perennial importance. Myths are, moreover, remembered because the need for them persists. . . . As the culture retells the myth over time, it constantly reinterprets it, however much the culture may claim that the myth has been preserved intact. . . . In fact, "true" and "false" are woefully inadequate words to apply to myths. . . . The problem of the truth of myth becomes even more irrelevant, I think, when we consider the fact that a major part of the impact of any myth lies not in its argument or *logos* (true or false) but in its imagery, its metaphor. The power of a myth is as much visual as verbal. The myth combines the functions of philosophy (the plot of the myth: what happens, and why) with the symbolism of ritual or cosmology (the actors in the myth: gods, animals, elemental powers). Myths are both events and images, both verbs and nouns. To analyze a myth in terms of either element alone (the verbal/philosophical event or the visual/symbolic image) is to reduce and distort it. (28)

Calling the Tooth Fairy a myth, then, cannot be termed derogatory, since cultural myth deals with "human questions of perennial importance." Certainly the Tooth Fairy fits into the other parts of the definition—it is as much visual as verbal, it is recurrent and is shared by a large portion of the American population, and it is philosophical as well as ritualistic. This symbolic aspect and the pervasiveness of the Tooth Fairy are more than evident when the works of one of America's most prolific writers is analyzed.

Stephen King, acknowledged by *Time Magazine* as the "indisputable king of horror," writes one best seller after another. He has found the Tooth Fairy to be a very useful device. In *The Tommyknockers,* he used it primarily as a visible sign of the loss of teeth, one of the symptoms of change in the people in Haven, Maine as they slowly turn into something non-human.

But in *It,* the Tooth Fairy and Santa Claus become a symbol of the innocence of childhood, a time when great things can be accomplished because of belief. So, it is when the adults of the story prepare to battle once again the epitome of evil they thought they had killed when children, and the Ritual of Chüd is about to begin, Bill, one of the major characters, says in his mind:

> Chüd, this Chüd, stand, be brave, be true, stand for your brother, your friends; believe, believe in all the things you have believed in, believe that if you tell the policeman you're lost he'll see that you get home safely, that there is a Tooth Fairy who lives in a huge enamel castle, and Santa Claus below the North Pole, making toys with his trove of elves, and that Captain Midnight could be real, yes, he could be in spite of Calvin and Cissy Clark's big brother Carlton saying that was all a lot of baby stuff, believe that your mother and father will love you again, that courage is possible and words will come smoothly every time . . . believe in yourself, believe in the heat of that desire. (1012)

When Bill shouts "I BELIEVE IN ALL THOSE THINGS!" his strength returns and he is able to fight the evil which up to this moment had been winning.

The denouement of the story demands the reader suspend what he knows is reality and enter the minds of the characters where they are transported back to their childhood before growing up had forced them into disbelief in magic.

It is really not surprising the Tooth Fairy enters at this important moment. The dedication of the book to King's wife and his three children—aged fourteen, twelve and seven—ends with: "Kids, fiction is the truth inside the lie, and the truth of this fiction is simple enough: *the magic exists*." And what is more magic to kids than the Tooth Fairy!

The Tooth Fairy as Icon

The Tooth Fairy is so prevalent in contemporary American culture and so pervasive an influence in family life, that it would not be surprising if, in the not too distant future, the Tooth Fairy became an American icon. To a certain extent, it already is.

> Icons are symbols and mindmarks. They tie in with myth, legend, values, idols, aspirations. . . . Icons still move men, even when they are not recognized as such in supermarkets, discotheques, used car lots, and funeral parlors. They pop up on billboards, magazine covers, and TV commercials. . . . Every age is compulsively creative. With each, mythology is transformed into history, history into life, and life into icons. (Browne and Fishwick)

Popular culture has taken the Tooth Fairy to heart and has created a living myth of her/him and is developing an icon which has great social as well as biological significance. As with any myth, the onset is not known, but that is immaterial. The need for children to believe—and for parents to continue—the tradition perpetuates it. When someone mentions "Tooth Fairy," there is instant and universal recognition from any native born American.

Thus the Tooth Fairy and the Ritual of Replacement accompanying it are at once a *myth of childhood* when the believer is the one acted upon, and an *act of adulthood* when again the ritual is brought to life, with the past participant now the active perpetrator. Its prevalence in American culture is assuring its place as an ever changing "pop" icon of family life.

This double role, then, accounts for the polarized comments about the Tooth Fairy quoted at the beginning of this article. If you believe in the impossible, then you must believe in the Tooth Fairy too, a myth with cultural acceptance. But to call forth the myth you also call out all the complex meanings that myth has for a culture. To some, that might signify deception and falsehood, but to others, perhaps many others, the myth can also mean a "richness" beyond measure. It encompasses children and adults of all ages, and no one can escape its influence.

When asked to define "rich," how significant that the writer Ross-Michau was not addressing young parents with children, but senior citizens who had lived through the double stages of Tooth Fairy existence and were starting on yet another phase, the grandparent stage. In a popular magazine designed for those over fifty-five, the author wrote:

> Rich is many things. It's having faith in the Easter Bunny, Santa Claus, the tooth fairy and God. It's a rocking chair that has been handed down for five generations and a child's laughter.

References

Aiken, Joan. 1985. J. Aiken, ed. *The Last Slice of Rainbow*. New York: Harper and Row.

Bate, Lucy. 1975. *Little Rabbit's Loose Tooth*. New York: Scholastic Book Services.

Berenstain, Stan and Jan Berenstain. 1981. *The Berenstain Bears Visit the Dentist*. New York: Random House.

Birdseye, Tom. 1988. *Airmail to the Moon*. New York: Holiday House.

Blair, John R., et al. 1980. "Children's Belief in Santa Claus, Easter Bunny and Tooth Fairy." *Psychological Reports* 46: 691–4.

Browne, Ray B., and Marshall Fishwick, eds. 1978. *Icons of America*. Bowling Green, Ohio: Popular P.

Buller, Jon and Susan Schade. 1989. *No Tooth, No Quarter*. New York: Random House.

Carter, William, et al. 1987. *Ethnodentistry and Dental Folklore*. Overland Park, Kansas: Dental Folklore Books of Kansas City.

Clark, Cindy. 1989. "'Flight' Towards Maturity: The American Tooth Fairy Custom as a Rite of Passage." Unpublished paper. U of Chicago.

Cole, Joanna. 1988. *The Missing Tooth* (A Step-into-Reading, Step 2 Book). New York: Random House.

Creighton, Helen. 1968. *Bluenose Magic: Popular Beliefs and Superstitions in Nova Scotia.* Toronto: Ryerson P.

Davidowitz, Esther. 1990. "Is Honesty the Best Policy?" *Parents* (April).

Dodge, Dan F. 1963 *Tu-Tu and the Joy Bell: The Story of How the Tooth Fairy Came to Be.* Fort Dodge, Iowa: Fort P.

Eriksson, Eva. 1985. *The Tooth Trip* (Roehrdanz, Barbro Eriksson, Trans.). Minneapolis, MN: Carolrhoda Books, Inc.

Feagles, Anita. 1962. *The Tooth Fairy.* Reading, MA: Addison-Wesley.

Forbes, Thomas R. 1971. "Verbal Charms in British Folk Medicine." *Proceedings of the American Philosophical Society* 115.4: 293–316.

Gabriel, Michelle. 1979. "Letters to the Tooth Fairy." *Family Circle* (May 15): 134.

Gunther, Louise. 1978. *A Tooth for the Tooth Fairy.* Champaign, IL: Garrard.

Haden, Bea. 1986. "The Legend of the Tooth Fairy." *Current Health* 9 (April): 22–4.

Hoban, Russell. 1965. *What Happened When Jack and Daisy Tried to Fool the Tooth Fairies* (4th printing, January 1973 ed.). New York: Scholastic Book Services.

Kaercher, Dan. 1984. "Is There Really A Santa Claus?" *Better Homes and Gardens* (December): 45, 47.

Kanner, Leo. 1928. *Folklore of the Teeth.* New York: Macmillan.

Karlin, Nurit. 1985. *The Tooth Witch.* New York: J.B. Lippincott (hardback), Harper and Row

King, Stephen. 1986. *It.* New York: Penguin.

———. 1987. *The Tommyknockers.* New York: Penguin.

Kroll, Steven. 1984. *Loose Tooth.* New York: Holiday House.

Lewis, Harvey A. 1958. "The Effect of Shedding the First Deciduous Tooth upon the Passing of the Oedipus Complex of the Male." *Journal of the American Psychoanalytical Association* 6.1 (January): 5–37.

McAllister, Frank and Fran McAllister. 1976. *The Tooth Fairy Legend.* Dallas, TX: Block Publishers.

McCloskey, Robert. 1952. *One Morning in Maine.* New York: Viking.

Melton, William C. 1989. "Making Money Off a Depression." *West of Wall Street* [newsletter].

Nerlove, Miriam. 1989. *Just One Tooth.* New York: Macmillan.

O'Flaherty, Wendy Doniger. 1988. *Other Peoples' Myths: The Cave of Echoes.* New York: Macmillan.

Ockene, Dr. Ira S. 1981. Letter to the author (15 July).

Opie, Iona, and Moira Tatem, eds. 1989. *A Dictionary of Superstitions.* Oxford, England: Oxford UP.

Original Tooth Fairy Ltd. [jewelry company], 1990. Ruislip, Middlesex, England. Letter to Barry Irving.

Park, W.B. 1977. *Jonathan's Friends.* New York: G.P. Putnam's Sons.

Peterson, Clarence. 1981. "Sellmates: The Dynamic Duo of Funny Radio Ads." *Chicago Tribune, Tempo* (4 February): 1, 3.

Prentice, Norman, and David Gordon. 1987. "Santa Claus and the Tooth Fairy for the Jewish Child and Parent." *Journal of General Psychology* 148: 139–51.

Prentice, Norman M., Martin Manosevitz, and Laura Hubbs. 1978. "Imaginary Figures of Early Childhood: Santa Claus, Easter Bunny, and the Tooth Fairy." *American Journal of Orthopsychiatry* 48.4: 618–28.

Radbill, Samuel X. 1964. "The Folklore of Teeth." *Kentucky Folklore Quarterly* 9.4: 123–43.

Radford, E., and M.A. Radford. 1961. "Teeth." *Encyclopaedia of Superstitions*. Ed. Christina Hole. London: Hutchinson. 336–9.

Rogow, Lee. 1949. "The Tooth Fairy." *Colliers* 124: 26.

Rooth, A.B. 1982. *The Offering of the First Shed Tooth and the Tooth-Formula: A Study of a "Physiological" Custom*. Uppsala, Sweden: Ethologiska Institutionem.

Ross, Pat. *Molly and the Slow Teeth*. 1980. New York: Lothrop, Lee and Shepard Books.

Ross-Michau, Lynn. 1990. "Gold Dust and Star Dust." *Mature Outlook* (September–October): 88.

Scheibe, Cynthia Leone. 1987. "Developmental Differences in Children's Reasoning about Santa Claus and Other Fantasy Characters." Diss. Cornell U.

Silvestro, John R. 1977. "Second Dentition and School Readiness." *New York State Dental Journal* 43 (March): 155–8.

Snyder, Barbara. 1987. "Tooth Fairy's Magic Makes Kids Believe." *The Boston Herald* (13 January): 27.

Sobel, Dava. 1988. "The Tooth Fairy Cometh." *Ladies Home Journal* (February): 86–8.

"Teeth and African Folklore." 1986. *Dental Journal of Zambia* 1.1: 22.

Townend, B.R. 1963. "The Non-therapeutic Extraction of Teeth and Its Relation to the Ritual Disposal of Shed Deciduous Teeth." *British Dental Journal* 115.8–10: 312–5, 354–7, 394–6.

Tuleja, Tad. 1989. "The Tooth Fairy: Perspectives on Money and Magic." Paper delivered at American Folklore Society Annual Meeting. Philadelphia, 18 October; see his revised essay in this volume.

van Gennep, Arnold. 1960. *The Rites of Passage*. Chicago: U of Chicago P.

Wells, Rosemary. 1979. "The Tooth Fairy: Part I. The Tooth Fairy and the Fairy World." *cal* 43.6: 2–7.

———. 1980a. "The Tooth Fairy: Part II. The Tooth Fairy and the Literary, Artistic and Commercial Worlds." *cal* 43.8: 18–24.

———. 1980b. "The Tooth Fairy: Part III. Folk Culture and the Dental World." *cal* 43.9: 12–25.

———. 1982. "Tooth Fairy Update." *cal* 45.12: 6–9.

———. 1983a "Tracking the Tooth Fairy: Finding the Trail." *cal* 46.12: 1–8.

———. 1983b "Tracking the Tooth Fairy: Blazing the Way." *cal* 47.1: 18–25.

———. 1983c. "Tracking the Tooth Fairy: Conclusion." *cal* 4.2: 25–31.

———. 1983d. "The Expanded Duty Tooth Fairy: Needlework and Sewing: Kits and Patterns." Paper delivered to Northwestern University Dental School, Evanston, Ill.

Whittle Communication. 1990. *Word of Mouth*. Knoxville: Whittle Communication.

Wichita District Dental Auxiliary. 1987. *Letters to the Tooth Fairy*. Wichita: Wichita District Dental Auxiliary.

Ziolkowski, Theodore. 1976. "The Telltale Teeth: Psychodontia to Sociodontia." *PMLA* 91 (January): 9–22.

VI. Semantics and Epistemology

In the last section of this book Noel Williams and Peter M. Rojcewicz ponder fundamental questions of semantics and epistemology. Benjamin Lee Whorf once observed, "We are all mistaken in our common belief that any word has an exact meaning."[1] Moreover, when words refer to extraordinary beings and events having no denotative, concrete referents in everyday life, semantic enigmas are compounded. In examining the documented usages of *fairy* and its variations over a five hundred year period, Williams notes the direct influence of literary tradition on oral tradition and the continuity of "fatedness" as a "central concept . . . that characterizes the *fairy* concept from its first use." His examination is also a corrective to folklorists who have habitually referred to "vague processes of confusion" when discussing the usages of *fairy* by medieval authors. These authors, Williams argues, were using a fashionable word that was attracting and taking over "the associative meanings of its rivals" (e.g., "elves").

It can be argued that fairy societies today are paralleled by at least two "significant other" societies: satanic cults and the alien occupants of "unidentified flying objects" (UFOs). Satanic panics exhibit social fears of the "enemy within." They prompt continuing anxieties concerning evil forces capturing the minds of youth, and as with changelings, kidnapping infants. It is no wonder that this is an area of recent folkloristic inquiry.[2]

UFO aliens, however, appear to bear a closer relation to fairies than human cultists. Unlike the completely negative stereotype of satanic cultists, aliens like fairies are *liminal personae* from unknown, *liminal space*.[3] They can be helpful, kind, indifferent, threatening, or malevolent. Moreover, as Peter M. Rojcewicz perceives, "tradition notes the extraterrestrial nature of some fairies." Given these similarities, it is somewhat surprising that folklorists have not examined these phenomena as thoroughly as might be expected. Perhaps this lack of inquiry can be linked to what the author calls the "questionable nature" of this kind of anomalous lore.

Rojcewicz approaches the similarities of fairy and UFO phenomena from a comparative and a Jungian perspective, first examining corresponding phenomena such as "shape-shifting" and "luminous entities" and then arguing that the archetypal structures of such anomalous folkloric forms "intimately relate" to structures "inherent in nature."[4] In turn, he believes that this understanding can assist humanity by illuminating the "pivotal role we play in the participatory enterprise we call reality," an antidote to the alienation brought on by "the relativity of knowledge," a "scientific worldview" that "rob[s] the universe of spirit and purpose."

A point that Rojcewicz raises in stressing the importance of studying anomalous folklore strikes a chord which rings though the many essays in this anthology, namely fairylore as a special kind of human *experience*, a kind that Jung linked to *unusual emotions*.[5] It is hoped that in gaining more understanding about the fairy of tradition we might all benefit, for the unusual emotions induced by fairy experiences have been measured responses to the needs of the human condition.

Notes

1. Benjamin Lee Whorf, "Language, Mind, and Reality," *Language, Thought, and Reality: Selected Writings of Benjamin Lee Whorf*, ed. John B. Carroll (Cambridge: M.I.T. P, 1956) 246–70.

2. Bill Ellis, "The Devil-Worshippers at the Prom: Rumor-Panic as Therapeutic Magic," *Western Folklore* 49.1 (1990): 27–49; Jeffrey S. Victor, "Satanic Cult Legends as Contemporary Legend," *Western Folklore* 49.1 (1990): 51–81.

3. For a fascinating material culture demonstration of popular beliefs regarding outer space see Douglas Curran, *In Advance of the Landing: Folk Concepts of Outer Space* (New York: Abbeville P, 1985).

4. For an appraisal of the relevance of C.G. Jung to folklore see Carlos Drake, "Jung and His Critics," *Journal of American Folklore* 80 (1967): 321–33.

5. C.G. Jung, *Flying Saucers: A Modern Myth of Things Seen in the Sky*, trans. R.F.C. Hull (1959; London: Routledge and Kegan Paul, 1977) 3.

The Semantics of the Word *Fairy:* Making Meaning Out of Thin Air

Noel Williams

Supernatural names have long fascinated both folklorists and linguists, not least because they name things that do not exist. It is a difficult question, semantically, to define the meaning of a word such as *fairy*, or even to delimit the boundaries of its significance within the language. I devoted a substantial study (Williams 1983) to the problem of defining the meaning of supernatural names, exploring every ramification of the word fairy from its earliest use to the beginnings of the nineteenth century (by when its meaning had, largely, settled down into the set of meanings we still use).

We find, of course, that defining a name that refers to nothing is a complex problem. It is complicated by the ease with which such a word can be used in almost any context imaginable and still bring to bear vague connotations and associations, hints of half-belief, which a word that "labels a thing" (such as *mountain, road, dog*) does not have.

It is complicated also by the habit folklorists have of mentioning vague processes of "confusion" in the minds of the medieval writers who first recorded the word, whenever the question of the derivations or origins of *fairy* are raised.

So in this essay I want to try and clarify a little of this confusion, to tease out some of the strands that were woven into the name *fairy*. I want to argue that *fairy* in particular, but more generally *any* supernatural name, is necessarily amorphous, and to show that from its earliest use in English, from the earliest occurrences of fairies in England, no single meaning has ever been paramount. At the same time, I will also argue that there is a central concept, that of "fatedness" which antedates the earliest occurrences of *fairy* and is captured by both the earliest and much later use of the word, and that this central concept perhaps best characterizes the *fairy* concept from its first use.

Modern commentators are reasonably certain that *fairy* has a clear and single meaning and a reasonable etymology which established (or retrospectively supports) that meaning. However, the fact that *fairy* has a reasonably fixed meaning today does not mean that it did so yesterday.

Nor, of course, does the general contemporary acceptance of a plausible etymology mean that the etymology is correct, or more importantly, that early users of *fairy* in English were influenced by a "correct" etymology. Rather it seems to be the case both that the meaning of *fairy* has varied a great deal within the period 1320–1829 (the period of the study I conducted), and that its early use, the foundation for much subsequent variation, was not simple or single but potentially at least influenced by a large number of factors extant before its first use in written English. Such variation is also evident in the form of the word, so much so that one cannot define that form absolutely. So the word is itself neither an object with clear boundaries nor possessed of a meaning with clear boundaries. Examination of this inherent vagueness and confusion is crucial to an understanding of the word, hence to the phenomena it is used to name.

Supernatural names in the period of transition from Old English to Middle English deserve fuller study, and the early development of *fairy* can only fully be understood against such a background, but that is beyond the scope of this paper. Rather, an attempt is made to show some of the meanings that may have accrued to *fairy* prior to its first recorded occurrence in English, in particular the central notion of "fatedness," to indicate the reasons why the etymology is not as straightforward as might be supposed, and to show that even if we can assign a simple history to the origin and development of the form, so many traditions may be involved in that development that the meanings attached to that form are already varied and complex.

Before proceeding to issues of meaning, however, I wish to make a brief examination of the form of the word, as even this is a matter of some complexity that affects the semantic problem to some degree.

The Form of Fairy

The form of a word may have important stylistic implications, which can in turn affect stylistic meaning and may also have an influence on other semantic areas, e.g., if the word frequently occurs as the last word in a rhyming couplet, its phonological form will influence collocation, particularly if the range of rhymes for the word within the language is limited. In order to study this word I built a corpus of occurrences in English prior to 1829, which is as comprehensive as such a corpus can be: 2,064 tokens of the word *fairy* from 468 texts, associated with context (i.e. words immediately linked with *fairy* in the text) totalling 30,283 words.

In this corpus the form of *fairy* has only two important aspects, the phonemic/graphemic and the syntactic. As it is a written corpus it is concerned with types that have graphemic rather than phonemic shape. However, purely graphemic description would suggest that this corpus contains ninety-three different forms of the same word, as shown in Figure 1. Even allowing for syntactic marking (generally for plurality) there are at least fifty different forms within the corpus which we would regard as a single word.

Figure 1
Total Occurrences

1	Fae	1	Faee	1	Faerey
49	Faerie	37	Faeries	2	Faerily
131	Faery	1	Faerye	18	Faeryes
5	Faerys	1	Fai	5	Faie
7	Faierie	6	Faieries	8	Faiery
6	Faies	1	Fair	2	Faire
1	Fairees	1	Faires	1	Fairfolkis
4	Fairi	52	Fairie	477	Fairies
1	Fairly	724	Fairy	9	Fairye
7	Fairyes	4	Fairyism	12	Fairyland
128	Fairys	1	Fare	1	Faree
1	Fares	1	Farey	1	Fareys
20	Farie	9	Faries	7	Fary
3	Farye	2	Faryes	1	Faryies
24	Fay	4	Faye	1	Fayeree
14	Fayerie	1	Fayeri	1	Fayeriy
4	Fayery	8	Fayerye	2	Fayeryes
4	Fayes	4	Fayre	3	Fayree
1	Fayrees	3	Fayres	39	Fayrey
1	Fayri	44	Fayrie	67	Fayries
1	Fayrre	1	Fayrrey	55	Fayry
19	Fayrye	1	Fayryes	1	Fayry e
25	Fays	1	Fearie	3	Fearrie
1	Fee	1	Fees	1	Feire
1	Feirie	1	Feiries	3	Feries
1	Fery	1	Ferye	1	Feyrie
1	Feyrrye	1	Ffair	2	Ffarye
1	Ffayeries	2	Ffayre	2	Ffayrees
1	Ffayrie	1	Ffey	1	Ffeyre
1	Ffeyrye	5	Phairi	1	Phareis
4	Pharie	2	Pharies	1	Phary

The most efficient and elegant means of describing these forms as types of one lexeme is to define the lexeme phonemically and regard each graphemic token as a particular realization of the stated phonemic shape. Thus all of the forms shown in Figure 1 can be regarded as graphemic variants of the phonemic words /fɛəri/ and /fei/. However there are in addition to the forms recorded in the corpus a number of borderline cases found in other texts which seem related to *fairy* but cannot be generated by the figure. These include farrisee,[1] pharisee,[2] farisee,[3] pharises,[4] farises,[5] fairisees, fairish, vaairy, faireen, fairesses,[6] ferishers,[7] fareeses,[8] feriers, ferrishyn,[9] fairises,[10] ferrish,[11] ferish,[12] frairy,[13] fraries,[14] vairies,[15] fairney,[16] and farefolkis.[17]

Most of these additional forms cannot be accounted for by any simple rules for graphemic realization of the defined phonemic shape. For *fairy* these forms thus represent the kind of confusing periphery found for many supernatural names, such as *bog* and *boo* (See Williams 1980 and below). Such a form as *farefolkis* would certainly seem to be derived from *fair* and *folk*,[18] the *fair folk* being a common euphemism for fairies,[19] yet it may well be formed with the underlying /fɛəri/ in mind, as the meanings or denotata of *farefolkis* and *fairy* would pretheoretically seem to be identical.

We can fairly assume, however, that *fairy* entered the language with one recognizable phonemic shape and was subsequently pronounced differently in different dialects of English. The two phonemic words are thus best regarded as descriptions of an underlying or original form, rather than a precise description of the pronunciation represented by each token. In most cases it would appear that graphemic variation is a result of the lack of universal orthographic conventions in Middle English, as the majority of graphemic variants disappear with the advent of printing.

Even the form of the word from its earliest is therefore unclear, and the collocations and connotations that may result from such forms (such as the attractiveness of *fair* and the lightness of *air*) accrue from the earliest date.

The Etymology of Fairy

Many words used to refer to the supernatural are of uncertain or obscure origin, often existing in an imprecise matrix of relations with groups of other words either related in form but differing in meaning, or different in form but related in meaning. This problem is central to the study of supernatural names. Groups which best demonstrate this confusion are those centering on bog, bug, and puck.[20] One could describe these three groups as one, based on the formula:

/bilabial plosive + back vowel + velar fricative/

which encodes such meanings as "frightening" and "revolting." However such a description must on the one hand account for possible relations with words such as *boghost (barghest)*, *phooka*, *bugalug*, *boobagger*, *tantarabogus* and on the other for the meanings of homonyms, such as "scarecrow," "nightjar," "soft land," "pimple," "nest of caterpillars," "boastful," and "railway truck." Clearly an examination of these interrelations must consider not only standard etymology but also folk etymology, and a complex series of relations between homonyms and homophones. In principle, such an explication might be possible; in practice it is not. To account for the meaning "nightjar," for example, which might be postulated as a separate lexeme from puck, meaning "demon," one must be aware of the folk belief that the nightjar attacked cattle and drank their blood and/or caused disease, as did demons called pucks.

The nightjar is called *goatsucker* for a similar reason. However, such an explication also must be aware that elves, witches, hares, hedgehogs, fairies and other creatures were held to be responsible either for nocturnal attacks on cattle or for taking the nourishment from them.[21] Thus not only is the question of the separateness of the lexemes difficult to determine, but also the meaning(s) of those lexemes are part of a larger set of relationships between the behavior of real creatures, beliefs about the behavior of supernatural creatures and words used to refer to all these phenomena.

Similarly, the meaning "scarecrow" for *bug(ge)* might be treated as a separate lexeme from the meaning "object of dread," were it not for the fact that scaring crows is obviously related to frightening people. Yet if bug = "scarecrow" is regarded as the same lexeme as bug = "demon," what is the status of the forms *bugalug*, *bucca*, *bucca-bo*, *bogle*, *boggart* and *boggy-bo*[22] which all mean "scarecrow," but only some of which are recorded as also having a meaning approximating "demon"?

Furthermore, many other words denoting the supernatural or similar to words denoting the supernatural also mean "scarecrow." How are we to decide which forms are derived from "demon" or vice versa, or if both are derived from an ur-form meaning "frightening object"; which word should be listed as "the same lexeme" and which separated; or whether it is necessary to explicate the relations between other supernatural names and "scarecrow" in order to obtain a full understanding of the (possible) relations in these groups?

The problem is not even as straightforward as this account suggests as there are identical forms with other meanings, forms which seem related to *bug* which have those meanings, some of which also mean "demon" and some of which do not, and the same meanings are encoded by forms which are only distantly related to *bug*.

Similar problems can be found in many other areas of lexis, particularly in vocabularies drawn largely from oral rather than written varieties. Indeed it may be true that the notions of distinct lexemes and "etymological laws" may be more artificial than the lexicographer might like to believe. It would certainly seem that the closer a dictionary or word list comes to recording the actual oral vocabulary currently in use, the greater are such problems. Oral language makes use of many nonce-forms, lexical items subject to fashion, slang, colloquialism and vocabularies drawn from areas of casual or temporary interest, many of which, unsurprisingly, are never collected in dictionaries and, if they are collected, are often recorded with meanings somewhat more restricted than those found in usage, for usage often employs words with very vague application.

Fairy is one word which enters into such a complex of relations. In the first place its etymology is by no means clear, although one etymology now seems to be generally accepted. Etymologies for *fairy* have generally been derived from words denoting female supernatural creatures in other languages. Thus it has been derived from the last syllable of Latin *nympha*,[23] and from Arabic *peri*.[24] Alternatively it has been derived from words with supernatural associations, or words connoting properties regarded as attributes of fairies. Amongst these are derivations from *fair*,[25] Old English *fagan*,[26] and Latin *fatua*.[27]

The accepted etymology also follows the pattern of derivation from a word taken to mean female supernatural creatures.[28] Ultimately it would seem to be derived from Latin *fatum* = "thing said." This gave *fata* = "fate," a neuter plural which, it is supposed, was misinterpreted in the Dark Ages as feminine singular, *fata* = "female fate, goddess," and these goddesses of fate were supposedly identified with Greek Lachesis, Atropos and Clotho and subsequently, following the Roman conquest of the Celtic peoples, further identified with various Celtic female deities manifested as tripartite. The evidence for such goddesses (known collectively as *matronae*) is largely archaeological and generally in Roman stonework.

Several examples may be seen in museums along Hadrian's Wall, such as a stone relief at Housesteads, Northumberland depicting three identical hooded deities;[29] other examples can be found at Ancaster, Lincolnshire; Kirkham, Lancashire; and Cirencester, Gloucestershire,[30] which suggest a general adoption of the tripartite goddess(es) by the Roman invaders. It is presumed therefore that *fata* became attached to the Celtic goddess(es) in vulgar Latin and, as that language became Old French, the /t/ was dropped to give *fa'a*, thence *fae*. There seems to be no written evidence for these changes.

The first recorded Old French forms occur in Old French and Anglo-Norman romances of the twelfth century and later, and in collections of tales and anecdotes made in Latin, also in the twelfth and thirteenth centuries. It is presumed either that the association of classical and Celtic goddesses is preserved in these romances (i.e., the fays of romance are derived from older Celtic goddesses) or that a further identification was made, this time by the romanciers, between Celtic goddesses called *fa'a and creatures in romance. In support of such an argument one could point to such features as the frequency with which Celtic females appear in multiples of three, their gifts of prophecy, their association with spinning or their association with the world of the dead. There are many scholarly works which seek to prove that the Arthurian cycle of romances and some related romances are derived from Celtic religion or myth.[31]

This identification firstly gives a noun *fai, fae, fay* referring to an individual female with supernatural powers, probably best translated as "enchantress," so that we must suppose that the substantive *faierie* is derived from this, meaning "enchantment." Later, this was again misunderstood or perhaps extended to signify "fairyland," and as a plural "enchantresses," whose singular was then mistakenly taken to be not *fay* but *fairie*. At this stage of development, perhaps at about the middle of the thirteenth century, this complex of meanings was carried into romances written in Middle English, the first recorded examples occurring in the Auchinleck manuscript (ca. 1330).[32]

There are clearly many imperfections and difficulties in this, the most generally accepted, etymology. In the first place different commentators give different accounts of the precise development of the word and of the interrelations supplied by the evidence. All agree that *fata* was interpreted as feminine and eventually gave four distinct meanings in Old French which passed into English, namely (1) enchantment, illusion; (2) fairyland, land of illusion; (3) human with special powers; (4) supernatural beings; but they differ as to which came first, and which developed from which. Although this etymology seems plausible in essence, it necessarily relies rather heavily upon vague processes of "identification" and "misunderstanding." Most important is the fact that many if not most of the occurrences of Old French *fee* and Middle English *fay*, or *fairy* are not nouns and if nouns, frequently do not denote or refer to "enchantress" or "female spirit." In a sample survey of one Anglo-Norman and six Old French works which use the word, of fifteen occurrences ten are adjectival, four nouns and one doubtful, being in noun form but used adjectivally (Orva la fee).[33] Three of the nouns occur in one work.[34] By far the most popular phrase is *c'est chose faee*, which is used six times of these fifteen. The *Dictionnaire de L'Ancienne Langue Francaise*[35] is able to quote many examples of *faer*, "to enchant," almost all of which are of the past participle *fae,* i.e., an "adjectival" form, but offers very few examples of fee, noun, "enchantress."

This would suggest that the notion of *fairy* in its earliest uses is not primarily to denote creatures, but a quality of phenomena or events which may or may not be associated with creatures. In Middle English before 1400 only two of thirty-five occurrences seem certainly to refer to creatures and both these are plural (or possibly collective):

> Prosepina and al hire fayerye
> Disporten hem and maken melodye[36]

> This maketh that they ben no fayeryes[37]

Certainly many of the other occurrences in this period could be interpreted as referring to creatures (a further fourteen) but none are singular nouns referring to individual creatures and when reference to any individual creature is made, *fairy* takes the form of an adjective which modifies a noun which denotes "creature," e.g.,

> A fairy knit herin is[38]

There is no instance of *fay* or *fairy* being used in Middle English to mean "enchantress" before *Morgne la Fay* [39] and the only other probable examples are *Galathe was a fairye* and *Galathe, þe which was a fairye*[40] and *by Nygromancye of a Faee.*[41] Even here *la Faye,* as in *Orva la fee* above, may perhaps be better translated "the magical," "the strange," "(of) unusual power," or "(of) the strangeness" than "the fairy," the appellation being probably attributive rather than defining, as in *Sir Brennor le Noire* or *Balin le Savage.*[42]

Thus, though it is certainly true that *fay* is used on some occasions to mean "enchantress" it does not seem to have been the most frequent or most central use of the more frequent term *fairy.* Although the meanings seem intuitively to be related, it has never been made clear precisely how a word meaning "fate" in an abstract or general sense could come to mean "enchantress," and thence give a further generic word "enchanted." It seems more in accord with the evidence, and also more likely, that the notion of fate "degenerated" into that of enchantment, and that this notion of "fatedness" is the central connotation of *fairy,* with *fay* being derived from, or developed parallel to this conceptual development. It seems likely that the generally accepted etymology, in following previous etymologies and attempting to derive Modern English *fairy* from an earlier form meaning "unusual female creature," is committing an error made by those earlier attempts, that of reading the later meaning into earlier forms. However, the more evidence one considers the more likely it seems that the idea of a female supernatural being as specifically *faee* does not antedate the general idea of *fairie*, hence the etymology may not be based upon *fata* giving *fa'a*, but on an original term for the general concept.

Such a concept may lie in the vague idea of "fatedness," a quality in the world which can control and direct the actions of humanity, and hence is more powerful than humanity. For example, there is clearly a link between the idea of fate and that of death. Death is perhaps the one mystery for which people feel they can never have an explanation fully adequate to their experience and the supernatural, in its widest sense, has always been connected with death, and is probably universally so.

A similar connection can be found in Old English. The word *faege* meaning "fated, doomed to die" was a commonplace of Old English poetry. It often seems to carry with it a semi-supernatural idea of "the marked man," such as is still evident in the modern notion of "the bullet with my number on it." Perhaps such fatalism was a response to frequent warfare and violent death. Certainly it is an expression of the central place of battle in the Anglo-Saxon scheme of things. The notion is retained in the Scottish word *fey*. By extension it was used to mean "destined," "dead," "accursed," "feeble," "cowardly." It is easy to see how the notion of some form of supernatural or divine selection could accompany use of this word, as part of its associative meaning, especially in relation to the denotational meanings "fated" and "accursed."

In this connection one might suggest that the notion of female supernatural beings who mark or select the dead may have been an important one in Anglo-Saxon pagan belief and may therefore have added a connotation to *faege* which encouraged this association. The word *waelcyrge* (valkyrie) meaning "choosers of the slain," is used to gloss *Bellone, Allecto, Venus, erinys* and *tisifone*[43] and is regarded by a least one commentator as a "fierce and vengeful spirit of the underworld."[44] Judith, shortly before she kills Holofernes, is called *ides aelfscinu*.[45] *Ides* is also used of Grendel's mother "apparently as a synonym with *aglaecwif*, a 'formidable' or 'terrifying woman.'"[46]

Aelf means "supernatural" and *scinu* has supernatural connotations, belonging to a group of related words concerned with "appearance," "shining" and "skin." *Scinn* means both "skin" and "phantom, illusion, magical image"; *scinncraeft* is "sorcery, magic"; *scinnes* is "radiance"; *scinan* "shine"; *sciene* "beautiful, brilliant, light"; *scinnhiw* "specter, illusion." The two groups are separable only by virtue of the long and short vowels but, as Storms says, the length of the vowel in *scinn* is uncertain:

> It is uncertain whether we have a long or a short vowel. The etymology points to a long vowel, the form *scinn* with double *n* to a short one.[47]

Insofar as all examples seem connected by the notion of "visual appearance" it seems reasonable to suggest that Anglo-Saxons were aware of a group of supernatural beings having a shining appearance.

Whether this group was evil or not before the advent of Christianity cannot be determined. In Salomon and Saturn a fiend (*feond*) is called *scines*. *Scinn* is used to gloss *fantasia, portentum, imaginatio, praestigium, monstrum, nebula* and *necromantia,* and is used in the Leechdoms to mean "affected by apparitions, haunted."[48] It seems to differ from sickness caused by devils, elves or dwarfs in that there is an implication of hallucination. Storms relates *scin* to the ignis fatuus, which may be one source of the conception of supernatural radiance or nimbus:

> The magical connotation of *scin* probably arose from flames appearing in decaying trees or in marshy districts and caused by the phosphorescent effects of the rotting process. The flame and the light produced in this way flares up in continually varying spots, thus creating an impression of dancing spirits.[49]

Judith, therefore, is given all the connotations of a death-dealing, supernatural female. In one charm mention is also made of bees called *sige-wif,* i.e., "victory-women," who have supernatural power.[50] Thus the bees in this charm, Judith, *waelcyrge* (which normally denotes "witch") and Grendel's mother are all described as females who are connected with death and have supernatural power. Though the evidence is slight, one might conclude that this conception was available to speakers of Old English, though by the time of the importation of *fairy* such an association could hardly have been a central one, for those speakers had long been Christian.

One might wish to argue therefore that even if the notion of the "fatal woman" was the central one in Old French (and this does not seem to be the case) in Middle English sufficient similarity between the connotations, forms and sounds of Old English *faege* and Anglo-Norman *faierie* existed to promote the connotation "fatedness" to the central semantic position. That *faierie* took over some of the connotations of *faege* may particularly seem to be the case in view of the fact that Layamon's *Brut,*[51] one of the last works to use *faege* extensively is also one of the first to use material from the romance cycles. Furthermore Layamon uses *aluen*[52] to describe creatures associated with the birth, weapon and death of Arthur (hence his "fate"), creatures whose functions are later fulfilled by Morgan la fee, the Lady of the Lake, and other fays in later versions. This suggests that the notion of "fatedness" was associated with the romance material, but had not yet been encapsulated in the word *faierie.*

Thus at the close of the twelfth and beginning of the thirteenth centuries occur the following recorded phenomena. Firstly Old French *faer* has produced Anglo-Norman *faee* in a romance of ca. 1170[53] which is almost certainly derived from an Old English story. Twenty years later we have a romance in early Middle English whose immediate source is French (Wace's *Brut*) but which also appears to have incorporated some local, probably Celtic, tales for which an Old English word *alven* is used, and which also employs a word similar both in form and meaning to Old French/Anglo-Norman *faee*, including the forms *faeie, feie, faei, faie,* and *feye*.[54]

By 1320 the three traditions have sufficiently intermingled so that one word, *faierie,* may do duty in stories from any source, and *faege* is diminished in use (though not totally redundant). There can thus be no clear demonstration of the possible influences of Old English *faege* on Old French *faer,* and the point should not be pressed, but there remains a strong possibility that the associative meaning of the Old English word is in part transferred to that of the import. However this may be, the notion of "fatedness" does seem to be a strong one in the development of *fairy* in English from its earliest occurrences, and this is particularly evident in the development of later associations such as "death," "hurt," "sickness," "birth," and "love,"[55] all of which appear as strong collocations later in my corpus.

The hypothesis of *faierie* preceding *fai* in Old French would be happier if there were an intermediary Medieval Latin form **fatalia* or **fataria,* for which there is no evidence and the forms themselves seem unlikely. Keightley says:

> In the Middle Ages there was in use a Latin verb, *fatare,* derived from *fatum* or *fata,* and signifying to enchant.[56]

However, the only recorded examples of this verb seem to be twelfth century or later, by which time Old French *fae* existed, and those Latin examples all appear to be participles. It would therefore not contravene the evidence to suggest that the recorded Latin forms are latinate borrowings of a previously extant popular word. Grimm quotes a thirteenth century manuscript:

> Aquisgrani licitur Ays, et dicitur eo, quod Karolus tenebat ibi quandam mulierem fatatam, sive quandam fatam, quae alio nomine nimpha vel dea vel adriades.[57]

Latham[58] cites *fatalitatis, fatatus* and *fatata,* which are translated as "fairy nature," "haunted" and "fairy" respectively. Although no specific source is cited these seem to come from Walter Map's *De a Curialum* (ca. 1190)[59] and Gervase of Tilbury's *Otia Imperialia* (ca. 1212),[60] in which case these three texts seem to constitute the entire evidence for the Latin verb *fatare.* As these texts all seem to be later than the earliest Old French sources, the evidence is not clear cut. The Latin forms may, as Keightley argues, represent an earlier Latin verb which became Old French *faierie*, or they may represent an attempt to express in Medieval Latin a concept already current in vulgar speech.

In either case Old French *faee* may be derived from these or may have developed along parallel lines as Gervase also uses *fadus* and *fadae* with what appears to be a nominal function, so that they may represent a noun (= "a fairy") rather than a participle (= "enchanted"). The contexts of use are translated by Ritson as:"some of this kind of larvae, which they named *fadae*, we have heard to be lovers" and "I know not if it were a true horse, or if it were a fairy (*fadus*), as men assert."[61] Here in the earliest uses there exists the same ambiguity that persists throughout the period examined. It is seldom clear if *fairy* (or *fee*, or *fadus*) is being used as a nominal or with a modifying function of some kind, i.e., whether the Entity described is regarded as an Object or an Item.

The evidence of the cognate forms Italian *fada*[62] and Spanish *fada*, *hada*[63] affirm the accepted etymology of *fay*.[64] It seems at least possible, therefore, that the two forms *fay* and *fairy* did not develop one from the other, but each under the influence of the other from Medieval Latin roots which were themselves related, and both were used to characterize a particular quality in experience which can be called "fatedness" and was probably felt to be a particular feature of Celtic tales. The invention or increased use of *fairy* in the twelfth century can be explained as the adoption of a generic term used to cover a set of tales and beliefs for which the Welsh themselves seem to have had no term. For it seems that Welsh names for supernatural beings tend either to be specific, unique to a particular place or circumstance, or euphemistic, such as *Tylwyth Teg* (the fair family).[65] Old French *faierie* seems to be a more objective term, less culturally restricted than these names. The Celtic peoples possessed a series of beliefs not felt to be totally homogenous by the culture to which they belonged, but appearing so to a culture which found each belief alien. In a similar manner Christianity seems to have grouped together multifarious creatures of Teutonic belief under the term devils.

Thus, despite possible origins in oral vocabulary, *fairy* is best regarded as primarily a literary word, and therefore not initially an item in the vocabulary of the illiterate in Medieval England. To express their supernatural beliefs medieval peasants in England almost certainly retained Old English words. Some of these passed out of usage; some were emptied of specific meaning and equated with the Christian devil; some occasionally occur in literature but most seem to go underground for a long period, preserved largely in oral tradition, to re-emerge in records of later folk belief.

Of the first kind Old English *scin, scinlac, drymann, ent, orc* and *aeglaeca* seem to disappear by the fifteenth century.[66] Of the second, most aspects of Anglo-Saxon pagan belief seem to have been regarded by Christians as evil and therefore devilish. Many Old English words used about the supernatural have come to characterize generic evil, or personified evil, i.e. devils, or the specific source of evil, the Devil. *Elf* (Old English *alven*) seems occasionally to be used in this sense. *Feond* and *deoful* are the words most frequently used. *Puca*, *bugge* and *schucke* are also used with these senses, particularly in Early Middle English. Those Old English supernatural names preserved in literature are generally those in the latter group; used to characterize evil. Their occurrence correlates well with alliterative traditions. In *St Juliana* and *Seinte Marharete*, *schucke* may well have been chosen for its alliterative value,[67] as may *pouke* in several occurrences in Piers Plowman,[68] and *thurse* in *Morte D'Arthur* and *Seinte Marharete*.[69] It seems that the change in literary fashion from traditional alliteration to French rhyme not only caused a certain conflict between rival vocabularies for one semantic area (resulting in, for example, the tendency for *fairy* to replace *elf*, or *gobelyn* to replace *thurse* and *schuck*), but also a reduction in alliterative verse reduced the need for a rich vocabulary of synonyms. Conversely one can see that the alliterative revival tended to reintroduce such synonyms. In addition one could note that in Old French and Anglo-Norman it is easy to rhyme on /ɪ/ or /iː/,[70] and this facility was useful to Middle English writers adopting the French style,[71] tending therefore to reinforce the use of *fairy* (and perhaps supporting the contention that it is primarily a literary word).

Yet, although the records indicate that Old English supernatural names declined in Middle English, both in frequency of use and in specificity of meaning, many of the displaced words seem to have been alive in oral traditions. *Bugge* becomes part of a complex and widespread set of meanings.[72] *Schucke* seems to preserve its original meaning of "phantom" in East Anglian dialect *Shuck* and *Shock*.[73] *Pouke* is recalled into literature in the late sixteenth century with a modified sense, but is probably preserved in the dialect names *Hodge Poker*, *Tom Poker*, *Old Poker*, and *Mum-poker*.[74] *Thurse* is retained as a component in many dialect supernatural names.[75]

It seems likely, therefore, that as the literary vocabulary of French superseded that of English in this area, although the words must have been felt to be equivalent in the central meaning, the new vocabulary would tend to be modified by connotations inherited from the old. There was not, as folklorists tend to express it, a "confusion" of fairies and elves in medieval belief but a tendency of the more generic and more fashionable word to attract and take over the associative meanings of its rivals. Chaucer, for example, uses *fayerye* predominantly to characterize a kind of place or experience[76] but *elf* for a kind of creature.[77] Although on four occasions he uses *fayerye* collectively of creatures, he never uses the word for an individual.

In addition to those aspects of meaning which *fairy* may have acquired from displaced Old English lexemes a number of disparate elements seem to have been attracted by the word from its earliest occurrences in English, largely from Classical and Celtic traditions. Insofar as *fairy* may represent a development of a classical word to accommodate a set of Celtic beliefs then the traditions certainly combine, but to ask whether the traditions were "identified" or "confused" would be to ask a meaningless question. In the romances the important feature was the exotic itself, not its source. Details would be assimilated and combined by individual tale-tellers in accord with their own sense of the degree of the exotic to be incorporated, the amount of familiar detail to be reiterated, the degree to which the familiar could be heightened or exaggerated, and the appropriateness of the relationships of these details to the particular idiom, form and tone of the work. These would be modified by the author's knowledge and abilities, the demands and capabilities of his audience, and the accidents of transmission. Probably in very few cases would only one consideration apply in the adoption of a detail. There would be a complicated balance to achieve between recognition of the familiar and the enjoyment of novelty. Hence there can be no single explanation for the complete form of any romance as we have inherited it.

As romance is the genre in which most of the earliest occurrences of *fairy* are to be found it is worth examining one example in detail to indicate the degree of complexity of the texts in which *fairy* may be embedded, and thus both the complex semantic net which surrounds it and the fact that we are not dealing with a word which begins with a simple meaning which is later expanded and confounded but one which from its earliest uses is problematic. *Sir Orfeo* is a good example as it has been much discussed as one of the best and most intriguing of the short metrical romances. It was probably based on an Old French source, the lai d'Orphey which may have been written by Marie de France, being similar to the *Lai de Freine* and *Sir Landeval*. If so it may well be based on an original Breton lay.[78] This Breton lay may have influenced or conversely been influenced by Walter Map.[79] The Middle English author may have introduced modifications extant in Anglo-Saxon tradition as found in King Alfred's translation of Boethius. The original tale may have been derived from Boethius, Virgil or Ovid[80] or all three, and might have been a deliberate attempt at welding the classical myth to a Celtic one (such as the *Wooing of Etain*[81]) or may simply represent the rewriting of the classical along familiar lines. The Auchinleck romance may therefore contain elements from Classical Latin, Medieval Latin, Old French, Old English, Breton and Irish as well as Middle English traditions, and there are also possible analogies with Welsh and continental tales. A final statement of the "source" of *Sir Orfeo* is thus impossible, and any attempt to isolate the constituent elements of the traditions it embodies seems certain to fail.[82]

Those features in *Sir Orfeo* which might be interpreted as belonging to or contributing to the experience of *fairy* constitute about half the poem. It is unclear which, if any, of those features properly belong to that experience whether from the characters', the author's or the audience's point of view. There are no details that can be isolated and treated as the distinguishing features of what constitutes *fairy* for the Orfeo poet. There are two ways of attempting to overcome this problem. One is to regard the poet's treatment of *fairy* as the reproduction of a typification, then to search out other statements of the supernatural which contain that same typification. From the point of view of literature this is a search for themes and parallels; from the point of view of folklore it is a search for motifs; from the point of view of language it is a search for cognates, etymologies and parallel terms. The second approach is to regard the poet's attitude as in some sense metaphorical, i.e., he is trying to convey an idea of *fairy*, his own subjective understanding of the term, not in any detail or series of details but in the subjective response those cumulative details arranged in that way may arouse in the reader.

This is essentially a romantic interpretation of the poetic method and as such is somewhat suspect when applied to writing in Middle English.

In general, however, if any writer is concerned to convey an experience and s/he cannot rely on reference to external details of that experience adequately to recreate it for a reader he must resort to an evocative method. In literature this resides in metaphor and image; in language in the associative meaning of words; and in folklore in the levels of irrational belief certain human situations demand.

From the earliest date *fairy* seems to be used both as a typification of experience (i.e., denotationally or referentially, applied to a real experience) and as a metaphor for experience (i.e., associatively, connotatively) meshing both kinds of meaning, as can be seen from the unclear etymology, from the vagueness and ambiguity of early uses and from the number of contributory influences on romances such as *Sir Orfeo*.

Conclusion

So the relation between supernatural name and putative referent is a loose one, such that the form of the word may vary whilst the referent remains constant (in some sense), or the referent may vary for a word of fixed form, or both may vary, as shown also by the *bog* and *puck* examples. The meaning and origin of *a* may be nothing like as precise as we might imagine or as dictionaries might lead us to believe. Nor is *fairy* either unique or distinct from other names such as *elf, pixy, puck,* and *goblin*. It has no precisely specifiable form, but shades into forms such as *frairies*, *ferrishers*, and *fairfolk*.

The meanings it possesses are not specific to the chosen language nor period, and are dependent on, or related to meanings of other words and similar words in other languages in other periods.

We may conclude that *fairy* exists as a fuzzy point on not one but several intersecting continua, and while analysis of that point does pare much of the fuzziness away, it serves only to disguise the continua and distort the object of study. Thus no matter how precise our description of the meaning of *fairy* it must be no more than a model.

For example it is clear that *fairy* begins in English with a complex meaning. It acquires that meaning not merely by virtue of the texts in which it is used, but probably by virtue of those texts in which it is not used. It acquires meaning by virtue of extant words which are similar and may or may not be used in similar texts. It acquires meaning by virtue of its previous history, of the traditions and beliefs its different users are aware of, of rhetorical constraints on usage and fashions in diction, such as the preference for rhyming "French" verse over alliterative "English." And it acquires meaning by virtue of complex cultural interactions concerning the supernatural. Thus one of the key notions which links usage of *fairy* from its earliest proto-usage seems to be that of "fatedness" but we cannot trace this notion to any particular culture, tradition, style, register or period, and we cannot even specify what that notion entails. "Fatedness" is itself a vague concept. How then are we to define the vague concept *fairy* if we can only appeal in turn to other vague concepts? As a word, it remains as ephemeral as the phenomena it names.

Notes

1. Wright 1898–1905, s.v. fairy ; Moor 1970, s.v.
2. Rye 1895, s.v. frary; Briggs 1976, s.v.; Simpson 1976, 75.
3. Wright 1898–1905, s.v. fairy; Keightley 1900, 306; Briggs 1976, s.v.; Briggs 1977, 217.
4. Hartland 1890, 89.
5. Briggs 1977, 98.
6. Wright 1898–1905, s.v. *fairy*.
7. Wright 1898–1905, s.v. *fairy*; Briggs 1976, s.v.
8. Simpson 1976, 75.
9. Briggs 1976, s.v; Briggs 1977, 217.
10. Briggs and Tongue 1965 34; Tongue 1970, 78–9.
11. Moore 1971, 34.
12. Moore 1971, 36.
13 Rye 1895, s.v.
14. *Folklore* VII (1896): 3–4; Keightley 1900, 306; Briggs 1976, s.v.

15. Briggs and Tongue 1965, 33.

16. Heslop 1892, s.v.

17. Jamieson 1808, s.v.

18. See for example Douglas 1854, Edwards 1974, 25–6 suggests that it is not derived from fair but Old English *faran* = "to go." This may have been the original euphemism but if so it seems to have developed into the more common *fair folk*. In the corpus *fair* collocates forty-five times with *fairy*, and *folk* twenty-one times, both totals being significantly above average.

19. Examples of *fair folk* are Pitcairn 1833, 49, 1.5; Jamieson 1808, s.v. A similar euphemism is the Welsh *Tylwyth Teg*, i.e., "the fair family."

20. Wasson 1957; Henry 1959.

21. See for example: Willan 1811, s.v. toad-bit; Cockayne 1864, II, 14–5, 16–7, 156–7, 174–5, 290–1, 304–5; Courtney 1887, 177; Atkinson 1891, 87–9 and 93; Hole 1945, 50, 56, 95; Stewart 1970, 134–5; Moore 1971, 95, 147–8; Sternberg 1971, 133; Rudkin 1973, 73–5; Evans 1974, 156–8; Hackwood 1974, 150 col. 2; Kirk 1976, 53–4; White 1976, 46; Andrews 1977, 81; MacNeil 1977, 108.

22. These forms can be found in Wright (1898–1905) and Murray (1933).

23. See Keightley 1900, 4 for this and other unlikely etymologies.

24. Keightley 1900, 4–5; Edwards 1974, 15–7.

35. Brand 1853, II 477; Keightley 1900, 4.

26. Keightley 1900, 4; Edwards 1974, 26.

27. Coote 1879.

28. Maury 1896; Keightley 1900, 5–11; Edwards 1974, 4–5; Chambers n.d., 150–1.

29. Birley 1976, 49

30. Ross 1974, 269–70 and plate X.

31. Such as Nutt 1897; Cross 1914; Loomis 1936, 1945, 1956, 1959, 1974; Paton 1936; Newstead 1946.

32. It seems likely that the manuscript was a compilation of stories including romances originating in different places; see Hibbard 1924. Thus it is probably evidence of a relatively widespread use of the word in Middle English before 1330. The occurrences of *fairy* are: *Kyng Alisaunder* 1 occurrence (Smithers 1952, Auchinleck, l. 41); Lai le Freine 1 occurrence (Sands 1966, 235, l. 10); *Reinbrun* 2 occurrences (Zupitza 1969); Degare 2 occurrences (French and Hale 1964); *Sir Orfeo* 5 occurrences (Bliss 1954).

33. The romances examined were: Benoit de Sainte-Maure: *Le Roman de Troie*, ca. 1155–1160; Thomas: *The Romance of Horn* (Anglo-Norman), ca. 1170; *Les Enfances Guillaume*, ca. 1205; *Aiol: chanson de gest*, ca. 1205–1215; Guillaume de Lorris and Jean de Meun: *Le Roman de la Rose*,ca. 1275–80; Jean Froissart: *Meliador*, ca. 1280; *Guillaume de Palerne*, 13th century.

34. Froissart 1895, *Meliador*, ls. 7968, 28366, 30343. Notice furthermore that this is one of the latest of these works.

35. Godefroy 1884.

36. Chaucer 1970, 123, l.2039.

37. Chaucer 1970, 84, l.872.

38. Zupitza 1969, 655, l.29.

39. Tolkien and Grodon 1970, l. 2446.

40. Scrope 1970, Bk LIX, l.6; Bk LIX, l. 13.

41. Watson 1937, 133, l. 20.

42. These are both taken from Malory (1969). As Malory seems to have collected a large number of such names from disparate sources his collection provides a good illustration of the vagueness of connection between name and epithet, as in: I, 12 Sir Uwain le Blanchemains; I, 33 Melot de la Roche; I, 40 Griflet le Fise de Dieu; I, 44 Balin le Savage; I, 162 Sir Sagramoure le Desirous; I, 283 Sir La Cote Male Taile; I, 284 Sir Uwain les Avoutres; I, 319 Hebes le Renoumes; I, 369 Sir Nabon le Noire; I, 370 Sir Nanowne le Petite; I, 370 Isoud la Blanche Mains; I, 398 Sir Breunor le Noire; I, 454 Sir Uwain le Fise de Roi Uriens.

43. Serjeantson 1936.

44. Chadwick 1959.

45. Chadwick 1959.

46. Beowulf 1954.

47. Storms 1948, 114.

48. *Scin-seoc.* Cockayne 1864–6, I.364.

49. Storms 1948, 114.

50. Storms 1948, 140.

51. Layamon 1847.

52. Layamon 1847, II, ls. 384, 385, 463, 489, 500; III, ls. 144, 145

53. Thomas 1964.

54. Clearly there is sufficient similarity with Old French/Anglo-Norman forms to suggest a connection in the minds of anyone knowing both languages. For detailed references see Layamon 1847, glossary.

55. See below *Orfeo* (Bliss 1954); Chaucer's *Merchant's Tale* (Chaucer 1970); *Launfal* (French and Hale 1964) and perhaps *Reinbrun* (Zupitza 1969) seem to connect *fairy* with the dead.

56. Keightley 1900, 6.

57. Grimm 1883–8, I, 405. He cites the source as "Isodori etym. 8, 11 92."

58. Latham 1965, s.v.

59. Map 1923, Dist. II Cha XII.

60. Gervase 1856.

61. Ritson 1831, 13.

62. Battaglia 1961–75, s.v.

63. Boggs et al. 1948, s.v.

64. For additional corroborative examples see Buck 1949, 1499–1500.

65. On the Tylwyth Teg see Briggs 1976, s.v.; Briggs 1977, 120–1, 142, 146, 223.

66. Serjeantson 1936.

67. *Seinte Marhete* 1866, 9, 17; *St Juliana* 1872, 56.

68. Langland 1867–73: A text, X.62, XI.158; B text, XVI.51; C text, XIX.279, XIX.282.

69. *Morte Arthur* 1847, l.1100. *Seinte Marherete* 1866, 12.

70. For a good example employing *faee* see Thomas 1964, ls. 437–454.

71. E.g., Chaucer 1970, *Wife of Bath* ls.859–69 *fayerye/compaignye*; ls.871–2 *dayeryes/fayeryes*; *Sir Thopas* ls. 799 and 802 *espye/Fairye*; ls. 814–5 *Fayerye/symphonye*. Gower 1901, *Confessio Amantis* I, ls. 2316–17 *faie/assaie*; II, ls. 963–4 *certifie/faierie*; II, ls. 1019–1020 *faie/a*; V, ls. 7073–4 a/ a.

72. For discussion of *bugge* and its cognates see Allen (1935–6) and Henry (1959).

73. These names have been recorded as dialectal for devil and various forms of apparition. See: Chambers (1866) II 434; Scott (1895) 145; Briggs (1977) 362.

74. These names can be found in Scott (1895). Although he comments, "This word . . . seems to be identical with the Swedish *pocker, pokker,* the devil, the deuce," he does not mention the possibility of a derivation from *pouke.* Indeed I have not seen such an etymology suggested in any source. Briggs (1977) includes *Mum-poker* and *Pokey-Hokey.* Henry (1959) discusses *puca.*

75. *Thurse* seems to survive in many recent dialect supernatural names. See Scott (1895) on *Guytrash, Hob Thurse, Hob Thurst, Hob Thruss, Hob Thrust, Hob Thrush, Hob Truss, Hob-trash, Hob-dross, Hob Hurst, Thurse, Thurst, Thrust, thruss, Thrush* and *Trash.* See also Clarke (1935) and Dickins (1942). Both *shock* and *trash* seem to be names for black dogs. See Broen (1970) and Briggs (1977) s.v.

76. Chaucer 1970, *Sir Thopas* 1.802 and *Squire's Tale* 1.96 seem to refer to places. *Merchant's Tale* 1.1743 and *Squire's Tale* 1.183 are not clear, probably meaning "illusion."

77. Chaucer 1970, *Man of Lawe's Tale* 1.754, *Wife of Bath* 1.873 refer to individual creatures, and *Miller's Tale* 1.3479 has *elven* as a plural noun. Chaucer also uses *elf* in the compound *elf-quene* (*Wife of Bath* 1.860 and *Sir Thopas* ls. 788, 790, 795 as other later authors use *fairy queen*).

78. Davies 1936.

79. Loomis 1936.

80. Severs 1961.

81. Hibbard 1924.

82. In addition one could note that many elements in this as in other romances are analogous to folk motifs in widely disparate cultures and that, perhaps, one must look to psychological universals for any final account of "sources."

References

Allen, Hope Emily. 1935. "The Influence of the Supernatural on Language." *Proceedings of Modern Language Association of America.* L.63: 1033–46.

———. 1936. "The Influence of the Supernatural on Language." *Proceedings of Modern Language Association of America.* LI.60: 904–20.

Andrews, E. 1977. *Ulster Folklore.* 1913. East Ardsley,Wakefield: EP Publishing.

Atkinson, J.C. 1891. *Forty Years in a Moorland Parish.* London: Macmillan.

Battaglia, Salvatore. 1961–75. *Grande Dizionario Della Lingua Italiana.* 8 vols. Torino: Unione Tipografico.

Birley, A.R. 1976. *Hadrian's Wall.* London: Her Majesty's Stationery Office.

Bliss, A.J., ed. 1954. *Sir Orfeo.* London: Oxford UP.

Boggs, R.S., et al., comps. 1946. *A Tentative Dictionary of Medieval Spanish.* Chapel Hill, North Carolina: U of North Carolina P.

Bond, Warwick, ed. 1911. *Early Plays from the Italian.* Oxford: Clarendon P.

Brand, John. 1853. *Observations on Popular Antiquities.* Enlarged by Sir Henry Ellis. 3 vols. London: Bohn.

Briggs, K.M. 1976. *Dictionary of Fairies.* Harmondsworth: Allen Lane, Penguin Books.

———. 1977. *The Fairies in Tradition and Literature.* London: Routledge and Kegan Paul.

———. 1978. *The Vanishing People.* London: B.T. Batsford.

————, and R.L. Tongue, eds. 1965. *The Folktales of England*. London: Routledge and Kegan Paul.

Brown, Theo. 1970. "The Black Dog in the North Country." *Lore and Language* 1.2: 6–8.

Buck, Carl D. 1949. *A Dictionary of Selected Synonyms in the Principal Indo-European Languages*. Chicago: Chicago UP.

Chadwick, Nora K. 1959. "The Monsters and Beowulf." *The Anglo Saxons*. Ed. P. Clemaes. London: Bowes and Bowes. 171–203.

Chambers, E.K. n.d. "The Fairy World." Appendix A. *A Midsummer Night's Dream*. London: Blackie and Son.

Chambers, R., ed. 1866. *The Book of Days: A Miscellany of Popular Antiquities in Connection with the Calendar*. 2 vols. London: W. and R. Chambers.

Chaucer, Geoffrey. 1970. *Complete Works*. Ed. F.N. Robinson. London: Oxford UP.

Clarke, E.D. 1935. "Obthrust in North Lincolnshire." *Leeds Studies in English* IV: 78–9.

Cockayne, Rev. O., ed. 1864–66. *Leechdoms, Wortcunning, and Starcraft of Early England*. 3 vols. Record Commission IV, Rolls Series 35. London: Longman, Green.

Cockayne, O., and E. Brock, eds. *St. Juliana*. 1872. London: Early English Text Society.

Coote, Henry Charles. 1879. "The Neo-Latin Fay." *Folklore Record* II.

Courtney, M.A. 1887. "Cornish Folk-lore, Pt III." *Folk-Lore Journal* V: 177–186.

Cross, T.P. 1914. "The Celtic Elements in the Lays of Lanval and Graelent." *Modern Philology* XII: 585–644.

Davies, Constance. 1936. "Notes on the sources of 'Sir Orfeo.'" *Modern Language Review* XXXI: 354–7.

Dickins, Bruce. 1942. "Yorkshire Hobs." *Transactions Yorkshire Dialect Society*, vii.

Dobbie, E. van Kirk, ed. 1954. *Beowulf and Judith*. London: Routledge and Kegan Paul.

Douglas, Gavin. 1896. *Poetical Works*. Ed. J. Small. 1874. Edinburgh: Paterson.

Edwards, Gillian. 1974. *Hobgoblin and Sweet Puck*. London: Geoffrey Bles.

Evans, George Ewart, and David Thomson. 1974. *The Leaping Hare*. London: Faber.

Folklore. 1890– .

French, W.H., and C.B. Hale, eds. 1964. *Middle English Metrical Romances*. 2 vols. New York: Russell and Russell.

Froissart, Jean. 1895. *Meliador*. Ed. A. Longnon. 3 vols. Paris: Société des Anciens texts Français.

Gervase of Tilbury 1856. *Otia Imperialia*. Hanover: von Felix Librecht.

Godefroy, Frederic, ed. 1881. *Dictionnaire de L'Ancienne Langue Française*. Paris: F. Vieweg.

Gower, John. 1901. *Complete Works*. Ed. G.C. Macaulay. Oxford: Clarendon P.

Grimm, J. 1883–88. *Teutonic Mythology*. 4 vols. Trans. J.S. Stallybrass. London: George Bell and Sons.

Hackwood, F.W. 1974. *Staffordshire Customs, Superstitions and Folklore*. 1924. East Ardsley, Wakefield: EP Publishing.

Hartland, E.S., ed. 1890. *English Fairy and other Folk Tales*. London: Walter Scott.

Henry, P.L. 1959. "The Goblin Group." *Etudes Celtiques* VIII.2: 404–16.

Heslop, R.O. 1892. *Northumberland Words*. London: English Dialect Society.

Hibbard, Laura A. 1924. *Mediaeval Romance in England: A Study of the Sources and Analogues of the Non-Cyclic Metrical Romances*. New York: Oxford UP.

Hole, Christina. 1945. *Witchcraft in England*. London: B.T. Batsford.

James I, King. 1924. *Daemonologie*. ed. G. B. Harrison. London: The Bodley Head.

Jamieson, John. 1808. *An Etymological Dictionary elucidating National Rites, Customs and Institutions of Scotland*. Edinburgh: The UP.

Keightley, Thomas. 1900. *Fairy Mythology*. 1870. London: George Bell and Sons.

Kirk, Robert. 1976. *The Secret Common-Wealth and A Short Treatise of Charms and Spells*. Ed. S. Sanderson. Cambridge: D.S. Brewer.

Langland, William. 1867. *Piers Plowman: A Text*. Ed. W.W. Skeat. London: Early English Text Society.

——. 1869. *Piers Plowman: B Text*. Ed. W.W. Skeat. London: Early English Text Society.

——. 1873. *Piers Plowman: C Text*. Ed. W.W. Skeat. London: Early English Text Society.

Latham, R.E., ed. 1965. *Revised Mediaeval Latin Wordlist from British and Irish Sources*. London: Oxford UP.

Layamon. 1847. *Brut*. 3 vols. Ed. Sir Frederic Madden. London: The Society of Antiquaries of London.

Loomis, R.S. 1936. "*Sir Orfeo* and Walter Map's *De Nugis*." *Modern Language Notes* 51: 28–30.

——. 1945. "Morgain La Fee and the Celtic Goddesses." *Speculum* XX: 183ff.

——. 1956. *Wales and the Arthurian Legend*. Cardiff: U of Wales P.

——. 1959. "Morgan la Fee in Oral Tradition." *Romania* 80.3: 337–67.

——, ed. 1974. *Arthurian Literature in the Middle Ages. A Collaborative History*. Oxford: Clarendon P.

MacNeil, F. Marian. 1977. *The Silver Bough*. Glasgow: Maclellan.

Malory, Thomas. 1969. *Le Morte D'Arthur*. 2 vols. Harmondsworth: Penguin.

Map, Walter. 1923. *De Nugis Curialium*. Trans. M.R. James. Ed. E.S. Hartland. London: Cymmrodorion Society.

Maury, L.F.A. 1896. *Croyances et legendes du moyen age*. Paris: n.p.

Montgomerie, Alexander. 1885–86. *The Poems*. Ed. J. Cranstoun. Edinburgh and London: Scottish Text Society and Blackwood.

Moor, Edward. 1970. *Suffolk Words and Phrases*. 1823. Newton Abbot: David and Charles.

Moore, A.W. 1971. *The Folk-lore of the Isle of Man*. East Ardsley, Wakefield: S.R. Publishing.

Morte Arthur. 1847. Ed. J.O. Halliwell. London: Early English Text Society.

Murray, J.A.H., et al., eds. 1933. *The Oxford English Dictionary and Supplement*. 12 vols. Oxford: Clarendon P.

Newstead, H. 1946. "The Traditional Background of Paronopeus de Blois." *Proceedings of the Modern Language Association of America* LXI: 916–46.

Paton, Cyril I. 1936. "Belief in Fairy Fishermen." *Folklore* 49: 50.

Pitcairn, R. 1833. *Ancient Criminal Trials in Scotland*. 7 vols. Edinburgh: Ballantyne.

Ritson, Joseph. 1831. *Fairy Tales, Now First Collected*. London: T. Davidson.

Ross, Ann. 1974. *Pagan Celtic Britain*. London: Sphere Books.

Rudkin, E.H. 1973. *Lincolnshire Folklore*. East Ardsley, Wakefield: EP Publishers.

Rye, Walter. 1895. *A Glossary of Words Used in East Anglia*. English Dialect Society No. 75. London: English Dialect Society.

Sands, Donald B., ed. 1966. *Middle English Verse Romances*. New York: Holt, Rinehart and Winston.

Scott, Charles P.G. 1895. "The Devil and his Imps." *Transactions of the American Philological Association* XXVI: 77–146.

Scrope, Stephen. 1970. *Epistle of Othea*. Ed. C. F. Buhler. London: Early English Text Society.

Seinte Marherete, the Meiden ant Martyr. 1866. Ed. O. Cockayne. London: Early English Text Society.

Serjeantson, Mary. 1936. "The Vocabulary of Folklore in Old and Middle English." *Folklore* 47: 42–73.

Severs, J. Burke, ed. 1967. *A Manual of the Writings in Middle English 1050–1500*. New Haven: Connecticut Academy of Arts and Sciences.

Simpson, Eve Blantyre. 1976. *Folklore in Lowland Scotland*. 1908. East Ardsley, Wakefield: EP Publishing.

Sinclair, George. 1685. *Satan's Invisible World Discovered*. Edinburgh: John Reid.

Smithers, G.V., ed. 1952. *Kyng Alisaunder*. London: Early English Text Society.

Sternberg, Thomas. 1971. *The Dialect and Folklore of Northamptonshire*. 1851. London: SR Publishers

Stewart, W. Grant. 1970. *Popular Superstitions of the Highlands*. 1823. London: Ward Locke.

Storms, G. 1948. *Anglo-Saxon Magic*. The Hague: Martinus Nijhoff.

Thomas. 1964. *The Romance of Horn*. 2 vols. Ed. M.K. Pope. Oxford: Blackwell.

Tolkien, J.R.R., and E.V. Gordon, eds. 1970. *Sir Gawain and the Green Knight*. Oxford: Oxford UP.

Wasson, V.P., and R.G. Wasson. 1957. *Russia, Mushrooms and History*. New York: Pantheon Books.

Watson, Henry, trans. 1937. *Valentine and Orson*. Ed. A. Dickinson. London: Early English Text Society.

White, Carolyn. 1976. *A History of Irish Fairies*. Dublin and Cork: The Mercier P.

Willan, Dr. 1811. *A Glossary of Words Used in the West Riding of Yorkshire*. n.p.: n.p.

Williams, Noel. 1981. "Semantic Variation and Fictional Reference in Oral Tradition." *Aspects of Linguistic Variation: Proceedings of the Conference on Language Varieties*. CECTAL Conference Paper Series 1. Ed. S. Lander and K. Reah. Sheffield: U of Sheffield P.

———. 1983. "The Semantics of the Word 'Fairy' in English between 1320 and 1829." Ph.D. dissertation. Sheffield U.

Wright, J., ed. 1898–1905. *The English Dialect Dictionary*. 6 vols. London: Henry Frowde.

Zupitza, J., ed. 1969. *Guy of Warwick*. 1883, 1887, 1891. London: Early English Text Society.

Between One Eye Blink and the Next: Fairies, UFOs, and Problems of Knowledge[1]

Peter M. Rojcewicz

> I readily believe that there are more invisible than visible Natures in the universe. But who will explain for us the family of all these beings, and the ranks and relations and distinguishing features and functions of each? . . . I do not deny that it is helpful sometimes to contemplate in the mind . . . the image of a greater and better world, lest the intellect, habituated to the petty things of daily life, narrow itself and sink wholly into trivial thoughts. But at the same time we must be watchful for the truth and keep a sense of proportion, so that we may distinguish the certain from the uncertain, day from night.
>
> Adapted by Samuel Taylor Coleridge from Thomas Burnet,
> *Archaeological Philosophicae*

Folklorists have shown minimal interest in UFOs. Since the appearance of the first UFO article in *Hoosier Folklore* fifty years ago, only three dissertations have been written on the topic.[2] UFOs have been treated directly or indirectly as topics more often in sociology and psychology.[3] The *Journal of American Folklore* has published but two UFO articles, despite the emergence in America of the modern age of "flying saucers" as early as 1947.[4] Scholarly articles have in fact appeared elsewhere in folklore publications, but it is difficult to explain the relative paucity of work given the rich and plentiful nature of the material. A phenomenon possessing (1) international motifs and tale types found in the Aarne-Thompson indexes, (2) informants in the roles of active and passive tradition-bearers, (3) presumed supernatural and psychic effects, (4) a rapidly emerging body of memorates, legends and proto-legends, and (5) existing bodies of information in related disciplines available for fruitful interdisciplinary and comparative study, I would think would be attractive to many. It would be most unfortunate to fail to monitor, record, and analyze this example of folklore in the making.

The time is proper for observing how powerful events generate beliefs and memorates that circulate through the printed media and orally via multi-channeled conduits in the formation of legends and "proto-legends."[5] We may even be able to observe at the ground level how

479

powerful regional and national myths incubate, emerge, develop, and expire.

Perhaps folklorists find unacceptable the prevailing attitude concerning the investigation of truth-claims of anomalous folklore. Some folklorists have pronounced the issue of the reality basis of anomalous claims to lie outside folklore's domain.[6] Perhaps this is because they fear that the questionable nature of anomalous lore might reflect undesirably upon them or because they lack the interdisciplinary skills necessitated by the complex UFO phenomenology. Elsewhere I have challenged this position in regards to a cryptic area of the UFO phenomenon known as the "Men in Black" (MIB).[7]

At any rate, the grip of the dominant position appears to be loosening. A major force in this development comes from the work of David J. Hufford. Hufford's study of supernatural assault traditions, *The Terror That Comes in the Night,* is a landmark work in the field. While it is true that "haggings" (the Newfoundland term for the classical nightmare) have connections to ghosts, witches, and UFOs, Hufford demonstrates that the assaults occur to healthy people of all types who are independent of knowledge of the "hagging" tradition. He argues that an authentic, although often perplexing experience, not culture, is the source of beliefs. Hufford concludes that psychology, pathological medicine, and dream research all fail to account for the stable nature of the content of the phenomenon.[8]

Belief-oriented folklorists are receiving further encouragement from the work of Felicitas D. Goodman who has produced compelling works on glossolalia (i.e., "speaking in tongues"), demonic possession and exorcism, and ecstasy and alternate realities. Among her findings relevant to folk anomalies studies, Goodman writes that humans apparently use the same trance state for ritual purposes the world over as part of our genetic endowment. She is not surprised, therefore, that people continually discover this cognitive mode independent of any ecstatic tradition.[9]

There are also early folklorists who deserve mention here for their important work, including Andrew Lang and Walter Yeeling Evans-Wentz. Lang argued for a reality basis to ghost lore and rejected as unsound all physicalistic explanations of fire-walking.[10] Evans-Wentz maintained that entities of discarnate consciousness lay behind the fairy faith of the Celts.[11]

This article is not the first work that considers together fairy and UFO lore. The first was Jacques Vallee's *Passport to Magonia, From Folklore to Flying Saucers* (1969). Abandoning the extraterrestrial hypothesis he held in earlier works, Vallee argues that modern UFOs are "nothing but a resurgence of a deep stream in human culture known in older times under various names." His basic contention is that "the modern, global belief in flying saucers and their occupants is identical to an earlier belief in the fairy faith."[12] In addition, Thomas E. Bullard and Peter M. Rojcewicz systematically arrange the numerous parallels between fairy and UFO traditions in sections of their doctoral theses. Assuming the orthodox position that the "folklorist's basic unit of concern is reports rather than objective phenomena behind them," Bullard concludes that "UFOs are a modern manifestation of an age old category of mysterious aerial phenomena that are akin to accounts in folklore, mythology and religion."[13] Rojcewicz explores in a tentative vein the notion of a common underlying psycho-physical trigger for extraordinary encounters and posits an unbroken continuum of folk imagination and reality.[14] Recently Linda Milligan has written her dissertation on UFOs, focusing, however, on "our culture's inconsistent response to UFOs and how that varied response has influenced legend making."[15]

As far as I know, this work at hand is the first to deal directly with the philosophical issue of knowledge in light of fairy and UFO comparisons.[16] Because tradition notes the extraterrestrial nature of some fairies, comparisons with UFO occupants are not spurious. For example, some Irish believe that the "Gentle Folk" were not earthly, having originated on other planets. Among the Welsh some maintained that "Tylwyth Teg" were only visitors to earth. As special forms of creation, they can fly about at will. According to the *Book of Dun Cow*, no one knows the exact origin of the "Tuatha De Danann," but it is likely that they come from heaven on account of their great intelligence.[17] I shall indicate here how a consideration of salient features indicates that the problem of the knowable and the real are major concerns in both traditions. Building upon this fact, I shall explore the hypothesis that the archetypal structure of folklore reflects the mind's deep core, and interacts together with the unseen archetypal structure in nature to construct our knowledge of the world. My primary goal here is to explore issues involved in the study of fairies and UFOs which force us to face the problems of the relativity of knowledge and human estrangement from the world. In this writing I am not arguing one way or another concerning the validity of the unusual accounts I discuss.[18] The reader should keep the words "alleged," "ostensible," and "presumed" in mind concerning all extraordinary accounts discussed here. I shall utilize anomalous folk beliefs in an exploration of problems of reliable human knowledge. My hope is that this discussion will encourage more folklorists to engage in speculative inquiries of anomalous belief materials. Belief in spiritual entities is universal. No culture known to anthropology is without a body of beliefs and narratives concerning the human interaction with nonhuman others. This complex lore is so rich in details that our taxonomies can never be more than inexact organizing tools. Still, it is easy to observe repeating story patterns. I do not propose to be offering here an exhaustive phenomenological picture of either fairies or UFOs and their occupants.[19] I shall simply choose some salient features with epistemological significance.

The "Subtle Body"

The belief that the human body is but the outer manifestation of an invisible, subtle, and more dynamic embodiment of the soul is very old. The astral or sidereal religion of classical antiquity held as its central notion the existence of an intimate correspondence between a mortal's psychic and sensible powers and the subtle nature of the universe. The relative locations of celestial bodies in space at any moment were regarded by the most advanced thinkers as indications of the harmonious interactions of invisible spheres with fields of vital energy. The primary tenet of the astral religion was the existence in man of a subtle organon of nature, an interior model of the world soul. Man's subtle nature was a miniature of nature at large.[20] Humans are not the only beings with a subtle embodiment.

The fairies, for example, are entities "betwixt man and angel," with light changeable bodies, neither fully flesh nor purely spirit, capable of altering their forms at will. Fairies have something of the nature of a mist or condensed cloud, having been called "astral," "crazed," or "sidereal." By comparison, angels are not usually considered to be mortal, although they are capable of sexual intimacy with humans. Some traditions point to the physical or semi-physical nature of angelic bodies but they generally are more spirit than flesh. Fairies, on the other hand, are more animal and elemental (i.e., of the spirit of the earth, air, fire and water) than angels. Fairies are closer to the everyday concerns of humans than are angels. Late in the sixteenth century the Reverend Robert Kirk observed that fairy bodies are "so pliable through the subtlety of the spirits, that agitate them, that they can make them appear or disappear at pleasure."[21] From the two thousand year old *Surya Siddhanta*, a compilation of ancient Indian astronomy, one learns that below the moon and above the clouds are found the "Siddhas" (perfected beings), capable of becoming very heavy at will or as light as a feather, and which travel through space and disappear from sight. In March 1966, mathematician Ogilvie Crombie asserted that he contacted fairies and elemental entities at the Findhorn Community, Scotland. According to Crombie, "Their primary state is in what may be termed a 'light body.' Not easy to describe in words, it is nebulous like a fine mist, being a whirl or a vortex of energy in constant motion."[22]

Mention of the paradoxical nature of UFOs and their occupants is plentiful in the literature. Computer specialist and UFO researcher Jacques

Vallee has noted the space-time distortions experienced by witnesses of craft-like objects which "appear or fade away on the spot, in ways that are reminiscent of descriptions of 'dematerializations' in the spiritualist literature."[23] Parapsychologist D. Scott Rogo has asserted that UFOs are neither purely physical nor mental, existing at the momentary interface between mind and matter.[24] Jerome Clark and Loren Coleman write that the apparent objective aspects of UFOs are "subsidiary" features whose sources can be traced to certain extrasensory operations of the brain. From this perspective, UFOs are psychokinetically generated by-products of unconscious processes.[25] Similarly, Michael Talbot argues that UFOs are ontologically ambiguous phenomena, neither completely objective nor subjective, but possessing attributes of both states, a condition he calls "omnijective."[26] Vallee, Rogo, Coleman and Clark and Talbot all describe a phenomenological oxymoron that C.G. Jung called "psychoid," or quasi-psychic. UFOs as manifestations of the psychoid unconscious are as much material as they are mental, and as such, can be grasped only in hints since they are partially transcendental.

Shape-Shifting

Fairies manipulate their forms at will. They assume the appearance of animate or inanimate objects, but every time they resume their proper shape they are a little smaller than they were before. The "Hadley Kow," "Pictree Braq," and all counterfeiting "bogey-beasts" accomplish this feat. The "Brown Dwarfs" and "Black Dwarfs"of Scandinavia use their hats to induce invisibility. Shape-shifting is universal among fairies with the exception of the Japanese "Kappa," a malignant entity which consistently appears as a goblin boy with a saucer-like cavity in his head.[27]

A peculiar feature reported by witnesses to UFOs which violates principles of physics is their ability to modify their form. UFOs manifest this ability in several dramatic ways. UFOs often split into two or more parts, or two or more whole UFOs all identical to the original, a characteristic reminiscent of holograms. Some accounts describe all or some of the fractioned parts reuniting. Disc-shaped UFOs often regenerate their forms from a larger "mother ship." In addition, UFOs are sometimes observed passing through physical objects unaffected. The following case contains most of the above-mentioned traits.

On a dark rainy night late in January 1972, four teenage boys from Ball Ferry, California, on their way to Battle Creek to fish, observed a spectacular glowing object pass over their car. Later, parked at the Battle Creek bridge, the boys heard a disturbance and a terrible scream coming from some bushes. Pointing his flashlight in the direction of the scream, John Yeries beheld a dark, "lumpy" beast approximately seven feet tall, walking toward him in a hunched up position. As the boys fled their car, the youth observed fiery blue, white, orange and red objects moving haphazardly over the open field. The boys noticed that two of the "glowing balls" merged in the sky. Another globe shot straight up in the sky and disappeared. A third glowing object assumed the outlines of a human being and hovered along the road.[28]

Reports of UFOs and their occupants suddenly vanishing without leaving the witnesses' field of vision, a trait duplicated by fairies, can readily be found in the literature. In the Maurice Masse case that occurred in Valensole, France, June 1965, Masse testified that he saw creatures less than four feet tall in tight fitting, gray-green clothing who went "bubbling up" a ladder of light into a space craft. Masse saw the occupants look at him through the windows of the craft as it ascended to a height of approximately twenty meters before disappearing. Landing gear impressions were found in the soil. Witnesses verified Masse's claims.[29] Very few UFO investigators suspect a hoax.

A case of a suddenly disappearing UFO occupant took place on September 30, 1954, at Marcilly-sur-Vienne, France. Seventeen witnesses saw the entity "dissolve." The UFO produced a heavy fog into which the object vanished. The frequency with which UFOs are reported along with clouds was noted by the late astronomer J. Allen Hynek who stated that "Time and time again a cloud develops around it, and the object either changes shape or completely dematerializes."[30]

This peculiar presence of fogs and clouds also appears in the fairy faith. In Scotland, the most formidable of the fairy tribe, the "Sluagh," or "hosts," spirits of deceased mortals, fly about in great clouds, up and down the face of the earth, and come back to the scenes of their earthly transgressions.[31]

Fairies often travel about the skies in cloud-like aerial boats called "fairy boats" or "spectre ships." Mysterious specter ships have been sighted in America from colonial days to the present.[32] The lights of these ghost ships often lure mortal sailors to their death. Count John De Salis of Balliot College noted: " . . . fairy boats appear across Lough Gur . . . there are four of these boats. . . . Boats and occupants seem to be transparent and you cannot see exactly what their nature is."[33] Of interest in the above account is the description of transparency of the fairy boat and its occupants. Some photographs of UFOs and related anomalous phenomena like ghosts and apparitions, display dark and light areas of what looks like energy forms, as if parts of the UFO are absorbing photons while other parts are releasing photons. Thus UFOs appear to be in transition between a solid and a pure energy state.

Shining, Luminous Entities

Fairies, like angels, demons, ghosts, and apparitions, assume forms of luminous, glowing light. Light is a constant feature in occult, mystical, and religious experience.[34] Even Lucifer, the "Prince of Darkness," once shined brightest of all the angels. In addition, the confrontation with "beings of light" is a standard feature of close encounters with death.[35]

Among fairy tribes, the "Peries" of Persia possess bodies of fire. The Hindi of India speak of "Devas," the "Shining Ones." The "Genii" or "Jinn" of Arabia consist of the "smokeless fire" of the wind Simoon. Related phenomena include "corpse candles," "ghosts," whose astral bodies glow, and the "spirits of the wilderness," strangers who use lights for work purposes. "Spectral men" carry lanterns or torches such as the "Jack-o'-Lantern" and the "Will-o'-the-Wisp." A "spectral woman" such as "Joan-in-the-Wad" walks about enveloped in flaming clothes and appears like a column of fire. Also related are the "Ignes Fatuus" and the "revenants" who come from hell or purgatory dressed in fiery clothes. A glowing or shining appearance can also be construed as demonic emanations of the devil or his animals or goblins. A terrifying light often emanates from evil or unredeemed souls and is referred to as the "light of Nature" or "Luciferion light."[36] Demonic light also shines from werewolves and firedrakes.

UFO occupants have been described on numerous occasions as shining or fluorescent. On October 18, 1973, in Falkville, Alabama, Police Chief Jeff Greenhaw encountered a shining, metallic-clad suited figure, resembling someone completely covered with aluminum foil.[37] In 1973, Patty Price was "abducted" by beings she described as "slightly over four feet tall, very thin, with large slanted eyes." They wore what appeared to be fluorescent clothing with Sam Brown belts.[38]

Discussion

Fairies and UFOs and their occupants possess quasi-physical natures that challenge common sense wisdom. Because of their subtle malleable bodies, fairies are extremely protean. They pass effortlessly through material objects and instantly dematerialize. Similarly, UFOs and their occupants display an apparent omnijective nature by splitting into two or more complete UFOs identical to the original, reuniting into a single object, and passing through physical objects with no apparent negative effects. Like fairies, UFOs and their occupants dematerialize before one's eyes. Both are often sighted with or in close proximity to clouds or fogs, vanishing into cloud formations often described as much smaller than the size of the reported "craft." The witness's comprehension of these mind boggling features is further complicated by overwhelming luminous visual effects. What explanation is there for these traits?

I propose that an existential reading of the key motifs mentioned above will reveal the problem of the subjective nature of human knowledge that gnaws at the postmodern mind. Stated simply, the mind can know directly only its own internal phenomena and not the world as it is in itself. Knowledge is what results when we try to order the seemingly endless flow of experiences by establishing patterns among them. This is to say that the "real" world manifests itself only when our constructions, our maps of reality, break down. But as we can only describe and interpret these breakdowns in terms of the same principles used to construct the now crumbling structure, we can never possess a picture of the world we can blame for the breakdown.[39] The subjectivity of our knowledge further complicates the study of anomalous folklore which is by its ontologically uncertain subject matter already suspect.

First, the nature of the "subtle body," a hybrid state between matter and spirit, is most difficult for us to comprehend in terms of everyday living. It engenders fundamental questions: What is a concrete object? Is an object any less physical because it is invisible? Are our sensory capacities and instruments of measurement the only criteria for physicality? Apparently not, since subatomic particles may exist beyond the range of our most sensitive equipment. The point here is that a notion we hold to be axiomatic is called into question in fairy and UFO accounts. Possessing a nature at least partially ethereal and abstract, and capable of volitional metamorphoses, fairies and UFOs and their occupants are not "things" in any absolute sense. Rather, they are multiple presence phenomena that will always withstand the monocular eye of materialistic science which can only see the most conspicuous physical aspects. Because we are not trained to see "no-things," we do not see accurately, or see nothing at all. Because fairies and UFOs exist as if on the border between fact and fiction, it is unlikely they can be easily perceived in their totality.

This uncertainty of understanding produced by the ontologically ambiguous nature of the "subtle body" is supported by the presence of cloud and fog motifs. The clouds which stand in the way of UFOs and into which fairies and UFO occupants disappear are suggestive of our "cultural maps" of reality, inherited pictures of what is possible in the world.[40] Our observations of the world come not simply from sense data but from an inherent organization which compares, matches, and interprets information. The more ambiguous an event is with one or more unknown or apparently mysterious features, the more active the role of this inherent structure. The world of human experience is constructed by those who experience it, and so our knowledge of the world is our interpretation. Our cultural lenses color our perceptions according to values we generally agree on.

The theme of human understanding is again suggested by the motif of light, perhaps the most noted feature of fairy and UFO encounters, and a constant detail of mystical and religious experience. Light is suggestive of direct revelation, and of prophecy or precognition. It is related to what some call the "Aha!" or "Eureka!" experience, that is, an illumination event. The Greeks referred to this cognitive and spiritual conversion as "metanoia."[41] Expressions of everyday speech point to the assumed connection between light and consciousness. We say "he is enlightened; she sees the light." The expression "to see" (as by light) connotes understanding. The idea of divine illumination can be found in the work of Plato, where it played, for the first time in its lengthy history, a major role. Plato, like many contemporary artists, prophets, mystics and thinkers spoke of sudden flashes of understanding as a flood of light. In the Christian tradition, the theory of illumination received its most developed treatment in the work of St. Augustine of Hippo. Like Plato, Augustine thought of understanding as analogous to seeing. Intellectual sight or understanding is contingent upon illumination just as physical sight is, but here the light is the intelligible light of God's mind that endows a human mind with understanding. Comprehension results from the inherent cooperation of the human mind with the divine.[42]

The light we so readily link to our illumination may be based on more than figures of speech or philosophical discussion. It is true that our pineal gland, the organ of the brain some researchers call the "seat of consciousness," consists of the same light-sensitive material as does the retina of the eye. It may actually be the case, therefore, that during moments of creative insight, a flash literally occurs in the brain.[43] This "bioluminescence" may be the experiential basis for the above mentioned figures of speech and philosophical discussion. My point here is that the motifs of light, subtle bodies, and cloud and fogs in fairy and UFO accounts may be linked to the theme of the attainment of human knowledge and consciousness.

And so it is that among North America Eskimo (Inuit), the "Angokok," an enlightenment-giving spirit, visits the tribal shaman during the rites of initiation. The "Angokok" assumes the form of a mysterious light which fills the shaman's body and enables him to see accurately in the dark. Being possessed by the "Angokok" grants the shaman the prophetic visions of future events and knowledge of the secrets of another's heart.[44] During Betty Andreasson-Luca's UFO abduction, Betty was told by her captors: "We are going to measure you for light. . . . You have not understood the word that you have. You've misunderstood some places. . . . You are not completely filled with light." Betty protested: "I believe I am filled with light. I believe—I believe that I'm filled with the light."[45] Betty, a devout born-again Christian, uses the word "light" as a descriptor for God's presence within her, suggesting what members of metaphysical churches know as "Christ-consciousness."

Superior Beings: Positive Effects

Throughout the Middle Ages people claimed frequent contact with subtle beings who neither identified themselves as angels nor offered spiritual advice or divine revelations. The average citizen assumed the possibility of interaction with luminous entities called "daemons," positive demons, or one's personal creative spirit. Belief in daemon spirits can be found also in the Greco-Roman world of antiquity. For example, in his "The Daemon of Socrates," Plutarch writes that the Roman gods eventually became detached from human emotional concerns. The gods, after all, were pure spirit. "Daemons" were neither wholly spirit nor wholly flesh, and served as intermediaries between gods and mortals, giving voice to the Romans' petitions before the gods. Every Roman citizen possessed a personal daemon or "genius" (Latin), as do Christians a "guardian angel," the Scots a "reflex man," the Norwegians a "vadogr," the Germans "der doppelganger," and the Jews the "mashal." If a Roman was attentive to a "genius" during life, he or she became a "lar" or household god from whom the surviving family could win favor. If a Roman ignored his creative spirit while alive, he or she became an evil and menacing entity called a "larva." Such malignant beings caused havoc inside the household, often floating over sleepers in their beds at night, or driving people insane.[46]

Fairies are part of the daemon tradition. As beings intermediary between mortals and angels, fairies have powers over human affairs and natural phenomena, and thus can render great service to mortals, provided they compensate their benefactors. Fairies assist mortals in the fields, around the house, and on country roads. They produce bountiful harvest and healthy livestock. They guarantee the uninterrupted flow of springs and the activity of wells. This fairy assistance centered around a universal system of reciprocity.

For example, in central Australia the Arunta tribes believe in ancestral "Alcheringa" and "Iruntarinia," spirit races raised in invisible fairy worlds. These beings must be propitiated if humans wish to secure their goodwill. They are beneficial guardian beings when not offended and if adequately accommodated, attach themselves to individual mortals assuming a role parallel to the Christian "guardian angel."[47] Among the Igbo of Southeast Nigeria, spiritual entities closely interact with mortals. The system of reciprocity here requires that ancestors be honored and offered regular sacrifice. Feeding crumbs from each meal to ancestral spirits guarantees family prosperity, as those spirits stand allied with the family against wicked men and malignant forces.[48]

Special Skills and Gifts

Some people receive extraordinary talents from nonhuman entities. Tradition refers to these recipients as "fairy men," "charmers," "wizards," "conjurers," "fairy doctors," "cunning men," "wise women," or "fairy mediums." Ancient Druids believed that their interaction with fairies and demons could produce power to master natural phenomena and animal processes, as well as to cast spells and see the future. In addition, mortals receive cures from beneficent fairies. A case well known in the fairylore involves the hunchback Lusmore. Because Lusmore offered fairies an acceptable ending to a fairy song, they cured him of his deformity.[49] Frequent mention is made in fairylore of a secret fairy book that contains the cures of all human disease. Similarly, UFO abductee Betty Andreasson-Luca claims her captors gave her a book of universal truths and secrets which she possessed for several days before it mysteriously disappeared without her committing any of its information to memory.[50] In addition, contacts with angels and apparitions of the Virgin Mary also produce miraculous cures. As a result of fairy contacts, mortals sometimes develop psychic or extrasensory abilities that include telepathy, precognition, and even invisibility.[51]

Continuities between fairies and UFO occupants extend to healings and special gifts. The literature contains accounts of people claiming cures from beams of light from UFOs. Such a case involves "Doctor X," cured of partial paralysis after his UFO close encounter in September 1969. "Doctor X," forty-three at the time of the encounter, had been a gifted pianist prior to the Algerian War when he stepped on a field mine which partially paralyzed both of his limbs on the right side of his body. The doctor's music career ended, and he walked thereafter with a considerable limp. Three days before his close encounter, the doctor's axe slipped while he chopped wood, opening a wound just above the ankle of his left leg. On the night of November 1–2 the doctor saw through his window intense flashes of light produced by two luminous disc-shaped "objects." The doctor observed the UFOs merge into one and then proceed toward his house. A beam of light hit him and the "object" dematerialized with a bang. When he returned upstairs, the doctor's wife pointed out that her husband walked normally. In addition, the swelling in his leg dissipated and the axe wound healed completely. That night the doctor uncharacteristically talked in his sleep: "Contact will be re-established by falling down the stairs on November second." The next morning the doctor recalled nothing of the night. His wife informed him of everything except the statement he made while asleep. That afternoon the doctor fell, hit his head, and recalled his entire UFO encounter. All sequelae of his Algerian War wound, which had remained unchanged for ten previous years, disappeared. The doctor resumed playing his piano as well as ever.[52] Cases of cures of hepatitis and even the development of new teeth can be found in the UFO literature.[53] Less concrete, but perhaps as significant to the individual involved, are instances of dramatic personality change. After a UFO encounter, witnesses sometimes develop a greater appreciation of life, an effect common to illumination experiences discussed earlier. People have reported the intercession of "helping apparitions"[54] not only in the modern age of flying saucers but throughout history.

Superior Beings: Negative Effects

The superior powers of fairies and UFO occupants do not always produce positive effects on witnesses. Human encounters with fairies have resulted in the ruin of health, property, and personality. Because they have always feared the superiority of fairies, mortals refer to them euphemistically as the "Good People," the "Gentle Folk," and the "People of Peace." Parents in the British Isles taught their children to say "God bless them!" whenever they mentioned fairies. These apparently benevolent appellations exemplify how people speak well of that which they fear. This is but a single example of using apotropaisms to protect oneself against evil. Likewise, the "Furies" are eventually called the "Eumenides" which means "the well disposed." The Black Sea is called the "Hospitable Sea." According to an early seventeenth century report, Lake Mjösa is a dangerous Norwegian body of water feared because it "takes many people away." Great whirlwinds and squalls make sailing here more dangerous than sea travel because fresh water is more easily agitated than salt water. For these reasons whenever people sail upon Mjösa, they never refer to it by name, but speak instead of "the fjord."[55] In Act II, Scene 5, Part II, Goethe's Faust protects himself against the mention of "the old heathen race" of the Goddesses by exclaiming: "The Mothers! The Mothers! It sounds so strange." C.G. Jung observed how the German people speak to each other in the plural, as a protective formality. Perhaps it is for similar reasons that people refer to UFO occupants as the "Space Brothers."

W.B. Yeats believed that some aspects of the fairy faith might be dangerous for mortals to explore. The message of fairies, he thought, was clear: "Be careful, and do not seek to know too much about us."[56] Parents instructed children never to fix their gaze on fairies. English tradition insists that safety results only if a mortal sees the fairy first. Perhaps Alan

Bruford summed up the matter best when he wrote that "The fairies can be helpful, but in an unpredictable way; the safest advice is to have as little as possible to do with them."[57]

Ample reasons exist to fear fairies. Mortals receive bodily injury and paralysis from the "fairy blast." When the "fairy host" travels about, it stirs up a whirlwind of leaves and dust. When confronting the host, a mortal must make the sign of the cross, since fairies may strike anyone along the way.[58] People who suffer "fairy blast" fall immediately into a state of unconsciousness. Travelers can also be "pixie-led," that is, have their senses confused by the strange lights of pixies, hobgoblins, and bogies. These creatures play havoc with familiar paths and roads, so that even longtime residents wander about aimlessly.[59]

Fairies are most feared for their tendencies to assault, torture, and abduct humans. Fairies steal children left unattended in their cradles, substituting a stunted and ugly fairy creature called a "changeling." This creature is a fully grown and mature demon who seeks access to mortal lives. Telltale signs of a changeling include its wan and wrinkled appearance, long fingers, bony development, fractious behavior and voracious appetite.[60] Infantile paralysis, or any disease that suddenly alters the appearance and abilities of a child are reasonable grounds to suspect a fairy substitution.

Antidotes against the "changeling" terror include brewing beer in egg shells over a fire, throwing the "changeling" into a pool, river or ford, or into a fiery hearth.[61] A "changeling" tossed into a fire disappears quickly up the cottage chimney and the mortal child is instantly returned.

In addition to "taking" children, fairies also abduct mortal women to serve as midwives or mothers for their race. Some fairy abductees suffer severe depression and catastrophic mental effects lasting a lifetime. Fairy abductees have died subsequent to their ordeals. In the famous Llewellyn and Rhŷs case, Rhŷs, abducted and later rescued from a "fairy dance," could barely be convinced by his mortal rescuers that an entire year had passed since he began to dance. Confused and depressed, his reality construct dismantled, Rhŷs took to his bed, rapidly deteriorated, and died. It is seldom "that captives in Fairyland recover from their experience."[62]

What is interesting to note here is that all of the negative effects of fairy contact are duplicated in UFO lore. Instances of paralysis, burns, and disorientation are plentiful. Temporary conjunctivitis and blindness can result from a UFO encounter.[63] Maurice Masse[64] and Herb Shirmer[65] both experienced a paralysis after being "hit" by something from a circular object. Like those who receive the "fairy blast" Travis Walton was "gunned down" by a brilliant beam of bluish white light that lifted him a foot into the air before laying him out on the ground, his head thrown back, his arms and legs wide apart.[66] A beam of green light rendered

Inacio de Souza unconscious. Police sergeant Charles Moody felt "numb" after he saw a UFO.[67]

While it is certainly true that some UFO contactees have their lives revitalized as occurs in the illumination and shamanic traditions, as many people, if not more, become "puppets," either of their own little understood psychic processes or some diabolical external agency. This ruin of contactees occurs so frequently that pioneer UFO researcher John A. Keel coined the term "used person."[68] Emotional collapse and mental disorders have followed UFO encounters. Mysterious deaths and even murders are suspected.[69]

Dependent Beings: They Need Us

Fairies and UFOs and their occupants possess powers superior to mortals. This superiority produces both beneficial and detrimental effects: people yearn for other worldly intercession in unsolvable life problems; they also know the dehumanizing terror of having one's will "taken." Despite their unequivocally superior powers, fairies and "extraterrestrials" alike apparently dislike and fear humanity. In 1888 W.B. Yeats remarked that fairies "have an aversion to self-conceited persons, such as dogmatists, scientists, drunkards and gluttons and against vulgar and quarrelsome people of all kinds . . . and the less there is of vanity and hypocrisy in a man, the easier it will be to approach them. . . ."[70] UFO occupants, on the other hand, reportedly fear us due to our continual destruction of the planet and our atomic tests which release radiation into the universe.[71]

The primary reason why fairies fear mortals, however, is because they need us. For reasons still unclear, fairies need us to recharge their fairy powers and guarantee their overall socio-psychological well-being. For example, fairies are always grateful for human assistance in making or mending fairy utensils. They also need the cooperation of humans to win their fairy wars. If unable to meet their foes with equal force, the Persian "Peries," for example, enlist a mortal whom they sit on a wild and fabulous fairy steed, and arm with enchanted talismans and weapons.[72] Human intervention thus ensures a "Peri" victory. Human intervention also ensures the quality of their leisure, recreation, and sport.

In addition, fairies need human food. They imperceptibly steal vitamins and nutrients called "foyson" from our milk or cheese or grain. This food now robbed of its wholesomeness is unsuitable for human consumption, and mortals fated to eat it will themselves become fairies never to return to their former lives. Fairies cast spells over cows to secure the nourishment of their milk for their offspring.[73]

Clearly the most significant form of fairy dependence upon mortals involves their genetic evolution. Humans are essential to fairies for a healthy bloodline. Fairies "take" mortal women to act as midwives at fairy births. In addition, mortals "taken" to fairyland as wives and mothers, themselves need the aid of mortal midwives, since these mothers never lose their mortal mixture.[74]

Hybrid children, part human and part fairy, are stronger and healthier than fairy offspring. For example, in Scandinavian folklore fairies are partially human in origin and are not creatures of another order like angels. Icelandic lore has the "Huldre" folk, the hidden children of Eve. From these unwashed products of Eve's great fecundity hidden from God, descend all subterranean creatures, including some fairies.[75] The substitution of "changelings" for healthy mortal babies is a major way fairies eliminate their physically and psychologically defective members at human expense. It should now be clear that humans are often unwillingly involved with fairies in a symbiotic relationship essential to their very physical and psychological life.[76]

UFO occupants display the same paradoxical independent-dependent, love-hate relationship with mortals displayed in the fairy faith. For example, UFO abduction researcher Budd Hopkins has proposed "that an ongoing genetic study is taking place and that the human species itself is the subject of a breeding experiment" with extraterrestrials (ETs).[77] According to the general pattern described by Hopkins, an individual, male or female, is first abducted as a child, perhaps as early as the third year. During the abduction a small incision is made in the child's body, apparently for sample testing purposes. The ETs conduct a physical examination of the child. A series of contacts or abductions extending through puberty often follows. Sperm and ova samples are sometimes taken. Some women are abducted on the night they conceive a child and later, despite initial confirmation by positive urinalysis and blood test, they suddenly learn that they are not pregnant without any sign of fetal tissue or miscarriage visible, as if the E.T.s removed the fetus for their own purposes. In cases of suspected artificial insemination of abducted human women, they are allegedly re-abducted after two or three months of pregnancy, and the fetus is removed from the uterus. When a woman is "taken" during ovulation, the ova are removed, fertilized and ostensibly brought to term outside the womb.[78]

The children produced from these interspecies unions bear resemblance to fairy "changelings." They look "tiny and pathetic" with limbs so thin their human mothers are surprised the babies are alive. Like the fairy "changelings," the hybrid bodies are disproportional, and also like the "changeling," they seem "wise."[79] Women are not the only ones forced to have other-species sex. Mortal men have been forced to have sex with alien females as well, after which sperm samples are collected.

Sodomy is reported.[80] Unlike the classic other-sex abduction of Antonio
Villas-Boas[81] where the sexual act proceeded in terms of general human
intimacy, recent abductees do not enjoy any erotic quality in their ordeal.
Elsewhere I have discussed the tradition of human dalliance with nonhuman beings.[82] The reason for this planetary breeding experiment, as
discussed by Hopkins, is similar to that of fairies. Extraterrestrials need
humans to invigorate their bloodline and "experimentally alter their
genetic structure."[83]

It has already been noted that mortal women "taken" into "fairyland"
to be wives and mothers to the "Gentle Folk" retain some of their mortal
mixture and thus require the assistance of human midwives to help nurse
their young. In the case of UFO abductions, women who are either
impregnated by ETs or have their humanly conceived embryos "taken,"
are later re-abducted in order to nurture their pathetic changeling-like
children. According to Hopkins, the ETs seem unable to give warmth to
their children. Extraterrestrials need humans to teach them how to express
and understand emotions.

> In this unexpected scenario the UFO occupants—despite this obvious
> technological superiority—are desperate for human genetic material and
> the ability to feel human emotions. Unlikely though it may seem, it is
> possible that the very survival of these extraterrestrials depends upon
> their success in absorbing chemical and psychological properties received
> from human abductees.[84]

This emotional dilemma described above is not without precedent in
fairylore. Every time fairies shift their shape, and perhaps, manifest any of
their considerable powers, they grow somewhat smaller and gradually
lose their capacities of enjoyment and suffering, so that eventually they
have only the memory of feelings they once had.[85] The paradox here is
that fairies need to utilize their powers to ensure the future success of their
failing genetic line, but in doing so, they desensitize themselves further,
necessitating still more use of their declining powers. We see here a
desperate fairy attempt to avoid an undesirable state of complete
insentience. Is there a meaningful connection between fairy and
extraterrestrial breeding practices? Will fairies eventually fade from the
earth?

Fairies have always disappeared and reappeared. This process is an
unchanging aspect of fairy tradition. When field workers find traces of the
fairy faith, they are considered mere cultural survivals of previous ages,
the endangered fragmented possessions of the latest generation. These
traces are hailed as the "last leaves of tradition," a term implying their
imminent demise. Nevertheless, the tradition proceeds onward, even if in
the face of adjustments to superficial features. If this is true, then why do
we not meet more people who have confronted fairies, or hear and read

about them more frequently in the mass media? It is a mistake to presume that because ideas and beliefs are not instantly familiar to the general public or cited in printed sources they are not traditional. Tradition is more resilient. A living tradition may never emerge into popular or elite social awareness, perhaps simply because it is not financially exploitable or of sufficient interest to be reworked by the high culture. This is particularly the case for anomalous folklore in literate, postmodern society.[86] Katharine Briggs noted that "As for Ireland and the Highlands of Scotland, they do not even pretend to think that they (fairies) have gone, though fewer people now believe in them."[87] The fairy faith is not dead but different. Fairies, remember, are fugitives from casual sight, chameleons playing hard at hiding.

We have noted numerous features of UFO lore that have precedent in fairy tradition. This fact is not surprising. Human beings traditionally return to the traditional. "Tradition" is not to be understood here in some limited antiquarian sense, but rather as a "functional prerequisite of social life."[88] People everywhere always traditionalize aspects of their meaningful experiences. Belief in UFOs and their occupants is part of the extraordinary encounter tradition and points to a continuum of folk imagination and reality.[89] Tradition, from this perspective, is the naming of an active and ongoing process that is universal. The movement of this traditional process from fairies to UFOs is not backward into a hoary past, but forward through the present to the future. Kathleen Raine has noted that "Where the ancestors saw the 'Sidhe' mounted on horses with silver bells on their harness, the Age of Aquarius sees flying saucers."[90] Raine is not saying that people do not continue to see fairies, or that "flying saucer" occupants are merely fairies by another name. Her statement raises important questions about what can reasonably be seen and known inside a particular "cultural map" of reality.

Seeing Fairies

The major features inherent in human confrontations with fairies and UFOs and their occupants raise important questions about human perception and understanding. Earlier we looked at four motifs: (1) luminescence, (2) the subtle body, (3) shape-shifting, and (4) the cloud-fog. The luminescent nature of fairies and UFOs and their occupants engenders questions of enlightenment and seeing. It relates to the witnesses' perceptions, memories, and conscious states. In addition, the issue of what we can reasonably grasp of an extraordinary encounter is raised by the subtle bodied nature of fairies and UFOs and their occupants. How can we accurately comprehend an entity whose nature is too material to be spiritual and too ethereal to be concrete? Furthermore, complications to our understanding come from the shape-shifting ability. What can reliably be known of entities that completely transform their physical appearance at will, even to the point of invisibility? Finally, the problem of gaining reliable information is suggested by the occurrence of the cloud-fog motif reported in many fairy and UFO accounts.

The difficult tasks of seeing and knowing fairies are made more difficult still because of fairy "glamour" or "pishogue," the fairy ability to make us see only what they want us to see. Not only do fairies render themselves invisible, but they also render people, animate and inanimate things invisible. They can make a dark and forbidding woodland mound appear like a glorious castle of light. We are tricked by fairy "glamour." Fairies put "pishogue" on us. These terms imply a spell, an illusion, a visual display wherein things are not simply what they seem. These spells are often of a grim kind, and by a kind of poetic justice they are put generally on people of ill merit.[91] Accurate cognition of fairy encounters is further clouded by the fairy power to supernaturally alter the passage of time.[92] What may subjectively seem to a mortal like one hour dancing in fairyland may actually be a year or more in our everyday time. Perhaps the epistemological dilemma raised by extraordinary encounters with nonhuman beings is best summed up in the ancient belief that fairies can only be seen "Between one eye blink and the next."[93]

Human witnesses may actually play an unwitting role in how, or even if, they see fairies. Tradition suggests a symbiotic or participatory relationship between the human perceiver and the entity perceived. From this perspective a fairy encounter is a mutually constructed reality. Poet and mystic W.B. Yeats once commented on this interdependent function: "Many poets and all mystics and occult writers, in all ages and countries, have declared that behind the visible are chains and chains of conscious beings, who are not of heaven but are of earth, who have no inherent form, but change according to their whim, or *the mind that sees them*" (my emphasis).[94] This is true for other types of extraordinary beings as well. The devil of tradition is said to assume whatever defect men and women ascribe him.[95] The devil, who is forever in mortal minds, likes to be modern. Today, the devil tradition assumes one of its many metamorphoses in the "Men in Black" experience where dark sinister figures, who often reveal an evil air and strong omniscience, warn UFO witnesses and researchers not to seek to communicate or understand fully their UFO encounters.[96] Support for the idea of a symbiotic or mind-matter connection comes from the fact that both fairies and UFO occupants seem desperately to need humans primarily to guarantee the future well-being of their genetic lines. Mortals, on the other hand, need the kindly if capricious endowment of the fairies' considerable powers.

An interactive human-UFO equation has been noted. Parapsychologist Harold Cahn has argued that we should view "the UFO experience as the product of an interaction between the anticipation of the percipient and the nature of what is perceived." The extraordinary encounter, according to Cahn, "is a composite function of how we and the UFOnauts think."[97] If matter, space-time, and mind form an unbroken continuum, then thought is reality, and all thinkable relationships exist. From this perspective, UFOs may substantially be our own creation, but we may be equally the creation of UFOs. The human mind is a mirror of the universe mirroring the human mind, though the process is subtle and apparently unfathomable.

Similarly, D. Scott Rogo maintains that UFOs constitute a "cosmic interface between mind and matter; a form of momentary conjunction between hyperdimensions and our world."[98] If fairies seem to disappear and UFO occupants referred to in the literature as "aliens," "extraterrestrials," "UFOnauts," and "visitors," are presently among us, do we play a significant if unwitting role in the type of entities we see? Perhaps we ourselves, supported both by inherent structures of mind and culture, actively shape the traditionalizing process of extraordinary encounters.

The epistemology of a society derives from and maintains its own social construction of reality. This interpretation of the world defines how "reality" works and why it is as it is. Whatever the case, to help answer questions engendered by extraordinary encounters, peoples of the British Isles, for example, developed over time systems for seeing and better understanding their relationships with fairies. For example, it was learned that one can generally see fairies if one has a four leaf clover in hand, or steps inside a fairy ring. Still another way to gaze safely at fairies is to step on the foot of a peasant seer or "cunning man." As he places his hands on your head, you are to look over the seer's right shoulder.[99] The most common way a mortal gains a glimpse into fairy reality is by rubbing on one's eyelids a special ointment used on fairy infants after birth. Still, all attempts at "seeing" fairies and gaining knowledge of their fundamental nature is risky business. When a fairy realizes that a human, most often a midwife, can see it, the fairy invariably asks "With which eye do you see me," and on receiving the answer, swiftly strikes out the offending eye.[100] As effective as the above mentioned methods are, they are ultimately only limited tools. Fairies dislike being discussed or viewed. They prefer privacy and initiate contact with mortals only when they choose.

No such system as yet exists relative to humans and UFOs and their occupants. How can we, and how should we see contacts with fairies, UFOs, and the entire continuum of extraordinary entities of folk tradition? We presume, even if tacitly, a determinable lawfulness of cause and effect in human affairs. This presumption is so strong as to meaningfully shape our expectations and deeds. Our sense of the world's lawfulness, however, is seriously challenged by fairy and UFO encounters. These contacts are a creative and powerful collaboration between perceiver and something perceived, and if Polanyi is correct, creative human acts have an emergent quality: the "whole is greater than the sum of the parts."[101] Systems of understanding strange encounters developed by previous cultures may indeed be useless to us today.

Problems of Human Knowledge

It is well known that folklore deals with the predominant concerns of mainstream life. Its great value lies in part in its ability to touch the pressure points of high and popular cultural thought and present them in unpretentious ways. Today, the great preoccupation of the postmodern mind centers around the criterion for what we say we know. We witness this Western mental preoccupation in accounts of extraordinary contacts with fairies and UFOs. The modern mind sees itself alienated from a world that it can never ultimately know as a reality independent of itself, and which apparently is indifferent, if not at times hostile, to its attempts for meaningful existence. How has the Western mind come to this present dilemma? Can we observe and gain reliable knowledge of the world?

The alienation of the Western mind from the world is a result of a series of paradigmatic revolutions in the West beginning with Copernicus.[102] With the theories of Copernicus we witness a cosmological shift away from a geocentric perspective where the earth is the center of the universe and man has a predominant place, to a heliocentric perspective in which the sun becomes the center, and the earth and man are wholly unexceptional. Perhaps even more significant is Copernicus' recognition that the movement of the heavens could be explained in terms of the movement of the observer. It is with this discovery that the observed condition of the outer world is unwittingly determined by the observing subject that the Copernican revolution becomes the dominant metaphor for the modern worldview. Men and women, displaced from the center of things, stand by themselves with their subjective knowledge in a contingent universe.

The Copernican cosmological crisis and its alienating effect on the mind received support and philosophical development from René Descartes. Starting with a position of fundamental doubt before the world and moving to his *cogito ergo sum* (I think therefore I exist), Descartes set into motion a number of important developments in philosophy visible in works from Locke to Berkeley to Hume and culminating in the epistemological crisis of Kant. The autonomous modern self becomes, after Descartes, distinct and separated from the world it seeks to know and dominate. A human is a conscious, personal observer facing an unconscious, impersonal, material universe. This estrangement of humans from the world produced by the Cartesian ontological revolution received support and epistemological expression from Immanuel Kant. It was Kant who pointed out that all human knowledge is radically interpretive. That is to say, there can be no photographic-like knowledge of the objective world, for the world apprehended by the mind is already arranged by its own internal structure. The mind can have a direct knowledge only of its own internal phenomena and not of external things. Human knowledge is not so much a collection of objective facts about the world as it is interpretation; the universe is a human construct. As a result of this relativization of human knowledge, we face an unbridgeable gap between ourselves and the world. The cumulative result of the Copernican, Cartesian, and Kantian schisms is that humans are minor and tangential agents adrift in the cosmos.[103]

The picture of reality that has dominated in the West for the last three centuries is of a predictable, mechanistic, and purposeless world devoid of human or spiritual qualities. But the lesson of Kant, supported by the findings of cognitive psychology, is that the world is never as described by our worldview. The meaning of reality rendered by the mind cannot be said to inhere in the world. First, we literally have to learn to see. We must organize sense data before the world as we know it appears.[104] We can only be certain that the universe is highly susceptible to our particular interpretations, for better or worse. We represent the world to ourselves as impersonal, mechanistic, and purposeless, and we respond to this representation, as if it were a cosmic law. The truth of the matter, perhaps, is that the impersonal, mechanistic, and purposeless qualities are in ourselves.

Toward Preliminary Understandings
of Anomalous Folklore

The anomalous folklore of extraordinary encounters with fairies and UFOs and their occupants, and perhaps all nonhuman beings, provides us not only unique depictions of questions of human knowledge, but also, with the help of depth psychology, an antidote to the dilemma. The point I want to argue here is that the archetypal patterns in anomalous folklore are intimately related to the structure inherent in nature itself.

I have argued throughout that the problematic nature of human knowledge that preoccupies the Western mind is manifested in the major recurring elements of fairy and UFO lore: the "subtle body," shape-shifting, clouds and fogs, luminous light, as well as abduction stories containing the motif of interspecies breeding and genetic revivification, and the themes of positive reciprocity (We Need Them; They Need Us) and negative reciprocity (We Fear Them; They Fear Us). When elucidated by the findings of depth psychology, all these elements together point to a participatory epistemological model that may be the answer to the mind's estrangement from the world.

Anomalous folklore arises from a source akin to mind and nature alike. C.G. Jung referred to this unitary background of mind and nature as the "Unus Mundus," an alchemical concept meaning "one world."[105] From this paradoxical psychophysical realm come "archetypes," structuring principles of mind comparable to a "pattern of behavior" in biology, that underlie typical human activities such as conception, birth, puberty, marriage, illness, death, and, functioning like an instinct, influence typical human relationships such as between mother and child, husband and wife, teacher and student, and so on. Because archetypes partake of the same paradoxical psychophysical nature of the Unus Mundus, Jung referred to them as "psychoid."[106] By this term Jung meant that archetypes are not purely psychic, but to a certain extent are physical and organic as well. So defined, the psychoid archetype is similar to the nature of "subtle bodies" discussed earlier. Archetypes possess "transgressivity," or the ability to cross over from the psychic to the physical realm. Because of their psychoid or psychophysical nature, archetypes honor no ultimate separation between matter and spirit since each transgresses the other. Because a psychoid archetype exists in both immaterial mind and material nature, it contains more than can be included in any conventional psychological system or explanation. The alchemical image for the ontologically ambiguous nature of the archetype is Mercurius who is both a material and spiritual being (Quicksilver), an elusive spirit of great power. He is "Mercurius duplex" or "utriusque capax," that is, capable of being masculine-feminine, good-evil, light-dark, conscious-unconscious, concrete-abstract, and as such, is a symbol for the psychoid unconscious.[107] The figure of Mercurius suggests the "coniunctio oppositorum," the union of opposites and the "hieros gamos," the wedding of sacred and profane qualities. Jung did not discover the sphere of the unitary world since mystics and religious intuitives have known it for millennia. Jung simply brought the concept to psychology at a time when physicists were exploring similar areas.

The psychoid archetype and psychoid unconscious have a parallel in subatomic physics. Jung wrote that "Microphysics is feeling its way into the unknown side of matter, just as complex psychology is pushing forward into the unknown side of the psyche."[108] Einstein's famous equation points in the direction of a unitary world or psychoid sphere: $E=mc^2$, that is, the total amount of energy "E" locked into a mass "m" is equivalent to that mass multiplied by the square of the speed of light "c." Energy and matter are not two faces of the universe but actually the two sides of the same face. Jung's concept of the psychoid archetype is to depth psychology what Einstein's theory of relativity is to physics.[109]

The subatomic units of matter display a paradoxical nature much like "Mercurius duplex." "Depending on how we look at them, they appear sometimes as particles, and sometimes as waves; and this dual nature is also exhibited by light which can take the form of electromagnetic waves or particles."[110] Wolfgang Pauli, a pioneer in quantum mechanics, posited the existence of a cosmic order both transcendental and objective that influences not only the perceiving subject but also the object perceived.[111] This is another way of saying that the psychoid level of the mind's core and the subatomic level of nature become one world, the Unus Mundus. It is from the intersection of this transconscious domain that synchronistic phenomena emerge.

The psychophysical nature of the archetype is closely related to Jung's concept of "synchronicity," an unexpected meeting of one or more psychic states with a physical event.[112] Because of an archetypes' transgressivity, its psychoid (i.e., polar) nature splits and appears in the mental realm as an image and in the world as an external event, and occasionally even as a quasi-physical "object." From this peculiar fusion of time and space and inner and outer-worlds, something of the original unity of life becomes visible and can be experienced. Synchronistic phenomena, like fairy and UFO encounters with their parallel mental and material aspects, must be regarded as the "coming-to-consciousness" of an archetype. A thing only becomes conscious when it becomes distinct from other things. Normally, coming-to-consciousness is an intrapsychic process: the distinction among things occurs in our dreams, thoughts and intuitions. With synchronistic phenomena, however, this process is different. According to Aniela Jaffe:

> Here the antinomies or parallelisms, the various facets of the archetype that is coming to consciousness, are torn asunder. They manifest themselves, psychically and non-psychically, at different times and in different places. This strange behavior may be explained by the fact that the psychoid archetype has not yet become fully conscious, but exists in a state that is half unconscious and half conscious. It is still partly in the unconscious, hence the relativization of time and space.[113]

This relativity of time and space is clearly visible in fairy and UFO abductions where temporal and spatial distortions are so common.[114]

Because the psychoid archetype arises from the timeless and spaceless realm of the Unus Mundus where causality has no hold, synchronistic phenomena are unpredictable and powerful. Sir James Jeans wrote that " . . . every mechanical model or image must represent things as occurring in space and time, whereas . . . the actual final processes in nature neither occur nor are able to be represented in time and space."[115] Synchronistic phenomena exist in the border zone between the conscious and the unconscious, the knowable and the unknowable, the visible world and the transcendent background of reality. Strange encounters with fairies and

UFOs and their occupants are "signals" from the unitary reality, challenging the validity of the subject-object estrangement discussed earlier.

In that worldview, recall, the inherent principles of mind that determine human knowledge belong exclusively to the perceiving human subject. But with the new epistemological model formed from a fusion of depth psychology, parapsychology and subatomic physics, those inherent ordering principles are also grounded in nature. The psychoid archetypes are as much in nature as in mind, and thus are also expressions of nature's own spirit. This means that man is involved in a symbiotic relationship with reality, a notion suggested by accounts of fairy and UFO contact.

"The human mind," according to Richard Tarnas, "is ultimately the organ of nature's own process of self-revelation, " and so "the essential reality of the world is not separate, self-contained, and complete in itself, so that the human mind can examine it 'objectively' and register it from without."[116] Instead, our knowledge of reality only emerges through the mind's full participation in the unfolding process of nature's evolving spirit. Nature's reality is not exclusively objective and independent of mind, rather it depends upon various acts of human cognition. Recall the statement of W.B. Yeats presented earlier that fairies "have no inherent form, but change according to their whims or the mind that sees them." The human mind does not simply interpret nature according to its inherent structure, as Kant maintained, "rather, the spirit of nature brings forth its own order through the human mind when that mind is employing its full complement of faculties—intellectual, volitional, emotional, sensory, and imaginative."[117] Nature reveals its own reality through human consciousness and thus, humans, rather than fundamentally estranged from the world, instead play an active role in the unfolding of life's meaning. This participatory epistemology, prefigured in fairy and UFO lore, reunites men and women with the universe, bridging a gap that has existed in our thinking for three centuries.

Implications for Future Folklore Studies

Scholars everywhere recognize the rich archetypal patterns in folklore, although disagreement exists as to the cause of its universality.[118] Folklore, because of its generally unschooled, informal, and conservative nature, more clearly presents the outlines of the mind's organization than does the more self-conscious and stylistically variable popular and elite arts. Having a more intimate relationship with their own archetypal roots, traditional societies have lived closer to the quintessential spirit of nature which employs the human mind as the context of its own "individuation."

Nature individualizes its spirit in all forms of cognition, human or otherwise.

I am not suggesting that the popular and high art communities are severed from their own archetypal foundations, but these structures are overlaid with much personal, conscious, and ever-changing stylistic material. Popular arts are more apt to be driven by the caprice of the marketplace and the "high" arts by the academic debates of competing schools. The archetypal framework of the human spirit is still present there, but is often less immediately available to consciousness.

If it is true that nature's essence is revealed in folklore, then this might mean that people living closer to nature, that is, to their archetypal or "imaginal" sources of creativity, more frequently experience fairy, UFO, and other types of extraordinary encounters. Anomalous folklore, as well as so-called parapsychological events, unusual healings, and the physical phenomena of mysticism as found in the lives of the Catholic saints,[119] would not, rightly speaking, point to a "supernatural " realm but toward a natural order that embraces all life. Folklore, from this perspective, does not bring us further away from the reality, but brings us through our "imaginal" archetypal roots to the nature's "truth." Folklore is never literally true, but it may always be fundamentally true.

Extraordinary experiences and their subsequent beliefs and narratives constitute folklore in the making and reveal in special ways nature's indivisible core. Because people are intimately involved with their folklore, it plays a role in the social construction of reality. Fairylore and the emerging lore of UFOs join together the subjective and objective, the seen and unseen, the factual and the imaginal as part of the ongoing culturally specific formulations of our unity with the world. The scientific worldview would rob the universe of spirit and purpose; fairies and UFOs re-enchant the world, not in the way of "glamour" or "pishogue," but in the sense that the world and our place in it is more and not less than it seems to the eyes.

Anomalous folk experiences must be re-evaluated and re-visioned. Whereas since the Enlightenment "anomalous" meant "contrary to nature or law," and today generally means in apparent contradiction to scientific fact, it meant something else indeed for the ancients. In Hellenistic times an anomaly like a strange aerial display or confrontation with one's "daemon," did not mean a violation of natural law, but its reverse. Anomalies and synchronicities established the fundamental order of nature and history, and were a "sign" of some overall design in reality. They were "portents" and "messages" from nature (i.e., the gods) and were not so interesting in themselves as for what they portended for the future. Anomalies of old were "signals" of a "New Age" in which archetypal (i.e., divine) principles inherent in nature manifested more frequently in the everyday world. Scholars have noted that today, as the millennium approaches, our consciousness is undergoing an "invasion of the archetypes"[120] in the form of "endtime anomalies."[121] Not since classical antiquity has life been so strikingly mythogenetic. For example, since World War II, there have been numerous international reports of UFO sightings, apparitions of the Virgin Mary, angelic visitations, spirit communications, and meetings with "Men in Black," to name but some strange events.

For the Greeks, such psychoid formulations of spirit and matter carried the spark of "divine" knowing (i.e., *imago dei* or image of god) simultaneously into human consciousness and into nature's own process of self-realization. This ancient teleological idea so central to classical thought and visible in anomalous folk belief systems of yesterday and today, is one of the most popular notions of what is erroneously referred to today as the "New Age."[122] Underlying the apparent chaos of competing folk belief and symbol systems lies the workings of a unitary, psycho-physical ground of being that has been slowly emerging into contemporary human awareness. This view, a staple notion of the Renaissance, is again being widely entertained. Notice its presence in the works of physicist David Bohm who posits an "implicate order" wherein consciousness and matter are aspects of the same indivisible reality,[123] and Robert G. Jahn and Brenda J. Dunne, who have demonstrated the role of consciousness in the physical world,[124] or in the study of Michael Murphy on the strange healing powers of the human body,[125] or Ken Ring's near-death studies,[126] or Michael Grosso's investigations into the parapsychology of religion,[127] and the serious consideration recently given by academics to UFOs and related phenomena.[128]

Anomalous folklore, more than "simply superstition," contains unique depictions of prevailing epistemological attitudes of mainstream culture and its rich archetypal patterns must be considered in any study of human knowledge. A more serious consideration of both its epistemological and ontological implications may produce important insights that shed light on the subtle embodiment of human beings and the pivotal role we play in the participatory enterprise we call reality. Certainly folklorists stand in the best position to further our understanding of anomalous folk belief and experience.

There is another reason why we should not leave this work to others. Anomalous folklore is too volatile to be left to those who do not empathize with the cultures they examine. Often people's illusions and fears dominate their lives, robbing them of the security of a free and purposeful will. History offers precedent. For example, slave owning classes during and following the era of American slavery manipulated Black fear of the supernatural into a system of psychological control to discourage the unauthorized assembly and movement of Blacks, especially at night, actions that were thought could lead to insurrection. From the post–Civil

War to World War I, that fear was used to halt Black migration from rural farming towns in the South to urban industrial centers in the North. Originally practiced during the time of slavery by white masters who dressed in white sheets to imitate ghosts, the control system was expanded later on into a system of mounted patrols called "patterollers," who provided a surveillance of slave movements in post Civil War days. During the Reconstruction era the Ku Klux Klan ran the system by continuing the old slave system of dressing in sheets and patrolling. Finally, the "night doctors" or body snatchers completed the system of black intimidation. Black victims referred to all the above groups as the "night riders." [129] During the seventeenth century, Scandinavian cultures used folklore to promote their own nationalistic glorification.[130] In addition, six years after the Kingdom of Sweden organized an extensive official investigation of folklore in 1667 called the "Antiquitets Collegium," a Swedish farm laborer at Markharads was sentenced to death by a court for admitting to "illicit intercourse with a wood or mountain spirit."[131] Folklorists do not want to manipulate, patronize or dismiss the truth claims of anomalous events to their own purposes, and thus fall prey to our own "traditions of disbelief."[132]

It is good to be a "skeptic" in the popular sense of one who doubts, or questions presumed truths. Blind faith and outright dismissal of the potential validity of anomalous claims are likewise antithetical to healthy skepticism, and approach dogmatism. There exists today the same potential for psychological exploitation of UFO, occult, satanic and mystical beliefs by special interest groups.[133] Even folklorists may treat the material in ways that favor their particular biases and vested interests rather than attend to the real and imagined fears of their informants. Recently Phillips Stevens, Jr., after examining widespread rumors of national satanic cults, and finding nothing behind them, chides folklorists for failing to bring their expertise "directly into the heart of social problems," reminding us that we have "a professional and moral responsibility" to share our knowledge about the alleged satanistic truth-claims with the public.[134] Folklorist Bill Ellis argues persuasively that we must recognize that folk "tradition includes serious threats to real life." Anomalous folk beliefs and narratives, for example, are not only "verbal texts to be collected, transcribed, and archived," but are also maps for possible "violent acts" like satanic murder and mutilation.[135] The mentally ill, sociopaths or the simply bored may, for example, pattern random thefts of children after traditional accounts of "changelings" and UFO abductions. This kind of "pseudo-ostension" wherein someone uses the popular images of folklore to cover the traces of his or her illegal and violent acts is not uncommon.[136] Felicitas Goodman suggests that as contact with spiritual beings becomes a larger part of all encompassing reality, "it behooves us to treat what others experience with respect, and should we encounter the believers as suffering human beings, to confront them on their own terms and not on our own."[137]

Folklorists need to be more philosophically minded in regard to anomalous belief, that is, to give critical reflection of the justification of basic human beliefs and analysis of basic concepts in terms of which such beliefs are expressed. Folklore has always shown an odd resistance to speculative inquiry and to theory, however, generally transmuting the latter into methodology.[138] One purpose of this discussion is to suggest that critical reflection be given to the concept of "experience" itself, since strictly speaking, the word cannot be restricted to one usage. The philosophically minded folklorist studying anomalous experience will want to determine whether by "experience" the informant means, for example, an accumulation of information or skill over a period of time. In this case, it admits of degrees since one's experience may be more or less than another's. If an informant states he or she had a terrifying fairy encounter last week, we may be identifying "experience" with a quality of sensation or emotion. A UFO abductee once told me that she had the "experience of floating" up into the space craft. A celebrated abductee experienced sinking slowly into his bed. "Experience" in these cases could mean a psychological reaction, but it need not be so. In both cases experience does not admit of degrees; development is not implied, nor is accumulation. We do not rightly speak of more or less experience but of different experience. Each experience is unitary. Experience here is something qualitative. It is possible that to an informant "experience" means the entire field of conscious awareness. From this perspective merely to be conscious is to experience. In addition, "experience" can mean a conscious and systematic use of a method of observation as is implied by the phrase "Science resorts to experience." In this sense we are dealing with an established approach in policy that may be employed at any time. "Experience" can also mean objective reality. Experience here exists prior to and independent of an observing subject. Finally, we can speak of "experience" as an interaction or relation of a perceiver and something perceived within an encounter matrix. Here experience is never simply the world of "fact" but a transactional field of activity.[139] I intend the above discussion to make clear the need for a speculative perspective in dealing with truth-claims of strange events. For as Oscar Wilde once wrote, "The pure and simple truth is rarely pure and never simple."

We should concern ourselves with the truth-claims of anomalous folk belief, first, because explanation and interpretation are integral to folkloristics; second, because as humanistic social scientists we owe it to our informants, who are our collaborators in the folkloric enterprise, to share the knowledge we ourselves may gain; third, because a majority of the world's population holds, to some degree, some kind of anomalous belief; and finally, because such claims are extremely interesting and profoundly important. Merely collecting, describing, and cataloguing beliefs is not sufficient to our enterprise. "The project of all the humanistic disciplines," folklorist Roger D. Abrahams argues, "has been to discriminate between the real and unreal, the genuine and the fake, the realistic and the sentimental or fantastic, the veritable truth (all those things we call the 'facts') and illusions, the misleading, the mystified, and the mythical."[140] It is a matter of professional duty and personal courage, for as T.S. Eliot once wrote in the "Four Quartets," "Human kind/cannot bear very much reality." As folklorists, it is our task to try. We avoid solipsism and despair not by having right answers or correct methods, but by generating worthwhile humanistic activities. As humans we feel an inner imperative not only to know but also to act and feel and seek the beautiful and the good. Such nonscientific but real experiences give rise to valuable things unapproachable on scientific grounds: ethics, religion, and art. We cannot know with certitude higher realities independent of ourselves, but our nature demands a faith that they do exist, as a means to explain that which we experience daily. Folklore, along with ethics, religion, and art, is one "signal" of that faith.

Notes

1. I want to thank professors Michael Grosso and Ron MacKay and poet Ron Price for their careful readings of this text.
2. Howard H. Peckham, "Flying Saucers as Folklore," *Hoosier Folklore* 9 (1950): 103–7.
3. In sociology see Michael K. Schutz, "Organizational Goals and Support-Seeking Behavior: A Comparative Study of Social Movement Organizations in the UFO (Flying Saucer) Fields," PhD dissertation, Northwestern U, 1973. In psychology see June Parnell, "Personality Characteristics on the MMPI, 16PF, and ACL of Persons Who Claim UFO Experiences," PhD dissertation, U of Wyoming, 1986.
4. The first UFO article published was Peter M. Rojcewicz, "The 'Men in Black' Experience and Tradition: Analogues with the Traditional Devil Hypothesis," *Journal of American Folklore* 100.396 (1987): 148–60. This was followed by Thomas Eddie Bullard, "UFO Abduction Reports, The Supernatural Kidnap Narrative Returns in Technological Guise," *Journal of American Folklore* 102.404 (1989): 147–70.
5. Linda Dégh and Andrew Vázsonyi, "The Hypothesis of Multi-Conduit Transmission in Folklore," Dan Ben-Amos and Kenneth S. Goldstein, eds., *Folklore: Performance and Communication* (The Hague: Mouton, 1975).
6. See Linda Dégh, "UFOs and How Folklorists Should Look at Them," *Fabula* 18 (1977): 242–8; Donald Ward, "The Little Man Who Wasn't There: Encounters with the Supranormal," *Fabula* 18 (1977): 212–5; and Thomas E. Bullard, "Mysteries in the Eyes of the Beholder," PhD dissertation, Folklore, Indiana U, 1982.
7. Peter M. Rojcewicz, "The Folklore of the 'Men in Black,' A Challenge to the Prevailing Paradigm," *Re Vision* 11.4 (1989): 5–16.

8.   David J. Hufford, *The Terror That Comes in the Night, An Experience Centered Study of Supernatural Assault Traditions* (Philadelphia: U of Pennsylvania, 1982).

9.   Felicitas Goodman, *How About Demons?* (Bloomington: Indiana UP, 1988) 10. See also *The Exorcism of Anneliese Michel* (New York: Doubleday, 1981) and *Ecstasy, Ritual, and Alternate Reality: Religion in a Pluralistic World* (Bloomington: Indiana UP, forthcoming).

10.   Andrew Lang, *Magic and Religion* (1901; New York: Greenwood P, 1969) 270–94. See also *Cock Lane and Common Sense* (London: Longman's, Green, 1894).

11.   W.Y. Evans-Wentz, *The Fairy-Faith in the Celtic Countries* (1911; New York: Lemma Publishing, 1973).

12. Jacques Vallee, *Passport to Magonia, From Folklore to Flying Saucers* (Chicago: Henry Regnery, 1969). No folklorist feels comfortable saying that UFO occupants are fairies by another name. Such a position implies that the author is looking only for functional equivalents, failing to note the important phenomenological differences between the fairy and UFO traditions.

13.   Bullard, "Mysteries in the Eyes of the Beholder" ii–iii.

14.   Peter M. Rojcewicz, "The Boundaries of Orthodoxy, A Folkloric Look at the UFO Phenomenon," PhD dissertation, Folklore and Folklife, U of Pennsylvania, 1984.

15.   Linda Jean Milligan, "The UFO Debate: A Study of a Contemporary Legend," PhD dissertation, Folklore, Ohio State U, 1988.

16.   David J. Hufford has done the same for humanoids and strange lights. See "Humanoids and Anomalous Lights: Taxonomic and Epistemological Problems," *Fabula* 18 (1977): 234–41.

17.   Evans-Wentz 286.

18.   I have argued for the reality basis of anomalous folk claims in "The Folklore of the 'Men in Black,'" and "Signals of Transcendence: the Human-UFO Equation," *Journal of UFO Studies* 1 New Series (1989): 111–26.

19.   I have attempted to present a more exhaustive picture in "Boundaries of Orthodoxy," Chs. 4–7.

20.   G.R.S. Mead, *The Doctrine of the Subtle Body in Western Tradition* (1919; Wheaton, Ill: The Theosophical Publishing House, 1967).

21.   Robert Kirk, *The Secret Common-Wealth and A Short Treatise of Charms and Spels*, Mistletoe Series, ed. Stewart Sanderson (1893; Totowa, N.J.: Rowan and Littlefield for the Folklore Society, 1976) 50.

22.   Crombie's statement is found in Paul Hawken, *The Magic of Findhorn* (1975; New York: Bantam, 1980) 226.

23.   Jacques Vallee, *The Invisible College* (New York: E.P. Dutton, 1975) 6.

24.   D. Scott Rogo, *The Haunted Universe* (New York: New American Library, 1977) 31.

25.   Jerome Clark and Loren Coleman, *The Unidentified, Notes Toward Solving the UFO Mystery* (New York: Warner Books, 1975) 242. Clark has since divorced himself from the views expressed here.

26.   Michael Talbot, "UFOs Beyond Real and Unreal," Brad Steiger, ed., *Gods of Aquarius* (New York: Harcourt Brace Jovanovich, 1976) 28–32.

27.   Richard M. Dorson, *Man and Beast in American Comic Legend* (Bloomington: Indiana UP, 1982) 2.

28.   Jerome Clark and Loren Coleman, *Creatures of the Outer Edge* (New York: Warner Books, 1978) 46.

29. Ralph Blum and Judy Blum, *Beyond Earth: Man's Contact with UFOs* (New York: Bantam, 1974) 179–81.

30. J. Allen Hynek and Jacques Vallee, *The Edge of Reality* (Chicago: Henry Regnery, 1975) 34.

31. Katharine M. Briggs, *An Encyclopedia of Fairies* (New York: Pantheon, 1977) 373.

32. See Richard M. Dorson, *America Begins: Early American Writing* (New York: Pantheon, 1950) 158; Raymond Lamont Brown, *Phantoms of the Sea, Legends, Customs and Superstitions* (New York: Taplinger, 1972); and Horace Beck, *Folklore and the Sea* (Middletown, Connecticut: Wesleyan UP, 1973) 389–408.

33. Alexander Carmichael, *Carmina Gadelica*, vol. 2 (Edinburgh, 1928) 330.

34. See William James, *The Varieties of Religious Experience, A Study in Human Nature* (New York: Collier, 1961); also Evelyn Underhill, *Mysticism* (New York: E.P. Dutton, 1961) and Genevieve Foster, *The World Was Flooded With Light*, commentary by David J. Hufford (Pittsburgh: U of Pittsburgh P, 1985).

35. See Raymond Moody, *Life After Life* (Harrisburgh, Pa.: Stackpole, 1976); Ken Ring, *Life at Death* (New York: Coward, McCann and Geoghegan, 1980), and Ken Ring, *Heading Toward Omega* (New York: Morrow, 1984).

36. Aniela Jaffé, *Apparitions: An Archetypal Approach to Death, Dreams and Ghosts* (Irving, Texas: Spring, 1979) 33–4.

37. Blum and Blum 85–6.

38. Coral Lorenzen and Jim Lorenzen, *Abducted: Confrontations with Beings from Outer Space* (New York: Berkeley, 1977) 14.

39. E. Van Glasersfeld, "An Introduction to Radical Constructivism," P. Wutzlawick, ed., *The Invented Reality* (New York: Norton, 1984).

40. Lawrence Le Shan, *Alternate Realities, The Search for the Full Human Being* (New York: M. Evans, 1976) 32–3.

41. For an extended discussion of the metanoia process see Joseph Chilton Pearce, *The Crack in the Cosmic Egg* (1971; New York: Washington Square P, 1973). See also the chapter on "conversion" in James, *Varieties of Religious Experience*.

42. Plato discusses the relationship between physical and intellectual sight in 507f of *The Republic of Plato*, translated with Notes and an Interpretive Essay by Allan Bloom (New York: Basic, 1968). For a discussion of Augustine's ideas see R. Allers, "St. Augustine's Doctrine on Illumination," *Franciscan Studies* 12 (1952): 27–46.

43. This idea is discussed in Michael Talbot, *Mysticism and the New Physics* (New York: Bantam New Age, 1981) 56.

44. Mircea Eliade, *Shamanism, Archaic Techniques of Ecstasy*, trans. Willard R. Reask (Princeton: Princeton UP, 1964) 60–1.

45. Raymond E. Fowler, *The Andreasson Affair* (1979; New York: Bantam Books, 1980) 44. Fowler has written two more books on the Andreasson case: *The Andreasson Affair, Phase 2* (Englewood Cliffs, N.J.: Prentice-Hall, 1982), and *The Watchers, The Secret Behind UFO Abduction* (New York: Bantam Books, 1990).

46. Marie-Louise von Franz, *Projection and Re-Collection in Jungian Psychology*, trans. by William H. Kennedy (La Salle and London: Open Court, 1980) 109–10.

47. Evans-Wentz 227.

48. Victor C. Uchendo, *The Igbo of Southeast Nigeria* (New York: Holt, Rinehart and Winston, 1965) 14.

49. Thomas Crofton Croker, *Fairy Legends and Traditions of the South of Ireland,* eds. Neil C. Hultin and Warren U. Ober (1926–8; Lelmar, N.Y.: Scholar's Facsimiles and Reprints, 1983) 27.

50. Fowler 1980 16–9, 146–56.

51. For the relationships between fairies and psychic phenomena see Evans-Wentz: clairvoyance 58, 73, 140, 151, 205; telepathy 472–3, 484; poltergeists 67, 120, 156, 475–6; teleportation 73, 87, 104, 127; apparitions 67, 179; near-death experiences 142, 217.

52. Blum and Blum 147.

53. For the former case, see Steiger 156; for the latter, see Blum and Blum 144.

54. See Michael Grosso, *The Final Choice* (Walpole, N.H.: Stillpoint Publishing, 1986) 199–221.

55. Michel Meurger, *Lake Monster Traditions: A Cross-Cultural Analysis* (London: Fortean Tomes, 1988) 25.

56. Yeats's statement is found in Kathleen Raine's "Foreword" in W.B. Yeats, ed., *Fairy and Folk Tales of Ireland* (1888, 1892; New York: Macmillan, 1973) xvi.

57. Alan Bruford, "Introduction" in James MacDougal, ed., *Highland Fairy Legends* (1910; Totowa, N.J.: Rowman and Littlefield, 1978).

58. See Patrick Logan, *The Old Gods: The Facts About Fairies* (Belfast, Ireland: Appletree P, 1981) 97.

59. See Thomas Keightley, *The Fairy Mythology* (1850; New York: Haskell House Publishers, 1968) 300. On another related form of "blast" see article by Barbara Rieti in this volume. Also see article by Peter Narváez for "fairy-led" experiences.

60. Hannah Aitken, *A Forgotten Heritage, Original Folk Tales of Lowland Scotland* (Totowa, N.J.: Rowman and Littlefield, 1973) 13.

61. See E.S. Hartland, *The Science of Fairy Tales* (1890; Detroit: Singing Tree P, 1968) 113–5; Yeats 50; MacDougal 3, 9; John Rhys, *Celtic Folklore: Welsh and Manx,* vol. 2 (London: Wildwood House, 1980) 693.

62. Katharine M. Briggs, *The Vanishing People: Fairy Lore and Legends* (New York: Pantheon Books, 1978) 10. See also Aitken 4.

63. Coral Lorenzen and Jim Lorenzen, *Flying Saucer Occupants* (New York: New American Library, 1967) 103; John A. Keel, *The Eighth Tower* (New York: E.P. Dutton and Co., 1975) 8–9, and J. Allen Hynek and Jacques Vallee, *The Edge of Reality, A Progress Report on Unidentified Flying Objects* (Chicago: Henry Regnery, 1975) 159.

64. Lorenzen and Lorenzen, *Flying Saucer Occupants* 101.

65. Blum and Blum 115.

66. Bill Barry, "Kidnapped!" in D. Scott Rogo, ed., *UFO Abductions* (New York: New American Library, 1980), 30.

67. The De Souza case is mentioned by Keel 157; the Moody case is discussed by Jim Lorenzen in *Proceedings of the First International UFO Congress* (New York: Warner Books, 1980) 248.

68. For a lengthy discussion of the "used person," see Rojcewicz, "Boundaries of Orthodoxy" 586–606.

69. See Jacques Vallee, *Confrontations, A Scientist's Search for Alien Contact* (New York: Ballantine Books, 1990).

70. Yeats's comment is found in Evans-Wentz 287.

71. See Lorenzen, *Abducted* 42; George Adamski, *Inside the Flying Saucers* (New York: Warner Books, 1967) 68–9, and also Jay David, ed., *The Flying Saucer Reader* (New York: New American Library, 1967) 75.

72. See Keightley 16–8 and Evans-Wentz 44.

73. Briggs, *Vanishing* 125–6.

74. Hartland 43.

75. See Keightley 159 and Briggs, *Vanishing* 30–1.

76. The symbiosis goes both ways to form a relationship of mutual dependence. In the case of Lusmore, the hunchback cured by fairies, Lusmore possessed a sanguine, kindly personality and his interaction with fairies proved beneficial. But when Jack Madden, a "peevish and ill-tempered" hunchback confronted fairies, hoping to gain a fine new suit, he was kicked and beaten nearly to death by twenty fairies. See Briggs, *Vanishing* 42.

77. Budd Hopkins, *Intruders, The Incredible Visitations at Copley Woods* (New York: Random House, 1987) 27.

78. Hopkins 196.

79. Hopkins 172–84.

80. See Whitley Streiber, *Communion* (New York: William Morrow, 1987) 30.

81. Gordon Creighton, "The Amazing Case of Antonio Boas," Rogo (1980) 51–85.

82. Peter M. Rojcewicz, "Strange Bedfellows: The Folklore of Other-Sex," *Critique* 29 (1988): 8–12.

83. Hopkins 83.

84. Hopkins 190.

85. Briggs, *Vanishing* 38.

86. Gillian Bennett, *Traditions of Belief, Women, Folklore and the Supernatural* (New York: Viking Penguin Books, 1987) 75.

87. Briggs, *Vanishing* 8.

88. Dell Hymes, "Folklore's Nature and the Sun's Myth," *Journal of American Folklore* 88 (1975): 353.

89. Peter M. Rojcewicz, "The Extraordinary Encounter Continuum Hypothesis and Its Implications for the Study of Belief Materials," *Folklore Forum* 19.2 (1986): 131–52.

90. Raine's statement is found in Yeats xi.

91. Verre D. Shortt, "The Fairy-Faith in Ireland," *The Occult Review* 18 (1913): 70–8.

92. See Hartland cs.VII–IX, and Briggs, *Vanishing* 11–26.

93. Briggs, *Vanishing* 6.

94. Yeats 11.

95. Kurt Seligman, *Magic, Supernaturalism and Religion* (New York: Pantheon Books, 1948) 162.

96. See Rojcewicz, "The 'Men in Black' Experience and Tradition," and also "The Folklore of the 'Men in Black.'"

97. Harold A. Cahn, "Speculations on the UFO Experience" in Richard F. Haines, ed., *UFO Phenomena and the Behavioral Scientist* (Metuchen, N.J.: Scarecrow P, 1979) 142.

98. Rogo, *Haunted* 31.

99. Kirk 64.

100. Hartland 59–60.

101. Found in Donald M. Michael, "Forecasting and Planning in an Incoherent Context," *Technological Forecasting and Social Change* 36 (1989): 80.

102. Here I draw freely from the fine overview of the major paradigmatic shifts in Western consciousness by Richard Tarnas, "The Transfiguration of the Western Mind," *Re Vision* 12.3 (1990): 3–17. See also Alexandre Koyre, *From the Closed World to the Infinite Universe* (Baltimore, Md.: Johns Hopkins U, 1968) and Herbert Butterfield, *The Origins of Modern Science*, Rev. ed. (1957; New York: The Free P, 1965).

103. I do not want to misrepresent Descartes and Kant as men who themselves lacked faith or spirituality. Descartes's theory of knowledge is of a representational kind. Mind or soul is fundamentally different from the body and thus can have as its content only ideas, which at best are representatives of physical things. Whether the ideas of sense knowledge correspond to the physical objects perceived by the senses is moot. Descartes maintains that there is reason to think there is such a correspondence based on the assumption that God by definition is not a deceiver. We are thus justified to trust our senses. Far from demonstrating that an absolute doubt before the world is necessary, Descartes shows that it is ultimately self-defeating. He uses skepticism as a means to refute absolute skepticism. And as for Kant, while he believed that we cannot have knowledge about what transcends our experience, he nevertheless holds that we can have faith. If Descartes's skepticism is replaced by intuition, Kant's is replaced by faith. In the absence of knowledge faith is justifiable, although it is neither a substitute for nor a renaming of knowledge. For a look into Kant's character and the motivating forces behind his ideas, see his *Anthropology from a Pragmatic Point of View*, trans. Victor Lyle Dowdell, rev. and ed. Hans H. Rudnick (Carbondale: Southern Illinois UP, 1978).

104. J.Z. Young, *Doubt and Certainty in Science: A Biologist's Reflections on the Brain* (London: Oxford UP, 1960).

105. C.G. Jung, *Mysterium Coniunctionis*, 2nd ed., vol.14, *Collected Works* (Princeton: Princeton UP, 1970) 463–5, 537–9.

106. C.G. Jung, *Synchronicity: An Acausal Connecting Principle* (Princeton, N.J.: Princeton UP, 1973) 89–90, 99.

107. Aniela Jaffé, *From the Life and Work of C.G. Jung* (Am Klosterplatz, Einsiedeln, Switzerland: Daimon Verlag, 1989) 68–9; see also Eugene Monick, *Phallos, Sacred Image of the Masculine* (Toronto: Inner City, 1987) 81.

108. Jung, *Mysterium* 538.

109. This comparison has been made by Monick 64.

110. Fritjof Capra, *The Tao of Physics* (Berkeley: Shambala, 1977) 55. See also Werner Heisenberg, *Physics and Philosophy* (New York: Harper and Row, 1962) 160.

111. Wolfgang Pauli, "The Influence of Archetypal Ideas on the Scientific Theories of Kepler," Jung and Pauli, *The Interpretation of Nature and the Psyche* (New York: 1955) 152.

112. Jung, *Synchronicity* (1973). See also Marie-Louise von Franz, *On Divination and Synchronicity, The Psychology of Meaningful Chance* (Toronto: Inner City Books, 1980); Jean Shinoda Bolen, *The Tao of Psychology, Synchronicity and the Self* (New York: Harper and Row, 1979); Ira Progroff, *Jung, Synchronicity, and Human Destiny* (New York: Dell, 1973).

113. Jaffé, *Life and Work* 38.

114. This fact has already been noted for the fairy faith. For evidence in the UFO literature see Budd Hopkins, *Missing Time, A Documented Study of UFO Abductions* (New York: Richard Marek Publishers, 1981). See also Rogo, *UFO Abductions* 99–182 and Streiber.

115. Sir James Jeans, *Physics and Philosophy* (New York: Macmillan, 1943) 175.

116. Tarnas 12.

117. Tarnas 12.

118. Structuralists and analytical psychologists posit inherent structures of mind which they argue accounts for folklore's universality. Polygenesis, the independent origin of analogous forms, is their basis for assuming a "psychic unity of mankind." See Marilyn J. Schlitz, "Psychic Unity: A Meeting Ground for Parapsychology and Anthropology," paper presented at the Parapsychology Foundation Conference, October 1987. Most folklorists feel more comfortable with the idea of monogenesis and dissemination from a single point of origin. See Franz Boas, *Race, Language and Culture* (New York: The Free P, 1966) 397–400.

119. See Herbert Thurston, *The Physical Phenomena of Mysticism* (Chicago: Henry Regnery, 1952); Michael Grosso, "Padre Pio and Future Man," *Critique* 30 (1989): 26–34; Patricia Treece, *The Sanctified Body* (New York: Doubleday, 1987); John Henry Cardinal Newman, *Two Essays on Biblical and Ecclesiastical Miracles* (New York: Longmans, Green, 1890); and Ian Wilson, *Stigmata* (New York: Harper and Row, 1989).

120. Dennis Stillings, "Invasion of the Archetypes: Images of High Numinousity in Current Popular Culture," *Gnosis* 10 (1989): 29–39.

121. Michael Grosso, "Endtime Anomalies," *Critique* 31 (1989): 15–9.

122. Michael Grosso, "UFOs and the Myth of the New Age," *Cyberbiological Studies of the Imaginal Component in the UFO Contact Experience, Archaeus* 5, ed. Dennis Stillings (St. Paul, Minn.: Archaeus Project, 1989): 81–98.

123. David Bohm, *Wholeness and the Implicate Order* (1980; Boston: Routledge and Kegan Paul, 1982).

124. Robert G. Jahn and Brenda J. Dunne, *Margins of Reality: The Role of Consciousness in the Physical World* (San Diego: Harcourt Brace Jovanovich, 1987).

125. Michael Murphy, *The Future of the Body* (San Francisco: J.P. Tarcher, forthcoming in 1991). See also "Dimensions of Healing," *Sciences Review*, 4.3 (1987): 5–9.

126. Ring, *Life at Death* and *Heading Toward Omega*.

127. Michael Grosso, *Provocations, Prolegamena to Any Future Religion* (unpublished manuscript).

128. See the *Journal of UFO Studies* 1, New Series (1984) published by the Center of UFO Studies, Chicago, Illinois; and Stillings, *Cyberbiological*.

129. Gladys-Marie Fry, *Night Riders in Black Folk History* (Knoxville: U of Tennessee P, 1975).

130. Meurger 16.

131. Meurger 17.

132. For a discussion of this pitfall see David J. Hufford, "Traditions of Disbelief," *New York Folklore* 11 (1985): 47–56.

133. Jacques Vallee has argued this point in *Messengers of Deception: UFO Contacts and Cults* (Berkeley, C.A.: And/Or P, 1979) and also in *The Invisible College.*

134. Phillips Stevens, Jr., "Satanism: Where Are the Folklorists?," Editorial Essay, *New York Folklore* XV.1–2 (1989): 21.

135. Bill Ellis, "Death by Folklore: Ostension, Contemporary Legend and Murder," *Western Folklore* 48 (1989): 218.

136. See Linda Dégh and Andrew Vászonyi, "Does the Word 'Dog' Bite? Ostensive Action: A Means of Legend-Telling," *Journal of Folklore Research* 20 (1983):

5–34; see also Sylvia Grider, "The Razor Blades in the Apples Syndrome," *Perspectives on Contemporary Legend*, ed. Paul Smith (Sheffield: CETAL, 1984) 120–40.

137. Goodman 126.

138. As recently as 1973 Richard M. Dorson wrote that "The history of American folklore discloses no books of theory, no continuity, no consensus, no high order of polemics. . . ." See "Afterword," *Journal of the Folklore Institute* 10 (1973): 125–6.

139. John Herman Randall, Jr. and Justus Buchler, *Philosophy, An Introduction* (New York: Barnes and Noble, 1942) 85–8.

140. Roger D. Abrahams, "Ordinary and Extraordinary Experience," *The Anthropology of Experience*, eds. Victor Turner and Edward Bruner (Urbana: U of Illinois P, 1986) 65.

Contributors

Linda-May Ballard received her MPh from the University of Ulster in 1979. Her thesis was a comparative analysis of Irish variants (Gaelic and English) of an international folktale (AT 726). Having held various positions at the Ulster Folk and Transport Museum, she is currently Head of the museum's Textile Section. She has researched various aspects of oral tradition in Ulster, made an intensive collection of the lore of Rathlin Island, and studied the oral history of childbirth in Ulster. Her chief research interests now include the social history of local costume, Ulster embroidery, and motorcycle club art. Her articles have appeared in many journals including *Ulster Folklife*, *Lore and Language*, *Oral History*, *Fabula*, *Archaeology Ireland*, and *Crafts*.

Margaret Bennett possesses degrees in folklore (MA) and Scottish ethnology (PhD). From 1984 to 1995 she was a Lecturer at Edinburgh University's School of Scottish Studies. In January 1996 she was appointed Honorary Research Fellow at Glasgow University Post-Graduate School of Scottish and Celtic Studies. She presently works as an independent scholar and heads the Scottish Folk Culture Consultancy in Edinburgh. She has written three books: *The Last Stronghold: Scottish Gaelic Traditions in Newfoundland* (Michaelis Jena Prize, 1991); *Scottish Customs from the Cradle to the Grave*; and most recently *Oatmeal and Catechism*, which concerns Scottish Gaelic settlers in Quebec.

Alan Bruford (1937-1995) studied at Cambridge and Edinburgh (PhD). He was the Editor of the folklore journal *Tocher*, the Archivist, School of Scottish Studies, and a Reader at the University of Edinburgh. His numerous articles on Gaelic and Scots folktales, legends, folksong, folk music, and the folklore and ethnology of Orkney and Shetland, where he engaged in extensive fieldwork, appeared in major academic journals. His legacy of publications also includes two books, *Gaelic Folk-Tales and Mediaeval Romances* and *The Green Man of Knowledge and other Scots Traditional Tales*.

David Buchan (1939-1994) received his PhD from Aberdeen and taught at universities in Canada, the United States, and Scotland. He was the author and editor of highly acknowledged, major works in folklore studies including *The Ballad and the Folk, A Scottish Ballad Book, Scottish Tradition,* and *Folk Tradition and Folk Medicine in Scotland: The Writings of David Rorie.* He was a Folklore Fellow of the Finnish Academy of Arts and Sciences, Fellow of the American Folklore Society, Honorary Member of the Folklore Society, Vice-President of the Kommission für Volksdichtung, and University Research Professor, Memorial University of Newfoundland.

Gary Butler is an Associate Professor, Communications Programme, Division of Humanities, York University, Toronto, Ontario. He received an MA at the Université de Bordeaux and his PhD from Memorial University of Newfoundland. His major research area, the relation of folklore to conversation and communication, is the topic of his critically acclaimed book *Saying Isn't Believing: Conversational Narrative and the Discourse of Tradition in a French-Newfoundland Community.* His most recent monograph is *Histoire et traditions orales des Franco-Acadiens de Terre-Neuve.*

Susan Schoon Eberly has studied at the University of Iowa, where she is presently a PhD candidate in medieval literature. Her professional position is Program Associate, Publications Supervisor, Division of Developmental Disabilities, Department of Pediatrics, University of Iowa Hospitals and Clinics. She has published articles in *Folklore,* the journal of the British Folklore Society, and is the author of several works in the field of public health including *Iowans with Autism: Responding to the Need.* Most recently she has co-edited *Medical and Surgical Care for Children with Down Syndrome—A Guide for Parents* with Don Van Dyke, Philip Mattheis, and Janet Williams.

Robin Gwyndaf is the Assistant Keeper, Department of Social and Cultural History, Museum of Welsh Life, St. Fagans, Cardiff. He studied at the University College of North Wales, Bangor, where he is presently an Honorary Lecturer in Folklore. The author of numerous publications on Welsh folk culture, he is the Past-President and co-founder of Cymdeithas Llafar Gwlad, the Welsh Folklore Society. In 1988 he was made a Fellow of the Society of Antiquaries of London.

Richard Jenkins is a Professor of Sociology at the University of Sheffield. He was trained in social anthropology at the Queen's University of Belfast and the University of Cambridge. Among his books are studies of young people on a Belfast housing estate (*Hightown Rules and Lads, Citizens and Ordinary Kids*), the impact of unemployment in South Wales (*Taking the Strain* with Susan Hutson), and the nature of informal economic activity (*The Myth of the Hidden Economy* with Philip Harding). His current research is concerned with the transition to adulthood of young people with mental handicaps.

Patricia Lysaght is a native of County Clare, Ireland. She received her PhD from the National University of Ireland in 1982 and is currently a lecturer in the Department of Irish Folklore, University College Dublin. The second edition of her major work, *The Banshee: The Irish Supernatural Death Messenger*, appeared in 1996. She organized the biannual congress of the International Commission for Ethnological Food Research in 1994 and edited the proceedings, *Milk and Milk Products: From Medieval To Modern Times*; she is presently the Commission's President. Dr. Lysaght has been an Alexander von Humboldt Scholar at Westälische Wilhelms-Universität, Münster, Germany (1987-8), and Guest Professor of Folklore at Seminar fur Volkskunde, Georg-August-Univesität Göttingen, Germany (1996-7).

Joyce Underwood Munro has studied at the University of Michigan and Wayne State University. She was admitted to the State Bar of Michigan in 1975 and received the MA at Wayne State University in English and Folklore Studies. She practices law full-time while pursuing a doctoral program in English at Wayne State University. Her research interests include contemporary fiction, folklore and literature, and folklore and child abuse.

Peter Narváez received his PhD in folklore from Indiana University. He is a Professor in the Department of Folklore, Memorial University of Newfoundland, where he has taught for twenty-three years. A Past-President of the Association for the Study of Canadian Radio and Television and the Folklore Studies Association of Canada, his articles have appeared in a variety of academic anthologies and journals including *Western Folklore, Southern Folklore Quarterly, Canadian Folklore canadien, Canadian Literature, Lore and Language, American Behavioral*

Scientist, and the *Journal of American Folklore.* He is currently the Record Review Editor of the *Journal of American Folklore.* Previous to this book he co-edited *Media Sense: The Folklore-Popular Culture Continuum* with Martin Laba.

Diarmuid Ó Giolláin is College Lecturer in Folklore, Department of Irish History, University College, Cork, Ireland. He is the author of an extensive study of the leipreachán, which was published in *Béaloideas,* and his numerous articles have appeared in an array of European journals including *Ulster Folklife, Temenos, ARV,* and *Suomen Antropologi.* His current research interests include folklore and popular religion, and the relation of the state to popular culture.

Barbara Rieti received an MA in Folklore from the University of California at Berkeley and a PhD in Folklore from Memorial University of Newfoundland. Her book, *Strange Terrain: the Fairy World in Newfoundland,* published by ISER Books at Memorial University, was awarded the Raymond Klibansky Book Prize for 1993 by the Canadian Federation for the Humanities. She is presently completing a study of Newfoundland witchcraft tradition based on field research and archival sources.

Peter M. Rojcewicz, PhD, is a folklorist, Professor of Humanities, and Chairman of the Liberal Arts Department, The Juilliard School. He has taught and frequently lectures at the C.G. Jung Foundation for Analytical Psychology, New York City. He has published widely on anomalies and folk belief materials. He was invited to Dharamsala, India, by the Fourteenth Dalai Lama to speak on Jungian perspectives of religious miracles.

Ann Helene Bolstad Skjelbred, PhD, is an Adjunct Professor in folkloristics at the University of Tromsö, Norway. Her many published studies concern folk belief and custom, legends, folklore and religion, women's studies, and traditional health systems. She is also the author of an extensive index of Norwegian folklore and folklife collections, and the compiler of a comprehensive bibliography of alternative medicine, *Bibliografi over alternativ medisin og behandling i Norge til og med 1980.*

Paul Smith, PhD, is a Professor of Folklore and Head of the Department of Folklore at Memorial University of Newfoundland. He initiated the International Perspectives on Contemporary Legend seminars, held annually since 1982. Currently the Vice-President of the International Society for Contemporary Legend Research, he is the Editor of its journal *Contemporary Legend*. He has produced many articles, books, and monographs on folklore topics. In collaboration with Dr. Gillian Bennett, he edited the five-volume *Perspectives on Contemporary Legend* essay series (1984-90), wrote *Contemporary Legend: The First Five Years* (1990), and compiled *Contemporary Legend: An Annotated Bibliography* (1993) and *Contemporary Legend: A Reader* (1996). He is Co-Editor of the journals *Traditional Drama Studies, New Books in Folklore*, and *Current Contents in Folklore*.

Tad Tuleja took MA degrees at Cornell and the University of Sussex. A freelance writer for the past twenty years, he has published widely on American topics in both the trade and the academic presses. His scholarly papers have examined calendar customs, invented traditions, and folk etymology, while his recent books include *Curious Customs, American History in 100 Nutshells*, and *The Public Library Book of Popular Americana*. A doctoral candidate at the University of Texas at Austin, he is completing a dissertation on popular representations of Mexico and editing *Usable Pasts*, an anthology of papers on North American folk traditions.

Rosemary Wells earned her PhD from Northwestern University, Evanston, Illinois, and is a retired Assistant Professor in the now defunct Dental Hygiene Department of Northwestern University Dental School in Chicago, where she taught courses in scientific writing for eighteen years. Her Tooth Fairy research, which was inspired by a student's question over fifteen years ago, has resulted in many articles, several of which have appeared in *cal*, a dental trade journal, and other professional journals including the *Bulletin of the History of Dentistry*. She has presented papers for the American Dental Association, the Popular Culture Association, the Midwest American Culture Association, the American Association of Dental Schools, and the American Medical Writers Association, and to numerous libraries and tour groups who come to her Tooth Fairy Museum, which opened in her home in 1993 (1129 Cherry Street, Deerfield, Illinois 60015).

Noel Williams was educated at Magdalen College School, Oxford, King's College, Cambridge (MA) and Sheffield University (PhD). He is presently a Senior Lecturer in Communication Studies at Sheffield City Polytechnic. His research has centered on language, semantics and folklore, oral narrative, communication skills, computing, and the teaching of writing. He is the author or editor of *Exercises in Teaching Communication, The Intelligent Micro, Computers and Writing, The Computer, the Writer and the Learner,* and many scholarly and popular articles on computing, language, and communication.

Index